THE ENCYCLOPEDIA YEARBOOKS OF JAZZ

THE ENCYCLOPEDIA
YEARBOOKS OF JAZZ

BY LEONARD FEATHER

DA CAPO PRESS • NEW YORK

Library of Congress Cataloging in Publication Data

Feather, Leonard G.
    The encyclopedia yearbooks of jazz / by Leonard Feather.
      p.   cm.
    First work originally published: The encyclopedia yearbook
of jazz. New York: Horizon Press, 1956; 2nd work originally
published: The new yearbook of jazz, New York: Horizon
Press, 1958. With new introd.
    ISBN 0-306-80529-4
    1. Jazz—History and criticism. 2. Jazz musicians. 3. Jazz—
Discography. I. Title.
ML102.J3F43   1993   92-24116
781.65′09—dc20   CIP

First Da Capo Press edition 1993

This Da Capo Press paperback edition of
The Encyclopedia Yearbooks of Jazz is an unabridged
republication of *The Encyclopedia Yearbook of Jazz*
and *The New Yearbook of Jazz*, first published in
New York in 1956 and 1958 respectively,
supplemented with a new introduction by the author.
It is reprinted by arrangement with Leonard Feather.

Published by Da Capo Press, Inc.
A Subsidiary of Plenum Publishing Corporation
233 Spring Street, New York, N.Y. 10013

Manufactured in the United States of America

INTRODUCTION TO THE DA CAPO EDITION

The Encyclopedia Yearbook of Jazz was written immediately after publication of the original edition of *The Encyclopedia of Jazz*. The latter appeared in November, 1955, and as the first reference book of its kind in the English language it enjoyed such immediate success that it was decided to update it annually with a follow-up volume.

The first *Yearbook* appeared in November of 1956; there was another one a year later, but by then there was a need to bring the original book up to date. As a result, a revised edition of *The Encyclopedia of Jazz*, issued in 1960, came out as a replacement for all three previous books. It is still in the Da Capo catalogue.

The 1956 *Yearbook* included the first-ever biographies of such artists as John Coltrane and Jimmy Smith, as well as such questionable inclusions as Elvis Presley, Bo Diddley and Lavern Baker, and such long-forgotten names as Ralph Gari and Philip Darois.

It was a coup to persuade Benny Goodman to write the foreword. His comments about the relative places of jazz as music for dancing and listening still seem pertinent.

The Musicians' Musicians poll marked the first and only time any such attempt was made to corral the opinions of leading jazzmen. Even Duke Ellington and Miles Davis voted as I ran around from club to club collecting these opinions. The two lists of winners ("Greatest Ever" and "New Stars") stand up amazingly well. It is sad to recall that the "New Stars" winner on trumpet, Clifford Brown, died just before the book went to press.

The list of recordings of favorite tunes is of interest in that almost every one of these compositions remains in the jazz repertoire of most musicians today.

The chapter analyzing the jazz fans is indicative of radical change: today's aficionado is considerably older, possibly a little wiser, spends more money on records, and is more broadminded. Some of the remarks about rock'n'roll in this chapter (including my own) seem very naive; the comment that this was a "passing fad" shows how badly clouded was my crystal ball.

The second *Yearbook* (originally issued as the *New Yearbook of Jazz*) is of special interest in retrospect, mainly on the strength of such chapters as "Meet The Critics," "The Jazzman As Critic," and the tabulation of international polls culled from *Down Beat*, *Metronome* and several European publications.

"Meet The Critics" consists of biographies of 28 writers who were then prominently engaged in analyzing jazz, mainly in print but also, as in the case of Willis Conover, on the air. It is sad to note that 18 of these pundits either have died or are no longer active in the field; however, their number has multiplied enormously, since, in 1958, very few newspapers had any specialized jazz coverage. A similar chapter today could easily run to many hundreds of listings.

"The Jazzman As Critic" is subtitled "The Best of the Blindfold Test" and comprises segments from various installments of that feature which I had originated in 1948 in *Metronome*, transferred in 1951 to *Down Beat*, and have been continuing in an expanded form (as *Before and After*) since 1989 in *Jazz Times*. It is also still in *Down Beat*, contributed by other writers.

It remains my contention that with some exceptions, professional musicians' views tend to be more valid and valuable than those of professional critics, especially critics who are not musically literate. A case in point is the series of reactions to various recordings by Jelly Roll Morton, who has been canonized by many critics despite having been put in his place by no less an authority than Duke Ellington.

Of five Morton records played, only one received a four star rating (from Louis Armstrong, who was reluctant to criticize anything). The others range from no stars (by Willie The Lion Smith, who said: "Those guys should be driving trucks!"), to one and one-and-a-half (Jimmy and Marian McPartland), to two stars (Coleman Hawkins, George Wallington). On the other hand Louis Armstrong, whose records I played for everyone from Miles Davis to Leonard Bernstein, received almost unanimously favorable comments.

One of the introductory chapters, "Jazz Overseas," dealt with the state of health enjoyed by jazz in Britain, France, Sweden and Germany. Today it seems odd that I did not include Japan, which presently outstrips any of those countries in the quantity of music it has absorbed, imported, created, or written about. *Swing Journal*, which in a typical month runs anywhere from 350 to 400 pages, is by far the biggest jazz publication in the world.

The essays by Bill Russo, Charles Graham and the late Martin Williams have stood up well despite the vast changes in their respective areas over the past 35 years.

Ira Gitler, who worked as my assistant on the original Encyclopedia and became a full partner with the 1976 publication of the *Encyclopedia of Jazz in The Seventies*, has been working with me since 1991 on a new, complete book which Oxford University Press will publish in 1994. Meanwhile I hope much of the information in these pages will be of interest to a new generation, unborn when the first two or three books appeared. I am grateful to Bea Friedland, Yuval Taylor and everyone else at Da Capo who has helped to make my books available again.

—Leonard Feather
Sherman Oaks, California
1993

THE ENCYCLOPEDIA YEARBOOK OF JAZZ

ACKNOWLEDGMENTS

A workman who enjoys his job is the one who does it best. I was fortunate in having the assistance, while the *Yearbook* was in production, of Ira Gitler, who had rendered similar services for *The Encyclopedia Of Jazz,* and who clearly was as fascinated as I was by the news, opinions and facts in the ballots and questionnaires as they came in.

Thanks are also due to Howard Lucraft, of Jazz International in Hollywood, for acting as West Coast representative in the collecting of ballots and biographical material, and to Jean Barnett, one of those rare stenographers who can combine complete efficiency with a thorough knowledge of and love for jazz.

My sincere thanks also to Herman Leonard and Chuck Stewart for supplying me with some superb examples of their work in jazz photography, as well as to Carole Reiff Galletly, Victor Tanaka, Richard Schaefer and the other photographers who contributed to the visual aspects of the *Yearbook.*

CONTENTS

ILLUSTRATIONS

FOREWORD
by
Benny Goodman

Since the readers of this book are already familiar with the subject, I suppose it will come as no revelation when I point out that many changes, many advances, have taken place in jazz during the past few years. Once ignored or looked on with condescension by laymen who were willing to accept all the other contemporary art forms on an esthetic level, jazz has at last undergone a number of important changes, both in the channels of creation and in the way it is being appreciated.

For one thing, jazz is no longer looked on merely as dance music. I am sure there will always be people who will dance to it, but there is no longer any need for the best jazz musicians to perform primarily in dance halls or cater only to the demands of dancers. Carnegie Hall in New York, Symphony Hall in Boston, and scores of other concert halls both in America and overseas, have opened up to jazz during the past decade. Today there are a dozen concert "packages" making cross-country and Transatlantic tours, playing all the halls that once were completely closed to jazz.

Similarly, many of the night clubs, those that cater to big bands as well as the spots that use only small combos, are tending more and more to eliminate dancing and to use the extra floor space for spectators who simply want to listen to the music, and listen with an intelligent, critical ear. This is another of the many signs that jazz and its audiences have come of age. Some of those audiences may be the fans who once danced the Lindy Hop, the Shag and the Big Apple to jazz, and now prefer to sit and listen. Others are youngsters just developing an appreciation for the music and learning from the start that this is music for the ears, not merely for the feet.

At one time, back in the years when my band was first becoming known, our audiences consisted chiefly of youngsters in their teens and early twenties who reacted directly and very emotionally to our music; they thought it was stimulating and exciting, and great for dancing. They never analyzed this emotional response, the happiness and enjoyment they experienced. The kids didn't read or write books about the music; they just liked it.

Today, as I say, those kids may still be around, listening to the same music with a feeling of nostalgia. But although these same people constituted a segment of our audiences in the spring of 1956, when I reorganized the band for the Waldorf Astoria in New York and a series of out-of-town dates, there was an even larger part of the audiences that consisted of a new generation who found the music as fresh and exciting as their parents had in the 1930's. Their reaction, again, was direct and emotional, but today it takes place against a different background. Swing music, in fact all forms of jazz, may be said to have been adopted by the intellectuals.

Since jazz is, in my opinion, one of our most original contributions to Twentieth Century culture and seems likely to go down in history as the real folk music of our country, it is a commendable thing that it has enjoyed this degree of intellectual acceptance. But although we have many competent critics in the newspapers, magazines and the book world writing capably about the subject, among them my brother-in-law John Hammond, the fact remains that there are a number of others who tend to go overboard, approaching the subject as if it were some kind of occult science. One of them, as a matter of fact, seems to be incapable of writing anything in words of less than four syllables, and he doesn't always get the syllables right either. Once he used the word "contrapointal." What does he mean by that? Contrapuntal? I wonder what his readers get out of reading that kind of stuff; my own reaction is simply bewilderment and a touch of dismay, because there seems to be no really deep emotional feeling in this sort of writing; there is nothing but pompousness behind this over-intellectual approach. The same situation exists in Europe, where a number of critics have gone about the business of analyzing and criticizing jazz from the most complicated and didactic standpoint, even though they themselves cannot create any of the music they discuss, and in the vast majority of cases the truly important jazz talents continue to come out of this country. The general public in those overseas countries continues to react to the music with a happy and healthy enthusiasm, as I found out firsthand when we toured Europe in 1950.

The jazz fans in those countries are quite amazing. I remember once meeting a Greek youth, from Athens, who was about 21 years old when he first came to America. He knew so much about me and my records that I had to ask *him* questions! He told me he corresponded regularly with record collectors in other countries.

Similarly, a year or so ago, I met Count Bernadotte's son, Bertil, who was not more than seventeen, and he turned out to be a jazz fan. He asked me so many questions about records I had made and forgotten about many years ago that I was actually embarrassed. Yet it is heartening to know that in Sweden, France, England and so many other countries, youngsters like this are growing up with a real and avid interest in the music and a desire to help foster its growth. The record collector represents an amazing and unique breed, sometimes as fanatic as any stamp collector or other hobbyist, but it certainly is a healthy trend.

This trend, in these past years, led to the publication of Leonard Feather's *Encyclopedia of Jazz,* which gave the fans, the musicians, and the whole music world a long-needed permanent reference work with its who's-who of more than a thousand musicians and its lists of records.

I am happy to know that the success of the first book led to the publication of *The Encyclopedia Yearbook of Jazz.* This book, and those following each year, will help to keep everyone up to date on the new personalities in jazz as well as supplying pertinent, last minute information for all those who are so vitally concerned about jazz and its progress.

I have known Leonard for many years and I know he has always been aware that facts, as well as opinions, are vitally important in the study of any art. I believe *The Encyclopedia Yearbook of Jazz* will add a wealth of important facts to the fast growing library of information about the most internationally popular branch of American music.

STAMFORD, CONN.
1956

THE ENCYCLOPEDIA YEARBOOK OF JAZZ

WHAT'S HAPPENING

in Jazz

Thou hast no sorrow in thy song,
No winter in thy year.
—John Logan (*To The Cuckoo*)

The past year, and the months that preceded it, may be remembered by posterity as the time of the great jazz gold rush. The simplest and truest answer to the inquiry: "What happened in jazz last year?" would be: "Everything."

For jazz by 1956 had not merely stepped into the sunlight of full respectability, of recognition on higher artistic, social and economic planes than ever before; it had also shown, within itself, a noteworthy degree of maturation as an art form.

In terms of overall achievement for the good of jazz, the most important event was the long-awaited decision of the United States Government to take official cognizance of jazz. Realizing that the global interest in our foremost musical export might be turned to patriotic advantage, the State Department authorized the American National Theatre Academy, as part of its $2,500,000 propaganda program, to send a jazz unit abroad as one of its numerous entertainment offerings.

Fortunately, Prof. Marshall Stearns, long a dedicated spokesman for jazz, was in charge of the selection of talent, and America's first group of jazz envoys was a new, big band under the leadership of John (Dizzy) Gillespie, for which Quincy Jones wrote the arrangements and acted as musical director. The choice could scarcely have been happier. The band, which included four white musicians and thus served to illustrate democracy effectively at work, was composed of first-class jazzmen playing everything from impressions of earlier styles to a wide survey of contemporary aspects.

The difference between the tour's cost and the receipts was underwritten by ANTA. The band played in Iran, Pakistan, Lebanon, Syria, Turkey, Yugoslavia and Greece during a two-month tour. Playing sometimes for the relatively initiated, sometimes for audiences so unsophisticated that they neither knew what jazz was nor had even heard of Louis Armstrong, the Gillespie band accomplished its mission triumphantly. Typical comments by ambassadors and United

States Information Service representatives were: "Maybe we could have built a new tank for the cost of this tour, but you can't get as much goodwill out of a tank as you can out of Dizzy Gillespie's band." "People are tired of words, of speeches about democracy: they want living people demonstrating it." "You people are making our job out here much easier, and without any flag-waving." As a result of the Gillespie tour, ANTA announced that plans would be formulated shortly for further jazz expeditions, and that India and other countries might be covered on future missions.

The 1955-6 concert season saw other overseas expeditions successfully launched on a more conventional commercial basis. Thanks largely to the tireless efforts of Stan Kenton, a Musicians' Union ban that had kept British and American orchestras from each other's countries for twenty years was at last modified, after a series of discussions between Kenton and James C. Petrillo, head of the American Federation of Musicians. Kenton's thus became the first civilian U.S. band to visit England since the 1930s; the successful Kenton tour of Great Britain in the spring of 1956 was accomplished under an exchange arrangement between the two countries' unions that brought Ted Heath's band to the U.S. for a concert tour. Heath's band ended its visit with an evening at Carnegie Hall and enjoyed what was probably the greatest ovation accorded a bandleader there since Duke Ellington's most luxuriant days. Shortly afterward, a similar transatlantic exchange took Louis Armstrong's sextet to Britain and introduced Freddy Randall's British Dixieland combo to American audiences.

In the area of recorded jazz, a ludicrous situation began to arise during 1955 and assumed alarming proportions in 1956. Jazz recording reached a quantitative peak with which the qualitative level could not possibly keep pace. By early 1956 every record company, large and small, had plunged into the production of long playing jazz discs. Many were made on a shoestring basis by companies that had to watch the clock, in fear of having to pay the musicians overtime, instead of paying attention to the quality of the performances.

Any sideman, even a bass player or a drummer, who could claim either an aggressive nature or a few years' publicity in name bands, could become a bandleader on his own LP. Moreover, for trade reasons, the dealers and distributors decided to make it economically unwise for the public to buy 10-inch LPs, with the result that by 1956 virtually every LP was a 12-inch item containing, in most cases, from 35 to 50 minutes of music by the same group. This usually strained the imagination of the musicians and the patience of many listeners. Nevertheless, jazz continued to sell profitably while the average jazz fan was left with an incredibly large choice of releases from which to select his purchases.

Radio and television continued to serve jazz, though by no means with the same loose-pocketed enthusiasm as the record industry. In television there were frequent guest appearances on major programs by Louis Armstrong, and occasionally Dave Brubeck and others were seen on variety shows. Dramatizations of plays with jazz themes appeared more and more frequently, affording Jimmy McPartland, Vic Dickenson and others a chance to display histrionic as well as musical ability. Most valuable of all was the contribution of Steve Allen, who continued to feature as guests on his nightly NBC telecast artists normally considered "too uncommercial," including Miles Davis, the Jazz Messengers and many others. NBC was also responsible for the dissemination of jazz, both live and recorded, through the medium of a patchwork program known as *Monitor,* in which Al (Jazzbo) Collins played a large role. Fuller details will be found in the chapters on disc jockeys and the average jazz fan.

Count Basie became the first Negro bandleader in a decade to find a sponsor for a full series of broadcasts, on a program run by Alan Freed and broadcast every Saturday night over CBS, mainly for teen-aged rock-and-roll fans, with rhythm-and-blues guest artists occupying much of the allotted time. Similarly a CBS television series, seen in the summer of 1955 with Stan Kenton's orchestra, featured one number a week by the band itself, with guest stars taking up the rest of the half-hour.

The motion picture industry, in a mood of myopic but benign expansiveness, acknowledged the inroads of jazz on the American psyche by incorporating jazz sound tracks in feature films that did not actually call for them. Shorty Rogers, Shelly Manne and other modern West Coast jazzmen played a significant part, aurally and visually, in the successful Frank Sinatra picture *The Man with the Golden Arm.* Rogers, virtually adopted by a number of Hollywood powers, even supplied the sound track music, along with Bob Cooper and others, for several animated cartoon shorts made by United Productions of America, and set a remarkable precedent by writing and playing what was, in effect, a jazz score for a short entitled *Sappy Homiens,* commissioned by the American Cancer Society. The achievement of a tasteful and appropriate score on such a grim subject was a tribute both to Rogers' ability and to the long-hidden flexibility of modern jazz.

Other feature films that had jazz themes or undercurrents were *The Benny Goodman Story,* in which, in addition to Goodman, such strangers to celluloid as Teddy Wilson, Lionel Hampton and Buck Clayton were participants; and *High Society,* with Louis Armstrong well to the fore in a vehicle originally designed to accommodate Bing Crosby, Frank Sinatra and Grace Kelly.

The strangest and least logical step taken by jazz was its sudden involvement with religion. Father Norman J. O'Connor, a chaplain at Boston University, became increasingly active as a moderator at jazz forums and even took to writing album notes for jazz LP records. Rev. A. L. Kershaw, pastor at Holy Trinity Episcopal Church in Oxford, Ohio, became a national celebrity when his avocation as a jazz fan enabled him to win $32,000 on a television quiz show called *The $64,000 Question* over CBS in the fall of 1955. (The incongruous tie-up achieved a corollary benefit when Rev. Kershaw gave part of the proceeds to the N.A.A.C.P.) The bond between the jazz laity and the church was further strengthened when such Sunday television shows as

Look Up and Live and *Frontiers Of Faith* began to feature jazz groups such as Dave Brubeck's and Marian McPartland's, justifying their innovations with some slightly tenuous dialogues about freedom of expression and happiness through music, as well as with the more valid thesis that jazz is a vital force in fighting racial prejudice.

In the press, there were developments that afforded jazz a new cachet. It was now not only newsworthy and respectable but even, from the viewpoint of the women's magazines, downright chic. Such publications as *Vogue, Glamour, Harper's Bazaar* and *Mademoiselle,* in whose pages jazz hitherto had been *infra dignitatem* and consequently tabu, went to great expense to stage special jam sessions at which the spirit of a trumpet solo could somehow be linked photographically with the mood of a new Paris gown. One lipstick manufacturer placed in every drugstore window, and in every major advertising outlet, a picture showing a luscious model dropping her cigarette ash into a grand piano and clearly making an effort (no doubt successful) to distract Dave Brubeck's mind from his music. The name of the lipstick was "Red, Hot and Cool." Musicians and fans all over America, when they saw this advertisement, felt that jazz must really have arrived. Madison Avenue, the last commercial bastion, had been stormed and conquered.

An accomplishment that would have appeared fantastic to any prophet in the 1930s is the achievement of jazz on the academic level as a subject for college courses. Jazz courses have been offered at schools intermittently since the early 1940s, but only in the past few years have they earned such stature as the *Development of Jazz* series given by Nesuhi Ertegun at UCLA, which was worth a two-unit credit toward a college degree, or George Wein's similar two-unit credit series at Boston University.

As a result of such lecture courses as these, along with Gene Hall's at North Texas State Teachers' College (a course in improvisation and arranging rather than an historical survey), America's music educators belatedly decided in 1956 that jazz was worthy of closer inspection. At the Music Educators' National Conference in St. Louis in April 1956, the potential value of jazz in all curricula for music students was outlined to the conference by Father Norman O'Connor and George Wein, both of Boston U., and by Dave Brubeck and George Avakian. As Avakian later commented in *Down Beat,* "they could have been flip, or obviously polite, about paying lip service to an unscrubbed but unavoidable stepchild. Instead, they were genuinely interested. . . . it was obvious that jazz already had made a great impression on the thinking of our leading music educators."

In addition to the courses, there were many special jazz seminars, sometimes combined with miniature jazz festivals featuring live music, at dozens of universities throughout the United States.

In the concert field, jazz continued to attract the many devotees who found this medium a desirable substitute for, or adjunct to, the customary night club setting. Norman Granz's Jazz at the Philharmonic unit toured the U.S. in the fall of 1955 and Europe in early 1956. Louis Armstrong's concert route took him, within three months, all the way from Australia to England to the Gold Coast of Africa. Newport, Rhode Island, was the scene of a jazz festival for the third and probably final time in July, 1956 (it was planned to move it to a more suitable location in future years); the festival motif, conceived in 1954 by Mr. & Mrs. Louis L. Lorillard and George Wein, had begun to spawn a series of imitators in Bridgeport, Conn., Lenox, Mass. and other communities. Established festivals of the arts in Stratford, Ontario and elsewhere added jazz to their schedules.

For the first time, some of the money in the Musicians' Union trust fund, derived from royalties paid by record companies, found a jazz outlet when Local 802 of the A.F. of M. presented concerts of modern jazz in New York halls such as Cooper Union and Hunter College.

All this activity in so many media could not fail to broaden the artistic scope of jazz. A glance at the new biographies in another chapter, notably those of Friedrich Gulda, Gunther Schuller and Willie Ruff, will give the reader an idea of the increasing rapprochement between jazz and "classical" music. Extended forms, as used by John Lewis, Schuller and other musicians both from inside and outside jazz, combined with the increasing frequent use of atonalism and twelve-tone rows, reduced the line between jazz and other music forms almost to invisibility. Most of these new developments were founded on a healthier and sounder knowledge of the essence of jazz, and of classical forms, than earlier attempts such as those of George Gershwin or even of Igor Stravinsky, whose *Ebony Concerto* for Woody Herman was not considered completely successful by critics on either side of the falling fence.

Just as the demarcation between jazz and classical music was fading, so were the lines separating jazz from Latin-American music, from popular music and from rhythm-and-blues. While it is possible to state that the majority of compositions and performances in all three of these categories cannot be considered valid as jazz, there is a fringe area that gives all of them enough kinship to make it very difficult, at times, to determine where one ends and the other begins.

Though it has long been a complaint of musicians and fans that the critics tend, as the author tends here, to categorize and pigeonhole music, the intention is not to stigmatize any branch or to brand it as jazz or non-jazz, but simply to point out that it becomes more of a problem every day to decide, for instance, which names belong and which do not belong in the biographical section of this book. Why, one might ask, is Elvis Presley included and analyzed while Villegas is shrugged off? If Beverly Kenney belongs in a book about jazz, why not Roberta Sherwood, Peggy King or a hundred other popular singers?

It is in the vocal department that this problem becomes insoluble. Most of the singing that has been accepted by jazz fans in recent years has been part of a minor art, a miniaturist subdivision in which the all-important factor of improvisation has been restricted by a fixed melody and a set of lyrics (usually of low calibre) from which the performer cannot deviate far. It might arguably be maintained that with such rare exceptions as Joe Williams and Carmen McRae none of the singers whose biographies are included in the *Yearbook* deserved to be included. Yet they have been presented on records accompanied by jazz musicians, and on labels that cater predominantly to the jazz market; ergo, the jazz fans take them into the fold. In most cases there is little or nothing to separate them from, or put them on a higher plane than, such singers as Martha Raye, Dick Haymes, Judy Garland and others who happen to move in a non-jazz world and are thus not considered a part of the jazz scene.

The situation is further confused by the fact that the musicians themselves do not consider the existence of any line between popular and jazz singing. The *Yearbook* poll showed that very few of the 100 voters gave their male vocal votes to such unmistakable jazz timbres as Louis Armstrong's or Jimmy Rushing's. Instead, most of them voted for Frank Sinatra. As far as the biographical chapter was concerned, the author solved this problem by taking the line of most resistance; that is, by eliminating all those "pop singers" who have not chanced, by their musical associations, to acquire a heavy following among jazz fans.

Despite the great advances made in jazz, esthetically and in terms of world-wide prestige, there was one development during 1955-6 that gave pause to many critics, fans and performers to whom the future course of this music was of vital importance. This was the unprecedented commercial success of an old body with a new face: the brand of music now nationally hailed and reviled under the guise of rock 'n' roll.

THE TRUTH ABOUT ROCK 'N' ROLL

A story, probably apocryphal, has been circulating among musicians concerning a noted jazz star who sat in a music publisher's office listening to the latest rock 'n' roll hit.

"Isn't it amazing," said the publisher, "to think that a song like that should have been written by a 13-year-old boy?"

"Frankly, yes," replied the musician. "I thought a song like that would have been written by a *six*-year-old boy."

Not legendary but factual is an incident that took place in California when a world-famous jazz drummer decided to jump on a potentially profitable bandwagon by making some records for the rock 'n' roll market. "We got a big band together," recalls one of the musicians, "and a vocal group. But it wasn't an easy session; the vocal group was composed of good singers, so at first they couldn't get the authentic sound. It took quite a while to get them to sing out of tune."

Perhaps most significant of all was the report in the New York *Daily News,* in a series on rock 'n' roll, concerning a publisher who played his latest hit for the reporter. "Awful, isn't it?" he said. "If I had my way I'd publish only good music, but this is the stuff the kids want, and they buy the records."

The only reason for the relating of these anecdotes, and for commenting on the rock 'n' roll mania in general, is that in the course of its leap to popularity among American teenagers during the past year it has often been mistakenly branded as an offshoot of jazz. Although it is true that some jazz artists appeal, either deliberately or accidentally, to rock 'n' roll audiences, most of the music has little in common with jazz. The phrase "rock 'n' roll" itself has only acquired a generic connotation in recent years; originally this was simply a phrase found frequently in the lyrics or titles of rhythm and blues songs. Rock 'n' roll is nothing more than the baser manifestations of rhythm and blues music, the present day counterpart of what was known in the 1920s and '30s as "race music," because it was aimed at the segregated Negro market.

As usually happens with entertainment forms of Negro origin, rock 'n' roll has expanded into the white area both in its exponents and its audiences. White artists who normally work entirely in the field of popular (Tin Pan Alley) music have sold hundreds of thousands of records simply by imitating performances of the same tunes by Negro artists such as LaVern Baker.

The most successful rock 'n' roll music, in terms of public acceptance, is almost always vocal, and most frequently is sung by males. A recent list, in the trade publication *Billboard,* of the ten top sellers in the rhythm and blues market showed only one girl singer, Ruth Brown; only two white artists, Elvis Presley and Carl Perkins; five other male singers—Little Richard, Fats Domino, Joe Turner, Clyde McPhatter and Ray Charles—and two vocal groups: the Platters and the Teen-Agers. Of all ten, only two (Ruth Brown and Joe Turner) have earned any recognition as jazz artists.

The uncrowned king of rock 'n' roll is a white disc jockey, Alan Freed, who broadcasts over WINS in New York City. Freed has made a fortune out of his concentration on this brand of entertainment, sometimes presenting his own shows in local theatres. At one stage presentation, in Brooklyn, the acts included The Rover Boys, The Willows, The Royaltones, The Jodimars, The Flamingos, The Valentines and the Cleftones. There was also a band that included two tenor sax men formerly considered to be jazz musicians, Sam (The Man) Taylor and Big Al Sears, who before their rock 'n' roll reincarnation were simply Sam Taylor and Al Sears.

The material performed by rock 'n' roll artists consists of three general types: traditional twelve-bar blues (such as *Corrine Corrina,* which enjoyed a big revival through Joe Turner's record in the summer of 1956, and *Blue Suede Shoes,* as popularized by Elvis Presley and Carl Perkins); low-grade rhythm songs, based on elementary harmonic patterns; and ballads, most of which are simply amateurish reproductions of some of the poorer ballads in the general pop music field.

The reason for the success of this esthetically impoverished music is the heart-on-sleeve sentimentality of the slower numbers and the steam-roller incisiveness of the rhythmic beat on faster ones. The primitive appeal of the latter has prompted many newspaper headlines during the past year: "Teeners

Riot In Massachusetts And Cause Rock 'N' Roll Ban" (*Down Beat*). "Rock 'N' Roll Vandals Rip Subway Car" (New York *Post*). "Rock 'N' Roll Ban By White Citizens' Council" (New York *Herald Tribune*). The Negro weekly news magazine, *Jet,* tying up the White Citizens with the frequent (until recently) Communist attacks on jazz, summed up the whole thing with: "Reds And Whites Ask For Boycott Against Blues."

The extent to which rock 'n' roll and jazz overlap is governed mostly by the willingness or reluctance of jazz musicians to cater to the atavistic demands of youthful rock 'n' roll audiences. Lionel Hampton's policy has concentrated largely on this kind of mass-hysteria appeal, with results that have, in the main, redounded to his great financial advantage though occasionally to his physical discomfort. *Newsweek* reported on one instance after a typical demonstration at the Concertgebouw in Amsterdam (*"audience wildly prancing, flinging arms, screaming. . . . saxophonist lying on back during solo, copulates with his shimmering instrument . . . two black-booted city cops turn up, grab Hampton, take him off stage into dressing room. 'What did I do? Arrested for jazzing,' he moans. 'Call the ambassador!' "*). Hampton, of course, equates performances of this type with jazz. Most musicians do not. Many modern jazzmen passing through the Hampton ranks, among them Quincy Jones, Clifford Brown and dozens more, expressed mortification at this continual reduction of a potentially fine jazz orchestra to a wild rock 'n' roll bacchanal.

The social problems raised by the rock 'n' roll hysteria are tangential and often lead to a confusion between cause and effect. If the teen-agers who respond to the erotic appeal of this music had no such outlet, they would undoubtedly find another one; rock 'n' roll is more the slave than the master of their adolescent emotions. Nevertheless, the music has been made the scapegoat for a multitude of sins. Under the headline "Rock 'N' Roll Called Battle Cry of Rebellion," the New York *World-Telegram* quoted Dr. Francis J. Braceland, psychiatrist-in-chief of the Institute of Living: "Rock 'n' roll is a cannibalistic and tribalistic form of music . . . a communicable disease . . . appealing to adolescent rebellion and insecurity." But he conceded: "If it isn't rock 'n' roll, it's something else."

To sum up: rock 'n' roll bears the same relationship to jazz that wrestling bears to boxing. The distress felt by fellow-musicians and fans on finding such superior jazz artists as Emmett Berry, Lou Donaldson and Herbie Nichols forced to work in rhythm-and-blues bands is exactly comparable with the reaction of fight fans to the sight of Joe Louis in the wrestling arena.

Rock 'n' roll not only is very rarely jazz; it is very rarely music. Its present popularity is a passing fad about which the parents of America need hardly concern themselves. The only two factors in its favor are, first, that it may tend to some degree to bring whites and Negroes closer together, though one can easily imagine a meeting ground somewhat farther above sea-level; and second, that from its less frenetic supporters an occasional jazz fan may grow.

JAZZ COLLIDES WITH THE INTELLECTUALS

An inevitable corollary of the stepped-up public interest in jazz in the mid-1950s was a rapidly expanded bibliography. To the list of books printed in the *Encyclopedia Of Jazz* can be added a longer line of additions than any previous year could have offered. Among the more important works have been *Jazz: Evolution and Essence,* by André Hodeir, the first work by a modern critic musically literate enough to analyze jazz improvisation with actual musical illustrations; *The Eddie Condon Treasury of Jazz,* an anthology edited by Richard Gehman; *Lady Sings The Blues,* Billie Holiday's autobiography as told to Bill Dufty; *The Story Of Jazz* by Marshall Stearns; and several novels with jazz as a main theme or an undercurrent, including *Sideman* by Osborn Duke and *Second Ending* by Evan Hunter.

The rapprochement between jazz and literature had a curious counter-revolutionary effect. Writers who had ignored jazz for decades while it was growing and flourishing in their midst now found it acceptable only to the degree that it could be aligned with their preconceived notions of its place and stature in the American cultural scene. More often than not they preferred to assess jazz in terms of a contentedly playful little subculture, the product of unlettered souls who could speak eloquently only through their horns. (The leftists, of course, never missed an opportunity to oversimplify the entire culture in terms of "music of protest," as if a flatted fifth could be equated with a revolt against indignity.)

As Nat Hentoff pointed out in an admirable inspection of the intellectuals' nervous flirtation with jazz (*The Chicago Review,* Fall 1955), the "frequent preference, by the small number of American intellectuals who care about jazz at all, for early blues, New Orleans, later Dixieland, and 'revivalist' jazz is yet another example of that odd ambivalence toward jazz (and particularly the Negro jazzman) that is shown by many intellectuals." Modern jazzmen are too unpure for them, too infused with European influences, he adds; it is difficult for them to conceive of an American Negro musical innovator of Charlie Parker's freshness, originality and complex power.

"Parker, the most important modern jazz influence in many years, was ignored when *Time* finally decided to 'recognize' jazz," Hentoff recalls. "*Time,* instead, gave its cover story to Dave Brubeck, a highly individualized modern jazz pianist of considerable resources but at some distance from Parker's attainments. Brubeck, however, was 'respectable' enough for *Time* because he had studied with Milhaud, was a favorite among collegians—and was white." Not that *Time* is Jim Crow, he adds; it is simply the preconcepts of what a Negro jazz musician should stand for that interferes with his acceptance on certain levels.

The intellectuals, as far as one can generalize about them, may be said to tend toward any jazz form that sequesters itself as folk music, offering no challenging comparison with contemporary classical forms, no emotional values beyond those of the mainly improvisational and instinctive inspirational qualities they have already ascribed to it. In almost every novel about jazz, the musician has been type-cast. There is the jazzman torn between complete freedom of expression in a small improvising group and financial security in the confines of a big "commercial" band; there is the innocent youngster drawn into a narcotics net; there is the colorful illiterate pouring out his soul in a dive in New Orleans. Only in rare cases does there seem to be a deeper understanding of the jazzman's effort to find his way out of the esthetic paper bag to which the intellectuals have long consigned him. (A notable exception, admittedly on the dope theme but written with a relatively keen insight into the workings of a musician's mind, was Elliott Grennard's short story *Sparrow's Last Jump,* published in May 1947 in *Harper's Magazine.*)

Fortunately writers like Whitney Balliett of the *Saturday Review,* and others who are willing to accept the music on its own terms, instead of crying inflation every time the terms are raised a little, typify a new generation that will ultimately wipe out the stigma left on jazz by the deliberately myopic approach of their predecessors. It seems that jazz and the intellectuals, whose wedding at first appeared to have been a shotgun affair, were never basically incompatible. All they needed was a good marriage counselor.

THE JAZZ FAN

*I*n the Spring of 1956, the writer framed twenty questions for use in a column in *Down Beat* in an effort to determine, from the readers' answers, some idea of the nature, habits and preferences of the typical jazz fan.

The mail produced by the column came from all over the United States and elicited a number of letters from abroad. Altogether, between 500 and 1,000 answers were used (varying according to the degree and clarity of the responses to each question) as a representative sampling for the compilation of the following facts and figures.

The first question established the age of the reader. (See figure 1.) The years of college age clearly provide the largest percentage, with the graph reaching its peak at 20 years, declining during the twenties and dropping off sharply in the thirties. The oldest respondent, 55-year-old Robert C. Sandison of Denver, Colorado, could be the grandfather of some of the youngest, who included several thirteen-year-olds. The Denver veteran, whose life as a fan began when he went to the Five Points district to hunt for Armstrong and Oliver records thirty years ago, enthuses over Dixieland, swing music, Latin rhythms, and such modernists as Art Farmer, Chet Baker ("when he doesn't sing"), the Howard Rumsey group and Shelly Manne. But he adds "I don't dig Dave Brubeck" and feels that rock-and-roll "is a lot closer to the fundamental Negro jazz than the slick presentations on Prestige or Fantasy. . . . thirty years ago the now hallowed jazz of Satchmo, the Original Dixieland Band, even Beiderbecke, was being denounced in the same terms used for rhythm and blues today. . . . is it, then, inconceivable that Paul Williams, Hal Singer or Joe Turner may be revered prophets in 1970?"

On the other hand a thirteen-year-old fan from Fall River, Mass., says of rock-and-roll "I neither enjoy nor patronize that type of entertainment," and of Latin rhythms: "these forms contain a good deal of interest when well expounded, but their relative novelty should not be allowed

Figure 1. How old are you?

Years

||||||||||||| 13 (1.3%)

|||||||||||||| 14 (1.5%)

||||||||||||||||||||||||||||||||||||||||||| 15 (4.4%)

||||||||||||||||||||||||||||||||||||||||||||||||||||||||||||||| 16 (6.7%)

||||||||||||||||||||||||||||||||||||||||||||||||||||||||||||||||||| 17 (7.1%)

||||||||||||||||||||||||||||||||||||||||||||||||||||||||||||||| 18 (6.7%)

||||||||||||||||||||||||||||||||||||||||||||||||||||||||||||||||||| 19 (7.3%)

|||||||||||||||||||||||||||||||||||||||||||||||||||||||||||||||||||||||||| 20 (8.2%)

||||||||||||||||||||||||||||||||||||||||||||||||||||||||||||||||||||||| 21 (7.7%)

||||||||||||||||||||||||||||||||||||||||||||||||||||||||||||||||||| 22 (7.3%)

|||||||||||||||||||||||||||||||||||||||||||||||||| 23 (5.5%)

||||||||||||||||||||||||||||||||||||||||||||| 24 (5.0%)

|||||||||||||||||||||||||| 25 (2.9%)

||||||||||||||||||||||||||||||||||||||||||| 26 (4.8%)

|||||||||||||||||||||||||| 27 (2.9%)

||||||||||||||||||||||||||||||| 28 (3.4%)

|||||||||||||||||||||||||||| 29 (3.1%)

|||||||||||||||| 30 (1.5%)

|||||||||||||||| 31 (1.7%)

|||||||||||||||||| 32 (2.0%)

|||||||||| 33 (0.9%)

|||||||||||||||| 34 (1.7%)

|||||||||||| 35 (1.3%)

|||||||||||||||||||||||||||||||||| 36 to 40 (3.7%)

||||||||||||| over 40 (1.4%)

to dominate the jazz field." The youngster, like several of the other teen-aged respondents, subscribes to the Jazztone Society. He describes himself as "both a jazz enthusiast and an audiophile" and is an amateur trombonist. Of his musical preferences he says: "mainly modern jazz, though I recognize traditional jazz as an important stepping stone to the present and future."

Question No. 2 was: How many hours do you spend listening to jazz in an average week? (See figure 2.) Many of the replies made it clear that the listening time was spread among many media, mainly phonograph records, radio, and in-person performances at nightclubs and concerts. A sizable percentage mentioned that their listening hours were temporarily restricted by school or college studies or by army service, but that they would make up for lost time as soon as possible. Chief honors went to a young woman from Hamden, Conn., whose answer stated: "Every waking moment I am on the lookout for a good jazz radio show. If at any time the radio proves to be a disappointment, I turn to the phonograph. I try for at least 112 hours per week." If this fan sleeps the normal eight hours a day, it must be assumed that she eats to music, never answers the telephone and never leaves home in an effort to keep up her 16-hours-a-day quota. Not far behind her is Lois Hewett of Rockford, Ill., who dedicates herself to jazz 84 hours a week and to classical music for a further 24 hours.

Figure 2.   How many hours do you spend listening to jazz in an average week?

IIIIIIIIIIIIIIIIIII 1–5 Hrs.   6.8%

IIIIIIIIIIIIIIIIIIIIIIIIIIIIIIIIIIIIIIIIIIIIIIIIIIIIIIIIIIIII 5–10 Hrs.   22.2%

IIIIIIIIIIIIIIIIIIIIIIIIIIIIIIIIIIIIIIIIIIIIIIIIIIIIIIIIIIIIIIIIII 10–15 Hrs.   26.4%

IIIIIIIIIIIIIIIIIIIIIIIIIIIIIIIIIIIIIIIIIIIIIIII 15–20 Hrs.   18%

IIIIIIIIIIIIIIIIIIIIIIIIIIIIIIIIII 20–25 Hrs.   12%

IIIIIIIIIIIIIIIIIIIIII 25–30 Hrs.   7%

IIIIIIIIIIIII 30–40 Hrs.   4.2%

III 40–50 Hrs.   1.1%

IIIIIII 50 and up   2.3%

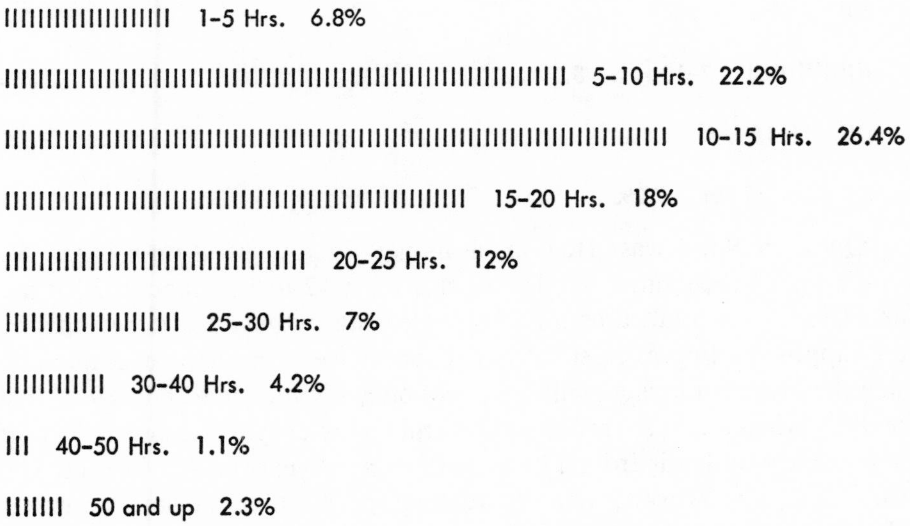

Question No. 3 investigated the readers' extra-jazz tastes: How many hours do you spend listening to classical music in an average week? (See figure 3.) The answers here revealed that almost half the jazz fans spend a bare hour or less a week with classical music and that ⅘ of this segment confesses to no listening at all. Scarcely anyone gave a figure for classical music listening that was as high as that given for jazz. An exception was a modern jazz fan from Detroit, Mich., who allots 14 hours apiece to jazz and classical music every week. Nicola Covara, a 30-year-old Manhattan resident, is interested mainly in traditional jazz, to which she devotes 15 hours per week, but spends a second 15 hours with classical music, including *Breakfast Symphony* and weekend afternoon operas on radio.

Of the 39.2% who admitted listening to no classical music at all, many were frank to admit that it did not interest them; others prefaced their remarks with "I am ashamed to admit . . ." or "Because my time is limited . . ." Very few expressed any intention of increasing their classical listening time.

Figure 3.   How many hours do you spend listening to classical music in an average week?

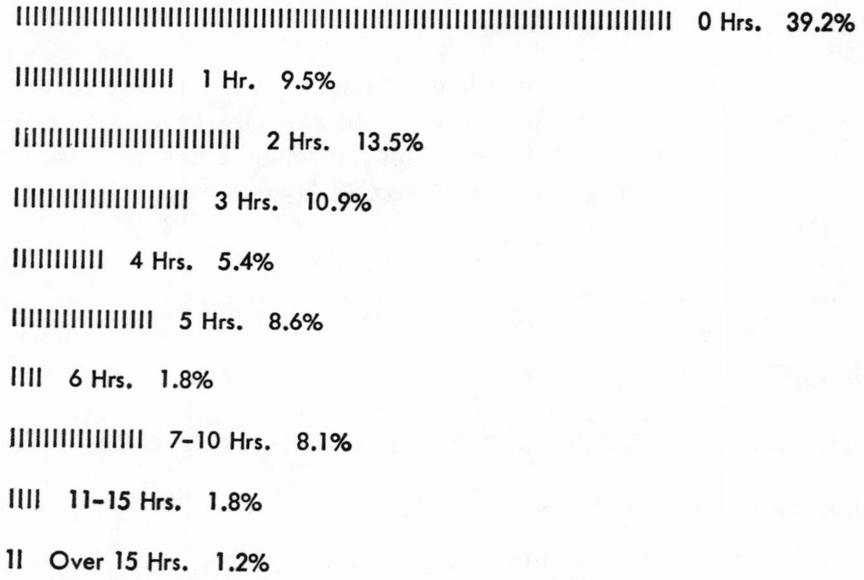

IIIIIIIIIIIIIIIIIIIIIIIIIIIIIIIIIIIIIIIIIIIIIIIIIIIIIIIIIIIIIIIIIIIIIIIIIIIIIII   0 Hrs.   39.2%

IIIIIIIIIIIIIIIIIII   1 Hr.   9.5%

IIIIIIIIIIIIIIIIIIIIIIIIIII   2 Hrs.   13.5%

IIIIIIIIIIIIIIIIIIIIII   3 Hrs.   10.9%

IIIIIIIIIII   4 Hrs.   5.4%

IIIIIIIIIIIIIIIII   5 Hrs.   8.6%

IIII   6 Hrs.   1.8%

IIIIIIIIIIIIIIII   7–10 Hrs.   8.1%

IIII   11–15 Hrs.   1.8%

II   Over 15 Hrs.   1.2%

Question No. 4 was: How much money do you spend on records in an average week? (See figure 4.) The figures from $2 to $5 accounted for more than 60% of the total; thus the ever-increasing output of jazz records, currently approximating at least 20 new issues a week, must meet a market in which the average fan is unwilling or economically unable to buy 19 of them. The 99% who cannot share his good fortune may envy a Pensacola, Fla., fan whose weekly outlay is from $25 to $30, or a 17-year-old fan in West Hartford, Conn., who, working in a record shop, gets a discount on his purchases and can acquire about $28 worth a week. At the other end of the economic scale are a dozen fans who, unable to buy records at all, rely on radio or on the bounty of parents and friends. A couple of them have tape recorders which, presumably, they use to copy their favorite records off the air.

Question No. 5 asked: Do you think there are too many jazz records coming out? This produced the following figures: Not too many records—46.5%; Yes, too many records—36.0%; Qualified—17.5%.

Figure 4. How much money do you spend on records
             in an average week?

||||||| $0 1.7%

|||||||||||||||||||| $1 8.2%

|||||||||||||||||||||||||||||||||||||||||||||||||||||||||||||| $2 16.4%

||||||||||||||||||||||||||||||||||||||||||||||||||| $3 12.7%

||||||||||||||||||||||||||||||||||||||||||||||||||||||||| $4 16.1%

||||||||||||||||||||||||||||||||||||||||||||||||||||||||| $5 16.2%

||||||||||||||||||||||| $6 5.0%

|||||||||||||||||| $7 4.0%

||||||||||||||||||||| $8 4.5%

||||||||| $9 1.7%

|||||||||||||||||||||||||||| $10 6.2%

||||||||||||||||||||||| $11–15 4.6%

||||||||||||| $16–20 1.7%

||||| $25–50 1.0%

"I welcome the so-called flooding of the market with jazz LPs," was one typical reaction. "The jazz fan should know what he wants and the many releases should not bother him." One reader in Paris commented: "I know few jazz enthusiasts who are not partial to one specific style, so I do not think you need be a millionaire to buy most of the best records within your own preferences." Al Smith of Wheaton, Maryland answered the question with another question: "Do you think there are too many cars on Broadway during rush hour?"

Whether their answer was a yes, a no or a maybe, hundreds of readers pointed out that the quality, rather than the quantity, is their main concern. Typical comments: "It seems like every performer who gets a one-line rave in a trade paper goes out, grabs a bunch of musicians and makes an LP." "It drives the retailers nuts—they refuse to keep that many labels in stock." "Too much jazz, both bad and good, is being recorded; so I must often rely on critics for recommendations of what to buy, and I frequently disagree with those gentlemen." "There are too many pseudo-jazz records being released— that is, records that are not real jazz but are billed as such—particularly in regard to vocalists." "There are not enough jazz records on the market, only too many that have been erroneously labeled so."

The possible advantages of the glut were also pointed out: "It has succeeded in selling the country at large on the virtues of jazz . . . disc jockeys, bowled over by the number of jazz records they receive, and by stacks of requests for jazz selections, are at last getting hip."

Question No. 6: Do your jazz interests tend to be (a) mainly traditionalist, (b) mainly modern jazz, (c) both? The ratio was as follows: Mainly modern jazz—56.7%; Mainly traditionalist—10.6%; Both—32.7%.

This indicated a definite trend away from traditional jazz forms, since a similar poll 18 months earlier in *Down Beat* showed 46% for modern jazz, 44% for both, and 10% for traditional. The proportion for modern jazz might have been even higher had not some of the younger fans misinterpreted the adjective "traditional," which was intended to imply New Orleans, Dixieland, and in general, jazz of pre-1930 vintage. For example, Leslie Davis of Washington, D.C. wrote: "My tastes are traditional, if the Parker-Gillespie-Davis school can be regarded as such; modern in that I appreciate the MJQ, Bud Powell, the Jazz Messengers . . ."

Del Leaming of Newton, Iowa answered: "My jazz interests are in men who are living and with us, which is not too advanced when you remember that Louis, Duke and Basie are with us. I'm also interested in men who are gone, like Jelly Roll, Django, Charlie Christian and Charlie Parker. I believe in promoting living jazz talent, not in moaning about what was going good thirty years ago. I have two friends . . . Friend A has a magnificent collection that ends about the time Benny played Carnegie Hall. Everything after that has sinister shadings which he wishes to ignore. This man has great erudition. Friend B had to give up his record player because of economic exigencies, during the depression. His wife informed him that he should get rid of all those old records, so he did; pitched them into a cornfield from his car. Oliver's *Milneburg Joys,* the Red Hot Peppers . . . practically an unforgivable crime; but Friend B's love of jazz has kept right on growing instead of stopping at one era. The result is that he can grin and say 'I still like New Orleans best,' but he will listen with enthusiasm to Elliot Lawrence-Mulligan arrangements, Bob Gordon's baritone solos, anything that at least sounds like the boys were trying. Which man do you think is doing the more for the music? There's no doubt in my mind. You don't have to like it all to be sympathetic. Jazz needs lifelong friends."

A good point is raised by Vernon L. McCain of Wenatchee, Wash.: "My main interest is mainstream jazz: swing era . . . I am particularly interested in records made by stars in this era who have moved with the times . . . Hawk, Norvo, Ellington, etc. To a lesser extent I am interested in good new records by figures of that period who have *not* moved with the times . . . Goodman, Wilson and so on. But I strongly object to referring to this type of music as either modern or traditional jazz. I prefer to call it just jazz."

Question No. 7: How do you feel about rock 'n' roll, or rhythm and blues? Do you attend events, or buy records, devoted to this brand of music?

Benny Goodman Orchestra at the Waldorf-Astoria Hotel, New York City, Spring 1956. Hank Jones, piano; Irv Manning, bass; Steve Jordan, guitar; Mousie Alexander, drums; Mel Lewis, Jimmy Maxwell, Fern Caron, trumpets; Urbie Green, Rex Peer, trombones; Budd Johnson, Al Block, Walt Levinsky, Sol Schlinger, saxophones; Goodman, clarinet. *(Popsie)*

Louis Armstrong *(Chuck Stewart)*

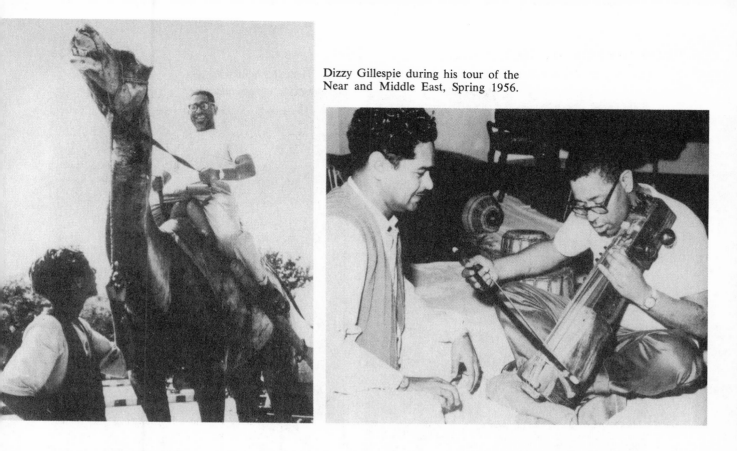

Dizzy Gillespie during his tour of the
Near and Middle East, Spring 1956.

The Gillespie trumpet section, L. to R.: Joe Gordon, E. V. Perry, John Gillespie,
Carl Warwick, Quincy Jones.

Bob Scobey *(Good Time Jazz Records)* Dick Collins *(Richard Schaefer)*

Conte Candoli *(Chuck Stewart)*

Art Farmer *(Carole Galletly)*

Thad Jones (right); Billy Mitchell in background *(Francis Wolff)*   Nat Adderley *(Herman Leonard)*

Jimmy Cleveland *(Herman Leonard)*

Chet Baker *(Herman Leonard)*
Jay Jay Johnson (left) and Kai Winding *(Herman Leonard)*

Roy Eldridge *(Herman Leonard)*   Turk Murphy *(Columbia Records)*

L. to R.: Ruby Braff, Vic Dickenson, Sam Margolis *(Vanguard Records)*

Upper left: Julian "Cannonball" Adderley *(H'erman Leonard)*

Lower left: Lennie Niehaus

Right: Herb Geller *(Herman Leonard)*

The percentages were: Dislike Rock 'n' Roll—78.6%; Like Rock 'n' Roll—4.2%; Qualified—17.2%.

This produced the longest and most violent replies of the entire 20 questions. Beyond any doubt, the rhythm-and-blues fan and the jazz fan are two different species, scarcely ever overlapping. One G.I. respondent bridled and answered: "I was quite taken aback that you bothered to ask the question . . . This low music form has been forced upon the public." A fan in La Mesa, Calif. remarks that several of his friends who worked with him in a band have switched to playing lucrative rhythm-and-blues dates while he himself makes coffee and cakes playing jazz with a beat—"I still say that I will not start playing rhythm-and-blues just for money." One reader tried to distinguish between rhythm-and-blues, which "has a deep feeling when performed as it should be," and rock 'n' roll, "which is nauseating . . . People like Pat Boone and Gale Storm ruin songs which should be done by Ray Charles and Ruth Brown." Most of the qualified answers were from readers who had detected the difference between legitimate blues artists with authentic jazz feeling, such as Joe Williams and Dinah Washington, and the spurious products of the current rock 'n' roll mania. Some of them regretted that artists who were formerly authentic country blues performers, such as T-Bone Walker, have to "resort to Elvis Presleyisms" in order to reach an audience; and that the teen-agers who applaud Sid Caesar's "Three Haircuts" satire of a rock 'n' roll vocal group on television are not even aware that Caesar is kidding.

Charles Martell of Watertown, N.Y. wrote: "I attend St. Lawrence University in Canton, just north of Watertown, and there I appear on a panel show over KSLU, the campus radio station. The show, called *Previews and Reviews,* plays the new record releases for the panel to review. Naturally much of the stuff we get is rock 'n' roll, and in all the records of this category that I have rated, I haven't liked one. Not only does it comprise a music on the incomparably low level of hillbilly, but it helps to glamorize and get more devotees to the leather jacket, switch-blade set, the kill-for-kicks crowd that I predict will become one of America's major social problems in the near future. I wouldn't be caught dead at a rock 'n' roll concert unless I was doing research for a paper on mass hysteria."

On the other hand, Lloyd F. Gossler boasted: "I not only like r and b—I *love* it. I like it for the insistent beat, for the things it has grown into musically, for the mass of teen-agers who at least know what a tenor sax looks like for the first time since the vocalists took over some years back. We have an 'interest-getter' in instrumental jazz, and these people who are learning to crawl with Earl Bostic, Red Prysock, et al will soon be learning to walk with Ted Nash, Paul Desmond, and others who represent a more musically advanced school."

Mr. Gossler may well be right, for a Harvard University student admitted: "I am getting tired of r and b, and I don't buy records or attend r and b events. The only thing I have to say for it is this. Back in 1948 I started to buy records. At the time I bought mostly popular records. But little by little I started to drift towards what was then called 'race records.' Within a year I was buying almost all race records, but all of a sudden I started to get tired of them and I turned to such artists as Kenton and Herman and some of the old Harry James and Frank Sinatra records. I really feel that I was finally led to jazz through these old r and b records and if they can do that for other people they are of some value."

Most of the teen-agers discussing this inflammatory subject were careful to point out that despite their tender years they had not been sucked into the vortex of the rock 'n' roll mania. Of the 4.2% that gave favorable opinions, typical answers were: "It's better than sloppy love songs. I attend events in town because they are the only ones that swing and sometimes they have nice musicians in the group." Another reader said: "To me, good rhythm-and-blues is the heart of good jazz. I am talking about the records by the Negro artists; I somehow can't endure the attempts of white musicians to play good r and b." "Granted many of the lyrics are inane—but whoever said 'Sister Kate' is an intellectual song?"

Question No. 8 was: How about mambos and related Latin-American forms? The answers were: Like Latin-American music—26%; Don't like—27%; Qualified—47%.

Though the pros and cons were almost matched mathematically, the large bulk of qualified opinions seemed to express the true reaction of the average jazz fan, who apparently finds pleasure in this type of performance when the artist is Cal Tjader, George Shearing or some other personality already more closely associated with jazz than with Latin-American music. Some pointed out its utilitarian value (as a later question revealed, most jazz fans are occasional dancers). Some stressed the audience-participation possibilities: "Ben Pollack's Restaurant down on the Strip in Hollywood has bongo sessions twice a week. Sooner or later, besides the performers on stage, everybody pulls out a set of bongos and starts playing. I make it down there every time I can."

Question No. 9 was: Do you have any special feeling for or against West Coast jazz? This produced the following figures: Like West Coast jazz—39.6%; Don't like—12.9%; Qualified—14.7%; Noncommittal—32.8%.

The wording of this question tended to imply, perhaps misleadingly, that the writer acknowledged the existence of a West Coast school of jazz, even though the presence of such a phenomenon has frequently been disputed by many musicians and by this reporter. Many of the replies ran along lines similar to the following: "West Coast jazz is also played on the East Coast and in the Midwest. They are the same, and I like it." Some took the question flippantly with retorts such as "How do you feel about Mason City, Iowa, jazz?"

On the other hand a few readers indulged in a detailed analysis of what they believed to be the meaning of the term: "West Coast jazz, a doubtful title, is characterized by a more happy 'sound' than the so-called East Coast type. It seems to 'swing' in a different manner; there are noticeable indigenous 'blocks of improvised notes' in the solo choruses of Shorty Rogers, Chet Baker, Giuffre, Cooper, et al, which seem to identify them as members of the Pacific Coast School . . . These 'blocks of notes' I mention are not hackneyed but, I feel, refreshing when used judiciously. . . . I will admit, however, that there is a tendency or compulsiveness on the part of many West Coast musicians to stick to a certain kind of arrangement and playing which is liable to assume habituated proportions in time and therefore give rise to adverse comments from music annotators, critics, etc."

Many of the fans, equivocal about West Coast jazz, carped at its esthetic approach—"At times these Californians tend to be more West Coast than they are jazz. Certain members of this school seem to display too much of an affinity for Bartok than Basie, sometimes losing the basic swing and funkiness in a search for 'sounds.' " "All the arrangements sound as though Shorty Rogers did them and all the altoists sound like Bud Shank. I could go on through all the other instruments, but why bother?"

Question No. 10 asked: How about your interest in dancing? (a) Expert dancer, (b) only dance occasionally, or (c) don't dance at all? The results of this question were: Expert dancer—3.9%; Only dance occasionally—60.9%; Don't dance at all—23.8%; Not expert but dance a lot—11.4%.

Obviously, dancing is not a serious consideration with most jazz fans. Typical answers were: "I dance occasionally at the Student Union which, excluding the Freshmen, blows the worst on wax every night." "Only when fortified by a stout Scotch or straight gin." From one saddened 36-year-old: "In the 1930s-40s 'a' (dance a lot); in 1950-51-52-53 'b' (only dance occasionally); in 1954-55-56, 'c' (don't dance at all)." Among the small minority of experts were such people as a gentleman in New Brunswick who said, "I am told I am a grand dancer, could dance seven nights a week. Give me the older tunes and a girl who likes ballroom dancing." And a lady in Monee, Ill. stated "I love to dance, but married a non-dancer; so I joined an interpretive dance class. . . ." (But she digs Art Tatum and Hank Jones.)

Question No. 11 was: Do you miss the dying 10-inch LP, or do you like to buy a whole 12-inch LP by one artist? This produced five categories of responses: Don't miss 10-inch LP—43.8%; Miss it—23.7%; Only play 45s— 1.5%; Qualified—15.1%; Noncommittal—15.9%.

Generally the fans seemed to feel that the 12-inch LP gave them better value in terms of minutes of music for each dollar invested. However, a number of recalcitrants qualified their answers by complaints about the monotony of too much continuous music by the same artist—"When I sit down to dig some records," complained Dick Sargis of Chicago, "I haven't got but an hour or two at a time. An LP takes 15 to 20 minutes and at that rate I could dig about three or four artists. With the 10-inch LP and the EPs you get a chance to hear a little from everyone." Another comment was, "I like variety in jazz, and on a limited budget it is extremely hard to get it by buying LPs exclusively." Generally speaking, though, jazz fans by 1956 appeared to have accepted as a *fait accompli* the virtual extinction of the 10-inch LP record.

Question No. 12 was: Do you believe you tend to buy an LP with an attractive cover, or don't you care? The results were: Don't care—53.1%; Prefer attractive cover—21.1%; Prefer but not influenced to buy—25.8%.

"If I bought for the covers, I'd probably own 90% of all the LPs released by Norman Granz," remarked Audrey Edwards of Bermuda. The general feeling here seemed to be that even if the potential purchaser's attention is drawn to an album with a more attractive cover it is unlikely that his decision to buy will be ultimately influenced by it. At least 100 of the respondents resorted to the "You can't judge a book by its cover" cliché.

Question No. 13 was: Do you believe you tend to buy an LP with detailed liner notes, or don't you care? Here the proportions differed slightly from those in Question No. 12: Liner notes helpful—39.9%; Helpful but can do without them—35.7%; Helpful but sometimes too wordy—6.6%; Don't care—17.8%.

A number of readers singled out certain companies for special mention: Columbia was praised by 6.3% for George Avakian's detailed liner notes, while Contemporary liners were applauded by 1.8%. Another 3.3% had harsh words for the alleged inadequacy of the information on Clef and Norgran records; RCA Victor came in for criticism from 2.4%. Some of the most amusing answers to this question were from the dissident 6.6% who objected to the verbosity of some liner notes. George E. Scott of Hartford City, Indiana wrote: "Although I buy first and always for the artist and the material, I have developed an aversion to long liner notes praising the recording artist, expounding the superiority of Brooks Brothers' clothes, or especially those that are catalogues of the label's other LPs." Another reader said, "If I wanted liner notes I would collect books instead of records."

Question No. 14 was: Which record labels do you find easiest to get in your vicinity? This produced the following figures: All labels easy to get—23.4%; All major labels—16.8%. Specific labels mentioned: Columbia—21.3%; RCA Victor—18.3%; Capitol—16.0%; Mercury (EmArcy)—12.8%; Decca—8.7%.

The fact that it was the independent labels that started to bring recorded jazz along the road to wider acceptance has not apparently prevented the major labels from cashing in heavily on their superior distribution, despite the tardiness of their big-scale entry into the field. Of the independent labels specifically mentioned as easy to obtain, none came near the five major labels mentioned above with the exception of Clef and Norgran, which had a combined total of 7%.

The other side of this picture was revealed in Question No. 15: Which records are hardest to find in your vicinity? The following figures are based on percentages of total mentions: Prestige—10.6%; Blue Note—10.0%; Savoy —8.6%; Bethlehem—8.2%; Clef and Norgran—6.5%; Pacific Jazz—

5.6%; Debut—5.0%; Roost—4.8%; Riverside—4.4%; Mercury (EmArcy) —4.2%.

These figures are, in a sense, a credit to the companies mentioned to the extent that they indicate fans' desire to obtain records on these labels. Other companies may have poorer distribution but are not listed above because very few of the readers were concerned with trying to find their products (similarly, such major labels as Coral and MGM, because they make so few jazz records, were not listed among the "easiest to get" in Question No. 14, despite their excellent distribution).

Answers to the last four questions (12, 13, 14, 15) were modified to some extent by the number of readers who buy their jazz records by mail and are therefore unaffected by attractive or unattractive covers, presence or lack of liner notes, and availability of specific labels.

The next question, No. 16, was: Do you subscribe to a jazz mail order record company? (See figure 5.) A few fans misinterpreted this to refer to record shops that supply through the mail. What was meant, of course, was the recently instituted "record club" system by which fans are offered monthly selections on a specific label designed exclusively for mail order business.

The first company to institute this method of jazz selling, the Jazztone Society, evidently had made a tremendous impact by the time the poll was conducted, since more than one-fourth of the respondents were members. Most of them expressed great satisfaction with the variety and quality of the Jazztone releases, though a number complained about the recording quality, the material of the records and envelopes, and particularly about the long wait between ordering and receiving the records they wanted. The Columbia Record Club, the only one of the three jazz mail order clubs directly connected with an already established label, showed signs of having made healthy inroads on this large potential market, while American Record Society, which had been instituted only a couple of months before this inquiry began, seemed likely to enjoy a similar success with its vast availability of material rented from the Norman Granz catalogues.

The general reaction among the 56% who were not subscribers to jazz mail order clubs was that they preferred to make their own selections rather than be forced to choose from a limited supply of records on one label only.

Figure 5. Do you subscribe to a jazz mail-order record company?

IIIIIIIIIIIIIIIIIIIIIIIIIIIIIIIIIIIIIIIIIIIIIIIIIIIIIIIIII No 56%

IIIIIIIIIIIIIIIIIIIIIIIIII Yes, Jazztone 25.3%

IIIIIIIIIIIIIII Yes, Columbia 15.7%

IIII Did but dropped 4%

III Yes, American Record Society 3.3%

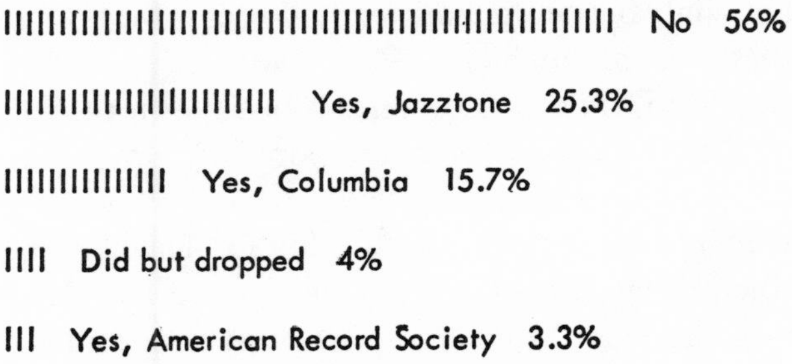

Question No. 17 was: Do you concern yourself much with hi-fi recording qualities, or do you tend to buy strictly for the musical values? The figures here were: Buy for musical values only—61.3%; Interested in hi-fi—8.4%; Qualified—27.3%; Noncommittal—3.0%.

This showed a slight increase in hi-fi interest over the figures two years earlier, when a similar question produced only 5% who tended to hi-fi specialization. Many of the letters pointed out that they would prefer an inferior recording of superior music to perfect recording of a less valuable performance—"You get a hi-fi effect by cupping your hands behind your ears in front of the speaker on any old Edison Gramophone," commented Lt. Robert C. Kriebel of Ft. McPherson, Ga.

Question No. 18 was: To what extent do disc jockeys influence your purchase of records—(a) very much, (b) slightly, (c) not at all? The proportions were as follows: Disc jockeys help considerably—13.3%; Help slightly—40.0%; Not at all—46.7%.

Evidently the inundation of the radio stations with jazz releases had forced the disc jockeys to consider jazz more frequently for inclusion in their programs, for the percentages were more favorable than in a 1954 poll, when 60% claimed that the D Js were little or no help. One reader in Miami reported a typical situation: "He advertises that every fourth record played is a jazz record," which, the reader commented, is a sort of reward for listening to the Cadillacs, the Platters and the other rhythm-and-blues groups that make up the rest of the program. Undoubtedly these figures will continue to change slowly and surely in favor of jazz.

Question No. 19 was: Which disc jockey do you think has done the most for jazz in the past year? (See figure 6.) The results constituted a remarkable tribute to the power and popularity of Al "Jazzbo" Collins, for whom votes came from all parts of the United States on the strength of his participation in a show called *Monitor* on the NBC network, to which he contributed frequent jazz moments during 1955 and 1956. In view of the distribution of the answers, which came from almost every state in the Union, the figure of 6.2% for listeners to Dick Martin in New Orleans is no less impressive. The tastes and beliefs of Collins and Martin are discussed elsewhere in the *Yearbook*.

Steve Allen can be particularly proud of the tribute to him reported in these figures, since those who voted for him must have been aware that actually he has not been a disc jockey for many years. Evidently his supporters were so conscious of the contribution he had made through the frequent live appearances of jazz guests on his nightly NBC network television program that they felt he was entitled to consideration on this basis; as a result, he tied for third place with Bob Garrity, conductor of the popular nightly "Birdland" show in New York.

The statistics also reflect great credit on "Daddy-O" Daylie, who virtually monopolized all the voting from Chicago, and on Mitch Reed, who, although he had been off the New York airwaves for several months at the time of the poll, was still missed by a number of listeners.

Figure 6.   Which disc jockey do you think has done the most for jazz in the past year?

Al "Jazzbo" Collins, NBC, New York   19.2%

IIIIIIIIIIIIIIIIIIIIIIIIIIIIIIIIIIIIIIIIIIIIIIIIIIIIIIIIIIIIIIIIIIIIIIIIIIIIIIIIIIIIIIIIIIIIIIIII

IIIIIIIIIIIIIIIIIIIIIIIIIIIIIII   Dick Martin, WWL, New Orleans, La.   6.2%

IIIIIIIIIIIIIIIIIIIIIIIIIII   Bob Garrity, WINS, New York   5.3%

IIIIIIIIIIIIIIIIIIIIIIIIII   Steve Allen, NBC, New York   5.3%

IIIIIIIIIIIIIIIIIIIIIII   Daddy-O Daylie, WJJD, Chicago   4.6%

IIIIIIIIIIIIIIIII   Willis Conover, Voice of America; WEAM, Arlington, Va.   3.3%

IIIIIIIIIIIIIII   Dick McDougal, CJBC, Toronto, Can.   3.3%

IIIIIIIIIIIIII   John McLellan, WHDH, Boston   2.9%

IIIIIIIIIIIII   Sleepy Stein, KFOX, Long Beach, Calif.   2.4%

IIIIIIIIIIII   Mitch Reed   2.2%

IIIIIIIIIII   Bob Raiford, WBT, Charlotte, N.C.   2.2%

IIIIIIIIII   Pat Henry, KROW, Oakland, Calif.   2.0%

IIIIIIIII   Jim Dunbar, CKLW, Windsor, Can.   1.8%

IIIIIIIII   Bill Williams, WNEW, New York   1.8%

IIIIIII   Symphony Sid Torin, WMBS, Boston   1.5%

IIIIIII   Gene Norman, KLAC, Hollywood, Calif.   1.5%

IIIIIII   Phil MacKellar, CKFH, Toronto, Can.   1.5%

IIIIIII   Bob Martin, WCOP, Boston   1.5%

IIIIIII   Tom Brown, WHK, Cleveland, Ohio   1.5%

IIIIIII   Harvey Husten, WKDN, Camden, N.J.   1.5%

Question No. 20 was: Which record company do you think has done the most for jazz in the past year? (See figure 7.) This was a very close race. Up to the last moment before the analysis of the mail was completed, it was uncertain whether Columbia or EmArcy would end in first place. Most of those who voted for Columbia paid tribute to the work of George Avakian in presenting such artists as Louis Armstrong, Dave Brubeck, Eddie Condon, and Kai and Jay, while those who voted for EmArcy (a subsidiary of Mercury) were in most cases unaware of a similar role played by Bob Shad, who remained very much in the background, though it was well known in trade circles that he was responsible for launching this jazz label and for the recording of such stars as Gerry Mulligan, Dinah Washington, Brown & Roach, Sarah Vaughan, Terry Gibbs, Cannonball and many others.

Most of the votes for Capitol apparently came from admirers of the big bands, since this label had produced many successful LPs by Ellington, Herman, Kenton, James, Les Brown et al, while its combo jazz releases (the "Kenton Presents" series) had been less successful and were dropped in late 1955. The high percentage of votes for Bethlehem is even more impressive in view of the fact that only 4% of the voters had singled out this label as easy to obtain, while more than twice as many found it generally hard to get.

Figure 7. **Which record company do you think has done the most for jazz in the past year?**

|||||||||||||||||||||||||||||||||||||||||||||||||||||||||||||||||| Columbia 13%

|||||||||||||||||||||||||||||||||||||||||||||||||||||||||||||| EmArcy 12.2%

|||||||||||||||||||||||||||||||||||||||||||||||||||||| Capitol 10.3%

||||||||||||||||||||||||||||||||||||||||||||||||| Bethlehem 9.8%

|||||||||||||||||||||||||||||||||| Pacific Jazz 7%

||||||||||||||||||||||||||||||||| Savoy 6.7%

||||||||||||||||||||||||||||||| Clef 6.4%

|||||||||||||||||||||||||| Prestige 5.5%

||||||||||||||||||||||||| Norgran 5.3%

|||||||||||||||| Blue Note 3.3%

|||||||||||||||| Contemporary 3.3%

|||||||||||| Victor 2.9%

|||||||||| Jazztone 2.3%

||||||| Vanguard 1.7%

In sum, the answers to the 20 questions tacitly provided a massive response to an imaginary 21st: "Do you like to write letters about jazz?" If the verbose and voluminous response to this inquiry is any yardstick, the answer was a resounding and enthusiastic "yes."

THE DISC JOCKEYS

In the 1920s and early '30s jazz received virtually no assistance from the radio industry. The esoterica of Louis Armstrong, Bix Beiderbecke and their contemporaries were virtually strangers to radio audiences; only through remote pickups from night clubs and dance halls, such as Duke Ellington's broadcasts from the Cotton Club, was there any wide dissemination of America's most important growing musical form.

During the swing era the situation improved perceptibly. Benny Goodman's participation in a sponsored series by the National Biscuit Company was followed by frequent regular airings of the bands of Artie Shaw, the Dorsey Brothers and Glenn Miller. The Negro bands, almost completely neglected by sponsors whose fear of antagonizing the southern white market was their governing emotion, found regular outlets on sustaining broadcasts, notably from the Savoy Ballroom in Harlem.

It was during this era that a new phenomenon emerged in the radio world, a species of personality which came to be known as the disc jockey (the name stemmed from a simple analogy: the records were his horses, the turntable was his racetrack). Al Jarvis and Martin Block, both pioneers of the *Make Believe Ballroom,* were quick to prove that a succession of baldly announced phonograph records had far less entertainment value than carefully planned programs in which the records were introduced with chatty, personal comments from the man behind the turntable. These pioneer disc jockeys immediately perceived that the fastest way to acquire mass audiences was to seek the lowest common denominator. Accordingly, their programming was based largely on *Hit Parade* psychology. They helped to build the public's top hit songs and the hit songs, in turn, helped to build the disc jockeys. Jazz, particularly in its more advanced small combo forms, got short shrift.

Not until the middle 1940s had radio reached the stage where it could afford to indulge itself in the luxury of such minority appeal programs as those of the disc jockeys' catering to the dedicated jazz fan. Time after time, announcers on small stations in remote areas who tried to slip in a jazz record now and then among the latest Tin Pan Alley outpourings would be reprimanded by the program director or even dismissed from their jobs. Little by little various stations came to realize that some of the minority groups were substantial enough to support products advertised on a record program in which Count Basie and Louis Armstrong replaced (or at least supplemented) such stars as Guy Lombardo and Perry Como.

Though today there are still many areas in which the jazz fans bemoan the comparative lack of good music on their local stations, the situation is far healthier than ever before, as can be deduced from the facts and figures detailed elsewhere in these pages in the chapter entitled *The Jazz Fan*. In order to give a clear picture of the impact of jazz-oriented disc jockeys on the contemporary radio scene, questionnaires were sent out by the author to several radio personalities in key cities, all of them men who have had the courage to feature jazz prominently in their programming. The disc jockeys who coöperated on this survey were: Al (Jazzbo) Collins of NBC in New York; Willis Conover of the Voice of America, who is also heard over WEAM in Arlington, Va. and Washington D.C.; Dick Martin of WWL in New Orleans; Bob Maxwell of WWJ in Detroit; John McLellan of WHDH in Boston; Jim Mendes of WICE, Providence; Gene Norman of KLAC in Hollywood; and Henry F. Whiston of CBM in Montreal, Canada.

Asked to name the bands featured most often on their broadcasts (and also to single out their own personal favorite), all the above jockeys mentioned Count Basie, Woody Herman, and Stan Kenton. Whiston, McLellan and Collins picked Basie as their favorite band; Martin and Conover named Herman. Conover named as his all-time favorite the Duke Ellington orchestra, which was mentioned by four of the jockeys on their "most played" list. Les Brown was named by five of the jockeys; Benny Goodman and Les Elgart were cited by two. Maxwell selected Buddy Morrow's band as his favorite. No personal favorites were selected by Collins or Mendes.

Answering a similar question concerning small combos, five of the jockeys (Whiston, McLellan, Martin, Collins, Conover) named the Modern Jazz Quartet; all of them picked this group as their personal favorite except Collins, whose vote went to Dave Brubeck. The latter group was included on six of the lists; the J. J. Johnson-Kai Winding quintet appeared on four and the George Shearing quintet on three.

All but Maxwell listed Ella Fitzgerald among the most played vocal artists, while Sarah Vaughan and Frank Sinatra each received five mentions; Carmen McRae and Chris Connor three apiece. Miss McRae is Whiston's favorite singer; McLellan selected Miss Fitzgerald; Dick Martin chose June Christy and Frank Sinatra. Collins and Conover also chose Sinatra as a personal favorite.

Five of the jockeys answered a question concerning their favorite instrumental soloist: Whiston voted for Lionel Hampton; McLellan and Conover for Charlie Parker; Collins for Benny Goodman; and Maxwell for Barbara Carroll.

In discussing the type of jazz preferred by themselves and by their listeners, the jockeys voted predominantly for modern jazz and indicated that their audiences were in agreement with this preference. However, Maxwell stated that he and his listeners liked the "gentle arranged" type of jazz; Mendes, though himself preferring the modern sounds, says that his listeners are equally enthusiastic about both Dixieland and modern jazz. Whiston prefers what he calls the Ruby Braff-Ben Webster school and adds: "75% of my listeners prefer modern jazz by Lester Young, Art Blakey, Milt Jackson, and Dave Brubeck. The rest are divided between Lionel Hampton's exhibitionistic style and the Dixielanders." Al Collins stated that he and his listeners prefer ballads and slow-tempo modern jazz in both combo and orchestral form.

The jockeys were asked what changes they have observed in listeners' tastes in recent years. Maxwell and Mendes have observed a significant revival of interest in big band jazz. Maxwell, hailing the return to swing, says "I personally ignore rock 'n' roll." Norman and Martin have both observed a strong increase in the interest in modern sounds, despite the general public's apparent interest in rock 'n' roll. "Requests for the honkers that made a bid for popularity in the '40s are now missing, thank goodness," says Martin, "and have been supplanted by requests for things involving well-arranged charts with well-played solos." Collins feels that there has not been much material change in tastes, which, he believes, are still generally on a simple level despite the increased interest in jazz.

A dual question next asked of the jockeys was "What changes do you feel you have personally effected in your listeners' tastes; what artists do you feel you have personally helped to 'make' through your broadcasts?" Following are excerpts from the answers:

Al Collins: "I have been trying to suggest that there be no snobbery in music. There are tasty things in every classification. I also am of the opinion the word 'jazz' in itself is a detriment to jazz, and that if you call it something else, like tasty music or whatever, you will have more acceptance. I feel that I have helped Brubeck, Mat Mathews, Herbie Mann, Carmen McRae, Urbie Green, Larry Sonn's orchestra, Art Van Damme."

Conover: "I hope I have contributed to the growing maturity, musical tolerance, eclecticism; a return to the beat; less inter-school antagonism; just a little less ignorance and malice among the anti-jazz element. Artists I've personally helped to 'make'—'The' Orchestra of Washington, D.C. . . . I feel I was responsible for Atlantic's signing of Ruth Brown."

Martin: "By bypassing much that is trite on the musical market it has been possible to maintain a format of sound that the listeners can depend on hearing for an hour and forty-five minutes daily . . . I wouldn't venture a guess as to what artists I have helped to 'make' . . ."

Maxwell, who mixes a great deal of popular music with his jazz, singles out Carmen McRae, Tennessee Ernie Ford, Harry Belafonte, Somethin' Smith.

Mendes says: "I expanded my listeners' horizons, by exposing them to a variety of music, with the emphasis on simplicity. Audience more aware of the following: Billy Taylor, Terry Gibbs, Chet Baker, and Gerry Mulligan."

John McLellan: "I hope that I have been able to improve some people's taste in music; by being exposed to a better product they probably become dissatisfied with an inferior product . . . I believe . . . I have materially helped Teddi King . . . Dave Brubeck, the Modern Jazz Quartet, Johnny Smith."

Gene Norman: "I have tried to expose my listeners to as much modern jazz as possible. Artists I have consistently featured most are Stan Kenton, Gerry Mulligan, Shorty Rogers, June Christy, and Woody Herman."

Whiston: "I feel, through my policy of always featuring *all* styles of jazz, limiting choice only by time and quality, I have shown more people in this area that there is a great deal of credit due in each general field of jazz. There is far too much bias shown among jazz fans who form a clique. This 'clique' attitude often causes those within it to criticize unfairly all those outside it. Tolerance is a big aim, a big objective, and not a thing that can be achieved overnight or by words alone. The jazz fan must be literally shown. Artist helped most: Modern Jazz Quartet."

The jockeys are optimistic about the possibility of jazz. Collins writes, "It is too vital an art form to die or decline; we become enriched as each era appears and then fades; the contributions of each will remain as part of the growth of jazz."

Conover: "Potential popularity of jazz: What determines 'popularity'? Listening? Buying records? Attending concerts and jazz clubs? Some listeners continue to enjoy their *favorites* as much as ever (for example, the late 1930s' Benny Goodman fans today), but can't enjoy anything which progresses beyond that point. Then there are listeners whose interest is superficial, having been developed *for* them by publicity experts, or having gone along with the gang to shout 'Saints!' at 'Dixieland' combos or 'Moon!' at 'boppers'; these will mature and advance, or drop out. One problem is keeping up with developments in all directions—forwards, backwards, and sideways. If you leave it for a few months, it's gone elsewhere by the time you return, and you're lost. A possible overall view: there's always a decline after a period of popularity (like now); but there's always another growth of interest in another decade; *and the next peak of interest is always higher and broader than the previous one.*"

Whiston: "The appreciation and toleration of jazz may reach into the psychological field even deeper than classical music, due to the importance of the musician's being able to express his own emotions primarily."

Finally, the jockeys were asked to name their recommendations to the artists or the record companies for maintaining or increasing the popularity of jazz. The chief recommendations here were that cultism should be avoided, along with the flooding of the record market with too many mediocre releases.

"Let the jazz critics be more charitable to artists," Al Collins advises.

"There are too many schools of thought being advanced and argued when all it amounts to is personal choice. Fact is not involved in taste. I feel the need in the jazz world for more charity and respect for others. Let us all enjoy all the music we can."

Martin: "What a shameful waste of talent it is when good artists are given inferior material to record."

Whiston: "Don't make so many LPs by the same artists . . . there are far too many records for any jazz jockey to cover fairly and effectively, let alone the poor record buyer, who is snowed under."

Willis Conover has the following recommendations: "To the artists: Make it while you can, but put some away for the drought. Recognize the equal pitfalls of being-narrow-but-deep and being-broad-but-shallow. Listen to the critics, but don't let them upset you; believe in yourself. Learn to speak English; 'hip' talk, even when it makes sense within the circle, can embarrass friends and further alienate the 'enemies' of jazz. At the same time, don't be afraid of showmanship; but keep it tasteful. Be dependable; be on time—if you're doing a disc jockey interview, don't make him sweat, wondering if you'll show; he has problems with the station manager already; if you're hired to blow, get to the stand when you're due: otherwise it isn't a gig, it's a ball, and look at it that way when the money is short. Particularly when you go overseas, you are America's best ambassadors; and drunkenness, junkiness, and rowdiness come close to treason. Be willing to think, feel, plan, and struggle—without self-pity. If you ignore all this, and make good records, I'll play them anyway."

"MUSICIANS' MUSICIANS" POLL

*I*t has always been the view of this writer that nobody is more entitled or better qualified to judge the artistic contribution of jazzmen, to assess the relative merits of the leading performers' esthetic impact, than the musician himself. Unfortunately the musician, not having constant access to the printed page, has had only intermittent opportunities to make his views known to the public.

Ten years ago, in the 1946 All American Jazz Poll conducted by the author for *Esquire,* a system was instituted of letting the previous poll-winning musicians themselves select the candidates for the "new star" division of the voting. The results proved significant: it was through this system that Charlie Parker, Sarah Vaughan and many others won their first polls. This offered them a form of recognition not afforded until several years later, in many cases, by the "public opinion" polls conducted in the music magazines.

In the Spring of 1956 it was decided to extend this system, using the medium of *The Encyclopedia Yearbook of Jazz,* by giving the musicians their first concerted chance to name not merely their selections for new stars, but also their all-time preferences.

Ballots were distributed among 120 leading musicians whose names were drawn principally from the lists of winners in numerous *Down Beat, Metronome* and *Esquire* polls. Also included were several musicians who have been active as critics, such as John Mehegan, Bill Russo and Billy Taylor. One hundred and one musicians responded by mailing back their ballots, or by naming their selections in personal interviews.

The musicians were given considerable latitude in the method of voting. Though nominally their selections were to list the "greatest ever" in each category, many of them qualified their selections, either by adding comments (see below) or by making more than one choice in some categories (Miles Davis extended this privilege to the inclusion of no less than ten trumpet selections, including three "new star" choices). They were asked to leave a blank space wherever they felt it impossible to make a selection. In many cases, because they felt they had not had an adequate chance to hear all the younger talents, they made few, if any, selections in the "new star" half of the ballot.

Although the musicians had the presidential privilege of voting for themselves, very few availed themselves of this option. In the few cases in which they did, the poll results were in no way affected.

Following are the names of the voters: (The asterisks (*) denote that these musicians voted in the poll but are not listed in the tabulations, because they requested that their votes be kept confidential.)

Louis Armstrong, Georgie Auld

Chet Baker, Count Basie, Billy Bauer*, Sidney Bechet*, Louis Bellson*, Ruby Braff, Bob Brookmeyer, Clifford Brown, Lawrence Brown, Ray Brown*, Ralph Burns

Harry Carney, Benny Carter, Conte Candoli, Teddy Charles, Buck Clayton, Jimmy Cleveland, Al Cohn, Nat King Cole, Eddie Condon, Bob Cooper

Johnny Dankworth, Miles Davis, Buddy De Franco, Jimmy Dorsey, Tommy Dorsey

Roy Eldridge*, Duke Ellington, Don Elliott, Herb Ellis

Tal Farlow, Maynard Ferguson, Ella Fitzgerald*, Bud Freeman

Erroll Garner, Herb Geller, Stan Getz, Terry Gibbs, John "Dizzy" Gillespie, Jimmy Giuffre*, Benny Goodman, John Graas, Urbie Green

Bobby Hackett, Chico Hamilton, Bill Harris, Coleman Hawkins*, Percy Heath, Neal Hefti, Woody Herman, Johnny Hodges, Bill Holman

Milt Jackson, Osie Johnson, Jay Jay Johnson, Quincy Jones

Lee Konitz, Gene Krupa*

Stan Levey

Shelly Manne*, Jimmy McPartland, Marian McPartland*, Carmen McRae, Johnny Mehegan, Red Mitchell, Sam Most*, Gerry Mulligan

Lennie Niehaus*, Red Norvo*

Sy Oliver

Oscar Peterson, Oscar Pettiford, Flip Phillips*, Bud Powell, André Previn

Jimmy Raney, Max Roach, Howard Roberts, Frank Rosolino, Pete Rugolo, Bill Russo

Tony Scott*, Bud Shank, Charlie Shavers, George Shearing, Horace Silver, Sonny Stitt

Billy Taylor, Cal Tjader, Lennie Tristano

Charlie Ventura

George Wallington, Frank Wess, Randy Weston, Ernie Wilkins, Cootie Williams, Teddy Wilson, Kai Winding

Lester Young

MUSICIANS' CHOICES FOR "GREATEST EVER"
(those with under four votes are not listed)

Trumpet:
DIZZY GILLESPIE—45, Louis Armstrong—39, Roy Eldridge—19, Miles Davis—14, Bunny Berigan—5, Bobby Hackett—5, Fats Navarro—5, Harry Edison—4, Harry James—4

Trombone:
JAY JAY JOHNSON—30, Bill Harris—29, Jack Teagarden—20, * Bob Brookmeyer—8, Tommy Dorsey—7, Lawrence Brown—6, Jack Jenney—6, Vic Dickenson—5, Kai Winding—5, Trummy Young—5, Jimmy Harrison—4, Frank Rosolino—4, Earl Swope—4
  (* includes votes in miscellaneous instrument category, valve trombone)

Alto sax:
CHARLIE PARKER—76, Johnny Hodges—17, Benny Carter—14, Lee Konitz—6

Tenor sax:
LESTER YOUNG—52, Coleman Hawkins—34, Stan Getz—17, Ben Webster—10, Bud Freeman—5, Chu Berry—4, Al Cohn—4, Sonny Rollins—4, Zoot Sims—4

Baritone sax:
HARRY CARNEY—58, Gerry Mulligan—21, Bob Gordon—8, Ernie Caceres—5, Serge Chaloff—5, Cecil Payne—4

Clarinet:
BENNY GOODMAN—65, Buddy De Franco—20, Artie Shaw—12

Flute:
FRANK WESS—22, Herbie Mann—5, Bud Shank—5

Vibes:
MILT JACKSON—49, Lionel Hampton—41, * Red Norvo—10, Terry Gibbs—9
  (* includes one vote on xylophone)

Piano:
ART TATUM—68, Bud Powell—21, Teddy Wilson—10, Count Basie—7, Earl Hines—6, Erroll Garner—5, Oscar Peterson—4

Guitar:
CHARLIE CHRISTIAN—63, Tal Farlow—10, Freddie Greene—8, Barney Kessel—8, Django Reinhardt—5, Johnny Smith—5

Bass:
JIMMY BLANTON—43, Oscar Pettiford—28, Ray Brown—26, Milt Hinton—10, Red Mitchell—6, George Duvivier—5

Drums:
MAX ROACH—28, Buddy Rich—18, Jo Jones—17, Sid Catlett—12, Dave Tough—12, Chick Webb—9, Louis Bellson—8, Art Blakey—8, Kenny Clarke—8, Shelly Manne—8, Gene Krupa—5

Miscellaneous Instrument:
In this category, partly because of the wide variety of instruments available for consideration and partly because of the voters' reluctance to tackle the problem, the voting was so diffuse that the result has to be declared no contest.

Male Singer:
FRANK SINATRA—56, Nat Cole—13, Billy Eckstine—11, Louis Armstrong—9, Bing Crosby—7, Al Hibbler—5, Perry Como—4, Jimmy Rushing—4

Female Singer:
ELLA FITZGERALD—66, Billie Holiday—23, Sarah Vaughan—21

Arranger:
DUKE ELLINGTON—27, Fletcher Henderson—11, Ralph Burns—10, Billy Strayhorn—8, John Lewis—6, Gil Evans—5, Johnny Mandel—5, Gerry Mulligan—5, Jimmy Mundy—5, Bill Finegan—4, Eddie Sauter—4

Big Band:
COUNT BASIE—62, Duke Ellington—42, Woody Herman—9, Benny Goodman—7, Jimmie Lunceford—5

Combo:
BENNY GOODMAN—24, Gillespie-Parker—22, Modern Jazz Quartet—14, Miles Davis—8, Gerry Mulligan—7, John Kirby—6, Parker-Davis—4, Oscar Peterson—4

MUSICIANS' CHOICES FOR NEW STARS (those with under four are not listed)

Trumpet:
CLIFFORD BROWN—25, Donald Byrd—8, Miles Davis—8, Ruby Braff—4, Conte Candoli—4, Joe Newman—4

Trombone:
JIMMY CLEVELAND—20, * Bob Brookmeyer—14, Jay Jay Johnson—10, Frank Rosolino—7, Urbie Green—6, Carl Fontana—4
(* includes votes in miscellaneous instrument category, valve trombone)

Alto sax:
JULIAN "CANNONBALL" ADDERLEY—11, Phil Woods—11, Charlie Mariano—10, Paul Desmond—5, Sonny Stitt—5, Davey Schildkraut—5, Lee Konitz—4

Tenor sax:
STAN GETZ—14, Bill Perkins—13, Sonny Rollins—11, Al Cohn—6, Seldon Powell—4, Zoot Sims—4, Sonny Stitt—4

Baritone sax:
GERRY MULLIGAN—11, Bob Gordon—6, Lars Gullin—4, Cecil Payne—4

Clarinet:
TONY SCOTT—15, Jimmy Giuffre—14, Buddy De Franco—8

Flute:
FRANK WESS—8, Herbie Mann—5, Jerome Richardson—5, Buddy Collette—4

Vibes:
MILT JACKSON—10, Cal Tjader—7, Victor Feldman—4, Terry Gibbs—4

Piano:
HORACE SILVER—13, Hampton Hawes—8, Dave McKenna—6, Pete Jolly—5, Hank Jones—5, Oscar Peterson—4

Guitar:
TAL FARLOW—12, Jimmy Raney—10, Herb Ellis—6, Johnny Smith—4

Bass:
PAUL CHAMBERS—22, Red Mitchell—12, Ray Brown—4, Leroy Vinnegar—4

Drums and Miscellaneous Instrument:
No contest; too few votes cast in these categories.

Male Singer:
JOE WILLIAMS—34

Female Singer:
CARMEN MC RAE—25, Helen Merrill—5, Chris Connor—4

Arranger:
QUINCY JONES—14, Bill Holman—8, Ernie Wilkins—7, Jimmy Giuffre—5, Al Cohn—4, Johnny Mandel—4

Big Band:
COUNT BASIE—20, Woody Herman—5

Combo:
JAZZ MESSENGERS—12, Modern Jazz Quartet—10, Chico Hamilton—6, Clifford Brown-Max Roach—5

VOTER	TRUMPET	TROM-BONE	ALTO SAX	TENOR SAX	BARI-TONE SAX	CLARI-NET	FLUTE	VIBRA-PHONE
LOUIS ARMSTRONG	Berigan Hackett †Braff	Teagarden Young	J.Dorsey B.Carter	E.Miller	Caceres Carney			Hampton Norvo
GEORGIE AULD	Armstrong †Linn	Teagarden †Rosolino	Parker †Geller	Hawkins †Perkins	Carney †B.Gordon	Goodman †Giuffre	†Shank	M.Jackson
CHET BAKER	M.Davis †J.Gordon	Brookmeyer	Parker †McLean †Geller	Sims †Perkins	Mulligan †Cameron	Goodman	†Jaspar	M.Jackson †Tjader
COUNT BASIE	Armstrong	Harrison	Hodges	Hawkins	Carney	Goodman DeFranco	Wess †Wess	Hampton
RUBY BRAFF	Armstrong †J. New-man	Dickenson L.Brown	Hodges Parker	Freeman L.Young †Margolis	Caceres	P.Russell		Hampton
BOB BROOKMEYER	Armstrong	Teagarden B.Harris †Swope †JJ John-son	Parker †Konitz	L.Young †Cohn †Sims	Mulligan Carney	P.Russell Goodman E.Hall		
CLIFFORD BROWN	Gillespie	JJ John-son †Cleveland	Parker	L.Young †Rollins	Carney Payne			Jackson
LAWRENCE BROWN	Armstrong	T.Dorsey †U.Green		Hawkins	Carney	Goodman		Hampton
RALPH BURNS	Armstrong †D.Collins	Jenney	Parker †Schild-kraut	L.Young †Perkins	Carney	Goodman	Mann †Mann	Jackson
HARRY CARNEY	Armstrong †C.Brown	L.Brown †Sanders	Hodges	Hawkins		Goodman †Hamilton	Esy Morales †Wess	Hampton

PIANO	GUITAR	BASS	DRUMS	MISC. INSTRU.	MALE SINGER	FEMALE SINGER	ARRANGER	BIG BAND	COMBO
Kyle	F.Smith	Hinton Shaw	Cole Deems		Bing Crosby	Fitzgerald †Joni James		Basie	Tatum Trio
Basie †Drew	Christian †Kessel	Blanton †Comfort	Kahn †Payne		Sinatra †Andy Williams	Fitzgerald †Pat Kirby	B.May †B.May	Basie †Basie	Goodman †Mod. Jazz Qrt.
Monk †Twardzik	Farlow †Rene Thomas	R.Mitchell †Chambers	Roach †Littman	C.Touff (b.tpt.)	Sinatra	Holiday	Mulligan †Bob Zieff	Basie	Mod.Jazz Qrt. Brown- Roach †C.Hamilton
Tatum †Newborn	Greene	Blanton †E.Jones		B.Davis Doggett (org.)	Eckstine J.Williams	Fitzgerald Vaughan †McRae	Ellington †E.Wilkins †F.Wess †F.Foster †N.Hefti	Ellington	Mod.Jazz Qrt. †Mod.Jazz Qrt.
Sullivan Wilson Hines Basie Garner M.Powell	Reinhardt F.Greene	Blanton W.Page †J.Woode	Jo Jones Catlett Tough	E.South R.Nance (vlns.)	Armstrong Bing Crosby	Fitzgerald Holiday Wiley B.Smith	Ellington	Ellington Basie	
Basie Ellington Morton Tatum	Christian †Raney	Blanton †R.Mitch-ell	Catlett †G.Johnson		Rushing	Holiday	Ellington Strayhorn J.Mundy B.Harding F.Henderson †Mulligan †A.Cohn †G.Evans	Ellington Basie	Kansas City 6 Ellington †Mulligan †Mod.Jazz Qrt.
Tatum B.Powell †Dennard	Christian	Pettiford †Chambers	Roach †E.Jones	J.Watkins (Fr.h.)	Eckstine	Vaughan		Basie	Mod.Jazz Qrt.
Tatum	Segovia	Blanton	Bellson		Bing Crosby	Fitzgerald			
Tatum †Guaraldi	F.Greene	Blanton †Budwig	Bellson †Flores		Sinatra †J.Will-iams	Fitzgerald	Sauter †J.Mandel	Basie	M.Davis
Tatum	Christian	Blanton	Bellson †Woodyard		N.Cole	Fitzgerald †McRae	Strayhorn	Ellington	J.Kirby

†New Star Vote

VOTER	TRUMPET	TROM-BONE	ALTO SAX	TENOR SAX	BARI-TONE SAX	CLARI-NET	FLUTE	VIBRA-PHONE
TEDDY CHARLES	Gillespie Eldridge †M.Davis †A.Farmer	JJ Johnson †Brook-meyer	Parker †P.Woods †H.Stein	Hawkins L.Young †Getz	Carney	Goodman †DeFranco †Giuffre		Hampton
CONTE CANDOLI	Gillespie †C.Brown	B.Harris †Brook-meyer	Parker †P.Woods	L.Young †A.Cohn	Carney †L.Gullin	Goodman	Shank Wess	T.Gibbs †V.Feldman
BENNY CARTER	†C.Brown	†C.Fon-tana	†C.Adder-ley			†T.Scott	†S.Most	
BUCK CLAYTON	Armstrong †C.Brown	Fred Becket †Green	Parker Hodges	Hawkins L.Young Getz †A.Cohn	Carney †C.Fowl-kes	Goodman Hassel-gard	Wess	Hampton
JIMMY CLEVELAND	Gillespie †C.Brown	JJ Johnson	Parker	L.Thomp-son	C.Payne	DeFranco	J.Richard-son	M.Jackson Hampton
AL COHN	Armstrong †Candoli	Teagarden Brookmeyer †E.Swope	Parker †Schild-kraut	L.Young †B.Perkins	B.Gordon	Goodman Shaw	Wess †J.Rich-ardson	M..Jackson †D.Elliott
NAT COLE	Armstrong †J.New-man	J.Jenney †H.Coker	W.Smith †Desmond	L.Young B.Webster †Wess	Carney †Mulligan	Goodman †DeFranco	H.Klee †Wess	M.Jackson
EDDIE CONDON	Armstrong	Teagarden	J.Dorsey	B.Freeman	Caceres	P.Hucko		Hampton
BOB COOPER			Parker			Goodman		
JOHNNY DANKWORTH	Beider-becke	Teagarden	Parker	L.Young	Mulligan	Goodman		Hampton
MILES DAVIS	Armstrong Eldridge Gillespie B.Hackett H.James C.Terry F.Webster †C.Brown †D.Byrd †K.Dorham	JJ Johnson B.Harris	Parker Konitz †C.Add-erley	L.Young S.Rollins †J.Colt-rane	Carney Mulligan	Goodman Shaw †T.Scott	Shank	Hampton M.Jackson

PIANO	GUITAR	BASS	DRUMS	MISC. INSTRU.	MALE SINGER	FEMALE SINGER	ARRANGER	BIG BAND	COMBO
Tatum †Monk	Christian †Raney †Farlow	Mingus †Joe DeWeese	Manne †K.Clarke	Norvo (xyl.)	J.Paris †Sinatra	Holiday †Merrill	Ellington Monk †Giuffre †G.Russell	Ellington †Basie	Gillespie-Parker Davis
B.Powell †L.Levy	Christian †J.Raney	Blanton †Chambers	Roach †J.Morello	B.Cooper (oboe)	Sinatra †J.Williams	Vaughan †McRae	R.Burns †B.Holman	Basie	Gillespie-Parker †C.Tjader
†H.Hawes	†Farlow	†C.Counce	†S.Payne	†J.Thielemans (harm.) †P.Jolly (acc.)	†J.Williams	†McRae	†E.Wilkins	†Basie	†C.Hamilton
T.Wilson Tatum †Sir C. Thompson	Christian †S.Jordan †Farlow	Blanton M.Hinton W.Page †E.Jones	Jo Jones B.Rich	D.Elliott (mello.)	Sinatra †J.Williams	Fitzgerald Vaughan †T.King †C.Connor	S.Oliver	Ellington Basie	Goodman †D.Elliott
B.Powell	Christian	Pettiford C.Mingus	Roach	M.Mathews (acc.)	Eckstine	Vaughan	Q.Jones G.Gryce	Basie	Brown-Roach
Tatum B.Powell †D. McKenna	Christian †J.Raney	Blanton †R.Mitchell	Jo Jones Roach †A.Mardigan	D.Elliott (mello.)	Armstrong Sinatra †J.Williams	Holiday †McRae	Ellington F.Henderson J.Mandel Strayhorn †M.Albam	Basie †Basie	Gillespie-Parker †Messengers
Tatum †Peterson	Christian †Kessel	Blanton †G.Duvivier	B.Rich †S.Payne	B.Davis (org.)	Sinatra †J.Williams	Fitzgerald †McRae	Nelson Riddle †N.Hefti	Ellington Basie †T.Heath	Shearing †Peterson 3
J.Bushkin	Christian	A.Hall	Tough		Armstrong Eckstine	Wiley Fitzgerald	F.Henderson	Basie	Goodman
	Christian							Basie	
Tatum	Reinhardt	Blanton			Sinatra	Fitzgerald	Ellington	Ellington	
Tatum B.Powell Gillespie †A.Jamal †R.Garland †Tom Flanagan †H.Jones	Christian	Pettiford R.Brown †P.Chambers	Blakey Roach †Philly J.Jones	R.Nance (vln.) †Jimmy Smith (org.)	Sinatra Hibbler †Bobby Short	McRae J.Southern	Strayhorn G.Evans †J.Lewis	Ellington †Sauter-Finegan	Mod.Jazz Qrt. †Messengers

†New Star Vote

VOTER	TRUMPET	TROM-BONE	ALTO SAX	TENOR SAX	BARI-TONE SAX	CLARI-NET	FLUTE	VIBRA-PHONE
BUDDY DE FRANCO	Navarro	B.Harris	Parker	Getz	Chaloff	DeFranco		M.Jackson
JIMMY DORSEY	Berigan	Teagarden	Parker	Hawkins	Chaloff	DeFranco	Wess	T.Gibbs
TOMMY DORSEY	Armstrong C.Shavers Berigan	Teagarden M.Mole †T.Turk	B.Carter J.Hodges J.Dorsey †J.Dumont	Hawkins B.Freeman †B.Richman	Carney	Goodman †De Franco	Wess	Hampton
DUKE ELLINGTON	Armstrong	T.Dorsey L.Brown	J.Hodges	Hawkins	Carney	Goodman		Norvo Hampton
DON ELLIOTT	H.James	T.Dorsey B.Harris †Rosolino †JJ John- son	Parker †Desmond †S.Stitt	Hawkins †McKus- ick †Getz	Ventura †Mulligan	Goodman †H.McKus- ick	†H.Mann	M.Jackson Hampton
HERB ELLIS	Gillespie	B.Harris †JJ John- son	Parker †S.Stitt	L.Young †Getz	Carney	Goodman †Giuffre		Hampton
TAL FARLOW	Gillespie †C.Brown	B.Harris †Brook- meyer	Parker †P.Woods	Getz †B.Perkins	B.Gordon	DeFranco †T.Scott	†Collette	Norvo †E.Costa
MAYNARD FERGUSON	M.Ferguson	Rosolino	Parker Konitz †Shank	Getz †B.Perkins	B.Gordon †B.Gordon			
BUD FREEMAN	Armstrong †R.Braff	Teagarden †U.Green	B.Carter J.Hodges	Hawkins L.Young †Getz	Carney Caceres	Goodman P.Russell	†H.Mann	
ERROLL GARNER	Armstrong Eldridge Gillespie C.Shavers	Dickenson B.Harris Rosolino T.Young	B.Carter	Hawkins B.Webster L.Young	Carney L.Parker Mulligan †Mulligan	Shaw	Wess	Hampton M.Jackson

PIANO	GUITAR	BASS	DRUMS	MISC. INSTRU.	MALE SINGER	FEMALE SINGER	ARRANGER	BIG BAND	COMBO
Tatum †Newborn †P.Jolly	Farlow	R.Brown R.Mitchell	Bobby White		D.Allyn	Fitzgerald	Mulligan	Basie	M.Davis
Tatum	Kessel	M.Hinton	Bellson	†D.Elliott (mello.)	Sinatra	Fitzgerald	E.Wilkins	Basie	Peterson 3
T.Wilson †E.Costa	E.Lang Christian	Safranski †E.Jones	Bellson †S.Payne	J.Venuti (vln.) †B.Davis (org.)	Sinatra †J.Williams	Fitzgerald †McRae	S.Oliver F.Comstock †E.Wilkins	Basie †Elgart	Goodman A.VanDamme
Tatum	Reinhardt	Blanton Pettiford	Bellson Krupa †S.Woodyard	R.Nance (vln.) O.Pettiford ('cello)	Sinatra Bing Crosby	Fitzgerald Vaughan L.Horne			
N.Cole Tatum †Peterson †B.Taylor	Christian †J.Puma	R.Brown Pettiford †E.Furtado †V.Burke	B.Rich Roach		Sinatra †Sinatra †M.Torme	Fitzgerald †Morgana King	F.Henderson †Q.Jones	Basie †Basie	Goodman
Peterson	Christian †Gray †Kessel	Blanton †R.Brown	Jo Jones B.Rich †Blakey	A.Van Damme (acc.) †Brookmeyer (v.trom.)	Sinatra	Fitzgerald †Toni Harper	A.Stordahl †J.Giuffre	Basie †Basie	Goodman
Tatum †P.Jolly	Christian †J.Hall †Ed Bickert	R.Mitchell R.Brown †M.Budwig †L.Vinnegar	Roach †Dick Scott	Thielemans (harm.)	Sinatra †J.Paris	Fitzgerald †C.Connor	B.Finegan †J.Montrose	Basie	Gillespie-Parker †Messengers
Peterson †L.Geller	Kessel †H.Ellis	R.Brown †Moe Edwards	S.Manne Roach †Flores		Sinatra Eckstine †J.Williams	Fitzgerald †Merrill	J.Mandel †B.Holman	Basie Kenton †M.Ferguson	Peterson 3
Tatum Waller	Christian †G.Barnes	M.Hinton B.Haggart	Tough Wettling †K.Kiffe	D.Elliott (mello.)	Bubbles Rushing	B.Smith E.Waters	F.Henderson †D.Cary	Ellington	Goodman
B.Powell Hines Tatum F.Waller M.L.Williams T.Wilson	Christian	R.Brown Blanton C.Mingus Pettiford R.Callender	Catlett Roach C.Webb	F.Waller (org.)	D.Haymes Bing Crosby Sinatra	Fitzgerald J.Richmond Stafford Vaughan Washington †S.Syms		Basie L.Brown Ellington W.Herman	A.Cobb Goodman

†New Star Vote

VOTER	TRUMPET	TROM-BONE	ALTO SAX	TENOR SAX	BARI-TONE SAX	CLARI-NET	FLUTE	VIBRA-PHONE
HERB GELLER	Gillespie Navarro †D.Byrd	JJ Johnson †J.Cleveland †Milt Gold	Parker †S.Stitt	S.Rollins †H.Mobley †S.Stitt		Goodman		M.Jackson
STAN GETZ	Gillespie M.Davis	Brookmeyer	Parker Schild-kraut	L.Young Z.Sims A.Cohn S.Stitt	Mulligan	Goodman		M.Jackson Hampton
TERRY GIBBS	Armstrong Eldridge Gillespie †C.Brown	B.Harris JJ Johnson †Brook-meyer	Parker	L.Young Getz A.Cohn †S.Stitt	Carney Chaloff Mulligan	Goodman DeFranco	Wess	M.Jackson Hampton †Tjader †Pollard
DIZZY GILLESPIE	Armstrong M.Davis Eldridge B.Hackett F.Webster †C.Brown	JJ Johnson †Rosolino	B.Carter J.Hodges Parker †P.Woods	C.Berry D.Byas Hawkins L.Young †B.Mitch-ell	Carney	Goodman Shaw	Wess	M.Jackson
BENNY GOODMAN	H.James	U.Green	H.Schertz-er	Getz				Hampton
JOHN GRAAS	Armstrong Berigan †R.Braff †M.Davis	†JJ John-son †Enevold-son	Parker †Konitz	L.Young †Getz	Mulligan †Mulligan	Goodman †DeFranco		Norvo †M.Jack-son
URBIE GREEN	Armstrong M.Davis Eldridge Butterfield Gillespie B.Hackett H.James Grady Lock †Fager-quist	Teagarden B.Harris J.Jenney JJ Johnson Winding E.Swope T.Young Al Green M.McEach-ern T.Dorsey	Hodges Parker	L.Young E.Miller Getz †A.Cohn †Z.Sims	Mulligan	Goodman Shaw Fazola Hamilton		M.Jackson
BOBBY HACKETT	Armstrong †R.Braff	Teagarden †Winding †JJ John-son	Parker	B.Freeman †Getz	Carney Caceres Mulligan	Goodman †DeFranco †P.Hucko		Hampton †T.Gibbs

PIANO	GUITAR	BASS	DRUMS	MISC. INSTRU.	MALE SINGER	FEMALE SINGER	ARRANGER	BIG BAND	COMBO
Tatum B.Powell †H.Silver	Christian	Blanton R.Brown †P.Chambers	K.Clarke †Philly J. Jones		Hibbler †J.Williams	Holiday †McRae †Merrill	G.Fuller J.Lewis B.May G.Russell †A.Cohn	Gillespie	Mod.Jazz Qrt. †Messengers
Tatum H.Jones L.Levy	Farlow J.Raney Ronnie Singer	R.Brown L.Vinnegar M.Hinton	Blakey T.Kahn R.Haynes		Sinatra	Fitzgerald	J.Lewis G.Evans	Basie	Mod.Jazz Qrt. Mulligan
Tatum †T.Pollard	Christian †Farlow †J.Smith	Pettiford †R.Brown	B.Rich Roach T.Kahn †J.Morello	D.Elliott (mello.) †Thielemans (harm.)	Sinatra †J.Williams †J.Paris	Fitzgerald †McRae	J.Mundy F.Henderson Ellington †N.Hefti †J.Mandel †A.Cohn †M.Albam	Basie	Gillespie-Parker Goodman †Getz
Tatum †O.Dennard	Christian Reinhardt †H.Ellis	Blanton R.Brown Pettiford †P.Chambers	Blakey Catlett K.Clarke B.Rich Roach †C.Persip	S.Smith (vln.) †J.Smith (org.)	N.Cole	Fitzgerald Holiday Vaughan Washington †McRae	†Q.Jones †E.Wilkins †M.Liston	Basie Ellington Lunceford	K.Cole 3 †Mod.Jazz Qrt.
T.Wilson M.Powell	J.Smith		D.Lamond		Sinatra	Fitzgerald	F.Henderson	F.Henderson	
Tatum B.Powell †H.Silver	†H.Roberts	†C.Counce †C.Mingus	†L.Bunker †S.Manne	†S.Rogers (flueg.)		Fitzgerald Holiday †Fitzgerald		Basie †Basie †S.Rogers	M.Davis †Mod.Jazz Qrt.
B.Powell Tatum T.Wilson †D.McKenna		Pettiford P.Heath M.Hinton †R.Mitchell			Armstrong Sinatra	Holiday		Basie	Gillespie-Parker
Tatum †H.Jones	L.Almeida †J.Smith	B.Haggart †A.Fishkin	Krupa †J.Morello	A.Van Damme (acc.) †D.Elliott (mello.)	Sinatra Armstrong †J.Williams	Wiley P.Lee Vaughan Fitzgerald †McRae	B.Haggart †Mulligan †Rugolo	Ellington Basie †Herman	Peterson 3 †Getz

†New Star Vote

VOTER	TRUMPET	TROM-BONE	ALTO SAX	TENOR SAX	BARI-TONE SAX	CLARI-NET	FLUTE	VIBRA-PHONE
CHICO HAMILTON			Parker				†Collette	
BILL HARRIS	Eldridge	J.Jenney	Parker	L.Young	Carney	Goodman		T.Gibbs †V.Feldman
PERCY HEATH	Gillespie †C.Brown	JJ Johnson	Parker †S.Stitt	Hawkins L.Young	†Mulligan	†T.Scott		Hampton M.Jackson
NEAL HEFTI	Butterfield †E.Royal	B.Harris †S.Russo	Parker Hodges †P.Woods	L.Young †S.Powell				
WOODY HERMAN	Armstrong †H.Edison	J.Jenney B.Harris †C.Fontana	Hodges †Desmond	H.Evans †R.Kamuca †B.Perkins	Carney †B.Gordon	Goodman DeFranco	Esy Morales †Wess	R.Norvo †V.Feldman
JOHNNY HODGES	Armstrong	L.Brown	W.Smith	Hawkins	Carney	Goodman		Hampton
BILL HOLMAN	Gillespie M.Davis	E.Swope †J.Cleveland	Parker †C.Mariano	L.Young †S.Rollins	B.Gordon †Giuffre	Goodman †Giuffre		M.Jackson
MILT JACKSON	Gillespie Eldridge †C.Brown	JJ Johnson	Parker S.Stitt	L.Young Hawkins †S.Rollins	Carney C.Payne	Shaw	Wess	
JAY JAY JOHNSON	Gillespie †M.Davis †C.Brown	Fred Becket †J.Cleveland	Parker B.Carter	L.Young Hawkins	Carney †Mulligan			M.Jackson
OSIE JOHNSON	Gillespie †A.Farmer	JJ Johnson †J.Cleveland	Parker †C.Adderley	Hawkins †S.Rollins	Carney †C.Payne	Goodman †T.Scott	Wess †H.Mann †J.Richardson	Hampton †M.Jackson
QUINCY JONES	Gillespie C.Brown †D.Byrd †Bill Hardman †T.Jones	JJ Johnson †J.Cleveland †U.Green	Parker †P.Woods †C.Adderley	L.Young †S.Rollins †S.Powell	†C.Payne	†Giuffre	Wess †H.Mann †Shank	M.Jackson †V.Feldman

PIANO	GUITAR	BASS	DRUMS	MISC. INSTRU.	MALE SINGER	FEMALE SINGER	ARRANGER	BIG BAND	COMBO
Tatum	Christian †J.Hall	G.Duvivier	Jo Jones					Basie	
Tatum	F.Greene	Pettiford R.Brown	Tough	C.Touff (b.tpt.)	Sinatra	Fitzgerald	R.Burns	Basie	Goodman
Tatum	Christian	Blanton †R.Brown †Pettiford	C.Webb Catlett †B.Rich †K.Clarke	Thielemans (harm.)	Sinatra	Fitzgerald	Ellington	Basie Ellington	Gillespie-Parker
†D.McKenna		Blanton †John Drew	Jo Jones D.Tough †S.Payne †G.Johnson		Sinatra P.Como N.Cole	F.Wayne	Ellington Strayhorn †Nelson Riddle	Ellington Basie	
Tatum †V.Guaraldi	C.Kress †Farlow	Blanton †M.Budwig	Razz Mitchell B.Rich	†C.Touff (b.tpt.)	R.McKenzie †Bob Manning	Fitzgerald †J.Southern	L.Hayton R.Burns †B.Holman	B.Pollack †Basie	J.Kirby †Mod.Jazz Qrt.
Tatum	Christian	Blanton	Bellson		P.Como	Fitzgerald	Ellington	Ellington	L.Jordan
E.Garner †H.Silver	Christian †J.Raney	R.Brown †L.Vinnegar	Catlett †Philly J.Jones		N.Cole †J.Williams	Fitzgerald	F.Henderson †J.Montrose	Basie †The Orchestra (Willis Conover)	Mulligan †M.Davis
Tatum B.Powell H.Jones	Christian	R.Brown Pettiford	Blakey K.Clarke		N.Cole †J.Williams	Fitzgerald Vaughan	J.Lewis T.Dameron †Q.Jones †E.Wilkins	Basie	Parker Gillespie Davis
Tatum B.Powell †H.Silver	Christian	Pettiford R.Brown †P.Chambers	Roach K.Clarke	†Brookmeyer (v.trom.)	N.Cole Sinatra	Fitzgerald Vaughan Holiday †McRae	†J.Lewis	Basie Lunceford	Gillespie-Parker Parker-Davis †Mod.Jazz Qrt.
Tatum †H.Jones	Christian †B.Galbraith	Blanton †P.Chambers	C.Webb †Philly J. Jones	Pettiford ('cello) †D.Elliott (mello.) †J.Watkins (Fr.H.)	Eckstine †J.Williams	Fitzgerald †Etta Jones	Ellington †Q.Jones	Ellington †Basie	Goodman Gillespie-Parker †Messengers
Tatum †H.Silver †O.Dennard	Christian †B.Galbraith †J.Puma	Pettiford †P.Chambers †M.Hinton	K.Clarke Roach †O.Johnson †Blakey	Pettiford (cello) †J.Watkins (Fr.H.)	Sinatra †J.Williams †Austin Crommer	Vaughan †Merrill †Honey Gordon	Ellington Strayhorn †E.Wilkins †G.Gryce	Ellington †Basie †N.Hefti	Gillespie-Parker †Messengers †Brown-Roach

†New Star Vote

VOTER	TRUMPET	TROM-BONE	ALTO SAX	TENOR SAX	BARI-TONE SAX	CLARI-NET	FLUTE	VIBRA-PHONE
LEE KONITZ	Eldridge †Don Ferrara		Parker	L.Young †W.Marsh	Mulligan †L.Gullin	L.Young †Giuffre		M.Jackson
STAN LEVEY	Gillespie †M.Davis	Rosolino †C.Fontana	Parker †C.Mariano	L.Young †Getz	Carney †Giuffre	Goodman †Giuffre	Shank †Wess	M.Jackson
JIMMY McPARTLAND	Beiderbecke Armstrong †C.Baker	Teagarden Dickenson	†Desmond	B.Freeman Hawkins †Getz	†Mulligan	Goodman		Norvo †T.Gibbs
CARMEN McRAE	Navarro	JJ Johnson	Parker †C.Adderley	B.Webster	Carney	T.Scott	H.Mann	M.Jackson
JOHNNY MEHEGAN	Armstrong †C.Brown	Teagarden †Rosolino	Parker †P.Woods	C.Hawkins †B.Holman	Carney †B.Cooper	Goodman †Giuffre		Norvo †E.Costa
RED MITCHELL	Gillespie †D.Byrd †T.Fruscella	B.Harris Dickenson †Brookmeyer	Parker †C.Mariano †Schildkraut	L.Young †S.Rollins	Carney †V.Gonsalves	J.Hamilton		M.Jackson †Tjader
GERRY MULLIGAN	Gillespie R.Nichols †C.Baker	B.Harris E.Swope †Brookmeyer	Parker Konitz P.Brown †C.Mariano †Z.Sims	L.Young Z.Sims D.Byas †R.Kamuca	Mulligan Carney †L.Gullin	Fazola Goodman †Giuffre	†Shank	M.Jackson Norvo
SY OLIVER	Armstrong	L.Brown	Hodges	Jacquet	Carney	Goodman		Hampton
OSCAR PETERSON	Gillespie †C.Brown	B.Harris	Parker	L.Young	Carney	Goodman †Giuffre	H.Mann	M.Jackson
OSCAR PETTIFORD	Red Allen M.Davis Gillespie †Thad Jones †Art Farmer	L.Brown JJ Johnson †Brookmeyer †J.Cleveland	Hodges S.Stitt †C.Mariano †Frank Morgan †C.Adderley	B.Webster L.Thompson †Getz †S.Stitt	Carney Mulligan †S.Shihab †C. Fowlkes	J.Hamilton Harry Pettiford †T.Scott	J.Richardson H.Mann S.Most †Wess	M.Jackson T.Gibbs †Tjader

PIANO	GUITAR	BASS	DRUMS	MISC. INSTRU.	MALE SINGER	FEMALE SINGER	ARRANGER	BIG BAND	COMBO
Tristano B.Powell †S.Mosca	Christian	Blanton †A.Fishkin	Roach		Hibbler	Holiday	R.Burns	Basie	Parker-Davis Gillespie-Parker
B.Powell †H.Silver	Christian †T.Farlow	Pettiford †P.Heath	Roach †Blakey	R.Nance (vln.)	N.Cole †J.Williams	Fitzgerald †Vaughan	J.Lewis †B.Holman	Basie †Basie	Gillespie-Parker †Messengers
Tatum †McPartland	E.Lang	M.Hinton †B.Crow	Tough †J.Morello		P.Como	Fitzgerald			
T.Wilson	M.Lowe	Ike Isaacs	K.Clarke	M.Mathews (acc.)	Sinatra	Vaughan	J.Mundy	Basie	Mulligan
Tatum P.Jolly	Christian †L.Almeida	Blanton †E.Furtado	B.Rich †J.Campbell		Bing Crosby †M.Dennis	Fitzgerald †Merrill	F.Henderson †C.Mariano	Ellington †S.Rogers	Creole Jazz Band †C.Hamilton
E.Garner †H.Hawes	T.Farlow J.Raney †J.Hall	Blanton †L.Vinnegar †W.Mitchell	Catlett †C.Thompson	Pettiford ('cello) J.Watkins (Fr.H.) †B.Davis (org.)	Sinatra †J.Williams	Holiday †J.Southern †Ethel Lewis	J.Mandel †Brookmeyer	Basie †Herman	Parker-Davis †Hawes 3
Tatum E.Garner †A.Previn †R.Freeman †J.Williams	J.Collins J.Raney †J.Smith	Blanton Pettiford †R.Mitchell	Tough S.Greer S.Manne †O.Johnson	R.Nance (vln.) Brookmeyer (v.trom.) †H.Kookofsky (vln.)	Sinatra David Allyn †J.Williams	Holiday Bailey †McRae	Ellington R.Burns G.Evans B.Sherwood Sauter Finegan †B.Holman	Ellington Herman Goodman	Mulligan Gillespie-Parker †S.Manne 5 †C.Hamilton
Basie	Floyd Smith	G.Duvivier	J.Crawford		Sinatra	J.Stafford	Wm.Moore, Jr.	Goodman Ellington	Ray.Scott
Tatum †H.Hawes	Christian Kessel	Blanton R.Brown †R.Mitchell	B.Rich Jo Jones	J.Thielemans (harm.)	Sinatra	Fitzgerald	Ellington †Giuffre	Ellington	K.Cole 3 Goodman
Tatum Tom. Flanagan H.Jones †D. McKenna †H.Silver	J.Smith B.Galbraith †J.Raney	R.Brown †P.Chambers	Roach O.Johnson †G.Johnson	H.Lookofsky (vln.) M.Mathews (acc.)	Sinatra †J.Williams	Fitzgerald †Morgana King	Q.Jones G.Gryce E.Wilkins †G.Evans	Ellington Basie †Herman	Mulligan Mod. Jazz Qrt.

†New Star Vote

VOTER	TRUMPET	TROM-BONE	ALTO SAX	TENOR SAX	BARI-TONE SAX	CLARI-NET	FLUTE	VIBRA-PHONE
BUD POWELL	Gillespie †C.Brown	JJ Johnson	S.Stitt	S.Rollins	Leo Parker	S.Hassel-gard T.Scott		T.Gibbs
ANDRE PREVIN	Gillespie †C.Cand-oli †Stu Wil-liamson	B.Harris E.Swope †Rosolino	Parker †C.Mari-ano	Getz †B.Perk-ins	Mulligan	DeFranco †Giuffre		M.Jackson †Tjader
JIMMY RANEY	M.Davis C.Brown	Brookmeyer JJ Johnson	Parker Konitz	Getz A.Cohn	Mulligan B.Gordon	DeFranco		M.Jackson T.Charles
MAX ROACH	†C.Brown	†J.Cleve-land	†C.Adder-ley	†S.Rollins				†M.Jackson
HOWARD ROBERTS	M.Davis	JJ Johnson	Parker	Getz	B.Gordon	DeFranco	Harry Klee	M.Jackson
FRANK ROSOLINO	Gillespie †D.Byrd	JJ Johnson Bill Harris †J.Cleve-land	Parker	Getz	B.Gordon	Goodman	Shank	M.Jackson
PETE RUGOLO	Armstrong Gillespie †C.Cando-li †J.New-man	B.Harris Winding †Rosolino †C.Fon-tana	Parker B.Carter †L.Nie-haus †Shank	L.Young Getz †B.Perkins †B.Cooper	Carney †B.Gordon	Goodman †T.Scott †Giuffre	†H.Mann	Norvo Hampton †M.Jackson
BILL RUSSO	M.Davis	Teagarden	Parker Konitz	L.Young †H.Koller †Sandy Mosse	†B.Gordon	Goodman		
BUD SHANK	Gillespie †S.Will-iamson	Rosolino	Parker †C.Mari-ano	L.Young †B.Perkins	B.Gordon	Goodman †Giuffre	Harry Klee †S.Most	M.Jackson †L.Bunker
CHARLIE SHAVERS	Armstrong	Teagarden	B.Carter	Hawkins †Getz	Carney	Goodman		Hampton
GEORGE SHEARING	Armstrong Gillespie †C.Brown †D.Fager-quist	T.Dorsey †JJ John-son †J.Cleve-land	Parker †C.Adder-ley †Konitz	Hawkins †Getz	Carney	Goodman †DeFranco	Wess †Wess	Tjader †Tjader

PIANO	GUITAR	BASS	DRUMS	MISC. INSTRU.	MALE SINGER	FEMALE SINGER	ARRANGER	BIG BAND	COMBO
Tatum Monk †Dwike Mitchell	Christian	Pettiford	Roach		Sinatra	K.Starr	T.Dameron	Kenton	Shearing †Gibbs
Tatum †H.Silver †R.Free-man	Kessel	R.Brown †L.Vinne-gar	S.Manne †Gene Gammage		Sinatra †J.Will-iams	Fitzgerald †B.Bennett	J.Mandel S.Rogers †B.Holman †J.Giuffre	Basie †Basie	Mod.Jazz Qrt. †S.Manne
B.Powell A.Haig Tatum	Farlow Christian	R.Mitchell Pettiford	Blakey Roach K.Clarke		Sinatra	M.McCall Holiday	Brookmeyer J.Montrose Mulligan	Basie Herman	Mulligan Getz
†Richie Powell	†Farlow	†Geo. Morrow	†Philly J. Jones	†J.Watkins (Fr.H.)	†J.Will-iams	†McRae	†J.Lewis		†Brown-Roach
P.Jolly	Ray Chamber-lain	G.Duvivier	Manne		Sinatra	Fitzgerald	B.Holman	Basie	Mod.Jazz Qrt.
B.Powell †S.Clark	Farlow	R.Brown †P.Cham-bers	Roach		Sinatra	Vaughan		Basie	M.Davis
Tatum †L.Levy †P.Jolly †H.Hawes	Christian †H.Roberts †Farlow	Blanton R.Brown †R.Mitch-ell	Tough S.Manne †C.Ham-ilton †J.Mor-ello	J.Thiele-mans (harm.) †B.Cooper (oboe)	Sinatra	Fitzgerald	Ellington Sauter R.Burns †B.Holman †J.Mandel	Ellington Herman †Basie	Tristano M.Davis †Mod.Jazz Qrt.
Tristano	Christian †J.Raney	Pettiford	S.Manne	Brookmeyer (v.trom.)		Fitzgerald	R.Burns	Ellington	
Tatum †C.Will-iamson	Kessel †D.Over-burg	P.Heath †Don Prell	S.Manne †Flores		Sinatra	Fitzgerald	J.Mandel †B.Cooper	Basie †Basie	Goodman †Mod.Jazz Qrt.
Tatum †Peterson	Christian	G.Duvivier	Bellson	A. Van Damme (acc.)	Armstrong	Fitzgerald †McRae	B.Finegan	Ellington	Goodman
Tatum †H.Hawes	Christian †Eddie Duran	Pettiford R.Brown †R.Mitch-ell	B.Rich †R.Haynes †Roach	S.Smith (vln.) †J.Thiele-mans (harm.) †L.Sash (acc.)	Sinatra †J.Will-iams	Fitzgerald †McRae	B.Finegan †Q.Jones	Lunceford †Basie †L.Brown	Savoy Sultans J.Kirby †C.Hamilton †D.Pell

†New Star Vote

VOTER	TRUMPET	TROMBONE	ALTO SAX	TENOR SAX	BARITONE SAX	CLARINET	FLUTE	VIBRAPHONE
HORACE SILVER	M.Davis †D.Byrd	JJ Johnson †J.Cleveland	Parker †J.McLean	S.Rollins †H.Mobley	C.Payne	DeFranco	Wess †G.Gryce	M.Jackson †T.Pollard
SONNY STITT	Gillespie †M.Davis	JJ Johnson †J.Cleveland	Parker	L.Young †Getz	Carney †C.Payne	Goodman Shaw †F.Foster †J.Hamilton	Wess †Wess	M.Jackson †M.Jackson
BILLY TAYLOR	Gillespie †D.Byrd †C.Brown	JJ Johnson †J.Cleveland	Parker †G.Gryce	Hawkins †F.Foster †C.Rouse	Carney †A.Cohn	Shaw DeFranco †T.Scott	Wess †J.Richardson	M.Jackson †T.Pollard †Tjader
CAL TJADER	Gillespie B.Hackett †M.Davis	B.Harris †JJ Johnson †Winding	Parker †Shank	L.Young Getz †B.Moore †Z.Sims	Mulligan †B.Gordon	Goodman †DeFranco		Hampton †M.Jackson
LENNIE TRISTANO	Eldridge †Navarro	†Winding †JJ Johnson	Parker †Konitz	L.Young †W.Marsh	†L.Gullin			
CHARLIE VENTURA	Gillespie †C.Candoli	B.Harris †Rosolino	Parker †C.Mariano	C.Berry †A.Cohn	†Giuffre	DeFranco †T.Scott		M.Jackson
GEORGE WALLINGTON	Gillespie Beiderbecke Jerry Lloyd †C.Brown †D.Byrd	Teagarden Winding JJ Johnson †J.Cleveland †Brookmeyer	Parker †P.Woods	Ray Turner †S.Rollins	Chaloff Mulligan	Goodman †DeFranco		M.Jackson T.Gibbs †J.Roland
FRANK WESS	Gillespie †C.Brown	T.Dorsey †U.Green	Parker †P.Woods	L.Young †S.Powell	Carney	Shaw †T.Scott		M.Jackson
RANDY WESTON	Gillespie †I.Sulieman	JJ Johnson †J.Cleveland	Parker	Hawkins L.Young †S.Rollins †P.Gonsalves	Carney †C.Payne	L.Young	Wess	M.Jackson

PIANO	GUITAR	BASS	DRUMS	MISC. INSTRU.	MALE SINGER	FEMALE SINGER	ARRANGER	BIG BAND	COMBO
Tatum B.Powell †H.Hawes	Christian †J.Raney	Pettiford †P.Chambers	Blakey Roach †Philly J. Jones		Sinatra †J.Williams	Fitzgerald †Ernestine Anderson	G.Evans †Q.Jones	Basie	Mod.Jazz Qrt. †Messengers
Tatum †H.Jones	Christian †J.Raney †H.Ellis †B.Jennings	Blanton Pettiford †Pettiford	C.Webb Blakey †Roach		N.Cole Sinatra †J.Williams	Fitzgerald Washington †Lurlean Hunter	Ellington T.Dameron †Q.Jones	Lunceford Eckstine Ellington G.Miller †Basie	Gillespie-Parker †Brown-Roach
Tatum †H.Silver	Christian †K.Burrell †Farlow	Blanton †P.Chambers †Earl May	Jo Jones †Charlie Smith †Ed Thigpen	Candido (congo) †Doug Duke (org.)	Sinatra Eckstine †Sammy Davis, Jr. †J.Williams	Fitzgerald Vaughan †McRae	Ellington †Q.Jones	Ellington †Basie	Tatum Trio †Messengers †Peterson 3
T.Wilson †E.Larkins †J.Lewis	F.Greene Farlow	Blanton †R.Brown †R.Mitchell	J.Crawford Krupa †Roach		Sinatra †J.Williams	Fitzgerald †McRae	R.Burns †Mulligan	Goodman †Basie †Herman	Goodman †Mod.Jazz Qrt. †Mulligan
B.Powell	Christian	R.Brown	Roach			Fitzgerald Holiday		Herman	Gillespie-Parker
Tatum †H.Silver	Christian †J.Raney	R.Mitchell †Peter Ind	Tough †Blakey	J.Venuti (vln.) A.Van Damme (acc.)	Russ Columbo	Fitzgerald †McRae	R.Burns †S.Rogers †Giuffre	Basie †Herman	Gillespie †Messengers
Hines A.Haig B.Powell M.Powell †P.Jolly	Farlow †D.Garcia	Pettiford T.Kotick †P.Chambers	Roach S.Levey †N,Stabulas	J.Thielemans (harm.)	Sinatra	P.Lee †C.Connor †B.Kenney	J.Mundy G.Evans Mulligan †Q.Jones	Goodman E.Hines Basie	Shearing M.Davis †Wallington 5
Tatum †H.Silver	Christian †J.Smith	Blanton †P.Chambers	C.Webb †O.Johnson	B.Davis (org.)	N.Cole	Vaughan †Lurlean Hunter	Ellington †Q.Jones	Ellington †Basie	Mod.Jazz Qrt.
Tatum	Christian	Blanton Pettiford †P.Chambers	Roach Blakey †S.Woodyard	C.Pozo (conga) †J.Watkins (Fr.H.)	Hibbler †J.Williams	Holiday †McRae	Ellington J.Lewis †Q.Jones	Ellington †Ellington	Mod.Jazz Qrt. †Brown-Roach

†New Star Vote

VOTER	TRUMPET	TROM-BONE	ALTO SAX	TENOR SAX	BARI-TONE SAX	CLARI-NET	FLUTE	VIBRA-PHONE
ERNIE WILKINS	Gillespie †Thad Jones †J.New-man	JJ Johnson †J.Cleve-land	Parker †C.Adder-ley †P.Woods	L.Young †S.Rollins †L.Thomp-son	Carney	Goodman †T.Scott †Giuffre	Wess †Collette	M.Jackson
COOTIE WILLIAMS	Armstrong	J.Harrison	J.Hodges	Hawkins	Carney	Goodman		Hampton
TEDDY WILSON	Armstrong	J.Harrison	B.Carter	Hawkins	Carney	Goodman		Hampton
KAI WINDING	Gillespie M. Davis †T. Frus-cella	JJ Johnson †J. Cleve-land	Parker †J. Mc-Lean	Getz L.Young †S.Powell	Mulligan			M.Jackson †T. Gibbs
LESTER YOUNG	Gillespie M.Davis Eldridge H. Edison	B.Harris JJ Johnson	Parker Hodges B. Carter W. Smith	C.Hawkins B.Webster P. Gon-salves Getz	Carney Leo Parker Mulligan	Goodman DeFranco Shaw	Wess	T.Gibbs M.Jackson Hampton

MUSICIANS' COMMENTS

A number of the musicians appended comments to qualify or amplify their votes. The most frequent remarks were that the phrase "greatest ever" is an extremely difficult challenge to the voter, and that the "new star" selections were construed to include musicians who had risen to prominence in the past several years rather than during the past year.

Excerpts from some of the most interesting comments are quoted below.

CLIFFORD BROWN: Parker, Christian and Basie are without a doubt, in my estimation, "greatest ever"; all others are simply the closest yet to being the "greatest ever"; I do not consider it possible to make just selections in every field.

BOB COOPER: I have only been able to arrive at a few names for the "greatest ever" category. These are the ones who appear singularly outstanding to me. The other instrumental categories have *many* varied great contributors, so I prefer leaving the few on the list; thus they appear all the more outstanding in my eyes.

DON ELLIOTT: Many greats were way before my time. I limited my choices to those I have heard in person, omitting the greats of the bygone past. Some of my favorites are not necessarily outstanding in jazz but are musicians who have influenced me (such as Harry James) and made way for new jazz trends.

Since it is almost impossible to be completely objective about your fellow musicians when they play the same instrument as yourself, I have left the Trumpet and Vibraphone categories blank (for greatest new star). I have many favorites: Chet Baker, Clifford Brown, Miles Davis, Milt Jackson, Red Norvo, and Terry Gibbs, but I cannot pin-point it to one, since every one has some particular quality which is outstanding and different from the others. The same goes for Instrumental Combos.

Being a Miscellaneous man myself, I tend to favor other Miscellaneous men, thereby making it impossible to have only one choice.

It is good to realize that Jazz has risen in stature to the point where an *Encyclopedia Yearbook of Jazz* and polls of this type have found a place in American culture.

BENNY GOODMAN: My selections are people who could work together in an ideal all-star band: in some cases I did not think of the term "greatest ever" in making my selections. They represent, too, a combination of old and new influences.

JOHN GRAAS: This is a very difficult poll for me, since the longer I am in jazz, the more I appreciate the entire field . . . The present day, the jazz of the '50s, with its wonderful linear and group feeling—i.e. from the

PIANO	GUITAR	BASS	DRUMS	MISC. INSTRU.	MALE SINGER	FEMALE SINGER	ARRANGER	BIG BAND	COMBO
Tatum †H.Jones	Christian	Blanton †P.Chambers	Jo Jones †O.Johnson	Ray Perry (vln.) †P.Jolly (acc.)	Sinatra †J.Williams	Holiday †McRae	Ellington †Q.Jones †G.Gryce	Ellington †Basie	Mod.Jazz Qrt. †Messengers
Hines	Christian	Blanton	B.Rich		N. Cole	Fitzgerald	Ellington	Ellington	Goodman
Basie Tatum	Christian	M.Hinton J. Kirby Blanton	C.Webb Catlett Jo Jones	S.Smith (vln.)		Holiday Fitzgerald	Ellington	Henderson Ellington	Goodman J. Kirby Gillespie-Parker
B.Powell Peterson †D.Katz	J.Smith Farlow	Pettiford M. Hinton †P Chambers	Roach O.Johnson †B.Bradley	Brookmeyer (v. trom.)	Eckstine †J.Williams	Vaughan †B.Kenney	A.Cohn Hefti †Q.Jones	Basie	Gillespie-Parker
Hines Ellington Basie	F.Greene J.Smith J.Collins Christian	W.Page Pettiford Blanton	Jo Jones Krupa B.Rich	D. Elliott (mello.)	Sinatra Eckstine F.Laine	Holiday Vaughan Fitzgerald	Andy Gibson Strayhorn	Basie Ellington Kenton	Mod. Jazz Qrt. L.Young J.Hodges Mulligan

†New Star Vote

trios all the way through to Basie, who to me is a large group rather than a band—is a golden age of jazz, and is probably producing more than at any other time in jazz history.

PERCY HEATH: This is almost the hardest form I ever tried to fill out!

JAY JAY JOHNSON: The late Fred Beckett, once with Harlan Leonard's orchestra and shortly afterwards with Lionel Hampton, was the very first trombonist I ever heard play in a manner other than the usual sliding, slurring, lip trilling, or "gut bucket" style. He had tremendous facilities for linear improvisation; in general, Beckett's playing made a very lasting impression on me.

SHELLY MANNE: It's so hard to name the "greatest ever." Your tastes change; what you once said was the greatest is now replaced with someone new, who you think is the greatest ever at this time. In many categories I could not honestly pick only one . . . I tried to name those who I feel had the biggest influence on other musicians.

There are many more new stars, but the ones I have mentioned are those I have heard the most.

JOHN MEHEGAN: Selections of the "greatest ever" must rest upon consideration of two factors: first, of course, the evaluation of the musician's specific contribution to his instrument, but more important a consideration of the influence exerted upon musicians of his time in terms of conception and in reference to all instruments.

Some instruments have been excluded because they are not considered jazz instruments. The two touchstones of decision are swinging and conception.

RED MITCHELL: By being limited to "greatest ever" and "greatest new star," I feel forced to leave out several people whom I consider very influential but who don't quite fall into either category, like Miles Davis, John Lewis, and Oscar Pettiford. . . . as for my "greatest ever" small combo choice, I picked this particular band of Bird's over the one Bird and Diz had together mostly because of Duke Jordan, one of my favorite soloists on any instrument. My choice of Erroll Garner on piano was made after hearing a solo album of his where he not only romped and swung as only he can, but went off into some explorations I thought only Art Tatum was capable of. As for the flute, I must be an old fuddy-duddy, but none of these fellas has actually made me jump up and down yet.

GERRY MULLIGAN: Congratulations on an excellent idea. A poll exclusively for leading musicians can only have an interesting outcome.

In filling in my ballot I encountered a few difficulties and, I think, some possible omissions that I would like to pass on for future reference. Since only musicians are voting it's possible to make the poll much more comprehensive than the usual popularity poll; you can include categories and make distinctions in the categories that wouldn't be pertinent to non-musicians.

My main difficulty was with the headings: "Greatest Ever" and "Greatest New Star of the Past Year." A choice for the "greatest ever" on any given instrument is not necessarily the same choice I would make for my personal all-time favorite. So I think it would be a good idea to clarify whether you would like us to choose those musicians who have had the strongest impact and influence on music in general and ourselves in particular or from whom we derive the most personal pleasure and inspiration.

As regards the other heading, "greatest new star, etc.," it would seem that by restricting our choices to those musicians who have attained "star" status during the year, we might easily limit ourselves right out of any choices at all since it's too much to assume a new star will emerge in any category every year, and at the same time we could quite possibly overlook new talents who have not yet but might one day achieve both stardom and greatness. In fact, I think it is a most harmful practice for new, young musicians to be acclaimed "star" and "great" too early in their careers. Such is one of the evils of our current recording boom . . . I would like to suggest for an alternate heading, "Most Impressive New Talent (or Newcomer) During the Past Year."

(Ed.'s Note: The enclosed sample ballot listed 19 additional categories, including cornet, slide and valve trombones, jazz songwriter, standard or popular songwriter, jazz record, own record, critic, reporter, jazz night club, and three drum categories—big band, small band and soloist.)

LENNIE NIEHAUS: I have chosen the "greatest ever" artists for their greatness in their prime, for the fact that they are still great today, and also for the influence they exerted on other musicians either directly or indirectly.

OSCAR PETERSON: I have chosen a few youngsters, so to speak, because even though many people may say that their efforts haven't been tested by time, I feel that being a musician myself, and having mingled, listened to, and played with many of the greats, I am experienced enough to make these choices.

Music must progress, and it will do so through not only talent, but *great talent!*

OSCAR PETTIFORD: My reason for not voting for Charlie Christian, Charlie Parker, Django Reinhardt, Jimmy Blanton and many other jazz immortals is that I don't believe the dead can bring back the life in music; we have to think in terms of what is here, not what has been here and gone.

I hope nobody will get mad at my choices; I didn't mean to slight anyone, but merely to select some of my favorites.

ANDRE PREVIN: Stu Williamson, Charlie Mariano and Leroy Vinnegar are all members of Shelly Manne's new group, and are all imaginative, swinging, expert players, capable of playing both experimental and traditional jazz. Jim Giuffre is a serious and well-schooled musician, equally impressive as an instrumentalist and as an arranger. Basie's band is not only the greatest ever but will probably be the new star every year to come. Gene Gammage, who was on the road with me, is a flexible, interesting, swinging drummer; Bill Perkins has the most beautiful tone ever, and Bill Holman is a great big-band writer. As far as vocalists are concerned, none have impressed me as consistently during the past year as Joe Williams and Betty Bennett. Horace Silver is the essence of modern swinging, but I wish there were room to mention Lou Levy and Hampton Hawes.

BILL RUSSO: The absence of new stars on my list above has two explanations: (1) I dislike the category, and (2) I have not heard many new people in jazz who amount to very much. I have the feeling that the art of jazz improvisation, despite its current popularity and exploitation, is at a lower point than ever in its history. It has reached limits beyond which "natural" talent cannot go; it requires thinking and training and technique. These qualities were not necessary to an early and simpler art; jazz must either remain on an earlier plateau or degenerate, as it now is moving.

BUD SHANK: This is both a privilege and a difficult task. Most active jazz musicians, I am sure, have wanted a voice in the popularity polls.

There are several musicians in my "greatest ever" category that have been popular only recently (Rosolino, Gordon, Heath, etc.), because I feel there have been no previous players of these instruments that I can still appreciate today as readily as I can such masters as Tatum, Bird, Pres, etc.

You will notice a prevalence of musicians active in Los Angeles in the "new star" category. With the exception of Sam Most, I have worked with these musicians. . . . I would rather not attempt to judge younger musicians only by what I hear on phonograph records. These choices were not made because of any geographical prejudices.

BILLY TAYLOR: To say that *any* musician is the "greatest ever" is an over-simplification of a very complex art. In every period of jazz many musicians made important contributions for which they were not credited and of the ones who did receive recognition, who can honestly say which was the most important or the "greatest ever"? For instance, to me, the contribution of Dizzy Gillespie to jazz was fantastic in its scope, but

I realize that though his contribution means more to me it would not have been possible had not Louis Armstrong and Roy Eldridge preceded him. The same thing holds true in each case.

Therefore my list includes my *favorites,* first, of the past few years, then, of the last year and these are *favorites,* nothing more. I only voted for musicians I heard personally, so this limited the field.

RANDY WESTON: There should be a space for modern jazz composers. I strongly believe that Thelonious Monk should rank as one of the greatest jazz composers of all time. I certainly hope he will finally get the recognition due him.

ERNIE WILKINS: Dizzy was the first man to introduce an altogether new jazz trumpet style since Louis Armstrong first startled the jazz world . . . Carney isn't the most modern, but is so great! Without him, Duke's band wouldn't sound like Duke . . . Whenever I hear Benny Goodman on the old records I have to love the "old man." I think though, that Artie Shaw was the most inventive . . . Wess is head and shoulders above the rest for jazz flute.

I was fortunate enough to hear Ray Perry on violin shortly before he died; if he had lived, I know by now he would have had much recognition and would have been heard on records . . . Sinatra just gets greater and greater. . . . I was a lover of Lunceford's incomparable orchestra but I can't forget the Duke Ellington band of the late thirties and early forties.

Thad Jones has a clear, lyrical sound; he's fresh and original. Joe Newman is "Mr. Soul"; the paragon of consistency, and nobody can outswing him. I'd like to mention, too, the long underrated Harry Edison.

The Jazz Messengers are a swinging and very exciting group. They have originality and freshness and humor, and if you can't pat your foot to their music, you must be dead.

TEDDY WILSON: Not voting for new stars because of lack of familiarity with their work. Since the war, I have been most impressed with Erroll Garner for his originality and Bengt Hallberg for refinements he brings to jazz piano. Would like also to mention Ray Brown as favorite rhythm section bass player of this later period. . . . There are many fine new horn players but they are all too derivative of Diz and Charlie so far.

AUTHOR'S COMMENTS

In assessing the results of this, the first national jazz poll in which musicians alone were the voters, it is interesting to compare the results with those of the readers' polls conducted by music magazines.

Eight of the winners in the "greatest ever" voting were

also winners, a few months earlier, of *Down Beat* and/or *Metronome* readers' polls: J. J. Johnson, Milt Jackson, Dizzy Gillespie, Max Roach, Don Elliott, Count Basie, Ella Fitzgerald and Frank Sinatra. Three of the "new star" winners had enjoyed similar victories: Stan Getz, Gerry Mulligan and Joe Williams.

In a number of categories, however, there were striking contrasts. Dizzy Gillespie, winner of this poll and of the last *Metronome* plebiscite, has never won a *Down Beat* readers' poll; neither has Art Tatum, and neither, during his brief career in jazz, did the late Jimmy Blanton, one of the three deceased musicians remembered by the *Yearbook* voters. (Charlie Christian won five music magazine polls between 1939 and 1942 and Charlie Parker, of course, won a dozen *Metronome* and *Down Beat* awards between 1948 and his death in 1955.)

Several contrasts of an opposite nature apply in these comparisons. Dave Brubeck, a great favorite with the readers of U.S. music magazines and winner of several *Metronome* and *Down Beat* polls, did not receive a single vote here, either in the "greatest ever" or in the "new star" division. Stan Kenton, whose band has won innumerable readers' polls since 1947, and Chet Baker, whose trumpet playing won him four victories in *Down Beat* and *Metronome,* were almost completely neglected by the musicians voting in the present poll.

The inclusion of a flute division marked the first acknowledgment, in the form of a separate poll category, of the important role assumed lately by this instrument in jazz. Though many of the voters left this space blank on their ballots, Frank Wess, of the Basie band, scored a decisive advantage over his competitors. (Wess, Milt Jackson and Count Basie duplicated their victories by winning also in the "new star" division.)

There were several very close races. At one time during the arrival of the votes Bill Harris was ahead of J. J. Johnson, and it was not known until the last few days of the poll whether Goodman or Gillespie-Parker would win in the combo category, Adderley or Woods in the new star alto, Getz or Perkins for new star tenor, Scott or Giuffre for new star clarinet, Farlow or Raney for new star guitar.

The closest thing to a complete monopoly was scored by Joe Williams, the Basie blues singer who so completely dominated the male vocal new star voting that his nearest competitor only received three votes to Williams' 34.

The largest number of votes received by any musician in any one category was Charlie Parker's 76 on alto saxophone, followed by Tatum's 68 on piano, Goodman's 65 on clarinet, Christian's 63 on guitar and Basie's 62 in the big band category.

One of the most impressive sets of figures can be found in the "greatest ever" female singer category, for it developed that by and large the musicians felt there have been only three girl singers, the Misses Fitzgerald, Holiday and Vaughan. Nobody else earned more than two or three votes.

The individual votes make clear that an effort was made to include, among the voters, musicians of every school, style and age group, and that the result was a crossing of lines in all directions. Louis Armstrong voted for Tatum, Jimmy Dorsey for Charlie Parker, Bud Freeman for Stan Getz; on the other hand Gerry Mulligan's vote for Red Nichols, Wallington's for Bix and Bobby Brookmeyer's for Pee-Wee Russell and Jelly Roll Morton, may surprise many readers.

Clearly the results show that the 101 musicians whose opinions were reflected in these votes based their selections on a conscientious survey of the entire field of jazz. While no poll result can be said to be definitive or to prove anything conclusively, it may be said that in all those categories where a substantial number of votes was cast, the two or three artists who came out on top are certainly those whose reputations will last as long as jazz is remembered; for the surest proof of the value of their contributions to jazz is this trial by a jury of their peers.

INTERNATIONAL POLLS

Following are the results of several jazz polls conducted during 1955 and 1956 in the U.S., Great Britain, France and Germany.

In the *Down Beat Critics' Poll* listing, the fractional votes are due to split selections made by some of the experts. Thirty critics participated in the voting, including several from England, France, Sweden and Italy.

	Down Beat Readers' Poll December, 1955		Down Beat Critics' Poll August, 1956		Metronome Readers' Poll January, 1956	
MUSICIAN OF THE YEAR	Dave Brubeck Count Basie Stan Kenton		Category Not Included		Category Not Included	
ORCHESTRA	Count Basie Stan Kenton Woody Herman	1902 1763 433	Count Basie Duke Ellington Dizzy Gillespie	22.3 4.3 1.3	Stan Kenton Count Basie Woody Herman	
COMBO	Dave Brubeck Modern Jazz Quartet Shorty Rogers	1050 880 395	Modern Jazz Quartet Louis Armstrong All Stars Jazz Messengers, Roach–Brown each	14.5 3.0 1.5	Dave Brubeck Modern Jazz Quartet George Shearing	
TRADITIONAL COMBO	Category Not Included		Category Not Included		Category Not Included	
ARRANGER	Pete Rugolo Shorty Rogers Gerry Mulligan	683 644 602	Category Not Included		Category Not Included	
MALE SINGER	Frank Sinatra Nat Cole Perry Como	2155 670 462	Louis Armstrong Frank Sinatra Joe Williams	10.5 7.5 5.5	Frank Sinatra Sammy Davis, Jr. Jackie Paris; Chet Baker; Nat Cole	
MALE BAND VOCALIST	Joe Williams Tommy Mercer Don Forbes	1487 560 432	Category Not Included		Category Not Included	
FEMALE SINGER	Ella Fitzgerald June Christy Sarah Vaughan	1439 675 460	Ella Fitzgerald Billie Holiday Sarah Vaughan	14.0 6.5 2.0	Ella Fitzgerald; Carmen McRae Sarah Vaughan	
FEMALE BAND VOCALIST	Ann Richards Joanne Greer Lucy Ann Polk	792 642 390	Category Not Included		Category Not Included	
ALTO SAXOPHONE	Paul Desmond Lee Konitz Bud Shank	1220 691 467	Benny Carter Sonny Stitt Lee Konitz	6.5 6.0 5.5	Paul Desmond Lee Konitz Bud Shank	692 477 279
TENOR SAXOPHONE	Stan Getz Lester Young Al Cohn	1215 630 491	Lester Young Stan Getz Coleman Hawkins	10.3 7.8 4.3	Stan Getz Lester Young Zoot Sims	1254 249 150
BARITONE SAXOPHONE	Gerry Mulligan Harry Carney Serge Chaloff	2709 611 420	Harry Carney Gerry Mulligan Serge Chaloff	12.5 11.0 2.0	Gerry Mulligan Harry Carney Serge Chaloff	1686 228 186
CLARINET	Buddy De Franco Tony Scott Benny Goodman	983 796 672	Benny Goodman Tony Scott Edmond Hall	8.0 7.5 3.0	Buddy De Franco Benny Goodman Tony Scott	825 393 357

Melody Maker (London) Readers' Poll - March, 1955		Jazz Hot (Paris) Readers' Poll January, 1956		Jazz Echo (Hamburg) Readers' Poll - February, 1956		Encyclopedia Yearbook of Jazz, Musicians' Poll, 1956	
Gerry Mulligan	3403	Category Not Included		Category Not Included		Category Not Included	
Stan Kenton	2613						
Shorty Rogers	1938						
Stan Kenton	5120	Count Basie	2815	Stan Kenton	1848	Count Basie	62
Duke Ellington	3332	Duke Ellington	1781	Count Basie	1374	Duke Ellington	42
Shorty Rogers	3331	Stan Kenton	1012	Shorty Rogers	1075	Woody Herman	9
Gerry Mulligan	1140	Modern Jazz Quartet	2181	Modern Jazz Quartet	1692	Benny Goodman	24
George Shearing	726	Gerry Mulligan	1421	Dave Brubeck	1282	Gillespie-Parker	22
Milt Jackson	575	Louis Armstrong	904	Gerry Mulligan	1033	Modern Jazz Quartet	14
Louis Armstrong	989	Category Not Included		Louis Armstrong	1515	Category Not Included	
Humphrey Lyttelton	628			Dutch Swing College	592		
Kid Ory	571			Humphrey Lyttelton	552		
Shorty Rogers	871	Gerry Mulligan	2661	Bill Russo	1204	Duke Ellington	27
Stan Kenton	836	John Lewis	1243	Duke Ellington	721	Fletcher Henderson	11
Pete Rugolo	520	Duke Ellington	1147	Gerry Mulligan	606	Ralph Burns	10
Frank Sinatra	1229	Louis Armstrong	2787	Louis Armstrong	1907	Frank Sinatra	56
Billy Eckstine	646	Nat Cole	1449	Billy Eckstine	799	Nat Cole	13
Nat Cole	506	Billy Eckstine	643	Frank Sinatra	567	Billy Eckstine	11
Category Not Included		Category Not Included		Category Not Included		Category Not Included	
Sarah Vaughan	1241	Sarah Vaughan	2760	Ella Fitzgerald	1657	Ella Fitzgerald	66
Doris Day	1113	Ella Fitzgerald	1975	Sarah Vaughan	1314	Billie Holiday	23
Ella Fitzgerald	972	Billie Holiday	1923	June Christy	967	Sarah Vaughan	21
Category Not Included		Category Not Included		Category Not Included		Category Not Included	
Lee Konitz	1048	Lee Konitz	1840	Lee Konitz	2085	Charlie Parker	76
Earl Bostic	594	Johnny Hodges	1458	Paul Desmond	1119	Johnny Hodges	17
Charlie Parker	572	Benny Carter	1298	Bud Shank	581	Benny Carter	14
Stan Getz	1028	Lester Young	2498	Stan Getz	1997	Lester Young	52
Bob Cooper	449	Stan Getz	1815	Coleman Hawkins	879	Coleman Hawkins	34
Coleman Hawkins	434	Coleman Hawkins	1021	Lester Young	725	Stan Getz	17
Gerry Mulligan	1261	Gerry Mulligan	3418	Gerry Mulligan	2608	Harry Carney	58
Lars Gullin	582	Harry Carney	1883	Lars Gullin	1447	Gerry Mulligan	21
Harry Klein	419	Serge Chaloff	649	Harry Carney	751	Bob Gordon	8
Buddy De Franco	1158	Benny Goodman	2003	Buddy De Franco	1762	Benny Goodman	65
Benny Goodman	707	Buddy De Franco	1586	Benny Goodman	1408	Buddy De Franco	20
Woody Herman	461	Barney Bigard	1055	Tony Scott	651	Artie Shaw	12

	Down Beat Readers' Poll December, 1955		Down Beat Critics' Poll August, 1956		Metronome Readers' Poll January, 1956	
TRUMPET	Miles Davis	656	Dizzy Gillespie	9.8	Dizzy Gillespie	387
	Chet Baker	645	Ruby Braff	5.0	Chet Baker	345
	Dizzy Gillespie	631	Miles Davis	4.8	Miles Davis	339
TROMBONE	Jay Jay Johnson	999	Jay Jay Johnson	11.0	Jay Jay Johnson	720
	Bob Brookmeyer	667	Bob Brookmeyer	4.0	Bob Brookmeyer	414
	Kai Winding	591	Jack Teagarden	3.0	Kai Winding	273
VIBRAPHONE	Milt Jackson	1050	Milt Jackson	17.0	Milt Jackson	919
	Lionel Hampton	830	Lionel Hampton	5.0	Lionel Hampton	467
	Terry Gibbs	722	Red Norvo	3.5	Terry Gibbs	399
PIANO	Oscar Peterson	664	Art Tatum	9.0	Dave Brubeck	465
	Dave Brubeck	651	Bud Powell	7.0	George Wallington	363
	Art Tatum	540	Erroll Garner	5.0	Oscar Peterson	273
GUITAR	Johnny Smith	765	Tal Farlow	8.5	Johnny Smith	621
	Barney Kessel	660	Freddie Green	7.0	Tal Farlow	369
	Tal Farlow	552	Jimmy Raney	6.0	Jimmy Raney	287
BASS	Ray Brown	704	Oscar Pettiford	11.5	Ray Brown	396
	Oscar Pettiford	525	Charlie Mingus	6.0	Charlie Mingus	360
	Charlie Mingus	504	Milt Hinton	2.5	Oscar Pettiford	279
DRUMS	Max Roach	835	Jo Jones	6.5	Shelly Manne	585
	Shelly Manne	820	Art Blakey	6.3	Max Roach	576
	Gene Krupa	728	Max Roach	4.3	Buddy Rich	348
ACCORDION	Art Van Damme	1140	Category Not Included		Category Not Included	
	Mat Mathews	537				
	Pete Jolly	530				
VIOLIN	Category Not Included		Category Not Included		Category Not Included	
ORGAN	Category Not Included		Category Not Included		Category Not Included	
SOPRANO SAX	Category Not Included		Category Not Included		Category Not Included	
FLUTE	Category Not Included		Category Not Included		Category Not Included	
MISCELLANEOUS INSTRUMENT	Don Elliott (mellophone)	846	Category Not Included		John Graas	426
	John Graas (Fr. horn)	655			Don Elliott	297
	Bud Shank (flute)	488			Bud Shank	291
VOCAL GROUP	Four Freshmen	1517	Category Not Included		Four Freshmen	
	Hi-Los	731			Hi-Los	
	Mills Brothers	266			Mills Brothers	
DANCE BAND	Les Brown	1905	Category Not Included		Category Not Included	
	Les Elgart	950				
	Count Basie	582				

Melody Maker (London) Readers' Poll – March, 1955		Jazz Hot (Paris) Readers' Poll January, 1956		Jazz Echo (Hamburg) Readers' Poll, February, 1956		Encyclopedia Yearbook of Jazz, Musicians' Poll, 1956	
Chet Baker	1026	Dizzy Gillespie	1803	Chet Baker	1785	Dizzy Gillespie	45
Louis Armstrong	875	Louis Armstrong	1646	Dizzy Gillespie	849	Louis Armstrong	39
Dizzy Gillespie	798	Miles Davis	1575	Louis Armstrong	835	Roy Eldridge	19
Frank Rosolino	1020	Jay Jay Johnson	2781	Bob Brookmeyer	1273	Jay Jay Johnson	30
Bennie Green	519	Bob Brookmeyer	1338	Jay Jay Johnson	916	Bill Harris	29
Kid Ory	481	Trummy Young	772	Kai Winding	667	Jack Teagarden	20
Lionel Hampton	1212	Milt Jackson	2652	Milt Jackson	1715	Milt Jackson	49
Milt Jackson	732	Lionel Hampton	2578	Lionel Hampton	1672	Lionel Hampton	41
Vic Feldman	266	Terry Gibbs	818	Red Norvo	1423	Terry Gibbs	9
Oscar Peterson	997	Bud Powell	1825	Oscar Peterson	957	Art Tatum	68
George Shearing	650	Art Tatum	1618	Dave Brubeck	816	Bud Powell	21
Erroll Garner	583	Oscar Peterson	692	Art Tatum	673	Teddy Wilson	10
Barney Kessel	949	Jimmy Raney	2261	Barney Kessel	1666	Charlie Christian	63
Les Paul	873	Barney Kessel	1329	Jimmy Raney	918	Tal Farlow	10
Johnny Smith	536	Tal Farlow	1261	Tal Farlow	771	Freddie Green	8
Johnny Hawksworth	849	Oscar Pettiford	2147	Ray Brown	1246	Jimmy Blanton	43
Eddie Safranski	828	Percy Heath	1532	Red Mitchell	1039	Oscar Pettiford	28
Ray Brown	517	Ray Brown	1472	Charlie Mingus	907	Ray Brown	26
Shelly Manne	1016	Max Roach	2667	Shelly Manne	1465	Max Roach	28
Louis Bellson	750	Art Blakey	1578	Max Roach	1035	Buddy Rich	18
Gene Krupa	644	Kenny Clarke	1203	Gene Krupa	636	Jo Jones	17
Tito Burns	1031	Category		Category		Category	
Art Van Damme	842	Not		Not		Not	
Toralf Tollefsen	781	Included		Included		Included	
Stephane Grappelly	869	Category		Category		Category	
Ray Nance	424	Not		Not		Not	
Max Jaffa	211	Included		Included		Included	
Harold Smart	843	Category		Category		Category	
Count Basie	836	Not		Not		Not	
Jerry Allen	766	Included		Included		Included	
Sidney Bechet	1088	Category		Category		Category	
Frank Weir	570	Not		Not		Not	
Ronnie Chamberlain	308	Included		Included		Included	
Category		Category		Category		Frank Wess	22
Not		Not		Not		Herbie Mann	5
Included		Included		Included		Bud Shank	5
Category		Sidney Bechet	1904	Sidney Bechet	1290	Don Elliott	6
Not		Oscar Pettiford	618	Bud Shank	876	Jean Thielemans	6
Included		Stuff Smith	603	John Graas	567	Ray Nance, Stuff Smith	5
Four Aces	1576	Category		Category		Category	
Four Freshmen	579	Not		Not		Not	
Deep River Boys	490	Included		Included		Included	
Category		Category		Category		Category	
Not		Not		Not		Not	
Included		Included		Included		Included	

ABBREVIATIONS

ABC   *American Broadcasting Co.*
acc.   *accompanied*
addr.   *address*
AFM.   *American Federation of Musicians*
Alad.   *Aladdin*
All.   *Allegro*
Amer. Mus.   *American Music*
Ap.   *Apollo*
app.   *appeared*
A&R   *artists and repertoire*
arr.   *arranged, arranger, arrangements*
ARS   *American Recording Society*
ASCAP   *American Society of Composers, Authors and Publishers*
Atl.   *Atlantic*
b.   *born*
BBC   *British Broadcasting Corp.*
Beth.   *Bethlehem*
blrm.   *ballroom*
BN   *Blue Note*
Bruns.   *Brunswick*
bus.   *business*
Cap.   *Capitol*
CBS   *Columbia Broadcasting System*
cl., clar.   *clarinet*
Col.   *Columbia*
coll.   *college*
Comm.   *Commodore*
comp.   *composed, composer, compositions*
cons.   *conservatory*
cont.   *continued*
Contemp.   *Contemporary*
Cor.   *Coral*
d.   *died*
DB   *Down Beat Magazine*
Dec.   *Decca*
Disc.   *Discovery*
div.   *divorced*
dj   *disc jockey*
ea.   *each*
ed.   *educated*
Em.   *EmArcy*
EPs   *extended play records at 45 revolutions per minute*
Eso.   *Esoteric*
Esq.   *Esquire Magazine*
Fant.   *Fantasy*
fav., favs.   *favorite, favorites*
feat.   *featured, featuring*
fin.   *finished*
Folk.   *Folkways*
GN   *Gene Norman Presents (record label)*
GTJ   *Good Time Jazz*
harps.   *harpsichord*
Imp.   *Imperial*
incl.   *includes, including, included*
Jag.   *Jaguar*
JATP   *Jazz at the Philharmonic*
Jub.   *Jubilee*

KC *Kansas City, Missouri*
LA *Los Angeles*
Liv. *Livingston*
Lond. *London*
LPs *Long playing records at 33⅓ revolutions per minute*
Mac. *MacGregor*
MCA *Music Corporation of America*
Merc. *Mercury*
Met. *Metronome Magazine*
Moh. *Mohammedan*
mos. *months*
Mus. *Musicraft*
mus. dir. *musical director*
NBC *National Broadcasting Co.*
NJ *New Jazz*
NO *New Orleans*
Noct. *Nocturne*
Norg. *Norgran*
NORK *New Orleans Rhythm Kings*
NYC *New York City*
ODJB *Original Dixieland Jass Band*
orch. *orchestra*
Pac. Jazz *Pacific Jazz*
Per. *Period*
Phil. *Philharmonic*
pl. *played*
Pres. *Prestige*
quint. *quintet*
Rain. *Rainbow*
R&B *Rhythm and Blues*

R. Ch. *Record Changer Magazine*
rec. *recorded, recordings*
Rem. *Remington*
repl. *replaced, replacing*
rest. *restaurant*
ret. *returned*
River. *Riverside*
Sav. *Savoy*
sch. *school*
78s *records at speed of 78 revolutions per minute*
SF *San Francisco*
Sky. *Skylark*
South. *Southland*
st. *started*
Stin. *Stinson*
Story. *Storyville*
stud. *studied*
symph. *symphony*
tpt. *trumpet*
trom. *trombone*
U., Univ. *University*
USC *University of Southern California*
Van. *Vanguard*
Vict., Vic. *Victor*
vln. *violin*
Voc. *Vocalion*
w. *with*
West. *Westminster*
"X" *"X" records (RCA Victor subsidiary)*
yrs. *years*

BIOGRAPHIES

In a field so vast and, moreover, constantly changing, some omissions in The Encyclopedia of Jazz *were inevitable. Requirements of space alone prevent completeness. With the annual publication of* The Encyclopedia Yearbook of Jazz, *however, it is hoped that the biographies will eventually include every active figure in jazz.*

This chapter comprises (a) biographies of artists who rose to prominence after publication of *The Encyclopedia of Jazz,* or who were omitted from it because of lack of space or adequate information, (b) details of any important recent biographical developments in the lives of those whose biographies were included in the *Encyclopedia,* and (c) lists of important records, by all these artists, released after the *Encyclopedia* went to press in the summer of 1955.

ABNEY, Don LPs: Norg. 1015 (Benny Carter); Beth. 33 (Oscar Pettiford).

ACEA, Johnny LPs: EmArcy 26048 (Roy Haynes).

ADDERLEY, Julian "Cannonball", *alto sax* (also *tenor, trumpet, clarinet, flute*); b. Tampa, Fla., 9/15/28. Father a jazz cornetist; whole family musical. Studied brass and reed instruments at high school in Tallahassee 1944-8, forming first jazz group with band director Leander Kirksey as advisor. From 1948-56 Adderley was band director at Dillard High School in Ft. Lauderdale, Fla. During this time he also had his own jazz group in south Florida 1948-50. Serving in the Army '50-2, he became leader of the 36th Army Dance Band. In '52 he had his own combo in Washington, D.C., where he was studying at the U.S. Naval School of Music; later he led another Army band at Ft. Knox, '52-3. The nickname "Cannonball" evolved from "Cannibal," a name given by high school colleagues in tribute to his vast eating capacity. "Cannonball" first attracted attention when he sat in with Oscar Pettiford at the Bohemia, NYC in the summer of '55. Shortly after, he signed with EmArcy records. In the spring of '56, he and his brother Nat (see below) started touring with their own combo.

"Cannonball," who names Charlie Parker and Benny Carter as his favorites, sounds like a twin of the former on faster tempi and reflects, at least tonally, the influence of the latter on slow ballads. Many musicians and critics, including the author, considered him the outstanding new alto saxophonist of the year.

LPs: EmArcy 36043 (own group); Wing 60000 (Nat Adderley); Savoy 12018 (*Presenting "Cannonball"*), 12017 (*Bohemia After Dark*); EmArcy 36058 (Sarah Vaughan), 36063 (and strings).

Addr: 444 W. Pensacola St., Tallahassee, Fla.

ADDERLEY, Nathaniel "Nat", *cornet* (also *trumpet, mellophone, French horn*); b. Tampa, Fla., 11/25/31. Brother of Julian "Cannonball" Adderley (see above). Started as child singer; when his voice began to change, took up trumpet in 1946, switched to cornet in 1950. His career roughly paralleled that of his brother, including service in the 36th Army Band from '51-3. Additionally, he was in Lionel Hampton's band from July '54 to May '55, spending most of that period on an overseas tour in which Hampton toured the European continent and Israel. Adderley states that his brother Julian, who started as a trumpet player, gave him his early training along with their father and band director Leander Kirksey. He plays first-class modern jazz reflecting the influences of his favorites Dizzy Gillespie, Miles Davis, and Clark Terry.

LPs: Wing 60000 (own group); Em. 36043 (Cannonball Adderley); Savoy 12017 (*Bohemia After Dark*), 12018 (*Presenting "Cannonball"*); Em. 36034, 36035 (Lionel Hampton).

Addr. 444 W. Pensacola St., Tallahassee, Fla.

AKIYOSHI, Toshiko The Japanese jazz pianist arrived in Boston in January 1956 to study under a scholarship at the Berklee School and also privately with Mrs. Margaret Chaloff. She made several television appearances and appeared at Storyville in Boston, the club owned by George Wein, whose protégée she became. She showed a superb technique and an ever greater mastery of the Bud Powell style, of which she has become one of the outstanding disciples.

ALBAM, Manny During 1955-6 this exceptional modern jazz arranger enjoyed his busiest year, working as a free-lance writer in New York on innumerable recording dates, many of them for RCA Victor. Among these were several albums for Joe Newman (*All I Wanna Do Is Swing; I'm Still Swingin'*); Salute to Andy Kirk, Salute to Satch, and Osie Johnson's vocal sides. LPs: Vict. LPM 1107 (*Basses Loaded*); Beth. 15 (*Don Elliot*); Kapp 1007 (Morey Feld); Beth. 16, Vict. LPM 1164 (Hal McKusick), 1211 (*The Jazz Workshop: Manny Albam*), 1212 (arrs. for *New York Land Dixie*); EmArcy 36064 (Terry Gibbs).

ALCORN, Alvin LPs: Good Time Jazz 12008 (Kid Ory); South. 214 (Jack Delaney).

ALESS, Tony Still working as a radio staff musician in NYC, he also formed a sextet with Seldon Powell which was feat. several times at Birdland. LPs: Roost 2202 (*Long Island Suite*), 2205 (Seldon Powell); "X" LXA 1032 (George Handy).

ALEXANDER, Elmer "Mousie", *drums;* b. Gary, Ind., 6/29/22. Father played violin. Stud. in Chicago at Roy Knapp School, 1948. In NYC with Sam Ulano. Played w. Jimmy McPartland 1948-50, Marian McPartland '52-3, Sauter-Finegan '53-5, Johnny Smith '55 to Feb., '56, then joined new Benny Goodman

band. Favs: Buddy Rich, the late Joe Timer. LPs: Roost LP 2203 (Johnny Smith); Savoy 15021 (Marian McPartland); Vict. LM 1888, LJM 1003 (Sauter-Finegan).

Addr: 337 Beach, 148 Street, Neponsit, L.I., N.Y.

ALEXANDER, Robert, *trombone;* b. Roxbury, Mass., 11/23/20. Originally inspired by Tommy Dorsey. Stud. in high school in Portland, Me., 1936. Joined Fenton Bros. orch., '40; Joe Marsala and commercial dance bands in New York, '41-2, Coast Guard, '42-5, then joined Jimmy Dorsey. After 5 months w. Eddy Duchin in '49, took up free-lance studio work in NYC. Favs: Kai Winding, Bill Harris, Tommy Dorsey. LPs: Grand Award 33-325 (*Progressive Jazz*).

Addr: 82 Hazelton Terrace, Tenafly, N.J.

ALLEN, Steve Enjoyed added prestige when *The Benny Goodman Story,* in which he played the title role, was released in January, 1956. Cont. to feature jazz artists on his nightly NBC television show and to make plans for various jazz ventures, including a book and a recorded history of the subject. LPs: Coral 57018 (*Jazz for Tonight*), 57019 (*Steve Allen Sings*), 57028 (*Let's Dance*); Decca DL 8151, 8152 (*All Star Jazz Concert,* Vol. 1 & 2).

ALLEN, Red Spent another year at the Metropole on Seventh Avenue in Manhattan. LPs: Beth. 21 (*Jazz at the Metropole*); Jazztone 1211 (Jelly Roll Morton), 1215 (Tony Parenti).

ALPERT, Trigger LPs: Kapp 1004 (Benny Payne); River. 204 (Mundell Lowe); Grand Award 33-325 (Al Klink); Vict. LPM 1240 (Sauter-Finegan).

AMMONS, Gene LPs: Em. 36016 (*Advance Guard of the '40s*); Vict. LPM 1112 (Count Basie); Em. 36023 (*Battle of the Saxes*); EmArcy 36038 (w. Billy Eckstine in *Boning Up On 'Bones*); Pres. 7050 (Jam Session; Ammons vs Stitt), 7039 (Jam Session).

AMRAM, David Werner III, *French horn;* b. Philadelphia, Pa., 11/17/30. Cousin of conductor Otto Klemperer. St. on piano, tpt., stud. at Curtis Institute. Played w. National Symph. in Washington, D.C. 1951-52; formed jazz sextet w. Spencer Sinatra. Army, Aug. '52. 7th Army Symph. in Germany '53-4. After discharge, went to Paris, Dec. '54, played w. Henri Renaud, Bobby Jaspar et al and made record debut w. Lionel Hampton. Back in New York in Fall of '55, gigged with Sonny Rollins, Charlie Mingus, Oscar Pettiford. One of the most promising young artists on his instrument. Favs: Julius Watkins, Gunther Schuller, Jim Buffington. LPs: EmArcy 36034 (Lionel Hampton).

Addr: 319 E. 8th St., New York, N.Y.

Gerry Mulligan *(Herman Leonard)*

Upper left: Coleman Hawkins *(RCA-Victor)*

Lower left: Davey Schildkraut *(ABC-Paramount)*

Right: Frank Foster *(Richard Schaefer)*

Bill Perkins

Zoot Sims *(Herman Leonard)*

Paul Desmond *(Victor Tanaka)*

Stan Getz *(Robert Parent)*

Charlie Mariano *(Richard Schaefer*)

Count Basie (*Victor Tanaka*)

Opposite page: Bud Powell (*Carole Galletly*)

Thelonious Monk *(Herman Leonard)*

André Previn *(William James Claxton)*

Right: Jutta Hipp visits Horace Silver at Cafe Bohemia, New York City. *(Len Kovar)*

Left: Billy Taylor *(ABC-Paramount)*

Terry Gibbs and Terry Pollard
(James J. Pappas)

Cal Tjader

Lionel Hampton *(Herman Leonard)*

John Lewis *(Herman Leonard)*

Milt Jackson *(Herman Leonard)*

ANDERSON, Cat LPs: Cap. 679, Beth. 60 (Duke Ellington); Col. CL 872 (Rosemary Clooney and Duke Ellington).

ANDERSON, Ernestine Irene, *singer;* b. Houston, Tex., 11/11/28. Joined Russell Jacquet orch. in Texas, 1943. Toured w. Johnny Otis '47-9, Lionel Hampton '52-3. Record debut w. Gigi Gryce Nov., '55. Toured Scandinavia w. Rolf Ericson combo in Summer, '56. Fav: Mary Ann McCall. LPs: Signal 1201 (Gigi Gryce).

Addr: 448 W. 55th St., New York, N.Y.

ANTHONY, Bill, *bass;* b. NYC, 3/28/30. Mother st. him on piano; stud. cello and bass in high school, then stud. bass w. Clyde Lombardi. Worked w. Buddy DeFranco big band 1950, Geo. Auld quintette in '51, Charlie Spivak, '52, Jimmy Dorsey, '53, Gerry Mulligan, '54, Stan Getz, '55, Claude Thornhill, '56. Favs: Oscar Pettiford, Ray Brown. LPs: Atl. 1022 (Tony Fruscella); Norgran 2000 (Stan Getz); Story. 305 (Brookmeyer); EmArcy 36061 (Johnny Williams).

ANTON, Arthur, *drums, conga, timbales;* b. NYC, 9/8/26. Stud. 1942 w. Irving Torgman; majored in music at NYU '43-4, '46-7. Navy '44-6. Played w. Herbie Fields '47 and '51. Sonny Dunham, Bobby Byrne, '48; Tommy Reynolds, Jerry Wald, Art Mooney, Bud Freeman '52; Ralph Flanagan, '53; Jerry Gray, Charlie Barnet '54, then free-lanced in LA. Non-music jobs incl. vacuum cleaner salesman, private detective. Best solo performances are on Jimmy Giuffre LP listed below. Favs: Dave Tough, Gus Johnson, Art Mardigan, Tiny Kahn. LPs: Cap. T634 (Jimmy Giuffre); Decca 8156 (Jack Millman).

Addr: Route 1, Box 162, Las Vegas, Nev.

APPLEYARD, Peter, *vibes;* b. Cleethorpes, Lincolnshire, England, 8/26/28. Started on piano at 14; professional debut as drummer with British bands. Served in RAF for 2 yrs., then to Bermuda for 3 yrs. playing drums at Princess Hotel. After moving to Canada in '51 he took up vibes professionally, playing w. many leading groups around Toronto. Joined Calvin Jackson early 1954. LPs: Col. CL756 (Calvin Jackson).

ARCHEY, Jimmy LPs: River. 2516 (Sidney Bechet).

ARMSTRONG, Lil LPs: Jazztone 1213 (Sidney Bechet).

ARMSTRONG, Louis After triumphant tours of the Continent, Australia and the US, Armstrong took his sextet to Great Britain in May, 1956 for his first appearance there in 21 yrs. and was received w. unprecedented enthusiasm. His group had undergone slight personnel changes since '55, now including Trummy

Young, trom., Edmond Hall, clar., Billy Kyle, piano, Barrett Deems, drums, Jack Lesberg, bass, and vocalist Velma Middleton. Armstrong visited Calif. in Jan. '56 to take an acting and playing role in the picture, *High Society* w. Grace Kelly, Bing Crosby, and Frank Sinatra.

LPs: Col. CL708 (*Satch Plays Fats*); Decca DL8168, 8169 (*At the Crescendo* Vol. 1 & 2), DL8126 (*Satchmo Sings*); Col. CL840 (*Ambassador Satch*); The Louis Armstrong Story, transferred from Col. ML series, is now on Col. CL851 (Hot Five), CL852 (Hot Seven), CL853 (and Earl Hines), CL854 (Favorites); River. 101 (*Young Louis Armstrong*).

ARNOLD, Buddy (Arnold Buddy Grishaver), *tenor sax, clarinet, oboe;* b. NYC, 4/30/26. St. on soprano and alto saxes. Played w. Joe Marsala, Geo. Auld 1943; Will Osborne, Bob Chester '44; Army band '44-6. After discharge played w. Herbie Fields, Buddy Rich; entered Columbia U., took courses in music and economics. Played w. Geo. Williams, Claude Thornhill, then left music for 1½ yrs. Toured w. Buddy DeFranco orch. during '51, Jerry Wald '52, later w. Tex Beneke, Elliot Lawrence, Neal Hefti. Early solo on *Just Goofin'* with Gene Williams (Mercury). Favs: Al Cohn, Zoot Sims, Sonny Rollins. Despite periodic absences due to family influence, has shown great promise as musician, making own album for ABC-Paramount in '56. LPs: ABC-Par. 114 (own group).

Addr: Park Savoy Hotel, 158 W. 58th St., New York, N.Y.

ASHBY, Irving LPs: Clef 676 (Illinois Jacquet).

ASMUSSEN, Svend The Danish violinist made one brief visit to NYC in '55, but did not perform professionally. He continued to appear successfully in Scandinavian vaudeville. LPs: Epic 3210 (*Sköl!*).

AULD, Georgie Still residing in LA, Auld formed a big band with Lunceford style arrangements by Billy May, first for EmArcy records, then planned to organize it for personal appearances. LPs: Coral 57009 (*I've Got You Under My Skin*); Vict. LPM1112 (Count Basie); Col. CL652 (Charlie Christian); EmArcy 36021 (Maynard Ferguson); Contemp. 3513 (Barney Kessel); EmArcy 36060 (own orch.); Grand Award 316 (*Jazz Concert*); EmArcy 36065 (Dinah Washington).

AUSTIN, Claire LPs: Contemp. 5002 (*When Your Lover Has Gone*).

BABASIN, Harry LPs: Liberty 6007 (Jack Millman), 6009 (Buddy Childers).

BAGLEY, Don LPs: Cap. W724 (Stan Kenton).

BAILEY, Buster LPs: Beth. 21 (*Jazz at the Metropole*); River. 2516 (Sidney Bechet).

BAILEY, Pearl Scored a big hit with her appearance in a Bob Hope film, *That Certain Feeling*, 1956, and in nightclub appearance at Waldorf-Astoria, NYC, May '56, as well as on many television shows. LPs: Coral 57037 (*Pearl Bailey*).

BAKER, Chet Spent Sept., 1955 to Apr. '56 touring European continent, Iceland and England, then returned to US and played nightclubs w. his own quartet. Won polls in London Melody Maker and German Jazz Echo as No. 1 tpt. player. LPs: Pac. Jazz 1206 (own groups), 1203 (*Jazz at Ann Arbor*), 1202 (Sings and plays with strings), 1218 (*Quartet in Paris*).

BAKER, Lavern, *singer;* b. Chicago, Ill., 1928. Starting professionally in early teens, she worked as singer and dancer in Chicago clubs during '40s and early '50s; toured Europe in 1953. Her record of a novelty nonsense song, *Tweedlee Dee,* released in '54, elevated her overnight from $125-a-week obscurity to $1,500-a-week national fame as a rhythm and blues attraction. Originally known as "Little Miss Sharecropper," she is now billed as "Lavern Baker, the Tweedlee Dee Girl." From the jazz standpoint she is one of the better rock-and-roll performers, with a relaxed rhythmic style that rises above the level of her material. Records for Atlantic; mostly single releases, also an LP on Atl. 566.

BALES, Burton F., *piano* (also *mellophone, bar. sax*); b. Stevensville, Mont., 3/20/16. Private piano lessons 1928, theory and arranging at Tamalpais High School, '34. St. playing piano in speakeasies, '31, Santa Cruz, Calif. Jazz experience w. Lu Watters '42. Army, '43. Joined Bunk Johnson '43, Dude Martin, '44; own group and solo work '45-9; re-joined Watters '49, then worked w. Turk Murphy at Hangover Club in SF '49-50. Played w. Bob Scobey '50 and '53, Marty Marsala '54, but has worked mostly as single and w. own groups since '50. Favs: Jelly Roll Morton, Fats Waller, J.P. Johnson, Joe Sullivan, Don Ewell, Ralph Sutton. Won dj poll on west coast for ragtime piano '43. Record debut '49 on GTJ, in trio w. Ed Garland and Minor Hall.

EPs: Good Time Jazz 1001 (Benny Strickler), 1006 (*Ragtime Piano*) LPs: Good Time Jazz 17 (Bunk Johnson), 4, 5 (Turk Murphy), 9 (Bob Scobey), 19 (*After Hours Piano*); Cavalier (*On the Waterfront* incl. fav. own solo, *Mr. Jellylord*); GTJ (Albert Nicholas), (Darnell Howard).

Addr: c/o Musicians Union No. 6, San Francisco, Calif.

BALL, Ronnie Worked w. Jay and Kai quintet from Feb., 1956. LPs: Atl. 1217 (Lee Konitz); Savoy 12051 (Mike Cuozzo), 12064 (*The Jazz Message*), 12065 (Kenny Clarke).

BANK, Danny LPs: Grand Award 315 (Rex Stewart); Decca 8235 (Ralph Burns).

BARBARIN, Paul LPs: Jazztone 1205 (*New Orleans Jamboree*).

BARBER, Bill LPs: Col. CL689 (Pete Rugolo); Decca 8235 (Ralph Burns).

BAREFIELD, Eddie LPs: Beth. 21 (*Jazz at the Metropole*).

BARKER, Danny LPs: Jazztone 1205 (Paul Barbarin).

BARNES, George LPs: Col. CL717 (Garry Moore); Urania 1203 (Ernie Royal).

BARNET, Charlie LPs: Col. CL639 (Town Hall Jazz Concert); Decca 8098 (*Hop On the Skyliner*); Vict. LPM1091 (*Redskin Romp*); Cap. T624 (Charlie Barnet); Vict. LPM1146 (*Lullaby of Birdland*); Epic 3128 (Red Norvo).

BASIE, Count Enjoyed his greatest commercial success on records and in person, 1956, largely owing to the tremendous popularity of his vocalist, Joe Williams. Appeared every 2 or 3 months at Birdland, NYC; during these visits his sidemen were in constant demand for combo LP dates, esp. Joe Newman, Thad Jones, Frank Wess, Frank Foster, Freddie Greene (q.v.).

LPs: Clef 647, (*Dance Session Album #2*), 666 (*Basie*), 678 (*Count Basie Swings, Joe Williams Sings*); Vict. LPM1112 (*Count Basie*); Col. CL754 (*Count Basie Classics*); Epic 3168 (*Let's Go to Prez*), 3169 (*Basie's Back in Town*); Col. CL652 (Charlie Christian); Bruns. 54012 (band; late 30's); ARS402 (*Count Basie and His Band That Swings the Blues*); Clef 685 (*The Count!*); Van. 9006 (as "Apollo Band of the Year" in *A Night at the Apollo*).

BATEMAN, Charles, *piano;* b. Youngstown, Ohio, 9/12/21. Played w. Edmond Hall at Cafe Society Uptown 1946-8, then dates w. Sy Oliver, Lucky Millinder, Gene Ammons, Sonny Stitt; South American tour with Panama Francis '54. Worked w. Aaron Bell trio in upstate New York '54-6. Appeared w. Buffalo Phil. '38, Concord Symph. '55. Fav: Art Tatum. LPs: Herald 0100 (Aaron Bell); Pres. 111 (Sonny Stitt).

Addr: 538 W. 153 St., New York, N.Y.

BATES, Bob LPs: Col. CL622, CL699 (Brubeck).

BATES, Norman Louis, *bass* (also *piano, sax*); b. Boise, Idaho, 8/26/27. Mother, Emily Bates, professional pianist and organist. Brothers Bill, Bob, Jim all musicians. Stud. at home, inspired by music of Duke Ellington. Bass w. Jimmy Dorsey '45, Raymond Scott, '46, Henry King, Carmen Cavallaro '47, Dave Brubeck trio '48-9. Piano and bass w. Jack Sheedy Dixieland Band '50, followed by 4 yrs. in the Air Force (not as musician) '51-5. Bass w. Wally Rose Dixieland Band '55, then repl. his brother Bob in the Dave Brubeck quartet. Favs: Jimmy Blanton, Red Mitchell. LPs: Col. (Wally Rose).

Addr. 2335 45th Ave., San Francisco, Calif.

BAUER, Billy LPs: Roost. 2202 (Tony Aless); Vict. LJM1024 (Al Cohn); Kapp 1007 (Morey Feld); Atl. 1217 (Lee Konitz).

BEAN, Floyd R., *piano, arranger;* b. Ladora, Iowa, 8/30/04. Played w. Bix Beiderbecke at Linwood Inn in Davenport, 1923; w. Bunny Berigan in Cy Mahlberg band '26; w. Jack Jenney in Earl Hunt band 1930. Own combo in Davenport, '33 and in Chicago '43-4 and '48. Wide experience w. both commercial bands and jazz groups. Best known associations are w. Jimmy McPartland, Bob Crosby '39; "Wingy" Manone '40; Boyd Raeburn '43; arranger and second piano w. Jess Stacy '45; Paul Mares and Sidney Bechet in '48, all in and around Chicago. After working w. "Big Sid" Catlett and "Miff" Mole, he toured with "Muggsy" Spanier '51-2, then worked with Geo. Brunies '53-5. Fav. and greatest influence: Earl Hines. LPs: Decca 8029 (w. Jimmy McPartland in *Chicago Jazz Album*); EmArcy 26011 (Muggsy Spanier).

Addr: 4878 N. Magnolia Ave., Chicago 40, Ill.

BECHET, Sidney Continued to reside in France and to enjoy great success in vaudeville and concert appearances. LPs: Blue Note 1201, 1202 (*Jazz Classics*), 1203, 1204 (*Giant of Jazz*); Jazztone 1213 (*Jazz à La Creole*); River. 2516 (own groups); GTJ 12013 (*King of the Soprano Saxophone*).

BEIDERBECKE, Bix LPs: *The Bix Beiderbecke Story* has been transferred from Col. ML to Col. CL844 (*Bix and His Gang*), CL845 (*Bix and Tram*), CL846 (*Whiteman Days*).

BELL, Aaron Led his own trio at Concord Hotel in upstate New York w. Charlie Bateman, piano and Charles Smith, drums. LPs: Herald 0100 (*Three Swinging Bells*).

BELLSON, Louis Featured with Dorsey Brothers orch. Aug. '55-Aug. '56. LPs: Norg. 1020 (*The Driving Louis Bellson*), 1028 (Ralph Burns); Clef 656 (*Jam Session #6*), MG17 (JATP Vol. 17); Clef 682 (Lawrence Brown).

BENJAMIN, Joe LPs: EmArcy 26048 (Roy Haynes).

BENNETT, Betty, *singer;* b. Lincoln, Neb., 10/23/26. Mother, a pianist, had jazz band in 1920s. 12 yrs. of piano study in Hamburg, Iowa, 2 yrs. legitimate voice study. Sang w. Geo. Auld 1943. While in WAVES, 1945, was MC of CBS show, *WAVES on Parade.* Worked w. Claude Thornhill '46, Alvino Rey, '47, Charlie Ventura, Kenton All-Stars '49, Woody Herman small band '50, Charlie Barnet '52. Married to Andre Previn, who in recent years has played, arranged and conducted for her records. An excellent pop singer, she made her solo debut in an album for Trend, Hollywood, '53. Favs: Ella Fitzgerald, early Sarah Vaughan, Martha Raye. LPs: Atl. 1226 (*Nobody Else But Me*); Trend 1006 (incl. fav. own performance *Time After Time*).

Addr: 833 Napoli Drive, Pacific Palisades, Calif.

BENNETT, Max LPs: Beth. 25 (Charlie Mariano), 48 (own septet).

BENSKIN, Sammy LPs: Period 1115 (Josh White).

BERIGAN, Bunny LPs: Epic 3128 (Red Norvo).

BERMAN, Sonny LPs: Grand Award 318 (*Jazz Concert*).

BERNAL, Gilbert, *tenor sax, etc.;* b. LA, 2/4/31. Mainly self-taught. Met Lionel Hampton through former high school English teacher and toured w. the band 1950-2. Aside from this, has always fronted his own combo, but worked w. Spike Jones as featured singer and soloist '56. Of Castilian, Spanish-Gypsy origin, Bernal, whose parents were born in Mexico, has many other interests incl. boxing, sketching, short story writing. Favs: Ch. Parker, early Lester Young. LPs: Col.6288 (Dan Terry).

Addr: 1874 Redondo Blvd., Los Angeles, Calif.

BERNHART, Milt LPs: EmArcy 36009, 36021 (Maynard Ferguson); Vict. LPM1146 (*Lullaby of Birdland*); Decca 8257 (*The Man with the Golden Arm*); Vict. LPM1123 (*Modern Brass*); Cap. W724 (*Stan Kenton*), T683 (*Four Freshmen*); Vict. LG1000 (*Boots Brown*).

BERRY, Chu LPs: Jazztone 1218 (*Prez and Chu*); Epic 3128 (Red Norvo).

BERRY, Emmett Toured Continent and North Africa with Sammy Price combo early 1956. LPs: Vict. LPM1112 (Count Basie); Em. 36023 (w. Corky Corcoran); Concert Hall 1201 (Coleman Hawkins); Van. 8503 (Jo Jones), 8505 (Jimmy Rushing).

BERT, Eddie LPs: Savoy 12015 (*Musician of the Year, Eddie Bert*), 12007 (Clarke-Wilkins Septet); Con. Hall 1201 (*Coleman Hawkins*); Fant. 206, 219 (Elliot Lawrence); Signal 1202 (Duke Jordan); Savoy 12019 (*Encore*), 12029 (*Montage*); Urania 1201 (Coleman Hawkins); Jazztone 1223 (*Modern Moods*).

BEST, Clifton "Skeeter", *guitar;* b. Kinston, N.C., 11/20/14. Stud. w. mother, a piano teacher. Professional debut w. Abe Dunn's local band in early 1930s. Worked mainly w. Slim Marshall in Philadelphia 1935-40. Joined Earl Hines late 1940. Navy 1942-5. Played w. Bill Johnson combo 1945-9. USO tour of Japan and Korea w. Oscar Pettiford 1951-2. Since then, has free-lanced in NYC w. own trio and w. Paul Quinichette, Jesse Powell, Kenny Clarke. Rec. solos on *Swingin' the Blues* w. Quinichette; *Best by Test* w. Sir Charles Thompson. Has also had considerable experience as arr., esp. w. Navy band. Underrated and first-class modern guitarist. LPs: Van. 8018 (Sir Charles Thompson); Decca 8176 (Paul Quinichette); Van. 8506 (Mel Powell).
Addr: 151 W. 140 St. (No. 51), New York 30, N.Y.

BIGARD, Barney LPs: Col. CL708 (Louis Armstrong); Decca DL8168, 8169 (Louis Armstrong).

BISHOP, Walter Jr. LPs: Savoy 12061 (Milt Jackson).

BLAKEY, Art Toured successfully with his own group, the Jazz Messengers, 1955-6. Other members included Hank Mobley, ten. sax; Kenny Dorham (later repl. by Don Byrd), tpt.; Horace Silver, piano; Doug Watkins, Bass. LPs: Em. 36007 (Clark Terry); Blue Note 1507, 1508 (*The Jazz Messengers, At the Cafe Bohemia*); Signal 1201 (Gigi Gryce), 1202 (Duke Jordan); EmArcy 36071 (*Drum Roll*); Trans. 4 (Donald Byrd); Blue Note 5062 (Horace Silver).

BLEY, Paul LPs: Wing 60001 (Paul Bley).

BLYTHE, Jimmy Epic 3207 (Johnny Dodds and Kid Ory).

BO DIDDLEY (Ellas McDaniel), *guitar, singer;* b. McCombs, Miss., 12/30/28. Parents moved to Chicago when he was an infant. Faced his first audience at age of 10 on a street corner as leader of combo comprising two guitars and washboard. No formal training. Professional debut 1951 at "708 Club" in Chicago. Scored hit in rhythm-and-blues record circles on Chess and Checker labels with such tunes as *Bo Diddley* and *I'm a Man,* 1955. Appeared in rock 'n' roll concert in Carnegie Hall.
Bo Diddley, a singer and electric guitarist, capable of producing some of the earthiest and most authentic sounds since the earliest days of primitive blues artists, is one of the few performers in the so-called rock 'n' roll field blessed with genuine artistic value. In effect, he is an authentic parallel for more widely acclaimed artists such as Elvis Presley.
Addr: c/o Shaw Artists Corp., 565 Fifth Avenue, New York 17, N.Y.

BOWMAN, Dave LPs: Grand Award 313 (Bud Freeman); Beth. 29, Weathers 5501 (Bud Freeman).

BRADLEY, Bill Played with Woody Herman, Jan. to Apr., 1956. LPs: Atl. 1220 (Tony Fruscella), Epic 3199 (*The House of Bradley*); Keynote 1102 (Harvey Leonard).

BRADLEY, Will LPs: Grand Award 310, 313 (own band in *Dixieland Jazz*); Epic 3199 (*The House of Bradley*); Grand Award 322 (*A Musical History of Jazz*).

BRAFF, Ruby Acting and playing role in Rogers-Hammerstein musical, *Pipe Dream,* 1955-6. LPs: Jazztone 1210 (*Swinging with Ruby Braff*); Van. 8504 (*The Ruby Braff Special*); Col. CL701 (Buck Clayton); Beth. 29 (Bud Freeman); Cap. 5706 (Benny Goodman); Atl. 1221 (George Wein); Keynote 1101 (Nat Pierce); Story. 908 (*Hustlin' and Bustlin'*); Van. 8506 (Mel Powell), 8507 (*2 x 2,* plays Rodgers & Hart w. Ellis Larkins); Vict. LPM1332 (*The Magic Horn*).

BREGMAN, Buddy, *arranger, conductor;* b. Chicago, Ill., 7/9/30. Brother of composer Jule Styne. Gave first piano recital at age of 12 in Chicago. Stud. harmony, composition, arranging at Chicago Conservatory, also learned many instruments incl. piano, clar., sax, flute. Later attended UCLA and stud. in LA w. Mario Castelnuovo-Tedesco. Living on West Coast, has orchestrated and conducted for NBC, CBS shows starring Jack Haley, Gary Crosby et al. Won "Emmy" nomination from Academy of Television Arts and Sciences for his scoring of NBC color show, *Anything Goes.* Wrote score for film, *Step Down to Terror,* 1956. Mus. dir. for Ella Fitzgerald and many other jazz artists on Norman Granz labels (principally Verve) 1956. LPs: Verve 2000 (Anita O'Day), 4001, 4002 (Ella Fitzgerald).

BRICE, Percy, *drums, conga, bongos;* b. New York City, 3/25/23. Stud. violin, piano under Works Projects Administration. First name band job w. Luis Russell Oct., 1944. Also worked w. Benny Carter, '45-6; concerts for Fran Kelley at UCLA; Mercer Ellington band '47, then rhythm-and-blues work w. Eddie Vinson, Tab Smith, Cootie Williams, Tiny Grimes. In '53-4 he worked w. Lucky Thompson, Oscar Pettiford and had own combo at Minton's Play House. Joined Billy Taylor trio June, '54. An expert jazz drummer, serious and ambitious musician. Favs: Max Roach, Buddy Rich, Kenny Clarke, Art Blakey. LPs: ABC-Par. 112 (Billy Taylor); Debut 8 (Oscar Pettiford); Prest. 194 (incl. fav. own solo, *How High the Moon,* Billy Taylor), 7001 (Billy Taylor).

Addr: 794 E. 158 St., Bronx, N.Y.

BROKENSHA, John Joseph "Jack", *vibes, drums;* b. Nailsworth, Adelaide, South Australia, 1/5/26. Father legitimate percussionist, gave him early tuition. As a child had xylophone act in radio and vaudeville. Australian Symph. Orch. 1942-4, Air Force, '44-6; own group touring in concert groups, broadcasts, etc. '47-53. Worked in Canada '54 where the Australian Jazz Quartet, of which he is a member, was formed. Made records in Australia w. Rex Stewart. Fav. own solo, *September Song* w. Australian Jazz Quintet (Bethlehem). Favs: Milt Jackson, Red Norvo. LPs: Beth. 39, 1031 (Australian Jazz Quartet), 51 (Joe Derise).

Addr: 16545 Mendota, Detroit, Mich.

BROOKMEYER, Bob Toured France and Italy w. Gerry Mulligan sextet, Spring, 1956. LPs: Pac. Jazz 1206 (Chet Baker); Clef 644 (*Bob Brookmeyer Plays Bob Brookmeyer and Some Others*); Pac. Jazz 1210 Gerry Mulligan); Pres. 214 (*The Dual Role of Bob Brookmeyer*); EmArcy 36056 (Gerry Mulligan); Dawn 1102 (Zoot Sims); Beth. 33 (Oscar Pettiford); Norg. 1029 (Stan Getz); Vict. LPM1211 (Manny Albam); Story. 907 (Bob Brookmeyer/Zoot Sims).

BROONZY, "Big Bill" Toured successfully in England and France. Autobiography, *Big Bill Blues,* as told to Belgian jazz writer Yannick Bruynoghe, was published by Cassell and Co. Ltd., London. LP: Period 1114 (*Big Bill Broonzy Sings*).

BROTHER MATTHEW—*See* BROWN, Boyce.

BROWN, Boyce The revelation, early in 1956, that the Chicago alto saxophonist had entered a monastery in 1953 and had become a member of the Servite Order earned widespread publicity. Together with Father Hugh Calkins, who played piano at sessions with him in the monastery, he earned more publicity than had ever been accorded him in his years as a lay jazzman. In Apr., '56 Brown, now known as Brother Matthew, took part in a New York television jam session, and in the LP listed below, royalties from which were turned over to missions of the Servite Order in South Africa. LPs: ABC-Par. 121 (*Brother Matthew with Eddie Condon's Jazz Band*).

BROWN, Clifford The brilliant young trumpet stylist was killed in an auto wreck June 26, 1956 on the Pennsylvania Turnpike while he was driving to an engagement in Chicago. The accident also took the life of Richard Powell (q.v.). Brown was 25 years old. A Clifford Brown Memorial Scholarship fund was started by the local musicians' union in Brown's home town, Wilmington, Del. An initial concert was held in September, 1956, to raise funds for musical scholarships in Brown's memory. LPs: EmArcy 36008 (*Brown and Roach Inc.*), 36006 (Helen Merrill), 36004 (Sarah Vaughan), 36039 (*Best Coast Jazz*), 36037 (*Study in Brown*), 36070 (Brown-Roach); Pres. 7038 (Sonny Rollins).

BROWN, Lawrence Left Johnny Hodges orch. and free-lanced in NYC, 1955-6, playing occasionally on radio and TV; house bands and theater pit band work. LPs: Col. CL 808 (Frankie Laine & Buck Clayton); Van. 8505 (Jimmy Rushing); Grand Award 315 (Rex Stewart), 322 (*A Musical History of Jazz*); Clef 682 (*Slide Trombone*).

BROWN, Les LPs: Cap. T657 (*College Classics*); Coral 57039 (*All-Weather Music*).

BROWN, Pete LPs: Em. 36018 (*Alto Altitude*); Jazztone 1207 (Sammy Price).

BROWN, Ray LPs: Norg. 1028 (Ralph Burns); Clef 642, 667 (Lionel Hampton), 656 (*Jam Session #6*), 677 (*Jam Session #7*), 648, 649, 650 (Oscar Peterson); Norg. 1031 (Buddy Rich); Clef MG17 (JATP Vol. 17); Savoy 12046 (Milt Jackson); ARS403 (Lionel Hampton).

BROWN, Vernon LPs: EmArcy 36013 (Bud Freeman); Coral 57028 (Steve Allen).

BRUBECK, Dave The Brubeck quartet toured in concert work and occasional nightclub dates in 1955-6; Brubeck returned at intervals to his home in Oakland, Calif. LPs: Col. CL622 (*Brubeck Time*), CL699 (*Jazz: Red Hot and Cool*); Fant. 210 (*Jazz at the Black Hawk*).

BRUNIS, George LPs: South. 210 (*And His Dixieland All Stars*).

BRYANT, Raphael "Ray", *piano;* b. Philadelphia, Pa., 12/24/31. Mother, sister play piano; eldest brother is bassist. St. on bass in junior high school. Professional debut through Jack Fields of Blue Note Club in Philadelphia. After working w. Billy Kretchmer band 1951-3, worked as a pianist at Blue Note accompanying Ch. Parker, Miles Davis and many other jazz men. Favs: Art Tatum, Teddy Wilson. LPs: Col. CL658 Jean Thielemans), Epic LN3202 (*Meet Betty Carter and Ray Bryant*); Pres. 7020 (Sonny Rollins), 7034 (Miles Davis).

Addr: 1923 N. 20th St., Philadelphia, Pa.

BUCK, Jack, *trombone, piano;* b. Keokuk, Ia., 10/6/11. Raised partly in SF, where he worked w. Ellis Kimball, Griff Williams; after touring w. Williams, worked in Oakland dance hall for several years, made record debut w. Frisco Jazz Band, 1946 on Pacific label, later played trom. and piano w. Bob Scobey. Appeared on regular TV series in SF, *Clancy's Corner* feat. Clancy Hayes, vocalist and banjoist with Scobey. Favs: Jack Teagarden, Kid Ory, Geo. Brunis. LPs: Good Time Jazz 9, 14, 12006 (Bob Scobey); GTJ (Albert Nicholas), (Darnell Howard).

Addr: 181 Taurus Ave., Oakland 11, Calif.

BUCKNER, Milt LPs: Cap. T642 (*Rockin' with Milt*); Gene Norman 15 (Lionel Hampton).

BUCKNER, Teddy Seen and heard in prologue to motion picture, *Pete Kelly's Blues.* LPs: South. 210 (George Brunis); Gene Norman 11 (own group).

BUDDLE, Errol Leslie, *tenor sax, bassoon, bar. sax, clar.;* b. Adelaide, Australia, 4/29/28. Stud. saxes and clar. at Adelaide College of Music 1936-41, bassoon at Sydney and Adelaide Conservatories '50-52. Radio studio work in Adelaide '46-7; Jack Brokensha quartet and other combos '47-50. Led own all-star group in weekly jazz concerts in Sydney '50-52. Arrived in Canada Oct., '52, played first bassoon w. Windsor Symph. and tenor w. local jazz bands. Worked w. Johnny "Scat" Davis on Detroit TV summer '54; own combo in Detroit, w. Elvin Jones on drums, July to Nov. '54. Joined Australian Jazz Quartet Dec. '54. Voted Musician of the Year by Australian *Music Maker* 1952. Also first-place winner on ten. sax. Fav. own solo, *These Foolish Things* on Bethlehem BCP 39. Favs: Stan Getz, Sonny Stitt, Zoot Sims. Buddle is the first musician in jazz to make extensive use of the bassoon as a medium for ad libbing. LPs: Beth. 39, 1031 (*Australian Jazz Quartet*), 51 (Joe Derise).

Addr: 15310 Grandville, Detroit, Mich.

BUDWIG, Monty Rex, *bass;* b. Pender, Neb., 12/26/29. Mother and father played piano and alto in band together. Stud. at high school in LA. Early experience w. Anson Weeks, 1950, Vido Musso '51, and various jobs around SF. During 36 months in Air Force went to band school and played in service band. In LA '54, worked w. Barney Kessel, Zoot Sims combos, then 14 months w. Red Norvo trio '54-5. Joined Woody Herman in fall of '55, first w. Herman combo in Las Vegas, then in Jan. '56 w. big band. Favs: Jimmy Blanton, Ray Brown, Red Mitchell.

LPs: Norg. 1030 (Tal Farlow); Contemp. 3503 (Lennie Niehaus); Disc. 3023 (Art Pepper); Contemp. 2514. 3510 (Barney Kessel) "X" LXA3034 (Red Norvo); Cap. (Woody Herman; incl. fav. own solo, *Bass Face*).

Addr: 1877 W. 94th Place, Los Angeles, Calif.

BUNKER, Larry This outstanding drummer began to concentrate more and more on vibes in 1955-6. During most of this time he was part of Peggy Lee's accompanying combo. LPs: Decca DL8104 (John Graas); Pres. 212 (Hamp Hawes); Beth. 44 (*Jazz City Workshop*); Liberty 6007 (Jack Millman).

BURKE, Joseph Francis "Sonny", *arranger;* b. Scranton, Pa., 3/22/14. Violin, piano from age five. All-state fullback during high school days. Mus. studies at Duke U., Durham, N.C., where he, Les Brown and Johnny Long all led student bands at one time. Took 15-piece college band for summer booking on transatlantic liner. Worked in department store in Detroit, then became free-lance arr. for Buddy Rogers, Joe Venuti, Xavier Cugat. To NYC, 1938; toured w. own dance band 1939-40; then, through Glenn Miller, got job as arr. for Ch. Spivak until '42. Three years as arr. for Jimmy Dorsey. Since 1949 has been recording dir. and bandleader for Decca Records in Los Angeles, scoring biggest hit with own arr. of *Mambo Jambo.* Among other numbers, he arr. *King Porter Stomp* for Jimmy Dorsey on Decca and *Everything I Have Is Yours* for Billy Eckstine, MGM. Fav. arr: Pete Rugolo, Nelson Riddle, Ralph Burns, John Graas, Shorty Rogers. LPs: Decca 8090 (mambo).

Addr: 342 N. Rockingham, W. Los Angeles 49, Cal.

BURKE, Raymond N. (Barrois), *clarinet, soprano and tenor saxes;* b. New Orleans, La., 6/6/04. Self-taught; whole family musical. Featured locally w. Sharkey's Kings of Dixieland, Johnny Wiggs' New Orleans Kings, Dukes of Dixieland, Geo. Hartman's New Orleans Jazz Band, Geo. Girard and His New Orleans Five. etc. Favs: Harry Shields, Leon Rappolo. LPs: Para. 107, S/D 1001 (Johnny Wiggs-Raymond Burke); South. 214 (Jack Delaney).

Addr: 905 N. Rampart St., New Orleans, La.

BURKE, Vinnie LPs: Savoy 12049 (Mehegan-Costa); Beth. 56 (Chris Connor); Savoy 12051 (Mike Cuozzo); ABC-Par. 106 (Don Elliott).

BURNS, Ralph LPs: Norg. 1028 (*Ralph Burns Among the JATPS*); Cap. T658 (Woody Herman); Norg. 1041 (Charlie Ventura); Atl. 1228 (arrs. & cond. for Chris Connor); Decca 8235 (*Jazz Studio #5*); Epic 3220 (cond. & arrs. for Don Heller, *Blame It On My Youth*).

BURRELL, Kenneth Earl, *guitar;* b. Detroit, Mich., 7/31/31. Three brothers, all musicians. Never studied except 1½ yrs. of classical guitar 1952-3. Bachelor of Music degree Wayne U., Detroit '55. Played w. Candy Johnson Sextet '48, Count Belcher, '49, Tommy Barnett '50, own combo and Dizzy Gillespie '51, then had own groups until Mar., '55, when he briefly repl. Herb Ellis in the Oscar Peterson trio. Moved to NYC and free-lanced with own group and other combos '55-6. Considered one of the most promising new guitarists of '56, he also sings and plays bass. Ambition: To become a college music teacher. Favs: Charlie Christian, Django Reinhardt, Oscar Moore. LPs: Dee Gee 1000 (Dizzy Gillespie); Blue Note 1513 (Thad Jones); Savoy (Frank Foster).

Addr: 355 Central Park West, New York, N.Y.

BUTTERFIELD, Billy LPs: Decca DL8151, 8152 (own band in Steve Allen's *All Star Jazz Concert* Vol. 1 & 2); Coral 57028 (Steve Allen); Essex 401, 402, 403, 404 (*At Princeton; At WYU; At Amherst; At Rutgers*); Jubilee 1019 (Lou Stein); Grand Award 331 (Peanuts Hucko); Vict. LPM 1212 (as "Gus Hoo" in *New York Land Dixie*).

BUTTERFIELD, Don., *tuba;* b. Centralia, Wash., 4/1/23. Entered Army 1942; after discharge early in '46, stud. at Juilliard, NYC. Professional debut with the Goldman Band. CBS and NBC studio work, numerous jobs with symph. orchestras, records w. Jackie Gleason and worked briefly w. Claude Thornhill orch., then became member of house orch. at Radio City Music Hall. Butterfield is one of the few musicians to make an outstanding contribution to jazz on the tuba. He took part in many concerts in the Jazz Composers Workshop Series with Teddy Charles and Charlie Mingus in '55-6. LPs: Atlantic 1229 (Teddy Charles); Blue Note 5063 (Gil Melle).

BYAS, Don LPs: Epic 3169 (Count Basie); EmArcy 36023 (Coleman Hawkins); Em. 36014 (Joe Turner-Pete Johnson); Storyville 906 (Mary Lou Williams).

BYERS, Billy After free-lancing extensively in NYC as arr. and trombonist on countless record dates, Byers left in Feb., 1956 for Paris to work for producer Ray Ventura as conductor, composer, arr. and soloist on various record, motion picture, and other projects.

LPs: Vict. LPM1107 (arr. & pl. in *Basses Loaded*); Jazztone 1210 (Ruby Braff); Vict. LJM1024 (Al Cohn); Beth. 12 (Don Elliot); Kapp 1007 (Morey Feld); Vict. LPM1146 (*Lullaby of Birdland*); Jazztone 1217 (*New Sounds in Swing*); Pres. 213 (Jim Chapin); Keynote 1101 (Nat Pierce); "X"1032 (George Handy); Vict. LPM1211 (Manny Albam); Decca 8235 (Ralph Burns); Story. 905 (Joe Newman); "X"LXA1032 (George Handy); Vict. LPM-1269 (*Billy Byers,* Jazz Workshop).

BYRD, Donald, *trumpet;* b. Detroit, Mich., 12/9/32. Father a Methodist minister and musician. Stud. Cass Tech High, Wayne University, and Manhattan School of Music. Played w. Air Force bands 1951-3. Geo.

Wallington combo at Bohemia, NYC Aug. to Oct. '55. Joined Art Blakey's Messengers Dec. '55. Acclaimed by New York musicians as jazz soloist with great future, he came into demand for free-lance recording work during '56. Favs: Dizzy Gillespie, Miles Davis.

LPs: Savoy 12017 (*Bohemia After Dark*); Prog. 1001 (George Wallington); Trans. 5 (*Byrd*); Savoy 12032 (*Byrd's Word*), 12037 (Hank Jones), 12044 (*Top Brass*); Ad Lib 6601 (Jackie McLean); Savoy 12029 (*Montage*); Beth. 33 (Oscar Pettiford); Savoy 12064 (*The Jazz Message*), 12065 (Kenny Clarke); Pres. 7035 (Jackie McLean), 7032 (George Wallington); Trans. 4 (*Byrd's Eye View*); Pres. 7043 (Elmo Hope).

Addr: 531 W. 187 St., New York, N.Y.

BYRNE, Bobby LPs: Grand Award 310, 313 (own band in *Dixieland Jazz*); MGME3286 (*Hot Vs Cool*); Grand Award 322 (*A Musical History of Jazz*).

CACERES, Ernie LPs: Col. CL717 (Garry Moore); ABC-Par. 121 (*Brother Matthew*); Vict. LPM1332 (Ruby Braff).

CAIN, Jackie LPs: Vict. LPM1135, Em. 36015 (Charlie Ventura); Story. 904 (*Jackie and Roy*); ABC-Par. 120 (*The Glory of Love*).

CALLENDER, Red LPs: Modern 1201 (*Swingin' Suite,* own octet).

CAMERON, Jay, *baritone sax;* b. NYC, 9/14/28. Stud. alto in Hollywood, '43-7. Played w. Ike Carpenter '46-7, Rex Stewart in France and Italy '49, various bands in Germany, Belgium, Scandinavia '50-4. Spring of '55 w. Sadi orch. at Rose Rouge, Paris, then joined Henri Renaud July '55 for 4 months. Back in US, joined Woody Herman Dec. '55. Favs: Gerry Mulligan, Lars Gullin, Bob Gordon.

Addr: c/o Abe Turchen, 200 W. 57th St., New York 19, N.Y.

CANDIDO Continued to free-lance in New York; made first album under his own name, Spring, 1956, for ABC Paramount. LPs: Decca DL8176 (Bennie Green); Pres. 7039 (Gene Ammons), 7051 (Billy Taylor), 7052 (Bennie Green); ABC-Par. 125.

CANDOLI, Conte LPs: Beth. 30 (own quintet); EmArcy 36021 (Maynard Ferguson); Vict. LPM1121 (*The Five*); Norg. 1032 (Stan Getz); Decca DL8104 (John Graas); Pac. Jazz 1208 (Jack Montrose); Gene Norman 12 (Frank Morgan); Contemp. 3504 (Howard Rumsey); Vict. LPM 1135 (Charlie Ventura); Beth. 37 (Stan Levey); EmArcy 36040 (Herb Geller); Savoy 12045 (Shelly Manne); Beth. 38 (Red Mitchell).

CANDOLI, Pete LPs: Decca 8257 (*The Man with the Golden Arm*); Beth. 52 (Mel Tormé); Atl. 1230 (Bobby Short); Cap. W724 (Stan Kenton).

CARISI, John E., *arranger, trumpet;* b. Hasbrouck Heights, N.J., 2/23/22. Stud. tpt., theory in high school, composition with Stephan Wolpe, 1948-50, tpt. with Carmine Caruso, '53-4. After working w. Babe Russin, Geo. Handy, Herbie Fields and several pop dance bands 1938-43, entered Glenn Miller's US Air Force Band also playing in Ray McKinley, Lou Stein contingent '43-6. Later played tpt. w. Skitch Henderson, Claude Thornhill, Charlie Barnet; arr. for Vincent Lopez and various jazz combos (see LP listings). Had works for chamber groups performed at various concerts incl. music symposium at Yale U. Best-known in jazz circles as composer of *Israel*, recorded by Miles Davis. Favs: Miles Davis, Dizzy Gillespie, Billy Butterfield, tpt.; Gil Evans, Geo. Russell, Gerry Mulligan, arr. LPs: Comps. & arrs. for: Cap. H459 (incl. *Israel*); Epic 3148, Jub. 1019, Coral 57003 (Lou Stein); Vict. (own band).
Addr: 1 E. 198th Street, Bronx 58, N.Y.

CARNEY, Harry Entered his 30th year in the Duke Ellington orchestra, 1956. LPs: EmArcy 36023 (Coleman Hawkins); Cap. 679 (Ellington); Norg. 1055 (*Ellingtonia '56*); Beth. 60 (Duke Ellington); Col. CL872 (Rosemary Clooney & Duke Ellington).

CARROLL, Barbara LPs: Vict. LJM1137 (*Have You Met Miss Carroll?*), LPM1146 (*Lullaby of Birdland*).

CARTER, Benny Continued to free-lance in Hollywood, writing and playing; seen and heard in movie, *View from Pompey's Head.* LPs: Norg. 1035 (*Alto Saxes*), 1015 (*Benny Carter Plays Pretty*); Clef 669 (*Billie Holiday*); Norg. 1044 (*New Jazz Sounds*); Cap. 707 (*Session at Midnight*).

CARTER, Bob LPs: Epic 3148 (Lou Stein); Grand Award 33-325 (Bob Alexander).

CARY, Dick LPs: Col. CL719 (Eddie Condon).

CASEY, Al LPs: Grand Award 318 (Earl Hines).

CATHCART, Charles Richard "Dick", *trumpet;* b. Michigan City, Ind., 11/6/24. Father played cornet; 3 brothers have all been prof. musicians. Started on clar. at 4 yrs., switched to tpt. at 13. Later stud. w. Geo. Wendt and Louis Maggio. First job w. Bob Barnes at Indiana U. Worked w. Ray McKinley, Alvino Rey, 1942, USAAF Radio Orchestra '43-6, Bob Crosby Feb.-Dec. '46. After 3 yrs. of studio work, mostly at MGM, he played in Ben Pollack's combo '49-50, Ray Noble '50-51, Frank DeVol '51-53; since '51, has worked off and on with his own jazz combo,

best known as Pete Kelly's Big 7, incl. 1951 radio show, *Pete Kelly's Blues* and '55 film bearing same title. Other movies, *Dragnet*, '54, *Battle Stations*, '55; dubbed solos for Billy May in *Nightmare.* Cathcart, who has been compared with Bix Beiderbecke, actually has hardly ever heard any records by Bix. His favorites are Louis Armstrong, Bobby Hackett, and Billy Butterfield. LPs: Vict. LPM1126, Col. CL690 (*Pete Kelly's Blues*); Cap. 677 (Billy May); Disc. 3008 (Ben Pollack; incl. fav. own solo: *I Can't Give You Anything but Love*).
Addr: 12329 Huston St., No. Hollywood, Calif.

CATLETT, Sid LPs: Norg. 1041 (Charlie Ventura).

CHALOFF, Serge LPs: EmArcy 36016 (*Advance Guard of the '40s*); Cap. T6510 (*Boston Blow-Up*).

CHAMBERS, Paul Laurence Dunbar, Jr., *bass;* b. Pittsburgh, Pa., 4/22/35. Started on bar. horn and tuba around Detroit, '49, working w. Kenny Burrell and other combos until Apr. '54. He then left Detroit w. Paul Quinichette, working w. him for about 8 months. In '55 he was heard with the combos of Benny Green, Joe Roland, Jay Jay Johnson and Kai Winding, Geo. Wallington and Miles Davis, remaining w. Davis through much of '56. Chambers, who has a phenomenal technique and whose improvisations are equally exciting both arco and pizzicato, is the most talented new bassist to enter the jazz scene in recent years. Favs: Jimmy Blanton, Oscar Pettiford.
LPs: EmArcy 36043 (Cannonball Adderley); Wing 60000 (Nat Adderley); Savoy 12017 (*Bohemia after Dark*), 12018 (*Presenting Cannonball*); Prog. 1001 George Wallington); Savoy 12032 (Donald Byrd); Prestige 7014 (Miles Davis); Jazz: West (own group).
Addr: 260 Berriman St. #5, Brooklyn 8, N.Y.

CHAPIN, James Forbes, *drums;* b. New York City, 7/23/19. Piano at 6, clar. at 10; left college at 18 to take up drums. Worked with many commercial groups from '38. Principal jazz jobs w. Red Norvo, 1943, Barbara Carroll trio briefly in '51, Woody Herman Sep.-Dec., '51; Tommy Dorsey, Feb. '52; also played many Monday night sessions at Birdland '54-56 with own group. Author of *Advanced Techniques of the Modern Drummer.* Favs: Max Roach, Jo Jones, Buddy Rich, Joe Morello. LPS: Pres. 213 (*Jim Chapin Ensemble*); Kapp 1015 (Art Harris), 1011 (Harris-Leigh).
Addr: 50 Morningside Drive, New York City.

CHARLES, Teddy LPs: Debut 120 (Miles Davis); Atlantic 1229 (own tentet); Pres. 7028 (*Collaboration: West*).

CHEATHAM, Doc LPs: Atl. 1219 (Wilbur DeParis).

CHEVALLIER, Christian, *piano, arranger;* b. Angers, France, 7/12/30. Father a pianist, mother a singer. Stud. Nantes Conservatory 1936-44. Worked with New Orleans style jazz band at Kentucky Club '49; w. Don Byas at Tabou, 1950. In '54-5 worked at Rose Rouge w. Geo. Daly, Michel de Villers. Own band w. Sadi, Bobby Jaspar, et al. Elected best French arr. in Jazz Hot Poll '55. Favs: John Lewis, Gerry Mulligan. Ambitions: To have Europe's best big jazz band; to arrange for Kenton; to play with his idol, Milt Jackson. LPs: Angel 60009 (*French Toast*).
Addr: 35 Avenue Gambetta, Paris, France.

CHILDERS, Buddy LPs: Liberty 6009 (*Sam Songs*).

CHRISTIAN, Charlie LPs: Col. CL652 (*Charlie Christian with the Benny Goodman Sextet and Orchestra*), CL820 (Benny Goodman).

CHRISTY, June LPs: Cap. T656 (*Duet* with Stan Kenton).

CLARK, Sonny Joined Howard Rumsey's Lighthouse All Stars, Jan., 1956. LPs: Fant. 211 (Cal Tjader); 213 (Jerry Dodgion); ABC-Par. 110 (piano & vibories in *Swingin' on the Vibories*).

CLARK, Walter Jr. "Buddy", *bass;* b. Kenosha, Wis., 7/10/29. Stud. piano, brass instruments, bass in Kenosha; general music courses at Chicago Musical College 1948-9. Doubled on trom. and bass in first jobs. Worked in Chicago w. Bud Freeman, Bill Russo combos, '50; on the road w. Tex Beneke '51-4. Moved to LA, worked w. Bob Brookmeyer, Kenny Drew groups '54, traveled w. Les Brown orch. '55-6. Night clubs w. Peggy Lee group '56. Ambition: To divide time between jazz, symphony and motion picture studio work. Favs: Ray Brown, Red Mitchell, Percy Heath. LPs: Vict. LPM1121 (*The Five*); Clef 644 (Bob Brookmeyer); Gene Norman 9 (Lyle Murphy); Cap T6511 (Claude Williamson); Atl. 1216 (Dave Pell); Cap. T659 (*Les Brown All Stars*).
Addr: 1428 North Sierra Bonita Ave., Hollywood 46, Calif.

CLARKE, Kenny Free-lancing in New York, took part in virtually every LP session for Savoy records, some of which are listed below.
LPs: EmArcy 36043 (Cannonball Adderley); Savoy 12015 (Eddie Bert), 12017 (*Bohemia after Dark*), 12018 (Presenting Cannonball), 12007 (*Clarke-Wilkins Septet*), 12022 (*Flutes and Reeds*), 12023 (*The Trio*); Atl. 1217 (Lee Konitz); Savoy 12028 (John Mehegan); Riv. 12-201 (Thelonious Monk); Signal 1201 (Gigi Gryce); Savoy 12042 (own sextet in *Roll 'em Bags*), 12046 (Milt Jackson), 12064 (*The Jazz Message*), 12065 (*Klook's Clique*); Dawn 1104 (Mat Mathews).

CLAYTON, Buck Featured in motion picture, *The Benny Goodman Story,* 1956. LPs: Col. CL754 (Count Basie); Epic LN3168, 3169 (Count Basie); Col. CL701 (*Jumpin' at the Woodside; A Buck Clayton Jam Session*), CL808 (*Jazz Spectacular* with Frankie Laine), CL778 (*Cat Meets Chick*); Storyville 906 (*Messin' 'Round in Montmartre*); Jazztone 1225 (*American in Paris*); Decca DL8252, 8253 (*Benny Goodman Story* sound track).

CLEVELAND, Jimmy LPs: Em. 36043 (Cannonball Adderley); Contemp. 3502 (Lionel Hampton); Em. 36007 (Clark Terry), 36011 (Dinah Washington); Signal 1201 (Gigi Gryce; as "James Van Dyke"); EmArcy 36066 (own groups); Pres. 7031 (Art Farmer); ARS 405 (Dizzy Gillespie); ABC-Par. 111 (Lucky Thompson).

COBB, Arnett LPs: Decca DL8088 (Lionel Hampton).

COHN, Al Under contract to RCA Victor 1955-6, he worked on innumerable record albums, as tenor saxophonist, arranger, or both, in addition to making sessions for various other labels as listed below.
LPs: Vict. LPM1107 (arr. & pl. in *Basses Loaded*); Col. CL701 (Buck Clayton); Vict. LJM1024 (*Mr. Music*), LPM1116 (*The Natural Seven*), LPM1161 (*Four Brass, One Tenor*), LPM1162 (*The Brothers*); Beth. 15 (Don Elliott; as "Ike Horowitz"), 14 (Urbie Green; as "Ike Horowitz"); Wing 60002 (Art Mardigan); Vict. LPM1147 (Teddi King); Fant. 219, 206 (Elliot Lawrence); Vict. LPM1146 (*Lullaby of Birdland*); Kapp 1004 (Benny Payne; as "Phil Flatbush"); Vict. LPM1118, LPM1198 (Joe Newman); Pres. 7022 (*The Brothers*); Savoy 12048 (*Al Cohn's Tones*); ABC-Par. 106 (Don Elliott); Vict. LPM1210 (Freddie Greene); LPM1211 (Manny Albam); LPM-1269 (Billy Byers); ABC-Par. 125 (Candido).

COKER, Henry LPs: Clef 647, 666 (Count Basie); Vict. LPM1210 (Freddie Greene); Pres. 7037 (Tadd Dameron).

COKER, Jerry LPs: Fant. 214 (*Modern Music from Indiana University*).

COLE, Cozy LPs: Jazztone 1207 (Sammy Price); EmArcy 36071 (*Drum Roll*).

COLE, Nat "King" Acting and singing role in motion picture, *Istanbul;* also in short feature based on his career, *The Nat "King" Cole Story.* LPs: W689 (piano solos acc. by Nelson Riddle Orch.), T332 (*Penthouse Serenade,* quartet); Decca 8260 (*In the Beginning*—King Cole Trio).

COLLETTE, Buddy Took leave of absence from his regular job as member of house band on Groucho Marx TV show to go on tour w. Chico Hamilton quintet, Spring, 1956. Made first album under his own name for Pacific Jazz.

LPs: Decca DL8130 (*Blow Hot, Blow Cool*); Pac. Jazz 1209 (Chico Hamilton); Decca 8156 (Jack Millman); Contemp. 3506 (Lyle Murphy); Liberty 6007 (Jack Millman); Pac. Jazz 1216 (Chico Hamilton); MGM 3390 (*West Coast Jazz vs. East Coast Jazz*).

COLLINS, Dick LPs: Cap. T658 (Woody Herman); Vict. LPM1146 (*Lullaby of Birdland*).

COLTRANE, John William, *tenor sax;* b. Hamlet, N.C., 9/23/26. Father, a tailor, played several instruments as hobby. Stud. E-flat alto horn, clar., then saxophone in high school; later at Granoff Studios and Ornstein School of Music in Philadelphia. Professional debut with cocktail combo in Philadelphia, 1945. Navy band in Hawaii, '45-6. Toured w. Eddie Vinson r & b band '47-8; Dizzy Gillespie, '49-51; Earl Bostic, '52-3; Johnny Hodges, '53-4; Miles Davis, '55-6. Several record dates in 1956 w. Paul Chambers group for Jazz: West in LA; w. Miles Davis for Prestige, Columbia in New York, etc. Favs: Sonny Stitt, Dexter Gordon, Sonny Rollins, Stan Getz. LPs: Pres. 7014 (Miles Davis); Jazz: West (Paul Chambers); Pres. 7043 (Elmo Hope).

Addr: 1511 N. 33rd St., Philadelphia, Pa.

CONDON, Eddie LPs: Col. CL632 (*Chicago Style Jazz*), CL719 (*Bixieland*); Jazztone 1216 (*Dixieland Classics*); Savoy 12055 (*Ringside at Condon's*); ABC-Par. 121 (*Brother Matthew*).

CONNOR, Chris LPs: Beth. 20 (*This Is Chris*); 56 (*Chris*); Atl. 1228 (*Chris Connor*).

COOK, Willie LPs: Beth. 60 (Duke Ellington); Col. CL872 (Rosemary Clooney and Duke Ellington).

COOPER, Bob Still working regularly at the Lighthouse in Hermosa Beach, Calif., this outstanding West Coast musician continued to double on tenor sax and oboe, remaining virtually the only jazz musician to use the latter effectively for improvisation.

LPs: EmArcy 36009 (Maynard Ferguson); Contemp. 3504, 3509 (Howard Rumsey); Decca 8257 (*The Man with the Golden Arm*); Cap. 6513 (own band: *Shifting Winds*); Savoy 12045 (Shelly Manne); Beth. 52 (Mel Tormé); Pac. Jazz 1219 (Bud Shank), Contemp. C 3512 (oboe w. Barney Kessel).

COPELAND, Ray M., *trumpet, arranger;* b. Norfolk, Va., 7/17/26. Four years tpt. study at Wurlitzer School of Music. Further studies with Prof. Middle-

ton, concert tpt. artist. Started gigging around Brooklyn with local groups. Joined Cecil Scott at Savoy Ballroom, NYC in 1945. After working w. Chris Columbus at Small's Paradise throughout '46, toured w. Mercer Ellington band '47-8 and w. Al Cooper's Savoy Sultans '48-9. In '50, took day job with paper company, remaining there for 5½ years and gigging in spare time w. Andy Kirk, Lucky Millinder, Lucky Thompson, Sy Oliver et al. Played lead tpt. on Frankie Laine-Buck Clayton session for Columbia, October, '55. Best solo work on Savoy and Prestige LPs listed below. Favs: Ernie Royal, Clifford Brown, Joe Wilder, Jimmy Nottingham. Ambitions: To expand activity as arr., make name as good lead tpt. and gain staff employment in radio or TV. LPs: Savoy 12044 (*Top Brass*); Prestige 7053 (Thelonious Monk).

Addr: 138-12 Linden Blvd., Jamaica 36, N.Y.

CORCORAN, Corky LPs: Em. 36023 (*Battle of the Saxes*), 36018 (Willie Smith); Gene Norman 15 (Lionel Hampton).

COSTA, Edwin J., *piano, vibes;* b. Atlas, Pa., 8/14/30. Stud. piano with brother, then with private teacher. Self-taught on vibes. After finishing high school, left for NYC. At 18 joined Joe Venuti. After 2 yrs. of Army service, worked in night clubs w. Sal Salvador, Tal Farlow combos, free-lanced around New York w. Kai Winding, Don Elliott et al. In addition to being a very capable vibraphonist, Costa plays piano in a unique style in which octave unison work is a strikingly characteristic feature. LPs: Kapp 1007 (Morey Feld); Savoy 12049 (*A Pair of Pianos*), 12051 (Mike Cuozzo); Cap. 6505 (Sal Salvador).

Addr: 153-10 75th Ave., Kew Garden Hills, N.Y.

COSTANZO, Jack LPs: Decca 8156 (Jack Millman); Col. CL689 (Pete Rugolo); Beth. 44 (*Jazz City Workshop*).

COUNCE, Curtis Joined Stan Kenton orch., Jan., 1956, touring England and Continent with him, March to May, '56. LPs: Decca DL8130 (*Blow Hot, Blow Cool*); Clef 676 (Illinois Jacquet); Decca 8156 (Jack Millman); Contemp. 3506 (Lyle Murphy); Atl. 1212 (Shorty Rogers); EmArcy 36039 (*Best Coast Jazz*); Beth. 44 (Jazz City Workshop); MGM 3390 (*West Coast vs East Coast*).

CRAWFORD, Jimmy LPs: EmArcy 36042 (Eddie Heywood); Period 1115 (Josh White).

CROSBY, Bob LPs: Coral 57005 (*The Bobcats Ball*); Col. CL766 (*The Bob Crosby Show*).

CROTTY, Ron LPs: Fant. 210 (Brubeck); 213 (own trio in *Modern Music from San Francisco*).

CROW, Bill Joined Gerry Mulligan in time for Spring, '56 tour of France and Italy. LPs: Cap. T699 (Marian McPartland).

CUOZZO Mike, *tenor sax;* b. Newark, N.J., 1925. Played in many name bands 1943-9 incl. Tommy Reynolds, Joe Marsala, Shep Fields, Elliot Lawrence. Since then, has free-lanced around New Jersey. LPs: Savoy 12051 (*Mighty Mike Cuozzo*).

CUTSHALL, Cutty LPs: Col. CL719 (Eddie Condon); ABC-Par. 121 (*Brother Matthew*).

DAMERON, Tadd LPs: Pres. 7037 (*Fontainebleau*).

D'AMICO, Hank LPs: Coral 57018 (Steve Allen).

DAROIS, Philip Neri, *string bass, tuba;* b. Lynn, Mass., 2/23/19. Stud. at school in Charlotte, N.C., later with private teachers and at Loyola U. Local bands in Charlotte and Boston; Dean Hudson, 1941-2, Ray Herbeck, '42, then served 4 yrs. in the Army, playing in symphony, dance and military bands. Worked again briefly w. Dean Hudson in '46, then w. Ray Eberle, Johnny Blowers. Living in New Orleans, worked w. Leon Prima, Louis Prima and his own combo '47-9, then w. Peter Toma orch. at Roosevelt Hotel '50-3. Since then has been employed at WDSU-TV (NBC) in New Orleans as staff musician, also working with Pete Fountain and His Three Coins. Favs: Bob Haggart, Walter Page. LPs: South. 217 (Monk Hazel), 213 (Santo Pecora), 210 (Pete Fountain).
Addr: 2418 Pressburg St., New Orleans, La.

DAVENPORT, Charles "Cow Cow" Pioneer boogie-woogie pianist died in Cleveland, Ohio, 12/2/55.

DAVIS, Eddie "Lockjaw" LPs: Roost 1203 (*The Battle of Birdland*).

DAVIS, Lem LPs: Col. CL701 (Buck Clayton).

DAVIS, Miles LPs: Pres. 7007 (*The Musings of Miles*); Blue Note 1501, 1502 (own groups); Pres. 7013 (*Conception*), 7012 (*Dig*), 7025 (*Miles Davis and Horns*), 7014 (*The New Miles Davis Quintet*); Debut 120 (*Blue Moods*); Pres. 7054 (quartets, quintet), 7034 (w. Jackson, McLean).

DAVIS, Richard LPs: Cadence 1004 (Don Shirley).

DAVISON, Wild Bill LPs: Col. CL719 (Eddie Condon); EmArcy 36013 (Bud Freeman); Col. CL717 (Garry Moore); Savoy 12055 (*Ringside at Condon's*); ABC-Par. 121 (*Brother Matthew*).

DEDRICK, Lyle F. "Rusty", *trumpet, arranger;* b. Delevan, N.Y., 7/12/18. Brother, Arthur, played trom. w. Red Norvo. Attended Fredonia State Teachers College; studied privately with Paul Creston and Stephan Wolpe. Worked w. Dick Stabile 1938-9, Red Norvo '39-41, Claude Thornhill '41-2. After Army service '42-5, he spent 3 months in Ray McKinley's band then rejoined Claude Thornhill '46-7, after which he settled in New York doing NBC-TV shows, records, etc., and arranging for Richard Maltby and others. Though not well-known as a jazzman, he has an exceptional tone and pleasant ad lib style. Favs: Louis Armstrong, Bunny Berigan, Miles Davis, Don Elliott. Fav. own solo, *You Are Too Beautiful* in Keynote album. LPs: Kapp 1004 (Benny Payne); River 2517 (*Six Valves with Don Elliott*); Esoteric 9 (*Rhythm and Winds*), 534 (Larry Carr); Keynote (own group).
Addr: 3 Tenth St., Carle Place, L.I.

DEEMS, Barrett LPs: Col. CL708, Decca DL8168, 8169; Col. CL840 (Louis Armstrong).

DE FRANCO, Buddy Featured in motion picture, *Wild Party,* Feb., 1956. LPs: Norg. 1016 (*De Franco and Peterson Play Gershwin*), 1026 (own quartet); Clef 642, 667 (Lionel Hampton), 656 (*Jam Session #6*); MGM E3286 (*Hot vs Cool*); Clef MG17 (JATP Vol. 17).

DELANEY, Jack Michael, *trombone;* b. New Orleans, La., 8/27/30. Studied Southeastern Louisiana College. Played w. Johnny Reininger 1949-51, Sharkey Bonano, '51-3, Tony Almerico '53-4, then rejoined Bonano. Also worked as staff member of WDSU—TV station in New Orleans. Rec. with Raymond Burke, Geo. Girard, Monk Hazel, and own group, for Southland; Eileen Barton for Coral; Lizzie Miles and Sharkey for Capitol; Johnny Reininger for Wright, and Tony Almerico for Crescent City. Fav. own solo, *Blues for Joe* w. Raymond Burke. Fav: Jack Teagarden. LPs: South. 217 (Monk Hazel); 214 (*New Orleans Jazz Babies*), 209 (Raymond Burke); Cap. T266 (Sharkey Bonano).
Addr: 3223 Dante St., New Orleans, La.

DENNIS, Matt Spent most of 1955-6 in New York; featured first on his own television program, then on the daily Ernie Kovacs Show, playing and singing. LPs: Vict. LPM1134 (*Dennis, Anyone?*); Kapp 1024 (transferred from Trend).

DE PARIS, Sidney LPs: Atl. 1219 (Wilbur De Paris).

DE PARIS, Wilbur LPs: Atl. 1219 (*New New Orleans Jazz*); River. 2516 (Sidney Bechet).

DESMOND, Paul LPs: Col. CL622, CL699 (Brubeck); Fant. 210 (Brubeck).

DEVITO, Frank Albert, *drums;* b. Utica, N.Y., 8/14/30. Stud. locally in 1942, then with Jim Chapin in NYC, 1948. Inspired by seeing Leo Gorcey in drum sequence in picture *Blues in the Night,* he made professional debut at 12. Played w. Bob Astor 1947, Ben Ventura '48, Buddy DeFranco '49 and '51, then w. Glen Gray and Hal McIntyre. Featured w. Terry Gibbs Quartet off and on '53-5. Featured in a film, *Step Down to Terror* (or *Wild Party*) with Buddy DeFranco, Feb. '56. Favs: Max Roach, Buddy Rich, Gene Krupa. LPs: Bruns. 54009 (Terry Gibbs); Beth. 1015 (Terry Pollard).

Addr: 1300 Steuben St., Utica, N.Y.

DICKENSON, Vic LPs: EmArcy 36038 (*Boning Up On 'Bones*); Van. 8504 (Ruby Braff); Jazztone 1207 (Sammy Price); Decca 8202 (Eddie Heywood); Norg. 1056 (*The Jazz Giants '56*); Jazztone 1227 (Jimmy McPartland); Story. 908 (Ruby Braff); Vict. LPM-1332 (Braff).

DODDS, Baby LPs: Epic 3207 (Johnny Dodds and Kid Ory).

DODDS, Johnny LPs: Epic 3207 (Johnny Dodds and Kid Ory).

DODGE, Joe LPs: Col. CL622, CL699 (Brubeck).

DOMINIQUE, Natty LPs: Epic 3207 (Johnny Dodds and Kid Ory).

DONALDSON, Lou LPs: Pres. 7050 (Gene Ammons).

DORHAM, Kenny After working for some months with Art Blakey's Jazz Messengers, Dorham left to form his own group, the Prophets, in early 1956. LPs: Norg. 1035 (w. Charlie Parker in *Alto Saxes*); Blue Note 1507, 1508 (*The Jazz Messengers at the Café Bohemia*); Savoy 12042 (Milt Jackson); Blue Note 5062 (Horace Silver), 5065 (*Afro-Cuban Holiday*); Pres. 7037 (Tadd Dameron); Signal 1203 (Cecil Payne); ABC-Par. 122 (own group).

DORSEY, Jimmy LPs: Epic 3128 (Red Norvo).

DORSEY, Tommy The Dorsey Brothers orch., led mainly by Tommy, but with Jimmy prominently featured, earned national publicity in 1955-6 through the Dorseys' own TV program *Stage Show,* seen every Saturday night over CBS. In addition, they spent several months in '56 on location at the Statler Hotel in NYC. Featured soloists with the band incl. Charlie Shavers, Lee Castle, and Louis Bellson.

DREW, John Derek, *bass;* b. Sheffield, Yorkshire, England, 12/23/27. Stud. piano as child, took up bass in Liverpool at 16. Stud. with private teacher. Later moved to London; worked with all kinds of pop and show bands incl. 2 yrs. w. Billy Ternent (BBC work, etc.). Immigrated to US, 1954. After working w. Les Elgart and others, went out to West Coast; w. Gene Krupa as first permanent bassist to augment trio to quartet size. Also made records w. Neal Hefti, appeared w. Hefti's band at Birdland; other records w. Nat Pierce, Dick Garcia et al. Original inspiration was Jimmy Blanton. Present favs: Ray Brown, Red Mitchell, Milt Hinton. Polished and promising modern bass man. LPs: Clef 668 (Gene Krupa); Epic 3187 (Neal Hefti); Dawn (Dick Garcia-Tony Scott).

Addr: 29 W. 65th St., New York 23, N.Y.

DREW, Kenny LPs: Norg. 1026 (Buddy De Franco); EmArcy 36039 (*Best Coast Jazz*); Jazz: West 4 (*Talkin' and Walkin' with the Kenny Drew Quartet*), 5 (quartet with Jane Fielding); ABC-Par. 110 (piano & vibories in *Swingin' On the Vibories*).

DUNCAN, Henry James "Hank", *piano;* b. Bowling Green, Ky., 10/26/96. Stud. Central High School, Louisville, Fisk U., Nashville. Had own combo in Louisville incl. Jimmy Harrison, trom. Coming to NYC, he worked w. Fess Williams at the Savoy Ballroom and w. Charles "Fat Man" Turner at the Arcadia Ballroom, 53rd and Broadway. Toured US w. Fats Waller's big band, then spent 8 yrs. as solo pianist at Nick's in Greenwich Village. W. Louis Metcalf and Zutty Singleton at the Metropole, NYC, '56. Many early records w. Fess Williams et al on Victor, Vocalion, Okeh, Columbia, Brunswick, Harmony, and other extinct labels. Also recorded w. King Oliver and Fats' big band on Victor. Fav. own record, *Maple Leaf Rag* w. Sidney Bechet's Original Feetwarmers on Victor. An authentic and expert traditional-style pianist, he names Fats Waller, J. P. Johnson, Teddy Wilson, and Earl Hines as his favorites. LPs: Jazztone 1215 (Tony Parenti).

Addr: 112-46 Dillon St., Jamaica 33, N.Y.

DURAN, Edward Lozano, *guitar;* b. San Francisco, 9/6/25. Brothers, Carlos, bass and Manual, piano, play w. Cal Tjader. Stud. piano in 1932, took up guitar in '37. Stud. for 7 months, but mainly self-taught. As child, sang in amateur hours with brother Manual in Fanchon & Marco reviews, winning first prizes. Aside from 2 yrs. in the Navy, has spent most of his time in SF where he has worked w. Freddie Slack, Flip Phillips, Charlie Parker, Stan Getz, George Shearing, Vince Guaraldi, Red Norvo, and Earl Hines. LPs: Fant. 211 (Cal Tjader), 213 (*Modern Music from San Francisco*), 217 (Earl Hines).

Addr: 1400 Jones St., San Francisco, Calif.

EAGER, Allen LPs: Em. 36016 (*Advance Guard of the 40s*); Atl. 1220 (Tony Fruscella); Pres. 7006 (Gerry Mulligan).

EARDLEY, Jon Featured mainly since Fall of 1954 in Gerry Mulligan combo, with which he toured Europe early '56. LPs: EmArcy 36056 (Gerry Mulligan); Pres. 7033 (*The Jon Eardley Seven*).

EATON, John Charles, *piano, arranger;* b. Philadelphia, Pa., 3/30/35. Extensive studies; began playing at local resorts in Poconos from age 9. Gave concerts, accompanied singers, etc. Summer resort work w. Clem Wiedenmyer, 1949-53; Stan Rubin, '54-5. Also had own group '53-6, recording for Columbia, but limited in other activities as all members were students at Princeton. Fav. own solo, *The Nearness of You* in own album. Ambitious modernist musician whose goal, he says, is "To express myself as an individual by the use of sounds, silences, motions, and time." Favs: Bud Powell, Lennie Tristano, Earl Hines. Fav. arr., Ralph Burns. LPs: Col. CL737 (*College Jazz: Modern*).
Addr: 83 South Courtland St., East Stroudsburg, Pa.

ECKSTINE, Billy Toured the US in vaudeville, paying another successful visit to England and France in Spring of 1956. LPs: Em. 36016 (own band in *Advance Guard of the '40s*), 36038 (valve tromb. with own band in *Boning Up On 'Bones*); MGM E3176 (*Mr. B with a Beat*).

EDISON, Harry LPs: Vict. LPM1112, Col. CL754 (Count Basie); Epic LN3168, 3169 (Count Basie); Clef 669 (Billie Holiday), 676 (Illinois Jacquet); Pac. Jazz 1211 (Cy Touff); Norg. 1038 (*Buddy and Sweets*); Contemp. 3513 (Barney Kessel); Cap. 707 (*Session at Midnight*).

ELDRIDGE, Roy LPs: Norg. 1028 (Ralph Burns); Clef 641, 671 (*Roy and Diz*), 683 (*Little Jazz*), MG17 (JATP Vol. 17), 684 (*Krupa and Rich*); Norg. 1056 (*The Jazz Giants '56*); Verve 2008 (Gene Krupa).

ELGART, Larry LPs: Decca 8034 (*Music for Barefoot Ballerinas*).

ELLINGTON, Duke Ended his affiliation with Capitol records in late 1955. In early '56, he rec. an album for Columbia with Rosemary Clooney, and 2 instrumental albums for Bethlehem. His band continued to tour mostly in night clubs with the same featured soloists as before, except that Johnny Hodges rejoined him during 1955 and a new drummer, Sam Woodyard, featured frequently in solos, earned considerable publicity and popularity.
LPs: Bruns. 54007 (Early Ellington); Vict. LPM-1092 (*The Duke and His Men*); Cap. T637 (*Dance to the Duke*); Cap. T679 (*Ellington Showcase*); Norg. 1055 (*Ellingtonia '56;* Duke's band under the leadership of Johnny Hodges); Beth. 60 (*Historically Speaking, the Duke*); Col. CL872 (*Blue Rose;* Rosemary Clooney and Duke Ellington); Cap. T477 (trio).

ELLIOTT, Don LPs: Beth. 15 (*Don Elliott Sings*), 12 (*Don Elliott: Mellophone*); Kapp 1007 (Morey Feld); MGM E3286 (*Hot vs Cool*); ABC-Par. 106 (own sextette); Coral 57035 (*East Coast Jazz Scene*, Vol. 1); River. 206 (Marty Bell/Don Elliott).

ELLIS, Herb LPs: Clef 667 (Lionel Hampton), 656 (*Jam Session #6*), 648, 649, 650 (Oscar Peterson), 637 (Flip Phillips); Verve 2001 (Toni Harper); Clef MG17 (JATP Vol. 17); Norg. 1044 (*New Jazz Sounds*); ARS 403 (Lionel Hampton).

ELMAN, Ziggy Though seen in the motion picture, *The Benny Goodman Story*, playing *And the Angels Sing*, Elman did not record the sound track. The music for this passage was rec. by Manny Klein. Elman continued to work as a studio musician on the West Coast. LPs: Vict. LPM1099 (Benny Goodman); Atl. 1225 (Jess Stacy).

ELWOOD, John (Stapleton), *bass;* b. Welland, Ontario, 3/9/27. Bass in high school; professional at 15. Became interested in radio engineering, worked in many radio stations. Went to Toronto, 1943; stud. at conservatory and appeared at leading local clubs accompanying name singers, then joined Calvin Jackson quartet, touring US and Canada, 1955-6. LPs: Col. CL756 (Calvin Jackson).

ENEVOLDSEN, Bob LPs: Norg. 1030 (Tal Farlow); Decca 8156 (Jack Millman); Contemp. 3503 (Lennie Niehaus); Beth. 19 (Bobby Troup); Cap. 6513 (Bob Cooper); Beth. 52 (Mel Tormé); Liberty 6008 (*Smorgasbord*); ABC-Par. 110 (tenor, valve trombone, bass in *Swingin' On the Vibories*); Contemp. 3514 (Duane Tatro); MGM 3390 (*West Coast vs East Coast*).

ERWIN, Pee Wee LPs: Grand Award 310, 313 (Bobby Byrne); Bruns. 54011 (*The Land of Dixie*); Urania 1202 (*Accent on Dixieland*); Grand Award 322 (*A Musical History of Jazz*); Cadence 1011 (*At the Grandview Inn*).

EVANS, Doc LPs: Col. CL793 (Turk Murphy).

EWELL, Don LPs: Good Time Jazz 12008 (Kid Ory).

FAGERQUIST, Don This excellent jazz trumpet artist joined the staff at Paramount Studios Jan. 1956. LPs: Cap. T659 (*The Les Brown All Stars*); Decca DL8104 (John Graas); Keynote 1101 (Nat Pierce); Beth. 52 (Mel Tormé); MGM 3390 (*West Coast vs East Coast*).

FARLOW, Tal LPs: Norg. 1027 (*The Interpretations of Tal Farlow*), 1030 (*A Recital by Tal Farlow*), 1033 (*Swing Guitars*); Fant. 218 (Red Norvo).

FARMER, Addison Gerald, *bass;* b. Council Bluffs, Ia., 8/21/28. Twin brother of trumpeter, Art Farmer. Stud. bass with Fred Zimmerman; piano and theory at Juilliard and Manhattan School of Music. Has worked w. Jay McShann, Art Farmer, Benny Carter, Howard McGhee, Gerald Wilson, Teddy Charles, Lucky Thompson, Ch. Parker, Miles Davis. Record debut in L. A., 1949 w. Teddy Edwards. Favs: Oscar Pettiford, Ray Brown, Percy Heath. LPs: Herald 0101 (Anthony Ortega); Prestige 193, 209, 7017 (Art Farmer), 7039, 7050 (Gene Ammons).

Addr: 134 W. 95th St., New York 25, N.Y.

FARMER, Art Led own quintet with Gigi Gryce, 1955-6; also feat. with Lester Young and other combos around New York. LPs: Fant. 209 (Sandole); Signal 1201 (Gigi Gryce); Prestige 7017 (own quintet); Atl. 1229 (Teddy Charles; as "Peter Urban"); Dawn 1104 (Mat Mathews); Pres. 7031 (own septet, *Plays the Compositions and Arrangements of Gigi Gryce and Quincy Jones*), 7039, 7050 (Gene Ammons), 7041 (Bennie Green).

FAZOLA, Irving LPs: EmArcy 36022 (*New Orleans Express*).

FEATHER, Leonard LPs: MGM 3390 (own groups in *West Coast vs. East Coast Jazz*); ABC-Par. 110 (own groups in *Swingin' on the Vibories*); Period 1909 (harps., arr. w. Maxine Sullivan), 1975 (arr. for *The Jones Boys*); Jazztone J-1229 (sup. *Flow Gently Sweet Rhythm*), J-1222 (piano w. Jack Teagarden in *Big T*); Decca 8088 (piano w. Dinah Washington in Lionel Hampton concert).

FELD, Morey, *drums;* b. Cleveland, O., 8/15/15. Self-taught. Played w. Ben Pollack, '36; Joe Haymes, '38; Benny Goodman, '44-5; Eddie Condon, '47; Billy Butterfield, '52; Bobby Hackett, '53; Peanuts Hucko, '54; was staff musician at ABC studios in New York for several years. Made record debut 1940 with Jess Stacy combo; many sessions in mid-'40s with Slam Stewart, Red Norvo et al. Film: *Sweet and Lowdown* with Goodman. Favs: Buddy Rich, Don Lamond. LPs: Kapp 1007 (own group in *Jazz Goes to Broadway*); Decca 5213 (Bud Freeman); Col. 6052 (Benny Goodman).

Addr: 81-06 34th Ave., Jackson Heights 72, N.Y.

FELDMAN, Victor Stanley, *vibes, drums, piano, arranger;* b. London, England, 4/7/34. Mainly self-taught through listening to his three brothers rehearsing with local musicians and played his first gig in the Rhythm Club, London, at the age of 7. He was hailed in the *Melody Maker* as a child genius. During the next few years he took up piano (at 9), studied music, tympani, etc. at London Coll. of Music; vibes at 14 with Carlo Krahmer. Self-taught as arranger. Feldman's

cousin Max Bacon, ex-Ambrose drummer, helped introduce him in music circles; in 1942 he appeared in a Jazz Jamboree at the Palladium; from '41 to '47 had his own trio with two brothers. At 10, guest star with Glenn Miller AEF band in London. Other appearances with Vic Lewis, Ted Heath; to Switzerland with Ralph Sharon group at 15. Paris Jazz Festival 1952; to India with Eddie Carroll '53-4. Movie: *King Arthur Was a Gentleman* (at age 8), etc. Five magazine awards from *Melody Maker* and *Musical Express* as Britain's No. 1 vibes man. Left for US Oct. '55; joined Woody Herman Jan. '56 and was soon recognized by American musicians as an exceptional jazz-man. Favs: Milt Jackson, Norvo, vibes; Tatum, John Lewis, piano; Sid Catlett, Tiny Kahn, Max Roach, Buddy Rich, Kenny Clarke, Art Taylor, drums; Ellington, Mulligan, Lewis, arrangers. Records: made debut at 8 in London, recorded with own groups and with Ronnie Scott, for local Esquire and Tempo labels. First US recordings with own combo for Keynote LP.

FERGUSON, Maynard LPs: EmArcy 36009 (*Jam Session*), 36021 (own octet); Decca 8156 (as "Tiger Brown" with Jack Millman); EmArcy 36046 (*Hollywood Party*), 36060 (Georgie Auld); Beth. 46 (*Four Horns and a Lush Life*); Cap. W724 (Stan Kenton).

FIELDS, Herbie LPs: Decca DL8130 (*Blow Hot, Blow Cool*), DL8088 (Lionel Hampton).

FINEGAN, Bill LPs: Vict. LPM1051 (*Concert Jazz*), LPM1240 (*Adventure in Time*).

FITCH, Mal, *singer, piano, composer;* b. Cleveland, O., 1927. Stud. with Cleveland Philharmonic conductor and others; 2 yrs. at Bethany College. Entered service '45, later continuing studies until '50. During Army career was leader of 2nd Army Band at Ft. Meade, Md., '46-8, also acting as disc jockey on Armed Forces station. Formed duo with wife, Betty, a singer, working in Dallas hotel for more than a year. Joined Crewcuts, pop vocal group, in May, 1955, as pianist and arr. Fitch has an attractive vocal style recalling at times some of the characteristics of Nat Cole and Bobby Troup. LPs: EmArcy 36041 (own quartet).

FITZGERALD, Ella Late in 1955 Ella Fitzgerald ended her twenty-year affiliation with Decca Records and began to record for Norman Granz on his new Verve label. Under the personal management of Granz, she began to play better-class hotel jobs, etc., and to earn even wider general recognition. Her first featured film appearance, in *Pete Kelly's Blues,* gave her added attention in late 1955. LPs: Decca DL8155 (*Sweet and Hot*), DL8166 (*Pete Kelly's Blues*), 8149 (*Lullabies of Birdland*); Verve 4001, 4002 (*Sings the Cole Porter Songbook*).

FLAX, Marty (Martin Flachsenhaar), *baritone sax;* b. New York City, 10/7/24. Has worked with Woody Herman, Louis Jordan, Raymond Scott, Lucky Millinder, Perez Prado. After playing some dates with Les Elgart in 1956 he joined the band assembled by Quincy Jones for an overseas tour under the leadership of Dizzy Gillespie. LPs: Van. 8014, Beth. 18 (Sam Most).

Addr: 3070 48th St., Astoria, L.I., N.Y.

FLEMING, Herb LPs: Beth. 21 (*Jazz at the Metropole*).

FLORES, Chuck LPs: Vict. LPM1162 (Al Cohn); Pac. Jazz 1211 (Cy Touff), 1215 (Bud Shank); Beth. 54 (Claude Williamson).

FONTANA, Carl LPs: Cap. T666, W724 (Stan Kenton); Pac. Jazz 1221 (Bill Perkins); Beth. 48 (Max Bennett).

FOSTER, Frank LPs: Clef 647, 666, 678 (Count Basie); Jazztone J-1220 (*The Count's Men*); Savoy 12029, 12032 (Donald Byrd); Story. 905 (Joe Newman); Pres. 7021 (*Hope Meets Foster*).

FOSTER, "Pops" Toured Continent and North Africa with Sammy Price combo early 1956.

FOUNTAIN, Peter Dewey, Jr., *clarinet, saxes;* b. New Orleans, La., 7/3/30. Father played drums and violin with jazz bands around Biloxi, Miss. Started on clarinet in school band, 1942; played with Junior Dixieland Jazz Band, '48-9; Phil Zito, '49-50; Basin Street Six, '50-4; since then, featured with his own group, Pete Fountain and his Three Coins. Has worked mainly in New Orleans but also made several trips to Chicago for jobs at Jazz Limited and the Blue Note, '49-53. Favs: Irving Fazola, Eddie Miller. LPs: South. 217 (Monk Hazel), 214 (Jack Delaney), 210 (*and his Three Coins*).

Addr: 409 Sena Drive, New Orleans, La.

FOUR FRESHMEN LPs: Cap. T683 (*with Five Trombones*).

FOWLKES, Charlie LPs: Clef 666 (Count Basie); Col. CL701 (Buck Clayton).

FREEMAN, Bud LPs: Col. CL 632 (*Chicago Style Jazz*); Grand Award 310, 313 (Will Bradley; also own trio on 313); EmArcy 36013 (*Midnight at Eddie Condon's*); Beth. 29 (own quintet); Weathers 5501 (*George Wettling*); Grand Award 322 (*A Musical History of Jazz*); Jazztone 1227 (Jimmy McPartland).

FREEMAN, Russ LPs: Pac. Jazz 1206 (Chet Baker), 1203 (Chet Baker), 1202 (Chet Baker), 1211 (Cy Touff); Contemp. 3516 (Shelly Manne); Pac. Jazz 1212 (trio).

FRIGO, John Virgil, *bass, violin, trumpet;* b. Chicago, Ill., 12/27/16. Stud. with Nathan Oberman, Ludwig Becker. Tuba, bass viol, in high school. Member of 4 Californians cocktail unit, 1934-40. In Chico Marx band 1943-5 as musician, comedian; singer in Mel Tormé group. Bass, violin w. Jimmy Dorsey band, '45-7; then left, with Dorsey pianist Lou Carter and guitarist Herb Ellis to form the Soft Winds Trio, a delightful instrumental and vocal group. Their compositions, *Detour Ahead* and *I Told Ya I Love Ya, Now Get Out* earned some popular success. Since '52, Frigo has free-lanced in Chicago on TV and records mostly, teamed with pianist Dick Marx. He is one of the few modern musicians to experiment successfully with ad lib violin. Fav. own record: *Polka Dots and Moonbeams*, violin solo in Marx LP (see below). Favs: Ray Brown, bass; no fav. on violin. LPs: Coral 57022 (Buddy Greco); Bruns. 54006 (Dick Marx); Jubilee 1017 (Dave Remington).

FRUSCELLA, Tony, *trumpet;* b. Orangeburg, N.J., 2/4/27. Lived in orphanage until age of 14; stud. with Jerome Cnuddle. At 18, entered Army and played in 2nd Division Band. Later worked w. Lester Young, Gerry Mulligan, Stan Getz, playing at Newport Jazz Festival in 1954 w. Mulligan. Married to singer, Morgana King. Promising new tpt. stylist in modern idiom. Favs: Joe Thomas, Phil Sunkel, Dizzy Gillespie, Don Joseph. LPs: Atl. 1220 (own group); Coral 57035 (*East Coast Jazz Scene*, Vol. 1).

GALBRAITH, Barry LPs: Beth. 12 (Don Elliott); Beth. 16, Vict. LPM1164 (Hal McKusick); Em. 36011 (Dinah Washington); Urania 1204 (Jimmy Hamilton); EmArcy 36066 (Jimmy Cleveland); Beth. 18 (Sam Most).

GARCIA, Richard Joseph, *guitar;* b. New York City, 5/11/31. Great-grandfather played command performance for King of Spain; grandfather and father both guitarists. Started playing by ear at 9; one year's study 1944-5. Terry Gibbs, hearing him at jam session in Greenwich Village, recommended him to Tony Scott, with whose combo he first played in 1950. While with George Shearing quintet, Feb.-Dec. 1952, toured US and Honolulu, recorded *Lullaby of Birdland*, etc. Free-lanced around New York, worked with Joe Roland '55, back with Tony Scott off and on '55-6. Fav. own recs. w. own quartet in *Jazzville USA, Vol. II* on Dawn; also feat. in ABC-Paramount LP with Jimmy Raney, Chuck Wayne, Joe Puma. Favs: Farlow, Kessel, Raney. Garcia is an extraordinarily gifted guitarist, fleet in technique and unusually fluent in phrasing and style. Other LPs: Cap. T642 (Milt Buckner), Col. CL757 (Lenny Hambro); Beth. 17 (Joe Roland);

Vict. LPM1268 (Tony Scott); ABC-Par. 109 (*Greatest Guitarists in the World*).

Addr: 21-62 25th St., Astoria, L.I., N.Y.

GARCIA, Russ, *arranger, trumpet, French horn;* b. Oakland, Cal., 4/12/16. Oakland High, San Francisco State College; private studies w. Edmund Ross, Mario Castelnuovo-Tedesco and others. Trumpet and arr. with high school and local dance bands; later played with Horace Heidt, Al Donahue, Al Lyons at Orpheum Theatre in LA; NBC staff work in Hollywood. Motion picture scores for Universal-International, Warners, Disney, etc. Although mainly concerned with the field of popular music, Garcia has provided appropriate accompaniments for many jazz soloists and for semi-jazz as well as for pop singers. LPs: Beth. 23 (Frances Faye), 40 (*Herbie Mann-Sam Most Quintet*); Verve 2002 (Oscar Peterson); Beth. 46 (*Four Horns and a Lush Life*); Beth. 1040 (*Wigville*); Norg. 1016 (Buddy De Franco-Oscar Peterson).

GARI, Ralph (Ralph Garofalo), *alto sax, clarinet, flute, piccolo, English horn;* b. New Castle, Pa., 7/15/27. Stud. in New Castle, Pittsburgh and NYC. Pl. w. Eddie Rogers in NYC 1945; Frankie Carle '49; settled in Las Vegas, '50, working in concert and jazz groups; organized own quartet '54, playing at El Rancho Vegas, sidemen being Hank Shank, piano; Danny Sherrett, bass; Eddie Julian, drums. Gari's work, though clever and complex, is not of the type usually considered to be legitimate jazz. LPs: EmArcy 36019 (own quartet).

Addr: 1916 Howard St., Las Vegas, Nev.

GARLAND, Ed LPs: Good Time Jazz 12008 (Kid Ory).

GARLAND, William M. "Red", *piano;* b. Dallas, Tex., 5/13/23. Started on clar., stud. with Prof. A. S. Jackson and alto saxophonist Buster Smith. Discovered by Hot Lips Page when the latter was passing through Dallas. Has worked with many name jazz-men since 1945, among them Charlie Parker, Coleman Hawkins, Roy Eldridge, Charlie Ventura, Billy Eckstine Band, Sonny Stitt, Ben Webster, Eddie Davis, Benny Green, Lou Donaldson, Hot Lips Page; w. Miles Davis in '56. Favs: Art Tatum, Bud Powell and Hank Jones. Ambitions: To record solo album with strings, and to lead big band. LPs: Pres. 7007, 7014 (Miles Davis).

Addr: 1528 N. 17th St., Philadelphia, Pa.

GARNER, Erroll LPs: Col. CL 651 (*Music for Tired Lovers*); Col. CL 2540 (*Garnerland*); EmArcy 36069 (solos); Modern 1203 (*Singin' Kay Starr, Swingin' Erroll Garner*).

GEE, Matthew LPs: Keynote 1101 (Nat Pierce).

GELLER, Herb LPs: EmArcy 36009, 36021 (Maynard Ferguson); Decca DL8130 (*Blow Hot, Blow Cool* under the name of "Bert Herbert"); EmArcy 36024 (*The Gellers*); Decca 8156 (as "Bert Herbert" with Jack Millman); EmArcy 36039 (*Best Coast Jazz*), 36040 (own sextette), 36065 (Dinah Washington).

GELLER, Lorraine LPs: EmArcy 36024 (*The Gellers*), 36040 (Herb Geller).

GETZ, Stan While on a visit to Stockholm in the fall of 1955, Getz was taken seriously ill and for the next 6 months he did not work, recuperating in Scandinavia and Africa. On his return, he resumed touring night clubs with a quartet. He was feat. in motion picture, *The Benny Goodman Story*, released early '56.

LPs: Norg. 1032 (*West Coast Jazz*), 1037 (*Hamp and Getz*), 1034 (*Tenor Saxes*); Pres. 7022 (*The Brothers*), 7013 (*Conception*), 7002 (quartets); Norg. 1029 (*Interpretations #3*), 1040 (*Modern Jazz Society*); Roost 2207 (*The Sound*), 2209 (*at Storyville*); Decca DL8252, 8253 (*Benny Goodman Story* sound track); Jazztone 1230 (quartet; quintet).

GIBBS, Terry LPs: Bruns. 54009 ("*Terry*"); EmArcy 36047 (own quartet); 36064 (*Vibes on Velvet*).

GILLESPIE, Dizzy In Feb.-Mar., 1956, while Gillespie was touring Europe w. Norman Granz's JATP, Quincy Jones, in New York, assembled a big band for Gillespie, wrote the arrangements and conducted rehearsals, then took the band to join Gillespie in Rome. Under Dizzy's leadership, this orch. made a tour, from Mar. to May, '56 of Pakistan, Lebanon, Syria, Turkey, Yugoslavia, and Greece.

The tour was subsidized by the US State Department. This was the first time the US Government had ever accorded official recognition and economic aid to jazz. The move was made as a result of the State Department's realization that jazz had become an international force for creating good will for America. Prof. Marshall Stearns, the jazz expert, accompanied Gillespie on most of the tour. After returning to the US, Gillespie retained the big band format, playing Birdland, NYC, May-June, '56, and the Newport Jazz Festival in July, then toured S. America.

LPs: Clef 641, 671 (*Roy and Diz*); Norg. 1003 (*Afro*), 1023 (strings); Decca DL8088 (one no. with Lionel Hampton); Clef 656 (*Jam Session #6*), 677 (*Jam Session #7*); MGM 3286 (*Hot vs. Cool*); Clef MG17 (JATP Vol. 17); Grand Award 318 (*Jazz Concert*); Clef 684 (*Krupa and Rich*); Norg. 1044 (*New Jazz Sounds*); ARS 405 (*Jazz Creations of Dizzy Gillespie*).

GIUFFRE, Jimmy LPs: Cap. T634 (*Tangents In Jazz*); Vict. LPM1105 (Pete Jolly); Decca 8156 (Jack Mill-

Joe Puma *(left)* and Dick Garcia *(ABC-Paramount)*

Tal Farlow

Perry Lopez *(Francis Wolff)*

Howard Roberts *(Howard Lucraft)*

Lou Mecca *(Francis Wolff)*

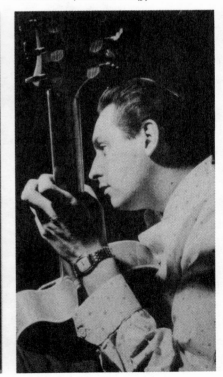

Upper left: Paul Chambers *(Herman Leonard)*
Upper right: Milt Hinton *(Chuck Stewart)*
Lower left: Chuck Flores *(Richard Schaefer)*
Lower right: Joe Morello *(Richard Schaefer)*

Upper left: Buddy Rich *(Victor Tanaka)*
Lower left: Max Roach *(Herman Leonard)*
Right: Osie Johnson *(Chuck Stewart)*

Top left: Teo Macero and Teddy Charles *(Richard Schaefer)*

Top middle: Quincy Jones *(Herman Leonard)*

Top right: Ernie Wilkins

Center left: Shorty Rogers and Pete Jolly *(RCA-Victor)*

Bottom left: Norman Granz and Manny Albam *(Herman Leonard)*

Center right: New sounds: the vibories played by Kenny Drew *(ABC-Paramount)*

Bottom right: Don Elliott, mellophone *(ABC-Paramount)*

Upper left: New Sounds: Jimmy Smith at the organ *(Francis Wolff)*
Lower left: Julius Watkins, French horn *(Herman Leonard)*
Right: New Sounds: Cy Touff, bass trumpet, with Richie Kamuca *(William James Claxton)*

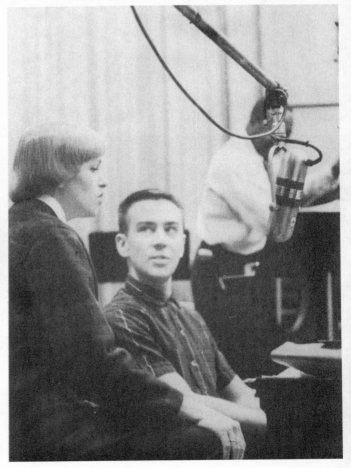

Left: Joe Williams *(Herman Leonard)*
Upper right: Mel Torme *(Dave Pell)*
Lower right: Jackie Cain and Roy Kral *(Carole Galletly)*

Above: The Blue Stars, Paris vocal group whose record of *Lullaby of Birdland* sung in French was a surprise hit in the U.S. Clockwise, starting at top: Christiane Legrand, Jeanine de Waleyne, Nadine Young, Blossom Dearie, Jean Mercadier, Roger Guerin, Fats Sadi, Christian Chevallier *(Jean-Pierre Leloir)*

Upper left: Chris Connor *(Carole Galletly)*

Right: Ray Nance *(Herman Leonard)*

Ella Fitzgerald *(Herman Leonard)*

Anita O'Day *(Herman Leonard)*

Carmen McRae *(James J. Kriegsmann)*

Billie Holiday *(Victor Tanaka)*

man); Contemp. 3503 (Lennie Niehaus); Atl. 1212 (Shorty Rogers); Cap. 6513 (Bob Cooper); Savoy 12045 (*Jazz Composers Workshop*); Liberty 6007 (Jack Millman); Pres. 7028 (*Collaboration: West*); Contemp. 3514 (Duane Tatro); Vict. LG1000 (Boots Brown).

GLASEL, Johnny LPs: Beth. 28 (*The Six*).

GLENN, Tyree LPs: EmArcy 36038 (w. Milt Hinton in *Boning Up On 'Bones*); Jazztone 1215 (Tony Parenti).

GOLD, Sanford Toured US and Europe as piano accompanist for Eartha Kitt, 1955-6. LPs: Vict. LJM-1024 (Al Cohn); Pres. 7019 (*Piano d'Or*; solos).

GONSALVES, Paul LPs: Vict. LPM1112 (Count Basie); Cap. T637 (Duke Ellington); Wing 60002 (*The Jazz School*); Norg. 1055 (*Ellingtonia '56*); Col. CL-872 (Rosemary Clooney and Duke Ellington).

GOODMAN, Benny To coincide with the release of the motion picture *The Benny Goodman Story*, Goodman reassembled a band, the first he had fronted in 2 yrs. After opening at the Waldorf-Astoria Hotel, NYC, Feb., 1956, he retained the group for a series of college dates. He also made jazz and classical concert appearances. The appearance of the Goodman film resulted in a flood of issues and re-issues of recordings. Goodman, without signing a contract to record exclusively for any company, was represented by many new releases (see list below).
   LPs: Epic 3128 (Red Norvo); Col. CL652 (Charlie Christian with Goodman), CL821 (*The Vintage Goodman*), CL820 (*The Great Benny Goodman*); Vict. LPM1099 (*The Benny Goodman Story*); Cap. 5706 (*Mr. Benny Goodman*); Dec. 8252, 8253 (sound track of *The Benny Goodman Story*); Vict. LPT6703 (*Golden Age of Swing*), LPM1239 (*This Is Benny Goodman*); Col. CL2572 (sextet & trio & Rosemary Clooney, *Date with the King*).

GOODWIN, Henry LPs: River. 2516 (Sidney Bechet).

GORDON, Bob Shortly after this brilliant baritone saxophonist had been elected New Star of the Year in a Down Beat critics' poll, he was killed in an automobile accident in Calif., 8/28/55. LPs: Cap. T659 (Dave Pell); Norg. 1030 (Tal Farlow); EmArcy 36009, 36021 (Maynard Ferguson); Decca DL8130 (*Blow Hot, Blow Cool*), 8156 (Jack Millman); Atl. 1223, Pac. Jazz 1208 (Jack Montrose); Col. CL689 (Pete Rugolo); Savoy 12045 (Shelly Manne); Contemp. 3510 (Lennie Niehaus); Liberty 6003 (Herbie Harper, Bud Shank); Contemp. 3514 (Duane Tatro).

GORDON, Dexter LPs: Em. 36016 (*Advance Guard of the '40s*); Beth. 37 (Stan Levey); Dootone 207 (*Dexter Blows Hot and Cool*).

GORDON, Joe Toured the Middle East with Dizzy Gillespie's band March-May, 1956. LPs: Wing 60002 (*The Jazz School*); Trans. 4 (Donald Byrd).

GOZZO, Conrad LPs: Vict. LPM1124 (*Goz the Great*).

GRAAS, John LPs: Decca DL8104 (*Jazz Studio 3*); Col. CL689 (Pete Rugolo); Cap. 6513 (Bob Cooper).

GRAY, Wardell LPs: Gene Norman 12 (Frank Morgan); Pres. 7008, 7009 (*Memorial*, Vols. 1 & 2).

GRECO, Buddy LPs: Coral 57022 (*Buddy Greco at Mister Kelly's*).

GREEN, Bennie LPs: Col. CL701 (Buck Clayton); Decca DL8176 (*Blow Your Horn*); Van. 8503 (Jo Jones); Em. 36015, Vict. LPM1135 (Charlie Ventura); Pres. 7023 (*Trombone by Three*); 7041 (own band w. Farmer), 7052 (*Blows His Horn*).

GREEN, Urbie In addition to extensive radio and recording work in New York, Green spent a month in Benny Goodman's band at the Waldorf-Astoria, Feb.-Mar. '56. Seen and heard in motion picture, *The Benny Goodman Story*, 1956.
   LPs: Coral 57018 (Steve Allen); Col. CL701 (Buck Clayton); Cap. 5706 (Benny Goodman); Beth. 14 (*Urbie*); Col. CL808 (Frankie Laine and Buck Clayton); Vict. LPM1146 (*Lullaby of Birdland*); ABC-Par. 101 (*Blues and other Shades of Green*); Vict. LPM1198 (Joe Newman), 1211 (Manny Albam); Fant. 219 (Elliot Lawrence); Vict. LPM1269 (Billy Byers); Decca DL8252, 8253 (*Benny Goodman Story* sound track).

GREENE, Freddie The popular guitarist, in his 20th year w. Count Basie, recorded his first album as a leader entitled *Mr. Rhythm* (see below). LPs: Vict. LPM1116 (Al Cohn); Van. 8503 (Jo Jones), 8505 Jimmy Rushing); Vict. LPM1118, LPM1198 (Joe Newman); Norg. 1056 (*The Jazz Giants '56*); Roost 2208 (Sonny Stitt); Vict. LPM1210 (*Mr. Rhythm*).

GRYCE, Gigi Worked chiefly as co-leader with Art Farmer in quintet 1955-6; also active as arr. for many avant garde jazz groups. LPs: Signal 1201 (own orch. & quartet); Beth. 33 (Oscar Pettiford); Prestige 7017 Art Farmer); Atl. 1229 (Teddy Charles); Dawn 1104 (Mat Mathews); Pres. 7031 (arrs. for Art Farmer).

GUARALDI, Vincent Anthony, *piano;* b. San Francisco, Calif., 7/17/28. Working on SF Daily News as apprentice in 1949, he almost lost a finger in an accident; as a result he decided to get into music on a full-time basis. He is a nephew of Muzzy Marcellino, TV musical director and Joe Marcellino, SF band leader, both of whom helped him start in music. Played w. Cal Tjader trio in SF '50; Bill Harris, Chubby Jackson orch., '53, Geo. Auld, '53, Sonny Criss, '55. Toured w. Woody Herman, '56. LPs: Fant. 213 (own group in *Modern Music from San Francisco*), 9 (Cal Tjader).

Addr: 696 27th Avenue, San Francisco, Calif.

GULDA, Friedrich, *piano;* b. Vienna, Austria, 5/16/30. Stud. piano from age 7 with Prof. F. Pazofsky. Entered State Academy of Music, 1942, stud. with Prof. B. Seidlhofer until '47. In '46 he won international music competition at Geneva. Played at festivals in Prague, '47, Vienna, '48. Many concerts throughout the Continent and South America. Made New York debut in Fall of 1950 at Carnegie Hall and was hailed by critics as one of the greatest new classical piano talents of this generation. Gulda, who has spent many hours visiting jazz clubs during his trips to New York, soon developed a talent for jazz piano and composing. In '56, after sitting in with the Modern Jazz quartet and other groups, he decided to take a combo into Birdland and to appear as a jazz musician at the 1956 Newport Jazz Festival. He is represented by many classical recordings, principally of Beethoven, on the London label. Jazz LP: Vict. LPM1355 (*At Birdland*).

Addr: c/o Hurok Attractions, Inc., 711 5th Avenue, New York 22, N.Y.

GULLIN, Lars LPs: EmArcy 36012 (*Lars Gullin*); 36059 (*With the Moretone Singers*).

HACKETT, Bobby LPs: Col. CL719 (Eddie Condon; under name of Pete Pesci); Cap. T575 (*In a Mellow Mood*), T692 (*Coast Concert*), and numerous LPs with Jackie Gleason.

HAFER, Dick LPs: ABC-Par. 118 (Don Stratton).

HAGGART, Bob LPs: Decca DL8151, 8152 (Lawson-Haggart Band in *Steve Allen's All Star Jazz Concert* Vol. 1 & 2), 8182 (*Jelly Roll's Jazz*), 8198 (*Windy City Jazz*).

HALE, Corky (Merrilyn Cecelia Hecht), *piano, harp, singer* (also *flute, piccolo, 'cello*); b. Freeport, Ill., 7/3/31. Started piano at 3, harp at 8, flute at 10, 'cello at 12. Stud. mostly in home town; a few lessons at Chicago Music Conservatory and 5 summers at Interlochen, Mich. She has worked mainly with commercial groups, started w. Freddy Martin in 1950, Dave Rose in '51, and toured w. Liberace '51-5. Sang and played harp w. Harry James '55; pianist and vocalist briefly w. Ray Anthony early '56. Appeared in motion pictures

The Benny Goodman Story, Sincerely Yours. The first album on which she was prominently featured w. Kitty White, Dec. '54, revealed her exceptionally modern approach to the harp. Favs: Dorothy Ashby, harp; Oscar Peterson, Billy Taylor, piano. LPs: Verve 2000 (Anita O'Day); Pacifica 2002 (Kitty White); Gene Norman 17 (own album).

Addr: Apt. 16, 1350 N. Crescent Hts., Hollywood, Calif.

HALL, Al LPs: Beth. 29 (Bud Freeman); EmArcy 36041 (Mal Fitch); Period 1115 (Josh White).

HALL, Edmond Replaced Barney Bigard in the Louis Armstrong combo, 1955, touring U.S., Australia, England, etc. LPs: Col. CL719 (Eddie Condon); EmArcy 36013 (Bud Freeman); Col. CL840 (Louis Armstrong); Story. 908 (Ruby Braff).

HALL, James Stanley, *guitar;* b. Buffalo, N.Y., 12/4/30. Bachelor of Music degree from Cleveland Institute of Music; stud. guitar privately. Started working local bands at 13. Moved to LA March, 1955. Worked w. Bob Hardaway Quartet, Ken Hanna's band, and Dave Pell octet. Toured w. Chico Hamilton quintet '55-6. A versatile guitarist capable of creating a wide variety of moods, he became a key member of the Hamilton group. Film: *Cool and Groovy*, a short, w. Hamilton quintet. Favs: Tal Farlow, Jimmy Raney, Barney Kessel, Howard Roberts. LPs: Pac. Jazz 1220, 1209, 1216 (Chico Hamilton); Cap. T6512 (Ken Hanna); Pac. Jazz 1217 (*Two Degrees East—Three Degrees West*).

Addr: 5320 W. Olympic Blvd., Los Angeles, Calif.

HALL, Minor LPs: Good Time Jazz 12008 (Kid Ory).

HALLBERG, Bengt LPs: EmArcy 36059 (Lars Gullin).

HAMBRO, Lenny LPs: Col. CL757 (*Message from Hambro*).

HAMILTON, Chico During 1956, this drummer's unusual quintet enjoyed increasing popularity, first on records and in Calif. night clubs, later on a national level after a visit to New York in the spring. The group comprised Hamilton w. Buddy Collette on saxophones and flute, Jim Hall on guitar, Carson Smith on bass, and Fred Katz on 'cello. The Hamilton quintet was featured in a short movie for Universal-International, *Cool and Groovy*. LPs: Decca DL8130 (*Blow Hot, Blow Cool*); Pac. Jazz 1209, 1216 (own quintet); Decca 8156 (Jack Millman); Pac. Jazz 1220 (own trio), 1217 (*Two Degrees East—Three Degrees West*).

HAMILTON, Jimmy LPs: Norg. 1028 (Ralph Burns); Cap. T637, 679 (Duke Ellington); Urania 1204 (*Ac-*

cent on Clarinet; with New York Jazz Quintet); Norg. 1055 (Ellingtonia '55); Beth. 60 (Duke Ellington); Col. CL872 (Rosemary Clooney and Duke Ellington).

HAMPTON, Lionel In October of 1955, the Hampton orch. was involved in a bus accident in New Mexico resulting in serious injury to most members of the band, incl. Hampton. After long hospitalization, the orch. was reassembled with only 5 personnel changes and played at Cafe Society in NYC, then embarked on another extremely successful European tour. Film: The Benny Goodman Story.

LPs: Col. CL652 (Charlie Christian); Col. CL820, Vict. LPM1099 (Benny Goodman); Contemp. 3502 (Hampton in Paris); Clef 642 (quintet), 667 (quartet; quintet); Decca DL8088 (All American Award Concert); Gene Norman 15 (Lionel Hampton with the Just Jazz All Stars); Col. CL711 (Wailin' at the Trianon) Clef 670 (Big Band); EmArcy 36032 (Hamp in Paris); Norg. 1037 (Hamp and Getz); Clef 677 (Jam Session #7), 681 (Krupa, Hampton, Wilson); EmArcy 36034 (Crazy Rhythm), 36065 (Jam Session in Paris); Clef MG17 (JATP Vol. 17), 709 (Hampton, Tatum, Rich Trio); ARS403 (The Swinging Jazz of Lionel Hampton, with Oscar Peterson Trio); Decca 8230 (Moonglow); Decca 8252, 8253 (The Benny Goodman Story, sound track).

HANDY, George LPs: "X" 1032 (By George!).

HANNA, Ken LPs: Cap. T6512 (Jazz for Dancers).

HARDAWAY, Robert Benson, tenor sax, etc.; b. Milwaukee, Wis., 3/1/28. Father is J. B. "Bugs" Hardaway, creator of movie cartoon characters Bugs Bunny and Woody Woodpecker. Darrell Caulker, film composer and friend of the family, helped Bob get started in music. Joined Air Force band as first clarinetist at 18; wrote and conducted Air Force Frolics of 1947, which toured Caribbean. Stud. Los Angeles City Coll. '49-50, played w. Ray Anthony, 1952 and '55; Hal McIntyre, '53; made solo record debut w. Billy May band in Bacchanalia album on Capitol. Several solos w. Jerry Gray, 1955, incl. Thou Swell, Baby's Lullaby, Kettle Drum (Decca). Also feat. in Ken Hanna album on Capitol. Toured w. Woody Herman band in 1956. Favs: Lester Young, Al Cohn, Zoot Sims, Stan Getz. LPs: Beth. 1026 (Lou's Blue); Cap. H374 (Billy May), T6512 (Ken Hanna).

Addr: 1907 N. Highland Ave., Hollywood, Calif.

HARPER, Herbie LPs: Beth. 23 (Frances Faye); Beth. 44 (Jazz City Workshop); Liberty 6003 (Bob Gordon, Bud Shank); Beth. 46 (Four Horns and a Lush Life).

HARPER, Rocquelle Toni, singer; b. Los Angeles, Calif., 6/8/37. Uncle, Buddy Harper, guitarist, played w. Ben Pollack. Featured for years as a child star, she scored her first hit with Candy Store Blues on Columbia records in 1947. Later made several records incl. Blacksmith Blues w. Harry James; also rec. w. Paul Weston (Silly Heart). Films: Manhattan Angel, Make Believe Ballroom. Made her album debut on Verve records in 1955. Throughout her youthful recording career, she has shown a strongly jazz-influenced style reminiscent of Ella Fitzgerald's. LPs: Verve 2001 (Toni).

Addr: 1751 W. 36th Place, Los Angeles 18, Calif.

HARRIS, Arthur Sidney, piano, Fr. horn, etc.; b. Philadelphia, Pa., 4/3/27. Stud. Yale U. 1947-52. Played w. Buddy Williams, Philadelphia, '45; Jeff Stoughton Dixieland Band, New Haven, '50-52; own trio in New Haven, '52. Featured in '55-6 on a series of recordings purporting to be jazz, though not generally acknowledged as such by many musicians, and considered by some critics to be mainly of academic interest. Favs: Dave Brubeck, Art Tatum. Ambition: "To write a more serious kind of jazz. A kind of jazz that combines the intellectuality of serious music with the spontaneity of jazz." LPs: Epic LN3200 (Harris-Leigh: New Jazz in Hi-Fi); Kapp 1015 (Jazz Goes to Postgraduate School), 1011 (Jazz 1755), Epic LN3086 (Harris-Leigh group in Swingin' Trends in Chamber Sounds).

Addr: 160 W. 73rd St., New York, N.Y.

HARRIS, Bill After a long period of semi-retirement in Florida, Harris returned to full-time jazz activity when he rejoined the Woody Herman orch. in Jan., 1956. LPs: Em. 36016 (Advance Guard of the '40s), 36038 (Boning up on 'Bones); Norg. 1028 (Ralph Burns); Clef 656 (Jam Session #6); EmArcy 36015, Norg. 1041 (Charlie Ventura); Clef MG17 (JATP Vol. 17); Norg. 1044 (New Jazz Sounds).

HARRIS, Joe LPs: Atl. 1229 (Teddy Charles); EmArcy 36066 (Jimmy Cleveland).

HAWES, Hampton His trio, in which the leader's superb modern piano was assisted by Red Mitchell, bass and Chuck Thompson, drums, was featured in 1956 in night clubs throughout the US. Hawes gradually gained acceptance as one of the top two or three performers of the Bud Powell school. LPs: Contemp. 3505 (own trio); Pac. Jazz 1205 (Bud Shank); Contemp. 3509 (in Lighthouse at Laguna); Pres. 212 (own trio); Contemp. 3510 (Lennie Niehaus); 3515 (own trio); Beth. 38 (Red Mitchell); Contemp. 3512 (Barney Kessel).

HAWKINS, Coleman The tenor sax veteran continued to free-lance mostly around New York and was featured in a remarkable new album: The Hawk in Hi-Fi with a big band and strings on RCA Victor. LPs:

EmArcy 36023 (*Battle of the Saxes*); Col. CL701 (Buck Clayton); Con. Hall 1201 (*Improvisations Unlimited*); Decca DL8127 (*The Hawk Talks*); Norg. 1034 (*Tenor Saxes*); Urania 1201 (*Accent on Tenor*); Grand Award 318 (*Jazz Concert*); Coral 57035 (*East Coast Jazz Scene*, vol. 1); Vict. LPM1281 (*The Hawk in Hi-Fi*).

HAYES, Clancy LPs: Good Time Jazz 12006 (Bob Scobey-Clancy Hayes); Down Home 3 (Clancy Hayes-Lu Watters), 1 (Bob Scobey).

HAYNES, Roy LPs: Wing 60000 (Nat Adderley); Fant. 208 (Red Rodney); EmArcy 36058 (Sarah Vaughan), 36071 (*Drum Roll*) 26048 (*Busman's Holiday*).

HAYSE, Al LPs: Decca DL8088 (Lionel Hampton).

HAZEL, Monk LPs: South. 217 (own group), 214 (Jack Delaney).

HEALEY, Richard J., *alto sax, clarinet, flute;* b. Youngstown, Ohio, 7/5/29. Studied clar. for 2 yrs. Worked with local bands through high school; went on the road after graduation. Joined Bob Astor orch. in 1947, Burt Massengale '48-9, Al Belletto, June '49; Australian Jazz Quartet, Dec., '54. LPs: Beth. 39, 1031 (Australian Jazz Quartet), 51 (Joe Derise).
Addr: 1919 Elm St., Youngstown 4, Ohio.

HEATH, Percy LPs: Wing 60001 (Paul Bley); ABC-Par. 101 (Urbie Green); Pres. 7005 (The Modern Jazz Quartet); Beth. 42 (Howard McGhee); Signal 1201 (Gigi Gryce), 1202 (Duke Jordan); Savoy 12046 (Milt Jackson); Atl. 1231 (*Fontessa/the Modern Jazz Quartet*); Pres. 7031 (Art Farmer); Norg. 1040 (*The Modern Jazz Society*).

HEATH, Ted The Heath orch. spent the month of April, 1956 on a concert tour of the US. Also featured: Nat "King" Cole, June Christy and the Four Freshmen. The tour ended with an appearance (without Cole) at Carnegie Hall, NYC on May 1. Shortly before Heath's tour, the Stan Kenton band had toured in England under a new reciprocal agreement arranged between the musicians' unions of the two countries. Heath's was the first English jazz orch. ever to play the US. He was extremely well received and it was planned to bring him back again in '57 to play many key cities that were omitted from the first tour, as well as return dates in the areas (mostly Southern) where he had enjoyed such resounding success.
LPs: London LL1000 (*100th Palladium Concert*), LL1217 (*Gershwin for Moderns*), LL1279 (*Kern for Moderns*), LL1211 (*At the London Palladium, Vol. 3*), LL1379 (*At the London Palladium, Vol. 4*).

HEFTI, Neal Giving up the trumpet entirely and switching to piano, Hefti assembled a band occasionally for appearances at Birdland, NYC, etc. in 1956, but concentrated mostly on free-lance arranging for records, radio and TV work in New York. LPs: Epic 3187 (*Hefti, Hot 'n Hearty*), 3222 (Frances Wayne).

HELM, Bob Col. CL650 (Turk Murphy).

HENDERSON, Skitch Cedric, *piano, conductor;* b. Halstad, Minn., 1/27/18. Studied piano with Malcolm Frost of Portland, Ore., Roger Aubert of Paris; conducting with Albert Coates and Fritz Reiner; harmony with Schoenberg. Early work with territory bands, then theater orchestras; film and radio studios on West Coast 1939-40; pilot in US Air Force '41-5, piano soloist on Sinatra and Crosby radio shows '46. Toured with own dance band '47-9, then resumed radio work. Since '51, he has been under contract to NBC in New York, appearing as pianist, conductor and playing versatile role as leader and comedian on the Steve Allen TV show, *Tonight* 1955-6. Many appearances as guest conductor with New York Phil., Minneapolis Symph., etc. Though not a jazz musician, he has featured such excellent jazzmen as Doc Severinsen in his NBC orch. Favs: Art Tatum, Teddy Wilson. Ambition: To become conductor in opera, concert work. LPs: Cap. H110 (*Sketches*), L502 (*Man and His Music*).
Addr: 245 E. 61 Street, New York, N.Y.

HENDRICKSON, Al LPs: Em. 36023 (w. Babe Russin); Decca 8131 (André Previn); Atl. 1225 (Jess Stacy).

HENKE, Mel LPs: Col. CL717 (Garry Moore); Contemp. 5003 (*Now Spin This*).

HERMAN, Woody For a few months in late 1955, Herman led a small band in Las Vegas. Reorganizing with numerous personnel changes, he went on tour with a large orch. in Jan., '56 featuring soloists Victor Feldman, vibes, Bill Harris, trom., Vince Guaraldi, piano, and Bob Hardaway, Richie Kamuca, Arno Marsh, tenor saxes. LPs: Col. CL701 (Buck Clayton); MGM E3176 (Billy Eckstine); Decca DL8133 (*Woodchopper's Ball*); Col. CL651 (*Music for Tired Lovers*); Cap. T658 (*Road Band!*).

HEYWOOD, Eddie LPs: EmArcy 36042 (own trio); Decca 8202 (*Lightly and Politely*).

HIBBLER, Al LPs: Verve 4000 (*Sings Love Songs*).

HIGGINBOTHAM, J. C. LPs: EmArcy 36038 (*Boning Up On 'Bones*).

HINES, Earl Settled in SF, 1956. LPs: Grand Award 318 (own septet); Epic 3223 (*Oh, Father!*); Fant. 217 (*Fatha Plays "Fats"*; quartet).

HINTON, Milt LPs: Vict. LPM1107 (*Basses Loaded*); Em. 36038 (*Boning Up On 'Bones*); Jazztone 1210 (Ruby Braff); Vict. LJM1024, LPM1116 (Al Cohn); Vict. LPM1164, Beth. 16 (Hal McKusick); Jazztone 1217 (Byers-Newman), 1207 (Sammy Price); Vict. LPM1118, (Joe Newman); Jazztone 1215 (Tony Parenti); Dawn 1102 (Zoot Sims); Vict. LPM1210 (Freddie Greene), 1211 (Manny Albam); Decca 8235 (Ralph Burns); Vict. LPM1212 (as "Junior Hifitz" in *New York Land Dixie*).

HIPP, Jutta The German pianist arrived in the US 11/18/55. In March, 1956 she opened with a trio at the Hickory House, NYC, and remained there for several months. Featured with her were Peter Ind, bass and Edmund Thigpen, drums. Her style underwent a change as a result of her enthusiasm for Horace Silver, which destroyed some of the individuality she had shown in her work in Germany. LPs: Decca 8229 (*"Das" is Jazz!*); Blue Note 1515, 1516 (*At the Hickory House*).

HODGES, Johnny The alto saxophone star gave up his own band, worked in NYC on the daily Ted Steele TV show in the summer of 1955, then rejoined the Duke Ellington orch. LPs: Norg. 1035 (*Alto Saxes*); Em. 36018 (*Alto Altitude*); Clef 677 (*Jam Session #7*); Grand Award 318 (Earl Hines); Norg. 1055 (*Ellingtonia '56;* as leader of Ellington band); Beth. 60 (Duke Ellington); Verve 4000 (Al Hibbler); Col. CL872 (Rosemary Clooney and Duke Ellington).

HOLIDAY, Billie LPs: Col. CL821 (Benny Goodman); Jazztone 1209 (reissues from Commodore); Clef 669 (*Music for Torching*); Decca 8215 (*The Lady Sings*); Clef 686 (*Recital by Billie Holiday*).

HOLMAN, Bill LPs: Beth. 30 (Conte Candoli); EmArcy 36021 (arrs. for Maynard Ferguson); Cap. T666 (arrs. for Stan Kenton); Contemp. 3503 (Lennie Niehaus); Contemp. 3514 (Duane Tatro).

HOPE, Elmo LPs: Pres. 7010 (*Meditations*, own trio), 7035 (Jackie McLean), 7021 (*Hope Meets Foster*), 7043 (sextet).

HORNE, Lena LPs: Vict. LPM1148 (*It's Love*).

HOWARD, Darnell LPs: Epic 3223 (Earl Hines).

HUCKO, Peanuts LPs: Grand Award 310, 313 (Bobby Byrne); Kapp 1007 (Morey Feld); EmArcy 36013 (Bud Freeman); Epic 3148 (Lou Stein);

Grand Award 325 (Bob Alexander); Jubilee 1019 (Lou Stein); Grand Award 322 (*A Musical History of Jazz*); Grand Award 331 (*A Tribute to Benny Goodman*); Vict. LPM1332 (Ruby Braff).

HUNTER, Lurlean, *singer;* b. Clarksdale, Miss., 12/1/28. Worked w. Red Saunders at Club De Lisa, Chicago; heard in numerous Chicago clubs. Came to New York to make first album for RCA Victor, Oct., 1955. Good pop singer, not particularly related to jazz. Favs: Sarah Vaughan, Carmen McRae, Connie Russell. LPs: Vict. LPM1151 (*Lonesome Gal*).
   Addr. 6227 South Park Ave., Chicago, Ill.

HURLEY, Clyde L. Jr., *trumpet;* b. Ft. Worth, Tex., 9/3/16. Mother, Esther B. Temple, was pioneer radio singer and pianist in Texas. Studied piano briefly, then taught self to play tpt. by listening to Louis Armstrong records. Solo trumpet w. TCU jazz band 1932-6. Joined Ben Pollack in Dallas, '37, went to Hollywood with him and did radio work there until Glenn Miller sent for him. After working w. Miller, '39-40, Tommy Dorsey, '40-1, Artie Shaw, '41, he free-lanced in film studios in '42-3, then was under contract to MGM from '44-9. Joined staff at NBC in Hollywood in '50 remaining until '55, then free-lanced for Columbia records, radio and TV shows, etc. Hurley played the tpt. solo on Glenn Miller's famous record *In the Mood*. Favs: Bunny Berigan, with whom he recorded in Tommy Dorsey's band, and Louis Armstrong. LPs: Col. CL785 (*Dixieland, My Dixieland*), CL693 (Paul Weston), CL648 (*Rampart and Vine*).
   Addr: 4245 Bellaire Ave., N. Hollywood, Calif.

HYMAN, Dick Still on staff at NBC in New York, Hyman enjoyed tremendous success with his commercial-style piano trio records, one of which, *Moritat* (theme for the *Threepenny Opera*) was a best-seller in the Spring of 1956. However, he continued to remain active in jazz on numerous record sessions, listed below. LPs: Period 1909 (Maxine Sullivan); River. 204 (Mundell Lowe); MGM E3280 (*Dick Hyman Trio Swings*); Grand Award 325 (Al Klink), 322 (*A Musical History of Jazz*); Jazztone 1229 (Maxine Sullivan); Grand Award 331 (Peanuts Hucko); MGM 3390 (*West Coast vs East Coast*).

IGOE, Sonny LPs: Cadence 1012, 1013 (Billy Maxted).

IND, Peter LPs: Wing 60001 (Paul Bley); Atl. 1224 (Lennie Tristano); Blue Note 1515, 1516 (Jutta Hipp).

ISOLA, Frank LPs: Pac. Jazz 1210 (Gerry Mulligan); Norg. 1029 (Stan Getz); EmArcy 36061 (Johnny Williams).

JACKSON, Calvin LPs: Col. CL756, CL824 (own quartet).

JACKSON, Chubby Living in Chicago, the former Woody Herman bassist made an unexpected new name for himself as master of ceremonies of a daily children's program which became one of the most popular afternoon TV shows in Chicago. For many months this was his only activity; he did not play bass at all. However, he took part intermittently in other shows featuring instrumental work by himself and other local Chicago musicians. LPs: Em. 36016 (*Advance Guard of the '40s*); Wing 60002 (Paul Gonsalves).

JACKSON, Mahalia LPs: Col. CL644 (*The World's Greatest Gospel Singer*), CL702 (*Sweet Little Jesus Boy*).

JACKSON, Milt LPs: Pres. 7003 (own quartet), 7005 (*Concorde;* The Modern Jazz Quartet); Savoy 12036 (*Opus de Jazz*), 12042 (*Roll 'em Bags*), 12061 (*Meet Milt*), 12046 (own quartet, pre-MJQ); Grand Award 318 (Dinah Washington); Atl. 1231 (*Fontessa/The Modern Jazz Quartet*); Pres. 7029 (Sonny Rollins); Blue Note 1509 (own group, and with Thelonious Monk); Pres. 7034 (Miles Davis).

JACKSON, Quentin LPs: Cap. T637, Beth. 60 (Duke Ellington).

JACQUET, Illinois, *tenor sax;* correct birth details: b. Broussard, La., 10/31/22. Moved to Houston, Tex. at 6 months. Jacquet continued to tour with his own combo in 1955-6, enlarging it occasionally to full size for theater dates. LPs: Col. CL754 (Count Basie); Clef 676 (own group), 677 (*Jam Session #7*); Grand Award 315 (*Uptown Jazz*); Norg. 1034 (*Tenor Saxes*); Clef 684 (*Krupa and Rich*).

JACQUET, Russell, *trumpet;* correct birth details: b. Broussard, La., 12/3/17. Played with Floyd Ray, 1939, stud. Wiley College, Texas, '40-4, then went to Calif. with brother Illinois' band. Had own band at Cotton Club in Hollywood. Rejoined Illinois Jacquet in '46 and worked either with him or with various groups of his own for the next decade.

JAMAL, Ahmad LPs: Epic 3212 (own trio).

JAMES, Harry After being featured in *The Benny Goodman Story,* James played with reduced personnel in Las Vegas, then enlarged the band again for engagements on the West Coast. Juan Tizol and Willie Smith continued to work as members of the James orch. LPs: Vict. LPM1099, Col. CL820, Cap. S706 (Benny Goodman).

JASPAR, Robert B., *tenor sax* (also *clar., flute*); b. Liège, Belgium, 2/20/26. Grandfather, father, were musicians. Stud. piano in Liège, 1937-9; clar. at 16. Worked for American Army Special Service in Germany. Played w. Henri Renaud in Paris, '50, later w. Bernard Peiffer, Aime Barelli. Had own quintet, '54-6, played at Club St. Germain in Paris; also made many record sessions in Paris w. Jimmy Raney, Henri Renaud, Chet Baker, Bernard Peiffer, Andre Hodeir, David Amram, and sessions under his own name for Vogue and Blue Star. Won first place for tenor sax and for small combo in *Jazz Hot* poll, '55. Came to US April, 1956 and made first American appearance w. Gil Fuller's band at concert in NYC. Married to American singer, Blossom Dearie. Jaspar is one of the finest jazz musicians produced on the European scene in recent years. His style and sound have often been compared with those of Stan Getz. LPs: Angel 60009 (*French Toast*); EmArcy 26036 (Bernard Peiffer). Jaspar toured w. J. J. Johnson combo, fall '56.

JEFFERSON, Hilton LPs: Em. 36023 (Jonah Jones); Col. CL808 (Frankie Laine & Buck Clayton); Grand Award 315 (Rex Stewart), 322 (*A Musical History of Jazz*); Period 1909 (Maxine Sullivan).

JEFFERSON, Roland Parris "Ron", *drums;* b. New York City, 2/13/26. Stud. at New York School of Music and w. private teacher. Played w. Roy Eldridge 1950, Coleman Hawkins, '51, later with many small combos in NYC, incl. Sonny Rollins, Charlie Parker, Lester Young, Sonny Stitt, Horace Silver, Joe Roland, Tal Farlow, Paul Bley, Oscar Pettiford. Favs: Max Roach, Art Blakey, Kenny Clarke, Philly Joe Jones. LPs: Beth. 17 (Joe Roland); Pres. 197 (Freddie Redd); Savoy 12039 (Joe Roland); Beth. 1003 (Oscar Pettiford).

Addr: 289 Convent Ave., New York, N.Y.

JEFFERSON, Thomas "Little Tom", *trumpet;* b. Chicago, Ill., 6/20/20. Started on drums, then French horn and trumpet. First played in Jones' Home (now the Municipal Boys' Home) Band with Peter Davis, who had taught Louis Armstrong, Kid Rena, and Red Allen. Worked w. Celestin Tuxedo Orch. 1936, later w. Sidney Desvignes, Jimmy Davis, Jump Jackson, John Casimir; also did TV work in New Orleans. Motion picture, *Pete Kelly's Blues.* Favs: Louis Armstrong. Ambition: To front his own band, and to sing and to play like Louis Armstrong. LPs: South. 213 (Santo Pecora), 215 (Johnny St. Cyr).

Addr: 2536 Conti St., New Orleans, La.

JENNEY, Jack LPs: Epic 3128 (Red Norvo).

JOHNSON, Budd Joined Benny Goodman's orch. at Waldorf-Astoria, NYC, Feb., 1956. LPs: Col. CL808

(Frankie Laine and Buck Clayton); Epic LN3223 (Earl Hines); ARS 405 (Dizzy Gillespie).

JOHNSON, Bunk LPs: Jazztone 1212 (*New Orleans Classics*); Col. CL829 (band; transferred from GL series).

JOHNSON, Gus LPs: Dawn 1102 (Zoot Sims); Story 907 (Zoot Sims-Bob Brookmeyer).

JOHNSON, James P. The jazz piano pioneer died in NYC, 11/17/55 after a long illness. He had been almost completely paralyzed since 1951. Full biographical details on Johnson can be found in the *Encyclopedia of Jazz*.

JOHNSON, Jay Jay LPs: Em. 36043 (Cannonball Adderley); Roost 2202 (Tony Aless; under name of "Joe"); Col. CL754 (Count Basie); Beth. 20 (Chris Connor); Norg. 1003, 1023 (Dizzy Gillespie); Col. CL742 (*Trombone for Two*), CL808 (Frankie Laine & Buck Clayton); Blue Note 1505 (*The Eminent Jay Jay Johnson*); Beth. 56 (Chris Connor); "X" LXA-1040 (*An Afternoon at Birdland*); Pres. 7023 (*Trombone by Three*), 7024 (with Sonny Stitt); Norg. 1040 (*The Modern Jazz Society*). Johnson ended partnership w. Kai Winding, formed own quintet, Aug. 1956.

JOHNSON, Osie In addition to free-lancing extensively in New York as drummer and arr., Osie Johnson made a series of records as vocalist for RCA Victor. LPs: Vict. LJM1024, LPM1116, LPM1161 (Al Cohn); Col. CL742 (J. J. and Kai); Vict. LPM1164, Beth. 16 (Hal McKusick); Jazztone 1217 (Byers-Newman); Dawn 1101 (Quill-Sherman); Epic 3238 (one number as vocalist in *Gentlemen, Be Seated*, minstrel show); ABC-Par. 106 (Don Elliott); Vict. LPM1210 (Freddie Green), 1211 (Mannv Albam); Decca 8235 (Ralph Burns); MGM 3390 (*West Coast vs East Coast*).

JOHNSON, Pete LPs: Em. 36023 (w. Ben Webster in *Battle of the Saxes*), 36038 (w. J. C. Higginbotham in *Boning Up On 'Bones*); Van. 8505 (Jimmy Rushing); Em. 36014 (*Joe Turner and Pete Johnson*).

JOLLY, Pete (Peter A. Ceragioli), *piano, accordion;* b. New Haven, Conn., 6/5/32. Father plays and teaches accordion. Started on accordion at age 3, piano at 9. Father helped him get started; after playing with school band and local groups, he settled in LA, working w. Geo. Auld '52, Shorty Rogers '54-6, Buddy De Franco Quartet, '56, and his own trio. Movies: *Man with the Golden Arm, Wild Party*. In addition to being an extremely facile pianist of the Horace Silver school, Jolly has shown promise of becoming almost the only important modern jazz accordionist in the single note

solo style. Favs: Horace Silver, Bud Powell, Geo. Wallington.

LPs: Vict. LPM1121 (*The Five*), LPM1105 (*Jolly Jumps In*), LPM1146 (*Lullaby of Birdland*); Contemp. 3503 (Lennie Niehaus); Atl. 1212 (Shorty Rogers); Pac. Jazz 1211 (Cy Touff); Pres. 205 (Jon Eardley); Vict. LPM1125 (duo, trio, quartet).

Addr: 136 N. Hamilton Drive, Beverly Hills, Calif.

JONES, Burgher William "Buddy", *bass, tuba;* b. Hope, Ark., 2/17/24. Met Ch. Parker in Kansas City at the age of 17; under his influence decided to enter music. Took up string bass in Navy; worked w. Charlie Ventura in 1947, then moved to LA, gigging in small jazz groups incl. Joe Venuti trio, '49, later joined Ina Ray Hutton. Came to NYC in '50; worked with Gene Williams, Lennie Tristano Quintet, Buddy De Franco, Elliot Lawrence. Joined Jack Sterling morning show on CBS Radio Dept., '52 (others in group were Elliot Lawrence, Tiny Kahn, Mary Osborne) and was still w. Sterling in '56. Favs: Walter Page, Milt Hinton, Jimmy Blanton. LPs: Vict. LJM-1024, LPM1161 (Al Cohn); "X" LXA1032 (George Handy); Fant. 206 (Elliot Lawrence); Beth. 18 (Sam Most).

Addr: 208 Woodhampton Drive, White Plains, N.Y.

JONES, Claude LPs: EmArcy 36038 (*Boning Up On 'Bones*).

JONES, Eddie LPs: Savoy 12022 (*Flutes and Reeds*); Vict. LPM1198 (Joe Newman); Jazztone 1220 (*The Count's Men*); Savoy 12036 (*Opus de Jazz*), 12037 (Hank Jones); Period 1210 (*The Jones Boys*).

JONES, Elvin Ray, *drums;* b. Pontiac, Mich., 9/9/27. Brother of Hank and Thad Jones. Self-taught; played in school band. Entered Army in 1946 and played in military band. Released in '49, spent 3 yrs. at the Bluebird in Detroit w. Thad Jones, Billy Mitchell et al. Played Newport Jazz Festival, Summer, '55, w. Teddy Charles, Ch. Mingus. Moved to NYC Spring '56, worked w. Bud Powell trio. Considered by musicians to be future star. Favs: Max Roach, Art Blakey, Kenny Clarke, Philly Joe Jones, Roy Haynes. LPs: Debut 120 (Miles Davis).

JONES, Hank In addition to making innumerable jazz LPs, mainly for Savoy, Jones worked w. Benny Goodman, whose band and trio he joined Feb., 1956. LPs: Savoy 12015 (Eddie Bert), 12017 (*Bohemia After Dark*), 12018 (*Presenting Cannonball*), 12007 (Clarke-Wilkins); Vict. LPM1162 (Al Cohn); Savoy 12022 (*Flutes and Reeds*), 12023 (*The Trio*); Vict. LPM1146 (*Lullaby of Birdland*); Herald 0101 (Anthony Ortega); Clef 645 (Artie Shaw); Grand Award 315 (Rex Stewart); Roost 2204 (Sonny Stitt);

Savoy 12037 (own quartet & quintet), 12032 (Donald Byrd), 12036 (*Opus de Jazz*), 12044 (*Top Brass*); Roost 2208 (Sonny Stitt); Savoy 12063 (Joe Wilder); Clef 682 (Lawrence Brown); Savoy 12058 (*Meet Marlene*); Story. 907 (Zoot Sims-Bob Brookmeyer).

JONES, Jimmy LPs: Em. 36004, 36058 (Sarah Vaughan); Period 1210 (*The Jones Boys*).

JONES, Jo LPs: Jazztone 1210, Van. 8504 (Ruby Braff); Van. 8503 (*The Jo Jones Special*), 8505 (Jimmy Rushing); Roost 2204 (Sonny Stitt); Period 1210 (*The Jones Boys*); Norg. 1056 (*The Jazz Giants '56*); Vict. LPM1210 (Freddie Greene).

JONES, Jonah LPs: Kapp 1004 (Benny Payne); Jazztone 1207 (Sammy Price); Weathers 5501 (George Wettling); Groove 1001 (*Jonah Jones at the Embers*); GTJ 12013 (Sidney Bechet).

JONES, Philly Joe LPs: Pres. 7007, 7014 (Miles Davis); Beth. 42 (Howard McGhee); Pres. 7017 (Art Farmer), 7043 (Elmo Hope).

JONES, Quincy One of the busiest free-lance arrangers in New York throughout 1955, Quincy Jones was conductor and arr. for countless LPs, many of them on EmArcy and Epic. Early in '56 he again took up tpt., which he had not played for almost 2 yrs., and became arr., trumpeter and mus. dir. for a big band that toured the Near East March through May, '56 under Dizzy Gillespie's leadership.

LPs: Vict. LPM1146 (*Lullaby of Birdland*); Roost 2204 (arrs. for Sonny Stitt); Period 1210 (fluegelhorn in *The Jones Boys*); ABC-Par. 106 (arrs. for Don Elliott); Pres. 7031 (arrs. for Art Farmer); EmArcy 36066 (arrs. for Jimmy Cleveland), 36007 (Clark Terry), 36006 (Helen Merrill); Verve 2008 (arrs. for Gene Krupa).

JONES, Reunald LPs: Period 1210 (*The Jones Boys*).

JONES, Thad LPs: Clef 647, 666 (Count Basie); Vict. LPM1161 (Al Cohn; under name of Bart Valve); Norg. 1031 (Buddy Rich); Roost 2204 (Sonny Stitt); Period 1210 (*The Jones Boys*); MGM 3390 (*West Coast vs East Coast*); Blue Note 1513 (*New York-Detroit Junction*).

JONES, William "Willie", *drums*; b. Brooklyn, N.Y., 10/20/29. Started w. Thelonious Monk; has worked w. Cecil Payne, Joe Holiday, Ch. Parker, Kenny Dorham, Ch. Mingus, Jay Jay Johnson. Favs: Max Roach, Kenny Clarke, Art Blakey. LPs: Pres. 7010 (Elmo Hope), 166 (Thelonious Monk); Atlantic (Charlie Mingus).

Addr: 77 Lefferts Place, Brooklyn, N.Y.

JORDAN, Duke LPs: Beth. 42 (Howard McGhee); Signal 1202 (own trio and quintet); Blue Note 5064 (Julius Watkins); Prestige 7017 (Art Farmer), 7039 (Gene Ammons); Signal 1203 (Cecil Payne).

KAHN, Tiny LPs: Fant. 219 (arrs. for Elliot Lawrence).

KAMINSKY, Max LPs: Jazztone 1208 (*Chicago Style*).

KAMUCA, Richie LPs: Vict. LPM1162 (Al Cohn); Cap. T658 (Woody Herman); Pac. Jazz 1211 (Cy Touff); Keynote 1101 (Nat Pierce).

KATZ, Dick LPs: Vict. LPM1161 (Al Cohn); Col. CL742 (J. J. and Kai); Vict. LPM1198 (Joe Newman); Dawn 1101 (Quill-Sherman); "X" LXA1040 (Johnson-Winding); Dawn 1104 (Mat Mathews); ABC-Par. 125 (Candido).

KATZ, Frederick, *'cello, piano, arranger*; b. Brooklyn, N.Y., 2/25/19. Grandfather was violinist; mother played drums; father (Dr. Hyman Katz) played many string instruments. Stud. piano and 'cello under scholarship at Third Street Music Settlement—'cello with pupil of Pablo Casals. Made his living for years as concert 'cellist; while overseas in Army after VE Day, was mus. dir. of 7th Army Hdq. After leaving the service, he worked for several years as piano accompanist for Vic Damone, Mindy Carson, Lena Horne, Tony Bennett, Jana Mason et al. As 'cellist, first real jazz job was w. Chico Hamilton quintet 1955-6. Katz is the first musician to put the 'cello to full use both in arco and pizzicato solos. A member of ASCAP, he has also done considerable writing for the Hamilton Quintet. Fav. own solo: *The Sage*. LPs: Pac. Jazz 1209, 1216 (Chico Hamilton).

Addr: 1814 S. Cochran Ave., Los Angeles 19, Calif.

KAY, Connie (Conrad Henry Kirnon), *drums*; b. Tuckahoe, N.Y., 4/27/27. At 6, stud. piano with mother. Self-taught on drums at 10; private lessons at 15. Played w. Sir Charles Thompson and Miles Davis at Minton's, NYC, 1944-5; also worked w. Cat Anderson, '45; Lester Young off and on '49-55, and club dates w. Ch. Parker, Coleman Hawkins, Stan Getz. Repl. Kenny Clarke in Modern Jazz Quartet, '55. A tasteful, discreet and flexible modern drummer. Favs: Sid Catlett, Art Blakey, Max Roach, Kenny Clarke, Shelly Manne. LPs: Pres. 7005 (*Concorde: The Modern Jazz Quartet*); Atl. 1231 (*Fontessa/The Modern Jazz Quartet*), 1228 (Chris Connor); Norg. 1022 (Lester Young), 1040 (*The Modern Jazz Society*).

Addr: 431 Bronx Park Ave., Bronx 60, N.Y.

KELLY, Wynton LPs: Em. 36011 (Dinah Washington).

KENNEY, Beverly, *singer;* b. Harrison, N.Y., 1/29/32. No formal training. Worked for Western Union singing "Happy Birthday" telegrams in 1953. Prof. career started Miami Beach, Fla. Sang w. Tommy Dorsey, Jan. through May, '55; since then has worked as single. Favs: Billie Holiday, Frank Sinatra, Mel Torme. LPs: Roost 2206 (*Beverly Kenney Sings for Johnny Smith*).
    Addr: 315 W. 4th St., New York, N.Y.

KENTON, Stan In Jan., 1956 Kenton organized a new band in LA and took it to England in March for a highly successful concert tour. Owing to union restrictions, his was the first big American jazz band to play for civilian audiences in Britain since Teddy Hill's in '37. He appeared there under a reciprocal union arrangement that enabled Ted Heath to tour the US in Apr., '56. Kenton followed the British tour with a series of dates on the Continent, returning to the US in May. Principal soloists in the band incl. Bill Perkins, tenor sax, Lennie Niehaus, alto sax, Sam Noto, tpt., Mel Lewis, drums, Curtis Counce, bass. LPs: Cap. T666 (*Contemporary Concepts*), T656 (*Duet* with June Christy); Decca 8259 (*The Formative Years*); Cap. W724 (*Stan Kenton in Hi-Fi,* new recordings of old hits).

KERSEY, Ken LPs: Beth. 29 (Bud Freeman), 21 (*Jazz at the Metropole*); Herald 0103 (Sol Yaged); Story. 908 (Ruby Braff).

KESSEL, Barney LPs: Norg. 1033 (*Swing Guitars*); Decca 8156 (Jack Millman); Contemp. 3509 (*Lighthouse at Laguna*); Norg. 1038 (Buddy Rich & Harry Edison); Contemp. 3513 (*To Swing or Not to Swing*); Verve 2000 (Anita O'Day); Good Time Jazz 12008 (Kid Ory); Contemp. 3512 (*Kessel Plays Standards*); Story. 904 (Jackie Cain-Roy Kral); Cap. T683 (Four Freshmen); Contemp. 5002 (Claire Austin).

KING, Morgana (Mary Grace Fruscella), *singer;* b. Pleasantville, N.Y., 6/4/30. Father played guitar and sang. Stud. at Metropolitan School of Music. Appeared at Basin Street and other NYC clubs in 1956; signed with Wing Records. Married to tpt. player Tony Fruscella. One of the best jazz inclined pop singers of the year. Ambition: To become dramatic actress. LPs: Wing 60007 (*Helen Morgan Songs*).
    Addr: c/o Lenny Lewis, 307 E. 44th St., New York 17, N.Y.

KING, Teddi LPs: Vict. LPM1147 (*Bidin' My Time*); Story. 903 (*Now in Vogue*).

KLINK, Al LPs: Cap. S706 (Benny Goodman); Coral 57028 (Steve Allen); Grand Award 325 (*Progressive Jazz*), 331 (Peanuts Hucko).

KOLLER, Hans LPs: Decca 8229 (*"Das" Is Jazz!*).

KONITZ, Lee Played successful series of concerts in Germany late 1955 with Hans Koller, Lars Gullin, et al. LPs: Atl. 1217 (*Lee Konitz with Warne Marsh*), 1224 (Lennie Tristano); Pres. 7013 (*Conception*); Atl. 1217 (Konitz-Warne Marsh), 1224 (Tristano); Pres. 7004 (w. Tristano, Marsh and Bauer).

KOTICK, Teddy LPs: Wing 60002 (Art Mardigan); Dawn 1101 (Quill-Sherman); Keynote 1102 (Harvey Leonard); Norg. 1029 (Stan Getz); Pres. 7018 (Phil Woods); Atl. 1229 (Teddy Charles); Pres. 7033 (Jon Eardley); Signal 102 (Hall Overton); Vict. LPM1268 (Tony Scott).

KRAL, Roy LPs: Em. 36015, Vict. LPM1135 (Charlie Ventura); Story. 904 (*Jackie and Roy*); ABC-Par. 120 (*The Glory of Love*).

KRUPA, Gene Toured Europe with JATP, Feb., 1956, then resumed night club work with his own quartet. LPs: Col. CL821, CL820, Vict. LPM1099 (Benny Goodman); Clef 627 (*The Rocking Mr. Krupa*), 668 (Quartet); Jazztone 1219 (*Jazz Concert*); Clef 681 (Krupa, Hampton, Wilson); Verve 2008 (*Drummer Man*); Decca 8252, 8253 (*Benny Goodman Story,* soundtrack).

KYLE, Billy LPs: Col. CL708 (Louis Armstrong); Decca DL8168, 8169 (Louis Armstrong); Col. CL701 (Buck Clayton); Col. CL840 (Louis Armstrong).

LAMB, Robert Valentine, *trombone;* b. Cork, Ireland, 2/11/31. Toured with circus band in Ireland. Played w. Roy Fox 1952-3, Teddy Foster part of '53, and 2 yrs. w. Jack Parnell in England, '53-5, then immigrated to US. Joined Woody Herman Jan., '56. Favs: Bill Harris, Urbie Green, Jimmy Watson.
    Addr: 101-50 111th St., Richmond Hill, New York, N.Y.

LAMOND, Don LPs: Kapp 1004 (Benny Payne); MGM 3280 (Dick Hyman); Vict. LPM1212 (as "Zane Grudge" in *New York Land Dixie*); Fant. 206 (Elliot Lawrence).

LANG, Ronny LPs: Cap. T-659 (*The Les Brown All Stars*).

LA PORTA, John Signed with Fantasy Records, April, 1956. LPs: Fant. 209 (Sandole); Savoy 12064 (*The Jazz Message*), 12065 (*Kenny Clarke*).

LARKINS, Ellis LPs: Beth. 56 (Chris Connor); Van. 8507 (*2x2,* plays Rodgers & Hart w. Ruby Braff).

LAWRENCE, Elliot LPs: Fant. 207 (*The Honey Dreamers Sing Gershwin*), 206 (plays Gerry Mulligan Arrangements), 219 (plays Tiny Kahn and Johnny Mandel Arrangements).

LAWSON, Yank LPs: Decca DL8151, 8152 (own band in *Steve Allen's All Star Jazz Concert*, Vols. 1 & 2), 8182 (*Jelly Roll's Jazz*), 8198 (*Windy City Jazz*).

LEE, Charles Freeman, trumpet; b. New York City, 8/13/27; Stud. at Wilberforce Acad. and pl. w. Wilberforce Collegians. Piano with Snooky Young, 1950; piano and tpt. w. Candy Johnson, '51; trumpet w. Eddie Vinson and Sonny Stitt, '52; Joe Holiday, '53. Free-lanced in New York '54-5. With James Moody, '56. Holds a B.S. in biology from Central State College. Favs: Dizzy Gillespie, Kenny Dorham, Fats Navarro. LPs: Prestige 7021, Blue Note 5044 (Elmo Hope).
Addr: 366 W. 29th St., New York, N.Y.

LEE, Peggy Recipient of an Academy Award nomination for her remarkable acting and singing role in the motion picture, *Pete Kelly's Blues,* Peggy Lee remained mostly in Calif., playing night club dates in LA and Las Vegas. She was married 4/28/56 to actor Dewey Martin. LPs: Decca DL8166 (*Pete Kelly's Blues*).

LEGGE, Wade LPs: Col. CL757 (Lenny Hambro); Epic 3199 (Junior Bradley); Savoy 12042, 12061 (Milt Jackson); EmArcy 36066 (Jimmy Cleveland); ARS 405 (Dizzy Gillespie).

LEIGH, Mitch (Irwin S. Michnick), bassoon, etc.; b. Brooklyn, N.Y., 1/30/28. Studied High School of Music and Art, NYC; Yale U, Bachelor of Arts '51, Master of Arts '52. Featured on daily radio show w. Art Harris (q.v.) on WOR, NYC. LPs: Epic LN3200 (Harris-Leigh: *New Jazz in Hi-Fi*); Kapp 1011 (*Jazz 1755*); Abbot (*Into the Unknown* w. Jean Shepherd incl. fav. own solo *Molière's Meditation*); Epic LN-3086 (Harris-Leigh group in *Swingin' Trends in Chamber Sounds*).
Addr: 12 E. 66th St., New York 21, N.Y.

LEIGHTON, Bernie LPs: Grand Award 33-325 (Bob Alexander).

LEONARD, Harvey LPs: Keynote 1102 (*Jazz Ecstasy;* own trio, sextet).

LEVEY, Stan LPs: Norg. 1027 (Tal Farlow); Contemp. 3504, 3509 (Howard Rumsey); Beth. 37 (*This Time the Drum's On Me*); Cap. 6513 (Bob Cooper); Beth. 46 (*Four Horns and a Lush Life*); ABC-Par. 110 (*Swingin' On the Vibories*); MGM 3390 (*West Coast vs East Coast*).

LEVITT, Al LPs: Wing 60001 (Paul Bley); ABC-Par. 102 (Bobby Scott).

LEVY, Lou Emerging from retirement, this outstanding modern jazz pianist moved to LA in 1955 and worked mainly as accompanist to Peggy Lee; also recorded his own solo album for RCA Victor. LPs: Beth. 30 (Conte Candoli); Norg. 1032 (Stan Getz), 1037 (*Hamp and Getz*); Beth. 37 (Stan Levey); Vict. LPM1267 (solos).

LEWIS, George LPs: Jazztone 1212 (*New Orleans Classics*); Empirical 107 (*Spirituals in Ragtime*).

LEWIS, John During 1956, the Modern Jazz Quartet, of which John Lewis was the founder, achieved new heights of popularity as a favorite combo in night clubs, on records and in concerts. In addition, he took part as composer and arr. for several other ventures, incl. the Modern Jazz Society LP listed below, concerts by specially organized groups at Cooper Union, NYC, etc.
LPs: Pres. 7005 (*Concorde;* The Modern Jazz Quartet); Savoy 12046 (Milt Jackson); Atl. 1231 (*Fontessa/The Modern Jazz Quartet*), 1228 (Chris Connor); Pres. 7029 (Sonny Rollins); Story. 905 (Joe Newman); Pac. Jazz 1217 (*Two Degrees East—Three Degrees West*); Norg. 1040 (*The Modern Jazz Society*).

LEWIS, Mel (Melvin Sokoloff), drums; b. Buffalo, N.Y., 5/10/29. Father has been prof. drummer for over 35 yrs. Prof. debut at 15. Played w. Lenny Lewis 1946-8, Boyd Raeburn, July-Nov., '48; Alvino Rey to Mar., '49, then a year w. Ray Anthony, 3 yrs. w. Tex Beneke, then back w. Anthony for a year to Aug., '54. Two yrs. w. Stan Kenton, '54-6, except for brief membership in Frank Rosolino quintet and Hamp Hawes trio, early '55. Favs: Tiny Kahn, Jo Jones, Max Roach, Shelly Manne, etc.
LPs: Clef 644 (Bob Brookmeyer); Vict. LPM1121 (*The Five*); EmArcy 36024 (*The Gellers*); Cap. T666 (Stan Kenton); Beth. 25 (Charlie Mariano); Prest. 214 (Bob Brookmeyer); Pac. Jazz 1221 (Bill Perkins); Beth. 48 (Max Bennett).
Addr: 13424 D Huston St., Sherman Oaks, Calif.

LINN, Ray LPs: EmArcy 36060 (Georgie Auld).

LOCO, Joe LPs: Col. CL760 (*Loco Motion*); Fant. 215 (under real name, Jose Esteves Jr., with Pete Terrace).

LOMBARDI, Clyde LPs: Col. CL757 (Lenny Hambro); Kapp 1015 (Art Harris); Savoy 12019 (Eddie Bert).

LONDON, Julie, singer; b. Santa Rosa, Calif., 9/26/26. Parents, both singers, had their own radio show. Self-taught. Sang briefly with trio as teen-ager. Two weeks w. Matty Malneck's orch. in 1943. Gave up singing for acting until Bobby Troup interested Liberty records in making her first album. Her initial release, *Cry Me a River,* was a big popular hit in '55. As actress under contract to major studios, she made 9 movies, the latest being *The Great Man* with José Ferrer, released Fall, '56. Favs: Ella Fitzgerald, Peggy Lee, Johnny Mercer. LPs: Liberty 3006 (*Julie Is Her Name* incl. fav. own perf. *Laura*).

Addr: c/o Liberty Records, 1556 N. La Brea Ave., Hollywood, Calif.

LOPEZ, Perry LPs: Blue Note 5064 (Julius Watkins).

LOVETT, Leroy LPs: Verve 4000 (Al Hibbler); Clef 682 (Lawrence Brown).

LOWE, Mundell LPs: Decca DL8173 (Carmen McRae); Kapp 1004 (Benny Payne); River. 204 (own quartet); Grand Award 325 (Al Klink), 322 (*A Musical History of Jazz*); River. 208 (*Guitar Moods*); EmArcy 36072 (Joe Saye); Vict. LPM1268 (Tony Scott).

LYON, Jimmy LPs: Beth. 14 (Urbie Green).

MACERO, Teo A new experimental work by the saxophonist-composer, entitled *Fusion,* was commissioned and performed by the Columbia U. orch., Spring, 1956. LPs: Fant. 209 (Sandole); Col. CL842 (*What's New*).

MAHONES, Gildo LPs: Dawn 1101 (Rouse-Watkins).

MAINI, Joseph Jr., *alto and tenor saxes (also clar. and flute);* b. Providence, R.I., 2/8/30. Father, guitarist; brother, mandolinist (Italian folk music). Stud. alto with Joe Piacitelli, toured w. Alvino Rey, Johnny Bothwell in 1948, Jimmy Zito, '49. During a few weeks spent w. Claude Thornhill in '51, Ch. Parker gave him a tenor sax which Maini still plays. Gigs, record dates and short movie w. Dan Terry, '54. During past 2 yrs. has gigged in Hollywood w. Jack Sheldon, Lorraine Geller, et al. Promising Parker-inspired musician. LPs: EmArcy 36039 (*Best Coast Jazz*); Beth. 38 (Red Mitchell); Contemp. 3514 (Duane Tatro); Jazz: West 4 (Kenny Drew), 5 (Jane Fielding); Pac. Jazz (Jack Sheldon).

Addr: 826 Kodak Drive, Los Angeles 26, Calif.

MANCE, Junior LPs: Wing 60002 (Paul Gonsalves).

MANDEL, Johnny LPs: Fant. 219 (arrs. for Elliot Lawrence).

MANGIAPANE, Sherwood, *bass, sousaphone;* b. New Orleans, La., 10/1/12. Self-taught. Worked in New Orleans with Blue Parody Orch., Johnny Wiggs, Papa Laine; several seasons on steamboat w. Dutch Andrus; played with servicemen's combo while in Army in England, 1944. Has been a bank employee for 24 yrs., playing music as a side line. Fav: Bob Haggart. LPs: Para. 107 (Johnny Wiggs-Raymond Burke); South. 214 (Jack Delaney), S/D1001, 200 (Johnny Wiggs), 209 (Raymond Burke).

Addr: 2516 Leonidas St., New Orleans, La.

MANN, Herbie The talented flutist wrote and directed the music for several TV dramas in New York in the Spring of 1956. LPs: Beth. 20, 56 (Chris Connor), 24 (own quartet), 40 (*Herbie Mann-Sam Most Quintet*); Decca DL8173 (Carmen McRae); Em. 36004 (Sarah Vaughan); ABC-Par. 106 (Don Elliott); Beth. 47 (Terry Morel); Decca 8235 (Ralph Burns); Dawn 1104 (Mat Mathews); Savoy 12058 (*Meet Marlene*).

MANNE, Shelly After his successful appearance in *The Man with the Golden Arm,* for which he instructed Frank Sinatra in the drumming sequence as well as appearing himself, Manne formed his own combo, which played in night clubs on the West Coast and then in the East in the Spring and Summer of 1956.

LPs: Norg. 1032 (Stan Getz), 1037 (*Hamp and Getz*); Decca 8156 (Jack Millman); Atl. 1223, Pac. Jazz 1208 (Jack Montrose); Contemp. 3506 (Lyle Murphy), 3503 (Lennie Niehaus); Atl. 1212 (Shorty Rogers); Contemp. 3509 (Hampton Hawes); Decca 8257 (*The Man with the Golden Arm*); Cap. 6513 (Bob Cooper); Savoy 12045 (*Jazz Composers Workshop*); Contemp. 3516 (Shelly Manne, Vol. 4); EmArcy 36071 (*Drum Roll*); Pres. 7028 (*Collaboration: West*); Contemp. 3514 (Duane Tatro), 5002 (Claire Austin), 5003 (Mel Henke).

MARABLE, Lawrence Norman, *drums;* b. Los Angeles, Calif., 5/21/29. Not related to Fate Marable. Father plays piano. Prof. debut, 1947. Heard around LA for several years in various combos incl. Ch. Parker, Dexter Gordon, Wardell Gray, Stan Getz, Hamp Hawes, Zoot Sims, Herb Geller. Favs: Kenny Clarke, Art Blakey.

LPs: Beth. 30 (Conte Candoli); Norg. 1030 (Tal Farlow); Gene Norman 12 (Frank Morgan); Pres. 212 (Hamp Hawes); Dootone 211 (Carl Perkins); Pres. 7008, 7009 (Wardell Gray); Jazz: West 4 (Kenny Drew), 5 (Jane Fielding); ABC-Par. 110 (*Swingin' On the Vibories*); EmArcy 26045 (Herb Geller).

Addr: 2804 5th Ave., Los Angeles, Calif.

MARDIGAN, Art LPs: Wing 60002 (*The Jazz School*); Liberty 3003 (Jimmy Rowles).

MARES, Paul LPs: Col. CL632 (*Chicago Style Jazz*).

MARGOLIS, Samuel, *tenor sax, clarinet;* b. Dorchester, Mass., 1924. Brother is classical critic and composer. Principally self-taught, first on clar. then on tenor. Played with most of the name combos around Boston; longtime friend and roommate of trumpeter Ruby Braff. Favs: Bud Freeman, Lester Young, Babe Russin, Ben Webster. LPs: Jazztone 1210, Vanguard 8504 (Ruby Braff); Keynote 1101 (Nat Pierce).
    Addr: 340 Cabrini Blvd., New York, N.Y.

MARIANO, Charlie LPs: Decca DL8104 (John Graas); Cap. T666 (Stan Kenton); Beth. 25 (own quartet); Contemp. 3516 (Shelly Manne); Beth. 48 (Max Bennett).

MARMAROSA, Dodo LPs: Decca 8098 (Charlie Barnet); Em. 36023 (w. Corky Corcoran).

MARRERO, Lawrence LPs: Empirical 107 (George Lewis); Jazztone 1212 (Bunk Johnson; George Lewis).

MARSH, Warne LPs: Atl. 1217 (*Lee Konitz with Warne Marsh*).

MARSHALL, Wendell LPs: Vict. LPM1107 (*Basses Loaded*); Norg. 1020 (Louis Bellson); Savoy 12015 (Eddie Bert); Cap. T642 (Milt Buckner); Savoy 12007 (Clarke-Wilkins); EmArcy 36042 (Eddie Heywood); Savoy 12023 (*The Trio*); Roost 2208 (Sonny Stitt).

MATHEWS, Mat LPs: Decca DL8173 (Carmen McRae); Dawn 1103 (Bob Stewart), 1104 (*The Modern Art of Jazz by Mat Mathews*); Bruns. 54013 (own quintet).

MATLOCK, Matty LPs: Vict. LPM1126, Col. CL690 (*Pete Kelly's Blues*); Col. CL785 (*Dixieland, My Dixieland*); Cap. 677 (Billy May); T692 (Bobby Hackett); South. 210 (George Brunis).

MAXTED, Billy LPs: Grand Award 310, 313 (Bobby Byrne); Urania 1202 (Pee Wee Erwin); Grand Award 322 (*A Musical History of Jazz*); Cadence 1012 (*Jazz at Nick's*), 1013 (*Dixieland Manhattan Style*), 1011 (Pee Wee Erwin).

MAY, Billy Film: acting role in *Nightmare,* also arrangements. His solos, however, were played by Dick Cathcart. LPs: Vict. LPM1091 (arrs. in *Redskin Romp*, Charlie Barnet); Cap. T677 (*Sorta-Dixie*).

MAY, Earl LPs: ABC-Par. 112 (Billy Taylor).

McEACHERN, Murray LPs: Vict. LPM1124 (Conrad Gozzo).

McGARITY, Lou LPs: Coral 57028 (Steve Allen); Grand Award 331 (Peanuts Hucko); Vict. LPM1212 (as "Erskine Tearblotter" in *New York Land Dixie*).

McGHEE, Howard LPs: Beth. 42 (*The Return of Howard McGhee*).

MacKAY, Stuart, *misc. woodwinds;* b. Montreal, Can., 12/10/09. Stud. Ithaca Conservatory, Univ. of Mich., Columbia U. Played w. Isham Jones in mid '30s, Les Brown, '37-8, Red Norvo, '39-40, Eddy Duchin, '40-2, in service, '42-5. Later with Mark Warnow, Russ Case and various musical comedy bands. Since Aug., '54, working in production department at WTVJ, Miami, Fla. Has experimented off and on with his own groups featuring an unusual instrumentation. Favs: C. Hawkins, Benny Carter, Stan Getz. LPs: Vict. LJM1021 (*Reap the Wild Winds*).
    Addr: 1475 N.E. 138th St., N. Miami, Fla.

McKENNA, David J., *piano;* b. Woonsocket, R.I., 5/30/30. Mother pianist and violinist; father a drummer. Started with nuns in Woonsocket, later in Boston w. Sandy Sandiford. Prof. debut w. Boots Mussulli, with whom he also worked in Ch. Ventura combo for several months in 1949. After a year and a half w. Woody Herman, '50-1, he entered the Army and was in Korea for much of the next two years. Discharged in '53, he rejoined Ventura for 18 months, then worked w. Gene Krupa combo for two months in '56. An original and fertile solo stylist, he showed, in his first LP, his ability to swing without any accompanying rhythm section. Favs: Teddy Wilson, Art Tatum, Nat Cole. LPs: ABC-Par. 104 (*Dave McKenna, Solo piano*), 101 (Urbie Green), 118 (Don Stratton); Beth. 48 (Max Bennett); Norg. 1013, 20 (Charlie Ventura); Coral 56067 (Ventura).
    Addr: 47 Cold Spring Place, Woonsocket, R.I.

McKENZIE, Red LPs: Col. CL632 (*Chicago Style Jazz*).

McKIBBON, Al LPs: Fant. 211 (Cal Tjader).

McKINLEY, Ray The drummer-vocalist was commissioned by the widow of the late Glenn Miller to organize a new orch. under Miller's name, using the band's original library and style. McKinley, who had played in Miller's band overseas and had assumed the direction of it after Miller's death, initiated this venture in May, 1956. LPs: Decca DL8151, 8152 (*Steve Allen's All Star Jazz Concert* Vol. 1 & 2); Camden 295 (*One Band, Two Styles*).

McKUSICK, Hal LPs: Vict. LPM1107 (*Basses Loaded*), LJM1024 (Al Cohn); Beth. 12 (Don Elliott); Fant. 206 (Elliot Lawrence); Beth. 16 (own quartet); Vict. LPM1164 (*In a Twentieth Century Drawing*

Room), 1211 (Manny Albam), 1212 (as "Fefe Phophum" in *New York Land Dixie*).

McLEAN, John Lenwood "Jackie", *alto sax;* b. NYC, 5/17/32. Father, John McLean, played guitar w. Tiny Bradshaw. Played w. Sonny Rollins, Kenny Drew, Andy Kirk, Jr. in neighborhood band, stud. w. Bud Powell after school. Worked mainly w. Paul Bley, George Wallington and Ch. Mingus, 1955-6. Favs: Ch. Parker, Sonny Rollins. LPs: Blue Note 1501, 1502, Pres. 7012, 7034 (Miles Davis); Prog. 1001 (George Wallington); Ad Lib 6601 (*The New Tradition*); Pres. 7035 (*Lights Out*), 7039 (Gene Ammons).
    Addr: 484 E. Houston St., New York, N.Y.

McPARTLAND, Jimmy LPs: MGM E3286 (*Hot vs Cool*); Jazztone 1227 (*The Middle Road*); Vict. LPM1332 (Ruby Braff).

McPARTLAND, Marian LPs: Cap. T699 (*After Dark*); Jazztone 1227 (Jimmy McPartland).

McRAE, Carmen LPs: Decca DL8173 (*By Special Request*).

McSHANN, Jay LPs: Decca 5503 (*Kansas City Memories*).

MEHEGAN, John LPs: Savoy 12028 (*Reflections*), 12049 (*A Pair of Pianos*), 12029 (*Montage*).

MENDELSON, Stanley J. Jr., *piano;* b. New Orleans, La., 6/23/33. Father played violin, sousaphone. Stud. piano and violin at Loyola U. Got into jazz through Dr. Souchon, Johnny Wiggs and other New Orleans jazz-men. Worked with Melody Lads 1947-9, Johnny Wiggs, '50, Dukes of Dixieland, '51, Sharkey Bonano, '52-6. Fav: Jelly Roll Morton. LPs: South. 214 (Jack Delaney), 200 (Johnny Wiggs), 205, 216 (Sharkey Bonano), 209 (Raymond Burke).
    Addr: 4433 Gen. Pershing St., New Orleans 25, La.

MERRILL, Helen LPs: EmArcy 36006 (*Helen Merrill*), 36057 (with strings).

METTOME, Doug LPs: Beth. 14 (Urbie Green); Col. CL689 (Pete Rugolo); Keynote 1101 (Nat Pierce).

MEZZROW, Mezz LPs: Jazztone 1225 (Buck Clayton).

MILLER, Eddie LPs: Vict. LPM1126, Col. CL690 (*Pete Kelly's Blues*); Col. CL785 (*Dixieland, My Dixieland*); Cap. 677 (Billy May).

MILLMAN, Jack Maurice, *arranger, trumpet, fluegelhorn;* b. Detroit, Mich., 11/21/30. Father was pianist

in Canada. Stud. violin from 1939, bass briefly, then trumpet. Majored in music at Compton Jr. College and Los Angeles City College. Played w. Glenn Henry, Sept., '51 to Feb., '52; a few weeks with Stan Kenton, then in Army to Mar. '54. Since then has had his own combos and worked briefly w. Perez Prado, Dec., '55. Favs: Dizzy Gillespie, Fats Navarro, Miles Davis, Clifford Brown. Ambition: To record a jazz symphony he has written. LPs: Decca 8156 (*Jazz Studio 4*); Liberty 6007 (*Shades of Things to Come*).
    Addr: 7719½ Hampton Ave., Hollywood 46, Calif.

MINGUS, Charlie LPs: Savoy 12059 (*Jazz Composers Workshop #2*); Debut 120 (Miles Davis).

MITCHELL, Billy, *tenor sax;* b. Kansas City, Mo., 11/3/26. Stud. Detroit at Cass Tech. and was an early associate of Lucky Thompson, Sonny Stitt, Julius Watkins, Milt Jackson. After playing w. Nat Towles' orch., came to New York w. Lucky Millinder, '48, worked briefly w. Jimmie Lunceford, Milt Buckner, Gil Fuller, and for five months in '49 w. Woody Herman. Returning to Detroit, had his own combo which at one time or another featured Thad and Elvin Jones, Terry Pollard, and Tommy Flanagan; also worked locally with organist Levi Mann. Toured w. Dizzy Gillespie on State Dept. sponsored visit to Middle East, Spring, '56. Excellent modern tenor stylist. Favs: Sonny Stitt, Sonny Rollins, Hank Mobley, Coleman Hawkins, Lester Young. LPs: Savoy 12042, 12061 (Milt Jackson); Blue Note 1513 (Thad Jones).
    Addr: 2240 Antoinette Ave., Detroit, Mich.

MITCHELL, Dwike (note, this is correct spelling), *piano;* b. Jacksonville, Fla., 2/14/30. Stud. Philadelphia Music Academy. Toured US and Europe w. Lionel Hampton 1953-5, then teamed up with another Hampton sideman, bassist and Fr. horn soloist, Willie Ruff, to form the Mitchell-Ruff duo which attracted immediate attention in New York night clubs and on records. A skilled musician, capable of first-rate performances in all idioms, Mitchell, though sometimes too pretentious in his approach, is capable of swinging very effectively. Favs: Art Tatum, Oscar Peterson, Hampton Hawes. LPs: Epic 3221 (*The Mitchell-Ruff Duo*); Col. CL711, Clef 670 (Lionel Hampton).
    Addr: 1150 Chapel St., New Haven, Conn.

MITCHELL, George LPs: Epic 3207 (Johnny Dodds and Kid Ory).

MITCHELL, Gordon B. "Whitey", *bass;* b. Hackensack, N.J., 2/22/32. Father plays pipe organ in local churches, brother, Red Mitchell, is bassist w. Hampton Hawes trio. Stud. clar., then tuba, then bass in school. After playing w. the Elinor Sherry Quartet, he spent 1951 and most of '52 w. Shep Fields Orch., then entered the service, playing in the 392nd Army Band.

After discharge, June, '54, settled in New York. Has gigged w. Boyd Raeburn, Tony Scott, Jay and Kai; toured w. Pete Rugolo, Sept. to Dec., '54, Ch. Ventura, Dec. '54-May '55, Krupa to Nov. '55, then several months with house combo at the Cameo, NYC. Made own LP for ABC-Paramount, Spring, 1956. An enterprising and gifted musician, he shows signs of following in the successful footsteps of his brother. Favs: Oscar Pettiford, Geo. Duvivier, Red Mitchell. LPs: Beth. 1004 (Bobby Scott); Col. CL689 (Pete Rugolo); ABC-Par. 126 (own group), 125 (Candido).

Addr: 79-10 35th Ave., Jackson Heights, L.I., N.Y.

MITCHELL, Red Regular member of the Hampton Hawes trio, 1955-56. LPs: Norg. 1027 (Tal Farlow); Beth. 23 (Frances Faye); EmArcy 36024 (*The Gellers*); Decca DL8104 (John Graas); Contemp. 3505 (Hamp Hawes); Decca 8156 (Jack Millman); Atl. 1223 (Jack Montrose); Fant. 19 (Red Norvo); Pac. Jazz 1210 (Gerry Mulligan); Contemp. 3509, 3515 (Hampton Hawes); EmArcy 36040 (Herb Geller); Fant. 218 (Red Norvo); ABC-Par. 110 (piano, bass, vibories in *Swingin' on the Vibories*); Beth. 38 (own quintet); Contemp. 3512 (Barney Kessel).

MOBLEY, Hank LPs: Blue Note 1507, 1508 (*The Jazz Messengers at the Cafe Bohemia*); Blue Note 5064 (Julius Watkins); Savoy 12064 (*The Jazz Message*); Trans. 4 (Donald Byrd); Blue Note 5062 (Horace Silver), 5069 (own quartet); ARS 405 (Dizzy Gillespie); Pres. 7043 (Elmo Hope).

MOER, Paul (Paul E. Moerschbacher), *piano, arranger;* b. Meadville, Pa., 7/22/16. Theory and composition at U. of Miami, grad. cum laude, 1951. Played w. Benny Carter, Vido Musso, '53; Zoot Sims, Stan Getz, '54; Jerry Gray, Bill Holman, '55. Enjoys teaching as well as playing and says he hopes some day to do some serious writing. Favs: Horace Silver, Russ Freeman, Lou Levy. LPs: Atl. 1223, Pac. Jazz 1208, 1214 (Jack Montrose), 12 (Bob Gordon).

Addr: 9323 Kester Avenue, Van Nuys, Calif.

MOLE, Miff The veteran trombonist free-lancing in New York; recovered from a serious illness early 1956. LPs: Col. CL632 (*Chicago Style Jazz*); Jazztone 1208 (Max Kaminsky).

MONK, Thelonious LPs: Pres. 7027 (trio); Riv. 12-201 (*Plays Duke Ellington*); Signal 1201 (Gigi Gryce); Blue Note 1509 (Milt Jackson), 1510, 1511 (*Genius of Modern Music*); Pres. 7053 (quintets).

MONTEROSE, J. R. (Frank Anthony Monterose Jr.), *tenor sax;* b. Detroit, Mich., 1/19/27. Family moved to Utica, N.Y., 1928. Clar. in grammar school band at 13, tenor at 15. Legit. clar. with Utica Jr. Symph. After working with territory bands 1948-9, he joined Henry Busse in '50. Came to New York, worked w.

Buddy Rich in '52, then worked around Syracuse, N.Y., '52-4, then ret. to NY w. Claude Thornhill. In '55 he gigged around New York w. Dan Terry, Teddy Charles, etc.; in '56 w. Ch. Mingus and Kenny Dorham. Record debut Jan., '55 w. Teddy Charles on Prestige. Favs: Ch. Parker, Sonny Rollins, Sonny Stitt. LPs: Epic 3199 (Junior Bradley); Savoy 12019, 12029 (Eddie Bert); Atl. 1229 (Teddy Charles); ABC-Par. 122 (Kenny Dorham); Pres. 206 (Teddy Charles), 207 (Jon Eardley).

Addr: 15501 Horace Harding Blvd., Flushing, L.I., N.Y.

MONTROSE, Jack LPs: Decca DL8130 (*Blow Hot, Blow Cool*), 8156 (Jack Millman); Atl. 1223 (*Jack Montrose with Bob Gordon*); Pac. Jazz 1208 (own sextet); Beth. 52 (Mel Tormé); Pac. Jazz 1214 (*Arranged by Montrose*).

MOODY, James LPs: Prest. 7011 (*Hi Fi Party*), 7036 (*Wail, Moody, Wail*).

MOORE, "Big Chief" Russell LPs: Jazztone 1225 (Buck Clayton).

MOORE, Brew LPs: Fant. 211 (Cal Tjader).

MOORE, Oscar LPs: Norg. 1033 (*Swing Guitars*); Decca 8260 (King Cole Trio).

MORELLO, Joe LPs: Epic 3148 (Lou Stein); Cap. T699 (Marian McPartland); Grand Award 33-325 (Bob Alexander); Jazztone 1227 (Jimmy McPartland). Joined Dave Brubeck Oct. '56.

MORRIS, Marlowe, *piano, organ;* b. Bronx, N.Y., 5/16/15. Uncle, Tommy Morrison, well-known jazzman of 1920s; father a music teacher. Self-taught; encouraged greatly by Art Tatum. Worked w. Eric Henry and Coleman Hawkins in 1940; record debut w. Lionel Hampton, '40. Army, '41-2, then played and arr. for Al Sears band at Renaissance Ballroom, NYC. Later toured in USO for Sears. Worked w. Big Sid Catlett in '44, moved to Calif. and appeared in Norman Granz's movie short, *Jammin' the Blues*. Back in New York, worked w. Doc Wheeler, Eddie South, Tiny Grimes. Has appeared mainly as soloist since '46. Took day job with Post Office, '49-50, but has been back in music full-time since then. Stud. classical music and arr. Favs: Art Tatum, Teddy Wilson; organ, Wild Bill Davis. EP: Epic 7009 (Buck Clayton). LPs: Decca 8176 (Paul Quinichette).

Addr: 2310 7th Ave., New York, N.Y.

MORRISON, John A. "Peck", *bass;* b. Lancaster, Pa., 9/11/19. Stud. trumpet, drums, bass, New Rochelle High School and Hartnett School of Music. Overseas in Special Services Band in Italy, 1946. Worked w.

Lucky Thompson octet at Savoy Ballroom, NYC, Dec. '51-Jan. '53, then toured w. Tiny Bradshaw. With Bill Graham's combo at Snookie's, NYC, Apr. '53-June '54, then gigged w. Horace Silver, Gigi Gryce, Art Farmer. Night club dates w. Jay and Kai quintet Oct., '54-Jan., '55. Briefly w. Duke Ellington, Jan., '55, Lou Donaldson, Apr., '55, Gerry Mulligan, Aug.-Dec., '55; Johnny Smith quartet '56. Favs: Milt Hinton, Oscar Pettiford, Clyde Lombardi. LPs: EmArcy 36056 (Gerry Mulligan); "X" LVA 1040, Pres. 7030 (Winding-Johnson).

Addr: 471 Swinton Ave., Bronx 65, N.Y.

MORSE, Ella Mae, *singer;* b. Mansfield, Tex., 9/12/24. Mother, a pianist, father played drums. After singing with father's jazz band, joined Jimmy Dorsey, 1939; scored first hit w. Freddie Slack when she recorded *Cow Cow Boogie,* '42. Has worked mostly as single since then, and had several other hits incl. *Mr. Five by Five,* '42; *House of Blue Lights,* '46. After several years' retirement, scored again with *Blacksmith Blues,* '51. Good pop singer whose style reflects her jazz background. Fav: Ella Fitzgerald. Ambition: To become actress in movies and TV. LPs: Cap. T513 (*Barrelhouse, Boogie, Blues*).

Addr: 2475 Arlington, Reno, Nevada.

MORTON, Benny LPs: EmArcy 36038 (*Boning Up On 'Bones*).

MORTON, Jeff LPs: Atl. 1224 (Lennie Tristano).

MORTON, Jelly Roll LPs: Jazztone 1211 (own group).

MOSCA, Salvatore Joseph, *piano;* b. Mt. Vernon, N.Y., 4/27/27. Stud. in Mt. Vernon and NYC. Is authorized teacher of the Schillinger System. Stud. piano, composition, conducting at New York College of Music, also w. Lennie Tristano. Played with Army Band, 1945-7, Saxie Dowell, '47, various society and jazz jobs, '47-'51. Intermittently w. Lee Konitz, '51-5, also working as part-time driving instructor, '53-6. One of the best disciples of Tristano, whose piano style his own strongly resembles. Favs: Lennie Tristano, Art Tatum, Bud Powell. LPs: Atl. 1217 (Lee Konitz); Pres. 7004 (Konitz), 7013 (Konitz in *Conception*).

Addr: 35 Rochelle Terrace, Mt. Vernon, N.Y.

MOST, Abe LPs: Liberty 6004 (*Mr. Clarinet*).

MOST, Sam LPs: Beth. 40 (*Herbie Mann-Sam Most Quintet*), 18 (own group).

MULLIGAN, Gerry Formed an excellent new sextet in the Fall of 1955 with which he played successful engagements early in '56 in Italy and at the Olympia Theater in Paris. LPs: Decca DL8104 (John Graas);

Fant. 206 (arrs. for Elliot Lawrence); Pac. Jazz 1207 (own quartet), 1210 (Quartet, *Paris Concert*); Pres. 7013 (*Conception*); EmArcy 36056 (sextet); Pres. 7006 (old "ten-tette"); Vict. LG1000 (Boots Brown).

MURPHY, Lyle LPs: Contemp. 3506 (own 12-Tone compositions and arrangements).

MURPHY, Turk LPs: Col. CL793 (*New Orleans Jazz Festival*), CL650 (*Dancing Jazz*).

MUSSO, Vido LPs: Atl. 1225 (Jess Stacy); Cap. W724 (Stan Kenton).

MUSSULLI, Boots LPs: Cap. T6510 (Serge Chaloff); Vict. LPM1135 (Charlie Ventura).

NANCE, Ray LPs: Cap. T637 (Duke Ellington); Grand Award 318 (Earl Hines); Norg. 1055 (*Ellingtonia '56*); Beth. 60 (Duke Ellington); Col. CL872 (Rosemary Clooney & Duke Ellington).

NAPIER, William James, *clarinet;* b. Asheville, N.C., 8/9/26. Parents both in show business. Self-taught. Led own trio in Sausalito, Calif., 1949. Played w. Turk Murphy, '50-2, then with various Dixieland groups, mainly around SF, but also in Chicago and Eastern cities. With Dixieland Rhythm Kings, '52-4; worked at Hangover Club, SF w. Wingy Manone, Joe Sullivan, Marty Marsala, '54; Bob Scobey, '54. Favs: Barney Bigard, Jimmie Noone et al. LPs: Pax 6002, River. 2504 (*Dixieland Rhythm Kings*); GTJ 5, 7 Turk Murphy), 12009 (Bob Scobey), 12006 (Bob Scobey-Clancy Hayes).

Addr: 920 Taylor St., San Francisco, Calif.

NAPOLEON, Marty LPs: Jazztone 1210 (Ruby Braff); Herald 0105 (Mickey Sheen).

NAPOLEON, Teddy Clef 627 (Gene Krupa).

NASH, Ted LPs: Em. 36023 (*Battle of the Saxes*); Cap. 677 (Billy May).

NAVARRO, Fats LPs: EmArcy 36016 (*Advance Guard of the '40s*).

NERO, Kurt Paul, *violin, arranger;* b. Hamburg, Germany, 4/29/17. Father a violin teacher in New York, founder of Violin Teachers Guild. Extensive studies incl. scholarship to Curtis Institute, arr. w. Johnny Warrington, conducting w. Fritz Reiner. Has worked with dance bands incl. Jan Savitt, 1937 and Gene Krupa, '45; symphony orch. incl. Pittsburgh Symph., '39, soloist with New York Phil., '45. Leader of US Navy dance band in Washington, D.C., '42-4. Since '48, has been in commercial radio, etc. on West Coast. Active intermittently writing and playing in jazz; has

been a licensed pilot since '37 and says, "I enjoy flying, with or without an airplane." Favs: Joe Venuti, Johnny Frigo, Eddie South. LPs: Sunset 303 (*Paul Nero and His Hi-Fiddles*); Cap. H236 (*Nero Fiddles*).
Addr: P.O. Box 691, North Hollywood, Calif.

NEWBORN, Edwin Calvin, *guitar (also piano, flute, piccolo, trombone, bar. horn)*; b. Memphis, Tenn., 4/27/33. Father is band director; brother, Phineas, pianist and quartet leader; wife, Wanda, trombonist. Stud. Booker T. Washington High School in Memphis, Le-Moyne College. Played w. Tuff Green's Rocketeers 1951-2; father's band and Roy Milton, '53; again with father '54-6, then joined quartet formed by brother, Phineas. Record debut in Memphis with his brother on Peacock label. Favs: Barney Kessel, Tal Farlow.
Addr: 613 Exchange No. 4, Memphis, Tenn.

NEWBORN, Phineas Jr., *piano (also trumpet, ten. sax, vibes, Fr. horn, bar. horn)*; b. Whiteville, Tenn., 12/14/31. Father is drummer and leader; mother plays piano, sings. Stud. privately, also at high school and Tenn. State U. Played w. Saunders King, 1947; many local bands in Memphis, '45-50, Lionel Hampton, '50 and '52, Tennessee State Collegians, '50-52, Willis Jackson, '53, Army, '53-5; toured state of Florida making radio and TV appearances for recruiting drive. After many years mainly in rhythm and blues and under his father's influence, he broke away to make what he considered his real start in jazz with his own quartet, '55-6, bringing it to New York for an appearance at Basin Street in May, '56. Newborn has an exceptional technique and an unusually active left hand. Despite a tendency to become florid and pretentious at times, he shows signs of becoming a major jazz talent. Fav: Art Tatum. LP: Atl. 1235.
Addr: 582 Alston, Memphis, Tenn.

NEWMAN, Joe LPs: Clef 647, 666 (Count Basie); Col. CL701 (Buck Clayton); Vict. LJM1024, LPM-1116, LPM1161 (Al Cohn), LPM 1147 (Teddi King), LPM1146 (*Lullaby of Birdland*); Jazztone 1217 (*New Sounds in Swing*); Norg. 1031 (Buddy Rich); Vict. LPM1198 (*I'm Still Swinging*), LPM-1118 (*All I Wanna Do Is Swing*); Jazztone J-1220 (*The Count's Men*); Vict. LPM1210 (Freddie Greene), 1211 (Manny Albam); Decca 8235 (Ralph Burns); Story. 905 (*I Feel Like a Newman*).

NEWTON, Frankie LPs: Em. 36014 (Joe Turner-Pete Johnson).

NICHOLAS, Albert LPs: Jazztone 1211 (Jelly Roll Morton).

NICHOLAS, George Walker "Big Nick", *tenor sax;* b. Lansing, Mich., 8/2/22. Stud. piano, clar. saxophone, 1933-9; theory, harmony, Boston Conserva-

tory, '44-6. Father, a saxophonist, helped him get started with local bands '39-40. Worked w. Kelly Martin at Club Congo in Detroit, 1942, also 3 months w. Earl Hines and 6 months w. Tiny Bradshaw. In Boston w. Sabby Lewis, '44-6, then settled in New York, working w. Claude Hopkins, J. C. Heard, Lucky Millinder, '46-7. Toured Europe w. Dizzy Gillespie Jan.-Mar. '48. Led his own combo at the Paradise, NYC, '50-53. Featured on Dusty Fletcher record of *Open the Door, Richard* (National), *Manteca* w. Dizzy Gillespie (Victor), *La Danse* w. Hot Lips Page (Columbia). Fav. own solos: *Baby, Baby All the Time, Sposin'* w. Frankie Laine. Capable tenor man of the big tone Hawkins school. Favs: Hawkins, Young, Byas, Webster, Getz. LPs: Col. CL808 (Frankie Laine & Buck Clayton); Pres. 7023 (Bennie Green); Vict. 3046 (with Dizzy Gillespie in *Crazy and Cool*).
Addr: 114-36 139th St., Jamaica, L.I., N.Y.

NICHOLS, Bobby LPs: Vict. LPM1240 (Sauter-Finegan).

NICHOLS, Herbert Horatio, *piano, composer;* b. New York City, 1/3/19. Uncle, Walter Nichols, trumpeter with old Paramount Stompers group. Stud. w. Chas. L. Beck 1928-35; Army, '41-3. An early associate of Thelonious Monk, Nichols was sidetracked into jobs that prevented his modern jazz style from being heard widely. He played during the '40s w. groups led by Snub Mosely, Rex Stewart, Milt Larkins, and w. many rhythm and blues bands. Not until '55, when he made his first solo records for Blue Note, was his harmonically venturesome style fully displayed. By this time he was ready to admit, "Music no longer holds the fascination for me that any business success would give me." Ambition: To study English literature, write novels or short stories. Favs: John Lewis; Vladimir Horowitz, classical piano; Duke Ellington, arr. LPs: Blue Note 5068, 5069 (own trio).
Addr: 850 Hewitt Place, Apt. E 1, Bronx 59, N.Y.

NICHOLS, Red The veteran trumpeter-band leader is to be the subject of a motion picture, *The Red Nichols Story*, with Danny Kaye in the title role. LPs: Bruns. 54008 (*The Red Nichols Story*).

NIEHAUS, Lennie Toured Europe w. Kenton in 1956. LPs: Cap. T666, W724 (Stan Kenton); Contemp. 3503 (own octet), 3510 (*The Quintet and Strings*), Contemp. 3514 (Duane Tatro).

NIMITZ, Jack Played in England and on Continent w. Stan Kenton, Feb., 1956. LPs: Cap. T658 (Woody Herman); Beth. 48 (Max Bennett).

NORIN, Carl-Henrik LPs: EmArcy 36012 (Lars Gullin).

NORVO, Red LPs: Fant. 19, 218 (own trio); Jazztone 1219 (*Jazz Concert*); Epic 3128 (*Red Norvo and His All Stars*).

NOTO, Sam LPs: Cap. T666, W724 (Stan Kenton).

NOTTINGHAM, Jimmy LPs: Roost 2204 (Sonny Stitt), 2205 (Seldon Powell); Vict. LPM1211 (Manny Albam).

O'DAY, Anita LPs: Verve 2000 (*Anita*), 2008 (Gene Krupa).

O'FARRILL, Chico LPs: Norg. 1003 (comps. for Dizzy Gillespie).

OLIVER, Sy LPs: Beth. 56 (Chris Connor).

ORTEGA, Anthony Robert, *saxophones, clarinet, flute;* b. Los Angeles, Calif., 6/7/28. Stud. with Lloyd Reese, 1945-8, then worked w. Earle Spencer. After two years in the Army, he toured w. Lionel Hampton's band, '51-3, worked briefly w. Milt Buckner trio in late '53, then led his own combo at the Red Feather in LA, '54. Visited Norway in '54 for concerts and combo jobs. Back in LA, Aug., '54, worked in mambo band; came East in Aug., '55 w. Luis Rivera. Since then, has free-lanced around New York. Fav. own solo: *We'll Be Together Again,* on Herald LP. Favs: Sonny Stitt, Gigi Gryce, Phil Woods. LPs: Herald 0101 (*A Man and His Horns*); Vantage 2 (own quartet).
Addr: 56 W. 91st Street, New York 24, N.Y.

ORY, Kid The veteran trombonist had an acting and playing role in *The Benny Goodman Story.* LPs: Good Time Jazz 12008 (*Creole Jazz Band, 1955*); Epic 3207 (Johnny Dodds and Kid Ory).

OVERTON, Hall LPs: Signal 102 (Jazz Laboratory Series, Vol. 2).

PACE, Salvatore, *clarinet, saxophones;* b. White Plains, N.Y., 8/10/10. Stud. clar. and started playing w. street marching bands. Crescent City Five in New York, 1924-8, RKO theater band in White Plains, 1929-31. During '30s and '40s, he worked in many commercial dance bands incl. Joe Haymes, '36-7, Al Donahue, '40, Frankie Masters, Teddy Powell, Bunny Berigan, '41, Charlie Spivak, '42. Active in Dixieland jazz work since '49, when he joined Phil Napoleon. From '51-3, he was heard with groups led by Pee Wee Erwin, Billy Butterfield, Yank Lawson, Jimmy McPartland. In '56, he was w. Billy Maxted at Nick's in Greenwich Village, NYC. Fav. own solo: *After You've Gone,* w. Pee Wee Erwin (Cadence). Favs: Goodman, Irving Fazola, Buddy De Franco. LPs:

Bruns. 54011, Urania 1202, Cadence 1011 (Pee Wee Erwin); Cadence 1012, 1013 (Billy Maxted).
Addr: 41-12 41st St., Long Island City 4, N.Y.

PAGE, Walter LPs: Van. 8504 (Ruby Braff), 8503 (Jo Jones), 8505 (Jimmy Rushing).

PAICH, Marty Shortly after the release of the successful Mel Tormé album for which he wrote and directed the accompaniment, Paich went to London as piano accompanist to Dorothy Dandridge, Spring, 1956. LPs: Decca DL8130 (*Blow Hot, Blow Cool*), DL8104 (John Graas); Beth. 52 (own "Dek-tette" acc. Mel Tormé), 44 (*Jazz City Workshop*), 46 (*Four Horns and a Lush Life*).

PARENTI, Tony LPs: Jazztone 1215 (*Happy Jazz*).

PARIS, Jackie LPs: Em. 36016 (*Advance Guard of the '40s*); Wing 60004 (*Can't Get Started with You*).

PARKER, Charlie Nine months after his death in March, 1955, the alto saxophonist was elected to the Hall of Fame in the *Down Beat* readers' poll. LPs: Norg. 1035 (*Alto Saxes*); Savoy 12009, 12014 (*Memorial albums*); Decca 5503 (Jay McShann); Roost 2210 (sextet w. Miles Davis, J. J. Johnson, reissued from Dial).

PARKER, Knocky LPs: Audiophile 28 (solos).

PASTOR, Tony LPs: Camden 296 (own band).

PAYNE, Cecil LPs: Em. 36043 (Cannonball Adderley); Savoy 12007 (*Clarke-Wilkins Septet*); Em. 36007 (Clark Terry), 36011 (Dinah Washington); Signal 1202 (Duke Jordan); EmArcy 36066 (Jimmy Cleveland); Pres. 7037 (Tadd Dameron); Signal 1203 (own group).

PAYNE, Sonny, *drums;* b. NYC, 5/4/26. Father, known as Christopher Columbus, is veteran drummer heard in recent years with Wild Bill Davis trio. Stud. w. Vic Berton 1936, played w. Bascomb brothers, '44, Hot Lips Page, '44-5, Earl Bostic, '45-7. Worked with bassist Lucille Dixon and her combo for 6 months, '48, then with Tiny Grimes until '50, when he began a three-year stint in Erskine Hawkins' orch. Led his own band in Larry Steele Revues, 1953-5, then in early '55 joined Count Basie. Favs: B. Rich, L. Bellson, Jo Jones, A. Blakey, M. Roach. LPs: Clef 678 (Count Basie); Coral 56061 (Erskine Hawkins); EmArcy 36072 (Joe Saye).
Addr: 1103 Franklin Ave., Bronx 5, New York.

PEACOCK, Burnie, *alto sax, clarinet,* etc.; b. Columbia, Tenn., 6/2/21. Stud. clarinet at 11, sax at 14. Attended Tenn. State College, 1936-8. Local groups in

Chicago and Detroit '38-42, incl. Jimmy Rachel's band which featured Wardell Gray, Howard McGhee, Milt Buckner. Played in Navy bands '42-5. With Lucky Millinder, Jimmie Lunceford, '45, Lionel Hampton, '46, Cab Calloway, '47, Count Basie, '48. Subbed as leader for Earl Bostic in '52 when latter was inactive owing to car crash. USO tour for Far East Command, '52. Many records w. Ruth Brown, Bull Moose Jackson and own combos. Favs: Benny Carter, alto; Buddy de Franco, clar.
Addr: 65 University Place, New York, N.Y.

PECORA, Santo LPs: Col. CL793 (Turk Murphy); South. 213 (own group), 216 (own group in *New Orleans Dixieland*).

PEDERSON, Pullman G. "Tommy", *trombone;* b. Watkins, Minn., 8/15/20. Stud. many instruments since age of 4, incl. drums, piano, violin. At 17, joined Don Strickland's territory band. During 1940s played w. many dance bands incl. Gene Krupa, '40-5, Red Norvo, Woody Herman, Tommy Dorsey, '43, Charlie Barnet, '44 and '46. For past decade has been free-lancing in Hollywood doing radio film and recording work. Since 1954 has stud. w. Mario Castelnuovo-Tedesco. Expert soloist showing the influence of his fav. trombonists, Tommy Dorsey, Bill Harris, Lou McGarity, Jack Teagarden, Frank Rosolino. Ambition: To write operatic and symph. music that will incorporate the color and phrasing of jazz. LPs: Beth. 46 (*Four Horns and a Lush Life*), 23 (Frances Faye); Cap. T683 (Four Freshmen).
Addr: 6141 Afton Place, Hollywood 28, Calif.

PEIFFER, Bernard The brilliant French pianist made his first American recording session in April, 1956 for the EmArcy label. LPs: EmArcy 26036 (*Le Most*); EmArcy 36080 (own trio and quartet).

PELL, Dave LPs: Cap. T659 (*The Les Brown All Stars*); Kapp 1025 (*Plays Rodgers and Hart,* transferred from Trend).

PEÑA, Ralph Raymond, *bass;* b. Jarbidge, Nev., 2/24/27. Father played traditional Spanish guitar. Stud. at San Francisco State Teachers College. Worked w. Nick Esposito, 1948-9; briefly w. Art Pepper, Vido Musso, Cal Tjader groups, '50; Billy May band, '51-2. Gigged frequently w. Barney Kessel around LA, '53-5, and local dates w. Stan Getz, Charlie Barnet, Jimmy Giuffre, Conte Candoli. Worked mainly w. Shorty Rogers '55-6. Talented modern musician whose best work, in his own opinion and the writer's, is on the Jimmy Giuffre *Tangents in Jazz LP.* Favs: Jimmy Blanton, Red Mitchell, Percy Heath. LPs: Cap. T634 (Jimmy Giuffre); Decca 8156 (Jack Millman); Pac. Jazz 1208 (Jack Montrose);

Decca 8257 (*The Man with the Golden Arm*); Pres. 202 (Zoot Sims); Contemp. 3514 (Duane Tatro).
Addr: 1139 N. Ogden Drive, Los Angeles 46, Calif.

PEPPER, Art LPs: Savoy 12045 (Shelly Manne).

PERKINS, Bill LPs: Vict. LPM1162 (Al Cohn); Norg. 1030 (Tal Farlow); Vict. LPM1121 (*The Five*); Cap. T658 (Woody Herman), T666 (Stan Kenton); Pac. Jazz 1205 (Bud Shank); Contemp. 3513 (Barney Kessel); Cont. 3510 (Lennie Niehaus); Pac. Jazz 1221 (own octet), 1217 (*Two Degrees East—Three Degrees West*).

PERKINS, Carl, *piano;* b. Indianapolis, Ind., 8/16/28. Not related to singer of same name. Brother, Ed. Perkins, is bassist. Self-taught. After working w. Tiny Bradshaw and Big Jay McNeely, 1948-9, he settled in Calif. Dec., '49 and has worked mostly as a single, also playing dates w. Miles Davis, '50. Army (saw action in Korea), Jan. '51 to Nov., '52. Spent '53 and Summer '54 w. Oscar Moore trio and worked with him again Sept.-Nov., '55. Own group from Feb., '56 at Strollers, Long Beach, Calif. Talented modern pianist. Favs: Art Tatum, Bud Powell, Hampton Hawes, Oscar Peterson, Erroll Garner. LPs: Norg. 1033 (Oscar Moore); Clef 676 (Illinois Jacquet); Gene Norman 12 (Frank Morgan); Dootone 207 (Dexter Gordon), 211 (own trio); Gene Norman Five (Max Roach-Clifford Brown).
Addr: 2535 Longwood Ave., Apt. 105, Los Angeles, Calif.

PERSIP, Charles Lawrence, *drums;* b. Morristown, N.J., 7/26/29. Stud. under Pearl Brackett in Springfield, Mass. First gigs in Newark, N.J. w. Billy Ford's rhythm and blues combo. Later worked w. Joe Holiday, also in Newark. Played in Tadd Dameron's band in Atlantic City, Summer, '53; joined Dizzy Gillespie, Sept., '53, touring overseas with him in Spring of '56. Favs: Max Roach, Art Blakey, Buddy Rich. LPs: Norg. 1003, ARS 405 (Dizzy Gillespie).
Addr: 2551 8th Ave., New York, N.Y.

PERSSON, Ake LPs: EmArcy 26048 (Roy Haynes).

PETERSON, Oscar With JATP, toured U.S., Fall 1955, and Europe, Feb., 1956. LPs: Norg. 1028 (Ralph Burns), 1016 (De Franco and Peterson Play George Gershwin); Clef 641, 671 (*Roy and Diz*), 642, 667 (Lionel Hampton), 656 (*Jam Session #6*), 677 (*Jam Session #7*), 648 (plays songs of Harry Warren), 649 (Harold Arlen), 650 (Jimmy McHugh), Norg. 1036 (*Piano Interpretations*); Clef 637 (Flip Phillips); Norg. 1031 (Buddy Rich); Verve 2002 (*In a Romantic Mood;* w. strings), 2001 (Toni Harper); Clef MG17 (JATP Vol. 17); Clef 708 (*Plays Count*

Basie), 684 (*Krupa and Rich*); Norg. 1044 (*New Jazz Sounds*); ARS 403 (Lionel Hampton).

PETTIFORD, Oscar LPs: Pres. 7007 (Miles Davis); Beth. 14 (Urbie Green); Atl. 1217 (Lee Konitz); Em. 36007 (Clark Terry); Roost 2204 (Sonny Stitt); Riv. 12-201 (Thelonious Monk); Beth. 33 (own octet); EmArcy 36066 (Jimmy Cleveland); Dawn 1104 (Mat Mathews); MGM 3390 (*West Coast vs East Coast*).

PHILLIPS, Flip Toured US and Europe with JATP, 1955-6. LPs: Norg. 1028 (Ralph Burns); Clef 656 (*Jam Session #6*), 677 (*Jam Session #7*), 637 (own quintet); Norg. 1034 (*Tenor Saxes*); Clef MG17 (*JATP Vol. 17*); Grand Award 318 (Earl Hines); Clef 684 (*Krupa and Rich*).

PIERCE, Nat Left Woody Herman, 1955, to free-lance in New York as arranger and pianist. LPs: Van. 8504 (Ruby Braff); Vict. LPM1116 (Al Cohn); Cap. T658 (Woody Herman); Van. 8503 (Jo Jones); Vict. LPM-1118 (Joe Newman); Keynote 1101 (*Jazz Romp*); Vict. LPM1210 (Freddie Greene).

PLATER, Bobby Badly injured in the Lionel Hampton band bus accident (see Hampton), the veteran reed man was described as the hero of the mishap, playing a major part in helping to rescue others more seriously hurt. He rejoined the band before its European tour, early 1956. LPs: Col. CL711 (Lionel Hampton).

POLLARD, Terry LPs: Bruns. 54009, EmArcy 36047 (Terry Gibbs); Beth. 1015 (own group).

POMEROY, Herb LPs: Cap. T6510 (Serge Chaloff); Trans. 1 (*Jazz in a Stable*).

POTTS, William Orie, *arranger, piano, accordion;* b. Arlington, Va., 4/3/28. Mainly self-taught. Organized jazz cocktail units, toured Southeast 1947-9 as accordionist-pianist-arranger. From '51, worked closely w. Willis Conover and the late Joe Timer with "The Orchestra" in Washington, D.C. Has entertained American troops in Iceland and Canada with jazz sextet every year since '52. Arr. for Tony Pastor, '54-5. Concurrent with playing and writing music, worked as audio engineer, '53-6. Ambition: To expand as composer in jazz and symphonic fields. Favs: John Mandel, Gerry Mulligan, Al Cohn, Tiny Kahn. LPs: Bruns. 54003 (Willis Conover, incl. fav. own comp. *Playground*); Beth. 28 (*The Six*); Vict. LPM1162 (Cohn, Perkins, Kamuca).
Addr: 862 N. Arlington Mill Drive, Arlington, Va.

POWELL, Benny LPs: Clef 666 (Count Basie); Jazztone 1220 (*The Count's Men*); MGM 3390 (*West Coast vs East Coast*).

POWELL, Bud LPs: Norg. 1036 (*Piano Interpretations*), 1017 (trio); Blue Note 1503, 1504 (*The Amazing Bud Powell*); Pres. 7024 (with Sonny Stitt).

POWELL, Mel LPs: Jazztone 1216 (*Dixieland Classics*); Cap. S706 (Benny Goodman); Van. 8506 (own septet and quintet).

POWELL, Richard, *piano, arranger;* b. NYC, 9/5/31. Died 6/26/56 in auto wreck (see Clifford Brown). Father, William Powell and brother, Bud Powell, both pianists. Stud. City College of New York, 1950-1, also privately with W. F. Rawlins; Jackie McLean, alto sax player, helped him get started. Played at Baby Grand Cafe, NYC w. Jimmie Carl Brown, '49-50. Worked around Philadelphia, '50-1. On the road w. Paul Williams rhythm and blues band, '51-2, and w. Johnny Hodges orch. '52-4. Joined Max Roach-Clifford Brown quintet, '54. An excellent small-group arranger, he did most of the writing for the quintet. Movie: *Carmen Jones*. Fav. own solos, *I'll String Along With You, My Funny Valentine*. Favs: Bud Powell, Calvin Jackson, Bobby Tucker. LPs: EmArcy 36008, 36037, 36070, 26043 (Brown-Roach), 36000 (Dinah Washington); Norg. 1009 (feat. on *Autumn in New York* w. Johnny Hodges); Pres. 7038 (Sonny Rollins).

POWELL, Rudy LPs: Van. 8505 (Jimmy Rushing).

POWELL, Seldon, *tenor sax;* b. Lawrenceville, Va., 11/15/28. Stud. Brooklyn and New York Conservatories, 1947-9; Juilliard '54-6. First job with Betty Mays and Her Swingtet, '49, Tab Smith at Savoy Ballroom, NYC, '49. Lucky Millinder, Dec., '49 to Jan., '51; Army, '51-2, playing with service bands in Germany and France. In past few years has remained in New York, playing dates and records w. Sy Oliver, Erskine Hawkins, Neal Hefti, Louis Bellson, Don Redman et al. Powell has a full but never lush tone, an extremely fluid style, and exceptional creativity. Musicians in the East considered him one of the important new tenor stars of '56. Ambition: To enter radio and TV staff work. Favs: Sonny Stitt, Lester Young. LPs: Roost 2202 (Tony Aless); Norg. 1020 (Louis Bellson); Epic 3187 (Neal Hefti); Roost 2205 (own group).
Addr: 1151 Lincoln Place, Brooklyn, N.Y.

PRADO, Perez LPs: Vict. LPM1101 (*Voodoo Suite*).

PRESLEY, Elvis, *singer, guitar;* b. Tupelo, Miss., 1/8/35. Self-taught. Drove a truck and stud. to be an electrician, also had some experience as furniture maker. Started with Sun Record Co., in Memphis. After first releases scored amazing success locally, RCA Victor bought his contract. His second release for Victor,

Heartbreak Hotel, sold well over a million records, and by early 1956 he had become the biggest new singing star since Johnnie Ray, enjoying his greatest success with teen-age and pre-teen-age audiences. Presley is a unique phenomenon. In his singing, as in his guitar playing, can be heard the influences of many fields of American music: country and western, rhythm and blues, jazz, and folklore origins in general. He acknowledges two Negro singers, Big Joe Turner and Bill Crudup, as the major influences on his style. Fav. own record: *Blue Suède Shoes* in LP. Ambition: To make headway in motion pictures (first movie due to be produced in Fall of '56). LPs: Vict. LPM1254 (*Elvis Presley*).

Addr: 1414 Getwell Road, Memphis, Tenn.

PREVIN, André The brilliant young pianist-arranger-conductor won an Academy Award nomination for his musical score for *It's Always Fair Weather.* It was his third nomination in four years. In early 1956 he took a leave of absence from the MGM Studios to return to jazz, leading his own trio in night clubs and participating in several jazz record sessions. In the Fall of 1956 he conducted a 12-week course in modern American music including jazz at the University of Calif., LA in the adult evening school. LPs: Decca DL8104 (John Graas); Vict. LPM1146 (*Lullaby of Birdland*); Contemp. 3506 (Lyle Murphy); Decca 8131 (*Let's Get Away From It All*); MGM 3390 (*West Coast vs East Coast*).

PRICE, Sammy On 12/16/55 the noted boogie-woogie pianist left for France under the auspices of the Jeunesse Musicale de France, taking with him a band comprising Emmett Berry, trumpet, Geo. Stevenson, trom., Herb Hall (brother of Edmond Hall) on clar., Freddy Moore on drums and Pops Foster, bass. This band toured in France, Belgium, Holland, Spain, and North Africa and made several record sessions, including one with Sidney Bechet for Vogue. Band returned to New York 5/22/56. LPs: Jazztone 1213 (Omer Simeon), 1207 (*Barrelhouse and Blues*).

PROCOPE, Russell LPs: Dot 3010 (*The Persuasive Sax of Russ Procope*); Beth. 60 (Duke Ellington).

PUMA, Joe LPs: Beth. 20, 56 (Chris Connor), 24 (Herbie Mann), 40 (Herbie Mann-Sam Most); Clef 645 (Artie Shaw); ABC-Par. 106 (Don Elliott); Dawn 1104 (Mat Mathews); ABC-Par. 109 (*Greatest Guitarists in the World*).

QUILL, Daniel Eugene "Gene", *alto sax, clarinet;* b. Atlantic City, N.J., 12/15/27. Joined union at 13, worked w. Alex Bartha's house band at Steel Pier, Atlantic City. Later toured with name bands incl. Jerry Wald, Art Mooney, Buddy De Franco, Claude Thorn-

hill, Gene Krupa, Dan Terry. Commendable alto sax stylist originally inspired by Ch. Parker, but rapidly developing his own personality. Favs: Phil Woods, Charlie Mariano, Herb Geller.

LPs: Vict. LJM1024 (Al Cohn), LPM1147 (Teddi King), LPM1146 (*Lullaby of Birdland*); Jazztone 1217 (Byers-Newman); Vict. LPM1198 (Joe Newman); Dawn 1101 (*Jazzville '56*); Coral 57035 (*East Coast Jazz Scene,* Vol. 1); Story. 905 (Joe Newman); Trend 1002 (Claude Thornhill); ABC-Par. 114 (Buddy Arnold).

Addr: 269 W. 72nd St., New York, N.Y.

QUINICHETTE, Paul LPs: Decca 8176 (*Blow Your Horn*); Em. 36004 (Sarah Vaughan); Em. 36011 (Dinah Washington); Decca 5503 (Jay McShann).

RAE, Johnny (John Anthony Pompeo), *vibes, drums, timbales;* b. Saugus, Mass., 8/11/34. Father, grad. of U. of Naples and U. of Milan, now a teacher in LA. Mother church org., piano and vocal teacher in Boston. Stud. piano 2 yrs. at New Eng. Cons.; tympani 2 yrs. Boston Cons.; drums, Berklee School. Pl. w. Herbie Lee R&B combo July, 1952-Aug., '53; Al Vega trio, Aug., '53 to Dec., '53 and July, '54-Jan., '55; Herb Pomeroy big band, Dec., '53-Apr., '54; Jay Miglori Jazz Workshop, Apr., '54-July, '54, all in Boston. Joined Geo. Shearing quintet Jan., '55, on recommendation of John Lewis. Fav: Milt Jackson; other influences, John Lewis, Horace Silver, Thelonious Monk. LPs: Cap. T648 (George Shearing).

Addr: 327 W. 56th St., New York, N.Y.

RAEBURN, Boyd After several years in semi-retirement, Raeburn resumed work as a bandleader, recording for Columbia in early 1956. LPs: Savoy 12040 (*Boyd Meets Stravinsky*).

RAGLIN, Junior The former Ellington bassist died in Boston, Nov. 10, 1955.

RAMEY, Gene LPs: Atl. 1224 (Lennie Tristano); Norg. 1056 (*The Jazz Giants '56*).

RANDALL, Frederick James, *trumpet;* b. London, Eng., 5/6/21. Mainly self-taught. Army, 1940-2. Early associate of Johnny Dankworth, who gigged with him before they both joined a group called Freddy Mirfield and His Garbage Men. After a year w. Mirfield, Randall organized his own group, which toured Germany four times, played concerts successfully throughout England and the Continent, and toured w. Teddy Wilson during the latter's visit to England. In May, '56, Randall brought his septet to the US and played a concert tour of Southern cities on an inter-union exchange arrangement that enabled Louis Armstrong to tour Great Britain. Favs: Armstrong, Bobby Hackett, Billy Butterfield, Charlie Teagarden.

Addr: 24 Chester Rd., Chigwell, Essex, London, England.

RANEY, Jimmy Remained in New York w. Jimmy Lyon trio at Blue Angel, 1955-6. LPs: Vict. LJM1024 (as Sir Osbert Haberdasher w. Al Cohn); Fant. 19 (Red Norvo); ABC-Par. 101 (Urbie Green); Pres. 214 (Bob Brookmeyer); Atl. 1229 (Teddy Charles); ABC-Par. 109 (*Greatest Guitarists in the World*).

REAY, Howard Thomas William, *drums;* b. Seamham Harbor, England, 10/10/30. Stud. Guildhall School of Music in London, served in the RAF, finishing his service as a disc jockey on the British Forces Network in Vienna. Played drums in band at the Elbow Beach Hotel in Bermuda, moving to Canada in 1951 and later joining the Calvin Jackson quartet. LPs: Col. CL756 (Calvin Jackson).

REDD, Freddie LPs: Beth. 17 (Joe Roland); Pres. 7050 (Gene Ammons).

REED, Lucy (Lucille DeRidder), *singer;* b. Marshfield, Wis., 4/14/21. Worked w. Ray Amicangelo quintet in Iron Mountain, Mich., 1949, Geo. Corsi trio in Milwaukee, and Woody Herman Sextet, '50. Record debut while w. Charlie Ventura's big band, '51. Resident in Chicago, she worked for some time at the Streamliner and at Lei Aloha w. Dick Marx and Johnny Frigo, '53-5, Village Vanguard, NYC, Jan., '56. Fav. own record, *It's All Right with Me* in Fantasy LP. Fav: Carmen McRae. LPs: Fant. 212 (*The Singing Reed*).

Addr: 4545 N. Clarendon Ave., Chicago 40, Ill.

REHAK, Frank James, *trombone;* b. Brooklyn, N.Y., 7/6/26. Navy, '43-7. Has played w. Art Mooney, Gene Krupa, Jimmy Dorsey, Ray McKinley, Claude Thornhill, Sauter-Finegan, Woody Herman. Toured overseas w. the Dizzy Gillespie band March to May, '56. Favs: Jay Jay Johnson, Earl Swope, Urbie Green. LPs: Vict. LJM1024, LPM1116 (Al Cohn); Beth. 21 (*Jazz at the Metropole*); Vict. LPM1118 (Joe Newman); Keynote 1101 (Nat Pierce), 1102 (Harvey Leonard); "X" 1032 (George Handy); Col. CL592 (Woody Herman); ABC-Par. 114 (Buddy Arnold).

Addr: Box 213, Bohemia, L.I., N.Y.

RICH, Buddy LPs: Clef 642, 667 (Lionel Hampton), 677 (*Jam Session #7*); Norg. 1031 (*Sing and Swing with Buddy Rich*), 1038 (*Buddy and Sweets*); Clef MG17 (JATP Vol. 17), 684 (*Krupa and Rich*), 708 (Oscar Peterson), 709 (Hampton, Tatum, Rich Trio); Norg. 1044 (*New Jazz Sounds*); ARS 403 (Lionel Hampton); EmArcy 36071 (*Drum Roll*); Verve 2009 (sings Johnny Mercer).

RICHARDS, Ann (Margaret Ann Borden Kenton), *singer;* b. San Diego, Calif., 10/1/35. Self-taught on piano, with mother's help, at age 10; private singing lessons. Local groups in Oakland and San Francisco, then four months w. Ch. Barnet combo, six months w. George Redman in Hollywood. Eddie Beal recommended her to Stan Kenton, with whom she toured in 1955. Married Kenton summer of '55; a few months later, shortly before winning *Down Beat* poll as No. 1 band vocalist, she gave up her career. One of the best band vocalists ever heard with Kenton, she expected to resume work for occasional record albums. Fav. own solo, *Winter in Madrid* w. Kenton.

Addr: 941 N. La Cienega, Los Angeles 46, Calif.

RICHARDS, Red LPs: Jazztone 1225 (Buck Clayton).

RICHARDSON, Jerome C., *tenor sax, alto, clarinet, flute;* b. Oakland, Calif., 12/25/20. Alto at 8, stud. music San Francisco State College. Local musicians, Ben Watkins and Wilbert Baranco, helped him get started in music profession at 14. Local bands and combos until 1941; Navy, '42-5, worked in Navy dance band under Marshall Royal. Toured w. Lionel Hampton band, '49-51, Earl Hines, '54-5, otherwise continued to free-lance. Had his own quartet at Minton's Play House, NYC, '55; played w. Lucky Millinder, Cootie Williams and expanded recorded activities in New York, '56, then joined house band at Roxy Theater, NYC. First flute solo was *Kingfish* w. Lionel Hampton. Played w. Chico Hamilton quintet at Basin Street May, '56. A fine tenor man, he is also one of the foremost jazz flutists. Favs: Frank Wess, flute; Ch. Parker, Sonny Stitt, Stan Getz, tenor.

LPs: Em. 36043 (Cannonball Adderley); Savoy 12017 (*Bohemia After Dark*), 12022 (*Flutes & Reeds*); Epic 3187 (Neal Hefti); Beth. 33 (Oscar Pettiford); EmArcy 36066 (Jimmy Cleveland); Jazztone 1223 (Eddie Bert).

Addr: 448 W. 55th St., New York, N.Y.

RICHMAN, Boomie LPs: Coral 57028 (Steve Allen); Grand Award 331 (Peanuts Hucko); Vict. LPM1212 (as "Mad Milt Summerblouse" in *New York Land Dixie*).

ROACH, Max LPs: Em. 36043 (Cannonball Adderley); EmArcy 36008 (*Brown and Roach Inc.*); EmArcy 36009 (Maynard Ferguson), 36039 (*Best Coast Jazz*), 36037 (*Study in Brown*); Pres. 7020, 7038 (Sonny Rollins); EmArcy 36070 (Brown-Roach), 36071 (*Drum Roll*).

ROBERTS, Howard LPs: Decca DL8104 (John Graas); Vict. LPM1105 (Pete Jolly); Gene Norman 12 (Frank Morgan); Col. CL689 (Pete Rugolo); Beth. 19 (Bobby Troup).

ROBINSON, Jim LPs: Jazztone 1212; Empirical 107 (George Lewis).

ROCHE, Betty After two years of semi-retirement, she returned via recordings made in New York and Calif. for Bethlehem. LPs: Grand Award 318 (with the Earl Hines Septet).

RODNEY, Red LPs: EmArcy 36016 (*Advance Guard of the '40s*); Fant. 208 (own quintet).

ROGERS, Shorty By 1956 Rogers was accepted as the most successful jazz musician in Calif., in terms of general acceptance on all levels—records, concerts, TV, night clubs, and especially motion pictures. He wrote and directed the scores for a number of cartoon shorts featuring such characters as Gerald McBoing Boing; he set a precedent by writing and playing a tasteful and effective score for a short film about cancer, *Sappy Homiens,* and was closely associated with such major features as *The Man with the Golden Arm.* In addition, he played night club engagements, mostly on the West Coast, with his own quintet featuring Jimmy Giuffre on clarinet. During this period, Rogers concentrated mainly on the fluegelhorn rather than on the trumpet.

LPs: Vict. LPM1121 (arrs. for *The Five*), LPM-1105 (Pete Jolly), LPM1146 (*Lullaby of Birdland*), LPM1101 (Perez Prado); Atl. 1212 (*The Swinging Mr. Rogers*); Pac. Jazz 1205 (Bud Shank); Decca 8257 (*The Man with the Golden Arm*); Savoy 12045 (*Jazz Composers Workshop*); Pres. 7028 (*Collaboration: West*); Vict. LG1000 (as "Boots Brown" in *Boots Brown and his Blockbusters*).

ROHDE, Bryce Benno, *piano;* b. Hobart, Tasmania, 9/12/23. Stud. Adelaide Conservatory, Australia. Worked as pastry cook until 1949, then led own trio in South Australia, '50-3, in radio, clubs, concerts. Moving to US, spent several months in radio and TV work then joined Australian Jazz Quartet. Fav: Art Tatum. LPs: Beth. 39, 1031 (Australian Jazz Quartet).
Addr: c/o ABC, 745 Fifth Ave., New York, N.Y.

ROLAND, Joe LPs: Beth. 17 (own quintet); Savoy 12039 (*Joltin' Joe Roland*).

ROLLINI, Adrian The jazz pioneer, who had played vibraphone since the early 1930s but who was originally famous as a bass saxophonist, died May 15, 1956 in Homestead, Fla., at the age of 51. He had lived for some years in Florida, where he was the proprietor of a hotel.

ROLLINS, Sonny Joined Clifford Brown-Max Roach combo Jan., 1956. LPs: Pres. 7013 (*Conception*), 7012 (Miles Davis), 7020 (*Worktime*), 7029 (*With the Modern Jazz Quartet*); EmArcy 36070 (Brown-Roach); Pres. 7038 (*Sonny Rollins Plus Four*).

ROOT, Billy LPs: Decca DL8176 (Bennie Green).

ROSE, Wally LPs: Col. CL650 (Turk Murphy).

ROSOLINO, Frank LPs: Contemp. 3504, 3509 (Howard Rumsey); Beth. 37 (Stan Levey); EmArcy 36060 (Georgie Auld); Beth. 46 (*Four Horns and a Lush Life*); Cap. T683 (*Four Freshmen*).

ROSS, Annie After spending two years singing with name bands in England, 1953-5, she scored a surprising hit in a London revue comedy, *Cranks,* and was hailed by critics as Britain's best new musical comedy bet.

ROUSE, Charlie Formed new combo, Les Modes, with Julius Watkins, French horn, Spring 1956. LPs: Wing 60002 (Joe Gordon); Dawn 1101 (*Jazzville '56*); Pres. 7031 (Art Farmer), 7052 (Bennie Green).

ROWLES, Jimmy LPs: Clef 644 (Bob Brookmeyer), 669 (Billie Holiday); Pac. Jazz 1205 (Bud Shank); Norg. 1038 (Buddy Rich & Harry Edison); Contemp. 3513 (Barney Kessel); Liberty 3003 (*Rare—but Well Done*); Norg. 1034 (w. Stan Getz in *Tenor Saxes*).

ROYAL, Ernie LPs: Savoy 12044 (*Top Brass*); Urania 1201 (Coleman Hawkins); Beth. 33 (Oscar Pettiford); Urania 1203 (*Accent on Trumpet*); Clef 682 (Lawrence Brown); EmArcy 36066 (Jimmy Cleveland); Fant. 219 (Elliot Lawrence).

ROYAL, Marshall LPs: Em. 36018 (*Alto Altitude*); Clef 647 (Count Basie).

RUBIN, Stan Rubin's Tigertown Five Dixieland group visited Monaco in April, 1956 to play at the wedding celebration of Prince Rainier and Grace Kelly. LPs: Vict. LPM1200 (*Dixieland Bash*); Jub. 1016 (Tigertown Five), 1024 (at Monaco).

RUFF, Willie, *bass, French horn;* b. Sheffield, Ala., 9/1/31. Bachelor of Music, 1953, Master of Music, '54, Yale U. While still studying, gigged w. Benny Goodman. Worked w. Lionel Hampton during Spring and Summer, '55, then teamed up w. Dwike Mitchell (q.v.). The Mitchell-Ruff duo, featuring Ruff mainly on bass, but with occasional Fr. horn solos, revealed Ruff's high standards of academic musicianship. His fav. musicians are Abe Kniaz, first horn with the Washington Symph.; Ray Brown, Oscar Pettiford. LPs: Epic 3221 (Mitchell-Ruff Duo).
Addr: 1150 Chapel St., New Haven, Conn.

RUGOLO, Pete Did free-lance recording work in LA until Spring, 1956, then signed exclusively with Mercury. Seen as bandleader in film *Meet Me in Las Vegas,* '56. LPs: Col. CL635 (*Introducing Pete Rugolo*), CL689 (*Rugolomania*); Cap. T683 (*Four Freshmen and Five Trombones*), W724 (*Stan Kenton*); MGM 3390 (*West Coast vs East Coast*).

RUMSEY, Howard LPs: Contemp. 3504 (Lighthouse All Stars); Decca 8259 (Stan Kenton); Vict. LG1000 Boots Brown).

RUSHING, Jimmy LPs: Col. CL754 (Count Basie); Van. 8505 (*Listen to the Blues*); Col. CL778 (*Cat Meets Chick*).

RUSHTON, Joe LPs: Col. CL785 (*Dixieland, My Dixieland*).

RUSSELL, George The former Gillespie arr. returned to jazz activities in 1956, writing arrangements for RCA Victor, etc.

RUSSELL, Pee Wee LPs: Jazztone 1208 (Max Kaminsky).

RUSSIN, Babe LPs: Em. 36023 (*Battle of the Saxes*); Col. CL820 (Benny Goodman); Atl. 1225 (Jess Stacy); Cap. T707 (*Session at Midnight*).

RUSSO, Anthony C. "Andy", trombone; b. Brooklyn, N.Y., 7/8/03. Played in Yerkes Happy Six, 1921; organized his own New Orleans Jazz Band, '22-4, then w. Mal Hallett, '25-30, Loew Theaters '30-1, followed by a decade of radio staff work. With Jimmy Dorsey band, '42-5; back in radio until '48. Since '49, he has worked mostly at Nick's in Greenwich Village, NYC, under such leaders as Phil Napoleon, Bobby Hackett, Pee Wee Erwin, Billy Butterfield, Yank Lawson, Jimmy McPartland. Fav. own solo: *Tin Roof Blues* w. Napoleon. Favs: Will Bradley, Tommy Dorsey, Eddie Kusby, Buddy Morrow, Jack Teagarden, Joe Yukl. LPs: Bruns. 54011, Urania 1202, Cadence 1011 (Pee Wee Erwin); Decca 5261 (Phil Napoleon).
Addr: 4746 40th St., Long Island City 4, N.Y.

RUSSO, Bill LPs: Savoy 12045 (*Jazz Composers' Workshop*).

RUSSO, Santo "Sonny", trombone; b. Brooklyn, N.Y., 3/20/29. Stud. with father, who plays tpt., violin, and grandfather, a trombonist. Played w. Buddy Morrow, 1947, Lee Castle, '48, Sam Donahue, '49, Artie Shaw, '49-50, Art Mooney, late '50. In '51 and '52 he was heard w. Jerry Wald, Tommy Tucker, Buddy Rich and Ralph Flanagan. Then w. Sauter-Finegan, 1953-5, after which he joined the Dorsey Brothers. Solos on *Everything I've Got, Scuttlebutt, Lucky Duck* in Neal

Hefti album, and many w. Sauter-Finegan (see below). Favs: Tommy Dorsey, Bill Harris, Urbie Green, Jack Teagarden. LPs: Fant. 209 (Sandole); Epic 3187 (Neal Hefti); Vict. LJM1003 (Sauter-Finegan); Herald 0105 (Mickey Sheen).
Addr: 938 McDonald Ave., Brooklyn 18, N.Y.

RUTHER, Bull LPs: Vict. LPM1107 (*Basses Loaded*); Fant. 210 (Brubeck); Story. 907 (Zoot Sims-Bob Brookmeyer).

SACHS, Aaron LPs: Norg. 1040 (*Modern Jazz Society*).

SAFRANSKI, Eddie LPs: Grand Award 322 (*A Musical History of Jazz*).

SAUTER, Eddie LPs: Vict. LPM1051 (*Concert Jazz*); Camden 295 (Ray McKinley); Vict. LPM1240 (*Adventure in Time*).

SAYE, Joe (Joseph Shulman), piano, accordion; b. Glasgow, Scotland, 2/25/23. Lost sight at age of two. Toured w. Roy Fox band playing accordion 1937-8, then spent 8 yrs. in vaudeville. Formed own group, '46. Arrived in US 12/8/55. Appeared at Bohemia, NYC. Favs: Tatum, Shearing, John Lewis, Duke Ellington. LPs: EmArcy 36072 (solos w. rhythm); Lond. LB-965.
Addr: Hotel Sussex, 116 W. 72nd St., New York 23, N.Y.

SCHAEFER, Harold Herman "Hal", piano, arranger; b. New York City, 7/22/25. Mainly self-taught as pianist; grad. of Music and Art High School, NYC, and stud. arranging w. Mario Castelnuovo-Tedesco. Gigged in the up-state New York "borscht belt" at 13. On graduating from high school, played w. Lee Castle, 1940; Ina Ray Hutton band, '41. Several months in Benny Carter's band, '42, then joined Harry James. Worked w. Boyd Raeburn, '43, Billy Eckstine, '44, later spent a year and a half as Peggy Lee's accompanist; arr., conducted for Gloria de Haven, and spent several years at motion picture studios as vocal coach and arr. Returned to NYC '55, led own trio at the Embers and wrote music for stage shows. An intelligent and articulate musician, Schaefer is a deft pianist and an arranger whose unusual ideas are well-displayed in the second album listed below. Fav: Art Tatum. LPs: Vict. LPM1106 (*Just Too Much*), LPM1199 (*The RCA Victor Jazz Workshop*).
Addr: 369 W. 56th St., New York, N.Y.

SCHILDKRAUT, David, alto sax; b. New York City, 1/7/25. Father, who used to play clar., bought him his first instrument. Stud. clar., alto at high school. Professional debut w. Louis Prima, 1941. Has worked off and on since '47 with various large and small groups led by Buddy Rich; also w. Anita O'Day combo, '47; European tour w. Stan Kenton, Summer, '53; Pete Rugolo band, '54, Geo. Handy combo, '55. Aside from these name-band jobs, he has free-lanced around New York, worked as floor manager for Woolworth's, '49, and had an office job at Decca in '52. Schildkraut at his best plays inspired jazz alto; he was once mistaken for Ch. Parker in a "blindfold test". Fav. own solo: *Solar* w. Miles Davis (Prestige) and *Case Ace* w. Geo. Handy (Label "X"). Favs: Ch. Parker, Benny Carter. LPs: Roost 2202 (Tony Aless); "X" 1032, 1004 (George Handy); Decca 8235 (Ralph Burns); Cap. H525, 526 (Kenton); Pres. 185 (Miles Davis).

Addr: 180 Chester St., Brooklyn, N.Y.

SCHLINGER, Sol, *baritone and tenor saxes;* b. New York City, 9/6/26. Stud. with Bill Sheiner, 1939. Prof. debut w. Henry Jerome, '40, playing ten. sax. While w. Shep Fields band, '41-3, toured Europe for USO. Switching to baritone sax, played w. Buddy Rich, '43, Tommy Dorsey, '43-6, Jimmy Dorsey, '47. During the next few years he was heard w. Ch. Barnet, Jerry Gray, Herbie Fields, Louis Jordan, Perez Prado. Joined Benny Goodman for concert tour playing tenor, '52 and again in '56 at the Waldorf-Astoria, NYC. First jazz records w. Al Cohn (see below). Favs: Bob Gordon, Gerry Mulligan. LPs: Vict. LPM1211 (Manny Albam); Atl. 1229 (Teddy Charles); Vict. LJM-1020, 1024 (Al Cohn), LPM1146 (*Lullaby of Birdland*).

Addr: 961 E. 181st St., New York, N.Y.

SCHNEIDER, Elmer Reuben "Moe", *trombone;* b. Bessie, Okla., 12/24/19. Father a violinist; 3 brothers, 4 sisters, all musically inclined. Started on banjo; trom. at 12. Moved to Calif., 1938. Played at Balboa Beach for a year, then w. Ken Baker, Ben Pollack, Gus Arnheim, Will Osborne, Alvino Rey. During 2 yrs. in service, played in Army band w. Ray Bauduc and Gil Rodin. After discharge in '46, rejoined Rey; toured w. Gene Krupa, '47, then settled in LA, worked w. Bob Crosby; Ben Pollack, '49, for 2 yrs; did radio version of *Pete Kelly's Blues* and also played in the movie. Began stud. in '47 to take up accounting and has had a practice since '51, alternating this work with musical activities. Fav. own solo: *Smiles* on Victor LP1126. Favs: Lou McGarity, Jack Teagarden, Ray Sims for jazz; Murray McEachern, Joe Howard for pretty solos. LPs: Cap. 677 (Billy May); Col. CL690, Vict. LPM1126 (*Pete Kelly's Blues*).

Addr: 3236 Bennett Drive, Hollywood, Calif.

SCHROEDER, Gene LPs: Col. CL719 (Eddie Condon); EmArcy 36013 (Bud Freeman); ABC-Par. 121 (*Brother Matthew*).

SCHULLER, Gunther, *French horn, composer;* b. Jackson Heights, N.Y., 11/22/25. Stud. with first Fr. horn

player of Metropolitan Opera and with Robert Schulze of Manhattan School of Music. Two years w. Eugene Goossens' Cincinnati Symph., then 10 yrs. w. the Metropolitan Opera. Although primarily a classical musician, Schuller has an exceptional knowledge and understanding of jazz and on numerous occasions has worked very closely with John Lewis and has appeared in jazz concerts. LPs: Norgran 1040 (*Modern Jazz Society*).

Addr: 98-26 64th Ave., Forest Hills, L.I., N.Y.

SCOBEY, Bob LPs: Good Time Jazz 12006 (Bob Scobey-Clancy Hayes); Down Home 1 (own band); Contemp. 5002 (Claire Austin).

SCOTT, Bobby The youthful ex-Gene Krupa pianist scored a surprise hit as a singer in 1955 in his first release for the ABC-Paramount label, *Chain Gang*. LPs: Clef 668 (Gene Krupa); ABC-Par. 102 (*Scott Free*).

SCOTT, Tony LPs: Vict. LPM1146 (*Lullaby of Birdland*); Norg. 1040 (as Anthony Sciacca in *Modern Jazz Society*); Vict. LPM1269 (*Both Sides of Tony Scott*).

SEDRIC, Gene LPs: EmArcy 36023 (*Battle of the Saxes*); Jazztone 1225 (Buck Clayton).

SEGAL, GERALD "Jerry", *drums;* b. Philadelphia, Pa., 2/16/31. Majored in music at Mastbaum High. Toured w. Benny Green combo, Pete Rugolo band, 1954; gigged in Philadelphia clubs, then joined Johnny Smith combo, Norma Carson quintet; Terry Gibbs quartet from Sept., '55. LPs: Roost 2201 (Johnny Smith); Pres. 206 (Teddy Charles); Decca 8176 (Benny Green); Col. CL689 (Pete Rugolo); EmArcy 36064 (Terry Gibbs).

Addr: 28 Macombs Pl., Apt. 12A, Philadelphia, Pa.

SEVERINSEN, Doc LPs: Coral 57019 (*Steve Allen Sings*); Cap. T624 (Charlie Barnet).

SHANK, Bud LPs: Pac. Jazz 1206 (Chet Baker), 1202 (Chet Baker), 1205 (own groups); Contemp. 3509 (Howard Rumsey); Decca 8257 (*The Man with the Golden Arm*); Beth. 52 (Mel Tormé); Liberty 6003 (Herbie Harper, Bob Gordon); Pac. Jazz 1215 (own quartet), 1219 (*Quartet at Cal-Tech*), 1221 (Bill Perkins); Pacifica 2002 (Kitty White); Vict. LG1000 (Boots Brown).

SHARON, Ralph LPs: Beth. 20, 56 (Chris Connor); 41 (own trio), 47 (Terry Morel).

SHAUGHNESSY, Eddie LPs: River. 204 (Mundell Lowe); Grand Award 33-325 (Al Klink).

SHAVERS, Charlie Rejoined Tommy Dorsey 1955-6. LPs: Coral 57018 (Steve Allen); Norg. 1020 (Louis Bellson); EmArcy 36013 (Bud Freeman); Gene Norman 15 (Lionel Hampton); Period 1909 (Maxine Sullivan); Em. 36015, Norg. 1041 (Charlie Ventura); Beth. 27 (*Gershwin, Shavers and Strings*); Grand Award 318 (*Jazz Concert*); MGM E3325 (*A Hi-Fi Salute to the Great Ones;* Leroy Holmes Orch.); Jazztone 1229 (Maxine Sullivan).

SHAW, Artie As he has intermittently since 1939, Shaw again announced his permanent retirement from music in '55. Aside from a tour of Australia, he was almost completely inactive as a musician. In '56 he spent some time in Spain, where he announced that he was working on a new book, and also visited England. His seventh marriage, to actress Doris Dowling, ended in divorce in '55. LPs: Clef 645 (*Gramercy Five #4*); Epic 3128 (Red Norvo); Vict. LPM1201 (*Both Feet in the Groove*).

SHAW, Arvell Left Louis Armstrong combo again in the Spring of 1956 to free-lance. LPs: Col. CL840 (Louis Armstrong).

SHEARING, George LPs: MGM E3176 (Billy Eckstine); Cap. T648 (*The Shearing Spell*).

SHELDON, Jack, trumpet; b. Jacksonville, Fla., 11/30/31. Stud. LA City College. Has worked in and around LA with Jack Montrose, Art Pepper, Dave Pell, Wardell Gray, Chet Baker, Dexter Gordon, Jimmy Giuffre, Herb Geller, and Howard Rumsey. Fav: Dizzy Gillespie. LPs: Cap. T634, T549 (Jimmy Giuffre); Jazz: West 1 (*Get Out of Town,* quartet), 2 (quintet).
    Addr: 5311 Hollywood Blvd., Los Angeles 27, Calif.

SHEROCK, Shorty LPs: Cap. T707 (*Session at Midnight*).

SHIHAB, Sahib LPs: Beth. 42 (Howard McGhee); EmArcy 26048 (Roy Haynes).

SHIRLEY, Don LPs: Cadence 1004 (*Piano Perspectives*), 1009 (*Orpheus in the Underworld*).

SHORT, Robert Waltrip "Bobby", singer, piano; b. Danville, Ill., 9/15/26. School in Chicago. Self-taught musically. A child prodigy, he was in vaudeville from the age of 10. Featured at the Blue Angel in NYC, the Haig in LA, and the Gala in Hollywood. Short worked also at clubs in Paris and London, 1952-3, and acquired a reputation among society people for his interpretation of sophisticated lyrics. Although this has been his main appeal, some of his work is of interest from a jazz standpoint. LPs: Atl. 1214 (*Songs by Bobby Short*), 1230 (Bobby Short).
    Addr: 5014 W. 20th St., Los Angeles 16, Calif.

SHU, Eddie LPs: Clef 668, 627 (Gene Krupa).

SHULMAN, Joe LPs: Vict. LJM1137 (Barbara Carroll).

SIGNORELLI, Frank, piano; b. New York City, 5/24/01. Stud. with a cousin, Pasquale Signorelli. A pioneer of jazz, Signorelli worked in the Original Dixieland Jazz Band, the Original Memphis Five, and w. Paul Whiteman, Bix Beiderbecke, Joe Venuti, Eddie Lang, and Red Nichols. An important jazz figure in the '20s and early '30s, he has also had great success as a songwriter and became a member of ASCAP in '33. His biggest hits were, *I'll Never Be the Same, Stairway to the Stars,* and *A Blues Serenade.* He has also written many piano solo pieces such as *Park Avenue Fantasy, Midnight Reflections, Caprice Futuristic.* Favs: Bob Zurke, Fats Waller. LPs: Kapp 1005 (*Ragtime Duo*); EmArcy 26008, 26009 (Phil Napoleon); Col. CL844 (Bix Beiderbecke); River. 1048 (Red Nichols); "X" LVA3036 (Joe Venuti-Eddie Lang).
    Addr: 1828 W. 5th St., Brooklyn 23, N.Y.

SILVER, Horace LPs: Wing 60000 (Nat Adderley); Savoy 12017 (*Bohemia After Dark*); EmArcy 36007 (Clark Terry); Blue Note 1507, 1508 (*The Jazz Messengers at the Cafe Bohemia*); Signal 1201 (Gigi Gryce); Savoy 12064 (*The Jazz Message*); Pres. 7031 (Art Farmer); Trans. 4 (Donald Byrd); Blue Note 5062 (quintet).

SIMEON, Omer LPs: Jazztone 1213 (*Jazz à la Creole*); Atl. 1219 (Wilbur De Paris).

SIMMONS, John LPs: EmArcy 36009 (Maynard Ferguson); Clef 679 (Art Tatum-Roy Eldridge); Norg. 1038 (Buddy Rich and Harry Edison).

SIMS, Ray LPs: Cap. T659 (*The Les Brown All Stars*).

SIMS, Zoot The tenor saxophonist joined Gerry Mulligan sextet, and toured Europe w. Mulligan, early 1956. He began doubling on alto at this time. LPs: Cap. T659 (Don Fagerquist); Decca DL8104 (John Graas); Pres. 7022 (*The Brothers*), 7013 (*Conception*); EmArcy 36056 (Gerry Mulligan); Dawn 1102 (*The Modern Art of Jazz by Zoot Sims*); Atl. 1228 (Chris Connor); Pres. 7033 (Jon Eardley); Fant. 219 (Elliot Lawrence); Story. 907 (Bob Brookmeyer/Zoot Sims); Jazz: West 2 (Jack Sheldon); Vict. LPM1146 (as "Jack Zoot" in *Lullaby of Birdland*).

SINATRA, Frank (Note: correct birth date is 12/12/15.) Received an Academy Award nomination for his performance in *The Man with the Golden Arm,* released early 1956. Also featured in *Guys and Dolls, The Tender Trap* and other movies. LPs: Cap. W653 (*Songs for Swingin' Lovers*).

SINGLETON, Zutty LPs: Jazztone 1213 (Sidney Bechet; Omer Simeon).

SLACK, Freddie LPs: Wing 60003 (*Boogie Woogie on the 88*).

SMITH, Bessie LPs: *The Bessie Smith Story* transferred from Col. ML to Col. CL855 (with Louis Armstrong), CL856 (*Blues to Barrelhouse*), CL857 (with Joe Smith and Fletcher Henderson's Hot Six), CL858 (with James P. Johnson and Charlie Green).

SMITH, Carson LPs: Pac. Jazz 1202, 1203 (Chet Baker); 1209, 1216 (Chico Hamilton); 1212 (Dick Twardzik).

SMITH, Charlie LPs: Herald 0100 (Aaron Bell).

SMITH, James Oscar, *organ;* b. Norristown, Pa., 12/8/25. Both parents pianists. At age of 9 won a Major Bowes Amateur Show, appeared as pianist on Philadelphia radio programs. In 1942 teamed with his father in song and dance routine for local night club work. Served with Navy in the Pacific; later had his first formal training in Philadelphia, stud. string bass at Hamilton School of Music, '48, and piano at Ornstein School '49-50. Joined a group called Don Gardner and His Sonotones, '52, playing first piano then organ. Formed his own trio, Sept., '55.

Jimmy Smith was perhaps the most extraordinary new instrumental jazz star to rise to prominence in '56. His relationship to previous jazz exponents of the Hammond organ parallels those of Ch. Christian and Jimmy Blanton to earlier guitarists and bassists. He uses a far greater variety of stops and has a unique gift for astonishing improvisations at fast tempi, producing unique tone colors and showing phenomenal technique with both hands and feet. His New York debut leading his trio at the Bohemia, early '56, was considered by many musicians an event of unprecedented interest. LPs: Blue Note 1512, 1514 (own trio).

SMITH, Johnny LPs: Roost 2201 (Plays Jimmy Van Heusen), 2203 (quartet), 2206 (Beverly Kenney).

SMITH, Paul LPs: Vict. LPM1124 (Conrad Gozzo); Verve 2000 (Anita O'Day).

SMITH, Tab LPs: EmArcy 36023 (Coleman Hawkins).

SMITH, Willie LPs: Norg. 1035 (*Alto Saxes*); Em. 36018 (*Alto Altitude*), 36023 (w. Corky Corcoran), 36038 (w. Juan Tizol); Gene Norman 15 (Lionel Hampton); ARS 405 (Dizzy Gillespie); Cap. 707 (*Session at Midnight*).

SONN, Lawrence "Larry", *arranger, trumpet, piano;* b. Long Island, N.Y., 1/17/24. Stud. Juilliard. Worked w. Teddy Powell, Bobby Byrne, Vincent Lopez. Had his own orch. for 8 yrs. in Mexico, playing before 80,000 people in the world's largest bullfight arena. Ret. to New York and organized new band July, 1955. Fav. own solo: *La Virgen de la Macarena* (*The Brave Bulls*) rec. by Columbia in Mexico. Favs: Ch. Shavers, Billy Butterfield. LPs: Coral 57035 (*East Coast Jazz Scene*, Vol. 1).

Addr: 229-03 Grand Central Pkwy., Bayside 64, L.I., N.Y.

SOUCHON, Edmond LPs: Para. 107, S/D1001 (Johnny Wiggs-Raymond Burke).

SOUTHERN, Jeri LPs: Decca 8055 (*The Southern Style*), 8214 (*You Better Go Now*).

SPANIER, Muggsy LPs: Jazztone 1216 (*Dixieland Classics*).

SPARGO, Tony LPs: Cadence 1011 (Pee Wee Erwin).

STABULAS, Nicholas, *drums;* b. Brooklyn, N.Y., 12/18/29. Stud. with Henry Adler, 1946-8. Work was confined to commercial music for some time, but in '54-6 he gigged and/or recorded w. Phil Woods, Jon Eardley, Jimmy Raney. Favs: Kenny Clarke, Art Blakey, Max Roach. LPs: Pres. 7018, 204, 191 (Phil Woods); Beth. 39 (Australian Jazz Quartet), 51 (Joe Derise); Pres. 7033, 207 (Jon Eardley); Pres. 199 (Jimmy Raney); Signal 102 (Hall Overton).

Addr: 205-10 35th Ave., Bayside, L.I., N.Y.

STACY, Jess LPs: Atl. 1225 (*Tribute to Benny Goodman*).

STARR, Kay LPs: Vict. LPM1149 (*The One—the Only Kay Starr*); Modern 1203 (*Singin' Kay Starr, Swingin' Erroll Garner*).

ST. CYR, Johnny LPs: Gene Norman 13 (*Dixieland Jubilee*); Epic 3207 (Johnny Dodds & Kid Ory); South. 215 (and his Hot Five).

STEGMEYER, Bill LPs: Grand Award 310, 313 (Will Bradley), 322 (*A Musical History of Jazz*); Jazztone 1227 (Jimmy McPartland).

STEIN, Lou LPs: Norg. 1020 (Louis Bellson); Grand Award 310, 313 (Will Bradley); Jazztone 1217 (Byers-Newman); Coral 57003 (*Sweet and Lovely;* own orch.); Epic 3148 (*The Lou Stein 3, 4 and 5*); Jubilee 1019 (*Eight for Kicks—Four for Laughs*); Grand Award 322 (*A Musical History of Jazz*).

STEVENS, Leith, *arranger, conductor;* b. Mt. Moriah, Mo., 9/13/09. Parents both piano teachers. Began stud. piano as soon as he could sit on the bench.

Earned first dollar at age of four playing the piano. Before he was twelve, played piano in movie theater in Kansas City. Stud. for three years at Horner Institute, during which time he played accompaniments for singers. Played with the Chicago Grand Opera Co. orchestra. He led a twenty-piece band on CBS' *Magazine of the Air* in the 1930s. At the height of the swing era, Stevens made an important contribution to jazz as bandleader on the CBS radio series, *Saturday Night Swing Session.* More recently, working in Hollywood as a musical director and arr., he has pioneered for jazz by introducing, as background music for dramatic films, themes with a jazz flavor, thus opening up a new avenue for jazz and the musicians in this field. He composed and conducted original music for *The Wild One, Private Hell 36* and *The Bob Matthias Story.* LPs: Decca DL8349 (*The Wild One*), Coral CRL-56122 (*Private Hell 36*).

Addr: 1966 Fitch Drive, Hollywood, Calif.

STEVENSON, George Edward Toured Continent and North Africa with Sammy Price combo early 1956.

STEWARD, Herbie LPs: Liberty 6009 (Buddy Childers).

STEWART, Rex LPs: Grand Award 310, 313 (Will Bradley), 315 (*Rex Stewart Plays Duke Ellington*), 322 (*A Musical History of Jazz*).

STEWART, Thomas, *tenor horn, trumpet;* b. Bridgeport, Conn., 12/26/31. Local groups in New England, 1946-9, and North Carolina, '49-51, Duke Ambassadors, '51-3, local groups around Conn., '53-5, Billy Butterfield, March, '56. Rec. for ABC-Paramount with own groups and w. Whitey Mitchell. Favs: Buck Clayton, Bobby Hackett, Dizzy Gillespie. LPs: ABC-Par. 117 (own group).

Addr: 301 W. 50th St., New York, N.Y.

STITT, Sonny LPs: Roost 1203 (*The Battle of Birdland*), 2204 (Plays Quincy Jones arrs.), 2208 (own quartet & quintet); Pres. 7024 (with Bud Powell; J. J. Johnson), 7050 (Ammons vs Stitt).

STOLLER, Alvin LPs: Clef 679 (Art Tatum-Roy Eldridge).

STRATTON, Donald Paul, *trumpet;* b. Woburn, Mass., 12/9/28. Stud. New England Conservatory and private tutors. Started in 1945 w. Ray Borden, out of whose group grew the Nat Pierce combo, '49-51; also worked w. Tommy Reynolds, '49, Victor Lombardo, '50, Dean Hudson, '51-2, Mal Hallett, '52, Tony Pastor, '52-3. Since '54 has worked w. Les Elgart, Elliot Lawrence, Tex Beneke, Boyd Raeburn, Buddy Morrow, Claude Thornhill and Jim Chapin. Originally influenced by Muggsy Spanier and Harry James. LPs:

Pres. 213 (Jim Chapin); ABC-Par. 118 (own group).

Addr: 570 J Grand St. (Apt. 1507-J), New York 2, N.Y.

STRAYHORN, Billy LPs: Norg. 1055 (*Ellingtonia '55*); Col. CL872 (Rosemary Clooney and Duke Ellington).

SULIEMAN, Idrees Dawud, *trumpet;* b. St. Petersburg, Fla., 8/27/23. Father plays piano and tuba. Stud. Boston Conservatory. Early experience w. Carolina Cotton Pickers Orch.; Fess Clark, in St. Petersburg. Featured during 1940s w. Tommy Reynolds, Gerry Mulligan, Cab Calloway, Mercer Ellington, Illinois Jacquet, Earl Hines, Count Basie, Lionel Hampton, Erskine Hawkins, Dizzy Gillespie. Jazz record debut on Blue Note w. Thelonious Monk. Favs: Rafael Mendez, Clifford Brown, Dizzy Gillespie. Ambition: To record with strings. LPs: Savoy 12044 (*Top Brass;* incl. fav. own solo *Imagination*); Blue Note 1510, 1511 (Thelonious Monk); King 265-85 (Mary Lou Williams).

Addr: 182 1st St., Englewood, N.J.

SULLIVAN, Joe LPs: EmArcy 36013 (Bud Freeman); Col. CL821 (Benny Goodman); Jazztone 1208 (Max Kaminsky); Riv. 12-202 (solos, 1953); Down Home 2 (*Mr. Piano Man*).

SULLIVAN, Maxine LPs: Period 1909 (*Maxine Sullivan—1956*); Jazztone 1229 (*Flow Gently, Sweet Rhythm*).

SUNKEL, Phillip Charles Jr., *cornet, trumpet, arranger;* b. Zanesville, Ohio, 11/26/25. Started on cornet at 14, switched to tpt. during Army service. Attended Cincinnati Conservatory of Music, graduated in 1950 and played with local bands around Ohio. Later worked with name bands incl. Tommy Tucker, Claude Thornhill, Ch. Barnet, Tony Pastor, Ray Anthony, Dan Terry, Sauter-Finegan, Les Elgart, Vincentico Valdez. First prominent in jazz w. Stan Getz combo, '55. Sunkel's use of the cornet, and his admiration for Bix Beiderbecke, have produced in him a stylistic blend of the old and the new. As an arr., he admires the work of Al Cohn, John Lewis and Thelonious Monk. LPs: Vict. LPM1161 (Al Cohn); Atl. 1220 (arrs. for Tony Fruscella); Epic 3199 (Junior Bradley); ABC-Par. 118 (Don Stratton); Clef 682 (Lawrence Brown).

Addr: 1011 Ocean Ave., Brooklyn 26, N.Y.

SYMS, Sylvia Scored her first commercial hit as a pop singer with her record of *I Could Have Danced All Night,* released on Decca, Spring, 1956. LPs: Decca DL8151, 8152 (*Steve Allen's All Star Jazz Concert,* Vols. 1 & 2), 8188 (*Sylvia Syms Sings*).

SYRAN, George (George Syrianoudis), *piano, arranger (also clarinet, tenor sax);* b. Youngstown, Ohio, 7/21/28. Stud. Youngstown College, 1946, Cincinnati

Conservatory of Music, '49-50, Manhattan School of Music, '53-6. Started on clar. and tenor, professional debut at 15. Jobs on saxophone w. Bob Astor, Bobby Sherwood, Hal McIntyre, '47-9; piano w. Cannonball Adderley, '52; Phil Woods, '53. Says, "I originally switched from saxophone to writing, and what better way to learn writing than by playing piano and analyzing all the great piano works and scores." Favs: Bud Powell, Randy Weston, Thelonious Monk. Fav. arr: Jon Eardley, Phil Sunkel. LPs: Pres. 7033, 207 (Jon Eardley), 204, 191 (Phil Woods).

Addr: 123 W. 75th St., New York, N.Y.

TATE, Buddy LPs: Col. CL701 (Buck Clayton); Van. 8505 (Jimmy Rushing).

TATRO, Duane Lysle, *arranger, tenor sax, clarinet;* b. Van Nuys, Calif., 5/18/27. Extensive studies including École Normale de Musique in Paris with Arthur Honegger; Darius Milhaud, 1948-51, Russ Garcia, '51-5. Played tenor saxophone in dance bands, started arr. while in Navy. Worked with a group led by Mel Tormé in '44, Stan Kenton, '45, Joe Venuti, '46, Dick Pierce, '47. Overseas, worked in Paris off and on, 1948-51 and in Knokke, Belgium, '49; Heidelberg, Germany and Tunis, Tunisia, '50. One of the best equipped and most stimulating writers among those who have tried to take jazz into atonal fields while retaining its basic rhythmic qualities. Favs: Jack Montrose, Gerry Mulligan, Bill Holman, Ralph Burns. LPs: Contemp. 3514 (*Jazz for Moderns*).

Addr: 7807 White Oak Ave., Reseda, Calif.

TATUM, Art Norg. 1036 (*Piano Interpretations*); Clef 657, 658, 659, 660, 661 (*The Genius of Art Tatum #6-10*), 679 (*Tatum, Eldridge, Stoller, Simmons Quartet;* Bruns. 54004 (*Here's Art Tatum*); Clef 709 (Hampton, Tatum, Rich Trio).

TAYLOR, Art LPs: Prog. 1001 (George Wallington); Atl. 1224 (Lennie Tristano); Dawn 1101 (Rouse-Watkins); Pres. 7035 (Jackie McLean), 7031 (Art Farmer), 7021 (Elmo Hope).

TAYLOR, Billy LPs: Con. Hall 1201 (Coleman Hawkins); Pres. 7001 (*A Touch of Taylor*), 7015, 7016 (trio); Urania 1203 (Ernie Royal); ABC-Par. 112 ("*Evergreens*"); Pres. 7051 (w. Candido).

TAYLOR, Samuel L. "Sam the Man", *tenor sax* (also *bar. sax, clarinet*); b. Lexington, Tenn., 7/12/16. Mother and sister pianists, father guitarist, brothers choir director and drummer. Started on clar., played with brother Paul Taylor's band in Gary, Ind. Worked w. Scat Man Crothers, 1937-8, Sunset Royal Orch. '39-41, Cootie Williams '41-3 and '45-6, Lucky Millinder, '44-5. From '46-52 he worked more or less

regularly w. Cab Calloway, touring South America with him in '51 and the Caribbean in '52. After this he began to find himself in great demand for rhythm and blues record sessions, and by '55-6 was frequently being featured on gigs with his own combo. Though often required to play exhibitionistically, he is a superior tenor man with a fine grounding in genuine jazz. Favs: Coleman Hawkins, Ch. Ventura, Ben Webster. LPs: EmArcy 36041 (Mal Fitch); Clef 682 (Lawrence Brown); MGM 3292 (*Blue Mist*).

Addr: 549 W. 144 St., Apt. 21, New York, N.Y.

TEAGARDEN, Charlie LPs: Col. CL821 (Benny Goodman), CL766 (*The Bob Crosby Show*).

TEAGARDEN, Jack LPs: Em. 36038 (*Boning Up On 'Bones*); Jazztone 1216 (*Dixieland Classics*) Col. CL821 (Benny Goodman); Urania 1205 (*Accent on Trombone*); Cap. T692 (Bobby Hackett); Jazztone 1222 (*Big T*).

TERRY, Clark LPs: Wing 60002 (*The Jazz School*); EmArcy 36007 (*Clark Terry*); 36011 (Dinah Washington); Cap. 679 (Ellington); Urania 1204 (Jimmy Hamilton); Norg. 1055 (*Ellingtonia '56*); Col. CL872 (Rosemary Clooney & Duke Ellington).

TERRY, Sonny LPs: Col. CL717 (Garry Moore)

THIELEMANS, Jean LPs: Cap. T648 (George Shearing); Col. CL658 (*The Sound—The Amazing Jean "Toots" Thielemans*).

THIGPEN, Edmund Leonard, *drums;* b. Chicago, Ill., 12/28/30. Father, Ben Thigpen, played drums for 17 yrs. w. Andy Kirk orch. Started on drums, piano in Los Angeles schools. Played w. Cootie Williams Sept., 1951 to Feb., '52; Army bands until Jan., '54, then toured w. Dinah Washington through Nov., '54. During the next year he was heard briefly w. Johnny Hodges, Lennie Tristano and Gil Mellé. Joined Bud Powell trio Sept., '55, Jutta Hipp trio Mar., '56. One of the most promising young drummers on the Eastern jazz scene. LPs: Herald 0101 (Anthony Ortega); Blue Note 1515, 1516 (Jutta Hipp).

Addr: 940 St. Nicholas Ave., New York, N.Y.

THOMAS, Joe, *tenor sax.* LPs: Em. 36023 (w. Jonah Jones in *Battle of the Saxes*).

THOMPSON, Charles Edmund "Chuck", *drums;* b. New York City, 6/4/26. Father was violin maker. Stud. piano in NYC, later 5 yrs. of drum study in Hollywood. While attending Jefferson High in LA, worked w. Charlie Echols band for 6 months, 1943, then played weekends w. Sachel McVea, father of Jack McVea. Worked w. Sammy Yates, 1945, Cee Pee Johnson, '46, Ch. Parker, Howard McGhee, Benny

Carter, '47, then intermittently w. Dexter Gordon, Wardell Gray, and various combos around the West Coast. Joined Hamp Hawes trio May, '55. Works smoothly w. Hawes and Red Mitchell as part of a tightly-knit unit that seems to think virtually as one man. Favs: Art Blakey, Philly Joe Jones, Kenny Clarke, Max Roach.

LPs: Contemp. 3505, 3515 (Hamp Hawes); Dootone 207 (Dexter Gordon); Clef 122 (Sonny Criss); Beth. 38 (Red Mitchell); Contemp. 3512 (Barney Kessel); Pres. 7009 (Wardell Gray).

Addr: 913 E. 118th St., Los Angeles, Calif.

THOMPSON, Lucky Visiting France in the Spring of 1956, Thompson found himself in great demand for record sessions, concerts, etc. He also worked w. Stan Kenton's band during the latter part of Kenton's European tour, playing baritone sax, and made some recordings with Kenton on tenor after their return to the U.S. in May '56.

LPs: Norg. 1003, 1023, (Dizzy Gillespie); Van. 8503 (Jo Jones); Savoy 12042, 12061 (Milt Jackson); Grand Award 318 (Dinah Washington); EmArcy 36066 (Jimmy Cleveland); Norg. 1040 (*Modern Jazz Society*); ABC-Par. 111 (own group).

THOMPSON, Sir Charles LPs: Col. CL808 (Frankie Laine and Buck Clayton); Jazztone J-1220 (*The Count's Men*); Story. 905 (Joe Newman).

TIZOL, Juan LPs: Em. 36038 (*Boning Up On 'Bones*); Cap. T637 (Duke Ellington).

TJADER, Cal LPs: Fant. 211 (*Tjader Plays Tjazz*).

TORMÉ, Mel LPs: Coral 57012 (*Mel Tormé at the Crescendo*); Beth. 34 (*It's a Blue World*), 52 (w. Marty Paich "Dek-tette").

TOUFF, Cy The bass trumpeter left Woody Herman's orch. Jan., 1956 to return to free-lance work in Chicago. LPs: Cap. T658 (Woody Herman); Pac. Jazz 1211 (own groups).

TOUGH, Dave LPs: EmArcy 36013 (Bud Freeman).

TRAVIS, Nick LPs: Roost 2202 (Tony Aless); Vict. LPM1161 (Al Cohn); Fant. 219, 206 (Elliot Lawrence); Vict. LPM1051 (Sauter-Finegan), LPM1211 (Manny Albam); Beth. 48 (Max Bennett); Vict. LPM1269 (Billy Byers).

TRENNER, Donald R. "Donn", *piano;* b. New Haven, Conn., 3/10/27. During school years stud. classical piano then played trom. Played with Yale Collegians, '43, Ted Fio Rito, '43-5, led Air Corps band, '46. In '47, he was in the Buddy Morrow orch. along with his wife, singer Helen Carr; the following year he and

Miss Carr had their own trio in SF, and in 1950-1 they worked w. Ch. Barnet. After playing w. Jerry Gray, Stan Getz, Ch. Parker, Geo. Auld, Jerry Fielding and Skinnay Ennis in '52-3, Trenner joined Les Brown's band for 2½ yrs. leaving him in Feb., '56. Favs: Peterson, Basie, Cole, Hawes, Tatum, Calvin Jackson. LPs: Cap. T659 (*The Les Brown All Stars*); Kapp 1025, Atl. 1216 (Dave Pell); Beth. 1027 (Helen Carr).

Addr: 7028 Beckford Ave., Reseda, Calif.

TRIGLIA, William E. "Billy", *piano;* b. Bronx, N.Y., 2/22/24. Parents both pianists. Stud. with an uncle, 1936-42; one year at Juilliard, '45-6, and a year at Louisville, Ky., '46-7. Professional debut after his return from the service in '45, playing jazz dates at Club Paradise in Nyack, N.Y. Name band experience incl. Les Elgart, '46; Alvino Rey, Sam Donahue, Johnny Bothwell, Geo. Auld, Terry Gibbs, Buddy Rich. Has played frequent club dates around NYC w. Davey Schildkraut, who helped him get started in jazz. He has also been active since '48 as piano teacher. Record debut '54 in Hank D'Amico album. Favs: Tatum, Bud Powell. LPs: Atl. 1220 (Tony Fruscella); Van. 8014, Beth. 18 (Sam Most). Beth. 1006 (Hank D'Amico).

Addr: 459 Kinderkamack Rd., Westwood, N.J.

TRISTANO, Lennie LPs: Em. 36016 (*Advance Guard of the '40s*); Atl. 1224 (own trio and quartet).

TROTMAN, Lloyd LPs: Clef 682 (Lawrence Brown).

TROUP, Bobby LPs: Beth. 19 (*Sings Johnny Mercer*); Cap. T484 (with Enevoldsen); Lib. 3002 (trio).

TRUMBAUER, Frankie The noted saxophonist, best known as an early associate of Bix Beiderbecke and featured on many jazz records of the late 1920s and early '30s, dropped dead June 11, 1956, in the lobby of a hospital in Kansas City. He was 55 years old. Employed by the Civil Aeronautic Authority off and on since 1940, Trumbauer had last worked regularly as a musician in the winter of 1945-6 as a staff member of Raymond Paige's orch. at the NBC Studios in NYC.

TURNER, Joe LPs: Em. 36014 (*Joe Turner and Pete Johnson*).

TWARDZIK, Richard, *piano;* b. Danvers, Mass., 1931; d. Paris, France, 10/21/55, during a tour with Chet Baker's quartet. Prof. debut in Boston, 1951 w. Serge Chaloff. Later worked in Boston w. Ch. Parker, Ch. Mariano, and toured for several months w. Lionel Hampton band. Twardzik's untimely death robbed jazz of a potentially great talent; he was developing into an outstanding individual modern stylist. LPs: Pac. Jazz 1212 (trio), 1218 (Chet Baker); Prest. 130, 153 (Charlie Mariano).

VAN EPS, George LPs: Col. CL785 (*Dixieland, My Dixieland*); Epic 3128 (Red Norvo).

VAN KRIEDT, David (David N. Kriedt), *arranger, tenor sax, etc.*; b. Berkeley, Calif., 6/19/22. Stud. flute, clar. in high school, composition w. Darius Milhaud at Mills College and in Paris. Worked with dance bands 1938-9; early associate of Dave Brubeck, '40. W.D.C. Band, Presidio, SF, '42-6. Assoc. with Jazz Workshop Ensemble early, '47 (later became Brubeck Octet); worked w. Jacques Diéval in Paris early '48 w. Kenny Clarke and Dick Collins, and other groups in France and throughout Continent, '47-8; Hal Mead, '49-52. Toured w. Stan Kenton summer, '55. Van Kriedt has free-lanced extensively around SF and was also active for six months as French teacher in SF City College. Ambition: To search for new forms, incorporate jazz into standard symphonic repertoire. Favs: Stan Getz, Zoot Sims; arr. Bill Holman, Shorty Rogers, Alec Wilder. LPs: Cap. T666 (Stan Kenton); Fant. 3, 16 (Dave Brubeck), 21 (Paul Desmond).
     Addr: 1139 N. Ogden Drive, Los Angeles 46, Calif.

VAUGHAN, Sarah LPs: Em. 36004 (*Sarah Vaughan*); Col. CL660 (*After Hours*), CL745 (*In Hi Fi*); EmArcy 36058 (*In the Land of Hi-Fi*); Merc. 20094 (*At the Blue Note*).

VENTURA, Charlie LPs: EmArcy 36023 (*Battle of the Saxes*), 36038 (*Boning Up On 'Bones*); Norg. 1034 (*Tenor Saxes*), 1041 (*Carnegie Hall Concert*); Em. 36015 (*Jumping with Ventura*); Jazztone 1219 (*Jazz Concert*).

VENUTO, Joe LPs: Vict. LPM1051, LPM1240 (Sauter-Finegan); LPM1269 (Billy Byers).

VILLEGAS, Enrique In 1955, this Argentinian pianist was introduced to American night club and record audiences purportedly as a jazz performer. He was aptly described in *Down Beat* by Nat Hentoff, who wrote: "I understate the case in pointing out that Villegas is the most appalling alleged 'jazz' pianist I have ever heard or could have imagined up to now." LPs: Col. CL787 (*Introducing Villegas*).

VINNEGAR, Leroy, *bass*; b. Indianapolis, Indiana, 7/13/28. Self-taught, first on piano, then bass. Started as pianist in Indianapolis jam sessions; played w. Jimmy Coles' local band. Moved to LA 1953; worked locally w. Stan Getz, Art Tatum, Herb Geller, Barney Kessel, Pete Candoli. Toured w. Shelly Manne combo, 1956. Rapidly acquiring reputation as one of the best new bassists on the West Coast. Favs: Ray Brown, Percy Heath, Oscar Pettiford.
     LPs: Beth. 30 (Conte Candoli); Norg. 1032 (Stan Getz), 1037 (*Hamp and Getz*); Gene Norman 12 (Frank Morgan); Pac. Jazz 1211 (Cy Touff); Beth. 37

(Stan Levey); EmArcy 36040 (Herb Geller); Dootone 207 (Dexter Gordon), 211 (Carl Perkins); Contemp. 3516 (Shelly Manne); Jazz: West 4 (Kenny Drew), 5 (Jane Fielding); ABC-Par. 110 (*Swingin' on the Vibories*).
     Addr: 6235 Primrose Avenue, Hollywood 28, Calif.

WALDRON, Malcolm Earl "Mal", *piano, arranger*; b. New York City, 8/16/26. Played alto first, then stud. at Queens College and received B.A. degree, later switching from saxophone to piano. Early experience from 1949 and club dates at Paradise Club, Cafe Society, etc. w. Ike Quebec, Big Nick Nicholas. Since '54 has worked off and on w. Ch. Mingus; also w. Lucky Millinder, Lucky Thompson, Allen Eager, '55. After stud. composition w. Karol Rathaus, composed modern ballet scores for Henry St. Playhouse dance group and others. Ambition: to develop these compositional techniques. Favs: Bud Powell, Thelonious Monk, Herbie Nichols; arr: John Lewis, Duke Ellington. LPs: Ad Lib 6601 (Jackie McLean); Savoy 12059 (Charlie Mingus); Atl. 1229 (Teddy Charles); Atl., Debut (Mingus).
     Addr: 107-39 166th St., Jamaica 33, N.Y.

WALLINGTON, George LPs: Prog. 1001 (*At the Bohemia*); Pres. 7032 (*Jazz for the Carriage Trade*).

WASHINGTON, Dinah LPs: Decca DL8088 (one no. with Lionel Hampton); Em. 36011 (*For Those in Love*); Grand Award 318 (*Sings the Blues*); Em. 36065 (*Dinah!*).

WATERS, Ethel LPs: "X" LVA1009.

WATKINS, Douglas, *bass*; b. Detroit, Mich., 3/2/34. Stud. Cass Tech High School, where schoolmates incl. bassist Paul Chambers, who is his cousin by marriage, and trumpeter Donald Byrd. Stud. in 1950 with Gaston Brohan. First left Detroit w. James Moody band Summer, '53. Worked mainly for next year w. Barry Harris trio, which backed visiting jazz stars incl. Stan Getz, Ch. Parker, Coleman Hawkins. Settled in New York, Aug., '54; first gigged w. Kenny Dorham, later at Minton's, etc. w. Horace Silver, Hank Mobley et al. Promising musician with agile technique. Favs: Percy Heath, Ray Brown, Slam Stewart.
     LPs: Epic 3199 (Junior Bradley); Blue Note 1507, 1508 (*The Jazz Messengers at the Bohemia*); Ad Lib 6601 (Jackie McLean); Savoy 12064 (*The Jazz Message*); Pres. 7035 (Jackie McLean); Trans. 4 (Donald Byrd); Blue Note 5058, 5062 (Horace Silver), 5069 (Hank Mobley).
     Addr: 531 W. 187th Street, Bronx, N.Y.

WATKINS, Julius Formed new combo, Les Modes, with Charlie Rouse, tenor sax, Spring 1956. LPs: Col. CL689 (Pete Rugolo); Dawn 1101 (*Jazzville '56*);

Savoy 12042, 12061 (Milt Jackson); Blue Note 5064 (own group); Dawn 1104 (Mat Mathews).

WATTERS, Lu LPs: Down Home 3 (Clancy Hayes-Lu Watters).

WAYNE, Chuck LPs: ABC-Par. 109 (*Greatest Guitarists in the World*).

WAYNE, Frances LPs: Epic 3222 (*Songs for My Man* with Neal Hefti's Orch.)

WEBSTER, Ben LPs: Em. 36023 (*Battle of the Saxes*); Clef 677 (*Jam Session #7*); Norg. 1031 (Buddy Rich), 1034 (*Tenor Saxes*), 1039 (*Music with Feeling;* w. strings); Clef MG17 (JATP Vol. 17); Grand Award 318 (*Jazz Concert*).

WEIN, George LPs: Atl. 1221 (*Wein, Women and Song*).

WELLS, Dicky LPs: Col. CL808 (Frankie Laine and Buck Clayton).

WESS, Frank LPs: Clef 647, 666, 678 (Count Basie); Savoy 12022 (*Flutes and Reeds*); Decca DL8176 (Bennie Green); Norg. 1031 (Buddy Rich); Jazztone J-1220 (*The Count's Men*); Savoy 12036 (*Opus de Jazz*); Story. 905 (Joe Newman); MGM 3390 (*West Coast vs East Coast*).

WESTON, Randy LPs: River. 203 (*Get Happy*).

WETTLING, George LPs: Col. CL719 (Eddie Condon); EmArcy 36013, Beth. 29 (Bud Freeman); Kapp 1005 (*Ragtime Duo*); Jazztone 1215 (Tony Parenti); Weathers 5501 (own group); ABC-Par. 121 (*Brother Matthew*).

WHITE, Josh The folk singer and guitarist again travelled extensively and successfully in England, 1956. LPs: Period 1115 (*Josh White Comes A-Visitin'*).

WHITE, Kitty, *singer;* b. Los Angeles, Calif., 7/7/24. Has been popular for a decade mainly in LA night clubs. Miss White has occasionally used jazz musicians in her record accompaniments, but is not a jazz artist. LPs: Em. 36020 (*A New Voice in Jazz*), 36068 (*Cold Fire*); Pacifica 2002.

WHITE, Robert E., *drums;* b. Chicago, Ill., 6/28/26. Stud. in Los Angeles, 1942 with Ralph Collier. Has played with many groups around LA incl. Vido Musso, Gerry Mulligan, Alvino Rey, Harry James, Ch. Barnet, Art Pepper, Chet Baker. Toured Europe in Buddy de Franco quartet Jan.-Feb., '54, and was the hit of the show nightly with his two-bass-drum solo specialty. First-class technician and modern drummer. Favs:

Art Blakey, Max Roach, Buddy Rich. LPs: Fant. 211 (Cal Tjader); Disc. 3019 (Art Pepper); Norg. 16, 1012 (Buddy De Franco); Pac. Jazz 3 (Chet Baker); Norg. 1016 (De Franco-Peterson).
Addr: 5140 Zakon Rd., Torrance, Calif.

WIGGINS, Gerry LPs: Beth. 23 (Frances Faye); Clef 676 (Illinois Jacquet); ABC-Par. 110 (*Swingin' on the Vibories;* piano & vibories).

WIGGS, Johnny LPs: Para. 107, S/D1001 (Johnny Wiggs-Raymond Burke).

WILBER, Bob The former Sidney Bechet protégé joined the house band at Eddie Condon's, NYC replacing Pee Wee Russell, May, 1956. LPs: Beth. 28 (*The Six*); River. 2516 (Sidney Bechet).

WILDER, Joe LPs: Vict. LPM1161 (Al Cohn); Kapp 1004 (Benny Payne); Savoy 12044 (*Top Brass*), 12063 (*Wilder 'n' Wilder . . . 'n' Wilder,* etc.), 12058 (*Meet Marlene*).

WILKINS, Ernie After giving up his saxophone chair in Count Basie's band, Wilkins settled in New York in 1955 and became a busy free-lance arr. writing for Count Basie, the Dorsey Bros. and for numerous recording groups. He continued to play alto and tenor saxes occasionally for night clubs and record dates. In March to May, '56, he toured the Middle East as saxophonist w. Dizzy Gillespie's orch. LPs: Savoy 12007 (Clarke-Wilkins Septet), 12022 (*Flutes and Reeds*); Vict. LPM1146 (*Lullaby of Birdland*), LPM1118 (Joe Newman); Savoy 12044 (arrs. for *Top Brass*).

WILLIAMS, Cootie LPs: Col. CL652 (Charlie Christian).

WILLIAMS, Joe (Joseph Goreed), *singer;* b. Cordele, Ga., 12/12/18. Lived in Chicago from the age of three. Professional debut in 1937, when he worked with the late Jimmie Noone. During the 1940s he worked around Chicago with local groups, also singing w. Coleman Hawkins' big band at Cafe Society, Chicago, in '41, and then w. Lionel Hampton band. He made a road tour w. Andy Kirk, spent a couple of months with the boogie-woogie piano team of Albert Ammons and Pete Johnson, and worked in local night clubs w. Red Saunders. During '50, when Count Basie led a septet at the Brass Rail in Chicago, Williams worked with him for ten weeks. He rejoined Basie Christmas day, '54, scoring his first big record hit with Basie a few months later in *Every Day,* an old blues which he had heard sung many years ago by Memphis Slim. During '55, his success w. Basie was so phenomenal that he elevated the entire band to a new plateau of commercial success.

Joe Williams is one of the few band vocalists of

outstanding merit to make his mark in jazz during the past decade and is certainly the first great blues singer to come to prominence in many years. His work combines an authentic earthy quality with a degree of musicianship and discreet, natural showmanship rarely found among contemporary singers. Although most of his big hits with Basie have been strictly blues numbers, he is a ballad singer of unusual talent.

Favs: Joe Turner, Nat Cole, and rhythm and blues singer Ray Charles. LPs: Clef 678 (*Count Basie Swings, Joe Williams Sings*); Amer. Rec. Soc. G402 (Basie).

Addr: c/o Willard Alexander, 30 Rockefeller Plaza, New York 20, N.Y.

WILLIAMS, Johnny, *piano;* LPs: EmArcy 36043 (Cannonball Adderley); Wing 60002 (Art Mardigan); Dawn 1102 (Zoot Sims); Norg. 1029 (Stan Getz); Pres. 7018 (Phil Woods); EmArcy 36061 (own trio), 36066 (Jimmy Cleveland).

WILLIAMS, Mary Lou The noted pianist-arranger was almost completely inactive musically in 1955 and '56, dedicating herself to welfare work and the rehabilitation of fellow-musicians. LPs: Jazztone 1206 (*A Keyboard History*); Storyville 906 (*Messin' 'Round in Montmartre*).

WILLIAMSON, Claude LPs: Cap. T624 (Charlie Barnet); Norg. 1027, 1033 (Tal Farlow); EmArcy 36009 (Maynard Ferguson); Contemp. 3504 (Howard Rumsey), 3509 (Rumsey); Pac. Jazz 1215, 1219 (Bud Shank); Cap. T6511 (trio); Beth. 54 (trio); Cap. T683 (Four Freshmen).

WILLIAMSON, Stu LPs: Decca DL8130 (*Blow Hot, Blow Cool*); Cap. T666 (Stan Kenton); Contemp. 3503 (Lennie Niehaus), 3504 (Howard Rumsey); Cap. 6513 (Bob Cooper); Contemp. 3510 (Lennie Niehaus); Contemp. 3516 (Shelly Manne), 3514 (Duane Tatro).

WILSON, Shadow LPs: Vict. LPM1118, LPM1198 (Joe Newman); Jazztone J-1220 (*The Count's Men*); Roost 2208 (Sonny Stitt); Story. 905 (Joe Newman); Vict. LPM1268 (Tony Scott).

WILSON, Teddy As a result of his appearance in an acting and playing role in *The Benny Goodman Story,* Teddy Wilson found himself in great demand for personal appearances. Early in 1956 he went out on a series of night club engagements with a trio featuring Jo Jones on drums and Gene Ramey on bass.

LPs: Col. CL821, Dec. 8252, CL820, Vict. LPM-1099 (Benny Goodman); Norg. 1036 (Piano Interpretations), 1019 (*The Creative Teddy Wilson*); Jazztone 1219 (*Jazz Concert*); Clef 681 (Krupa, Hampton, Wilson); Epic 3128 (Red Norvo); Norg.

1056 (*The Jazz Giants '56*); Decca 8252, 8253 (*The Benny Goodman Story,* soundtrack).

WINDING, Kai LPs: Roost 2202 (as "Moe" w. Tony Aless); Em. 36038 (*Boning Up On 'Bones*); Beth. 20 (Chris Connor); MGM E3286 (*Hot vs Cool*); Col. CL742 (*Trombone for Two*); Beth. 56 (Chris Connor); Pres. 7023 (*Trombone by Three*).

WISE, Buddy The tenor saxophonist, formerly with Gene Krupa, died in Las Vegas, Nev., July, 1955.

WOODE, James Bryant, *bass, piano;* b. Philadelphia, Pa., 9/23/28. Father, a music teacher, played baritone horn with Dixieland bands. Stud. piano at Philadelphia Academy of Music, Schillinger System under Clarence Cox, later at Boston U. School of Music, Boston Conservatory, and under bassist Paul Gregory on West Coast. Entered Navy as radar operator, transferred to Special Services in 1945 while in the Philippines; sang with Navy band. Started in music as pianist and vocalist with singing group, the Velvetaires, then formed own trio in '46. Living in Boston, spent 2 yrs. as house bassist at Storyville, then spent a year touring w. Flip Phillips and one year w. Sarah Vaughan and Ella Fitzgerald. Worked w. Nat Pierce trio and band off and on before Pierce left to join Woody Herman. Joined Duke Ellington Jan., '55. Ambition: to stop traveling, study a few years and then teach. A splendid musician, he expanded into the arr. field in '56 with occasional writing for the Ellington band. Favs: Ray Brown, Milt Hinton, Oscar Pettiford, George Duvivier.

LPs: Story. 301, 306 (Sidney Bechet), 310 (Serge Chaloff-Boots Mussulli); Cap. T679, Beth. 60 (Duke Ellington); Norg. 1055 (*Ellingtonia '56*).

Addr: 106-24 Ditmars Blvd., East Elmhurst, N.Y.

WOODMAN, Britt LPs: Cap. 679, Beth. 60 (Ellington); Debut 120 (Miles Davis).

WOODS, Phil Toured the Middle East w. Dizzy Gillespie March-May, 1956. LPs: Epic 3187 (Neal Hefti); Pres. 213 (Jim Chapin); Keynote 1101 (as "Phil Forest" with Nat Pierce); Pres. 7018 (*Woodlore*), 7033 (Jon Eardley); Signal 102 (Hall Overton); Vict. LPM1269 (as "Phil Funk" w. Billy Byers).

WOODYARD, Samuel, *drums;* b. Elizabeth, N.J., 1/7/25. Self-taught; no musicians in family. Earned his early experience by sitting in locally around Newark and North Jersey, then joined Paul Gayten, 1950-1. Played w. Joe Holiday, '51, Roy Eldridge, '52, Milt Buckner Trio, '53-5, then joined Duke Ellington. Considered by Ellington to be his best drummer since Louis Bellson, he has been featured prominently in the latter's old solo specialties such as *Skin Deep.* Favs:

Max Roach, Jo Jones, Art Blakey, Gene Krupa, Roy Haynes, Buddy Rich. LPs: Beth. 60 (Duke Ellington); Norg. 1055 (*Ellingtonia '56*); Col. CL872 (Ellington-Clooney).

Addr: 20A Washington Ave., Elizabeth, N.J.

WRIGHT, Eugene Joseph, *bass;* b. Chicago, Ill., 5/29/23. Stud. cornet at school; self-taught on bass until recent studies w. Paul Gregory in Los Angeles. Had own 16-piece band, the Dukes of Swing, 1943-6. Worked w. Gene Ammons, '46-8 and '49-51; Count Basie, '48-9, Arnett Cobb, '51-2; Buddy de Franco quartet, '52-5, touring Europe with him Jan.-Feb., '54. Went to Australia w. Red Norvo trio, '55. Made movie short w. Ch. Barnet. A serious, dependable and capable musician. Fav: Milt Hinton. LPs: Fant. 211 (Cal Tjader); Norg. 16, 1006, 1012 (Buddy De Franco); EmArcy 26031 (Gene Ammons).

Addr: 1189 W. 36th Pl., Los Angeles 7, Calif.

WRIGHTSMAN, Stan LPs: Gene Norman 13 (*Dixieland Jubilee*); Contemp. 5002 (Claire Austin).

YAGED, Sol LPs: Herald 0103 (*It Might as Well Be Swing*).

YANCEY, Jimmy LPs: River. 1061 (*Yancey's Getaway*).

YOUNG, Lee LPs: Gene Norman 15 (Lionel Hampton).

YOUNG, Lester Correct birthplace is Woodville, Miss.; the family moved to New Orleans after his birth and stayed there until he was 10. Young revealed in a *Down Beat* interview with Nat Hentoff that his original idol was Frankie Trumbauer, who played C melody saxophone; that he gained early experience playing for his father, who was in charge of a carnival band, before joining the Bostonians in Salina, Kans.

LPs: Epic LN3168 (*Let's Go to Prez*); Norg. 1034 (*Tenor Saxes*); Jazztone 1218 (*Prez and Chu*); Norg. 1056 (*The Jazz Giants '56*).

YOUNG, Trummy LPs: Col. CL708 (Louis Armstrong); Decca DL8168, 8169 (Louis Armstrong); Col. CL701 (Buck Clayton); Col. CL840 (Louis Armstrong).

ZELNICK, Melvin M., *drums;* b. New York City, 9/28/24. Stud. at Christopher Columbus High School, 1939-42; joined union in '42. Early associate of Arnold Fishkin and Shorty Rogers. Played w. Les Elgart, Bob Chester and Scat Davis, '45, Herbie Fields and Jerry Wald, '46, Chubby Jackson, '47, then back w. Fields. Benny Goodman sextet (w. Stan Hasselgard, Wardell Gray), '48; Lennie Tristano, '49, Boyd Raeburn, '50; since then has worked around New York w. Pete Rugolo, Eddie Bert, Marion McPartland, Don Elliott et al, and on staff w. Jerry Jerome at WPIX-TV. Fav. own records: three LPs listed below. Favs: Buddy Rich, Max Roach, Jo Jones. LPs: Col. CL757 (Lenny Hambro); Disc. 3020 (Eddie Bert); Beth. 12 (Don Elliott).

Addr: 64-34 102nd Street, Forest Hills 74, L.I., N.Y.

ZIMMERMAN, Roy Emile, *piano;* b. New Orleans, 10/23/13. Stud. privately. The late Fate Marable helped him get started in music. Has worked with many local groups in New Orleans incl. Geo. Hartman, '39, Monk Hazel, '41, Sharkey Bonano, '45, Irving Fazola, '46, Leon and Louis Prima, '47, Basin Street Six, '50, Phil Zito and Tony Almerico. Favs: Earl Hines, Fats Waller, Bob Zurke. LPs: South. 217 (Monk Hazel), 213 (Santo Pecora), 210 (George Brunis); EmArcy 36022 (George Hartman), 26012 (*Basin Street Six*); South. 211 (Al Hirt), 214 (Jack Delaney), 209 (Raymond Burke).

Addr: 4304 Dumaine St., New Orleans, La.

THE ENCYCLOPEDIA OF JAZZ
on Records

Under the title *The Encyclopedia of Jazz on Records,* an album of four twelve-inch LPs was assembled by the author for release by Decca in January, 1957 as a reference volume and musical parallel for *The Encyclopedia of Jazz.*

The first LP is entitled *Jazz of the Twenties.* Among the pioneer musicians featured are King Oliver and his orchestra in his original version of *Aunt Hagar's Blues;* Johnny Dodds' Black Bottom Stompers, featuring Louis Armstrong and Earl Hines in their 1927 recording of *Wild Man Blues;* James P. Johnson in one of his early piano solos, *You've Got to Be Modernistic;* Pinetop Smith in the original *Pinetop's Boogie-Woogie;* Red Nichols in the first and most famous of his "Five Pennies" items, the 1926 *That's No Bargain;* Jimmie Noone in *My Monday Date;* a 20-year-old Benny Goodman in *Muskrat Ramble;* the fabulous Jelly Roll Morton in his own *King Porter Stomp;* the New Orleans Rhythm Kings in *Tin Roof Blues,* the Eddie Lang-Joe Venuti All-Stars, with Jack Teagarden in *Farewell Blues,* Elmer Schoebel's Friars' Society Orchestra with Frank Teschemacher in *Prince of Wails* and the early Duke Ellington band in the Duke's original theme *East St. Louis Toddle-O.*

The second volume bears the name, *Jazz of the Thirties.* The artists featured are Count Basie and his original band in *Roseland Shuffle;* Bob Crosby's orchestra in *South Rampart Street Parade;* the Dorsey Brothers in *St. Louis Blues;* Sidney Bechet in *Blackstick,* Glen Gray's orchestra in *Chinatown, My Chinatown;* Fletcher Henderson's orchestra in *Down South Camp Meeting;* Jimmie Lunceford's orchestra in *Swanee River;* Andy Kirk's orchestra in *Walkin' and Swingin';* Glenn Miller's orchestra in *Moonlight Bay;* Chick Webb's orchestra with Ella Fitzgerald in *Sing Me a Swing Song;* Sister Rosetta Tharpe in *That's All* and John Kirby's *From A-Flat to C.*

On the third volume, which bears the title *Jazz of the Forties,* the artists are: Nat "King" Cole's trio in *Honeysuckle Rose;* Eddie Condon's All-Star Dixieland group in *Somebody Loves Me;* Roy Eldridge in *The Gasser;* Eddie Heywood in

How High the Moon, featuring Don Byas and Ray Nance; Lionel Hampton in *Flyin' Home;* Woody Herman's orchestra featuring Juan Tizol and Johnny Hodges in *Perdido;* Stan Kenton in his original version of *Gambler's Blues* (*St. James Infirmary*); Billie Holiday in *Lover Man;* Coleman Hawkins in *How Deep Is the Ocean?;* Jay McShann's orchestra featuring Charlie Parker in *Sepian Bounce* and Artie Shaw's orchestra in *I Get A Kick Out of You* and Art Tatum with Joe Turner in *Wee Baby Blues.*

In the final volume, *Jazz of the Fifties,* the artists are Louis Armstrong's All-Stars in *When the Saints Go Marching In;* Ralph Burns' orchestra in *Cool Cat on a Hot Tin Roof;* Les Brown's orchestra in *One O'Clock Jump;* Erroll Garner in *Sweet Lorraine;* Benny Green's combo in *Taking My Time;* Terry Gibbs' group with Don Elliott in *Now's the Time;* John Graas' group with Gerry Mulligan in *Mulliganesque;* Jimmy and Marian McPartland playing *In a Mist;* Red Norvo trio in *Good Bait;* Tony Scott's quartet in *Swootie Patootie;* Shorty Rogers' arrangement of *Frankie Machine* from *Man with the Golden Arm* played by Elmer Bernstein; Charlie Ventura with Jackie Cain and Roy Kral doing *I'm Forever Blowing Bubbles.*

It is the belief of the author that this album covers virtually every important development in the history of recorded jazz and incorporates, as leaders or sidemen, most of the principal figures who have proved to be the most influential through the years.

"The Encyclopedia Of Jazz On Records" is available in a special album on Decca DX 140, at $14.95. Individual volumes are also obtainable separately at $3.98 each as follows: Jazz of the Twenties: Decca DL 8398; Jazz of the Thirties: Decca DL 8399; Jazz of the Forties: Decca DL 8400; Jazz of the Fifties: Decca DL 8401.

52 BEST RECORDS
of the Year

Since no two people agree on a definition of jazz, it is impossible to estimate exactly how many jazz records were released in 1955 and 1956. Beyond a doubt, however, it can be claimed that measured in minutes of recorded music, more jazz reached this reviewer's desk in the average month than used to arrive in an entire year before the advent of long playing records.

An important development during this period was the virtual disappearance, by early 1956, of the 10-inch LP disc. The manufacture of 45 r.p.m. EP records for jazz fans had also slowed down almost to a halt by mid-1956. The following list, inevitably, consists entirely of 12-inch LPs offering about 35 to 45 minutes of music per disc.

The use of the chapter designation "52 Best Records Of The Year" does not indicate that one record was selected for each week; it was merely used to point up the fact that the flood of material coming to hand produced, on an average, at least one LP per week of outstanding musical value. The period covered is roughly from the summer of 1955 through the summer of 1956.

The records were chosen solely on the basis of the writer's personal reaction, without regard to the category into which they happened to fall. Many of the records are indicative of the trends and new forces that were at work. With the exception of the anthologies, none of the material selected had ever been released previously on LPs. A reissue might be considered a "record of the year" if a basic library were under consideration, but this list is not intended for a basic library. It is intended simply to remind the reader of some great jazz that was recorded during the past couple of years.

Few of the records of traditional jazz (New Orleans and other early forms) sent to the writer for review during this period managed to offer anything new, or, for that matter, anything excitingly old. At the other end of the spectrum, it was a lean year for big-band jazz. The few large orchestras left that specialized in jazz found little to say that they had not said at least as effectively in earlier years. Thus most of the selections in the list feature small combos, though the variety of sounds and styles produced made a colorful reflection of the resourceful ideation that took place both in improvisational patterns and in creative jazz writing.

BIG BANDS

COUNT BASIE. American Record Society G402. *Every Tub; Basie Goes Wess; Amazing Love; Magic; Lady in Lace; Down for the Count; She's Just My Size; Blues Inside Out; Lady Be Good; Paradise Squat; Sweety Cakes; New Basie Blues.*

Soloists include Joe Newman, Thad Jones, trumpets; Paul Quinichette, Frank Foster, Eddie Lockjaw Davis, tenor sax; Frank Wess, tenor sax and flute; Marshall Royal, alto sax and clarinet; Bill Graham, alto sax; Henry Coker, trombone; Buddy Rich, drums; Joe Williams, vocalist.

Though the band is still more exciting in person, something of its grandeur and power is communicated here. Like all releases on A.R.S., this is accompanied by a lengthy and excellent analysis of the brand of music involved, of the artists and of each title individually, written by Bill Simon. All tunes are by the full band except *Lady Be Good,* which features a nonet. Produced by Norman Granz.

DUKE ELLINGTON: HISTORICALLY SPEAKING. Bethlehem BCP60. *East St. Louis Toodle-O; Creole Love Call; Stompy Jones; The Jeep is Jumpin'; Jack the Bear; In a Mellow Tone; Ko-Ko; Midriff; Stomp, Look and Listen; Unbooted Character; Lonesome Lullaby; Upper Manhattan Medical Group.*

Personnel: "Cat" Anderson, Ray Nance, Clark Terry, Willie Cook, trumpets; Britt Woodman, John Sanders, Quentin Jackson, trombones; Johnny Hodges, alto sax; Russell Procope, alto sax, clarinet; Jimmy Hamilton, tenor sax, clarinet; Paul Gonsalves, tenor sax; Harry Carney, baritone sax, bass clarinet; Duke Ellington, piano; Jimmy Woode, bass; Sam Woodyard, drums.

Though by no means representative of the ultimate in Ellingtonia, this contains a high proportion of legitimate jazz, unspoiled for the most part by high note effects and other irrelevancies. The twelve titles are approximately a chronological rundown, starting with Duke's earliest theme song, written in 1926, and concluding with two new compositions. Though ten of the tunes have been performed in previous Ellington versions, some of them several times throughout three decades, there is enough engagingly swinging big band

jazz to give this new collection individual validity. Produced by Red Clyde.

WOODY HERMAN: ROAD BAND! Capitol T658. *Opus De-Funk; Gina; I Remember Duke; Sentimental Journey; Cool Cat on a Hot Tin Roof; Where or When; Captain Ahab; I'll Never Be the Same; Pimlico.*

Personnel: Dick Collins, Bernie Glow, Ruben McFall, Jerry Kail, Charlie Walp, Gerry LaFurn, trumpets; Cy Touff, bass trumpet; Dick Kenney, Keith Moon, trombones; Dick Hafer, Richie Kamuca, Art Pirie, tenor sax; Jack Nimitz, baritone sax; Billy Bauer, guitar; Nat Pierce, piano; John Beal, bass; Chuck Flores, drums.

This typical set by Woody Herman's "Third Herd" includes three Ralph Burns originals and one by Manny Albam. The band still has much of the vivid yet unpretentiously pulsating quality that earned Herman's band of the '40s a place in jazz history.

ELLIOT LAWRENCE BAND PLAYS GERRY MULLIGAN ARRANGEMENTS. Fantasy 3-206. *The Rocker; Bye Bye Blackbird; Happy Hooligan; Mullenium; My Silent Love; Bweebida Bwobbida; Apple Core; Elegy for Two Clarinets; The Swinging Door; But Not for Me; Mr. President.*

When Gerry Mulligan played and arranged for Lawrence in 1950, the band's jazz was kept largely under wraps. Many of the excellent arrangements of those days have now been disinterred by Lawrence and are interpreted here by a loose, Herman-like band that features such soloists as Al Cohn, tenor; Eddie Bert, trombone; Hal McKusick, alto; Dick Sherman, Nick Travis, trumpet; Don Lamond, drums; and Lawrence on piano. Produced by George T. Simon.

SMALL BANDS

MANNY ALBAM: THE JAZZ WORKSHOP. RCA Victor, LPM-1211. *Anything Goes; Headstrong; Black Bottom; The Changing Scene; The Turning Point; Charmaine; Diga Diga Doo; Royal Garden Blues; Swingin' on a Star; Intermezzo; Ferris Wheel; Urbanity.*

This series of standards and original compositions arranged by Albam was recorded in three sessions, each featuring octet with slightly varying personnels. The soloists include Nick Travis, Jimmy Nottingham, Joe Newman, trumpets; Bobby Brookmeyer, Billy Byers, Urbie Green, trombones; Hal McKusick, alto sax; Al Cohn, tenor sax; Sol Schlinger, baritone sax; Milt Hinton, bass.

The overall sound, comprising two trumpets, two trombones, two saxes, a bass and drums, achieves an attractive timbre, and the music swings consistently. Produced by Jack Lewis.

CLIFFORD BROWN AND MAX ROACH AT BASIN STREET. EmArcy 36070. *What is This Thing Called Love; Love* is a Many Splendored Thing; I'll Remember April; Powell's Prances; Time; The Scene is Clean; Gertrude's Bounce.

Personnel: Clifford Brown, trumpet; Sonny Rollins, tenor sax; Richie Powell, piano; Max Roach, drums; George Morrow, bass.

Modern jazz at its extrovert best is typified in this well-balanced collection, for which most of the arrangements were written by Richie Powell. Even Roach's individual passages come as close as is humanly possible to justifying the inclusion of a long drum solo on a jazz record. Produced by Bob Shad.

MILES DAVIS: THE MUSINGS OF MILES. Prestige LP7007. I Didn't; Will You Still Be Mine?; Green Haze; I See Your Face Before Me; A Night in Tunisia; A Gal in Calico.

Personnel: Miles Davis, trumpet; Red Garland, piano; Oscar Pettiford, bass; Philly Joe Jones, drums.

Davis's subdued muted performance in I See Your Face Before Me typifies the mood of this set, in which he again emphasizes the value of understatement, of a pensive horizontal line supported by sensitive harmonic understanding. Garland, a new pianist from Philadelphia, plays as if he has only two, but two very eloquent fingers. Produced by Bob Weinstock.

THE JAZZ MESSENGERS AT THE CAFE BOHEMIA, VOL. I. Blue Note 1507. Soft Winds; The Theme; Minor's Holiday; Alone Together; Prince Albert.

Personnel: Kenny Dorham, trumpet; Hank Mobley, tenor sax; Horace Silver, piano; Doug Watkins, bass; Art Blakey, drums.

This on-the-spot recording shows eloquently why the Yearbook jury of musicians voted this the best new combo of the year. The ensembles are simple but the group spirit and solo level can compare with that of any small jazz group in recent years. Art Blakey can be heard introducing the members of the band and the entire atmosphere combines the informality of a night club recording session with a surprisingly high level of recording quality. Produced by Alfred Lion.

MODERN JAZZ QUARTET: FONTESSA. Atlantic 1231. Versailles; Angel Eyes; Fontessa; Over the Rainbow; Bluesology; Willow Weep for Me; Woody'n You.

Personnel: John Lewis, piano; Milt Jackson, vibraharp, Percy Heath, bass; Connie Kay, drums.

In sharp contrast with the Messengers, the Modern Jazz Quartet moves to the other extreme of the small combo spectrum. Sometimes the men play as respectfully as if John Lewis were conducting them through a church, yet on occasion they swing naturally and, thanks to Milt Jackson, now and then achieve a "funky" quality that brings them closer to the roots of jazz. The title composition, an eleven-minute work by Lewis, is described by him as "a little suite inspired

by the Renaissance Commedia Dell'arte." It is a delicate, fragile work that hangs to jazz by a thread. Produced by Nesuhi Ertegun.

SAXOPHONES

INTRODUCING NAT ADDERLEY. Wing MGW-60000. Watermelon, Little Joanie Walks; Two Brothers; I Should Care; Crazy Baby; New Arrivals; Sun Dance; Fort Lauderdale; Friday Nite; Blues For Bohemia.

Personnel: Nat Adderley, trumpet; Cannonball Adderley, alto sax; Horace Silver, piano; Roy Haynes, drums; Paul Chambers, bass.

Despite its title, this LP belongs in the saxophone listing of recommendations since it is the most eloquent presentation to date of the alto sax of Julian "Cannonball" Adderley, though recorded under the nominal leadership of his cornetist brother, Nat. Because of the intimate quintet format there is more improvisation and less arranged interference than on Cannonball's own sessions for EmArcy. In addition, Yearbook poll winners Horace Silver and Paul Chambers are heard to an advantage. Produced by Bob Shad.

HAMP AND GETZ. Norgran 1037. Louise; Jumpin' at the Woodside; Gladys; Cherokee; Tenderly; Autumn in New York; East of the Sun; I Can't Get Started.

Personnel: Stan Getz, tenor sax; Lionel Hampton, vibraphone; Shelly Manne, drums; Lou Levy, piano; Leroy Vinnegar, bass.

This unlikely alliance, occasioned by the presence of both musicians in the studios where The Benny Goodman Story sound track was recorded, teams the assertive swinging style of Hampton with the cool understatement of Getz, which to some students may appear comparable with a meeting held somewhere between the Tropic of Capricorn and the Antarctic Circle. Nevertheless, the two mix most effectively and are accompanied by an exceptional rhythm section. The performances combine the finest characteristics of two eras. Produced by Norman Granz.

LEE KONITZ WITH WARNE MARSH. Atlantic 1217. Topsy; There Will Never Be Another You; I Can't Get Started; Donna Lee; Two Not One; Don't Squawk; Ronnie's Line; Background Music.

Personnel: Lee Konitz, alto sax; Warne Marsh, tenor sax; Sal Mosca, piano; Billy Bauer, guitar; Oscar Pettiford, bass; Kenny Clarke, drums.

Two saxophonists normally associated with the quiet, introverted personality of the Tristano school are here heard with a rhythm section that propels them to heights of eloquence and extroversion resulting in their most effective and happy collaboration to date. The cover photograph, showing them both in an exceptionally joyful mood, is symbolic of the album's achievement. Produced by Nesuhi Ertegun.

PRESENTING THE GERRY MULLIGAN SEXTET. EmArcy MG36056. *Mud Bug; Sweet and Lovely; Apple Core; Nights of the Turntable; Broadway; Everything Happens to Me; The Lady is A Tramp; Bernie's Tune.*

Personnel: Gerry Mulligan, baritone sax; Zoot Sims, tenor sax; Bob Brookmeyer, trombone; Jon Eardley, trumpet; Dave Bailey, drums; Peck Morrison, bass.

This is the new group formed by Mulligan in the fall of 1955 and subsequently, with a slightly changed personnel, heard in France and Italy. A modern, rocking beat is synonymous with any Mulligan group, but this unit is exceptional, even by Mulligan standards. Produced by Bob Shad.

THE MODERN ART OF JAZZ BY ZOOT SIMS. Dawn DLP-1102. *September in the Rain; Down at the Loft; Ghost of a Chance; Not So Deep; Them There Eyes; Our Pad; Dark Clouds; One to Blow On.*

Personnel: Zoot Sims, tenor sax; Bob Brookmeyer, trombone; Milt Hinton, bass; Gus Johnson, drums; John Williams, piano.

Sims' Young-inspired tenor stretches out even more effectively here than on the Mulligan sides, while Brookmeyer and the rhythm section members contribute valuably in solo and ensemble roles. Produced by Chuck Darwin.

SONNY STITT PLAYS ARRANGEMENTS FROM THE PEN OF QUINCY JONES Roost LP2204. *My Funny Valentine; Sonny's Bunny; Come Rain or Come Shine; Love Walked In; If You Could See Me Now; Quince; Star Dust; Lover.*

Personnel: Sonny Stitt, alto sax; Thad Jones, Jimmy Nottingham, Ernie Royal, trumpets; Cecil Payne, baritone sax; Seldon Powell, tenor sax; Freddie Greene, guitar; Oscar Pettiford, bass; Jo Jones, drums; Hank Jones, piano.

Better-known as a tenor man in recent years, Stitt reverts to alto sax for a set of tasteful, well-integrated performances for which Quincy Jones' arrangements provide a neat, unpretentious framework. Produced by Jack Hooke and Teddy Reig.

BEN WEBSTER WITH STRINGS: MUSIC WITH FEELING. MGN1039. *Chelsea Bridge; What Am I Here For?; Early Autumn; Willow Weep for Me; My Greatest Mistake; No Greater Love; Teach Me Tonight; Until Tonight; We'll Be Together Again; Blue Moon.*

The Ravel of the tenor saxophone is here comfortably cushioned against a soft, sympathetic background arranged and conducted by Ralph Burns (one title, *Chelsea Bridge,* was composed and directed by Billy Strayhorn). *Willow Weep For Me,* in particular, is a work of stark beauty. Produced by Norman Granz.

BRASS

LOUIS ARMSTRONG: AMBASSADOR SATCH. Columbia CL-840. *Royal Garden Blues; Tin Roof Blues; The Faithful Hussar; Muskrat Ramble; All of Me; Twelfth Street Rag; Undecided; Dardanella; West End Blues; Tiger Rag.*

Personnel: Louis Armstrong, trumpet; Trummy Young, trombone; Edmond Hall, clarinet; Billy Kyle, piano; Barrett Deems, drums; Arvell Shaw, bass.

Recorded during two concerts, one at a theater in Milan, the other at the Concertgebouw in Amsterdam, this has several advantages over Armstrong's previous few LPs. There are no vocals except by Louis himself; Barney Bigard's somewhat dispirited clarinet has been replaced by the plangent contributions of Edmond Hall; and the material includes a couple of items never before recorded by Louis. In addition, there are competent solo spots by the other sidemen. Produced by George Avakian.

JIMMY CLEVELAND AND HIS ALL STARS. EmArcy MG-36066. *Hear Ye! Hear Ye!; You Don't Know What Love Is; Vixen; My One and Only Love; Little Beaver; Our Love is Here to Stay; Count 'Em; Bone Brother; I Hadn't Anyone Till You; See Minor.*

Collective personnel: Jimmy Cleveland, trombone; Ernie Royal, trumpet; Jerome Richardson, Lucky Thompson, tenor sax; Cecil Payne, baritone sax; Wade Legge, Hank Jones, John Williams, piano; Barry Galbraith, guitar; Paul Chambers, Oscar Pettiford, bass; Joe Harris, Max Roach, Osie Johnson, drums.

Recording with three different octets, for which Quincy Jones wrote and directed the arrangements, the jet-propelled trombone virtuoso is set off to full advantage in the first LP under his own name. Produced by Bob Shad.

DIZZY GILLESPIE: JAZZ CREATIONS. American Recording Society G405. *'Bout to Wail; Flamingo; Rails; O Solow; Blue Mood; Devil and the Fish; Shout by Rail; Caravan.*

A pleasantly diversified grab-bag, this shows Gillespie in a variety of settings, including a regular reeds-brass-and-rhythm big band, on *'Bout to Wail* and *Shout by Rail;* a large orchestra with strings and woodwinds directed by Johnny Richards on *O Solow* (vaguely adapted from *O Sole Mio*); an octet featuring a flute and an all-Latin rhythm section on *Caravan,* a nonet on *Flamingo,* and a sextet on the other three titles. The ensemble is occasionally less than perfect, but Gillespie soars over it all in magnificent form, a constant reminder of the "greatest ever" selection by a jury of his peers. Produced by Norman Granz.

J. J. JOHNSON AND KAI WINDING: TROMBONE FOR TWO. Columbia CL742. *The Whiffenpoof Song; Give Me the Simple Life; Close as Pages in a Book; Turnabout;*

Trombone for Two; It's Sand, Man; We Two; Let's Get Away from It All; Goodbye; This Can't Be Love.

Personnel: J. J. Johnson and Kai Winding, trombones; Dick Katz, piano; Paul Chambers, bass; Osie Johnson, drums.

The twin founding fathers of modern jazz trombone have been heard on half a dozen LPs of approximately equal merit. This set has a slight advantage in its interesting variety of material. Six of the arrangements were by Winding, four by Johnson. The variety of mutes used produces enough variation of timbre to eliminate any danger of monotony; and the music never stops swinging. Produced by George Avakian.

THAD JONES: DETROIT-NEW YORK JUNCTION. Blue Note 1513. *Blue Room; Tariff; Little Girl Blue; Scratch; Zec.*

Personnel: Thad Jones, trumpet; Billy Mitchell, tenor sax; Kenny Burrell, guitar; Tommy Flanagan, piano; Oscar Pettiford, bass; Shadow Wilson, drums.

Jones' masterful trumpet leads a small parade of Detroiters who knock at the walls of New York fame here; for Mitchell, Burrell and Flanagan, it is their first adequate representation on an LP. *Little Girl Blue*, treated partly as a waltz, simply with guitar and bowed bass, is a striking example of Jones' ballad style. Produced by Alfred Lion.

JOE NEWMAN OCTET: I'M STILL SWINGING. RCA Victor LPM1198. *Top Hat, White Tie and Tails; You Can Depend on Me; We'll Be Together Again; It's Bad for Me; Exactly Like You; Shameful Roger; The Daughter of Miss Thing; Sometimes I'm Happy; Sweethearts on Parade; Slats; Lament for a Lost Love; Perfidia.*

Personnel: Joe Newman, trumpet; Urbie Green, trombone; Gene Quill, alto sax; Al Cohn, tenor sax; Freddie Greene, guitar; Shadow Wilson, drums; Eddie Jones, bass; Dick Katz, piano.

Chosen almost arbitrarily from a handful of equally effective Newman albums recorded during the past year or two, this set owes its success to a closely-knit little ensemble and perfectly tailored arrangements by Manny Albam, Al Cohn, and Ernie Wilkins. Newman's neutral trumpet draws effectively from bop and swing era concepts, while the group as a whole has something of a small band Basie quality. Produced by Jack Lewis.

TOP BRASS: FEATURING FIVE TRUMPETS. Savoy MG-12044. *58 Market Street; Trick or Treat; Speedway; Dot's What; Top Brass; Willow Weep For Me; Imagination; It Might as Well Be Spring; The Nearness of You; Taking a Chance on Love.*

Personnel: Joe Wilder, Ernie Royal, Ray Copeland, Idrees Sulieman, Donald Byrd, trumpets; Hank Jones, piano; Kenny Clarke, drums; Wendell Marshall, bass.

With Ernie Wilkins as conductor and arranger, five outstanding modern trumpet players are here presented in a track race for which all contestants found the ground perfect and the weather ideal. Fortunately the album notes provide identification of all solos in order. The Jones-Clarke-Marshall rhythm section, virtually a resident foundation at Savoy, leaves no room whatever for improvement. Produced by Ozzie Cadena.

JOE WILDER: WILDER 'N' WILDER. Savoy MG12063. *Cherokee; Prelude to a Kiss; My Heart Stood Still; Six Bit Blues; Mad About the Boy; Darn That Dream.*

Personnel: Joe Wilder, trumpet; Hank Jones, piano; Wendell Marshall, bass; Kenny Clarke, drums.

One of the five admirable trumpet men from the *Top Brass* LP is heard here in a session of his own, revealing a style, a tone and a general approach that are superbly personal. Wilder, an exceptionally skilled and versatile academic musician, makes his most unusual contribution as a jazzman in *Six Bit Blues*, which presents the traditional 12 bar theme effectively reconstituted as a waltz. Produced by Ozzie Cadena.

VOCAL

JACKIE CAIN AND ROY KRAL: JACKIE AND ROY. Storyville LP904. *Says My Heart; Let's Take a Walk Around the Block; Spring Can Really Hang You Up the Most; Mine; Bill's Bit; Lover; Tiny Told Me; You Smell So Good; Lazy Afternoon; Dahuud; Listen Little Girl; I Wish I Were in Love Again.*

Personnel: Roy Kral, piano; Shelly Manne, drums; Barney Kessel, guitar; Red Mitchell, bass.

The extent to which popular music and a jazz background can be effectively combined has never been more admirably illustrated than by this fascinating vocal duo. Kral and Miss Cain have the happy knack of being able to dig up unusual material and do unexpected things with it. Included in this set are compositions by Bill Holman, Clifford Brown, Rodgers and Hart, the Gershwins and others, all recast perfectly in the Cain-Kral mold. A joyous and unique set of performances. Produced by George Wein.

ELLA FITZGERALD SINGS THE COLE PORTER SONG BOOK. Verve MGV4001-2. Composed of two 12-inch LPs, this offers 32 of Porter's songs, ranging from the 1928 *Let's Do It* to the 1954 *All of You*. Miss Fitzgerald's performances are flawless. The backgrounds, by Buddy Bregman, are most effective on the numbers that simply employ a rhythm section. The latter, not credited in the album notes, is composed of Paul Smith, piano; Barney Kessel, guitar; Joe Mondragon, bass; Alvin Stoller, drums. Strings and woodwinds are heard on some numbers, brass and saxes on others. The overall results are commendable and this must be considered one of Ella's best albums, though with a looser setting she will do even better. Produced by Norman Granz.

CARMEN MC RAE: BY SPECIAL REQUEST. Decca DL8173. *Give Me the Simple Life; Sometimes I'm Happy; Love is Here to Stay; Something to Live For; I Can't Get Started; Yardbird Suite; Just One of Those Things; This Will Make You Laugh; My One and Only Love; I'll Remember April; Supper Time; You Took Advantage of Me.*

Personnel: Mat Mathews, accordion; Herbie Mann, flute; Dick Katz, piano; Mundell Lowe, guitar; Wendell Marshall, bass; Kenny Clarke, drums.

One of the few new jazz oriented vocal sounds to earn major significance in the past couple of years, Miss McRae's voice is displayed in a pleasantly unpretentious setting here. On *Something to Live For* the composer, Billy Strayhorn, takes over at the piano. On Irving Berlin's *Supper Time*, Miss McRae herself moves over to the keyboard. Produced by Milton Gabler.

HELEN MERRILL. EmArcy MG36006. *Don't Explain; You'd Be So Nice to Come Home To; What's New; Falling in Love with Love; Yesterdays; Born to Be Blue; 'S Wonderful.*

Collective personnel: Clifford Brown, trumpet; Danny Bank, flute; Barry Galbraith, guitar; Jimmy Jones, piano; Milt Hinton, Oscar Pettiford, bass; Osie Johnson, Bobby Donaldson, drums.

Miss Merrill's voice has a strange, husky quality that lends itself almost exclusively to slow, mournful ballads. Quincy Jones wrote the unobtrusive backgrounds. Produced by Bob Shad.

JACKIE PARIS: CAN'T GET STARTED WITH YOU. Wing MGW60004. *There Will Never Be Another You; Heaven Can Wait; Strange; That Ole Devil Called Love; Whispering Grass, Don't Tell the Trees; Heart of Gold; I Can't Get Started; Indiana; Cloudy Morning; Wrap Your Troubles in Dreams; Good Night My Love.*

Another great voice stranded on the no-man's-land between jazz and popular music, Paris sings, and selects his material, like a real musician. It is ironic that after a decade of first-class work in this idiom he has still to make any great commercial impact. Manny Albam wrote the backgrounds, which feature five saxophones and rhythm section on some numbers; five strings, harp, oboe and rhythm on others. Produced by Bob Shad.

JIMMY RUSHING: LISTEN TO THE BLUES. Vanguard VRS8505. *See See Rider; It's Hard to Laugh a Smile; Every Day; Evenin'; Good Morning Blues; Roll 'Em Pete; Don't Cry, Baby; Take Me Back, Baby; Rock and Roll.*

Personnel: Pete Johnson, piano; Rudy Powell, alto sax and clarinet; Lawrence Brown, trombone; Emmett Berry, trumpet; Buddy Tate, tenor sax; Walter Page, bass; Jo Jones, drums; Freddie Greene, guitar.

The sharp distinction between blues in the world of rock 'n' roll and those sung by the unspoiled artists who have survived from the great blues days of the 1930s is vividly demonstrated in this fine set of unabashed old-time performances by the former Count Basie vocalist. Kansas City memories are recalled by the Rushing reunion with such men as Pete Johnson, Jones and Page. (*Roll 'em Pete* is a Johnson piano solo.) Produced by John Hammond.

MEL TORMÉ WITH THE MARTY PAICH DEK-TETTE. Bethlehem BCP52. *Lulu's Back in Town; When the Sun Comes Out; I Love to Watch the Moonlight; Fascinating Rhythm; The Blues; The Carioca; The Lady is a Tramp; I Like to Recognize the Tune; Keeping Myself for You; Lullaby of Birdland; When April Comes Again; Sing for Your Supper.*

Personnel: Marty Paich, piano; Pete Candoli, Don Fagerquist, trumpet; Bob Enevoldsen, trombone; Bud Shank, alto sax; Jack Montrose, Bob Cooper, tenor sax; Jack DuLong, baritone sax; John Cave, Vince DeRosa, French horn; Albert Pollan, tuba; Red Mitchell, bass; Mel Lewis, drums.

Students of vocal jazz have seldom accorded Tormé the recognition due him as one of the most musical of the few genuine jazz-grounded singers on today's popular music scene. In this LP the accompaniment was designed by Tormé and Paich to simulate the sound of the old Gerry Mulligan Ten-tette as heard on a Capitol LP a few years ago. The result is a session reflecting all the best qualities of West Coast jazz and setting off Tormé's voice in a consistently swinging atmosphere. A dramatically effective performance is his interpretation of Duke Ellington's *The Blues* from *Black, Brown and Beige*. Produced by Red Clyde.

JOE WILLIAMS: COUNT BASIE SWINGS, JOE WILLIAMS SINGS. Clef MG C 678. *Every Day; The Comeback; All Right, Okay, You Win; In the Evening; Roll 'Em Pete; Teach Me Tonight; My Baby Upsets Me; Please Send Me Someone to Love.*

Personnel: Count Basie, piano; Reunald Jones, Thad Jones, Wendell Culley, Joe Newman, trumpets; Henry Coker, Bill Hughes, Ben Powell, trombones; Frank Wess, Bill Graham, Marshall Royal, Frank Foster, Charlie Fowlkes, saxophones; Sonny Payne, drums; Eddie Jones, bass; Freddie Greene, guitar.

Almost single-handed, blues singer Joe Williams expanded the audience of Count Basie's band to an unprecedented degree in 1955-6 through the success of his initial vocal hit with the band (*Every Day*, included in this collection). Though Williams' blues work is the essence of his striking and virile personality, a couple of pleasant examples of his ballad performances are also included here. Six of the nine arrangements are by Basie's tenor saxophonist, Frank Foster. Produced by Norman Granz.

RHYTHM, PERCUSSION

TAL FARLOW, BARNEY KESSEL, OSCAR MOORE: SWING GUITARS. Norgran 1033. *Lullaby of the Leaves; Stompin' at the Savoy; This Is Always; Tea for Two; Sonny Boy; Beautiful Moons Ago; A Foggy Day; Oscar's Blues; Heat Wave; East of the Sun; All the Things You Are; Crazy Rhythm.*

Personnel: Farlow with Red Mitchell, bass; Claude Williamson, piano; Kessel with Jim Wybee, guitar; Morty Corb, bass; Shelly Manne, drums; Moore with Carl Perkins, piano; Joe Comfort, bass; George Jenkins, drums.

Four performances apiece by three of the most eloquent exponents of modern jazz guitar, one of whom, Oscar Moore, has inexplicably disappeared from the limelight in recent years but must still be rated an artist of first rank. Produced by Norman Granz.

HAMPTON HAWES, VOL. 2: THE TRIO. Contemporary C3515. *You and the Night and the Music; Stella by Starlight; Blues for Jacque; Yesterdays; Steeplechase; 'Round Midnight; Just Squeeze Me; Autumn in New York; Section Blues.* Personnel: Hampton Hawes, piano; Red Mitchell, bass; Chuck Thompson, drums.

Hawes plays brittle yet facile piano in the Bud Powell tradition, with an occasional touch of Tatum in the ballads. He is particularly effective on blues at all tempi. Mitchell's solo contributions add considerably to the value of this pulsating set. Produced by Lester Koenig.

RED NORVO WITH STRINGS. Fantasy 3-218. *Who Cares; Let's Fall in Love; Old Devil Moon; Cabin in the Sky; How Am I To Know; That Old Black Magic; What Is This Thing Called Love; I Brung You Finjans For Your Zarf; My Funny Valentine; Lullaby of Birdland.* Personnel: Red Norvo, vibes; Tal Farlow, guitar; Red Mitchell, bass.

The title is mildly satirical, since the only strings involved are those employed by the guitarist and bassist in Norvo's trio. The group has a comfortable, lived-in quality that makes its music consistently listenable. The executives of Fantasy Records, never anxious to take themselves too seriously, insist that the cover and the whole production were conceived by Finjan W. Zarf.

BERNARD PEIFFER: BERNIE'S TUNES. EmArcy 36080. *Lover Come Back To Me; You Took Advantage of Me; Rhumblues; 'S Wonderful; Black Moon; Ah-Leu-Cha; Blues on the Wing; Bernie's Tune; Lullaby of the Leaves; Blues for Slobs.* Personnel, trio: Peiffer, piano; Joe Puma, guitar; Oscar Pettiford, bass. Quartet: Peiffer, Puma, Chuck Andrus, bass; Edmund Thigpen, drums.

Peiffer is by all odds the most original of the many talented immigrant pianists to brighten the U.S. jazz scene. He swings in his own ecstatic way, has an incredible left hand, and is given to occasional introspective forays into the atonal field, as on the piano solo item in this set, the provocative *Black Moon.* Produced by the author.

OSCAR PETERSON, BUD POWELL, ART TATUM, TEDDY WILSON: PIANO INTERPRETATIONS. Norgran MGN1036. Oscar Peterson: *Body and Soul; I Cover the Water Front; The Second Astaire Blues.* Bud Powell: *Tea For Two; Willow Weep For Me; Hallelujah.* Art Tatum: *Can't We Be Friends; The Man I Love; Stompin' At The Savoy.* Teddy Wilson: *Everything Happens to Me; Tea For Two; Oh, Lady Be Good.*

This happy collation presents three pace-setting pianists at peak form and a fourth, Bud Powell, slightly below his optimum capabilities, but still eminently listenable. Produced by Norman Granz.

OSCAR PETTIFORD VOL. 2. Bethlehem BCP33. *Another One, Minor Seventh Heaven; Scorpio; Kamman's A'Comin'; Don't Squawk; Oscalypso; Titoro; Bohemia After Dark.*

Personnel: Oscar Pettiford, bass; Don Byrd, trumpet; Ernie Royal, trumpet; Bobby Brookmeyer, trombone; Gigi Gryce, alto and clarinet; Jerome Richardson, tenor, clarinet, and flute; Don Abney, piano; Osie Johnson, drums.

Using a variety of arrangers including Ernie Wilkins, Tom Talbert, and Tom Whaley, Pettiford is well displayed in this pleasantly conceived set, which affords ample solo opportunities to all the sidemen. *Minor Seventh Heaven,* an Osie Johnson original, features Pettiford on 'cello. The album also provides a couple of demonstrations of the intelligent incorporation of Latin rhythms (*Oscalypso* and *Titoro*). Produced by Red Clyde.

NEW SOUNDS, NEW THOUGHTS

THE TEDDY CHARLES TENTET. Atlantic 1229. *Vibrations; The Quiet Time; The Emperor; Nature Boy; Green Blues; You Go to My Head; Lydian M-1.* Personnel: Teddy Charles, vibraharp; "Peter Urban" (Art Farmer), trumpet; Gigi Gryce, alto sax; J. R. Monterose, tenor sax; George Barrow, Sol Schlinger, baritone sax; Don Butterfield, tuba; Jimmy Raney, guitar; Mal Waldron, piano; Teddy Kotick, bass; Joe Harris, drums.

Operating within the rhythmic framework of normal contemporary jazz, Charles nevertheless breaks a few melodic and harmonic sound barriers in these performances, most of which, despite his denial in the album notes, might well be described as experimental. George Russell's *Lydian M-1* is based on the composer's new harmonic theory, which he calls the

Lydian concept of tonal organization. The first two titles are arranged by Mal Waldron and Jimmy Giuffre respectively; Gil Evans wrote the resourceful treatment of *You Go to My Head;* the other three titles are Charles' arrangements. The most successful session of its kind during the past year. Produced by Nesuhi Ertegun.

FLUTES AND REEDS. Savoy MG12022. *Shorty George; Bouncin' with Boots; That's a Woman; Doin' the Thing; Blues in a Cold Water Flat; Stereophonic.*

Personnel: Ernie Wilkins, alto sax; Frank Wess, tenor sax and flute; Jerome Richardson, tenor sax and flute; Hank Jones, piano; Eddie Jones, bass; Kenny Clarke, drums.

The full-scale arrival of the flute as a vehicle for jazz improvisation has never been more attractively presented than in this LP, for which Ernie Wilkins sketched a few simple arrangements. Wess and Richardson, whose solos on both tenor and flute are identified in each title for easy comparison purposes, both emerge with undivided credit for a series of first-rate performances. Produced by Ozzie Cadena.

THE JIMMY GIUFFRE FOUR: TANGENTS IN JAZZ. Capitol T634. *Scintilla One; Finger Snapper; Lazy Tones; Scintilla Two; Chirpin' Time; This Is My Beloved; The Leprechaun; Scintilla Three; Rhetoric; Scintilla Four.*

Personnel: Jimmy Giuffre, tenor sax, clarinet; Jack Sheldon, trumpet; Artie Anton, drums; Ralph Peña, bass.

Giuffre describes the unique music in this album as "Jazz, with a non-pulsating beat. The beat is implicit but not explicit . . . the two horns are the dominant but not domineering voices. The bass usually functions somewhat like a baritone sax. The drums play an important but non-conflicting role." Giuffre's concepts are as venturesome harmonically as rhythmically, dipping into atonality but never into excessive pretention and never to the point where an essential jazz undercurrent is lost. He has accomplished one of the few innovations capable of taking jazz forward, into new fields of its own, rather than sideways, into direct competition with the modern classicists.

CHICO HAMILTON QUINTET FEATURING BUDDY COLLETTE. Pacific Jazz 1209. *A Nice Day; Funny Valentine; Blue Sands; The Sage; The Morning After; I Want to Be Happy; Spectacular; Free Form; Walking Carson Blues; Buddy Boo.*

Personnel: Buddy Collette, flute, clarinet, tenor sax and alto; Jim Hall, guitar; Fred Katz, 'cello; Carson Smith, bass; Chico Hamilton, drums.

The unique timbre of the quintet is closely interrelated with the quality of the writing. All five members are represented as composer-arrangers. Katz's jazz work on the 'cello is masterful; Collette is fully exposed

as one of the two or three greatest musicians on the West Coast. Hamilton's own work is delightfully integrated into the whole. Produced by Richard Bock.

MAT MATHEWS QUINTET. Brunswick BL54013. *Bags' Groove; Yesterdays; There's a Small Hotel; Laura; Maya; The Nearness of You; Bernie's Tune; Spring It Was; Study in Purple; Owl Eyes; Night and Day; Lullaby of the Leaves.*

Personnel: Mat Mathews, accordion; Benny Weeks, guitar; Percy Heath, bass; Kenny Clarke, drums; Herbie Mann, flute.

Recorded in 1953 but not released on LP until 1956, these extraordinary sides are a reminder of a short-lived group that should have achieved musical and commercial recognition. Mathews' unique sound on a specially built button-key accordion blends with the flute of Herbie Mann for some luxuriant tonal effects. Produced by Bob Thiele.

MODERN JAZZ SOCIETY: A CONCERT OF CONTEMPORARY MUSIC. Norgran MGN1040. *Midsömmer; Little David's Fugue; The Queen's Fancy; Django; Sun Dance.*

Collective personnel: Stan Getz, Lucky Thompson, tenor sax; Tony Scott, Aaron Sachs, clarinet; J. J. Johnson, trombone; Gunther Schuller, French horn; Percy Heath, bass; Connie Kay, drums; and flute, bassoon and harp.

Two titles, *The Queen's Fancy* and *Django,* were arranged by Gunther Schuller; the other three are original compositions and arrangements by John Lewis, mentor of the Modern Jazz Quartet, who directed this session. There is extensive use of classical forms but the jazz solo voices are heard occasionally. The result is a stimulating synthesis that may, more than the Modern Jazz Quartet itself, show the direction Lewis's career will ultimately take.

PAUL NERO & HIS HI FIDDLES. Sunset LP303. *Scherzo-Phrenia; Street of Dreams; Just a Minuet; I Cover the Waterfront; That's Aplenty; Flew the Coop; Yes, We Have No Vibrato; Love is for the Very Young; Lullaby of the Leaves; Midnight Sun; A Foggy Day; Bridie Murphy, Won't You Please Come Home.*

Personnel: Paul Nero and Gerald Vinci, violins; Stan Harris, viola; Paul Bergstrom, 'cello; Rolly Bundock, bass; Bobby Gibbons, guitar; Milt Holland and Irv Cottler, drums.

Nero has been trying for years to prove that a string section can play jazz. Though the phrasing on a couple of the faster numbers comes perilously close to being corny, the balance is slightly on the plus side, especially in the writing. Marty Paich, Jimmy Giuffre, Bob Cooper, Jack Montrose, and Frank Comstock, of the West Coast jazz elite, contributed one arrangement apiece, while Nero himself wrote four. Produced by Ruby Raksin.

JIMMY SMITH AT THE ORGAN. Blue Note 1514. *The Champ; Bayou; Deep Purple; Moonlight in Vermont; Ready 'N Able; Turquoise; Bubbis.*

Personnel: Jimmy Smith, organ; Thornel Schwartz, guitar; Donald Bailey, drums.

Comments on the incredible Mr. Smith will be found under his name in the biographical chapter. On the basis of the up-tempo performances alone, this might well be called the most amazing jazz LP of the past year. It is an indispensable item for any jazz library. Produced by Alfred Lion.

LENNIE TRISTANO. Atlantic 1224. *These Foolish Things; You Go to My Head; If I Had You; Ghost of a Chance; All the Things You Are; Line Up; East Thirty-Second; Requiem; Turkish Mambo.*

Collective personnel: Lennie Tristano, piano; Lee Konitz, alto sax; Gene Ramey, Peter Ind, bass; Art Taylor, Jeff Morton, drums.

The first five titles were recorded in a New York restaurant where the Tristano-Konitz quartet was working. Far more important are the studio recordings, of which *Requiem*, a touching blues tribute to Charlie Parker, for which Tristano superimposed two piano tracks, is the most impressive, and deserves to rank as the most emotionally effective work Tristano has yet recorded. Trick recording techniques were again used on *Line Up* and *East Thirty-Second*. The bass and drum accompaniment was recorded at normal speed, after which Tristano recorded his piano ad libbing in the bass register of the piano, then superimposed it on the rhythm accompaniment, but at twice the speed at which he had played it. The effect, technically, was to bring the piano track an octave higher and to give the instrument a strange tone quality at the doubled-up tape speed; musically, the end justified the highly controversial means. Produced by Lennie Tristano.

MISCELLANEOUS

A NIGHT AT THE APOLLO. Vanguard 9006. Coles & Atkins, George Kirby, The Keynoters, Jackie "Moms" Mabley, and Amateur Show; Accompaniment by Count Basie band.

Though this is not basically a jazz LP, it is an invaluable social document in which jazz frequently is an important undercurrent. Recorded at the famous theater on 125th Street in Harlem, it presents for the first time on records the brilliant comedy routine of George Kirby, whose imitations of Pearl Bailey and Al Hibbler alone make the album indispensable. Count Basie, whose band provides the music for the acts, is heard in occasional dialogue with the earthy "Moms" Mabley. A couple of the less fortunate amateurs can be heard in all their ignominy as the audience boos them off the stage. As a documentary record of one of the principal

settings in which much great jazz and other Negro entertainment has been showcased, this is a welcome and unique disc. Produced by John Hammond.

BILLY MAY AND HIS ORCHESTRA: SORTA-DIXIE! Capitol T677. *Oh By Jingo!; South Rampart Street Parade; Down Home Rag; Sugar Foot Strut; The Sheik of Araby; Sorta Blues; Panama; Riverboat Shuffle; Five Foot Two, Eyes of Blue.*

Humor is an element too often lacking in jazz but always welcome when it is accomplished in good taste. On these sides Billy May leads a large orchestra, with innumerable woodwind and percussion doubles as well as harp, French horn, tuba, eight brass, and a four-man Dixieland front line (Dick Cathcart, trumpet; Matty Matlock, clarinet; Moe Schneider, trombone; Eddie Miller, tenor sax), through a series of delirious satires. In effect, May does for jazz what Spike Jones has long done for popular music; the result is a healthy catharsis in which, incidentally, legitimately superior jazz solo performances occasionally intervene.

ANTHOLOGIES

BETHLEHEM'S BEST. Bethlehem BCP13. Chris Connor, *Blue Silhouette;* Conte Candoli, *Tune for Tex;* Howard McGhee, *Tweedles;* Joe Derise, *My Romance;* Ruby Braff, *Easy Living;* Stu Williamson, *Slugger;* Frances Faye, *They Can't Take That Away from Me;* Milt Hinton, *Pick and Pat;* Max Bennett, *Just Max;* Bobby Troup, *Jamboree Jones;* Red Mitchell, *Kelly Green;* Oscar Pettiford, *Stardust;* Mel Tormé, *I've Got it Bad;* Kai and J.J., *Gong Rock;* Herbie Harper, *Angus;* Johnny Hartman, *September Song;* Charlie Mariano, *S'Nice;* Hal McKusick, *Blue Who;* Chris Connor, *Come Back to Sorrento;* Russ Garcia, *Wigville;* Bobby Scott, *Count Bill;* Helen Carr, *Down in the Depths;* Stan Levey, *West Coasting;* Bob Hardaway, *JR.;* Chris Connor, *Blame It on My Youth;* Ralph Sharon, *You Stepped out of a Dream;* Terry Pollard, *Emaline;* Rufus Smith, Betty Glamann, *Pulling Strings;* Australian Jazz Quartet, *The Girl with the Flaxen Hair;* Joe Roland, *Stairway to the Steinway;* Carmen McRae, *Easy to Love;* Urbie Green, *Mutation;* Don Elliott, *Summer Setting;* Julie London, *Motherless Child;* Charlie Shavers, *Ill Wind;* Herbie Mann-Sam Most, *Let's Get Away from It All.*

This album of three 12-inch LPS clearly mirrors the admirable variety of modern jazz performances recorded for this label since its inception in late 1953.

GIANTS OF JAZZ. American Recording Society G401. Count Basie, *Blues Backstage;* Johnny Hodges, *All of Me;* Roy Eldridge, Ray Brown, Jo Jones, *Dale's Wail;* Lionel Hampton, Oscar Peterson, *The High and the Mighty;* Dizzy Gillespie, Stan Getz, Max Roach,

It Don't Mean a Thing; Meade Lux Lewis, *Yancey's Last Ride;* Gene Krupa All-Stars, *Show Case;* Oscar Peterson Quartet, *Air Mail Special;* Billie Holiday, *Come Rain or Come Shine;* Lester Young, Nat Cole, Buddy Rich, *I Want to Be Happy;* Art Tatum, *Sunny Side of the Street;* Buddy De Franco Quartet, *Show Eyes.*

Many hidden virtues are contained in the above listing, for the sidemen include innumerable great jazz names. Produced by Norman Granz.

JAZZ DIGEST. Period SPL302. Charlie Shavers, *Flow Gently, Sweet Rhythm;* Osie Johnson, *Osie's Oasis;* Jack Teagarden, *Meet Me Where They Play the Blues;* Django Reinhardt, *Nuages;* Al Haig, *Woody'n You;* Josh White, *Evil Hearted Me;* Osie Johnson, *Johnson's Whacks;* Ralph Burns, *Bijou;* Maxine Sullivan, Charlie Shavers, *Loch Lomond;* Django Reinhardt, *Mélodie Au Crepuscule;* Charles Mingus-John LaPorta, *Abstraction;* Big Bill Broonzy, *Baby, Please Don't Go.*

The contrasts here are startling at times: the transition from the Mingus-LaPorta atonality to the primitive blues of Broonzy is an object lesson in jazz variegation. Anyone training to become the world's most broadminded jazz fan might use this set as his aural textbook.

The tunes selected for inclusion represent only a sampling of the hundreds of numbers that have become part of the standard jazz repertoire, and of the scores of versions of each that have been recorded through the years.

Since these lists may be of interest to collectors who are willing to go to a little extra trouble to secure little-known versions, it was decided to include a number of records that are on extinct or hard-to-get labels.

Readers are invited to suggest tunes that might be of interest for inclusion in subsequent editions of the *Yearbook*. No individual correspondence can be entered into.

FAVORITE VERSIONS
of Favorite Tunes

AIN'T MISBEHAVIN'. Andy Razaf, who wrote the lyrics to Fats Waller's music, recalls: "In 1929 we wrote the *Hot Chocolates* revue and it was so big they decided to produce it downtown. I remember one day going to Fats' house on 133rd Street to finish up a number based on a little strain he had thought up. The whole show was complete, but they needed an extra number for a theme and this had to be it. We worked on it for about 45 minutes and there it was—*Ain't Misbehavin'*." Publ. Mills Music, Inc.

Louis Armstrong (Decca; Columbia), Count Basie (Clef), Herman Chittison (Columbia), Duke Ellington (Decca), Dizzy Gillespie (Atlantic), Benny Goodman (Columbia), Bobby Hackett (Epic), Coleman Hawkins (Concert Hall), Ted Heath (London), Mel Henke (Contemporary), Earl Hines (Fantasy), Jutta Hipp (Blue Note), Harry James (Columbia), James P. Johnson (Decca), Gene Krupa (Victor), John Mehegan (Perspective), Jelly Roll Morton (Circle), Tony Pastor (Camden), Quintet of the Hot Club of France (Victor), Sonny Stitt (Prestige), Ralph Sutton (Columbia), Art Tatum (Clef), Sarah Vaughan (Columbia), Charlie Ventura (Norgran), Fats Waller (Victor), Dinah Washington (Mercury), Teddy Wilson (Columbia).

ALL THE THINGS YOU ARE. Music by Jerome Kern, lyrics by Oscar Hammerstein II, 1939. Introduced in an unsuccessful Broadway show *Very Warm for May*, the song became a popular hit in 1940 and was adopted by jazzmen a few years later. Publ. T. B. Harms, Inc.

Georgie Auld (Coral), Chet Baker (Pac. Jazz), Mildred Bailey (Columbia), Charlie Barnet (Capitol), Dave Brubeck (Fantasy), Billy Eckstine (National), Erroll Garner (Savoy), Dizzy Gillespie (Savoy; Debut), Lionel Hampton (EmArcy), Hampton Hawes (Contemporary), Elmo Hope (Prestige), Calvin Jackson (Columbia), Barney Kessel (Norgran), **Modern Jazz Quartet** (Prestige), Howard Rumsey (Contemporary), Hal Schaefer (Victor), Artie Shaw (Decca), Willie Smith (Monarch), Art Tatum (Clef), Billy Taylor (Roost; ABC-Paramount), Lennie Tristano (Atlantic), Charlie Ventura (Norgran).

BLUE SKIES. Lyrics and music by Irving Berlin; published in 1927. It was used as the title song of the Berlin picture in 1946 starring Fred Astaire and Bing Crosby. Publ. Irving Berlin Music Corp.

Count Basie (Columbia), Sid Catlett (Delta), Al Cohn (Victor), Tommy Dorsey (Victor), Duke Ellington (*Trumpets No End*) (Allegro), Erroll Garner (Mercury), Dizzy Gillespie (Dee Gee), Benny Goodman (Columbia; Bluebird), Ted Heath (*Blue Skies March*) (London), Jutta Hipp (Blue Note), John Kirby (Vocalion), John Mehegan (Savoy), Red Norvo (Brunswick), Oscar Peterson (Clef), Mel Powell (Commodore), Andre Previn (Monarch), Hal Schaefer (Victor), Artie Shaw (Epic), Maxine Sullivan (Vocalion), Art Tatum (Capitol; Clef), Dinah Washington (EmArcy), Ben Webster (Savoy), Mary Lou Williams (Disc).

BODY AND SOUL. Music by Johnny Green, lyrics by Edward Heyman, Robert Sour and Frank Eyton. Introduced by Libby Holman in the show, *Three's a Crowd*, 1930. Publ. by Harms, Inc.

Steve Allen (Coral), Louis Armstrong (Decca), Chu Berry (Jazztone), Beryl Booker (Cadence), Bob Brookmeyer (Pacific Jazz), Serge Chaloff (Capitol), Nat Cole (Capitol), Buddy De Franco (MGM), Billy Eckstine (MGM), Duke Ellington (Victor), Erroll Garner (Columbia), Stan Getz (Clef), Benny Goodman (Victor), Joe Gordon (in *The Jazz School*) (Wing), Al Haig (Esoteric), Coleman Hawkins (Victor), Earl Hines ("X"), Billie Holiday (Clef), Stan Kenton (Capitol), Howard McGhee (Hi-Lo), Charlie Mingus (Savoy; Debut), James Moody (Prestige), Oscar Peterson (Norgran), Bud Powell (Clef), Boyd Raeburn (Savoy), George Shearing (MGM), Art Tatum (Clef), Sarah Vaughan (Allegro; EmArcy), Charlie Ventura (Gene Norman), Teddy Wilson (Columbia), Lester Young (Aladdin).

HONEYSUCKLE ROSE. Music by the late Fats Waller, lyrics by Andy Razaf, 1928. Razaf writes: "We were at my mother's house in Asbury Park, N.J. working on a show, *Load of Coal,* for Connie's Inn, and I had just done half the chorus of a number when Fats remembered a date and said, 'Gotta go.' I finished up the verse, and gave it to him later over the telephone. The tune was *Honeysuckle Rose*." Publ. Santly-Joy, Inc.

Louis Armstrong (Decca; Columbia), Mildred Bailey (Decca), Count Basie (Decca), Vinnie Burke (Bethlehem), Nat Cole (Capitol), Dorsey Brothers (Decca), Duke Ellington (Capitol), Bud Freeman (EmArcy), Dizzy Gillespie (Capitol), Benny Goodman (Columbia), Coleman Hawkins (Decca), Earl Hines (Brunswick; Fantasy), Illinois Jacquet (Clef), Jazz Off the Air (Esoteric), Jazztime U.S.A. Vol. 2 (Brunswick), James P. Johnson (Decca), Jonah Jones (Angel), Gene Krupa (Victor), Red Norvo (Epic), Anita O'Day (Verve), Sammy Price (Brunswick), Joe Sullivan (Riverside), Art Tatum (Brunswick), Fats Waller (Victor), Ben Webster (Savoy).

HOW HIGH THE MOON. Music by William Morgan Lewis, lyrics by Nancy Hamilton, from their score for the Broadway production, *Two for the Show*. A mild popular hit in 1940, this began to become a jazz standard several years later when it was adopted by the first bop musicians. Publ. Chappell and Co., Inc.

Louis Armstrong (Decca), Dave Brubeck (Fantasy), Don Byas (Savoy), Al Casey (in *Then Came Swing*) (Capitol), Duke Ellington (Columbia), Ella Fitzgerald (Decca), Erroll Garner (Columbia), Dizzy Gillespie (in *Hot vs. Cool*) (MGM), Benny Goodman (Columbia; Capitol), Hampton-Tatum-Rich (Clef), Lionel Hampton (Decca; Columbia), Ted Heath (London), Eddie Heywood (Brunswick), Jazz at the Philharmonic (Stinson), Jazz at the Philharmonic (Clef), Jazz Off The Air (Esoteric), Stan Kenton (Capitol), Gene Krupa (Columbia; Clef), Howard McGhee (Hi-Lo), Jimmy McPartland (in *Hot vs. Cool*) (MGM), Oscar Peterson (Clef), Bud Powell (Norgran), George Shearing (MGM), Art Tatum (Columbia), Billy Taylor (Prestige), Sarah Vaughan (EmArcy), Charlie Ventura (Decca; EmArcy), Mary Lou Williams (Disc).

I CAN'T GET STARTED. Lyrics by Ira Gershwin, music by Vernon Duke (Vladimir Dukelsky), from *Ziegfeld Follies of 1936*. Popularized among jazzmen when the late Bunny Berigan sang and played it on his biggest hit record. Publ. Chappell and Co., Inc.

Georgie Auld (Grand Award), Paul Bley (Debut), Joe Bushkin (Atlantic), Billy Butterfield (in *Trumpet Stylists*) (Capitol); also in *Steve Allen's Jazz Concert* (Decca), Bunny Berigan (Victor; Epic), Ruby Braff (Bethlehem), Conte Candoli (Bethlehem), Benny Carter (Capitol), Buck Clayton & Ruby Braff (Vanguard), Dorothy Donegan (MGM), Douglas Duke (Herald), Roy Eldridge (Decca; Clef); also in *Jazz at the Philharmonic,* Vol. 16 (Clef), Roy Eldridge & Dizzy Gillespie (Clef), Ella Fitzgerald (Decca), Erroll Garner (Mercury), Dizzy Gillespie (Manor; Roost), Benny Goodman (Capitol), Lionel Hampton (Victor), Coleman Hawkins (Decca), Neal Hefti (Brunswick), Billie Holiday (Columbia), Jazz At The Philharmonic (Clef), Teddi King (Victor), Lee Konitz (Atlantic), Carmen McRae (Decca), Glenn Miller (Victor), Phil Moore (Clef), Gerry Mulligan & Lee

Above: Mood Indigo: L. to R.:
Duke Ellington, Quentin Jackson,
Harry Carney, Britt Woodman
(Herman Leonard)

Below: Duke Ellington
(Herman Leonard)

Below: Jazz for the Carriage Trade: George Wallington Quintet. L. to R., standing: George Wallington, Teddy Kotick, Bill Bradley; seated: Phil Woods, Donald Byrd *(Victor Tanaka)*

Opp. page above: The Jazz Messengers at one of their Blue Note recording sessions. L. to R., standing: Doug Watkins, Horace Silver, Kenny Dorham, Hank Mobley; seated: Art Blakey *(Francis Wolff)*

Opp. page below: Chico Hamilton Quintet. Buddy Collette, tenor sax; Jim Hall, guitar; Chico Hamilton, drums; Fred Katz, cello; Carson Smith, bass *(William James Claxton)*

Above: Louis Armstrong group in a scene from the motion picture *High Society*. L. to R.: Trummy Young; pianist Billy Kyle holding guitar; Barrett Deems, drums; Edmond Hall, clarinet; Arvell Shaw, bass.

Below: Hamp Hawes Trio. L. to R.: Red Mitchell, Hamp Hawes, Chuck Thompson

Above: Dave Brubeck Quartet: L. to R.: Joe Dodge, drums; Bob Bates, bass; Paul Desmond, alto sax and Brubeck (*Columbia Records*)

Below: Zoot Sims Quintet broadcasting from Cafe Bohemia. L. to R.: John Williams, Zoot Sims, Jerry Lloyd, Sonny Rollins, Kenny O'Brien (*Chuck Lilly*)

Top left: Newport Jazz Festival: The band shell at Freebody Park, during a matinee session, with Teddy Charles' Tentet on stage *(Robert Parent)*

Center left: Newport Jazz Festival: Some of the 20,000 who attended during three nights in July 1956 *(Robert Parent)*

Bottom left: Jazz forum at Newport. L. to R.: Hall Overton, Jimmy Giuffre, Friedrich Gulda, Bill Coss of *Metronome,* Nat Hentoff of *Down Beat,* David Broekman, Quincy Jones, Tony Scott *(Robert Parent)*

Right: Buck Clayton at Newport *(Robert Parent)*

Lower right: Newport's surprise hit: Paul Gonsalves of the Duke Ellington Orchestra *(Robert Parent)*

Left: At Newport: L. to R.: Charlie Mingus, Ernie Henry, Teo Macero, Bill Hardman *(Robert Parent)*

Lower left: Teddy Charles at Newport *(Robert Parent)*

Top right: Phineas Newborn Jr. at Newport *(Robert Parent)*

Center right: Toshiko at Newport *(Robert Parent)*

Bottom right: Friedrich Gulda at Newport *(Robert Parent)*

IN MEMORIAM
Top left: Richie Powell *(Herman Leonard)*
Top right: Clifford Brown *(Herman Leonard)*
Center left: "Cow Cow" Davenport
Center right: Frankie Trumbauer
Bottom left: Adrian Rollini
Bottom right: Bob Gordon

Konitz (Pacific Jazz), Anita O'Day (Verve), Jackie Paris (Wing), Charlie Parker (Clef), Oscar Peterson (Clef), Perez Prado (Victor), Max Roach & Clifford Brown (Gene Norman), Artie Shaw (Victor), Don Shirley (Cadence), Bobby Short (Atlantic), Jess Stacy (Brunswick), Sonny Stitt & Eddie Davis (Roost), Maxine Sullivan (International), Lennie Tristano (EmArcy), Sarah Vaughan (MGM), Dinah Washington (Mercury), Cootie Williams (Allegro), Mary Lou Williams (Folkways), Teddy Wilson (Columbia; Mercury; MGM), Lester Young (Aladdin; Norgran).

I GOT RHYTHM. Music by George Gershwin, lyrics by Ira Gershwin. Introduced in 1930 by Ethel Merman in *Girl Crazy,* the show that also included *Embraceable You* and *Bidin' My Time.* (The definitive biographical work on George Gershwin, *A Journey to Greatness,* by David Ewen, was published in 1956 by Henry Holt.) Publ. New World Music Corp.

Buddy De Franco (Norgran), Bud Freeman (Majestic), Erroll Garner (Blue Note), Dizzy Gillespie (Contemporary), Benny Goodman (Columbia), Lionel Hampton (Victor; Clef), Hampton Hawes (Contemporary), Horace Henderson (Vocalion), Pee Wee Hunt (Savoy), Jazz at the Philharmonic (Clef), Just Jazz (Modern), Metronome All Stars (Columbia), Red Norvo (EmArcy), Oscar Peterson (Victor), Ben Pollack (Savoy), Don Redman (Brunswick), Charlie Shavers (Bethlehem), Art Tatum (Brunswick), Dickie Wells (Signature), Teddy Wilson (Mercury; Jazztone), Lester Young (Commodore).

I'LL REMEMBER APRIL. Music by Gene de Paul, lyrics by Patricia Johnston and Don Raye, 1941. Miss Johnston was a model and this was her only song hit. De Paul collaborated with Raye on such hits as *Mr. Five by Five, Star Eyes,* and *He's My Guy.* Publ. Leeds Music Corp.

Count Basie (Epic), Johnny Bothwell (Brunswick), Louis Bellson (Norgran), Clifford Brown-Max Roach (EmArcy), Dave Brubeck (Fantasy), Conte Candoli (Bethlehem), Teddy Charles (Prestige), June Christy (Capitol), Miles Davis (Prestige), Kenny Drew (Norgran), Stan Getz (Norgran), Sanford Gold (Prestige), Lionel Hampton (Decca), Hampton Hawes (Prestige), Jutta Hipp (Blue Note), Thad Jones (Debut), Stan Kenton (Capitol), Lee Konitz (Roost; Storyville), Teo Macero (Debut), Herbie Mann-Sam Most (Bethlehem), Howard McGhee (Blue Note; Bethlehem), Carmen McRae (Decca), John Mehegan-Eddie Costa (Savoy), Modern Jazz Quartet (Prestige), Frank Morgan (Gene Norman), Red Norvo (Discovery), Charlie Parker (Clef), Bud Powell (Roost), Hal Schaefer (Victor), Ralph Sharon (London), Artie Shaw (Decca), George Shearing (MGM), Johnny Smith (Roost), Billy Taylor (Prestige), Trombone Rapport (Debut), Dick Twardzik (Pacific Jazz), George Wallington (Savoy).

INDIANA. (Back Home Again in Indiana). Lyrics by James Frederick Hanley, music by Ballard MacDonald; 1917. The writers died in 1942 and 1935, respectively. Among their other hits was *Rose of Washington Square.* Publ. Shapiro, Bernstein & Co., Inc.

Red Allen (Okeh), Louis Armstrong (Decca), Sidney Bechet (Storyville), Chu Berry (Epic), Dave Brubeck (Fantasy), Joe Bushkin (Savoy), Eddie Condon (in *Chicago Style Jazz*) (Columbia), Harry Edison (Pacific Jazz), Erroll Garner (Savoy; Columbia), Dizzy Gillespie (in *Hot vs Cool*) (MGM), Bengt Hallberg (Prestige), Bob Hardaway (Bethlehem), Art Hodes (in *Gems of Jazz*) (Decca), Barney Kessel (Contemporary), Gene Krupa (in *Jazz at the Philharmonic,* Vol. 16) (Clef), Jimmy McPartland (in *Hot vs Cool*) (MGM), James Moody (Prestige), Red Nichols (Brunswick), Jackie Paris (Wing), Bud Powell (Roost), Andre Previn (Modern; Victor), Ike Quebec (Blue Note), Jess Stacy (Brunswick), Art Tatum (Capitol), George Wettling (Columbia), Teddy Wilson (Mercury), Lester Young (Aladdin; Savoy; Norgran).

LULLABY OF BIRDLAND. Originally written by George Shearing as an instrumental theme for the Birdland night club in New York City, 1952. Lyrics were later added by B. Y. Forster. Publ. Patricia Music, Inc.

Charlie Barnet (Victor), Milt Bernhart (Victor), Billy Byers (Victor), Blue Stars Of France (sung in French) (EmArcy), Barbara Carroll (Victor), Al Cohn (Victor), Dick Collins (Victor), Chris Connor (Bethlehem), Bill Davis (Epic), Ella Fitzgerald (Decca), Erroll Garner (Columbia), Stan Getz (Roost), Urbie Green (Vanguard), Coleman Hawkins (Concert Hall), Calvin Jackson ("X"), Pete Jolly (Victor), Jonah Jones (Groove), Quincy Jones (Victor), Barney Kessel (Contemporary), Marian McPartland (Savoy), John Mehegan (Savoy), Gil Melle (Blue Note), Joe Newman (Victor), Red Norvo (Fantasy), Bud Powell (in *Jazz at Massey Hall,* Vol. 2) (Debut), Shorty Rogers-Andre Previn (Victor), Bobby Scott (Bethlehem), Tony Scott (Victor), George Shearing (MGM), Don Shirley (Cadence), Billy Taylor (Prestige), Mel Torme (Bethlehem), Sarah Vaughan (EmArcy), Ernie Wilkins (Victor), Kai Winding & Jay Jay Johnson ("X").

THE MAN I LOVE. Music by George Gershwin, lyrics by Ira Gershwin, 1924. Featured in two Gershwin shows, first, *Lady Be Good* and then in *Strike Up the Band.* Publ. New World Music Corp.

Mildred Bailey (Crown), Aaron Bell (Herald), Les Brown (Capitol), Don Byas (Atlantic), Teddy Charles (Prestige), Nat Cole (Capitol), Eddie Condon with Lee Wiley (Decca), Miles Davis (Prestige), Buddy De Franco (Norgran), Roy Eldridge (Discovery; Clef), Erroll Garner (Savoy), Dizzy Gillespie (Clef), Benny Goodman (Columbia; Victor), Al Haig (Period), Edmond Hall (Commodore), Lionel Hampton (Decca), Coleman Hawkins (Brunswick), Mel Henke (Contemporary), Woody Herman (MGM), Eddie Heywood (Decca), Billie Holiday (Columbia; Clef), Ada Moore (Debut), Anita O'Day (Clef), Oscar Peterson (Clef), Terry Pollard (in *Cats vs Chicks*) (MGM), Jazz At The Philharmonic (Clef), Just Jazz (Decca), Barney Kessel (Atomic), James Moody (Prestige), Red Norvo (EmArcy), Charlie Shavers (Bethlehem), Artie Shaw (Columbia), George Shearing (Capitol), Don Shirley (Cadence), Frankie Socolow (Duke), Art Tatum (Dial; Clef; Norgran), Clark Terry (in *Cats vs Chicks*) (MGM), Sarah Vaughan (MGM), Charlie Ventura (Imperial; Crystalette), Mary Lou Williams (Disc).

MUSKRAT RAMBLE. Written as an instrumental by trombonist Kid Ory and recorded by him with Louis Armstrong in 1926. Lyrics were added in 1950 by Ray Gilbert, and the number enjoyed a new revival as a popular hit. Publ. George Simon, Inc.

Louis Armstrong (Columbia; Decca), Basin St. Six (EmArcy), Ray Bauduc (Capitol), Sidney Bechet (Blue Note), Bobby Byrne (in *Dixieland Jazz*) (Grand Award), Bob Crosby (Coral), Wild Bill Davison (Commodore), Dixieland Jubilee (Decca), Jimmy Dorsey (Columbia), Roy Eldridge (Varsity), Don Elliott (in *Hot vs. Cool*) (MGM), Bud Freeman (Columbia), Benny Goodman (Brunswick), Bobby Hackett (Capitol), Lionel Hampton (Victor), George Hartman (Mercury), Woody Herman (Capitol), Pee Wee Hunt (Savoy; Capitol), Jonah Jones (Groove), Jimmy McPartland (in *Hot vs. Cool*) (MGM), Eddie Miller (in *Dixieland Stylists*) (Capitol), Phil Napoleon (EmArcy), Mel Powell (Capitol), Preacher Rollo (MGM), Bobby Sherwood (Mercury), Muggsy Spanier (Circle), Ralph Sutton (Columbia), Lu Watters (Good Time Jazz).

OH LADY BE GOOD. Music by George Gershwin, lyrics by Ira Gershwin, 1924. From the show, *Lady Be Good;* the cast included Fred Astaire, his sister, Adele, and Cliff "Ukulele Ike" Edwards. Among the other song hits from the show was *Fascinating Rhythm.* Publ. New World Music Corp.

Count Basie (Decca; Clef), Sidney Bechet (Victor; Storyville), Dave Brubeck (Fantasy), Joe Bushkin (Commodore), Billy Butterfield (Capitol), Eddie Condon (Decca), Ella Fitzgerald (Decca), Slim Gaillard (Clef), Erroll Garner (Disc; Columbia; EmArcy), Dizzy Gillespie (Dee Gee), Benny Goodman (Victor), Lionel Hampton (MGM; Decca), Jam Session, Vol. 4 (Clef), Jazz at the Philharmonic (Stinson), Jazz at the Philharmonic (Clef), Ken Kersey (Savoy), Yank Lawson (Brunswick), Glenn Miller (Victor), Phil Moore (Clef), Gerry Mulligan & Lee Konitz (Pacific Jazz), Red Norvo (Decca; Brunswick), Oscar Peter-

son (Clef), Andre Previn (Modern), Artie Shaw (Victor), Jimmy Smith (Blue Note), Eddie South (Columbia), Muggsy Spanier (Commodore), Charlie Ventura (EmArcy), Mary Lou Williams (Stinson), Teddy Wilson (Clef; Norgran), Lester Young-Count Basie (Epic).

ON THE SUNNY SIDE OF THE STREET. Lyrics by Dorothy Fields, music by Jimmy McHugh from the *International Revue,* 1930. One of many standards they wrote together, others being *I Can't Give You Anything but Love, I Must Have that Man, Exactly Like You, I'm In the Mood for Love.* Publ. Shapiro, Bernstein & Co., Inc.

Ivie Anderson (Black & White), Louis Armstrong (Decca), Svend Asmussen (Angel), Mae Barnes (Atlantic), Chu Berry (Jazztone), Herman Chittison (Columbia), Cozy Cole with Coleman Hawkins (Savoy), Nat Cole (Savoy), Duke Ellington (Columbia), Erroll Garner (Blue Note; Savoy), Terry Gibbs (in *Jazztime USA*) (Brunswick), Dizzy Gillespie (Dee Gee), Benny Goodman (Columbia), Benny Goodman with Peggy Lee (Columbia), Lionel Hampton (Victor; Clef), Glenn Hardman with Lester Young (Columbia), Coleman Hawkins (EmArcy), Eddie Heywood (Brunswick; Decca), Earl Hines (Victor), Johnny Hodges (Norgran), Billie Holiday (Jazztone), Illinois Jacquet (Clef), Jay McShann (Capitol), Jack Parnell (London), Oscar Peterson (Clef), Hazel Scott (Signature), Lou Stein (Epic), Art Tatum (Dial), Chick Webb (Decca), Lester Young (Aladdin; Norgran).

PERDIDO. Written as an instrumental by Juan Tizol, trombonist with the Duke Ellington band; recorded by Ellington, 1942. Lyrics were later added by Hans Jan Lengsfelder (Harry Lenk), noted Viennese-born author and playwright, and Ervin M. Drake. Publ. Tempo Music, Inc.

Louis Armstrong (Decca), Count Basie (Clef), Les Brown (Coral), Dave Brubeck (Fantasy), Bobby Byrne (in *Dixieland vs Birdland*) (MGM), Red Callender (Victor), Jimmy Dorsey (Decca), Duke Ellington (Victor; Columbia), Rolf Ericson (Discovery), Bud Freeman (Bethlehem), Erroll Garner (Atlantic), Terry Gibbs (in *Jazztime USA*) (Brunswick), Dizzy Gillespie (Debut), Lionel Hampton (Decca; Gene Norman), Hampton-Tatum-Rich (Clef), Neal Hefti (Epic), Woody Herman (Mars), Eddie Heywood (MGM), Johnny Hodges (Mercer; Norgran), Jazz at the Philharmonic, Vol. 8 (Clef), Jonah Jones (Angel), Gene Krupa (Clef), Howard McGhee (Hi-Lo), Oscar Pettiford (Mercer), Perez Prado (Victor), Red Rodney with Dave Lambert & Buddy Stewart (EmArcy), Stuff Smith (Commodore), Willie The Lion Smith (Urania), Sarah Vaughan (Columbia), Mary Lou Williams (Contemporary), Kai Winding (in *Dixieland vs Birdland*) (MGM).

'ROUND MIDNIGHT ('ROUND ABOUT MIDNIGHT). First written as an instrumental by Thelonious Monk, and recorded by Cootie Williams' orchestra, in 1944. Lyrics were later added by Bernie Hanighen. Publ. Advanced Music Corp.

Benny Carter (Norgran), Bob Cooper (Capitol), Jane Fielding (Jazz; West), Dizzy Gillespie (Dial), Babs Gonzales (Blue Note), Hampton Hawes (Contemporary), Milt Jackson (Savoy), Barney Kessel (in *Lighthouse at Laguna*) (Contemporary), Teddi King with Beryl Booker (Storyville), Thelonious Monk (Blue Note), John Mehegan (Savoy), Jackie Paris (EmArcy), Bud Powell (Norgran), George Shearing (Capitol), Jimmy Raney (Prestige), Dick Twardzik (Pacific Jazz), George Wallington (Prestige), Cootie Williams (Hit), Mary Lou Williams (Contemporary).

ST. LOUIS BLUES. Lyrics and music by W. C. Handy, 1914. Biography of Handy will be found in the *Encyclopedia of Jazz*. (An excellent blues book, with 67 songs, critical text by Abbe Niles and pictures by Miguel Covarrubias, is published by Charles Boni, distributed by Simon and Schuster. It is entitled *A Treasury of the Blues*.) Publ. W. C. Handy.

Louis Armstrong (Columbia; Victor; Decca; Vox), Svend Asmussen (Angel), Mildred Bailey (Vocalion), Pearl Bailey (Columbia), Charlie Barnet (Clef), Count Basie (Columbia), Billy Butterfield (Westminster), Don Byas (Savoy), Cab Calloway (Brunswick), Dorsey Brothers (Decca), Roy Eldridge (EmArcy), Duke Ellington (Victor), Ralph Flanagan (Rainbow), Herbie Fields (Decca), Stan Freeman (Columbia), Erroll Garner (Columbia), Terry Gibbs (in *Jazztime USA*) (Brunswick), Dizzy Gillespie (Victor), Babs Gonzales (Capitol), Benny Goodman (Victor), W. C. Handy (Varsity), Earl Hines (Victor; Dial), Billie Holiday (Columbia), Lena Horne (with NBC Chamber Music Society) (Victor), John Kirby (Victor), Metronome All Stars (MGM), Lizzie Miles (Cook), Glenn Miller (Victor), James Moody (EmArcy), Johnny Moore (Exclusive), Perez Prado (Victor), Hal Schaefer (Victor), Freddie Slack (Capitol), Bessie Smith (Columbia), Kay Starr (Lamplighter), Maxine Sullivan (Columbia; Period), Art Tatum (Decca; Brunswick), Jack Teagarden (Victor), Fats Waller (Victor), Mary Lou Williams (Circle).

STARDUST. Music by Hoagy Carmichael, lyrics by Mitchell Parrish. Originally an instrumental and recorded as such by Isham Jones in 1929; became a popular song in 1932. Publ. Mills Music, Inc.

Louis Armstrong (Columbia; Decca), Chu Berry (Commodore), Clifford Brown (EmArcy), Dave Brubeck (Fantasy), Billy Butterfield (Westminster), Don Byas (Atlantic), Hoagy Carmichael (Decca), Charlie Christian & Dizzy Gillespie (Esoteric), Cozy Cole (Candy), Bing Crosby (Decca), Tommy Dorsey (Victor), Billy Eckstine (MGM), Roy Eldridge (Bruns-

wick), Duke Ellington (Capitol), Ella Fitzgerald (Decca), Erroll Garner (Savoy), Dizzy Gillespie (Dee Gee), Benny Goodman (Columbia), Bennie Green (Prestige), Lionel Hampton (Columbia), Coleman Hawkins (Decca; Capitol), Edgar Hayes (Decca), Earl Hines (Mercury), Illinois Jacquet (Clef), Jack Jenney (Columbia), Just Jazz (Decca), Stan Kenton (Capitol), Gene Krupa (Clef), Howard McGhee (Hi-Lo), Benny Morton (Stinson), Red Norvo (Commodore), Ernie Royal (Urania), Tony Scott (Victor), Charlie Shavers (EmArcy), Artie Shaw (Victor), Sonny Stitt (King; Roost), Art Tatum (Brunswick; Clef), Trombone Rapport (Debut), Fats Waller (Victor), Mary Lou Williams (Stinson), Lester Young (Norgran).

STOMPIN' AT THE SAVOY. Written as an instrumental by Edgar Sampson, then a saxophonist in the late Chick Webb's band, with whom he recorded it in May, 1934. It was named for the Savoy Ballroom in Harlem, where Webb's band often played. Benny Goodman extended its popularity by recording it, first with his big band in Jan., 1936, then with his quartet in December of that year. Lyrics were later added by Andy Razaf. Publ. Robbins Music Corp.

Steve Allen (Coral), Louis Armstrong (Decca), Georgie Auld (Musicraft), Kenny Baker (Angel), Louis Bellson (Norgran), Eddie Bert (Savoy), Les Brown (Coral), Joe Bushkin (Atlantic), Charlie Christian (Esoteric), Dotty Denny (A440), Duke Ellington (Capitol), Tal Farlow (Norgran), Erroll Garner (Savoy; Columbia), Babs Gonzales (Blue Note), Benny Goodman (Capitol; Columbia; Victor; Decca), Brad Gowans (Victor), Lionel Hampton (Clef), Coleman Hawkins (Savoy; Concert Hall), Woody Herman (Mars), Eddie Heywood (MGM), Jam Session #6 (Clef), Stan Kenton (Capitol), Hans Koller (Discovery), Gene Krupa (Columbia; Clef; Jazztone), Howard McGhee (Hi-Lo), Glenn Miller (Victor), Oscar Peterson (Clef), Flip Phillips (Brunswick), Perez Prado (Victor), Ernie Royal (Urania), Sheboblou Trio (Chord), Eddie South (Columbia), Art Tatum (Brunswick; Clef; Norgran), Sir Charles Thompson (Vanguard), Charlie Ventura (Crystalette), Chick Webb (Vocalion), Teddy Wilson (MGM), Cecil Young (King).

SUMMERTIME. Music by George Gershwin from his 1935 folk opera, *Porgy and Bess,* for which Ira Gershwin and Du Bose Heyward collaborated on the libretto. Other songs from *Porgy and Bess* include *I Got Plenty o' Nuttin'* and *It Ain't Necessarily So*. Publ. Gershwin Pub. Corp.

Mildred Bailey (Crown), Sidney Bechet (Blue Note), Bob Crosby (Decca), Bill De Arango (EmArcy), Buddy De Franco (MGM), Tommy Dorsey (Victor), Kurt Edelhagen (Decca), Erroll Garner (Atlantic), Stan Getz (Norgran), Herbie Harper

(Nocturne), Al Hibbler (Sunrise), Billie Holiday (Columbia), Duke Jordan (Signal), Wynton Kelly (Blue Note), Gil Mellé (Blue Note), Ada Moore (Debut), Charlie Parker (Clef), Seldon Powell (Roost), Boyd Raeburn (Musicraft), Charlie Shavers (in *Jazz at the Philharmonic*, vol. 15) (Clef) (Bethlehem), George Shearing (MGM), Bobby Scott (ABC-Paramount), Joe Sullivan (Riverside), Maxine Sullivan (International), Swedish All Stars (Blue Note), Sarah Vaughan (Columbia), Charlie Ventura (Norgran), George Wallington (Blue Note), Dinah Washington (EmArcy), Randy Weston (Riverside).

SWEET GEORGIA BROWN. Music and lyrics by Maceo Pinkard, Kenneth Casey, 1926. Publ. Remick Music Corp.

Frank Assunto (Imperial), Max Bennett (Bethlehem), Brother Matthew (ABC-Paramount), Dave Brubeck (Fantasy), Joe Fingers Carr (Capitol), Barbara Carroll (Victor), Nat Cole (Capitol), Eddie Condon (Savoy), Buddy De Franco (MGM), Jimmy Dorsey (Columbia), Roy Eldridge (Clef), Firehouse Five Plus Two (Good Time Jazz), Benny Goodman (Capitol; Victor), Johnny Guarnieri (Admiral; Brunswick), Edmond Hall (Delta), Erskine Hawkins (Victor), Ted Heath (London), Art Hodes (Blue Note), Jam Session (Skylark), Jazz at the Philharmonic, vol. 3 (Clef), Jazz Off the Air, vol. 2 (Esoteric), Just Jazz (Modern), John Kirby (Columbia), Lawson-Haggart (in Steve Allen's Jazz Concert) (Decca), Jimmy Noone (in *Gems of Jazz*, vol. 5) (Decca), Oscar Peterson (Victor) (in *Jazz at the Philharmonic*, vol. 15) (Clef), Bud Powell (Clef), Preacher Rollo (MGM), Django Reinhardt (Angel), Stan Rubin (Victor), Eddie South (Victor), Muggsy Spanier (EmArcy), Billy Taylor (Prestige), Sir Charles Thompson (Vanguard), Charlie Ventura (EmArcy), Lu Watters (Clef), Bob Wilber (Circle), Teddy Wilson (Clef), Cecil Young (King).

TEA FOR TWO. Music by the late Vincent Youmans, lyrics by Irving Caesar; from the show *No, No, Nanette*, 1924. Publ. Harms, Inc.

Steve Allen (Coral), Louis Armstrong (Decca), Svend Asmussen (Brunswick), George Barnes (Mercury), Pete Brown (Bethlehem), Dave Brubeck (Fantasy), Nat Cole (Capitol), Baby Dodds (American Music), Tommy Dorsey (Victor), Pee Wee Erwin (Cadence), Tal Farlow (Norgran), Jerry Fielding (Trend), Bud Freeman (EmArcy), Terry Gibbs (Brunswick), Bob Gordon (Pacific Jazz), Al Haig (Period), Mel Henke (Contemporary), Earl Hines (Dial), Johnny Hodges (Clef), Jazz at the Philharmonic (Clef), Hank Jones (Clef), Stan Kenton (Capitol), Gene Krupa & Anita O'Day (Columbia), John Mehegan (Perspective), Charlie Mingus (Savoy), Joe Mooney (Decca), Gerry Mulligan (Pacific Jazz), Red Nichols (Brunswick), Bud Powell (Clef), Oscar Peter-

son (Clef), Clarence Profit (Brunswick), Django Reinhardt (Angel), Adrian Rollini (Mercury), Willie Smith (Norgran), Willie "The Lion" Smith (Commodore), Sylvia Syms (De Luxe), Art Tatum (Brunswick; Capitol; Clef), Charlie Ventura (Sunset), Fats Waller (Victor), Lee Wiley (Columbia), Teddy Wilson (Clef; Norgran), Cecil Young (King), Lester Young (Aladdin; Norgran), Bob Zurke (Victor).

WHAT IS THIS THING CALLED LOVE? Music and lyrics by Cole Porter from *Wake Up and Dream*, 1930. Full details concerning Porter and his songs can be found in *103 Lyrics of Cole Porter* published by Random House, edited by Fred Lounsberry. Publ. Harms, Inc.

Claire Austin (Contemporary), Clifford Brown-Max Roach (EmArcy), Dave Brubeck (Fantasy), Ray Bryant (Epic), Nat Cole (Capitol), Corky Corcoran (Keynote), Tommy Dorsey (Victor), Ella Fitzgerald (Verve), Russ Garcia (Bethlehem), Erroll Garner (Apollo; Roost), John Hardee (Blue Note), Hampton-Tatum-Rich (Clef), Mel Henke (Vitacoustic), Billie Holiday (Decca), Hollywood Jazz Session (Savoy), Jam Session No. 2 (Clef), Barney Kessel (Atomic), Marian McPartland (Savoy), Red Norvo (Fantasy), Anita O'Day (Coral), Les Paul (Capitol), Oscar Peterson (Clef), Artie Shaw and The Meltones (Allegro), Billy Taylor (Roost), Charlie Ventura (Imperial), Villegas (Columbia), Fran Warren (MGM).

WHEN THE SAINTS GO MARCHING IN. Originally published by Nazarene Publ. Co., 1896; lyrics are credited to Catherine E. Purvis, music to James M. Black. Long in the public domain, the work was revived by traditionalist jazz musicians during the 1940s.

Steve Allen's Jazz Concert (Decca), Gene Ammons (Prestige), Ray Anthony (Capitol), Louis Armstrong (Decca), Paul Barbarin (Jazztone), Sidney Bechet (Blue Note), Graeme Bell (Angel), Bobby Byrne (in *Dixieland Jazz*) (Grand Award), Pete Daily (Capitol), Wild Bill Davison (Pax), Wilbur de Paris (Atlantic), Dixieland Rhythm Kings (Pax), Pee Wee Erwin (King), History of Jazz (Grand Award), Mahalia Jackson (Columbia), Jamming At Rudi's (Circle), Jazz At The Metropole (Bethlehem), Jazz Dance (Jaguar), Bunk Johnson (Victor), Max Kaminsky (MGM), George Lewis (Jazz Man), Phil Napoleon (Decca), Santo Pecora (Southland), Preacher Rollo (MGM), Lu Watters (Clef), Bob Wilber (Circle).

YESTERDAYS. Music by Jerome Kern (died 1945); lyrics by Otto Harbach, who was elected president of ASCAP in 1950. Publ. in 1933 by Bourne, Inc.

Clifford Brown (EmArcy), Milt Buckner (MGM), Vinnie Burke (Bethlehem), Jackie Cain & Roy Kral (Storyville), Kenny Clarke (Savoy), Miles Davis (Blue Note), Wild Bill Davison (Circle); (in *Garry Moore Presents*) (Columbia), Buddy De Franco (Norgran), Dorothy Donegan (Continental), Kenny

Drew (Blue Note), Morey Feld (Kapp), Erroll Garner (Savoy; Blue Note; EmArcy), Stan Getz (Roost), Virgil Gonzales (Nocturne), Art Harris (Kapp), Coleman Hawkins (Grand Award), Eddie Heywood (Decca), Billie Holiday (Jazztone; Clef), Milt Jackson (Savoy), The Jazz Messengers (Blue Note), Hank Jones (Clef), Duke Jordan (Signal), Stan Kenton (Capitol), Lee Konitz (Prestige), Teo Macero (Debut), Helen Merrill (EmArcy), Charlie Mingus (Debut), Roger King Mozian (Clef), Oscar Peterson (Clef), Bud Powell (Clef), Tony Scott (Brunswick), Artie Shaw (Clef), George Shearing (Capitol), Johnny Smith (Roost), Sonny Stitt (Roost), Art Tatum (ARA; Columbia; Clef), Trombone Rapport (Debut), Charlie Ventura (Decca; Norgran), Villegas (Columbia).

WHERE TO HEAR JAZZ
in Night Clubs

The following list of jazz night clubs in leading American cities was originally printed in *Down Beat,* and with the permission of this publication it is reproduced below.

BOSTON

THE FIVE O'CLOCK, 78 Huntington Ave.; CO 6-0514. Open seven days a week. No cover or minimum. Barton Buckhalter, manager.

THE STABLE, 20 Huntington Ave.; KE 6-9329. Open seven days a week. No cover. Minimum: Tuesdays and Thursdays, $2. Harold Buchalter, manager.

STORYVILLE, 47 Huntington Ave.; KE 6-9000. Open seven days a week and Sunday matinee. No cover charge. Minimum: Monday through Thursday $2.50, weekends $3, Sunday matinee $2. George Wein, owner.

BUFFALO, N.Y.

TOWN CASINO, 681 Main St.; CL 7-388. Open seven days a week. No cover charge. Minimum: Saturday only, $3. Harry Altman and Harry Wallens, owners.

CANADA

CAMPBELLS', 100 Dundas St., London, Ontario; LO 3-4820. Open six days a week, closed Sundays. No cover or minimum. George and Ted Campbell, owners.

DAGWOOD'S RESTAURANT, 995 Montee St. Laurent, Ville St. Laurent, Montreal, Quebec; RI 7-6269. Open seven days a week. No cover or minimum. Lionel Paquette, owner.

TOWN TAVERN, 16 Queen St., Toronto, Ontario; EM 6-5363. Open seven days a week. No cover or minimum. S. Berger, manager.

CHICAGO

BLUE NOTE, 3 N. Clark St.; SPring 7-7876. Open Wednesday through Sunday, including Sunday matinee. No cover charge. Minimum: $3. Frank Holzfeind, owner.

BUDLAND, 6412 S. Cottage Grove Ave.; MUseum 4-6400. Open six days a week, closed on Tuesday.

Minimum: Friday, Saturday, Sunday, $2. Bob Lee, manager.

CLOISTER INN, 900 N. Rush St.; SUperior 7-0506. Open seven days a week. No cover or minimum. Paul Raffles, owner.

EASY STREET, in the alley, 1135 N. off Elm at State St.; WHitehall 4-4748. Open seven days. No cover or minimum. Howard Badgley, manager.

1111 JAZZ CLUB, 1111 Bryn Mawr Ave.; SUperior 4-1111. Open Wednesday through Sunday. No cover or minimum. Nick Alex, manager.

JAZZ, LTD., 11 E. Grand Ave.; SUperior 7-2907. Open six days a week, closed Sundays. No cover charge. Minimum: $2. Ruth and Bill Reinhardt, owners.

LONDON HOUSE, 360 N. Michigan Ave.; ANdover 3-6920. Open seven days a week. No cover or minimum. Oscar and George Marienthal, owners.

THE MAX MILLER SCENE, 2126 N. Clark St.; LAkeview 5-9591. Open Wednesday through Sunday. No cover or minimum. Max Miller, owner.

MISTER KELLY'S, 1028 N. Rush St.; WHitehall 3-2233. Open seven days a week. No cover or minimum. Oscar and George Marienthal, owners.

PREVIEW LOUNGE, 7 W. Randolph St.; ANdover 3-6908. Open seven days a week (Mondays and Tuesdays use "off-night" groups). No cover or minimum. Milt Schwartz and Ralph Mitchell.

RED ARROW, 6927 Pershing Rd., Berwyn, Ill.; GUnderson 4-9670. Open seven days a week. No cover or minimum. Otto J. Kubik, owner.

STAGE THEATER LOUNGE, 1524 E. 63rd St.; NOrmal 7-5757. Open seven days a week. No cover or minimum. Fred Mays, manager.

COLUMBUS, OHIO

GRANDVIEW INN, 1127 Dublin Rd.; HU 6-2419. Open six days a week, closed on Sunday. No cover or minimum. Mike Flesch, manager.

DAYTON, OHIO

APACHE INN, 5100 Germantown Pike; MElrose 0213. Open seven days a week. Cover charge: $1. No minimum. Jessie W. Lowe, owner.

DETROIT

BAKER'S KEYBOARD LOUNGE, 20510 Livernois; UNiversity 4-1200. Open seven days a week. Cover charge: $1. No minimum. Clarence H. Baker, manager.

ROUGE LOUNGE, 1937 Coolidge Highway, River Rouge; VInewood 3-9380. Open six days a week, closed on Monday. Cover charge: $1. No minimum. Ed and Tom Sarkesian, owners.

LOS ANGELES

BRUCE'S BIG TOP, 5336 Sunset Blvd., Hollywood; HO 9-6907. Open seven days a week. No cover or minimum. Earle Bruce, owner.

CLUB COSMO, 1952 W. Adams Blvd.; RE 2-5244. Open seven days a week. No cover or minimum. Eddie A. Wormly, manager.

CRESCENDO, 8572 Sunset Blvd., Hollywood; BR 2-0921. Open seven days a week. Cover charge: $1.50. No minimum. R. Forsley, manager.

400 CLUB, 3330 W. Eighth St.; DU 2-0330. Open six days a week, closed Mondays. No cover or minimum. Happy Koomer, manager.

THE HAIG, 638 S. Kenmore St.; DU 7-9356. Open six days a week. No cover charge. Minimum: Two drinks. John Bennett, manager.

JAZZ CITY, Hollywood Blvd. at Western; HO 4-8446. Open seven days a week. No admission or cover.

KEYBOARD SUPPER CLUB, 453 N. Canon Dr., Beverly Hills; CR 5-1244. No cover charge. Minimum: Two drinks. Earl Maltby, manager.

LIGHTHOUSE CAFE, 30 Pier Ave., Hermosa Beach; FR 4-9065. Open seven days a week. No cover or minimum. John Levine, manager.

THE MEL-O-DEE, 113 W. Broadway, Glendale; CL 2-9035. Open seven days a week. No cover or minimum. Sid Berk, owner.

ROYAL ROOM, 6700 Hollywood Blvd., Hollywood; HO 7-3032. Open seven days a week. No cover or minimum. Bernie Rudd, manager.

SANBAH ROOM, 4500 Sunset Blvd., Hollywood; NO 3-0996. Open seven days a week. No cover or minimum. Jimmie Maddin, manager.

CLUB STARLITE, 1520 W. Manchester; PL 1-6601. Open seven days a week. No cover or minimum. John and Stan Moustakas, managers.

TIFFANY CLUB, 3260 W. Eighth St.; DU 2-5206. Open six days a week, closed Mondays. No cover charge. Minimum: Two drinks. Jack Tucker, manager.

ZARDI'S JAZZLAND, 6315 Hollywood Blvd. (at Vine); HO 5-3388.

MIAMI

CIRO'S, 1827 Alton Rd.; JE 8-7277. Open seven days a week. No cover charge. Minimum: $1.50. Montrose Gardner, manager.

ONYX ROOM of the Coral bar, 1685 Alton Rd.; JE 8-1915. Open seven days a week. No cover or minimum. Freddy Sisk, manager.

CLUB WALLY, 151 S.E. Third Ave.; FR 4-4379. Open seven days a week. No cover or minimum. Wally Bros., owners.

NEW ORLEANS

DANNY'S INFERNO, 831 Bienville St.; MA 8531. Open seven days a week. No cover or minimum. Danny Price and Charlie McKnight, owners.

SID DAVILLA'S MARDI GRAS LOUNGE, 333 Bourbon St.; MA 8610. Open six days a week, closed Sundays. No cover or minimum. Sid Davilla, owner.

GORDON NATAL'S LOUNGE, 7716 Chef Menteur Highway; FR 9255. Open seven days a week. No cover or minimum. Gordon Natal, owner.

PADDOCK LOUNGE, 309 Bourbon St.; MA 9648. Open seven days a week. No cover charge. Minimum: 75 cents. Steve Valenti, manager.

CARL LILLER'S LOUNGE, 103 Airline Highway; VE 5-5281. Open seven days a week. Cover charge: Weekly nights $1.15; weekends $1.50. Carl Liller, owner.

NEW YORK

BASIN STREET, 209 W. 51st St.; PLaza 7-3728. Open six days a week. No cover charge. Admission: $1.80. Minimum: $2.50. Ralph Watkins, manager.

BIRDLAND, 1678 Broadway; JUdson 6-7333. Open seven days a week. No cover charge. Minimum: Tuesday through Sunday, $1.50 admission; dining room section, $2.50 minimum; lounge section and bar, no minimum;

Monday nights only (jam session), $1.25 admission, no minimum. Oscar Goodstein, manager.

CAFE BOHEMIA, 15 Barrow St.; CHelsea 3-9274. Open six days a week, closed Tuesday nights. No cover charge. No minimum at bar. Minimum at tables: $3.50 on Friday and Saturday, $2.50 other nights. Jimmy Garofolo, owner.

CENTRAL PLAZA, 111 Second Ave.; ALgonquin 4-9800. Open Friday and Saturday nights. No cover charge. Minimum: Friday admission $1.80, Saturday admission $2. Jack Crystal, manager.

CHILDS PARAMOUNT, 1501 Broadway at 44th St.; PEnnsylvania 6-3885. Open Friday, Saturday, Sunday. No cover or minimum. Bob Maltz, manager.

THE COMPOSER, 68 W. 58th St.; PLaza 9-6683. Open seven days a week. No cover charge. Minimum: $2.50. Cy Baron and Willie Shores, owners.

EDDIE CONDON'S, 47 W. Third St.; GRamercy 5-8639. Open six days a week. No cover charge. Minimum: $3. Eddie Condon, owner.

EMBERS, 161 E. 54th St.; PLaza 9-3228. Open seven days a week. No cover charge. Minimum: Monday through Thursday $3.50; Friday and Saturday $4; Sunday $3. Ralph Watkins, owner.

THE HICKORY HOUSE, 144 W. 52nd St.; JUdson 6-1150. Open seven days a week. No cover or minimum. John Popkin, manager.

NICK'S TAVERN, INC., 170 W. 10th St.; CHelsea 2-6683. Open six days a week. No cover charge. Minimum: $2.50. Frank Harvey, manager.

THE PLAYHOUSE, 208 W. 118th St.; UNiversity 4-9228. Open seven days a week. No cover charge. Minimum: $1. Teddy Hill, manager.

JIMMY RYAN'S, 53 W. 52nd St.; ELdorado 5-9600. Open six days a week. No cover or minimum. Jimmy Ryan, manager.

PHILADELPHIA

JACK FIELD'S BLUE NOTE, 15th and Ridge Ave.; ST 7-1730. Open Monday through Saturday. No cover or minimum. Jack Fields, manager.

PEP'S MUSICAL SHOW BAR, 516 S. Broad St.; PE 5-6206. Open six days a week. No cover or minimum. Bill Gerson, manager.

SHOWBOAT, Broad and Lombard Sts.; KI 5-9848. Open six days a week. No cover or minimum. Herb Kellar, owner.

SAN FRANCISCO

BLACKHAWK, 200 Hyde; GR 4-9567. Open seven days a week. No cover charge. Minimum: Two drinks. John Noga, Guido Caciniti, managers.

FACK'S II, 960 Bush St.; GA 1-9675. Open six days a week. Cover charge: $1. Minimum: Two drinks a show. George and Nick Andros, managers.

CLUB HANGOVER, 729 Bush St.; GA 1-0743. Open six days a week, closed Sundays. No cover or minimum. Doc Dougherty, manager.

THE TIN ANGEL, 987 Embarcadero; SU 1-2364. Open six days a week. Cover charge: $1. No minimum. Peggy Tolk-Watkins, owner.

JAZZ ORGANIZATIONS
and
RECORD COMPANIES

AMERICAN JAZZ FESTIVAL, NEWPORT, RHODE ISLAND. The jazz festival is a non-profit corporation organized "to encourage America's enjoyment of jazz and to sponsor the study of jazz, a true American art form." It came into being after Mrs. Louis L. Lorillard, attending a series of jazz classes given by George Wein at Boston University, became deeply interested in jazz. The officers are: Louis L. Lorillard, President; George T. Wein, Vice-President; Richard Sheffield, Secretary; Jeremiah P. Maloney, Treasurer. The directors are the officers and: John Hammond, Charles Bourgeois, Mrs. Louis L. Lorillard, Claiborne Pell, Prof. Marshall Stearns, Miss Terri Turner.

The first national jazz festival ever held in the United States was presented at Newport, Rhode Island July 17-18, 1954 in the Newport Casino. The 1955 and '56 festivals were presented at Freebody Park in Newport. Plans have been under discussion for similar presentations overseas under the auspices of the jazz festival organization.

Further details may be obtained by writing to The American Jazz Festival, Newport, Rhode Island, or c/o Miss Terri Turner, Copley Square Hotel, Boston, Massachusetts.

RECORD COMPANIES

Ad Lib, 20-43 19th St., Long Island City 5, N.Y.
Aladdin, 451 North Canon Drive, Beverly Hills, Calif.
Allegro, 510 22nd St., Union City, N.J.
American Recording Society, 100 6th Ave., New York, N.Y.
Angel, 38 West 48th St., New York 36, N.Y.
Apollo, 457 West 45th St., New York 36, N.Y.
Atlantic, 234 West 56th St., New York 19, N.Y.
Bethlehem, 1650 Broadway, New York 19, N.Y.
Blue Note, 767 Lexington Ave., New York 21, N.Y.
Brunswick, 50 West 57th St., New York 19, N.Y.
Cadence, 40 East 49th St., New York, N.Y.
Camden, 155 E. 24th St., New York 10, N.Y.
Capitol, Sunset and Vine, Hollywood 28, Calif.
Cavalier, 298 9th St., San Francisco 3, Calif.
Clef, 451 No. Canon Drive, Beverly Hills, Calif.
Columbia, 799 Seventh Ave., New York 19, N.Y.
Commodore, 147 East 42nd St., New York 17, N.Y.
Concert Hall Society Inc.: *see* Jazztone Society.
Contemporary, 8481 Melrose Place, Los Angeles 46, Calif.
Cook Laboratories, 101 Second Street, Stamford, Conn.
Coral, 50 West 57th St., New York 19, N.Y.
Dawn, 39 West 60th St., New York 23, N.Y.
Debut, 331 West 51st St., New York, N.Y.
Decca, 50 West 57th St., New York 19, N.Y.
Delmar, 5663 Delmar Ave., St. Louis, Mo.
Dootone, 9514 Central Ave., Los Angeles, Calif.
Down Home: *see* Clef.
EmArcy, 745 Fifth Ave., New York 22, N.Y.

Empirical, P.O. Box 52, Yellow Springs, Ohio.

Epic, 799 Seventh Ave., New York 19, N.Y.

Esoteric, 238 East 26th St., New York, N.Y.

Euterpean, 506 South Coast Blvd., Laguna Beach, Calif.

Fantasy, 654 Natoma St., San Francisco 3, Calif.

Folkways, 117 West 46th St., New York, N.Y.

Fraternity, 413 Race St., Cincinnati, Ohio.

Gene Norman Presents, 8600 Lookout Mt. Ave., Hollywood 6, Calif.

Good Time Jazz, 8481 Melrose Ave., Los Angeles 46, Calif.

Groove, 155 East 24th St., New York 10, N.Y.

Herald, 1697 Broadway, New York, N.Y.

HiFiRecord (High Fidelity Recordings, Inc.), 6087 Sunset Blvd., Hollywood 28, Calif.

Imperial, 137-139 North Western Ave., Los Angeles, Calif.

Jaguar, 1650 Broadway, New York 19, N.Y.

Jay-Dee, 1619 Broadway, New York 19, N.Y.

Jazz Man, 6420 Santa Monica Blvd., Hollywood 38, Calif.

Jazzology, 3918 Bergenline Ave., Union City, N.J.

Jazztone Society, Dept. E-3, 43 West 61st St., New York 23, N.Y.

Jazz: West, 451 No. Canon Drive, Beverly Hills, Calif.

Jubilee, 1650 Broadway, New York 19, N.Y.

Keynote, 267 Fifth Ave., New York, N.Y.

King, 1540 Brewster Ave., Cincinnati, Ohio.

Liberty, 1556 No. La Brea, Hollywood, Calif.

London, 539 West 25th St., New York 1, N.Y.

Mercury, 35 East Wacker Drive, Chicago, Ill.

MGM, 701 Seventh Ave., New York 36, N.Y.

Modern, 9317 West Washington Blvd., Culver City, Calif.

Norgran, 451 No. Canon Drive, Beverly Hills, Calif.

Pacific Jazz, 7614 Melrose Drive, Hollywood 46, Calif.

Paramount, 1637 North Ashland, Chicago, Ill.

Pax, 3918 Bergenline Ave., Union City, N.J.

Period, 304 East 74th St., New York 21, N.Y.

Prestige, 446 West 50th St., New York 19, N.Y.

Progressive, 25 Spruce St., Jersey City 6, N.J.

Rainbow, 767 Tenth Ave., New York 19, N.Y.

Remington, 551 Fifth Ave., New York 17, N.Y.

Riverside, 418 West 49th St., New York 19, N.Y.

Roost, 625 Tenth Ave., New York 36, N.Y.

Savoy, 58 Market St., Newark, N.J.

S/D, 1637 No. Ashland Ave., Chicago, Ill.

Seeco, 39 West 60th St., New York 23, N.Y.

Signal, 580 Fifth Ave., New York, N.Y.

Southland, 520 St. Louis St., New Orleans 16, La.

Starlite, 6671 Sunset Blvd., Hollywood 28, Calif.

Storyville, 75 State St., Boston, Mass.

Sunset, 6671 Sunset Blvd., Hollywood 28, Calif.

Tempo, 8540 Sunset Blvd., Hollywood 46, Calif.

Tico, 220 West 42nd St., New York 36, N.Y.

Transition, 6 Ashton Place, Cambridge, Mass.

Urania, 40 East 19th St., New York 3, N.Y.

Vanguard, 256 West 55th St., New York 19, N.Y.

Verve, 451 No. Canon Drive, Beverly Hills, Calif.

Victor, 155 East 24th St., New York 10, N.Y.

Vik (formerly "X"), 155 East 24th St., New York 10, N.Y.

Weathers Industries, 66 East Gloucester Pike, Barrington, N.J.

Westminster, 275 Seventh Ave., New York 1, N.Y.

Windin' Ball, 5207 South Kimbark Ave., Chicago 15, Ill.

HOW TO REACH THE STARS

*F*ollowing are the principal booking agencies that specialize in the handling of jazz talent, or of artists in closely related fields.

WILLARD ALEXANDER, INC., 30 Rockefeller Plaza, New York, N.Y., CIrcle 6-4224; 333 North Michigan, Chicago, Ill., CEntral 6-2395; c/o Harold Jovien, Premiere Attractions, 1046 North Carol Drive, Hollywood, Calif., CRestview 4-5488.

Artists: Count Basie, Matt Dennis, Tal Farlow, Bud Freeman, Urbie Green, Ray McKinley (directing Glenn Miller band), Phineas Newborn, Boyd Raeburn, Charlie Rouse-Julius Watkins (Les Modes), Jeri Southern, Joe Venuto.

ASSOCIATED BOOKING CORP., 745 Fifth Avenue, New York 22, N.Y., PLaza 9-4600; 203 North Wabash Ave., Chicago, Ill., CEntral 6-9451; 8619 Sunset Blvd., Hollywood 46, Calif., CRestview 1-8131.

Artists: Julian "Cannonball" Adderley, Henry "Red" Allen, Louis Armstrong, Lillian Armstrong, Australian Jazz Quartet, Georgie Auld, Chet Baker, Al Belletto, Les Brown, Dave Brubeck, Joe Bushkin, Conte Candoli, Barbara Carroll, Page Cavanaugh, Eddie Condon, Buddy De Franco, Dorothy Donegan, Duke Ellington, Don Elliott, Herbie Fields, Erroll Garner, Terry Gibbs, Jerry Gray, Buddy Greco, Bobby Hackett, Chico Hamilton, Lionel Hampton, Woody Herman, Earl Hines, Jutta Hipp, Art Hodes, Billie Holiday, Helen Humes, Lurlean Hunter, Calvin Jackson, Ahmad Jamal, Herb Jeffries, J. J. Johnson, Max Kaminsky, Lee Konitz, Roy Kral & Jackie Cain, Gene Krupa, Elliot Lawrence, Joe Loco, Wingy Manone, Joe Marsala, Marian McPartland, Carmen McRae, Helen Merrill, Gerry Mulligan, Rose Murphy, Vido Musso, Marty Napoleon, Paul Nero, Red Nichols, Anita O'Day, Kid Ory, Leo Parker, The Peters Sisters, Max Roach & Donald Byrd, Red Rodney, Frank Rosolino, Hazel Scott, Bud Shank, Ralph Sharon, George Shearing, Don Shirley, Bobby Short, Eddie South, Muggsy Spanier, Ralph Sutton, Sylvia Syms, Billy Taylor, Jack Teagarden, Dinah Washington, Teddy Wilson, Kai Winding.

GALE AGENCY INC., 48 West 48th Street, New York 36, N.Y., PLaza 7-7100; Milton Deutsch, 9157 Sunset Blvd., Hollywood, Calif., CRestview 4-7321.

Artists: Paul Barbarin, Lavern Baker, Eddie Bonnemere, Paul Bley, Eddie "Lockjaw" Davis, Wild Bill Davison, Ella Fitzgerald, Erskine Hawkins, Eddie Heywood, Al Hibbler, Joe Holiday, Illinois Jacquet, Buddy Johnson, Beverly Kenney, George Kirby, George Lewis, Gene Mayl (Dixie Rhythm Kings), Mitchell-Ruff, Turk Murphy, Bud Powell, Paul Quinichette, Jimmy Rushing, Johnny Smith, Cal Tjader, Mel Tormé, Sarah Vaughan, Enrique Villegas, Josh White, Lester Young.

GENERAL ARTISTS CORPORATION, The Americas Bldg., Rockefeller Center, New York 20, N.Y., CIrcle 7-7750; 8 South Michigan, Chicago, Ill., STate 2-6288; 9650 Santa Monica Blvd., Beverly Hills, Calif., CRestview 1-8101.

Artists: Tommy Alexander, June Christy, Nat Cole, Perry Como, Kenny Dorham, Maynard Ferguson, Ralph Flanagan, Stan Free, Four Freshmen, Georgia Gibbs, Art Hodes, Bobby Jaspar, Jazz Prophets, Louis Jordan, Kitty Kallen, Stan Kenton, Frankie Laine, Peggy Lee, Gloria Mann, Ralph Marterie, Billy May, Hal McIntyre, Milcombo, Art Mooney, Russ Morgan, Buddy Morrow, Helen O'Connell, Patti Page, Tony Pastor, Johnny Ray, Something Smith, Lennie Sonn, Kay Starr, Margaret Whiting, George Williams.

JAZZ ARTISTS MANAGEMENT, 15 East 48th Street, New York, N.Y., MUrray Hill 8-3724.

Artists: Paul Bley, Chris Connor, Don Heller, Jay Jay Johnson, Mitchell-Ruff, The Modern Jazz Quartet, Mark Murphy, Sylvia Syms, George Wallington, Kai Winding.

WILLIAM MORRIS AGENCY, INC., 1740 Broadway, New York, N.Y., JUdson 6-5100; 919 North Michigan Ave., Chicago, Ill., WHitehall 3-1744; 151 El Camino Drive, Beverly Hills, Calif., CRestview 4-7451.

Artists: Sammy Davis, Jr., Billy Eckstine, Eartha Kitt, Elvis Presley, Maurice Rocco, Bobby Scott.

MUSIC CORPORATION OF AMERICA, 598 Madison Avenue, New York 22, N.Y., PLaza 9-7500; 430 N. Michigan Ave., Chicago, Ill., DElaware 7-1100; 9370 Santa Monica Blvd., Beverly Hills, Calif., CRestview 6-2001.

Artists: Charlie Barnet, Tex Beneke, Billy Butterfield, Les Elgart, Harry James, Conrad Janis, Johnny Long, Shelly Manne, Kid Ory, Perez Prado, Shorty Rogers, Stan Rubin, Charlie Spivak.

SHAW ARTISTS CORP., 565 Fifth Ave., New York 17, N.Y., MUrray Hill 8-2230; 203 North Wabash Ave., Chicago, Ill., RAndolph 6-0131.

Artists: Sidney Bechet, Pia Beck, Art Blakey, Ruth Brown, Hadda Brooks, Milt Buckner, Don Byas, Candido, Benny Carter, Ray Charles, Buck Clayton, Cozy Cole, Chris Connor, Wild Bill Davis, Miles Davis, Joe Derise, Bo Diddley, Lou Donaldson, Bill Doggett, Roy Eldridge, Allen Eager, Slim Gaillard, Linton Garner, Stan Getz, Dizzy Gillespie, Johnny Hartman, Hampton Hawes, Coleman Hawkins, Johnny Hodges, Jazz Messengers, Jo Jones, Jonah Jones, Herbie Mann, Howard McGhee, Charlie Mingus, Modern Jazz Quartet, Oscar Peterson, Flip Phillips, Joe Roland, Sahib Shihab, Leon Sash, Charlie Shavers, Eddie Shu, Jimmy Smith, Rex Stewart, Slam Stewart, Sonny Stitt, Art Tatum, Jean Thielemans, Ben Webster.

UNIVERSAL ATTRACTIONS, 2 Park Avenue, New York 16, N.Y., MU 3-3282; 3984 Southwestern, Los Angeles, Calif., AX 2-0517.

Artists: Earl Bostic, Tiny Bradshaw, Teddy Charles, Arnett Cobb, Bennie Green, Willis Jackson, Big Jay McNeely, Jay McShann, James Moody, Tony Scott, Tab Smith, Sir Charles Thompson, Charlie Ventura, Randy Weston, Cootie Williams.

THE NEW YEARBOOK OF JAZZ

Erik Satie, the French composer, once said about American jazz, "Jazz cries out its soul and nobody cares." That is no longer true of America . . . Jazz is a contemporary, vital, immediate expression of the soul of the people. Therefore, we care.

—DAVE BRUBECK

CONTENTS

ILLUSTRATIONS

AUTHOR'S NOTE

Since the appearance of *The Encyclopedia of Jazz*, 1955 (Volume One in this series), and of *The Encyclopedia Yearbook of Jazz*, 1956 (Volume Two), there have been new developments not only in jazz but in our plans to keep the reader abreast of them.

Because there seemed to be an urgent need for a comprehensive guide-book with a chapter-by-chapter, instrument-by-instrument delineation of the story of jazz, and with actual musical examples of the work of the greatest soloists, much of 1957 was devoted to the writing and publication of *The Book of Jazz*, in which I attempted to fulfil this need. As a result, there was no additional volume in the *Encyclopedia* series.

To bridge the two-year gap, and to cover more fully than before every important aspect of the greatly expanded jazz scene, several additional features have been included in the present volume. Among them are contributions from representatives of four foreign countries where both native and imported jazz has flourished more prosperously than ever before; a discussion of the significant rapprochement between jazz and classical music; a survey of the relationship between jazz and other contemporary art forms; and a history of the important role played by the phonograph and other reproduction systems in preserving jazz.

I am deeply grateful to Benny Green, Daniel Filipacchi, Carl-Erik Lindgren and Joachim E. Berendt for the overseas reports; and to Bill Russo, Charles Graham and Martin Williams for the other chapters cited above. In the case of Martin Williams, my thanks are due not only for the chapter that carries his byline, but also for the very substantial assistance he offered in compiling the rest of the book, including the assembling and writing of a large proportion of the biographical section. He was not only a valued collaborator but a congenial and efficient associate.

Jean Barnett, whose presence made the work on Volume Two so much easier, was again tremendously helpful. Thanks are also due to my unabatedly patient wife for her general assistance; and to many who volunteered their help in collating material, notably Howard Lucraft, of Jazz International in Hollywood; Ira Gitler and Bob Bach in New York and Steve Race in London.

For the photographs I am indebted to the press departments of NBC, CBS and of individual television stations, as well as to Nat Hentoff, to Hanns E. Haehl, of *Jazz Im Bild*, and to the photographers whose names will be found adjacent to the pictures.

INTRODUCTION

by

John Hammond

*I*t has been almost a quarter of a century since I first came across Leonard Feather, that indefatigable chronicler of the jazz scene. Then, as now, our opinions about music were often in violent conflict; but his resourcefulness and industry could always be envied.

Leonard has had a quite unbelievable career in jazz. He once operated simultaneously as composer, arranger, instrumentalist, publicist and critic—a feat never duplicated, before or since. What's more, he has been effective in all these fields, except possibly as pianist. His energy is legendary, and his knowledge awesome. Both in his private and public life he has been a consistent and effective foe of Jim Crow.

All of us in jazz can be deeply grateful to him for *The Encyclopedia of Jazz*, without which only a few could pose as authorities on the subject. It is the *Who's Who*, *Webster's* and *Grove's* of the field, and it has been a motivating force in the appreciation of jazz as a serious art form.

How ironic it is that our leading writer on what is supposed to be America's most significant contribution to the arts is an ex-Britisher who arrived here in the middle thirties. The fact is that the English jazz fan of the early thirties was far better informed about America's improvising musicians than we were. At that time, there were a great number of Englishmen with even more knowledge than Leonard—but none with his energy or drive. Incidentally, I shall never forget that it was English Columbia that gave me my first job, in 1933, recording jazz for which there was a demand in Great Britain that the American companies were unwilling to satisfy.

Leonard Feather's first visit to America was in 1935, and I recall being on the pier waiting for the *Normandie* to dock. Within a few days, he had combed Harlem, placed some songs with Clarence Williams, and arranged to become (gratis) the London correspondent of the *New York Amsterdam News*. For the next four years he shuttled between the two countries; it was then that he acquired the experience that made him the unique figure he has become in American jazz. He wrote tunes for Irving Mills' publishing firm; later he became confidant and press agent to his idol, Duke Ellington; supervised recording sessions, wrote for every conceivable musical publication here and abroad, and in 1943 joined *Esquire* as a staff writer. During the war there was great interest in jazz, both among servicemen and civilians; Leonard was directly responsible, with Robert Goffin, for the yearly polls run by *Esquire*, the first non-specialized publication to take jazz seriously. Many writers and musicians voted for their favorite instrumentalists, singers, bands and arrangers; *Esquire* sponsored annual jazz concerts, the first of which was held at the Metropolitan Opera House, featuring the winners.

Up to 1949 Leonard was about the busiest man on the jazz scene, writing, promoting, recording, broadcasting, and becoming involved with various artists. Then his life suddenly changed. While crossing a street on a wintry day, he and his wife were run over by a driverless car whose parking brakes had slipped. For weeks he was on the brink of death.

Those months in the hospital transformed Leonard in many ways. In recent years his musical horizons have widened; today he is a great, constructive force on the musical scene, a selfless, considerate human being, eager to help others, and always working toward the elevation of jazz as an art form.

In the first volume of *The Encyclopedia of Jazz*, the author imposed the sensible limitation of biographies to those musicians whose work was available on long playing records. In 1955 many of the great performances of the earlier jazz stars had not been reissued on LPs, whereas now there is a really representative grouping of all types of jazz available at all speeds. With this third volume in the *Encyclopedia* series, it is safe to say that there is scarcely an important name omitted.

In the year 1958 it remains just as difficult as ever to agree on a definition of jazz. Certainly much of the tortured, cerebral gropings of the Tristano and Mingus schools have more to do with the League of Composers' concerts of the twenties and thirties than with the uninhibited improvisation of earlier days.

This new volume has many guideposts to the appreciation of jazz besides all the new biographies: the fascinating blindfold tests of famous musicians, results of polls, reports from overseas, history of the record business—and even a dissection of that curious breed, the jazz critic. He also has a chapter on jazz and classical music with which I take issue.

I may still disagree with Leonard about what constitutes jazz, but I will always be in his debt for his cataloguing of its achievements in the various volumes of *The Encyclopedia of Jazz*.

THE NEW YEARBOOK OF JAZZ

JAZZ U.S.A.

As far as can be determined from the often conflicting recollections of the surviving pioneers, jazz as a fairly distinct style of music has been with us since the turn of the twentieth century; yet it was not until this century was more than half over that it began to earn substantial acceptance both as an art form and as a part of the American Big Business tradition.

The esthetic recognition came a little sooner than the economic acknowledgment. The report in volume two, *The Encyclopedia Yearbook of Jazz*, in the chapter titled "What's Happening in Jazz," indicated in some detail the extent to which the music had matured artistically and earned social respectability. What held true in 1956 had multiplied many times in intensity by mid-1958. Jazz had extended its horizons, found important new media, and bigger and immeasurably better ways of channeling itself to the general public at home and abroad.

The tentative interest that had been shown by the United States State Department in 1956 in underwriting a tour of the Near East by John (Dizzy) Gillespie's orchestra developed into an almost continuous project. Further undertakings involved the dispatching of the Gillespie band to Latin America, later in 1956; the partial sponsoring of Benny Goodman's visit to the Far East in the winter of '56-7, the subsidizing of an African safari in 1957 by the Wilbur de Paris combo, which included appearances at the Ghana independence celebrations and a 16-week tour of successful visits to Nigeria, Liberia, the Belgian Congo, French Equatorial Africa, Tanganyika, Uganda, Ethiopia, Libya, Tunisia, Algeria and Morocco; and the planning for Woody Herman's orchestra of a similar 10-week invasion of the South American countries in late 1958.

Visits such as these, supplemented by the far more numerous non-subsidized tours made by name bands and combos and by individual musicians, showed more vividly than ever before the impact of American jazz as a treasured cultural import in dozens of countries. A few days after Vice-President Nixon had been stoned and spat upon in Caracas, Venezuela, somebody asked Mrs. Louis Armstrong how she and her husband had been treated on their visit to Caracas and elsewhere in Latin America. She replied that the crowds had mobbed them with such ecstatic enthusiasm that "they almost put us out of business with affection," and added, "You can win more friends with music than with politics."

Typical of the incidents that made these visits unforgettable for the musicians was the reception accorded Benny Goodman in Thailand when, at the Palace in Bangkok, his band played for King Phumipol Aduljej. Knowing that His Majesty was a jazz fan, and an amateur musician, Goodman presented him with a clarinet. During the command performance the King left his new horn untouched, but gingerly picked up a saxophone and ad libbed with Goodman and the rhythm section. Later, after Benny had left the stand, the King shyly took up the clarinet and began to play a tune long associated with the Goodman Sextet, *Memories of You*. According to a spectator, Hal Davis, who reported on the scene for *The Saturday Review*, "Diplomats present commented that there could be no better way of cementing friendly relations . . . it has been a proud time for Goodman and American music. Russia may match our atomic weapons and jet planes—but she will find it impossible to compete with hot jazz, Cold War or no."

While jazz continued to expand geographically (fuller details will be found in the *Jazz Overseas* chapter in this volume), it found new strength domestically in widely diverse areas. One was the lay press. A jam session at Carnegie Hall, or an appearance by the Modern Jazz Quartet in solemn recital at Town Hall, was just as sure of a long and sometimes ponderous review in the New York *Times* and *Herald Tribune* as was an appearance by a symphony or chamber group. Even tabloids like the New York *Daily News* had their built-in jazz critics, reporting at length on the esthetic values of the new combos at the Composer or Birdland. This was true not only in New York but of scores of papers in cities and towns across the country, many of which accorded considerable space to jazz record reviews as well as general commentary. This development is particularly remarkable if one bears in mind that not many years ago these newspapers were completely unaware of jazz, unless a juicy news story came along involving a musician with narcotics.

The intellectual magazines and slick periodicals also found jazz. *The New Yorker*, which for a quarter-century had limited its coverage to an occasional feature (such as the Profiles on John Hammond, Ellington and Gillespie) started a jazz department and ran it more and more often. *The Saturday Review*, which could have helped bring jazz out of the cellars decades earlier but had chosen virtually to ignore it, began to carry jazz features and record reviews twice a month. Various magazines aimed at hi-fi enthusiasts (*High Fidelity*, *Hi-Fi Music at Home*, *Hi-Fi and Music Review* and others) assumed a similarly benign attitude toward jazz. *Esquire*, which had been exceptionally prescient with its annual polls and monthly features from 1944-47 but had then climbed slowly off the jazz wagon, gradually climbed back on and by the summer of 1958 celebrated its return with a special jazz issue. Meanwhile, *Playboy* started a series of annual polls, the first of which, published in February 1957, showed a series of vote-totals that were staggering when compared with those of the music magazines to which jazz polls had previously been confined. The impact of the poll was supplemented by a two-volume album featuring the winners. Other magazines of the *Playboy* stripe followed its example in running occasional jazz features; one of them, *Escapade*, sponsored an unusual music-and-talk LP with Bobby Troup as moderator and Jack Teagarden heading the list of player-panelists.

Of course, there were further explorations into jazz by writers of the type that would be stigmatized in the tabloids as "eggheads." More often than not they were concerned with ancient jazz history; a story about the early jazz drummer, Baby Dodds, appeared in a *recherché* quarterly. But there were increasing signs, during 1956-58, of a split among the champions of jazz into intellectual (or pseudo-intellectual) and anti-intellectual forces. The split was, in fact, evident both in the music itself and in the writing devoted to it.

The anti-intellectual attitude was perhaps best expressed in 1957 by Douglas Watt, an experienced writer whose jazz reports have often been seen in the New York *Daily News* and *The New Yorker*. "The experts," he lamented, "have finally taken over, and the music that was distinguished by its spontaneity and gaiety has become . . . a carefully thought-out exercise." The Modern Jazz Quartet, in his opinion, is "one of the most unjazzlike units on the scene; it produces sensitive chamber music with echoes of jazz in it."

Less sensitive evaluations from approximately the same standpoint came from Robert Ruark in a syndicated column regretting the transference of Eddie Condon's night club from Greenwich Village to the fashionable East Side, and proclaiming: "Mr. Condon is a professional minstrel who specializes in jazz and is also a sort of bum like me . . . I don't care about all the cultured approaches to jazz . . . jazz calls for dim lights and lousy service and a bunch of worthless people to make it jump." Other such remarks came from the author and columnist, Robert Sylvester, who from time to time has issued such pronunciamentos as "most jazz musicians are irresponsible bums"; and from Arthur Godfrey, who in 1958 informed the world that he was ready to "rescue jazz from the intellectuals" and bring it "back to the man on the street level."

The attitudes of Watt, Ruark, Sylvester, Godfrey and of many others (among them Richard Gehman, Eddie Condon's ghost-writer, and the New York *Journal-American* TV columnist, Jack O'Brian) who love jazz and have helped to propagate it but are aggressively anti-intellectual, contrast sharply with both the viewpoints and the writing style of their adversaries. The following passage, for instance, is quoted from André Hodeir's *Jazz: Its Evolution and Essence*, which enjoyed a considerable *succès d'estime* in this country in 1956-57:

" . . . the theme phrase is more stripped, less diffuse, because it has less ornamentation than the variation phrase. The latter may be subdivided into two principal types, the paraphrase and the chorus phrase . . . unless we are greatly mistaken, the chorus phrase does not have an exact equivalent in European music. It behaves and looks like a variation, but it does not arise directly from any melodic theme. Its rhythmic equilibrium depends on the instrument by which it is expressed. Usually abundant, it can be ornamented to the same degree as a melodic phrase."

The following paragraph appeared in the album notes by Nat Hentoff for an LP by Gerry Mulligan and Paul Desmond:

"As for some of the songs, there is an intimation of a figurative coronary occlusion in *Standstill*; *Wintersong* is a litany for more mnemonic foolishness; *Battle Hymn of the Republican* . . . has at least enough Lapsang Souchong left for *Alice and the Mad Hatter*; and *Fall Out* is a hortatory celebration of natural genetics rather than an essay on possible genocide."

It is this writer's feeling that much of the lack of rapport between musicians and non-musicians, as well as between intellectuals and anti-intellectuals, can be attributed simply to the fact that there is an utter lack of any meeting of the minds between them. A non-jazzman writing for a quarterly review is no more capable of understanding what really goes through a musician's mind when he plays a solo than the musician is able to understand, or even take seriously, the pompous polysyllables with which his work is dissected. But there was ample evidence, during 1956-58, that intellectuals and anti-intellectuals alike were working, in effect, for the ultimate good of jazz, by stirring up interest in ever wider areas.

The intellectual adoption of jazz extended during these same years to other arts. In a later chapter, Martin Williams deals with the phenomenon of the poetry-with-jazz-background, which during 1957 was a localized fad and by 1958 had become a coast-to-coast curiosity. Still another oddity was the linking of the graphic arts with jazz. On NBC Gilbert Seldes pointed to a reproduction of a painting by the Dutch artist, Mondrian, called *Broadway Boogie Woogie*, "in which," he declared, "the critics find the snapping rhythms of modern American music." At the Vanguard in Greenwich Village, an artist and illustrator named Don Freeman clambered down to the basement night club to draw abstracts and scenes of New York night life with luminous chalk, to the accompaniment of jazz, both live and on records.

Bruce Mitchell, a painter and jazz enthusiast, is attached to the Fine Arts Department of the University of Pittsburgh. Early in his career he narrowly escaped jobs as vocalist with the bands of Paul Whiteman and Benny Goodman. In New Orleans with Doc Souchon's combo, at Music Inn with Randy Weston's quartet, and at New York University with Tony Scott's group, Mitchell illustrated his technique of drawing and painting to jazz; recently, he even tried it on a local TV show with the Oscar Peterson trio. "Whatever I do in painting relates to the sounds I hear," he says. "The entire painting area has to swing in relationship to the music before any individual area is particularized." Mitchell begins his appearances with a short discourse on line and curve—in harmony and contrast—pointing up the fact that music, too, has form relationships such as unison, counterpoint, etc.

It does not seem that too many intermediary steps are left before some enterprising promoter may invite Frank Lloyd Wright to design a new skyscraper to a background of an extended work by Teo Macero.

If jazz reached a new peak of acceptance among advocates of the other arts, it was no less successful in making inroads on a less predictable plane—the world of society. Following the lead of Mr. and Mrs. Louis L. Lorillard, who had converted to jazz many of the élite in their Newport, Rhode Island, social world, a socially prominent stockbroker-turned-jazz-pianist-turned-promoter, Fran Thorne, earned a new identity as the organizer of the very successful Great South Bay Jazz Festival in Long Island, New York. Lord Montagu of Beaulieu announced in the spring of 1958 that he would turn over the grounds of his estate in the New Forest to the staging of a two-day jazz festival.

In England similar associations have long been commonplace, with Lord Donegall a boisterous advocate of traditionalist jazz, and the Hon. Gerald Lascelles, a cousin of the Queen, busying himself as a jazz promoter and co-editor of an anthological book mainly devoted to early jazz styles.

In or out of society, the jazz festival (or, in some cases, the hastily-assembled, one-night stand palmed off as a festival) by 1958 had spread like a pyramid club. In the summer season, not only were there a four-day fiesta at Newport, marking the fifth year in an increasingly well-received series, and the above-mentioned Great South Bay event, but also a three-day jazz episode (organized by George Wein, of the Newport festival) as part of the four-week music festival in French Lick, Indiana; a jazz night at the annual Boston Arts Festival; five jazz concerts at the sixth annual drama, music, art and film festival in Stratford, Ontario; five concerts in the first International Festival of the Arts in Vancouver, British Columbia; jazz as part of the regular Ravinia music festival in Highland Park, Illinois; and a West Coast jazz festival planned for October 1958 in the fairgrounds on the Carmel-Monterey peninsula. All these were major events involving nationally known talent of the Ellington-Brubeck-Fitzgerald class. New York City has its own annual festival at Randall's Island, which began in the summer of 1956. In Europe, where the jazz festival idea had originated (the first were held in Nice and Paris in 1948), there was a similar eruption of interest as new festival sites were set. At the second National Jazz Festival in Rome (six straight nights in May 1958), the Modern Jazz Quartet seemed to be a main influence on many groups that came from small provincial towns to play in one of Rome's biggest theatres; the gala affair was a tremendous success.

The academic strides made by jazz in 1956-58 were without precedent and had the greatest possible significance for the future. The most important development was the foundation of an actual school of jazz as part of the summer activities at Music Inn in Lenox, Massachusetts. The first three-week course was given in August 1957 with 34 students enjoying tuition by a faculty comprising such figures as John Lewis, Dizzy Gillespie, Max Roach, Ray Brown, Oscar Peterson, Bill Russo, Jimmy Giuffre and Marshall Stearns.

The number of colleges offering jazz courses increased substantially each semester. They included Bradley University in Peoria, Illinois; Carleton College in Northfield, Minnesota; North Texas State in Denton, Texas; Boston University in Boston, Massachusetts; Northwestern University in Evanston, Illinois;

and many others. The Institute of Jazz Studies gave courses in adult education divisions in several areas in the East and offered a course for credit at Queen's College. When the Institute made available a syllabus of fifteen lectures on the history of jazz, containing an outline for each lecture plus a list of readings and records, the degree of interest shown in the teaching of the subject was indicated by the receipt of more than 400 requests for the syllabus.

As in previous years, there were numerous individual lectures on jazz at colleges in most parts of the country, though not very frequently in the South, where jazz presumably is too well-integrated an art to deserve close inspection. The Ford Foundation, however, made a $75,000 grant to Tulane University in New Orleans to collect an oral history of local jazz by tape-recorded interviews with survivors of the early era. The products of the research, to be kept in the archives at Tulane, were to be made available to everyone, regardless of race.

As jazz grew in every area of personal contact, its development in the scientific reproduction media expanded proportionately. The flood of jazz LPs, which in 1956 averaged about ninety a month, went well over the hundred mark in 1957; by 1958 the market was so badly glutted with good, bad and indifferent recorded jazz of every kind that signs of a recession began to set in. Verve, RCA Victor and other major labels decided to reduce the quantity of jazz LP releases. Even so, the number of new jazz records per month remained around a hundred, with at least a dozen or two more in the border zone between jazz and popular music. The small independent companies were able to cover their costs and perhaps make a small profit with the sale of a couple of thousand records, if a trio or union scale combo was involved. Production costs, however, were rising continually as cover designs tended to become more elaborate and expensive, and advertising had to be extended to numerous magazines; consequently, the break-even point generally was closer to five thousand, even for a small, economically run company.

Columbia, which probably now has as high an average sale as any company for its jazz releases, considered any record a flop that sold a mere ten thousand. Over an indefinite period of time, sales of twenty to twenty-five thousand were expected, even on LPs by the lesser artists, while several LPs by the top names such as Brubeck, Ellington and Garner each went well over the 100,000 figure. One of the biggest jazz hits of recent years, the album by Shelly Manne and André Previn on Contemporary of tunes from *My Fair Lady*, was also believed to have reached the 100,000 mark. Similarly impressive figures were achieved by Atlantic, Verve and several other labels well established in the jazz market.

The above figures are cited for the purpose of comparisons. Before the jazz boom began only five or six years ago, most jazz LPs were lucky to average a five to ten thousand sale.

Still another new method for the funneling of jazz to the public was opened up as more and more releases were scheduled in 1957 on stereophonic tape and also, beginning in 1958, on stereophonic discs. By mid-1958 stereophonic discs of modern jazz were available on Contemporary and Atlantic, and were being prepared for release on several other labels.

JIM CROW

By 1958 racial discrimination in American jazz was down for the count, but by no means out. A tacit quota system was still in force for most television bookings. In 1957-58 at least three well-known leaders switched to an all-white personnel for their combos; a couple of them were indiscreet enough to admit that this had been done in the interest of better-class bookings—a misguided and useless viewpoint, since by now there were few, if any, important clubs in America featuring jazz that had any objection to booking mixed groups. The West Coast jazz scene remained pretty much a white musicians' preserve, though Buddy Collette, Harry Edison and a few others nudged themselves into the élite circle that was grabbing off the juiciest studio assignments. And on both coasts, in June 1958, there was still not a single Negro musician on staff at NBC.

There were several curious developments on the racial front. Chauvinists complained to Chico Hamilton about his hiring of white sidemen; Eddie Condon's group at his club, which for years had been all-white and as such supposedly representative of this brand of Dixieland jazz, by 1958 included three Negro and three white sidemen. The general trend was toward mixed personnels, with bandleaders like Lionel Hampton and Benny Goodman, as well as combo leaders such as Charles Mingus, Teddy Charles, Gerry Mulligan, George Shearing and Tony Scott, choosing their sidemen without consideration of race. Segregation only held its ground, and in most cases this was more by chance than by design, in the big bands of Basie, Ellington and Herman, the combos of Max Roach, Art Blakey, and the Modern Jazz Quartet.

Perhaps because the South had more or less been written off as dead territory for musicians, there was a generally reduced tendency to appease it. Many artists simply refused to undertake any kind of Southern engagement. Norman Granz continued his aggressive policy of fighting Jim Crow with a musical boycott wherever and whenever it became necessary.

BOOKS

Like everything else in jazz, its bibliography multiplied at an incredible rate in 1956-58. A list of all the important books published on the subject will be found in the bibliography in this volume.

The best individual piece of writing directly connected with jazz during this period was a short article, *Joe Shulman Is Dead*, by Steve Allen. Originally published in *Down Beat*, it later appeared in a collection of short stories, *The Girls on the 10th Floor* (Henry Holt & Co.). Much of the rest of the book comprised fictional short stories, which unfortunately gave the impression that Allen's piece, written immediately after he had learned of the death of the young bassist, was also fictional. The article had all the qualities of warmth, sincerity and inside understanding of a musician's personality that have been lacking in practically all the fiction and non-fiction writing about jazz. If Allen ever took the time to write a novel about jazz musicians, there is little reason to doubt that it would be the first completely successful work of this nature.

RADIO

Radio was one of the few fields in which jazz made little or no progress. A few disc jockeys, such as those interviewed in the chapter on this subject in *The Encyclopedia Yearbook of Jazz* (Volume 2), continued to play jazz records. Some of them, however, had apparently ended their station affiliations in protest against the so-called "top forty" policy. Many radio stations required their disc jockeys to program only those records that had been reported among the top forty best sellers according to figures published in the trade papers. Since most of these reflect the taste of teen-agers, there was a strong tendency toward rock-'n'-roll tunes with infantile lyrics and a bare minimum of melodic line. As a result, the quality of popular music programs on radio deteriorated alarmingly.

It did not seem to occur to the executives of the radio stations that the teen-agers who made hits of these 98-cent records were not likely to be steady customers of the sponsors, whose wares included Cadillacs, refrigerators and washing machines. Thus the policy, though nominally decided in terms of popularity, actually was suicidal and seemed to be setting radio back twenty years. The process of grinding out programs of these records became so mechanical that many stations felt they no more needed disc jockeys than a jukebox does. As one New York radio-television columnist expressed it, "This can be the straw that breaks radio's back."

Of course, there were still a few jazz disc jockeys, but in most cases, even in New York and Los Angeles, they were heard through inconvenient outlets—on low-power or FM stations, or at an hour such as mid-afternoon or after midnight, when the audiences represented a mere fraction of the listening public available during the peak mid-evening hours.

As for live music on radio, the "remotes" from ballrooms featuring the better dance and jazz orchestras were a thing of the past. Live jazz continued to be used spasmodically on the NBC weekend program, *Monitor*. But to all intents, the one program that acted as the savior of jazz on radio was Mutual's *Bandstand USA*. Initiated July 6, 1956 at the Newport Jazz Festival, *Bandstand USA* was the creation of the clarinetist and bandleader Tommy Reynolds, who had gone into radio production at Mutual. Heard every Saturday evening for two hours, it comprised live broadcasts by leading jazz combos and bands from such New York clubs as Birdland, the Embers, the Bohemia and the Village Vanguard, as well as from jazz clubs in Boston, Camden (New Jersey), Washington and Philadelphia. The best measure of the reaction to the show was its expansion from the eighty-two stations that carried it at the outset to the more than three hundred Mutual outlets around the country that were taking it by the time it reached its second anniversary, in 1958. For all its popularity, *Bandstand USA*, after two years on the air, still had failed to acquire a sponsor and still was the only show of its kind in American radio.

TELEVISION

In strong contrast, the graph of jazz progress on television showed a continual upward curve. In fact, to many who were comparative newcomers to television, it seemed as though 1957 and 1958 were the years in which jazz was finally discovered on this medium.

Actually, this assumption is incorrect. In 1948-49, when television had not yet overtaken radio but was beginning to become a national institution, there were two network television jazz series. One was the Eddie Condon show, which Condon himself emceed and which featured mainly musicians who met Condon's somewhat special requirements. The Condon show was seen first on the NBC network; after its demise there, it was found for a while on WPIX, a local New York station. The other series was CBS' *Adventures In Jazz*, produced by Bob Bach, emceed at first by Freddie Robbins (later Bobby Sherwood and Bill Williams). This show was responsible for some of the most memorable jazz moments in the early television era: an appearance by Mildred Bailey; a nostalgic revival of the Artie Shaw-with-string-quartet format; a Dixieland-versus-modern battle; a fiftieth birthday celebration for Duke Ellington.

After these two shows went off the air, there was a long, jejune spell relieved only by an occasional glimpse of Louis Armstrong's handkerchief or by Duke Ellington playing "a medley of some of our award-winning compositions." Admittedly, these and a few other big jazz names edged their way into guest spots on some of the big network shows, but there was little or no regular jazz activity of any importance. Shows featuring such popular bands as the Dorsey Brothers or Ray Anthony made only incidental use of jazz.

In 1955 CBS presented ten shows entitled *Music '55* as a summer replacement series, with Stan Kenton moderating and leading an all-star New York band assembled and directed for him by Johnny Richards. The band usually only played one instrumental number per show, the rest of the half-hour being dedicated to various guest stars, the majority of whom were not jazz performers. A weekly show called *Stars of Jazz*, with Bobby Troup as moderator, began on the local ABC station in Hollywood in the summer of 1956 and was lucky enough to acquire a sponsor almost immediately. Also in 1956-57 there were the Sunday morning jazz-and-religion shows, such as *Look Up And Live*, discussed previously in Volume 2.

The story of how jazz finally eased itself into television as a commercially desirable entity rather than an occasional grudgingly welcomed visitor involved such steps as the series of courageous attempts by Steve Allen to disseminate jazz during his years in control of the NBC *Tonight* show; the use of "interviews in depth" with jazzmen (almost inevitably involving questions about narcotics, as when Stan Getz bared his soul to Mike Wallace in March 1957); and, at long last, the first television spectacular involving the partial use of jazz, Duke Ellington's *A Drum Is A Woman*, which was a full hour show sponsored by United States Steel and seen in color and black-and-white on CBS-TV on May 8, 1957.

The following September another color television show, *Crescendo*, showed Louis Armstrong guiding Rex Harrison, who played an exaggerated stage Englishman, through a supposed cross section of the American music scene. There was not too much music of value, and what there was suffered from poor audio balance, but the show did present Benny Goodman's band and vocal segments by Dinah Washington, Mahalia Jackson, Peggy Lee, Armstrong and others.

Probably the most important date in the resurgence of jazz on television was December 8, 1957, when, in a CBS series called *The Seven Lively Arts*, an hour-long program entitled *The Sound Of Jazz* presented for the first time to a large national audience an abundance of good music. This program was done with taste and dignity and, no less important, with excellent camera work and first-class sound balance. John Crosby, the emcee, was discreetly allowed to let the music speak for itself. The cast included an all-star band especially assembled under the leadership of Count Basie; Billie Holiday, Jimmy Rushing, Red Allen, Ben Webster, Coleman Hawkins and others.

Because it was part of a series already proclaimed a failure by critics and public (it went off the air a few weeks later), and because it was seen on a Sunday afternoon, *The Sound Of Jazz* did not earn a spectacularly high audience rating. But it did something perhaps as important: it demonstrated that jazz could be presented on a network as a medium of mass entertainment. It also came to grips with one of the two inhibiting factors that had certainly held jazz back ever since television had overtaken radio as a national entertainment medium.

One factor, which the show met head on with distinct success, was the race problem. For years agency executives and sponsors had felt uncomfortable about presenting to an audience that included the Southern states a racially-integrated combo or band (which by now included a majority of the most important groups). Their reticence had not been helped by the failure of the Nat King Cole show to find a national sponsor; in fact, almost immediately after *The Sound Of Jazz* was presented, the Cole show, having for more than sixty weeks flailed around in various time slots, went off.* But somehow this issue magically lost its importance in the light of the esthetic success of *Sound Of Jazz*. True, its cast was almost all Negro, but there was no discrimination in the selection of musicians, and such white performers as Mulligan, Giuffre and Pee Wee Russell were involved.

The second obstructive factor was the curious belief, on the part of agencies and network executives, that the public was not "ready" to accept the more

---

* Cole was widely publicized as the first Negro to have his own sponsored television series. This was incorrect. Hazel Scott had her own sponsored show for some months in 1949 and Billy Daniels had one at a peak Sunday evening hour two years later.

modern forms of jazz. When the Reverend Alvin Kershaw, in the fall of 1955, appeared as a contestant in the jazz category on *The $64,000 Question*, he was bombarded with questions about such antiquities as a thirty-year-old Louis Armstrong record and an obscure Kid Ory recording cut many years before Stan Getz, Gerry Mulligan *et al.* were born. In strange contrast, in the summer of 1956, on an almost identical program in Italy, a jazz fan was expected to (and did) know the answers to questions about John Lewis, Woody Herman's Four Brothers, Brookmeyer, Mulligan and other contemporary figures.

If the ice was cracked with *The Sound Of Jazz*, it was broken irrevocably with the *Timex All-Star Jazz Show*, emceed by Steve Allen and seen on NBC on December 30, 1957. Unlike *The Sound Of Jazz*, it was sponsored, aired at a peak evening hour, studded with big names of the quasi-vaudeville variety, including the ubiquitous Louis Armstrong; and it got rousingly enthusiastic reviews and a high rating. It was a perfect launching platform for the 1958 season. Within the next four months, there were two more jazz spectaculars, and NBC, in collaboration with the television educational center at Ann Arbor, Michigan, had launched its own 13-week series of educational shows entitled *The Subject Is Jazz* (a similar series, on a narrower scale, had successfully been achieved in Boston the previous fall by Father Norman O'Connor with the George Shearing Quintet).

For nine years it had not rained; now it poured. In May 1958, another weekly series, with Art Ford as emcee, began on a New York station, WNTA. The musicians were predominately Dixielanders and the atmosphere in the main was that of a night at the New York City club, The Metropole. Again the critics ransacked the dictionaries for laudatory adjectives; the attitude of the daily press during the whole course of this unexpected upsurge of jazz on television had been consistently and indiscriminately encouraging.

By the summer of 1958 plans had been set for eight more major network jazz spectaculars sponsored by a watch company and featuring mainly the extrovert type of performers, such as Louis Armstrong and Lionel Hampton. There were indications that less ambitious and perhaps more localized shows, probably on a regular weekly basis, were about to be set in motion on at least two or three more New York stations, as well as on various others in cities around the country. While rejoicing at the wonderful new exposure thus accorded to jazz, one was forced to hope that there would be no parallel of the situation in the recording field, in which initial success had led to a dangerous state of over-production. But at least it could be said, and said with relief and pride, that 1958 was the first golden year for jazz on television.

THE MOVIES

While television surged ahead in the wake of its new-found discovery of a mass audience for jazz, Hollywood continued to stagnate. The entire record of the motion picture industry throughout the history of jazz has been little short of scandalous. Even during the swing era, when the bands of Goodman, Shaw and Basie were carried along in the wave of a new national fad, the best Hollywood could do was insert them arbitrarily for a production number in grade B musical comedies. Usually, after the first eight measures, the cameras would cut away from the band and the sound would fade to make way for the superimposition of more important business, such as a conversation between the hero and the ingenue. Occasionally, there might be one- or two-reel shorts dedicated to some of the bands, but even these were grotesquely distorted with inept dancing, phony jive talk and other impedimenta.

One would think, in view of the fantastic change in the general American attitude toward jazz in recent years, that Hollywood would have made at least a half-dozen important pictures, such as *The Duke Ellington Story*, *The Count Basie Story*, etc., as well as a series of feature-length documentaries to preserve for posterity, aurally and visually, the contributions of the Mulligans, Brubecks, Modern Jazz Quartets and others. By now, instead, aside from a couple of features (and some UPA shorts) that used jazz background scores, the 1956-58 record of the movie industry included rock-'n'-roll-dominated features, such as *The Girl Can't Help It* (in which Benny Carter was restricted to backgrounds for a singer), *Hot Rod Rumble* and *Rock Pretty Baby*; the use of Ray Anthony as bandleader and very briefly as actor in *This Could Be The Night*; the incorporation of the Chico Hamilton Quintet in *The Sweet Smell of Success* (with, inevitably, a marijuana angle to the story); and exactly two pictures that might be said to have been directly connected with jazz: *The Benny Goodman Story* and *St. Louis Blues*. Because both the latter are symptomatic of what has been wrong all along with the Hollywood approach to jazz, they will be discussed here in detail.

In the first place, Hollywood has always been scared stiff of the race issue. For decades the Negro was hardly ever seen in any picture, except as a servant or some kind of buffoon (Hollywood was always kind to Louis Armstrong, who was used as an actor and singer from the mid-thirties on, and even reached documentary status in 1957 with *Satchmo the Great*). So terrified were the producers of offending the Southern market that on numerous occasions, where mixed groups had to be presented, they were retained intact for the soundtrack but changed to all-white or all-colored units for the camera. One does not have to go back farther than 1950 to recall that when Buddy DeFranco was a member of the Count Basie group he was not allowed to appear on the screen with Basie for a movie short. DeFranco recorded the track, but Marshall Royal took his place on screen. There are probably even more recent instances.

In a sudden access of boldness, the movie industry tackled the race problem, as such, in a series of movies a few years ago—*Home of the Brave*, *Lost Boundaries*, *No Way Out*, etc.—but most of these pictures were not very profitable and the film colony remained fearful of antagonizing white potential patrons in the Southern states.

Ironically, as a result of this myopic policy, *The Benny Goodman Story* had to sacrifice the one genuinely dramatic aspect that could have turned it from a routine motion picture biography into a valuable historic document: the role that Goodman played in breaking down the race line in jazz by hiring Teddy Wilson and forming the Goodman trio. This could have been a dramatically effective gambit, and might certainly have provided the pivotal moment of the picture. Instead, the producer and writers cooked up a conventional love story with the conventional counterposition of poor boy and society girl. As ever, much was made of the difference in social position between the hero and the heroine; as ever, unsubtle fun was poked at customs in high society; as ever, in any picture that purportedly shows an aspect of American-Jewish life, the hero's family was depicted in a one-dimensional shabby-genteel light; and, as ever, with any picture involving a band, the climax was a concert (Goodman's 1938 appearance at Carnegie Hall). The film was riddled with anachronisms (the actual Goodman romance did not take place until years after the 1938 finale of the picture); but this would have been unimportant if the producer had at least had the courage to grab hold of the one fact that, aside from Goodman's musicianship, gave him his real importance in jazz history. Instead, Teddy Wilson was found working with Goodman with no explanation; Lionel Hampton was discovered in a fictional and ridiculous scene that depicted him as a short-order chef; and Buck Clayton, who at the time of the events shown was actually a member of the Basie band and never really worked with Goodman at all during that era, was also seen as a member of the band. Admittedly, barriers had been removed to the extent of showing integration in a band, but the issue that this represented in Goodman's career was completely jettisoned in favor of the trite-and-true romance angle. Perhaps to the surprise of nobody but the producer, the picture was not the money-maker that had been expected; taking careful aim at a mass market, the creators of *The Benny Goodman Story* had unwittingly fired a boomerang.

The case of *St. Louis Blues* was even more pitiful. Here was a story that could have been inspirational, documentary, unique. The essence of Handy's story was the time and work he devoted to the study of the folk music he heard around him in the South, and the manner in which he documented some of these melodies and created new themes of his own. But here again Hollywood could think only in terms of a basic and puerile conflict. This time, instead of poor boy versus society girl, it was that other hardy Hollywood perennial, stern jazz-hating father versus jazz-loving son ("We don't want that kind of music in God's house—son, that's the devil's music!"). Every cliché associated with this situation was trotted out; at the performance attended by this writer in a Broadway theatre the audience was even laughing in the wrong places. Presumably angry at Handy for not looking enough like a Negro, the producer selected for the role of W. C. Handy a fine musician and capable actor, Nat King Cole, who looks as much like Handy as Louis Armstrong resembles Rep. Adam Clayton Powell, Jr. Handy was a cornetist and touring bandleader, not a singer or a pianist; Cole was shown occasionally going through the motions of playing a horn but, inevitably, was mainly depicted as a singer and pianist, and the years on tour all over the South with Mahara's Minstrels, probably the most important phase of Handy's life, were not shown at all. Some of the most important songs were sung by Eartha Kitt, who has never pretended to be a blues singer. Ella Fitzgerald and Mahalia Jackson were both relegated to minor roles. The part of Handy's father was as grotesque a caricature as that of Benny's father in the Goodman story. The laughable finale, again at the inevitable concert, carried with it the implication that the *St. Louis Blues* had finally achieved respectability and musical validity in being performed by a huge symphonic orchestra with no semblance of a beat. Hollywood had preserved the stereotype again. Not surprisingly, except for a couple of minor roles, the cast was all-Negro, and all concerned had bent over so far backwards to avoid any accusations of Uncle Tomism that Negro life in Memphis was portrayed with all the gentility and respectability of a bunch of Philadelphia mainliners. As a reviewer for *Variety* commented, "You might wonder why the Negroes ever sang the blues."

That's Hollywood. And that still will be Hollywood, it seems, for some time to come. At this writing, there is no indication that anybody has expressed the slightest interest in filming *The Duke Ellington Story*. On the other hand, *The Gene Krupa Story*, presumably including the brief and comparatively insignificant involvement of Krupa with a narcotics scandal many years ago, was announced for production with, of all people, Sal Mineo playing Krupa (one is reminded of the incredible television show a few years ago in which, portraying Mezz Mezzrow in a dramatization of *Really the Blues*, Jackie Cooper was shown in the alleged agonies of "withdrawal" from the marijuana habit!). Similarly, Billie Holiday's autobiography, which, according to John Hammond and many others who have known her closely through the years, bears about as much resemblance to her actual story as *Really the Blues* did to Mezzrow's, was bought for Hollywood—prostitution, dope addiction and all. If there is any attempt to produce *The Ella Fitzgerald Story*, it will come as a great surprise to those who are aware of Hollywood's attitudes; for Ella has led a life untorn by vice in any shape or form, though the story of her discovery and adoption by the late Chick Webb would alone make a more desirable and valuable basic theme than anything currently being planned by the powers of Beverly Hills.

Because Hollywood has not yet successfully taken the initiative, there has been talk that some motion pictures giving adequate treatment to jazz, either in fictional or documentary form, may be produced in Europe. There has already been substantial acknowledgment of the film value of jazz in France, where the Modern Jazz Quartet and Miles Davis were recently used for background music. Ironically, with the California movie industry on the skids and losing out rapidly to television, the realization has now come, too late, that the Jim Crow Southern market they were so afraid to offend—or, for that matter, the United States market as a whole—may be less important in the long run than the overseas market, where movies offering authentic treatments of jazz themes undoubtedly would enjoy an unprecedentedly enthusiastic welcome. Possibly we shall live to see the day when pictures of this kind will be produced on the

West Coast; the tragedy is that all the great developments of decades gone by that could and should have been preserved on celluloid can never be reclaimed.

In summing up the recent past in American jazz, an important point may be made as a corollary of the preceding observations on its progress in so many areas. Because today the market for jazz is infinitely greater than at any previous time, there has been a great reduction in the degree to which musicians are forced to work in fields that they find musically unsympathetic. The stories of the frustrated jazzman confined to work in a commercial dance band (another invariable favorite of the novelists and Hollywood script writers) could be found much more rarely in real life nowadays. If a musician has something to offer as an individual soloist, the chances are very good that before his career has gone very far he will find plenty of outlets of expression. Moreover, he will earn a living commensurate with his talents.

At the beginning of this chapter, it was observed that jazz had become big business; perhaps it might be appropriate to conclude with a few specific examples of the size of this business as concerns the musicians directly. By 1958 John Lewis, who only four years earlier had been forced to take a job as accompanist to Ella Fitzgerald, was able to command around $1,000 a night for his Modern Jazz Quartet. Combos such as Brubeck's and Garner's were able to earn salaries ranging up to $4,000 or $5,000 a week. A Lionel Hampton or a Louis Armstrong, playing a command performance at a private party on Park Avenue, might be paid, for himself and his group, as much as $3,500 for the night's work. Name singers like Ella Fitzgerald also reached up into the $5,000-a-week category. And two years ago Duke Ellington rejected an offer of $18,500 a week to take his band on a tour of one-nighters in Europe.

It has taken a long time, but one must be thankful that both in terms of material rewards and artistic recognition jazz today, both at home and abroad, has reached another peak, and can see ahead new mountains that it will have no difficulty in scaling. Granted there was not as much progress as could have been hoped for in some areas, notably radio and motion pictures; granted that some inequities still existed and racial discrimination still played a vicious, though diminishing, role in the progress of jazz; but if the millennium was not yet here, it was encouraging to know that by 1958 it was clearly visible on the horizon.

NBC *Timex Show*. Louis Armstrong and Steve Allen.

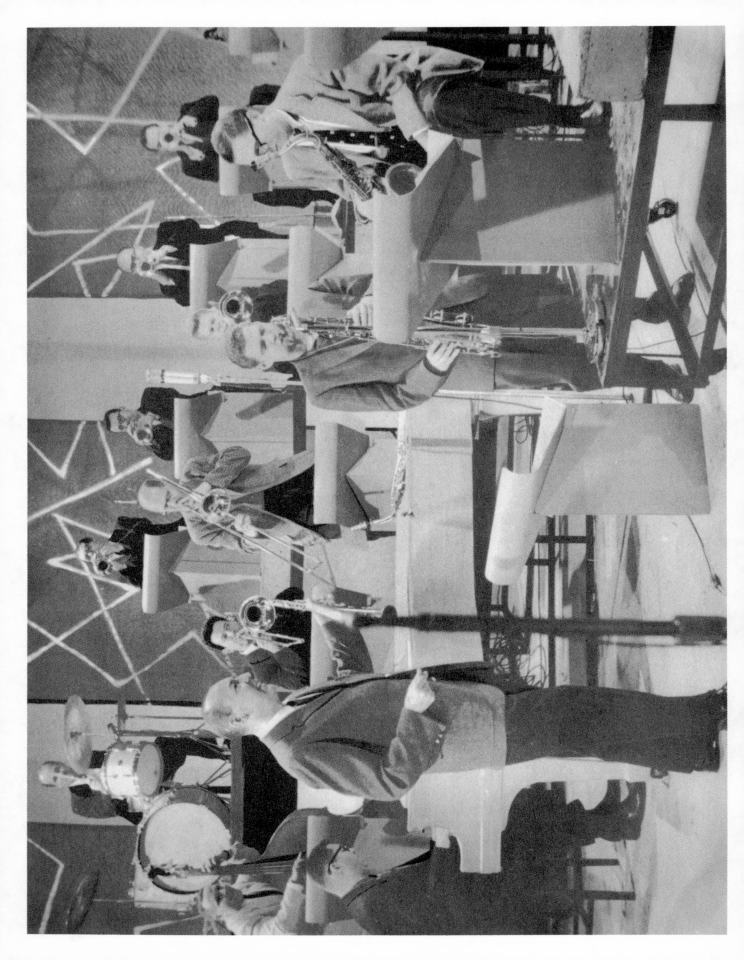

35

Opposite: NBC *Timex Show*. Woody Herman Orchestra. Soloists standing are: Bill Harris, Zoot Sims. Rhythm section: Nat Pierce, Chubby Jackson, Don Lamond.

Right: NBC *Timex Show*. Dave Brubeck and Paul Desmond.

Below: NBC *The Subject is Jazz*. Buck Clayton.

Above: NBC *The Subject is Jazz*. Duke Ellington and moderator Gilbert Seldes.

Opposite: NBC *The Subject is Jazz*. Eddie Safranski, Billy Taylor, Mundell Lowe, Osie Johnson.

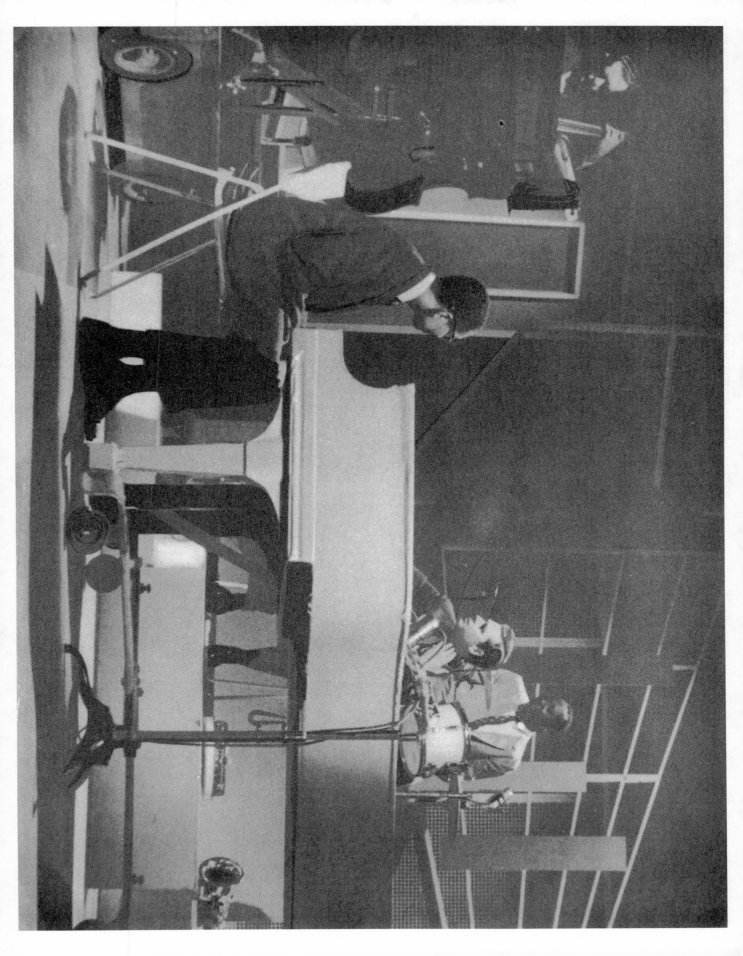

Left: NBC *The Subject is Jazz.* Tony Scott, Doc Severinsen, Jimmy Cleveland.

Below: NBC *The Subject is Jazz.* Jimmy Rushing.

Above: NBC *Swing into Spring*. Teddy Wilson, Arvell
Shaw, Benny Goodman, Red Norvo.

Below: NBC *Swing into Spring*. Harry James.

Above: CBS *The Sound of Jazz.* Jimmy Giuffre, Milt Hinton, Pee Wee Russell, Danny Barker, Jo Jones.

Below: The Sound of Jazz. Osie Johnson, moderator John Crosby; Thelonious Monk, Ahmed Abdul-Malik.

JAZZ OVERSEAS

A cartoon in the *New Yorker* Magazine dated April 19, 1958 showed a group of diplomats seated around a conference table earnestly listening to their chairman who was making a grave pronouncement. The caption read: "This is a diplomatic mission of the utmost delicacy. The question is, who's the best man for it—John Foster Dulles or Satchmo?".

There is something more than humor in the message of this cartoon. It is possible to infer correctly that jazz, unknown or ignored only a few years ago on most artistic and diplomatic levels in the United States, has become one of the few exports from this country than can be depended upon to be greeted with devotion and enthusiasm rather than with the uneasy resentment that has met many of our shipments in the recent past.

A glance at the biographical references in this volume under the names of many top American jazzmen will tell its own story. Despite the tremendous advances made by American jazz on the domestic front, there have been few events at home to match the warmth of the welcome accorded to Gerry Mulligan and the Modern Jazz Quartet and the Count Basie band in Europe, Benny Goodman in Asia, Louis Armstrong and Tony Scott and Wilbur de Paris in Africa, John Dizzy Gillespie in South America, Lionel Hampton in Australia. These names are a few taken at random from the dozens who have been among our unofficial ambassadors. Even the Iron Curtain has been penetrated with visits from Tony Scott, the Dave Brubeck Quartet and the Glenn Miller orchestra directed by Ray McKinley. It seems highly probable that this penetration within the next year or two will reach Soviet Russia itself, where the resistance to jazz is not expected to last much longer.

With the stepping up of these foreign tours, there has been a concomitant improvement in the jazz standards of local musicians in most countries. To point up the newly internationalized character of jazz, a tour of many countries was undertaken on behalf of the Newport Jazz Festival, in order to present, in July 1958, a specially assembled

"Tower of Babel" orchestra with one musician from each of the countries represented. Symbolically, these jazzmen, unable to communicate by the language of words, could make contact only through the international language of jazz; and there was no doubt from the first moment the project was undertaken that the sympathetic musical bond among them would transcend the handicaps of language. This unique project was directed by Marshall Brown.

In the following reports will be found a picture of the jazz scene in the four foreign countries generally considered to have become most important in jazz. The majority of musicians and experts have agreed (and a poll taken in late 1957 among *Down Beat* readers further indicated their concurrence) that England, France, Germany and Sweden have produced the best native jazz outside the United States; not unnaturally, they are also the four countries that have imported American jazzmen most frequently. I believe that these reports, each of which comes from a man who has long been a keen observer of the scene in his own territory, will be of value in documenting and clarifying the remarkable evolution of the international jazz movement.

GREAT BRITAIN

It is the proud boast of the British that in their country may be found the best jazz anywhere outside the United States. In the last two years, the claim has certainly had its application, though not quite in its intended sense. Since the British Musicians' Union lifted its unconditional ban on all foreign jazz artists publicly appearing in Britain, the élite of the jazz world has beaten a path to Britain's door. After Kenton had broken the ice in the spring of 1956, there followed at regular intervals the Count Basie band (twice, with a third tour already planned), the Mulligan Quartet, the Teagarden-Hines All-Stars, the Louis Armstrong All-Stars, the Lionel Hampton band, the Condon circus, the Modern Jazz Quartet, the Dave Brubeck Quartet, June Christy, Sarah Vaughan and, as an appropriate climax to the pilgrimage, *Jazz at The Philharmonic*, with Dizzy, Oscar, Ella, and Norman Granz trailing clouds of incandescent though vicarious glory.

British jazz audiences are invariably very generous, but as American jazzmen have lost their rarity value, there has been a noticeable stiffening of esthetic judgment. The Kenton concerts were conducted in an atmosphere of near-hysteria, no doubt because this was the first visit of an American band in twenty years. When I deputized for two concerts with the Kenton band on baritone saxophone, I found that people who knew of my feat held me in a new and unnatural regard. Illogical but understandable.

As the Harold Davison office continued with its band-exchange policy, the critical faculty began to reassert itself, until by the time Hampton came here a year later there were many who carped about the low jazz content in his concerts.

Almost every one of these tours was commercially successful, with triumph reaching its giddy climax as JATP tickets were hustled around with an expertise reminiscent of *My Fair Lady*. Even an artist like Jack Teagarden, perhaps in partial eclipse at home, brought a smile of relief to the faces of the entrepreneurs. However much Teagarden's reputation may have fluctuated in the States, he was still a legend in Britain and support for him was widespread.

Fears that all this competition would harm the cause of British jazz have proved only partly well-founded, and there have been compensations. It is naturally harder now to induce audiences to attend all-British concerts, but the influence on the scene in general has been a beneficent one. The touring band business in Britain, only three or four years ago such a staple part of every musician's livelihood, has disintegrated completely, shattered by the tide of shamateurism which has appeared in the form of the rock-'n'-roll and skiffle phenomena. By the end of 1957 there were barely half a dozen bands worthy of the name left on the road. With the Ted Heath orchestra confining itself more and more to studio performances and foreign tours, the first place in the big band polls has now passed to the Johnny Dankworth orchestra. The crown is Johnny's through sheer esthetic justice, for his is the only big band in Britain that plays a jazz program of any appreciable quality. Dankworth has become one of the leaders of the British jazz movement, particularly as a spokesman to the outside world. His appearances at the Oxford Union debates and his series of autobiographical pieces in the London *Star* (circulation 880,000) broke new ground in lay territory.

Another British jazz figurehead, Humphrey Lyttleton, has suffered in the past year something of a fall from grace with his once fanatically loyal fans. Lyttleton, for so long an adherent of the theory that musically, at least, time can be made to go backwards, suddenly stopped doing a Gatsby and began to remodel his band on more imaginative lines. The importation of a Hodges-style altoist to replace a Dodds-style clarinetist is a fairly accurate indication of the extent of his first advances. But the alto of Bruce Turner proved to be the thin end of the wedge of an entire saxophone section. Although the musical value of Lyttleton's band rose sharply as he imported more and more proficient musicians from the modern ranks, like ex-Dankworth drummer Eddie Taylor and modern-club star attraction Jimmie Skidmore, Humphrey's fan following took a drop in inverse proportion to the quality of the music, from which fact may be deduced a homily far too terrifying for this writer to acknowledge.

The developments in Lyttleton's band were some of the most interesting to take place in Britain last year, and Humphrey's comparative eclipse as the leader of British traditionalism, a position surely befitting one whose grandfather had once captained an English Test Match team, coincided with the phenomenal commercial success of rival traditionalist Chris Barber, an undistinguished trombonist surrounded by an undistinguished collection of traditionalist musicians and a surprisingly good blues singer called Ottilie Patterson, known to advertising copy-writers as "Utterly" Patterson. Barber, braving the circuits once confined to the big commercial orchestras now defunct, broke house records previously held by Ted Heath in almost every hall in the Four

Kingdoms. To date, Barber's ascendancy over all his rivals remains unchallenged, except perhaps for the even more primitive band of clarinetist Cy Laurie, snugly installed in his own club a stone's throw from the Eros Statue in Piccadilly Circus, with a several-thousand-strong membership of pencil-trousered poseurs and dangly-haired demi-mondaines.

For the moderns, as one door had closed, so another has opened. The touring bands, once the last resort of unemployed modernists, have, like the dodo and the brontosaurus before them, proved unable to adapt themselves to changing conditions and have paid the price. Which raises the subject of the Little Jazz Clubs phenomenon, one which distinguishes Britain, and particularly London, from all other jazz cities.

In London have survived for some years now establishments which are jazz clubs in every sense of the phrase. Holding four or five hundred people at most, and changing premises as circumstances dictated or rents rose, these clubs catered primarily to the jazz fan. The sale of alcohol in modern clubs is still an almost unknown phenomenon. There are no bars and drinking licenses. The programs consist of two groups and a *compère*, the amenities of tables and chairs and a small dance floor.

In the past two years, with interest stimulated by American visitors and the subsequent belated acknowledgment of the existence of jazz as something more than a source of delinquency and viciousness, the Little Clubs have gone from strength to strength, until today they are not so little. Crowds of a thousand are not unheard of at Jazz City, nor are club programs of four nights a week of music at the Flamingo. It is calculated that on a normal Saturday night in London, about five thousand people pay for admission into the Little Clubs, with an equal division between traditional and modern.

Most of the modern groups these fans hear when they get inside the building are the same groups they have been hearing for the past five years, or sometimes new groups composed of permutations of old faces. Currently accepted as the best of these are the Jazz Couriers, a five-piece unit co-led by tenorists Ronnie Scott and Tubby Hayes. Scott was for two years leader of the cooperative band which was the most successful modern group to have survived in Britain so far, and Hayes, doubling on vibes, broke up his own touring band to help form the Couriers, who recently appeared as the supporting attraction on the Sarah Vaughan bill.

Other outstanding personalities include West Indian altoist Joe Harriott, currently leading his own quintet, baritonist Ronnie Ross, selected to appear at the 1958 Newport Festival, trumpeter Dizzy Reece, currently flitting bewilderingly to and from the Continent, where he has been reported as playing with Kenny Clarke, and the inseparable three, Jimmie Deuchar (trumpet), Derek Humble (alto) and Ken Wray (trombone), at present enjoying self-imposed exile in Germany with the Kurt Edelhagen band.

Generally influential figures on the jazz scene, for instance commentators like Dankworth and Lyttleton, are able to wield a certain persuasive influence because of the existence of a genuine body of respectful jazz fans. Musician-columnist Steve Race, for example, was largely responsible for the successful booking in Britain of the Brubeck Quartet, for whom, by his consistent championing of the group in his weekly columns, he cleared the way.

Johnny Dankworth's action in rejecting the offer of a lucrative return appearance in South Africa, because of the racial angle, was another action typical of the man, which earned unanimous approval and lent a moral force to the voice of jazz that can only strengthen its position in the social life of the land. In the meantime, South Africa seems to be the first outpost of the Empire being opened up by the jazz pioneers, for since the Dankworth appearance there in 1954, the first ever in the Union by an imported jazz star, American jazzmen are beginning to include the Union as part of their world tour itineraries. Apart from a few traditional flutters from Australia from the Graeme Bell band, which toured Britain so successfully in the early '50s, the British Empire seems quiescent in the face of the advancing jazz muse. Perhaps that is because the sun never sets on the Empire and jazz is essentially the after-hours art.

—BENNY GREEN

FRANCE

France was without doubt the first country in the world to offer official acknowledgment to jazz as a genuine art form rather than a mere novelty. As early as 1928, Parisian intellectuals, headed by Jean Cocteau, proclaimed the right of jazz to recognition along with the motion picture and modern painting.

Only in recent years has jazz extended beyond the borders of a limited *succès d'estime* among a minority to reach into the great mass of the French people. Perhaps the most characteristic illustration of the trend can be found in the appearance, in the "pops" programs at the Olympia, the great Parisian music hall, of a large number of American and French jazzmen. During the past two years the Olympia has offered its stage to such figures as Louis Armstrong, Lionel Hampton, Gerry Mulligan, Miles Davis, Count Basie, Erroll Garner, J. J. Johnson, Earl Hines, Jack Teagarden, in addition to the annual visits of the Jazz at the Philharmonic tour.

Another popular music hall, the Alhambra, presented Harry James and his orchestra and the Stan Kenton band. The Modern Jazz Quartet enjoyed a triumphant success at the Théatre des Champs-Elysées. An increasing number of night clubs have offered on a regular basis the music of numerous jazz combos, some of them featuring American musicians residing in Paris, others especially imported from the United States: among the latter were Miles Davis, Bud Powell and the Modern Jazz Quartet.

Another aspect of the French jazz scene that points up significantly the increased respect in which jazz is held is its frequent use for motion picture sound tracks. For the film *No Sun in Venice*, Roger Vadim commissioned John Lewis to write the musical score, which was interpreted by the Modern Jazz Quartet. For another picture, *Elevator to The Gallows*—which, incidentally, enjoyed a great success in France—Louis Malle, the director, used Miles Davis' trumpet. According to experts, the music created by Miles was one of the major factors in the commercial success of the film. Other production companies are now frequently calling upon American and French jazzmen to provide the music for their movies.

Television in France is represented by a sole outlet, controlled by the Government. Clearly, this solitary network attempts to satisfy the most diversified popular tastes. Nevertheless, and this fact, too, may be considered symptomatic, a half-hour broadcast entitled *A la Recherche du Jazz*, seen once every month, explains the characteristics of this music to the uninitiated. In addition the Modern Jazz Quartet, during one of its visits to Paris, was accorded the privilege of occupying the small screen at a peak viewing hour—9 p.m.—with no production of any kind, except for a simple series of panels announcing the titles of the tunes. A performance of this kind might not be accomplished even in the United States; it is even more astonishing when one takes into consideration the fact that the audiences had no alternate program selection available to them, so that everyone in France and Belgium who owned a television set and had it turned on at that time was bound to see the Modern Jazz Quartet's performance. Moreover, the directors of the network received many congratulations for their "happy initiative."

Radio, as might be expected, offers a much more important place to jazz. Quite a large number of jazz broadcasts can be heard. For more than six years an American, Sim Copans, has been in charge of a very popular show heard every Saturday at 12.30 p.m. on France I, the official Government channel. Europe No. I, which in less than a year has become the most listened-to station in France, certainly owes a substantial part of its success to the fact that from the very beginning it dedicated a full hour every evening (two hours on Sunday) to jazz. These broadcasts bring in an extraordinarily large amount of mail, attesting to the quantity of the French jazz fan following, as well as to the quality and intensity of their enthusiasm.

Jazz record sales similarly have enjoyed a remarkable upsurge in the past two years. As many as 60 per cent of the jazz records published in the United States are released in France and are satisfactorily absorbed by the French market, an impressive fact when one takes into consideration the relative population (less than one-third that of the United States). Some companies, such as RCA Victor, prepare for release in France special LPs, some of which are not even available in the United States, such as reissues of old masters by Jelly Roll Morton, Lionel Hampton, Fats Waller and others.

The jazz magazines are faring especially well. *Jazz Hot*, the oldest, recently celebrated its twenty-fifth anniversary, while *Jazz Magazine*, after little more than three years of existence, has a circulation of twenty-five thousand. In addition, a number of larger daily newspapers, as well as several weekly publications, now offer a regular jazz department.

The tastes of the French public have evolved considerably in the past couple of years in the direction of a broader acceptance of all styles. During the period immediately after World War II, only Dixieland jazz (or New Orleans style, as it is called in France) had any real commercial value. Today, modern jazz is consistently becoming more fashionable.

Given these favorable conditions, the quality of jazz produced by French musicians has developed commendably in the course of the past two years. The performers are not only more numerous than ever, but find more opportunities for work as jazzmen. The performance level of the soloists has shown a sharp improvement; several outstanding artists, in the opinion of visiting American musicians who have heard them, are comparable if not superior to many of their distinguished and celebrated confrères across the Atlantic.

In the night clubs of Paris, it is possible today to hear such veterans as Stéphane Grappelly (one of the original members of the Quintet of the Hot Club of France with Django Reinhardt in the middle '30s), as well as many promising young stars. Among the latter are Barney Wilen, a tenor saxophonist who has emulated the styles of Sonny Rollins and John Coltrane; René Urtreger and Martial Solal, the pianists; Pierre Michelot, an outstanding bassist; and at least a dozen other talented musicians. Among the adherents of a more classical style, Guy Lafitte and Michel de Villers represent the "middle-jazz" era, while the Dixielanders still have Maxime Saury and Claude Luter as the local kings of this venerable genre.

As for the American colony in Paris, Sidney Bechet remains in a class by himself, a figure of national glory in France, on the same level of acceptance as Maurice Chevalier or Edith Piaf. Other American jazzmen resident in France include Albert Nicholas, Bill Coleman, Nelson Williams, Don Byas, Mezz Mezzrow, Quincy Jones, Jimmy Gourley, Kenny Clarke and many others.

To sum up all the happy developments of the past two years on the French jazz scene, it might be apt to quote a young American girl now living in Paris who remarked recently, "I had to come over here to live before I realized what an important part jazz could play in the artistic life of a country."

—DANIEL FILIPACCHI

SWEDEN

The Swedish interest in jazz, generally considered to be the greatest outside the United States, has undergone some significant changes during the last two or three years. Earlier, when our records were often warmly received by American critics and buyers, the interest was mostly concentrated around local talent like Bengt Hallberg and Lars Gullin. Now there appears to be a trend among younger jazz lovers and critics to minimize the importance of Swedish jazz in general. The reason could possibly be that stars like Hallberg and Gullin have been comparatively inactive in jazz in recent years. The former devotes more and more of his time to commercial studio work and Gullin has had to fight several personal problems, which have limited his musical capacities. One must also consider the enormously increased record output of American jazz.

Stockholm, the only real jazz center in Sweden (Gothenburg is more or less a dead city these days), has a unique place where jazz reigns during more than eight months every year. Nalen, a huge dance hall with five steadily employed bands, is the scene for jam sessions twice a week and generally adds American solo talent to its impressive artist roster. Among those who have appeared during the last two years are Tony Scott, Don Byas and Lucky Thompson. Scott was a tremendous hit, both with the musicians and the listeners.

There are no more clubs or dance halls in Stockholm that concentrate entirely on jazz. Several attempts have been made to start informal after-hours spots, but the Swedish police always keeps an eye on them and generally closes them after a few weeks. All over Sweden, however, there is a network of local jazz clubs which are knitted together in a federation with about 1,000 members.

If you want to listen to jazz in Stockholm, do not try to find it during the summertime. Most bands of importance are on the road playing open-air spots because, by tradition, the Swedish people always go outdoors from the end of April until the beginning of September, no matter what kind of weather it is.

Apart from records—most American LPs reach us rather fast and are often split up on EPs—there are two major factors that keep the jazz interest alive: radio, and concerts by visiting United States stars. Jazz on the radio— there are two networks, controlled by the Government—is built around one-hour spots on Monday nights. There are also several other programs on the other weekdays, although some of them are not so exclusively jazz orientated. On television, by the way, jazz is almost non-existent, but then TV is just under way here.

About half a dozen American attractions, big bands and small groups, and occasionally a single soloist, visit us every year with concerts in Stockholm, Gothenburg and sometimes two or three more cities. During the last two years the outstanding hits have been Count Basie and Gerry Mulligan. Basie and his band made a two-week tour (quite a long time here) in September 1956. Steady visitors are JATP; Lionel Hampton's band has returned to Sweden several times with most unpleasant riots as a result. Among the more successful concerts one must mention Dave Brubeck's appearance in early 1958. Big bands include Stan Kenton, Benny Goodman and Ray McKinley. Benny played to sell-out houses but was completely murdered by the critics. There are no jazz concerts during the summer.

Two bands, however, have toured Sweden in the summertime recently. The first, headed by Swedish trumpeter Rolf Ericson of Woody Herman fame, started travelling in June 1956, but Ericson had to reorganize the following month after some of the most scandalous events that ever took place in this country. Ericson had to send his men back to the States, enlisted three new musicians with the help of jazz correspondent Claes Dahlgren in New York, joined forces with Lars Gullin and was able to finish his contract with less disastrous results. Jay Jay Johnson presented his quintet in the summer of 1957 and made splendid performances throughout. Jazz fans here find it hard to understand why this group was not brought back the next summer, as both the music and the box office reports were excellent.

There are two magazines, devoted exclusively to jazz, that have been operating in Sweden for more than twenty years, *Estrad* and *Orkester Journalen*. The former also owns a concert bureau which stages just about every American guest appearance. Jazz is given big space in the morning and afternoon dailies and also in most weeklies.

Jazz in Sweden is almost entirely modern. Traditional jazz is fast losing its grip on the audiences and the amount of revival bands now in existence has decreased with astonishing speed. Concerning the modern influences, Swedish musicians have always been very alert to pick up and often accept new trends, but it definitely seems that our jazzmen are turning back to reliable sources of inspiration like Ellington and Basie. Of course, modern giants like Bud Powell, Miles Davis, Sonny Rollins, John Lewis and Milt Jackson, to name a few, are extremely popular, especially among the younger set, but actually very few musicians here play that way. The best, steadily organized band is by far the Arne Domnerus Orchestra, which seems inspired by a wide variety of styles, from Duke *via* Bird to West Coast jazz.

New talent is coming up in greater profusion than ever. One could mention at least fifty names, but this writer will limit himself to put tenor saxophonist Bernt Rosengren's name in print. Bernt, who follows the Sonny Rollins trend, was chosen as the Swedish representative in the European band that appeared during the 1958 Newport Jazz Festival.

Swedish jazz records are almost as scarce these days as in the '30s and '40s. The reason is mainly the flood of American releases drowning this country; furthermore, jazz records are almost never made here, except when ordered from a United States company, *e.g.*, the Atlantic label. There have, however, been some impressive albums, of which Bengt Hallberg's trio LP was warmly received and chosen with a huge majority of votes as the best album made in Sweden in 1957. American critics were obviously not as enthusiastic as their Swedish colleagues when the record was released in the States on the Epic label.

A story on Swedish jazz would not be complete without mentioning Harry Arnold and his Swedish Radio Studio Orchestra, a band composed of our leading talents and organized only for broadcasts, recordings and an occasional concert. As many American critics and musicians will verify, this band is quite something and the first LP by Arnold, released in the United States with the "Mystery Band" gimmick, is the best jazz seller this country has ever seen. Quincy Jones contributed to the second LP, due for release at this writing. During his hectic days here in Stockholm in April 1958, Quincy had only superlatives for the Swedish musicians and named the Arnold band as one of the very best in the world.

In short: Swedish jazz is better off than ever, with more promising newcomers, more good bands and a broader audience. It is getting more publicity in one year's time than it did during the whole previous decade. The record sales have been amazing for such a small country. Some of us, however, mourn the fact that the easily identified, national brand of jazz is dying out. Our music is entirely Americanized these days and it is hard to put your finger on a specific record made here now and state that it definitely was made in the land of the Midnight Sun. Don't let that fact prevent you from going to Sweden, though, if you have a chance and keen ears for our jazz. As our American visitors will gladly tell you, it's a swinging country!

—CARL-ERIK LINDGREN

GERMANY

"They take it so much as an art form—as what it really is; much more than we do in our country." John Lewis said this when he was touring Germany in the winter of 1957-58, expressing what he and the other members of his Modern Jazz Quartet thought about their overwhelming success and the appreciation they found in this country.

Many other famous American jazzmen have made similar comments. There seems to be, in this country, a kind of jazz appreciation which applies the famous German tendency to take everything very seriously. Nowhere else in Europe are there so many discussions on jazz. And the market for books on jazz is nowhere better than here. On the other hand, the market for jazz records is, compared to other European countries, just average—maybe not even that.

Lee Konitz and the Lennie Tristano school are the most important influence on jazz in Germany. When this writer, some months ago, in a television show, asked each musician in a German all-star group about his favorite American jazzmen, everyone named Lee Konitz. The musicians are fascinated by Lee's long, flowing lines, his harmonic conceptions, and—most important of all—by an attitude of playing which more often than not is reflected as being cerebral although, in fact, it is as "intuitive" as any good jazz from Oliver to Rollins.

Typically enough, highlights of all the German jazz festivals during the last few years were duos between one of the better known German hornmen—either Albert Mangelsdorff on trombone or Emil Mangelsdorff, his brother, on alto—and Atilla Zoller on guitar, reminiscent of the duos in the old Tristano days between Billy Bauer and Lee Konitz. There is a strong tendency to linearity in German jazz, but linearity in the conception of the nineteenth century Romantic style.

Tenor man Hans Koller and trombonist Albert Mangelsdorff are the best known jazz soloists in Germany. When Charles Delaunay in Paris asked a board of the German Jazz Federation to name a German representative for an all-star European band, they proposed Albert. George Wein, of the Newport Festival, and Marshall Brown, of the Farmingdale High School Band, also selected Albert as Germany's representative for their International Big Band to be presented at the Newport Festival in 1958. Albert plays a lyrical, sensitive, cool trombone. He says he formed his style by adopting the Lee Konitz way of playing to the trombone.

Hans Koller, also, comes from Konitz but, during the last few years, he has changed completely. He now is a great improviser on the Al Cohn-Count Basie "classicistic" line with all the Cohn "moanings" in his phrasing and a "down home" jazz feeling. Hans is a member of the big band that the American arranger, Eddie Sauter, built for the *Sudwestfunk*—the Southwestern German Radio Network in Baden-Baden.

Two other German radio networks have regularly employed jazz big bands: Radio Stuttgart has Erwin Lehn and Radio Cologne has Kurt Edelhagen. Sauter, of course, adapts all his brilliant arranging ability to his German band. Lehn has a very musicianly and clean playing, Basie-orientated orchestra. Kurt Edelhagen assembled what he calls "a U.N. in jazz" insofar as he has a kind of all-European big band with leading jazz improvisers from England, Belgium, France, Switzerland, Italy, Austria and, of course, Germany. That things of this kind are possible in jazz at a time when Europe still is full of borders and political jealousy is one of this music's most wonderful aspects.

All these bands have regular programs on the networks. In addition, the eight German radio networks have—about twice a week—regular jazz shows with commentaries by jazz critics, only the *Sudwestfunk*, however, having this kind of program every day of the week.

There are many jazz combos in Germany; it is impossible to name all of them. The Helmut Brandt Quintet and the Michael Naura Quintet—both from Berlin, but mostly playing in Western Germany—are outstanding. Baritone saxophonist Helmut Brandt is, even by American standards, a good arranger, fascinated by the Miles Davis Capitol band and astonishingly successful in adapting the feeling of this band's music to his own two-horn combo. Piano player Michael Naura acquired the most promising new jazz improviser for his Quintet: Wolfgang Schlüter, a vibes player with fluent ideas and very modern harmonic conceptions.

The most popular German jazz group is the Wolfgang Lauth Quartet from Mannheim. Wolfgang has the MJQ instrumentation. He might be called the German Dave Brubeck, arousing the same kind of discussion among German musicians as Brubeck does in America. The sensational success of his group seems to be typical for German jazz audiences.

In the German Jazz Poll, there is no "hard swinging" group or musician in the lead. Names like Blakey, Horace Silver, Sonny Rollins and Max Roach never seem to be able to get a better vote than, maybe, sixth or seventh place, leaving the top places to the MJQ, the Brubeck Quartet, John Lewis, Jimmy Giuffre, Chet Baker and the West Coast musicians.

All the professional musicians are assembled, each year, at the German Jazz Festival in Frankfurt. There is also an annual Amateur Jazz Festival in Düsseldorf. The number of amateur musicians is increasing rapidly. When the first amateur festival was held, three years ago, 26 groups applied for participation. Two years ago, we had about 60 groups, last year it was 150 and this year (1958) about 300 applications have been received covering more than 1,500 musicians.

To both festivals, jazz groups from the Eastern part of Germany are invited. Jazz, now, is tolerated there but not encouraged. Reginald Rudorf, the busiest jazz worker in the East, was condemned to two years of convict prison and forced labor, not officially because of his jazz work, but for "political conspiracy"; however, jazz, of course, had something to do with it. Many people in the East love jazz, and they love it so feverishly that you can feel how very much is in it, both of their love for the music and their love for the whole world of what jazz means for them. The musicians in the East are diligent and enthusiastic but they do not seem to get that feeling—especially in their way of phrasing.

Coming back to the Western part of this country, jazz had its biggest breaks in 1957 when it was presented at the Donaueschingen Music Festival and when both Protestant and Catholic Churches took a keen interest in it. The Donaueschingen Music Festival is the most important European festival for contemporary music, having made musical history since the twenties when Hindemith and many others had their works premiered there. It took this writer many years to convince the Donaueschingen Festival organizers that jazz is just as contemporary as any other "contemporary" music. But when, in late 1957, for the second time in its history, the Donaueschingen Festival had two jazz concerts on its program, they were a sensational success, overshadowing even Stravinsky conducting his brilliant Agon Ballet. The Modern Jazz Quartet, André Hodeir's experimental jazz group from Paris—an all-star band composed of the best known French and Belgian musicians—and the Eddie Sauter band were heard at the Festival.

Concerning the churches, many jazz meetings and jazz conventions were held in church seminars, Protestant academies and Catholic youth meetings. Attempts were made to incorporate jazz elements into church music. Heinz Werner Zimmermann, Director of the Protestant Church Musical Institute at the Heidelberg University, wrote a "Church Concerto" for Jazz Combo, leaving room for improvised solos, and a "Psalm Concerto" for Jazz Band and Singers, these works have been played in churches.

German hit (popular) music has become so ordinary that, in comparison, American hit songs are works of art. With this in mind, a church official explained what the reason for the church's jazz interest might be: "In a period where no real folk music lives in Germany anymore, where classical music is appreciated only by a minority of highbrow people, and even these people very often do not appreciate modern symphonic music, jazz is the only thing to keep the youth away from the banality and sentimentality of the *Schlager*."

—JOACHIM E. BERENDT

JAZZ AND CLASSICAL MUSIC

by Bill Russo

During the past two years there have been many hints of a coming rapprochement between contemporary symphonic (or classical) music and jazz. The most spectacular was the playing of Teo Macero's work, *Fusion*, by the New York Philharmonic. In this work, as the title suggests, jazz and symphonic techniques and materials were joined.

Gunther Schuller conducted three pieces by jazz composers (Jay Jay Johnson, John Lewis and Jimmy Giuffre) for a Columbia record released in 1957. On the other side of the same LP was Schuller's own work, *Symphony for Brass and Percussion*, played by the brass ensemble of the Jazz and Classical Music Society conducted by Dimitri Mitropoulos. This work is not jazz and does not use jazz materials, but is certainly sympathetic to the jazz idiom. The attempt at connection between jazz and symphonic music allows an abominable opportunism, however, and Mitropoulos' conducting of Lionel Hampton's *King David Suite*, at a Town Hall (New York City) concert in February 1957, provided a good example of this.

Jazz and symphonic music co-exist more frequently these days. The concerts that George Avakian presented at Town Hall in April and May 1957 provided a good illustration. Early in 1958 I wrote a series of pieces for Lee Konitz and string quartet, half of which used a four-player rhythm section also. In these pieces, jazz materials were used as desired rather than to fulfil a vague but rigorous idiomatic restriction.

More and more musicians have been active in both classical and jazz settings, among them Gunther Schuller, John Graas and several pianists: Dr. Roland Kovac, Hall Overton, Friedrich Gulda, Bengt Hallberg.

The late David Broekman was responsible for a series of concerts, starting around 1952, at Cooper Union in New York City, at which jazz compositions were played. Beginning in 1955, these concerts, known as *Music in the Making*, used a mixture of symphony musicians and jazzmen to interpret the music presented. There was no admission fee; the performances were sponsored

JAZZ AND CLASSICAL MUSIC

at various times by the Trust Fund of Local 802, by Broadcast Music Incorporated and by a number of other organizations. Among the writers whose works were performed (generally by an orchestra ranging up to fifteen or twenty men) were George Russell, Charles Mingus, Teddy Charles, Teo Macero, Gigi Gryce and Mal Waldron. Broekman also conducted Teddy Charles' *Word From Bird* at Newport.

For the Brandeis Festival in 1957, works were commissioned from Gunther Schuller, Charles Mingus, George Russell and Jimmy Giuffre and were performed by an orchestra composed of symphony and jazz musicians.

In Canada, Norman Simmons in 1956 wrote a work for full symphony orchestra combined with a jazz group. It was performed by the CBC Symphony Orchestra in Toronto.

Works by jazz writers were performed before representatives of six conservatories at Julliard in 1951. Since that time, there have been several Julliard concerts involving classical and jazz musicians in joint performances. During the past few months an album has been prepared for Bethlehem Records for which Teddy Charles composed and arranged music for himself, Sam Most on flute and clarinet, and a "legitimate" string quartet. On an LP for Jubilee, a chamber music-like background was provided for the singer Mary Ann McCall in arrangements by Bob Brookmeyer, Jimmy Raney, Teddy Charles and myself.

Before discussing the success or desirability of joining symphonic music and jazz, I think it would be best to point out three parallels. Jazz is closely related to Viennese classical music (*e.g.*, Haydn, and, to a lesser degree, Beethoven), in that jazz shares its chord progressions with this music. The chords of jazz are larger and denser but they are, in essential quality, not very different from Mozart's chords. Their root progressions, for example, are similar, and few of the altered harmonies of the nineteenth century are to be found.

Also, the jazz melodic line has much in common with the Viennese melody. Jazz melody is compact; that is, it is stepwise or chord-attached, and its skips are not shocking. In fact, it has almost no pointillistic flavor. Too, there is a significant use of sequences. Sectional music is made up of more or less articulated units which are often repeated almost exactly. Sectionalism allows an easily attained availability and comprehension to the listener. Mozart and Haydn are sectional, as is most written jazz.

Jazz has a connection with Baroque music, also, especially with J. S. Bach. Its chords are similar, perhaps even more so than to Viennese classical music. Surprisingly, though, the chord progressions in jazz are not nearly as adventurous as Bach's. This is partly due to the greater density of jazz chords; their implications are more specific and their weight is greater, not allowing as flexible a manipulation. The improvised jazz melody of the past fifteen years or so—from Lester Young on—is very close to Bach. If the syncopation and very personal interpretation of a Brookmeyer solo were omitted, the relationship of *approach* to the Baroque line would be immediately manifest.

Both Viennese classical and Baroque music have other qualities in common with jazz. There is a *general* degree of symmetry in all three. (Of course, Mozart is less symmetrical than he is thought to be. He uses many melodies made up of odd-numbered bars, etc.) In all three of these idioms there is a regularity, a connection between melody and harmonic cadence, a close correspondence between rhythm and melody and harmony—an ordered musical content. It has begun to disappear in modern jazz under the banner of a free melodic line. (Because the jazz improviser has laid on a procrustean bed of a pre-established harmonic framework, this tendency is somewhat justifiable. I would like to see the jazzman create his chordal structure and melody at the same time.)

The fact that improvisation is common to the three idioms in question is too well known to be discussed. This similarity, though, I think has been over-estimated. A remaining element in all three is the unvarying implied or stated pulse.

In contrast, contemporary symphonic music is steeped in the nineteenth century, especially in the tradition of the romantic expressionists—mixed with a large part of academic thinking and a rather introverted view of music's role in the world. As a result, much of today's music is cerebral and neurotic and self-consciously passionate (as opposed to the anti-intellectual neuroticism of mambo music—I have grabbed an example at random). Contemporary symphonic music is less related to the Baroque and Viennese periods than much of jazz is. Even neo-classicists are not as much like the Viennese school as might be imagined. Stravinsky's classicism is structural and formal; his melodies (which have never been impressive) continue to be acidulous and angular-puppetized. Hindemith is steeped in the power and majesty of the nineteenth century *expressive*. He is Teutonic, whereas Bach and Mozart are more Italian.

But what relationship can be seen between today's symphonic music and jazz? First, the symphony brass player's techniques have been greatly expanded by developments in jazz. Brass ranges are larger; a full and more dramatic tone quality is to be heard. The new symphony brass playing was vividly demonstrated when Rolf Lieberman's *Concerto for Jazz Band and Orchestra* had its United States premiere in Chicago. The Sauter-Finegan band, which is not a jazz band, although it certainly applies many jazz principles, formed the concertino within the Chicago Symphony Orchestra. To my amazement, the symphony brass section had the strength and bite and the Sauter-Finegan brass section was weak and enfeebled. On the whole, though, I feel that the symphony players have much to learn from the jazzman about an ensemble technique. An English composer friend of mine once told me that they don't strive for "that kind of accuracy." They should.

There has been some infiltration of the immense variety of jazz brass mutes into the symphony orchestra, although the straight mute is still basic and standard and resists competition. There has also been a slight renaissance of improvisation among today's classical musicians, with one of whom I improvised a four-handed minor blues recently (in Baroque style). On the other hand, the jazz player has made great strides in terms of velocity, purity of sound and smooth articulation because of his contact with "legit" teaching. Today's jazzman is much less mannered in his playing. Lennie Tristano and John Lewis feel that the playing techniques of jazz are sufficiently unusual enough to require jazz-oriented teaching.

Some symphonic music using jazz materials has been written. It has failed because of a lack of understanding of the contentual principle of Viennese classical music and jazz; it has failed because it has been incomplete. The use of one or two elements in the jazz idiom is superficial, and it is especially true of syncopation, which is not as endemic to jazz as people think. It has failed because some elements of jazz are far more subtle than classical composers realize. For example, jazz' eighth notes are more probably in the ratio of three to two or four to three than two to one. Also, the melodic curve, the organic structure, and the continuity of a Miles Davis solo, for example, cannot be perceived very easily by a classically trained musician.

In composition, many jazzmen have learned and applied symphonic techniques. Some have incorporated these techniques strictly within the field of jazz (Giuffre, Shorty Rogers, Jack Montrose, John Lewis and Tristano—the latter most successfully). Some have not cared about this incorporation (Teddy Charles, Charlie Mingus and myself).

Should jazz and symphonic music combine? In the relationships which I have outlined above, they already have. Should the fusion continue? I think not, unless the healthiest parts of both combine. Tendencies indicate to me a fusion of their worst elements: neuroticism, academia, and sensuality.

However, successful use of symphonic techniques in the jazz world and successful use of jazz materials in symphonic composition probably will be throttled by the bugaboo of "is it jazz?". If the music is meaningful and significant, its idiom seems totally irrelevant. It may lack the spontaneity of mainstream jazz but mainstream jazz is not enough, and I suspect that a good portion of the spontaneity is sheer primitivism and anti-intellectualism. Man must not be primitive and he must use reason.

JAZZ AND THE OTHER ARTS

by Martin Williams

During the spring of 1957 in San Francisco, the members of the artistic community, who (like many of their breed in other big cities) had long been almost fan-ish listeners to jazz, began to get into the act. In a club called the Cellar, poets began reading their poems while the musician-owners played in the background. The leader of this activity was Kenneth Rexroth, critic, translator, poet and a kind of father-overseer to several younger poets and novelists who have declared themselves voices of the "beat generation." Several people have maintained (not without certain mythological overtones) that the original idea for this activity came from Dylan Thomas. Soon poetry nights found the small club (capacity 150) bursting with patrons attired by everyone from Sweet-Orr to Brooks Brothers, from Capezio to Anne Fogarty. Saxophonist Bruce Lippincott was leading his men through backgrounds for Rexroth, Laurence Ferlinghetti, Kenneth Ford, and, soon, Kenneth Patchen.

The word spread, *Down Beat* reported, and records were made. The following fall, the Half Note, a small jazz club in lower Greenwich Village, New York City, was holding regular poetry nights when anybody with a verse could drop in and might even win a prize, and soon had employed a poet for other nights to declaim while Charlie Mingus vaguely ran arpeggios and made crescendos behind. In the spring, the Five Spot, across town where all the painters and writers have fled the high rents, was featuring Kenneth Rexroth, now touring and booked solid eight months in advance.

Meanwhile, Jean Shepherd, a New York radio personality who had largely abandoned discs and was jockeying verbal ruminations often interspersed with and accompanied by jazz records by everything from jug bands to Miles Davis, had recorded a piece with Mingus. And Ken Nordine was delivering a night club "stand up" comic's monologue over a musical background, calling it "word jazz."

For years "modern" dancers have flirted with jazz and near-jazz, and people like Katherine Dunham and Pearl Primus have done a bit more than flirt. Such things have usually had the dance recital as their center, but in the last two years dancer Lee Becker has come out of the Henry Street Settlement House in New York City to appear in jazz clubs and to dance before a gathering of jazz musicians and critics to recordings by Gerry Mulligan and the Modern Jazz Quartet at Music Inn in the summer of 1956. Eartha Kitt, who had been a student of Miss Dunham's, appeared with a dance group at the 1957 Newport Jazz Festival accompanied by Dizzy Gillespie's orchestra. In early 1958, Anneliese Widman was in a Broadway revue starring Mort Sahl dancing to the music of the Jimmy Giuffre trio. Some were speaking of "new forms"; some were remembering the blatant undulations on view on the floor of the old Cotton Club as Duke Ellington's musicians played *Black and Tan Fantasy* in the background, or remembering the times they had heard everything from *The Mooche* to *Groovin' High* at Minsky's.

One of Sahl's lines in the Broadway revue had been about the fellow in Greenwich Village who paints pictures to jazz. Of course, the gag, if it had not been a public performance, had long been a reality. Stuart Davis had done it since the thirties; Mondrian's last completed work (1943) was titled *Broadway Boogie Woogie*; and Bruce Mitchell was the most prominent of several men who have titled their paintings after jazz pieces.

In drama, some things had happened which were a different matter from the film writing of, say, Benny Carter and of Pete Rugolo (who has worked for Lili St. Cyr as well as MGM) and the backgrounds John Mehegan had supplied for Tennessee Williams. Hollywood had provided an "exploitation" quickie called *Hot Rod Rumble* with a stridently Kenton-esque background score sprinkled with solos by Barney Kessel, Pete Candoli, Frank Rosolino, Bud Shank and others. John Lewis did the score for a French film, *Sait-on Jamais* (called *No Sun in Venice* by its American distributors) and the Modern Jazz Quartet played it on the sound-track. Miles Davis had freely improvised background music for *L'ascenseur Pour L'Echafaud* (*The Elevator to the Gallows*) in early 1958.

It is particularly ironic that jazz, a music that has struggled so long against its functional role as a part of social dancing and social atmosphere, should take on at the same time that it was invading the concert hall as something other than a vaudeville show such decidedly functional tasks. The truism that Western concert music is the only "self-conscious" music, the only music that asks to be listened to on its own terms, is dramatized by the fact that only about two or three film scores are really worth listening to in themselves, that so many ballet scores are done in concert only as throw-aways, and that no one bothered to notate or even describe the lyre strummings with which the ancient bard accompanied his lays. Perhaps, too, the jazz musician was being asked to become less artistic and more arty—in some cases, even a handy-man for dabblers or publicists.

The appearance of Langston Hughes as poet-reader with jazz groups pointed to the irony and suggested solutions. If there was one kind of jazz that had not been so much a dance or atmosphere music in the past but had been listened to for the poetry that it was, it was the work of the blues singers. And Hughes, as far back as the middle twenties, had decided that the poetry of the blues and the gospel hymn was the tradition he would take to work in and from which develop his own poetic voice. Hughes reading with jazzmen was almost a natural development, certainly a legitimate alliance. And if today there exists no such creative participation as that which the dancing of the jitterbugs at the Savoy Ballroom in the thirties provided, there are jazz dancers who work naturally within the medium and whose art grows with it. Bunny Briggs (a regular at New York's Apollo Theatre), Jack Ackerman, Al Minns (who has worked on Broadway), the almost legendary "Baby" Lawrence (who had been nearly as much a figure around Minton's in the forties as had Dizzy Gillespie)— those are only a few names of men who seem to dance jazz as surely as Sidney Catlett played it. In the hands of such men as these, jazz seemed in no danger of being swallowed up as a set of devices or mannerisms by another artistic tradition but was sure of maintaining its own identity and finding its own way.

THE JAZZMAN AS CRITIC

THE BEST OF THE BLINDFOLD TEST, 1951-1958

If it sounds good, it is good

—Duke Ellington

*T*he simple truism often uttered by Duke Ellington and quoted above should be axiomatic not only among musicians and critics but among all who listen intelligently to music. Yet it is a yardstick applied only intermittently by the average listener, and very rarely by the critic. The latter has a subconscious variation of the Ellington slogan. It runs: "If it seems to sound good, before deciding whether it *is* good, I must first determine who is playing, how it compares with what I know of his other performances, whether the style is original or imitative, into what category it falls, and several other matters. Only then will I be sure that it sounded, and was, good."

There are few among us (and the author has been as guilty as any of his colleagues) who can claim never to have adopted this attitude, knowingly or unwittingly, in assessing a record or any other performance. It was for this reason, and for the hardly less important reason that most musicians are better qualified to be jazz reviewers than most of the men who hold those jobs, that I instituted the blindfold test. Immediately it became apparent that, without prior access to the label, the listener to a recorded performance might have an entirely different reaction. For, as I later pointed out in an article entitled *Canons for Critics* in *The Saturday Review*, such responses as "I'll have to listen to that a dozen more times before I can decide about it" (or "before I can understand it"), or "if this is the genuine article I enjoyed it; if it isn't, I found it dull and unoriginal" are palpably absurd.

Thus the objective of the blindfold tests was honesty of reaction. There were attendant issues such as the guessing game, but before commencing a test I always impress upon the blindfoldee that this is secondary, and that his estimate of the commercial value of the record is even less important; the factors that remain paramount are his emotional reaction and musical evaluation of what he has just heard.

The Blindfold Test has been running as a regular feature in *Down Beat* since March 1951, after having run as a monthly article in *Metronome* from September 1946. Instead of quoting entire tests in this chapter, I have used selected segments of various tests and arranged them in special groups that have some particular point in common. Usually only one blindfoldee at a time undertakes the test; occasionally, in the case of married couples or joint bandleaders, the test is given to two people simultaneously. Generally the interviews are conducted at the writer's apartment, under conditions that allow for complete, uninterrupted concentration. Incidentally, in twelve years of blindfold tests only two performers (Benny Carter and Frank Sinatra) have refused entirely to take the test, and only one (Lionel Hampton) has been unwilling to come back for a second test.

In the samples given here, the name of the musician interviewed appears in italics at the beginning of the paragraph of comments. In addition to musicians and singers, those who have taken the blindfold test include Hollywood and Broadway screen and stage stars, television personalities, gossip columnists and others, all of them with the bond of a special interest in jazz.

The interviewees were asked to rate the records according to the following system:

Five Stars	-	-	-	Outstanding
Four Stars	-	-	-	Very Good
Three Stars	-	-	-	Good
Two Stars	-	-	-	Fair
One Star	-	-	-	Poor

(Material quoted herein from various Blindfold Tests by special permission of *Down Beat* magazine, copyright 1957 by Maher Publications, Inc.)

REACTIONS TO LOUIS ARMSTRONG

Louis Armstrong. *Ole Miss* (Columbia). Trummy Young, trombone; Barrett Deems, drums.

Kai Winding: It's Louis and Trummy. Trummy was one of the first trombonists I ever really dug. He came through in great style here. And I liked Cozy very much. For the idiom that it's in, this made it; it swung all the way. Three stars.

Jay Jay Johnson: It had a relaxed feeling. But Trummy seemed to be forcing. He used to play easily, effortlessly; he sounds unnecessarily loud here. Pops was in very good form, as always. Three and a half.

Louis Armstrong. *Angel Child* (Decca).

Joe Newman: I liked the record very much. In fact, Louis Armstrong can do no wrong as far as I'm concerned. He's one of my idols. I think the record is very commercial. All in all, it's a good record. I'll give it four stars. This reminds me—when I was just a young boy, there was a young lady of whom I was very fond at one time. One day she was visiting me, and I played a record by Louis with him singing. She thought it was horrible.

It irked me for her to say this, and I immediately got angry with her; but I tried to hold my composure and I offered her some candy from a glass candy jar. She reached in to get some, and when she tried to get her hand out, it stuck. I thought this was very funny, and I laughed—it was my way of getting back at her for not liking Louis. I didn't like her anymore after that.

Louis Armstrong. *Pennies from Heaven* (Victor). Recorded at Town Hall, New York City.

Dave Garroway: Well, this record is what's wrong with Norman Granz. This is the Boston Symphony Hall concert, I think. You notice quickly that they don't try to have a climax every thirty seconds.

Actually Norman's are the best of the concerts that try to have a climax every thirty seconds, but you can't do that! Louis' band has maybe one or two big moments a night, and they work up to that. As incandescent as the man is, I don't see how he's going to get along without Teagarden and Hines. But he's done it before; he's never depended much on the band. Another thing, Louis' music is less non-arranged than most of the music at these concerts. These boys fit together. Four stars.

Louis Armstrong. *Ain't Misbehavin'* (Decca). Recorded 1938.

Terry Gibbs: That's Louis! I like the way he sings—he swings. I dig Louis' trumpet, too; lots of soul. Joe Bushkin's always talking to me about Louis—his favorite musician. If I'd taken this test ten years ago, I'd probably have said four stars. Today, I give it three stars—all for Louis.

Louis Armstrong. *Ain't Misbehavin'* (Victor).

Leonard Bernstein: Well, I love it, as long as Louis is around. It's so refreshing in the midst of all this contrived mental stuff—it's a breath of fresh air—warm and spontaneous, simple and meaningful, and besides he makes beautiful phrases on the trumpet.

Louis Armstrong. *Ain't Misbehavin'* (Victor). Bobby Hackett, Armstrong, trumpets; Jack Teagarden, trombone.

Miles Davis: I like Louis! Anything he does is all right. I don't know about his *statements*, though . . . I could do without them. That's Bobby Hackett, too; I always did like Bobby Hackett—anything by him. Jack Teagarden's on trombone. I'd give it five stars.

EARLY JAZZ

As a general rule, the primitive, folk music jazz forms fared poorly in the blindfold test, even when the musician interviewed was of an older generation. The following are typical reactions to some of the oldest recordings played, as well as to one record (Turk Murphy) representing the so-called "revivalist" school.

George Lewis. *Fidgety Feet* (Blue Note). Chester Zardis, bass; Edgar Mosley, drums.

Jimmy Giuffre: They were doing the same thing over and over. All of them were. Every once in a while they'd stop and the clarinet player would play by himself. I'm sure that was part of the background of what's happening now, and those guys were experimenting. They didn't show too much imagination and I've heard records that sounded like they were made as far back as this that had a lot of imagination. I won't say I've heard records that are perfect from that era or from this one, but, for instance, I remember a lot of Armstrong and Beiderbecke records where Louis and Bix were just terrific to me. This didn't have any imagination and the rhythm section played on the same level. Of course, the recording techniques were different. I don't know about the musicianship—I'd say one star. I didn't like the clarinet—it sounded like an exercise book.

Jelly Roll Morton. *Original Rags* (Commodore). Recorded 1939.

George Wallington: This is before my time. It could be a recent recording. I'm not sure. It reminds me of silent movies, because usually they played things like that behind them; but I would say it's definitely jazz, whoever it is. There is a feeling in there. It's a period I don't know much about. It has very little validity today. Two stars, I'd say.

Jelly Roll Morton. *Shake It* (Commodore). Red Allen, trumpet. Recorded 1940.

Jimmy McPartland: Must be Rex Stewart on the trumpet there, or cornet.

Marian McPartland: Whoever it is, it doesn't kill me.

Jimmy: They never did get going, it was chopped up too much for them to get into the groove. Sluggish.

Marian: The piano did nothing to me. I'd give it one and a half.

Jimmy: The trumpet tried, but he couldn't get it going. Give it one.

Jelly Roll Morton. *Black Bottom Stomp* (Victor). Recorded 1926.

Louis Armstrong: Put four on them. They played it too fast for five stars; they couldn't keep up with it. The trumpet player attacked his notes like Joe Oliver and Mutt Carey. The piano, if that ain't Buster Wilson, it's that other boy that went to California in the early days—it's one of the old-timers. It could be Harvey Brooks. Or Freddie Washington? From New Orleans? This is worth a hell of a rating over that bop stuff, but not a five-star rating for a cat that would like to dance by it. Give it four.

Jelly Roll Morton. *The Pearls* (Victor). Recorded 1927.

Willie The Lion Smith: Those guys should be driving trucks! There's a lot of guys who think they can play instruments, but this must be some guys that *never* knew. The word square is a modern term, but that's what those guys are . . . They never could hear and never could play. Didn't know how to wear pants, talk, or nothing . . . There's some of them still around. The phrasing is bad—old-fashioned, and they've never learned the formula of music. I don't give this any stars.

Jelly Roll Morton. *Grandpa's Spells* (Label "X"). Morton, composer; recorded 1926. Morton, piano; John Lindsay, bass.

Coleman Hawkins: Well, I suppose those fellows did the best they could with that piece . . . That's strictly Dixieland fellers . . . I really don't want to rate that at all. You know, all that Dixieland sounds alike to me. They're pretty precise, usually; take that boy Pee Wee Erwin, he's correct, he's real precise in his playing . . . This is a lot of hodgepodge; I wouldn't even be particular about listening to that any more. (*Feather:* Do you hear any musical value in it?) Actually, no. The piano? I didn't notice—wasn't that like the rest of it? The bass sounded like Pops Foster—was that Pops Foster? He's the only one I can even come close to identifying—because of that popping sound. Well, Dixieland is a type of music, you can't get away from it; if it's good, it's good—but I've heard a lot better than this. Fair is two? Well, give it two.

Turk Murphy-Wally Rose. *Tom Cat Blues* (Columbia). Murphy, trombone; Bob Short, tuba.

Kai Winding: They're playing our song! How did you know that was our groove? Jay, I'll let you go first.

Jay Jay Johnson: Ho, ho! Well . . . seriously, I can't give a fair judgment on that. Let's say three stars for the tuba solo and no further comment!

Kai: It's pretty corny, but it makes you tap your feet, anyway. The recording sounds recent; possibly it's a burlesque or re-creation of something. But for musical merit—I don't know much about ragtime, or whatever this is. I'd rather not rate it.

Bunk Johnson. *When the Saints Go Marching In* (Victor). Recorded 1945. George Lewis, clarinet.

Marian McPartland: All we need here now is Nat Hentoff!

Jimmy McPartland: Don't tell me this is Conrad Janis. The trumpet is sharp. I've heard Red Allen play this tune so much I always think it's him when I hear it . . . clarinet sounds like Omer Simeon; Johnny Dodds' style. It's so incongruous, the idea of 20-year-old boys playing in that style. Just like something coming out and speaking Latin!

Marian: It's like the study of antiques, isn't it?

Jimmy: It's living in the past. I think we used to sound a little like that; it sounds a little like the old King Oliver New Orleans style—which was good in its day, but nothing stands still in this world.

Marian: Well, it's like somebody who likes Bach and that's all they like. Or like the study of folk music. I'll give it one and a half for their enthusiasm. At least they all played loud.

Jimmy: One and a half's about right.

Kid Ory. *Milneburg Joys* (Good Time Jazz). Don Ewell, piano.

Shorty Rogers: Yeah! Happy New Year! . . . I think this is wonderful Dixieland. It has a very good spirit, honest performance, and they're swinging in their own way. I really appreciate it. I haven't heard any Dixieland records lately, but it's kind of a kick to hear it. I don't know any of the individuals—the piano player kind of gassed me. Four stars.

Kid Ory. *Tiger Rag* (Verve).

Jay Jay Johnson: Well! It was certainly a lively performance. Dixieland players playing Dixieland, and it came off as such, with lots of spirit. On the strength of that, I'd give it two and a half. I didn't recognize any of the players or soloists. They weren't particularly outstanding individually, but as a unit they were quite on the ball . . . Somehow I got the feeling that the trombonist had more than he could handle with the tempo. Any guess I would make would be a stab in the dark—was it Wingy Manone?

REACTIONS TO DUKE ELLINGTON

Duke Ellington. *Lady Mac*, from *Such Sweet Thunder* (Columbia). Russell Procope, alto; Clark Terry, trumpet.

Sonny Rollins: This record is immediately recognizable as having a Duke Ellington sound. The soloists sound like Russell Procope, possibly, and Clark Terry on trumpet. It's very important to have a sound that you can recognize immediately, and, of course, Duke is an institution now in music. He's one of my particular favorites. Always has been a great inspiration to me. This was very well arranged. All the parts have a significance to the whole thing. I'd rate this four and a half stars.

Duke Ellington. *Rose of the Rio Grande* (Brunswick). Lawrence Brown, trombone; Ivie Anderson, vocal. Recorded 1938.

Morton Gould: I'm neutral on this. I don't know, this seems to have some very interesting spots—towards the end there's an ensemble mixture of rhythms that's very interesting—there's some good solo work also; but, for some reason or other, this sounds dated to me—it doesn't make a point to me one way or another. The singer didn't particularly do anything to me. (It's probably somebody I should fall off my chair at!) There are patterns that were hot stuff some years back; I don't know whether this was done at that time or whether this is just a reflection of that kind of pattern but it just doesn't stimulate me. I would say one and a half.

Duke Ellington. *All Day Long* (Capitol). Billy Strayhorn, composer and arranger; Ray Nance, trumpet.

Woody Herman: It's either Duke, or somebody doing a Duke job. It's an interesting arrangement, and pretty well played, but if it is Duke's band, I can't understand why, other than the opening trumpet solo, there weren't any other solos. I liked it and I thought it was played cleanly; four.

Duke Ellington. *Stormy Weather* (Capitol). Harry Carney, baritone; Willie Cook, Ray Nance, Cat Anderson, trumpets; Billy Strayhorn, arranger.

Miles Davis: Oh, God! You can give that twenty-five stars! I *love* Duke. That sounded like Billy Strayhorn's arrangement; it's warmer than Duke usually writes . . . I think all the musicians should get together on one certain day and get down on their knees and thank Duke. Especially Mingus, who always idolized Duke and wanted to play with him; and why he didn't mention it in his Blindfold Test, I don't know. Yes, everybody should bow to Duke and Strayhorn—and Charlie Parker and Diz . . . Cat Anderson sounds good on that; Ray *always* sounds good.

The beginning soloist sounded real good, too. That's Harry Carney, too, in there; if he wasn't in Duke's band, the band wouldn't be Duke . . . They take in all schools of jazz . . . Give this all the stars you can.

Duke Ellington. *Satin Doll* (Capitol).

Leonard Bernstein: Well, that's about the quintessence of slick, professional, expert boring arrangement. I couldn't say offhand who it was. As I say, I haven't heard jazz for a year. I found it dull—methodical and extremely slick—the last word in polish and professionality—but dull.

Duke Ellington. *One O'clock Jump* (Capitol). Buck Clayton, arranger.

Jo Jones: Ha! Ha! Ha! . . . Now there's a record that you could get five different arrangements from. That was Duke, wasn't it? That's got to be Duke. I could tell from a little thing I heard coming out of his piano solo; and, again, right after the tenor, there was a brass figure in there that had just enough of that touch; and then again, I was trying to detect the actual humor of the whole tune.

Many people have tried to play the *One O'clock Jump*, but to do it right, they would have to have a very close association with the environment of its beginnings. It's a little older than we think, in its original form.

And that's why it's Duke, because he has captured the picture of what that tune is supposed to typify. It typifies a little word called LIFE. Spell that in capital letters, please . . . This is a little before Kinsey; and Kinsey would do well to take this record and dissect it, and he can write him another book. Just slow this record down and set it to words. You can give that five stars *any* day.

Duke Ellington. *Stompy Jones* (Bethlehem). Ellington, arranger; Jimmy Hamilton, clarinet; Cat Anderson, trumpet; recorded 1956.

Pete Rugolo: That's wonderful—a Duke Ellington thing. I don't know what period . . . It started off like a real old one. Must be Jimmy Hamilton on clarinet and Cat Anderson on trumpet. He almost sounded like Louis. I really like it but don't know if it's Duke's or Billy Strayhorn's arrangement.

I'd guess this is about eight or ten years old, but it's hard to tell. It sounds a little dated. I don't think it is a thing that was written today. This might have been re-recorded. For what it is, I'll give it four stars.

Pete Rugolo. *Early Duke* (Mercury). Don Fagerquist, trumpet; Rugolo, composer.

Bill Russo: It was beautiful . . . It was Duke Ellington. I'm getting tired of people accusing music of being pretentious when high brass is used . . . High brass sometimes, as in that record, really shows man's attempt to go beyond himself. Of course, there are indiscriminate uses, but I thought that was a wonderful use of a screaming trumpet.

There are a couple of absolutely absurd things and I don't know how there can be so much beauty and then some occasional silly things . . . But that's been true of almost everything I know of Duke's. Despite that, however, rather than because of it, the music is often very moving. I've never heard this before . . . I'll give it four and a half stars, and I would rate it the same way if it were a band imitating Duke Ellington.

Mary Lou Williams. *Mary's Waltz* (Storyville). Don Byas, tenor sax.

Sonny Rollins: That was Duke-flavored . . . I think it was Duke Ellington, and Paul Gonsalves on tenor . . . Very good execution on that record . . . I think I'll give this five stars . . .

FOREIGN MUSICIANS

On numerous occasions through the years records were played in the blindfold test on which the music was played by foreign performers. In the majority of cases the musician interviewed failed to guess this, usually identifying the record as the work of some American artist. Occasionally (as in the Gil Melle record below) the reverse occurred.

Hans Koller. *Beat* (Discovery), Germany. Koller, tenor.

Charlie Shavers: . . . I liked the tenor player very much. I figured possibly it might be Stan Getz or somebody Getzing Stan, which, of course, would be a derivative of Pres, but I still liked it. I'd give that at least four stars.

Roman New Orleans Jazz Band. *Muskrat Ramble* (Victor), Italy.

Charlie Shavers: If there's anything I hate worse than bad bop it's bad Dixieland! It sounded a little bit like Eddie Condon's group, and I'm a little surprised at him because usually he has some pretty good Dixieland musicians . . . Maybe it wasn't Eddie Condon, but if it was, I don't think he liked it either. It sounded like everybody was drunk—maybe everybody was. I'll give them credit for being drunk. Let's give them half a star.

Lars Gullin. *Holiday for Piano* (Prestige).

Sammy Davis, Jr.: I like that very, very much . . . I think it's Gerry Mulligan, isn't it? . . I love the record. I'd give it four.

Gil Melle. *October* (Blue Note). Melle, tenor.

Gerry Mulligan: It's not Brew Moore, is it? . . . It might be that German tenor, Hans Koller . . . I'd give it three stars.

Django Reinhardt. *Impromptu* (Decca).

Les Paul: Wow! Who that is it would be hard to say!

Mary Ford: I would never guess.

Les: I'm not one to speak of technique because I'm in favor of it, but commercially it doesn't mean an awful lot. I know that my mother and dad wouldn't flip. If you were there in person at this particular jam session, you might get enthused. But when you listen to it cold like this, it doesn't strike me as proving an awful lot.

Mary: Of course, I'm probably prejudiced, but the guitar work—I would very much rather hear Les Paul. It didn't sound clean to me. His technique wasn't very clean.

Les: Well, at that fast a tempo, it's hard to play.

Mary: It was out of tune, too.

Les: This is more of an exhibition type thing. Trying to prove something I guess . . . I'd give it two.

Mary: Two.

Hans Koller. *I Cover the Waterfront* (Discovery). Koller, tenor.

Illinois Jacquet: . . . Could it be Stan Getz? If not, it's in the same vein—

sounds like an alto, until the last part, then you can hear it's a tenor . . . Three stars.

Bernard Peiffer. *Slow Burn* (Roost).

> *Dave Brubeck:* It's Garner—for the first time today I'm really positive I know who it is. It's real relaxed, swings a lot. The effect is like you've got a guitar man playing the beat, only it's the pianist's left hand. If that isn't Erroll, somebody sure picked it up well. I'd rate it four.

EDDIE CONDON'S COMMENTS

Jazz musicians in general tend to be broadminded in their reaction to music of various schools. One of the least generous, and most uncompromising in his views, was Eddie Condon, some of whose typical reactions follow.

Stan Kenton. *Crazy Rhythm* (Capitol). Bill Russo, arranger; Lee Konitz, alto.

> *Eddie Condon:* That must be a big band. There's some very interesting voicing as little as I know about big band voicing. Saxophones sound very effective when they dashed in after that tornado was over. Is it Hampton? I thought it was a good record. Alto a bit on the bop side. That wouldn't be a style similar to Charlie Parker's, would it? I'm not too interested in that type of sax work. The arrangement required some effort, though. Three stars.

Milt Buckner with Terry Gibbs. *Trapped* (Brunswick).

> *Condon:* I sat through a hurricane in 1944 in Normandy Beach out in New Jersey and this is very remindful of it. They sound almost as powerful. That must be a tremendous light bill they run up, with the electric organ, the electric—how many string instruments? One? The electric guitar, the bells—now tell me, would a record like that sell? It might go good in a bowling alley, might equal the decibels down there. It's like nothing I've ever heard outside of that hurricane. Rating? How do you rate a hurricane?

Teddy Charles, *Composition for Four Pieces* (Prestige). Jimmy Raney, Composer.

> *Condon:* I heard the guitar, some bells, some brushes, I believe, or was it two guitars? Hard to tell when they've got that contrary action going. It could be six men for all I know. I never heard anything quite like that— do they expect to sell many of those? Jazz is like a sporting event: some pole vault, and some shot put and some are dash men. I don't know what sort of an entry we could make that group, but so many things are being called jazz nowadays I guess you could call that jazz, too, though I couldn't tell you what kind, other than that it's new and strange. I might be able to enjoy that after wearing out about sixty-five copies . . . I don't understand what those fellows are doing harmonically. I just heard it for the first time, and all I could consider was as it enters the ear, does it come in like broken glass or does it come in like honey? I don't know about rating this one.

REACTIONS TO DAVE BRUBECK

Dave Brubeck trio. *How High the Moon* (Fantasy).

Sy Oliver: This is the first Shearing record I've ever heard that I didn't like. In the first place, outside of *Body and Soul*, this is the most abused tune ever written, so I'm inclined to close my ears. If it is Shearing, and I'm convinced that it is, he must have been influenced by the fact that people are supposed to ad lib on this tune. The first, slow part is in very good taste. The last chorus shows touches of Shearing originality, but his heart isn't in it. Because it's Shearing, give it two stars anyway.

Dave Brubeck (piano solo). *My Romance* (Fantasy).

Toshiko: I don't know who it is . . . doesn't sound like Brubeck, but . . . I don't know. Just a piano, no rhythm; no swing, and nothing too fantastic in the harmony. Nice enough to listen to, but I don't think anything is happening there. Two stars.

Dave Brubeck. *St. Louis Blues* (Columbia). Paul Desmond, alto; Norman Bates, bass.

Willie The Lion Smith: I give them five, and if they were all put on the stage together, they would capture the prize anywhere—not only in a concert hall, but in a back room or any place. They upset me . . . The minute they start playing, that feeling and beat is there.

I like the piano because he plays like the guys I told you about at the brickyards in Haverstraw, New York, where the blues was born . . . He has heavy hands, but hits some beautiful chords . . . You could put this on at anybody's house, and they'd dance all night.

Dave Brubeck. *The Trolley Song* (Fantasy). Paul Desmond, alto.

Buddy DeFranco: That sounds like Dave Brubeck. I don't like the tune, never did go for *The Trolley Song*. Pretty clever, what they did with it. I don't think it actually gets off the ground. I like Paul Desmond very much, and I think he's sometimes inhibited with Dave's group. Maybe it holds him back. Paul saves this record; two and a half.

Dave Brubeck. *Rondo* (Fantasy). Brubeck, composer.

Benny Goodman: I should know this. I don't know who it is, but I'll take a guess. I know it's a jazz group playing it, and it sounds a little bit like Milhaud, I guess. Sounds a little bit like *Scaramouche* by Milhaud. I don't think it should be given a rating.

The performance isn't first class; not by any means. I don't think it's very good. I think that's the sort of thing that should be done by amateur groups . . . I don't think it should be put out on a commercial record. On the other hand, I won't criticize it because I think it's a good endeavour. If you're going to compete with the Boston Orchestra, with first-class classical musicians, "longhair musicians," playing this stuff, then that's bad.

Dave Brubeck quartet. *Me and My Shadow* (Fantasy). Paul Desmond, alto; Herb Barman, drums.

Nat Cole: I liked the ending best; that little countermelody idea against *Me and My Shadow* . . . Piano sounded as though there was too much going on behind him—the drummer was noisy. Piano didn't play too much himself, at that. He seems to be from the Thelonious Monk class, I would say. I don't know who's on the saxophone; sounded to me like Lee Konitz and several other guys . . . I'll give it one.

Dave Brubeck. *How High the Moon* (Fantasy).

Dorothy Kilgallen: Oh, that's wonderful! Whoever that is, I'd like to get that record. He's obviously a modern pianist, but what he did there in his progressions reminds me of a Scarlatti Toccata, especially toward the end; he became very seventeenth or eighteenth century. Could that be Dave Brubeck? Gee, I just love him! I heard him down at Birdland and thought he was great. You know, sometimes when a modern pianist takes a pop tune and does a lot of departures from it, they seem forced and artificial. But the way he does it, you forget that isn't the way the composer really wrote it. He elaborates on the theme without destroying. Five stars!

RIDDLE OF THE RACES

After returning from a long stay in France, where he had apparently been influenced by the reverse racial prejudice that then prevailed in French jazz circles (it survives to a lesser degree today), Roy Eldridge made a bet with me that he would be able, in a blindfold test, to distinguish white musicians from Negroes. The result was a unique blindfold test in which he attempted not only to evaluate the music, but also to guess the racial origin of the musicians. The examples that follow are typical of what happened.

George Shearing. *To Be or Not to Bop* (London). Shearing, piano; accompanied by white English musicans, Jack Fallon, bass; Norman Burns, drums.

Roy Eldridge: This could be three or four people I know . . . On this kind of playing it's hard to tell white from colored. The piano player *might* be white; the bass player, I think—yes, I think he's colored. The drummer's colored, too. It's very well executed, doesn't kill me too much, but gets going nicely when he goes into the block-chords stuff. Two stars.

Miles Davis. *Venus de Milo* (Capitol). Gerry Mulligan, baritone and arranger.

Eldridge: Haven't the slightest idea who this is; it's a nice-sounding thing . . . I couldn't tell whether this is white or colored. Most of these guys play with hardly any vibrato, and a sound without vibrato is an easier thing to capture than one with a distinctive vibrato. One minute I thought it might be Miles Davis, but it's not quite like his sound. The baritone I didn't care for. Arrangement very nice. Three stars.

Billy Taylor quartet. *All Ears* (Coral). All colored musicians.

Eldridge: This is a fair side, combining bop influences with boogie-woogie Sounded nice on the first chorus. I liked the pianist. Couldn't tell who was colored and who was white. They could be Eskimos for all I know. Two stars.

Billy Strayhorn-Duke Ellington. *Tonk* (Mercer).

Eldridge: This is a nice little ditty. Let's see now, what two-piano teams are there? White or colored? It's impossible to tell. Two stars.

Afterthoughts by Roy Eldridge: I guess I'll have to go along with you, Leonard—you can't tell just from listening to records. But I still say that

I could spot a white imitator of a colored musician immediately. A white musician trying to copy Hawkins, for instance. And, in the same way, I suppose I could recognize a colored cat trying to copy Bud Freeman. I can only talk about individual sounds that have made it, highly individual sounds. But you take a sound like Tommy Dorsey gets—any good musician could get that. Okay, you win the argument!

Eldridge was by no means the only musician vulnerable in the matter of racial identification. The following quotation comes from a blindfold test conducted in the summer of 1958:

Buddy Collette. *Cycle* (Contemporary). Collette, tenor sax.

Miles Davis: I can't tell . . . All those white tenor players sound alike to me.

THE GREAT ONES

If there is less in this chapter of Gillespie and Tatum, of Fitzgerald and Parker, than about other musicians who are of far less importance in jazz history, the reason is simple. From the very beginning of the blindfold test series, I found that there was a uniform tendency to accord unqualified praise to certain artists. This made for monotonous reading; one singer's views on Ella Fitzgerald, for example, would be completely interchangeable with another's. As time went by, I used fewer records by these unanimously praised performers and concentrated more on the artists about whom there was some disagreement.

The following is, to the best of my recollection, the only unfavorable reaction to Ella Fitzgerald ever recorded in the history of the blindfold test. Immediately after it are a few of the more provocative reactions involving Charlie Parker, who, like Ella, was not often used as a subject because of the conformity among the reactions.

Ella Fitzgerald. *My Heart Stood Still* (Verve).

Anita O'Day: Well, I guess if you are an Ella Fitzgerald fan, you would like this very much. However, this old version—dream up a story and sell it to Hollywood . . . Hollywood'll buy anything. Who dreamed up Ella singing "and then my heart stood still?" It's ridiculous. Here's a girl who sings good swing music . . . She reads very well on this and she's got the melody down. Dum, bum, bum, two-beat, ya, da da . . . boy! this is it for melody and everything, but classing Ella in this kind of a tune—I don't know. All I can say is, sell it to Hollywood—and they did.

The arrangement was pleasant, and Ella didn't sing badly on it. I'm not saying it's bad or good, but I think it's kind of silly—the entire tune with Ella. So much talent and how they've used it! As far as buying the record—I'm hung again as to how to class this. It wasn't so bad musically—it's a nice record, whatever "nice" is.

George Handy. *Crazy Lady* (Label "X"). Dave Schildkraut, alto; George Handy, composer.

Charlie Mingus: That old-fashioned writing could be Johnny Richards or somebody—at least, when he writes jazz it's old-fashioned. That could be Bird on alto . . . If it's not, it's a cat who sure loved him . . . I would give that five. For the solos, not for the writing.

Charlie Parker. *Cosmic Rays* (Clef). Recorded 1953.

Charlie Mingus: . . . If that wasn't Bird, I quit . . . You know what's funny? Now I know that Bird was progressing still. The other cats were the ones that were standing still and making Bird sound old, you know? Bird isn't just playing riffs on here, the way his imitators do. You know how he used to be able to talk with his horn, the way he could tell you what chick he was thinking about? That's the way he's playing here. How many stars? FIFTY!

Charlie Parker. *Relaxin' with Lee* (Mercury). Dizzy Gillespie, trumpet; Thelonious Monk, piano.

Sy Oliver: I don't know who this one is, but it's one of those bop records in the sense that I detest it. I am not equipped to distinguish one group of this kind from another. I don't like it. I feel there is nothing derogatory about commercial values; I think in the final analysis the music that lives is the music that the greatest number of people buy, and this isn't it.

If this form of musical expression makes them happy, okay. No musical effort is entirely wasted. Sure, they have tremendous talent. Hitler was one of the greatest orators and spellbinders who ever lived; but greatness does not mean goodness. For my personal preference, no stars.

Charlie Parker, with Dave Lambert Singers. *Old Folks* (Verve).

Bob Morse (of the Hi-Lo's): . . . The saxophone seemed so inappropriate with that song. It seems to go along with that group; I mean it's on a par with them. Is the saxophone player a famous player?

Gene Puerling (of the Hi-Lo's): It sounded like a member of the Charlie Parker school. I've never liked that school—it's one of those out-of-tune, honking-type things . . .

Lennie Tristano, in a 1951 blindfold test, observed: I want to say something about Charlie Parker, his importance in the picture. As great as we all think Bud Powell is, where would he be if it hadn't been for Bird? He's the first one that should remember it—he told me himself that Bird showed him the way to a means of expression.

George Shearing shows a good deal of personality, but it's still a take-off on Parker. You take *Groovin' High,* or pick at random any five records by well-known boppers, and compare the ideas and phrases. You'll see that if Charlie Parker wanted to invoke plagiarism laws, he could sue almost everybody who's made a record in the last 10 years. If I were Bird, I'd have all the best boppers in the country thrown into jail!

BATTLE OF THE SEXES

Female instrumentalists have often been mistaken for males in the blindfold test, and males have occasionally been mistaken for females. The myth of the alleged ability to distinguish a girl jazz pianist by her touch was totally destroyed by some of the reactions shown below:

Mary Lou Williams. *Harmony Grits* (Victor). Mary Lou, piano; Mary Osborne, guitar; Margie Hyams, vibes; June Rotenberg, bass; Rose Gottesman, drums.

Terry Gibbs: This must be Red Norvo's trio . . . no, wait, I hear piano, it can't be the trio . . . I hear drums, too. Guitar sounds like Tiny Grimes! No, it's not Red. This guy likes Lionel, but it's not him . . . one of those foreign records, maybe? Or Dave Brubeck? I'm completely baffled . . . now it sounds like a trio again . . . the solos all sound good. Three stars.

Johnnie Ray. *Gee But I'm Lonesome* (Columbia).

Faye Emerson: I love it. I don't know who it is; I would say it was Sarah Vaughan or somebody like that. For a minute I thought it was Johnnie Ray, but it couldn't be 'cause it's a woman's voice, isn't it? . . .

Hazel Scott. *That Old Black Magic* (Capitol).

Barbara Carroll: Don't know. Sounded like someone imitating Erroll Garner at times and Dave Brubeck. I didn't like it very much . . . I think he sounded unsure of himself—rushed and not musical. I'll give him one star to be kind.

Vivien Garry. *Body and Soul* (Victor). Ginger Smock, violin; Edna Williams, trumpet; Wini Beatty, piano.

Barbara Carroll: Violin sounded like Stuff Smith. I liked the trumpet solo. Was it Roy? I like the whole record, the piano solo, too. Three stars.

Terry Pollard. *Mamblues* (MGM). Corky Hale, harp; Norma Carson, trumpet.

Barbara Carroll: Very good record. Afro-Cuban with a good swing. I'm not familiar with the harpist. Trumpet player was in the Dizzy style, although it didn't sound like him. Sounded like some of those all-star groups. Four stars.

Cats and Chicks. *Anything You Can Do* (MGM). Norma Carson, Clark Terry, trumpets; Mary Osborne, Tal Farlow, guitars; Horace Silver, Terry Pollard, piano.

Barbara Carroll: I like that record. I like the tune done as a jazz tune. Very exciting record and I like the trumpets. One sounded like Dizzy. Piano player in the Bud Powell school . . . might be Horace Silver. Were there two guitars? I liked both of them. Very clever having double instrumentation. I expected to hear two piano players . . . maybe there were, but I didn't hear them. Four stars.

Afterthoughts by Barbara Carroll: Leonard Feather: What would you say if I told you that every solo you've heard on this blindfold test—piano, vibes, everything else—has been by a girl?

Barbara: Well, I'd say great. You mean every one was by a girl?

Leonard: Are you pleasantly surprised?

Barbara: I certainly am. That's what you get for working with male musicians, you don't know what the girls can do. All I can say is I'm proud of 'em.

Blossom Dearie. *More Than You Know* (Verve). Ray Brown, bass; Herb Ellis, guitar; Jo Jones, drums.

Horace Silver: . . . The group sounds to me like the Oscar Peterson trio, which I dig very much. This might be one of the things from his album, *Oscar Plays So and So.* They could have improvised a little more on it but it was beautiful—sort of like a mood thing. I'll give it three stars.

REACTIONS TO OSCAR PETERSON

A favorite gambit, one that usually produced amusing results, was the playing of a record with a vocal by Oscar Peterson, whose voice so closely resembles Nat King Cole's. In the examples below, Peterson is involved either as vocalist or instrumentalist, or as the man for whom another instrumentalist was mistaken.

Oscar Peterson. *Autumn in New York* (Verve). Peterson, vocal.

Jane Russell: Mmmmm . . . do you mind if I just go to sleep to that? That was Nat King Cole singing . . . I think that's a five. I love it . . . When you want to get in that mood, that's the best thing I know for it. What mood? Sleeping mood, of course!

Oscar Peterson. *Until the Real Thing Comes Along* (Mercury). Peterson, piano and vocal; Barney Kessel, guitar.

Dave Garroway: That sounds like Nat Cole after taxes . . . the way people are falling apart these days it might even *be* Nat Cole, but I sure hope not. It can't possibly be. A very dull imitation, vocally and piano-wise. He's stolen all the tricks and left none of the good things there. The guitar is kind of charming . . . Too bad about imitations; I resent them unless they're done in fun, as a humorous, frank imitation . . . but if we had never heard Nat Cole; suppose this fellow had grown up all by himself on an island someplace, never heard Nat Cole, and developed this style in the dark— well, it would be pretty sad for him to hear some guys like me say, well, this fellow's no good, because he imitates somebody of whom he had never heard. And that has probably occasionally happened . . . I'm embarrassed to have to rate this . . . one star.

Oscar Peterson. *Spring Is Here* (Mercury). Peterson, vocal.

Sammy Davis, Jr.: The first sixteen bars he had me fooled, but real good. I'd say offhand that that was Nat's brother, but he wouldn't use an echo chamber that harshly.

The first sixteen bars were a gas—wow!—but then he went off a little bit, I think, tonewise. I think he's trying to create a mood, and it almost sounded in the beginning that it might be something that Nat had cut four years ago with the trio, and that kind of flipped me. But then when I didn't hear the fiddles after the first eight bars, that kind of convinced me, along with the echo chamber, that it wasn't Nat. I'd say it was a fair record. Give it two stars.

Billy Taylor. *All Too Soon* (Prestige).

Duke Ellington: That's Peterson, isn't it? Wonderful record—such good taste . . . That's something rather new he's doing there, amplifying the hammers on the piano, or at least putting the mike extra close to the hammers. It's a device that came off very well. Peterson has good taste. Very good—four stars.

The playing of a record by A during the blindfold test of B sometimes seems to call for the use of a record by B during A's blindfold test, so that the reader could observe the two artists' reactions to each other. A couple of samples follow.

In addition, three examples are shown below in which the blindfoldee was unsure at first whether or not he himself was a participant on the record being played for him.

Oscar Peterson-Buddy DeFranco. *Strike Up the Band* (Verve).

Charlie Mingus: No stars! Because this is supposed to be a jazz review, and I don't think that's jazz—I think that's fascist music. Some cats that have listened and learned the lines and have no reason for playing them.

I don't know if they're foreigners or what they are. Fascist is a word I use for a certain kind of musician—they really don't dig it, but they'll do it anyway, and they'll act like it's better than anyone else is doing. I just heard a little of that in there; I've heard worse . . . I can't see any reason for that record.

Charlie Mingus. *Gregorian Chant* (Savoy). John LaPorta, alto sax and clarinet.

Buddy DeFranco: Whatever happened to jazz? First of all, everybody should have tuned up before making the session. I don't recognize these players. The sound of the alto is like Konitz, but there was so little of it that I can just about make it out. I didn't recognize the quality of the clarinet. With what he had to do, it could be any clarinet.

This was a feeble attempt to do something classical with modern sounds. It didn't mean anything to me at all—didn't get off the ground. This is nothing to me, so that's how I'll rate it—nothing.

Jane Russell, Connie Haines, Beryl Davis, Della Russell. *Do Lord* (Coral).

Dinah Washington: I don't care for that at all, because they seem to be playing with a sacred song. That *really* didn't kill me. It's in *very* bad taste. When I do a sacred song, I do it with sacredness. I think that's terrible. I don't give that *no* rating. And I don't know who it is! But they should all be punched in the face.

Dinah Washington. *The Lord's Prayer* (Mercury).

Jane Russell: Well, I didn't recognize the gal until the very end . . . the end was the part I liked. It's Dinah Washington. I like Dinah better singing things that are more her own typical style. Of course, I like the song very much, and possibly if I heard it in church, I'd think it was the greatest; but when I heard it just as a record, mixed in with a lot of other records, I'm not particularly impressed. Maybe it's just a mood you have to be in. It isn't because it's churchy, particularly; it's just a fair record. Two.

King Cole Trio. *Return Trip* (Capitol). Recorded 1947.

Nat Cole: Wait a minute, who is this? . . . Now that's not fair! You know, it took me a whole chorus before I realized who it was. That shows you how far I've gotten away from playing like myself . . . I'll give this two stars—put this in, don't change it, because I'm just as critical of my work as anybody else can be. I think if I made this over I could do a better job.

Jerry Gray. *Shine on Harvest Moon* (Decca). Eddie Safranski, bass.

Eddie Safranski: This is definitely a very Millerish-type band; I'd say probably Flanagan or Jerry Gray . . . it doesn't leave me with anything in particular. Very good bass, by the way; I thought I detected a few spots where he played double stops . . .

Afterthoughts by Safranski: Oh! I've just thought of something. You know, I think the bass player on that Jerry Gray record was me! If it was Jerry Gray, and if it was the date he made in New York, I'm sure it was—but I make so many sessions I can't always remember every tune. Anyway, I sure didn't know it when I reviewed the record!

Vic Lewis. *Everywhere* (English Esquire). John Keating, trombone; Bill Harris, composer.

Bill Harris: I haven't heard this in a long time . . . It doesn't even sound like me . . . Wait a minute. There's something wrong here. Who the hell made that thing? I noticed a couple of spots where the phrasing was different, and he goofed a little near the end . . . well, they say this is the sincerest form of flattery. It's a rather nice performance but who would want to repeat everything so closely? . . . Is it foreign? The guy'd do better to strike out for himself. After all, how far can you get imitating somebody? . . . Two stars.

REACTIONS TO STAN KENTON

Probably no artist in the records of the blindfold test has produced a broader variety of reactions than Stan Kenton. As a consequence, his provocative recordings have been used very frequently in the test, as well as a number of records (some of which are cited below) that led to the mistaking of another orchestra for Kenton's.

Stan Kenton. *Young Blood* (Capitol). Gerry Mulligan, arranger.

Leonard Bernstein: Speaking of pretentiousness! Is that a Kenton band? Strangely enough, what I liked about it was the beginning, and I like the ensemble parts better than any solo parts, which I found dry and ordinary—but there was a very nice quality to the beginning, even though it used all the stock-in-trade rhythmic and harmonic things I've heard for years; but as it progressed to the solos it lost interest, and at the end it became just a pretentious piece of big-bandism, which I just don't find amusing, or moving, or exciting—what else is there that it can be? Give it two stars.

Stan Kenton. *In Veradero* (Capital). Neal Hefti, composer and arranger; Bud Shank, flute; Bob Cooper, tenor sax; Harry Betts, trombone; Don Bagley, bass.

Friedrich Gulda: I really didn't like it so much—I don't think it's a jazz piece. I couldn't tell who it might be. I don't go for this kind of music very much, because I don't think it was jazz. There was nothing spectacular in any of the solos. I think the bass player could have learned his part better.

I never heard a record of Sauter-Finegan, and it could have been their band. It's hard to rate that, because I don't think it was jazz. The playing was actually good, but I don't think it belongs in a jazz blindfold test. No rating for this.

Stan Kenton. *Sweets* (Capitol). Buddy Childers, trumpet; Milton Gold, trombone; Bill Russo, composer.

Benny Goodman: I don't know whose band that is. It starts off kind of nice, and then it gets lost the last couple of choruses. I haven't the slightest idea who that is.

Some of the solos are good. The first trumpet solo is pretty good. I thought it got kind of shaky in spots there. To me, anyway. The trombone player sounds kind of amusing, I'll put it that way. *Marcheta, Marcheta,* is that what he's playing? Well, it's just fair.

Stan Kenton. *House of Strings* (Capitol). Bob Graettinger, composer and arranger.

Ralph Burns: Hmmm! I'd love to know what that's an extract from. It can't be a whole complete piece. Must be Schoenberg or Alban Berg or one of their disciples. I can't pretend to understand the 12-tone scale, I've never gotten that far. You have to hear something like this about ten times before you even know what's going on. But it sure is wonderful to hear music that can make your mind whirl in a spin. The performance is excellent, I'm sure, as little as I know about the music. According to what I've heard so far, I'd rate it four, but I'd better rate it three, because . . . why should I give it a perfect rating when I can't pretend to even understand it?

Jacques Helian. *A La Kenton* (Pathe), France. Jo Beyer, arranger.

Charlie Shavers: Evidently, I'm not a very good judge of who people are, but I must say that was well played with what they had to work with. It seemed to be quite a difficult arrangement, and I think that whoever the musicians were—and I'm almost afraid to take a chance on who I *think* they were—they most certainly played the arrangement very well—if you like that type of arrangement. (Personally, I like feet-pattin' music.)

It sounded an awful lot like Kenton . . . I'd even take a chance and say that it *was* Kenton. I'd give it three stars.

Boyd Raeburn. *Hip Boyds* (Savoy). Ralph Flanagan, arranger; Lucky Thompson, tenor; Dodo Marmarosa, piano.

Lester Young: That's the kind of music that I like. Swingin' eyes. Tenor sounds like Paul Gonsalves, as of today, and then, Ben Websterini, lot of times he sounds like that . . . I wouldn't be too sure of the band 'cause Duke has changed—his band sounds different—but he plays very nice piano. Piano tricked me; sounded like Stan Kenton, then like Duke. So you dig? I'm kinda lost. Nice eyes for that one. Four stars.

Count Basie. *Little Pony* (Columbia). Wardell Gray, tenor; Neal Hefti, arranger.

Lester Young: That's real crazy! I think I heard it once in Chicago. Onliest thing I would say would be Woody Herman or either Stan Kenton. I don't know the tenor, but it sure is crazy, the way the arrangement goes. I'm going to get the name from you so I can get the record. Four stars.

Kurt Edelhagen. *Tenderly* (German Brunswick). Franz von Klenk, alto.

Ted Heath: This is a misfit. It's got the trombones playing in the wrong register for the tune, but more important, it's a jazz arrangement of a standard tune that people love. Does anybody really want to hear *Tenderly* this way? This kind of performance has hurt the band business. We used to do that sort of thing but we gave it up two years ago. This could be Kenton. Nice alto player. It's well played, but the way they make jazz out of a pretty song is bad for the cause. Is it Kenton? On principle, because I'm against the whole idea, I'll give it one star.

Stan Kenton. *Thisbe* (Capitol). Bill Russo, arranger.

Kai Winding: Obviously a Stan Kenton production. Well executed. The material they had to work with was . . . well, one of those way out things, you have to be in a certain mood to listen to it. Jazzwise it didn't prove anything. Like so many Kenton things I've heard in the past few years, there's no message as far as jazz is concerned. Three stars for the performance, I guess.

Jay Jay Johnson: I go along with Kai, inasfar as it was executed well. The Kenton trombone section, as always, came through with flying colors. The arrangement sounds as though it was intended for a display of tonal and harmonic fabrics. A few interesting progressions, but I don't see any link between that and modern jazz, or *any* kind of jazz. If I were a student at Juilliard or something, maybe some kind of message would have come through. I'd say two and a half.

Stan Kenton. *Monotony* (Capitol). Pete Rugolo, arranger.

Norman Granz: This has got to be Stan . . . you know, I don't think even Kenton likes this! It must be that *Monotony*. If it isn't called *Monotony*, it should be. Take it off, I don't have to hear the rest. You know, I've been following the Kenton band for years, and the only things I ever liked were *Peanut Vendor, Lover, How High the Moon,* and things like that . . . It's a shame; this could have been a real swinging band, but it failed because Stan read a few books or something. He had some wonderful raw material, eager young musicians, and music; but as Stan is verbose, his band is the same way. If you have a musical idea to sell, you sell it on its own merits, you don't press-agent it with a lot of loud talk.

This band cheats; it uses gimmicks and advertising slogans. What did progressive mean, anyway? Goodman and Basie and Ellington never needed a slogan. I'd hate to hear Kenton try to mess with some of the swinging bands at the Savoy. Duke Ellington was the real pioneer in jazz concerts, and he can go into the Apollo or the Savoy and play the same music he plays at a one-niter for dancing and at his concerts—things like *Cotton Tail* and *Ko-Ko* are good anywhere.

      With Stan it's 20 men for dancing one year, 40 men for concerts the next. I guess next year he'll have to have 80 men, and the year after that 160. If he or Pete have anything to say, they can say it just as well with 16 men. Give the record no stars.

Stan Kenton. *Jump for Joe* (Capitol). Gene Roland, composer; Art Pepper, alto.

Billy Strayhorn: Sounds like Kenton . . . not a bad record; played very cleanly, but not too original, and keeps repeating the original theme. The solo is not too inspired, but in keeping with the rest of it . . . Kenton is trying to do a very wonderful thing with his band, but becomes too frantic about the whole thing; everything is a do-or-die struggle, there's no looseness, which I think is one of the great ingredients of good jazz. His more ambitious things are even more contracted, stringent. Tears me all up, makes me feel tense, and I don't like to feel tense about music. Two stars.

Stan Kenton. *Street of Dreams* (Capitol). Art Pepper, alto; Stan Kenton, arranger.

Eddie Safranski: When did Kenton make this? It's very much in the style of the band back in the days when I'd just joined it, in 1945 or so. The voicing sounds like one of Stan's own arrangements. Very good bass; needed more presence, but he played nice things. Art Pepper's solo was the only jazz feeling on the record. If I were to do a record like that, I might try to add a little more jazz feel here and there, with bass fills, for instance. It's a good record, though—three stars, and Art's solo is worth four.

      A thing like this means a lot to Stan as far as the public is concerned. The versatility of the men shows up in the concert things, then they can turn around and play the jazz things, too. But things like this are the kind that gave me a chance to express myself. Sometimes Stan and I would just start playing piano and bass with no particular pattern in mind, and we'd wind up having a record. A lot of our things were born that way, right on the bandstand.

Stan Kenton. *Round Robin* (Capitol). Shorty Rogers, composer, arranger, trumpet; Art Pepper, alto.

Eddie Sauter: I liked the way they played it—I don't like what they played. The material is pretty empty. Again, it's a sense of shape that isn't there . . . little chunks that stop and go.

Bill Finegan: I'm pretty much along with that. I liked the saxophone—that's all. Who it is isn't important to me, because, as I said, these guys have all molded into a thing. That could have been Charlie Parker as far as I'm concerned—it still could have been if I heard it again.

Sauter: I liked what he did. I liked the soloists, but I suppose I don't like that one-strain emotional content. It's not in a very—well, it's not a very deep record.

Finegan: I'll tell you one thing I don't like in general about that. In any of these large bands that play this style, it's an angry sound that the brass gets. I don't find that exciting—it's just ugly. Brass can sparkle and have an exuberant sound that seems to be intended without sounding like everybody's frowning and mad . . .

Finegan: I'd give this three.

Sauter: Three.

Stan Kenton. *Spring Is Here* (Capitol).

Sammy Kaye: Sounded like Kenton to me. I'll give it four stars for arrangement and execution and one star so far as personal taste is concerned. I don't go for that extreme type of music.

Stan Kenton. *Star Dust* (Capitol). Kenton, piano.

Ralph Flanagan: It's pretty hard to think of Stan's music without thinking of Stan, the guy. I think he is just about the warmest person you can find; he makes you feel real at ease when you talk to him. Everybody knows he is about the most sincere person in the world; but to get back to this record, *Star Dust* has been recorded so many times, I would never want my band to record it. But here's a guy comes out with a record that I think is among one of the three records I like of *Star Dust*. Everything is terrific.

There's some parts of Stan Kenton's band that I don't like; there were some fellows in Kenton's band this summer that I thought shouldn't be there. I have heard Kenton's band play the same arrangements, with different musicians, and sound a hundred times better. For anybody to stick their neck out by recording *Star Dust* these days, you've really got to come up with something, and I think this is it. Five stars.

ACROSS THE FENCE

As may have been observed from the comments by Leonard Bernstein and Morton Gould cited earlier, classical or symphonic music and musicians have been involved from time to time in the blindfold test. Here are two examples in which classical works were played for artists normally associated with the world of popular music.

Hollywood String Quartet. *Hindemith Quartet No. 3, Op.* 22 (Capitol).

Lena Horne: I don't know the soloist . . . it sounds a little like the lovely things Walton did for violin and cello. I like violin; I love cello . . . I fell in love with Walton, with that concerto he wrote for Heifetz . . . We have a violin trio of his, but I don't think it's this . . . I like Bartok, Hindemith, and we've loved Milhaud for a long time—some of his old jazz era ones from the 1920's . . . as far as rating, how would you rate something like this? Four stars?

Debussy. *Petite Piece* (Columbia). Played by Artie Shaw, clarinet, with orchestra conducted by Walter Hendl. Hershy Kay, arranger.

Gordon Jenkins: That's extremely well orchestrated. Beautiful, and well played. It had . . . a line that you can follow after hearing it for the first time. I've never heard the composition to my knowledge, but I like it very much. Three and a half.

MISCELLANY

Earl Hines. *Fine and Dandy* (Dial). Recorded 1951. Arvell Shaw, bass; Wally Bishop, drums.

Billy Taylor: No stars! Whoever it is, he committed the unpardonable sin—in this style—of lousing up his left hand. If this was recorded as early as it sounded, there was a little more harmonic thought than was usual, say in the '30s, if that's when it was done. Rhythm section and recording were horrible—no definition. That adds to my dislike of the record.

Lennie Tristano. *Yesterdays* (Capitol).

Earl Hines: I've got two sides on that. As to the general public . . . it's too far-fetched. Speaking from the public's viewpoint, I don't like the record.

As a musician, I think he's got some wonderful ideas, and he's trying to portray some of the things that he's been studying, or possibly heard or learned, as far as modern music is concerned. That's my conception of that particular record.

It's not actually from the soul, but more from the mechanical side of it. It's trying to knock the musicians out. That's what it appears to me. I think for the modern musician, the average guy will probably rave over it, but my viewpoint is—as a piano solo and musically speaking—I really don't care too much for it. I'd put two on that one.

Randy Weston. *I've Got You Under My Skin* (Riverside).

George Wallington: That I liked. That's Monk . . . I think Monk has developed a certain thing, where it's not the ordinary left hand like Teddy Wilson and a lot of piano players used to use; he's done something different. Artistically, I don't think this is that great. I'd give it about three. The piano on this needs an awful lot of fixing—the action, the tuning. They shouldn't have recorded at all on that piano.

Thelonious Monk. *Four in One* (Blue Note). Milt Jackson, vibes; Sahib Shihab, alto.

Count Basie: I know this from somewhere—it seems as though every time I turn on a radio this seems to slip in; and I've always liked it. It's cute, real cute; and although it's sort of not in my department and I don't know too much about that type of music, I like it an awful lot. Wonderful piano; vibes sound like what's-his-name, Gibbs, a little bit; and the alto, if it's not the Bird, he loves Bird. All the solos were wonderful. I've got to give it four stars.

Art Tatum. *You Took Advantage of Me* (Capitol).

Steve Allen: It sounds a little like Art Tatum if he'd had about four drinks (I don't even know if Art does drink) . . . his runs, descending runs particularly, are always characterized by a lacy, precise accuracy, and I could swear I could hear a few clinkers here and there. It could be somebody like Oscar Peterson or André Previn playing like Art on this one record, or it could be your Aunt Fanny, so I wouldn't swear . . . Sounds like the guy had a bit of trouble with the key action. But it had that fine, full chord treatment that characterizes Tatum's playing, and the powerful left hand with the occasional kind of Fats Waller heavy bit that Art uses. I like this. Give it four.

Art Blakey. *Mayreh* (EmArcy). Joe Gordon, trumpet; Gigi Gryce, alto; Walter Bishop, Jr., piano.

Buddy Rich: Well, sir—what can I tell you? Up until this storm I was having a very enjoyable evening. The music's all been good—I heard Basie, some good Dixieland . . . and now comes this mayhem. I don't understand it; there wasn't one difference in the attack of the soloists—piano, trumpet and alto could have been one man playing three different tracks.

There's no warmth in this kind of music at all. I know I'll get in a lot of trouble for this—it'll mean that I'm old hat or something, but . . . The drummer, for instance, why doesn't he make up his mind if he's going to play on the top cymbal, or bongo drums, or cross-sticks—there's so much going on that it doesn't swing at all. I don't like it. I won't rate it—I won't rate anything I wouldn't buy.

Sharkey and His Kings of Dixieland. *Temptation Rag* (Capitol).

Dave Garroway: That sounds like Brooks Brothers Dixie. The guys know they're supposed to have a good time with Dixie, but they're afraid somebody might hear them. This might be one of the young groups that are interested in Dixie. You don't have to be an old man to have a good time; but this is a pretty dull, dignified Dixie record. Sounds like Jazz Ltd. on a rainy night when everybody's feeling bad. One.

Bessie Smith. *Take Me for a Buggy Ride* (Okeh).

Patti Page: That sounds like an old record. I've never heard this singer before, not that I recall. I don't like it. I never cared too much for Dixieland jazz as they call it. One of my favorite artists is Louis Armstrong, but even his old records I don't like as much as the new ones. All I can say about this is, I just don't like it. One star.

Peggy Lee. *When the World Was Young* (Decca).

Raymond Scott: It must be Billie Holiday—but it's so accurate and so precise, it's so artistic that I can't believe it. That's the best I have ever heard her do. It's absolutely wonderful. I liked everything about it. That is the most exciting record I have heard tonight . . . Absolutely marvellous! Five and a half stars.

Mahalia Jackson. *I'm on My Way* (Apollo).

Gisele McKenzie: Is that a man or a woman? . . . I only understood one phrase of the entire lyric: "I'm on my way, hallelujah." I don't know much about rhythm and blues. It's got a great beat, but it's not my type of music. I don't know how to rate that but probably as a rhythm and blues record it's excellent. We might as well give it two stars because it's got a good beat . . .

Gerry Mulligan. *Makin' Whoopee* (World-Pacific).

Ralph Meeker: Oh, I love it. I think that's great. I recognize the instrumentation as being bass, drums, trumpet and baritone sax, which means Gerry Mulligan, and I think that this guy is so fine. This is the kind of stuff that

Bach would write if he wrote jazz—it's all wonderful counterpoint and a fine rhythm right behind it. It's such a nice sound. That's five.

Fats Navarro. *Nostalgia* (Savoy).

Harry James: That sounded a little like Fats; I'm not sure. I thought the cup mute and the tenor made a wonderful sound. It's pretty rough on anybody to try to play a cup mute in tune, so he deserves credit for being able to play the unison with the tenor in tune. I thought it was all well played, although not as well as I have heard him play other things. Fats has been one of my favorites of the so-called moderns, and it was very unfortunate that we had to lose him. Even though this isn't his best, give it three stars.

Liberace. *Jalousie* (Columbia).

André Previn: I'm going to have the first word on this one. I don't have any idea who it is, but I would go out and buy the record just to have the satisfaction of breaking it in the store. I think this has in it the worst aspects of society playing and the worst aspects of small-string groups' bad orchestrating. I just think this is horrible. No stars!

Sy Oliver. *Ain't She Sweet* (Decca). Recorded 1950. Hymie Schertzer, alto.

Ralph Burns: I don't know the band, but I know the whole arrangement— it's the exact same old Lunceford arrangement. Sy Oliver—only played like, ah, Frankie Trumbauer's orchestra or something. The alto was terrible. I remember the wonderful alto solo on the original—Buckner. This whole thing is just second-hand, a bad copy of what used to be one of my favorite records. It's cleanly played, but that's about all. One star.

Kenneth Patchen. *State of the Nation* (Cadence). Accompanied by the Chamber Jazz Quartet.

Annie Ross: Well, I'm speechless! Is that that new reading-poetry-with-jazz stuff? This is the first thing of that kind I've heard, but I kind of figured it would be that way—you know, like two people sitting at a table in complete despair and like nothing's going to happen anyway, so why waste time doing it? I don't agree with the philosophy at all . . . Like, you know, I thought when you first put it on I might put it on at a party as a novelty record, but it isn't that funny. I don't think the music has any relation to the reading . . . It's meaningless to me—I wouldn't rate it.

Annie Ross. *Farmer's Market* (Prestige).

Pearl Bailey: I've only got one thing to say, and that's just what was on my mind while I was listening: what in the world is *that*? I couldn't understand the lyrics; I didn't know what it was. I think the man in the street's going to be a little bit confused and I'm right in the street along with the man. Musically, I wouldn't give this anything. I'd leave the room.

MEET THE CRITICS

*T*he following biographies represent a sampling of the backgrounds of some writers, in the United States and abroad, who have been active at some time during the past two years as jazz critics. Material is now being gathered on others, who will be similarly profiled in the next edition of *The Encyclopedia of Jazz*.

"Main int." refers to a question I asked in which the critics were requested to name the types of jazz to which they now listen most often. "Mus. exp." refers to the critics' own empirical background in jazz and/or classical music. "Coll. rec." represents my attempt to dig back into the critics' memories and document the longevity of their experience as record collectors as well as the approximate present size of their disc libraries.

A common pattern found among many men who were once best known as jazz critics is the tendency to move on to an A and R job with a record company. This was the case in the 1940's with such men as Dave Dexter and George Avakian, who went to Capitol and Columbia respectively, and continued into 1958, when Jack Tracy joined Mercury. Reasons of space made it impossible to include many critics in this chapter. Critics who are better or equally well known as musicians (John Mehegan, André Hodeir *et al.*) were dealt with in Volume 1 of *The Encyclopedia of Jazz*.

AVAKIAN, GEORGE: b. Armavir, Russia, 3/15/19. Stud. piano, NYC, 1930. Got start as critic by subbing for Marshall Stearns, reporting for *Tempo Magazine* on Goodman-Basie concert at Madison Square Garden, Dec. 1937; as rec. supervisor by making Chicago Jazz album for Decca, 1939. Produced almost all jazz for Col. 1946-58; left to join World-Pacific, March '58. Frequent writer for jazz mags. in early '40s; contrib. ed. for *Mademoiselle, Pic*, 1946-8; co-editor of U.S. edition of Delaunay's *Hot Discography* 1947-8. Coll. rec. since 1934; 2,000 LPs, 3,000 78s. Stopped writing articles on jazz, 1948, but through work at Col. played important part in helping careers of Brubeck, Garner, Turk Murphy, Armstrong and others. Main interest: contemporary, experimental jazz. No mus. exp. Married to concert violinist Anahid Ajemian.
Addr: 10 W. 33rd St., New York 1, N.Y.

BALLIETT, WHITNEY L.: b. New York City, 4/17/26. Record and book reviewer for *Saturday Review*, 1952-7; *New Yorker*, 1956-8; has written poems for these publications and for *The Atlantic* magazine. Was musical advisor, with N. Hentoff, for CBS-TV show *The Sound of Jazz* in *Seven Lively Arts* Series, 12/8/57. Coll. rec. since 1940; 700 LPs, 1,200 78s. Professes equal interest in all types of jazz. Mus. exp.: pl. drum and piano as hobby ("Blues, in the key of C only").

Addr: *New Yorker*, 25 W. 43rd St. New York 36, N.Y.

BERENDT, JOACHIM-ERNST: b. Berlin, 7/20/22. Writer of six books on jazz publ. in Germany since 1949, incl. *Das Jazzbuch*, believed to be best-selling of all jazz books (235,000 copies to early '58); *Jazz-Optisch*, a pictorial survey; *Spirituals*; *Blues*. Co-ed. of German mag. *Jazz Echo*. Own jazz dept. at S.W. German radio network in Baden-Baden; runs more regular jazz programs there than are heard on any other European radio network. Has also had own TV series. Coll. rec. since 1939; 3,500 LPs, 1,800 78s. Supervised many rec. dates. Main int: mainstream, modern. No mus. exp.

Addr: Bluecherweg 5, Baden-Baden, Germany.

BLESH, RUDOLPH PICKETT: b. Guthrie, Oklahoma, 1/21/1899. Grad. U. of Cal., 1925, went into interior and industrial design. Lectures and articles on jazz in San Francisco, '43; to NYC, '44. First jazz book, *Shining Trumpets*, 1946. Had one-man show of abstract painting, '46; wrote book *Modern Art USA*, publ. '56. Wrote *They All Played Ragtime* w. Harriet Janis, '50. Ran Circle Rec. w. Harriet Janis, '46-52; supervised many sessions w. veteran musicians in New Orleans. Radio: *This is Jazz*, live series, WOR-Mutual, 1947. Presented first formal concert of New Orleans jazz, San Francisco, '43, broadcast by NBC and State Dept. On faculty at Queen's College, NYC, 1958, teaching jazz course there. Coll. classical records since 1910; jazz since 1917 after hearing Orig. Dix. Band. Jazz coll: about 650 LPs, 10,000 78s. Played major role in discovering or rediscovering Ralph Sutton, Jimmy Archey, Luckey Roberts, Chippie Hill *et al*. Main int.: "All types of jazz." Mus. exp.: stud. piano, then cello, at Mus. Arts Inst., Okla. City; harmony, counterpoint, theory; practice in pl. chamber music and in orch.

Addr: Hillforge, Gilmanton, New Hampshire.

CERULLI, DOMINIC P.: b. Winthrop, Mass., 2/7/27. From 1953, news editor, broadcaster, news and jazz reporter in Boston for WBZ, WLYN, United Press; Boston *Globe*, '54-6; to NYC '56 as Nat Hentoff's asst. on *Down Beat*, became NY editor, '57. Did occasional cartoons for *Globe*, '47-56. Main int: New Orleans jazz, swing-mainstream, bop, contemporary. Coll. rec. since 1939; 1,200 LPs, 350 78s. Active advocate of Johnny Richards and Herb Pomeroy bands. Mus. exp: stud. piano for three years in Boston, choral singing in high school, fronted band and sang in Navy, wrote and sang in musicals at Northeastern U., Boston.

Addr: 98-09 64th Rd., Forest Hills 74, N.Y.

CONOVER, WILLIS CLARK, Jr.: b. Buffalo, N.Y., 12/18/20. Active since 1938 as radio announcer, also writing occasionally for *Down Beat*, *Metronome*, etc., while living in Washington, D.C., where he has done ghost-writing for congressmen, written poetry and done narration for TV film commercials. Best known as producer and narrator of *Music USA* for Voice of America since Dec. '54, two-hour daily show, half jazz, half pop music, believed to have largest audience in world. Produced about 50 concerts, 1947-54; sponsored "The Orchestra," big band of Washington musicians. Member of board of directors of Newport Jazz Fest., which he emceed '57-8. Helped discover Ruth Brown, Farmingdale High School band. Coll. rec. since 1939: 4,000 LPs, 6,000 78s. Main int: swing-main stream, contemp.-experimental. No mus. exp. LP: The Orchestra (Brunswick).

Addr: Box 9122, Roslyn Station, Arlington 9, Virginia

DELAUNAY, CHARLES: b. Paris, France, 1/18/11. Parents both painters. Has been active since early 1930's in painting, and in promotion and publicity. Leading figure in founding of *Jazz Hot* Mag., Feb. 1935. Published first Vol. of *Hot Discography*, 1936; after visit to U.S. in 1946 (during which he supervised recording sessions at Victor), arr. for publication of U.S. edition of *Hot Discography*, major reference work covering almost every jazz record made until that time. As staff member of the Hot Club of France, promoted concerts, record dates and radio programs; supervised French recording sessions since 1935, incl. all early dates by Quintet of Hot Club of France, w. Django Reinhardt and Stephane Grappelly. As promoter, brought over many U.S. artists to France since 1946, incl. Gillespie, Bechet, Parker, Garner, Hawkins, JATP, Mulligan. Coll. rec. since 1929: now has well over 10,000. Main int: all types of jazz. Ran Swing Records, first European jazz label, from 1937. No mus. exp.

Addr: 14 Rue Chaptal, Paris, France.

FILIPACCHI, DANIEL: b. Paris, France, 1/12/28. Father a great jazz enthusiast and record collector. Began as reporter for *Paris Match*. To U.S., 1951, accompanying French President Vincent Auriol. Later became fashion photographer for women's magazine; returned to *Paris Match* as artistic director. After working as co-editor of *Jazz Magazine*, he became co-owner w. Frank Tenot in 1958; also shares w. Tenot a one-hour nightly broadcast over Europe #1. Consultant for numerous French recording companies, incl. representatives of RCA, Decca, London *et al*.

GITLER, IRA: b. Brooklyn, N.Y., 12/18/28. Cousin, Norman Gitler, trumpet w. name bands; cousin, Elie Siegmeister, composer and conductor. Attended U. of Missouri,

1946-50; Columbia U., '50. Worked for Prestige Records, 1950-55, and off and on since; asst. writer and researcher on *Encyclopedia of Jazz*, 1954-5, and *Yearbook* (Vol. 2), 1956; articles for *Jazz Magazine*, France; *Estrad*, Sweden; *Metronome, Jazz Today*, etc. Coll. rec. since 1942: 500 LPs, about 1,000 78s. Main int: bop, contemporary. Mus. exp: piano at 11 for two years; alto sax. 1947, mainly self-taught; still plays as hobby.

Addr: 277 West End Avenue, New York, N.Y.

GLEASON, RALPH J.: b. New York City, 3/1/17. Stud. piano in grammar school. During past twenty years, has written for many jazz magazines; in past decade, living in San Francisco, writing regularly on jazz for *S.F. Chronicle*. Has also worked for *Printers Ink*, ABC, CBS, several advertising agencies, and weekly and daily newspapers as reporter, rewrite man, publicist, etc.; also worked for Office of War Information during war, in Lisbon and London. Did publicity for variety of clients during past, incl. Shearing, W. Herman; worked with and promoted various jazz concerts in SF since late '40s. Editor and part-author of anthological book, *Jam Session*, publ. 1958. Coll. rec. since 1935: 4,000 LPs, 500 78s. Main int: swing-mainstream, bop, contemp.-experimental jazz. No mus. exp.

Addr: 2835 Ashby Ave., Berkeley 5, California.

GOLD, DONALD: b. Chicago, 3/13/31. Stud. piano as child. Joined *Down Beat*, Sept. '56; became assoc. editor, Sept. '57. Has devoted spare time to writing fiction. Coll. rec. since 1942: 800 LPs, 300 78s. Main int: "I listen to all types of jazz constantly."

Addr: 520 Oakdale Ave., Chicago 14, Illinois.

HAMMOND, JOHN HENRY, JR.: b. New York City, 12/15/10. Stud. at Hotchkiss, 1925-9; Yale, 29-31; studied music at Juilliard. Acquired ownership of a theatre on 2nd Ave. at 4th St., N.Y.C., in which he ran Negro shows with Fletcher Henderson, Luis Russell *et al.*, Mar. 1932; in May, persuaded Columbia Records to make session w. Henderson's band. Served as announcer, disc jockey and producer of live jazz shows on WEVD for six months in '32, using mixed bands.

As a writer, Hammond was associated through the 1930's with three British publications: *The Gramophone*, '31-3; *Melody Maker*, '33-7; and *Rhythm*, '37-9. In addition, he was music critic of the *Brooklyn Daily Eagle*, '33-5; assoc. ed. in '34-5 of *Melody News*, a house organ owned by publisher Irving Mills; columnist for *Down Beat*, '34-41, and intermittently since. His other writing affiliations have included *People's Voice*, '41-2; *Music and Rhythm* as co-editor and co-publisher, '43; *N.Y. Daily Compass*, '50-2; Sunday *Times*, '52-3; *Herald Tribune*, '55-6; music editor of *Gentry*, '56-7; contrib. *Hi-Fi Music at Home*, '58.

As a recording director, he produced U.S. masters for British release for Columbia and Parlophone, 1933-5; was recording director for Irving Mills in '34; sales manager, Columbia Masterworks, '37; supervised Teddy Wilson, Billie Holiday dates, etc., for Vocalion-Brunswick, '35-8; was associate recording director for Col. '39-43, and again briefly in '46; director of Keynote, '46; and recording director of Majestic, '47. Keynote subsequently merged with Mercury, of which he was vice-president, '47-52; director of jazz classics for Vanguard, '53-8.

Throughout his career, Hammond has always been intensely active in race relations (vice-president of NAACP, member of board since 1937); he covered the Scottsboro trial for *The Nation* and *The New Republic*, 1933 and 1935. He arranged interracial jobs, for public appearances as well as records and radio, in the early 1930's when such things were practically unheard of, and in 1935 was responsible for the formation of the Benny Goodman Trio, the first interracial jazz unit ever to tour the U.S.

Hammond served as the propulsive force for two major phases of jazz, overlapping each other in the late 1930's: the swing era and the boogie-woogie piano craze. He engineered the former through his association with Benny Goodman, with whom he worked closely in the formation of a band first for the *Let's Dance* radio series, later for public appearances. He revived the long-dormant boogie-woogie, never known to the white public, when, after a long search for the artist on a record of *Honky Tonk Train Blues* that had fascinated him, he located the performer washing cars in a Chicago garage, re-recorded the tune and launched him on a successful career. The artist was Meade Lux Lewis. Hammond similarly arranged for the other best boogie-woogie pianists of that time, Albert Ammons and Pete Johnson, most of their affiliations in records, night clubs and concerts.

He produced two memorable concerts, *From Spirituals to Swing*, in 1938 and '39, recordings of which were scheduled at last for release in 1958 on Vanguard records.

Hammond discovered and helped along to international acceptance, often at the expense of seemingly endless time and money, an impressive list of great jazz names, among whom the best known are Count Basie, Teddy Wilson, Charlie Christian, Billie Holiday and the musicians already named. A board member of the Newport Jazz Festival, he has continued to offer unofficial sponsorship to younger musicians and to rediscover older ones; many have been heard on Vanguard in the past five years, among them Ruby Braff, Sir Charles Thompson and Ronnell Bright.

A man of intense opinions on almost every subject— he has rarely been heard to express faint praise or mild displeasure at anything or anyone—Hammond has been not only the most important of all jazz writers but by far the most effective catalyst in the development of jazz. A member of a wealthy and socially prominent family, he has used his advantages to effect so much musical, racial and social good that a complete tribute to the work he has done would take a full book; fortunately, such a project is now in progress, as Hammond has been giving material for his biography to Willis Conover and it will be published, within the next year, by Horizon Press Inc.

Hammond has been collecting records since 1920 and now has well over 10,000 78s and several thousand LPs. His main interests are swing, mainstream jazz and the blues, though he has shown enthusiasm for some modern and experimental groups. An accomplished viola player, he has always played privately for pleasure; his Mozart clarinet quintet performance with Benny Goodman in 1935 led to Goodman's interest in classical music. In 1942 he became Goodman's brother-in-law when Goodman married one of Hammond's sisters, Alice.

Addr: 444 East 57th St., New York 22, N.Y.

HENTOFF, NATHAN IRVING (NAT): b. Boston, Mass., 6/10/25. Started on WMEX as news, sports announcer; own jazz show from 1945 for eight years. Historical series on jazz for WGBH, heard on 50 U.S. educ. stations. Occasional contrib. to *Down Beat* from late '40s; to NYC as assoc. ed., 1953-7. After leaving *Down Beat*, became contrib. ed. of *Metronome*, columnist for *Record and Sound Retailing*, reviewer of jazz and folk recordings for *Hi-Fi and Music Review*, free-lance writer on music and other subjects for *The Village Voice, The Reporter, Esquire, The Nation, Harper's*, etc. Wrote article on jazz for *Collier's Encyclopedia*, 1958. Appointed Eastern artists and repertoire rep. for Contemporary Records, Feb. '58. Helped organize *The Sound of Jazz*, in collaboration w. Whitney Balliett, for CBS-TV, 1957. Has served as emcee and lecturer at many jazz concerts and forums. Books: co-ed. w. Nat Shapiro of *Hear Me Talkin' To Ya*, 1955; *The Jazz Makers*, 1957. Coll. rec. since 1937: several thousand LPs, 2,000 78s. Main int: "As a reviewer, and by preference, all kinds of jazz." Mus. exp: clarinet (private instruction in Boston) for ten years; piano and theory at Chaloff Sch. of Mus. w. father of late Serge Chaloff for several months.

Addr: 245 W. 107th St., New York 25, N.Y.

JONES, RONALD MAXWELL (MAX): b. London, 2/8/17. He and his brother played saxophones in group known as Campus Club Band in early '30s. Began *Jazz Music* mag. w. Albert McCarthy in London, 1942; took part in Radio Rhythm Club and other BBC jazz shows; joined *Melody Maker* in '44. Edited booklet *Folk*, '45; wrote and compiled Jazz Photo Album, '47. Weekly record column for London *Daily Herald*, '55-7. Coll. rec. since 1931: 500 LPs, 250 EPs, 2,000 78s. Active in helping careers of leading British jazzmen, incl. Bruce Turner, Humphrey Lyttleton. Main int: mainstream and vocal jazz. Mus. exp: see above; self-taught, starting on sop. sax, then tenor and clarinet, sold tenor in '34 "when Hawkins played here and convinced me of the futility of continuing."

Addr: 26 Primrose Hill Rd., London N.W.3, England.

LINDGREN, CARL-ERIK: b. Lulea, Sweden, 2/18/26. Started out planning to be dentist, then worked in Simon Brehm's band while studying, '49-53. Copy writer for ad agencies. Several months w. Rolf Ericson band, '52. Various shows for Swedish Broadcasting Co. to '56; own shows since then, incl. *Flygpostjazz (Air Mail Special)*. Editor of *Orkester Journalen*, '50-56; editor of *Estrad* since '56. Reg. contrib. to *Stockholm Tidningen* daily and *Vi*, Sweden's biggest weekly. Coll. rec. since 1940: 800 LPs, 1,000 EPs, 2,000 78s. Main int: swing-mainstream, bop, contemp.-experimental, vocal. Mus. exp: see above. Pl. clarinet, '44-55; tenor, '52-5; self-taught. Wrote sev. tunes: *Kief* and *Forever Stoned* recorded by R. Ericson, Brehm.

MURAOKA, TEIICHIRO (TAY): b. Kyoto, Japan, 12/18/1897. Was first Japanese to write on Ellington ca. 1932 on strength of his records. Accredited correspondent for *Metronome*, late '30s. First president Hot Club of Japan ('47-57). Ed. advisor to *Juke Box*, recently founded monthly on jazz and pop music. Contrib. to *Swing Journal, Hot Club Bulletin*, many periodicals. Proprietor of a record shop. Coll. rec. since ca. 1920, but whole coll. reduced to ashes by bombing during World War II. Now has 100 LPs, 350 78s. Main int: early New Orleans jazz and Ellington.

Addr: 2 Jimbocho Nichome, Kanda, Tokyo, Japan.

O'CONNOR, FATHER NORMAN: b. Detroit, 1922. Stud. philosophy, theology at Catholic U., Paulist House of Studies; ordained a Catholic priest May '47. As youngster, often visited Fox Theatre, Detroit, to see name band stage shows. In recent years, serving as chaplain at Boston U., has become increasingly active as spokesman for jazz. Own radio series over WBUR-FM; weekly TV show, *Father O'Connor's Jazz*, on Boston's educational channel, WGBH-TV. On latter station, w. George Shearing, started series of half-hour shows called *Jazz Meets the Classics* for kinescoped use on educational channels, Oct. '57. Coll. rec. since 1936: 5,000 LPs, 400 78s. Main int: "Any kind of jazz, except Dixieland." Is on board of Newport Jazz Festival. Mus. exp: whole family musically inclined. Pl. piano w. bands, combos around Detroit as teenager.

Fuller details of Father O'Connor's activities were published in a two-part series in the issues of *Down Beat* dated 11/14/57 and 11/28/57.

Addr: 70 St. Stephen St., Boston, Mass.

POLILLO, ARRIGO: b. Pavullo, Italy, 6/12/19. Stud. law in Milan, '38-43; soon after World War II, joined forces w. Giancarlo Testoni, who had just started *Musica Jazz* mag.; has been exec. editor ever since; general secretary of Italian Jazz Federation since '47. Has organized many jazz concerts in Milan, also nine jazz festivals, incl. three international events in San Remo (Riviera) since '56. Arr. many recording sessions; articles for newspapers, magazines. Co-author *L'Enciclopedia Del Jazz* (Milan,

The Sound of Jazz. Vic Dickenson, Red Allen.

The Sound of Jazz. Roy Eldridge.

The Sound of Jazz. Billie Holiday.

Above: The Sound of Jazz. Coleman
Hawkins, Lester Young,
Ben Webster.

Right: The Sound of Jazz. Count
Basie.

Opposite: CBS *Timex Show*. Lionel
Hampton's Orchestra; Drummers,
rear to front: Gene Krupa, Cozy
Cole, Garry Moore.

CBS *Timex Show*. Louis Armstrong, Lionel Hampton (Gerry Mulligan, Jack Teagarden in background).

CBS *Timex Show*. Peanuts Hucko, Jack Teagarden.

NBC *Timex Show*. June Christy.

CBS *The Big Record*. Ella Fitzgerald.

CBS *Crescendo*. Mahalia Jackson.

CBS *Crescendo*. Lizzie Miles.

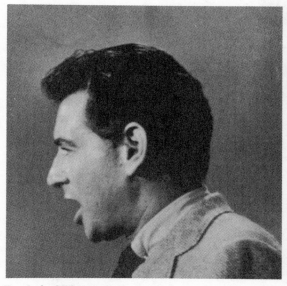

Top Left: CBS *Crescendo*. Peggy Lee.

Top Right: CBS *Omnibus*. Leonard Bernstein (*Roy Stevens*).

Below: German Television: The Eddie Sauter Orchestra's first TV show in Baden-Baden, Germany (*Hanns E. Haehl*).

Opposite: CBS *Omnibus*. *Foreground:* Indian drummer Chatur Lal and Jo Jones. *Background:* Urbie Green, Ruby Braff, Tony Scott, the late Walter Page, Ronnell Bright.

NBC *The Nat King Cole Show*. Mel Torme, Nat Cole.

1952); author of *Jazz Moderno, Musica del Dopoguerra,* '58. Coll. rec. since '35: 1,000 LPs, 2,000 78s. Main int: modern jazz of all kinds. Is a lawyer and journalist by profession. Mus. exp: is gen'l. sec'y. of UNCLA (National Union of Composers and Lyricists of Light Music), has written pop songs. Outside music, has written historical features for *Epoca* and a novel for children.

Addr: Corso Italia 6, Milan, Italy.

RACE, STEVE: b. Lincoln, England, 4/1/21. Weekly columnist for London *Melody Maker* for several years; occasionally contributes to other periodicals. Coll. rec. since late '30s: no estimate of size of coll. Main int: swing-mainstream, bop, contemp.-experimental. Mus. exp: piano studies at Royal Academy of Mus., London; active as pianist, composer, arranger and conductor; wrote a ballet (*Skyline*) and orchestral works, incl. film music. Staff conductor and mus. dir. for Associated Rediffusion, London, commercial TV contractors. Has also supervised British recording sessions, incl. London dates of Jimmy and Marian McPartland; several BBC disc jockey series, also broadcast in France, Iceland. Many radio, TV shows w. own orch. and quintet. Largely responsible for British acceptance of Brubeck quartet.

Addr: c/o Television House, Kingsway, London, W.C.2, England.

SCHULZ-KOEHN, DR. DIETRICH: b. Sonneberg, Thuringia, 12/28/12. While a student, founded first German jazz club, in East Prussia. Worked for Brunswick, Telefunken Records. In German Army, held as prisoner of war; released, '47; worked for Military Govt. Since then has been advisor to record companies, broadcaster, lecturer, writer. To U.S., 1957, to gather material for touring German museum of jazz. Has recorded German Jazz Festival annually since '53. Coll. rec. since 1932: 900 LPs, 5,000 78s plus classical coll. Mus. exp: stud. violin ten yrs.; piano, 12 yrs.; drums, trombone in high school band. Stud. music and languages at Univ., Freiburg and Frankfurt.

Addr: 24 Auer St., Cologne, Germany.

SHAPIRO, NATHANIEL M.: b. New York City, 9/27/22. Has written for *Down Beat, Jazz Hot,* many LP liner notes; supervised recording dates for Jazztone, Concert Hall, Vanguard, Columbia, Harmony. Publicity work for O. Peterson, Eckstine, JATP, etc., 1953. Though not mainly active as critic, made important contrib. as co-editor w. N. Hentoff of books *Hear Me Talkin' To Ya* and *The Jazz Makers.* Director of international artists and repertoire for Columbia, Epic, Harmony, '57-8. Coll. rec. since 1935: 3,000 LPs, 2,000 78s. Main int: swing, mainstream. No mus. exp.

Addr: 156 W. 86th St., New York, N.Y.

SIMON, GEORGE THOMAS: b. New York City, 5/9/12. One brother was music critic for *PM* and author of several books on classical music; another dir. of light music at WQXR; cousin, Robert, was mus. critic for *New Yorker* for 25 years. Editor of *Metronome,* '35-55. Producer-writer for NBC radio show *For The Record,* '44-5; writer for many TV shows since '55, incl. America's Greatest Bands, *The Music of Gershwin, Look Up and Live;* writer and assoc. producer for Timex All-Star TV Jazz shows, '57-8. Coll. rec. since 1928: 600 LPs, 8,000 78s. Main int: swing, contemporary. As recording supervisor, made majority of jazz dates for V Discs during World War II; Metronome All-Star sessions, '39-53; in recent years, dates for Grand Award, Jazztone, Victor. Radio show *World of Jazz,* WQXR, '55-7. Mus. exp: stud. piano; drum lessons w. Gene Krupa, Bill West; harmony w. Otto Cesana. Led own band at Harvard, '30-34. Pl. dr. on rec. date w. Glenn Miller for Decca, '37. Has also written blues lyrics and numerous pop tunes. Has been instrumental during past 20 years in aiding careers of many dance bandleaders and singers, esp. Glenn Miller, Elliot Lawrence, Paul Whiteman, Dinah Shore. Assoc. w. Glenn Miller AAF band, while both were in service, at New Haven; prod. weekly jam sessions during war at Stage Door Canteen.

Addr: Overbrook Dr., Stamford, Connecticut.

SIMON, WILLIAM LOUIS (BILL): b. Springville, N.Y., 6/1/20. Worked in record store, '40; managed own store in Buffalo in early '40s; salesman for Decca, NYC, '44; supervised recordings for National, '45; Gotham, '46-7. Writer for *Billboard,* '48-51, '55-7. Pop and jazz record reviewer for *Saturday Review,* '48-54. Wrote series of leaflets for American Recording Society accompanying its LPs, '56-7. Pl. important part in early careers of Tony Scott, Earl Bostic. Coll. rec. since 1933: 2,000 LPs, 2,000 78s. Main int: mainstream, bop, contemporary. Mus. exp: piano at 11, sop. sax at 12; stud. mus. at U. of Michigan, pl. in U. band. Pl. clarinet one summer season in Buffalo Prom Symphony, also some chamber music in early '40s. Stopped playing, '45; resumed, '55, and has been working regular jazz gigs since then on tenor sax.

Addr: 79 Prospect Dr., Chappaqua, N.Y.

SMITH, CHARLES EDWARD: b. Thomaston, Conn., 6/8/04. Grandfather, Leander Whiteman, pl. guitar, sang, inspired his love for music. Writing on jazz since 1930; first contrib. to *Esquire,* '34; books: *Jazzmen,* '39 (co-editor); *The Jazz Record Book,* '42 (editor); contrib. to *The Jazz Makers,* '57. Created script for first live network jazz radio series, *Saturday Night Swing Session,* in mid-'30s. With F. Ramsey, created *Jazz in America* short-wave programs for OWI during war. Wrote poem, *Blues Stanza,* publ. in *New Republic.* Supervised Jelly Roll Morton's *New Orleans Memories* for Commodore. Was founding member of Institute of Jazz Studies. Was one of first writers to interest record companies in recording or reissuing jazz, working on RCA Victor's Hot Jazz series in late 1930's. Wrote booklet for Riverside's *History of Classic Jazz*, '57. With Moses Asch, planned and completed documentary study of civil, human rights, a book-and-record project. Says he is "Not a record collector" and his coll. is "variable and negligible." Main int: small band jazz of all types, singers, and some big bands. No mus. exp.

STEARNS, MARSHALL WINSLOW: b. Cambridge, Mass., 10/18/08. Harvard B.S., '31; Yale Ph.D., '42. Has been teacher at U. of Hawaii, Indiana U., Cornell, NYU, New School, and, in recent years, at Hunter College, NYC. Awarded Guggenheim Fellowship in music, '50-1. Best known as president and exec. director of the Institute of Jazz Studies, Stearns has been for many years the most active of all jazz experts on the academic level; he has lectured on jazz at numerous colleges, is a faculty member of the School of Jazz in Lenox, Mass., board member and director of the critics' symposium at the Newport Jazz Festival and advisor to the State Department's ANTA Music Panel on its cultural exchange program. In this last capacity he toured the Near East in the spring of 1956 with Dizzy Gillespie's orchestra.

His book, *The Story of Jazz*, was published in 1956; he has contrib. to *Down Beat*, *Metronome*, *The Saturday Review*, *Variety*, *Esquire*, New York *Times*, *Harper's*, etc. He was consultant to the NBC educational TV series, *The Subject is Jazz*, March-June 1958.

Stearns began collecting records in 1922; the reference library of the Institute of Jazz Studies, housed in his New York home, now numbers over 15,000 78s and 5,000 LPs. He listens to all types of jazz, but is especially interested in the study and documentation of what he has called its "pre-history" and the ragtime and brass band origins. He studied music with Henry Cowell and played drums, saxophone and guitar in college bands.

Addr: 108 Waverly Place, New York 11, N.Y.

TENOT, FRANK: b. Mulhouse, France, 10/31/25. Started in 1944 as writer for *Jazz Hot* and disc jockey for Bordeaux station. Editor of *Jazz Hot*, '48-55, then editor-in-chief of *Jazz Magazine*. Worked in nuclear physics at French Atomic Energy Commission, '49-55. Supervised recording dates in France for Django Reinhardt, Zoot Sims, Lucky Thompson *et al.* Daily radio show on Europe No. 1. Coll. rec. since 1938: 3,000 LPs, 1,500 78s. Main int: swing, mainstream. Mus. exp: stud. sop. sax, Bordeaux, 1940.

Addr: 46 Rue St. Dominique, Paris 7, France.

ULANOV, BARRY: b. New York City, 4/10/18. Started as jazz writer while editing literary mag. at Columbia College, '35-9. Soon after graduation, he joined *Swing* mag., remaining until '41, when he joined *Metronome*, editing it w. George Simon or w. this writer until '55. On leaving *Metronome*, he became a columnist for *Down Beat*.

Ulanov's books have included *The Recorded Music of Mozart* ('41), biographies of Duke Ellington (*Duke Ellington*, '46) and Bing Crosby (*The Incredible Crosby*, '48); *A History of Jazz in America*, '52, and *A Handbook of Jazz*, '57. He was a teacher at Juilliard in the summer of '46; at Princeton U., '50-1; since '51 he has been at Barnard College, where he is now an Assistant Professor of English. He is assoc. editor of *The Bridge*, yearbook of the Inst. of Judaeo-Christian Studies; vice-president of Catholic Renascence Society, chairman of Conference of the Humanities. In 1958 he was completing work on a book to be called *Sources and Resources: Studies in the Literary Traditions of Christian Humanism*.

A collector of records since the early 1930's, he now has 3,000 LPs and uncounted 78s. His main interests in jazz are contemp.-experimental music. Mus. exp: stud. at home from age four w. father, a professional violinist, teacher and conductor; continued to play violin through college years.

Addr: 19 Bethune St., New York 14, N.Y.

WILLIAMS, MARTIN T.: b. Richmond, Va., 8/9/24. Began writing on jazz in prep. school newspaper. Contributor, record reviewer for *Record Changer*, '52-7 *Saturday Review*, '57; *American Record Guide*, *Down Beat*, '58. Contributor on jazz for various publications, incl. *Jazz Monthly* (England), *Just Jazz No.* 2 (England). Helped organize concerts on return to college (U. of Va.) after World War II. Has also written on literature for scholarly publications; worked as editor in book publ. and been an English instructor. Coll. rec. since 1937: size of coll. variable. Main int: all types of jazz. Mus. exp: stud. clarinet in teens, no professional experience. Contrib. to present volume in *Encyclopedia of Jazz* series.

Addr: 213 W. 66th St., New York 23, N.Y.

WILSON, JOHN S.: b. Elizabeth, N.J., 1/6/13. N.Y. editor *Down Beat*, '49-50; jazz reviewer for New York *Times* since '52 and *High Fidelity* since '53. Coll. rec. since 1923: lost count of size of coll. Radio: *The World of Jazz*, WQXR, weekly since '54. Listens to all kinds of jazz, claims no preferences. No mus. exp. but stud. piano as child in Elizabeth. Contrib. to *The Jazz Makers*, '57.

Addr: R.D. 1, Princeton, New Jersey.

INTERNATIONAL POLLS

*F*ollowing are the results of nine jazz polls conducted during 1957 and 1958 in the United States, Great Britain, France, Germany, and Holland.

In the *Down Beat* Critics' Poll a point system is used, ten points being awarded for each vote; two-way split votes are given five points and three-way split votes three points, etc. Thus a vote of 135 points for Ella Fitzgerald, for instance, indicates that she received a total of 13½ votes from the 31 critics who participated in the poll.

The *Playboy* Readers' Poll was inaugurated in the February 1957 issue of that publication. The results of the first poll did not differ substantially from those of the second, published here, with a few minor exceptions: Dave Brubeck was the winner on piano and Charlie Ventura placed second on tenor sax; thus the only names in the 1958 poll that had not appeared in the previous year's list of winners are Erroll Garner and Coleman Hawkins.

The *Melody Maker* Critics' Poll was conducted among 25 British jazz critics. The results are based on a point system: three points for a first place vote, two for a second place vote, and one for a third.

In the *Metronome* Readers' Poll, the reason for the omission of figures in the orchestra, combo, male singer, female singer and vocal group categories is that these were part of an earlier poll conducted in the fall of 1957 and the results were printed without any listing of votes.

	Down Beat Readers' Poll December, 1957		Down Beat Critics' Poll August, 1957		Metronome Readers' Poll February, 1958		Playboy Readers' Poll February, 1958	
MUSICIAN OF THE YEAR	Duke Ellington Modern Jazz Quartet Dizzy Gillespie		Category Not Included		Category Not Included		Category Not Included	
ORCHESTRA	Count Basie Duke Ellington Stan Kenton		Count Basie Duke Ellington Dizzy Gillespie	110 85 65	Count Basie Stan Kenton Duke Ellington		Stan Kenton Duke Ellington Count Basie	9268 3953 2401
COMBO	Modern Jazz Quartet 1109 Dave Brubeck Chico Hamilton	1109 667 560	Modern Jazz Quartet Gerry Mulligan Chico Hamilton	66 40 28	Modern Jazz Quartet Dave Brubeck Gerry Mulligan		Dave Brubeck Modern Jazz Quartet Louis Armstrong	5180 3598 1865
TRADITIONAL COMBO	Category Not Included		Category Not Included		Category Not Included		Category Not Included	
COMPOSER (ARRANGER)	Duke Ellington John Lewis Jimmy Giuffre	876 789 311	Category Not Included		Category Not Included		Category Not Included	
MALE SINGER	Frank Sinatra Nat Cole Joe Williams	3001 355 321	Frank Sinatra Louis Armstrong Jimmy Rushing	135 57 27	Frank Sinatra Mel Torme Joe Williams		Frank Sinatra Nat Cole Sammy Davis, Jr.	14674 2113 1981
FEMALE SINGER	Ella Fitzgerald Anita O'Day Sarah Vaughan	1969 610 499	Ella Fitzgerald Billie Holiday Sarah Vaughan	135 55 25	Ella Fitzgerald June Christy Sarah Vaughan		Ella Fitzgerald June Christy Chris Connor	6199 3981 2810
ALTO SAXOPHONE	Paul Desmond Art Pepper Sonny Stitt	1414 726 656	Lee Konitz Sonny Stitt Johnny Hodges	67 60 50	Paul Desmond Art Pepper Lee Konitz	830 326 227	Paul Desmond Bud Shank Johnny Hodges	12212 6860 5560
TENOR SAXOPHONE	Stan Getz Sonny Rollins Zoot Sims	1903 652 430	Stan Getz Sonny Rollins Coleman Hawkins	74 47 40	Stan Getz Al Cohn Zoot Sims	833 276 252	Stan Getz Coleman Hawkins Charlie Ventura	13802 4420 3720
BARITONE SAXOPHONE	Gerry Mulligan Harry Carney Pepper Adams	2960 490 236	Gerry Mulligan Harry Carney Serge Chaloff	148 93 13	Gerry Mulligan Harry Carney Bud Shank	1117 213 171	Gerry Mulligan Bud Shank Harry Carney	18306 1999 1742
CLARINET	Jimmy Giuffre Tony Scott Benny Goodman	1522 1391 454	Tony Scott Jimmy Giuffre Benny Goodman	116 45 43	Jimmy Giuffre Tony Scott Benny Goodman	713 679 385	Benny Goodman Buddy De Franco Jimmy Giuffre	8362 4507 3824

Melody Maker (London) Readers' International Poll November, 1957		Melody Maker (London) Critics' Poll November, 1957		Jazz Hot (Paris) Readers' Poll February, 1958		Jazz Echo (Hamburg) Readers' Poll February, 1958		Muziek Express (Holland) Readers' Poll January, 1958	
Count Basie	1365	Duke Ellington	32	Category		John Lewis	2945	Louis Armstrong	18%
Chico Hamilton	990	Count Basie	16	Not		Jimmy Giuffre	680	John Lewis	17%
Duke Ellington	738	John Lewis	11	Included		Gerry Mulligan	425	Milt Jackson	15%
Count Basie	5193	Duke Ellington	58	Count Basie	4317	Count Basie	3844	(Combined with " Combo" Category below)	
Duke Ellington	1131	Count Basie	51	Duke Ellington	2362	Stan Kenton	2244		
Stan Kenton	1122	Dizzy Gillespie	6	Dizzy Gillespie	2180	Duke Ellington	1247		
Modern Jazz Quartet	2685	Modern Jazz Quartet	38	Modern Jazz Quartet	2725	Modern Jazz Quartet	4593	Modern Jazz Quartet	32%
Chico Hamilton	1371	Louis Armstrong	21	Miles Davis Quintet	2712	Chet Baker	1608	Gerry Mulligan	20%
Gerry Mulligan	1269	Chico Hamilton	11	Jazz Messengers	1966	Gerry Mulligan	969	Count Basie	14%
Category		Category		Category		Louis Armstrong	4045	Chris Barber	47%
Not		Not		Not		Humphrey Lyttelton	1424	Louis Armstrong	21%
Included		Included		Included		Dutch Swing College	1215	Eddie Condon	11%
Pete Rugolo	786	Duke Ellington	50	Quincy Jones	2424	John Lewis	3370	John Lewis	30%
John Lewis	720	John Lewis	21	John Lewis	2404	Jimmy Giuffre	1464	Gerry Mulligan	21%
Duke Ellington	671	Neal Hefti	5	Duke Ellington	1163	Bill Russo	1224	Pete Rugolo	20%
Frank Sinatra	5619	Jimmy Rushing	32	Louis Armstrong	3206	Louis Armstrong	5143	Frank Sinatra	30%
Mel Torme	615	Louis Armstrong	30	Joe Williams	2218	Frank Sinatra	1238	Pat Boone	24%
Jimmy Rushing	486	Joe Turner	29	Frank Sinatra	1065	Billy Eckstine	1108	King Cole	5%
Ella Fitzgerald	5925	Ella Fitzgerald	49	Ella Fitzgerald	4157	Ella Fitzgerald	4787	Ella Fitzgerald	42%
Sarah Vaughan	450	Billie Holiday	25	Sarah Vaughan	2604	Billie Holiday	1737	Caterina Valente	12%
June Christy	381	Mahalia Jackson	18	Billie Holiday	1408	June Christy	1653	Doris Day	7½%
Paul Desmond	1875	Johnny Hodges	63	Sonny Stitt	2718	Bud Shank	3489	Bud Shank	27%
Johnny Hodges	1365	Benny Carter	20	Lee Konitz	2065	Lee Konitz	3041	Charlie Parker	25%
Lee Konitz	1065	Art Pepper	9	Johnny Hodges	1619	Art Pepper	753	Paul Desmond	17%
Stan Getz	2825	Coleman Hawkins	35	Sonny Rollins	2754	Stan Getz	3587	Coleman Hawkins	15½%
Coleman Hawkins	753	Lucky Thompson	24	Stan Getz	2122	Bob Cooper	2397	Zoot Sims	14%
Zoot Sims	738	Lester Young	15	Lester Young	1625	Lester Young	1036	Sonny Rollins	13½%
Gerry Mulligan	6696	Harry Carney	55	Gerry Mulligan	3781	Gerry Mulligan	5487	Gerry Mulligan	87%
Harry Carney	537	Gerry Mulligan	23	Harry Carney	1697	Jimmy Giuffre	1735	Cecil Payne	3%
Charlie Fowlkes	201	Charlie Fowlkes	9	Cecil Payne	1123	Lars Gullin	1139		
Buddy De Franco	1635	Edmond Hall	38	Jimmy Giuffre	2178	Jimmy Giuffre	2857	Benny Goodman	38%
Benny Goodman	1413	Albert Nicholas	15	Benny Goodman	2105	Tony Scott	2263	Tony Scott	27%
Jimmy Giuffre	1113	Tony Scott	11	Tony Scott	1377	Benny Goodman	2252	Edmond Hall	12%

	Down Beat Readers' Poll December, 1957		Down Beat Critics' Poll August, 1957		Metronome Readers' Poll February, 1958		Playboy Readers' Poll February, 1958	
TRUMPET	Miles Davis	989	Dizzy Gillespie	138	Miles Davis	673	Chet Baker	12551
	Dizzy Gillespie	950	Miles Davis	45	Louis Armstrong	411	Louis Armstrong	12008
	Chet Baker	570	Louis Armstrong	40	Dizzy Gillespie	352	Dizzy Gillespie	11771
TROMBONE	J. J. Johnson	1742	J. J. Johnson	137	J. J. Johnson	778	J. J. Johnson	21649
	Bob Brookmeyer	826	Bob Brookmeyer	42	Bob Brookmeyer	382	Kai Winding	17412
	Kai Winding	770	Bill Harris	25	Bill Harris	229	Bob Brookmeyer	10200
VIBRAPHONE	Milt Jackson	2344	Milt Jackson	212	Milt Jackson	1109	Category Not Included (See Miscellaneous Instrument)	
	Terry Gibbs	767	Lionel Hampton	37	Terry Gibbs	457		
	Lionel Hampton	439	Terry Gibbs	12	Lionel Hampton	333		
PIANO	Erroll Garner	954	Erroll Garner	100	Erroll Garner	411	Erroll Garner	5910
	Oscar Peterson	637	Oscar Peterson	35	Oscar Peterson	319	Dave Brubeck	5897
	Dave Brubeck	621	Thelonious Monk	25	Dave Brubeck	282	George Shearing	2141
GUITAR	Barney Kessel	1236	Tal Farlow	82	Barney Kessel	602	Barney Kessel	7041
	Tal Farlow	684	Freddie Greene	60	Les Paul	308	Eddie Condon	3057
	Jim Hall	533	Barney Kessel	57	Tal Farlow	279	Johnny Smith	2487
BASS	Ray Brown	752	Oscar Pettiford	95	Ray Brown	511	Ray Brown	4108
	Oscar Pettiford	736	Milt Hinton	60	Oscar Pettiford	365	Oscar Pettiford	3796
	Leroy Vinnegar	500	Charles Mingus	50	Leroy Vinnegar	312	Leroy Vinnegar	2208
DRUMS	Shelly Manne	1141	Max Roach	102	Shelly Manne	510	Shelly Manne	7160
	Max Roach	1010	Jo Jones	80	Gene Krupa	506	Gene Krupa	3935
	Joe Morello	416	Shelly Manne	50	Max Roach	493	Chico Hamilton	2417
ACCORDION	Art Van Damme	1444	Category Not Included		Art Van Damme	163	Category Not Included	
	Mat Mathews	865			Mat Mathews	142		
	Leon Sash	472			Leon Sash	109		
FLUTE	Herbie Mann	1344	Category Not Included		Category Not Included (See Miscellaneous Instrument)		Category Not Included	
	Bud Shank	1199						
	Frank Wess	832						
MISCELLANEOUS INSTRUMENT	Don Elliott (mellophone) 1105		Category Not Included		John Grass (Fr. Horn) 913		Lionel Hampton	7122
	Fred Katz ('cello)	519			Don Elliott (mellophone) 516		Milt Jackson	3277
	Bob Cooper (oboe)	420			Frank Wess (flute)	218	Cal Tjader	1818
VOCAL GROUP	Category Not Included		Category Not Included		Hi-Lo's		Four Freshmen	9625
					Four Freshmen		Hi-Lo's	7989
					Ray Charles Singers		Mills Brothers	1846

Melody Maker (London) Readers' International Poll November, 1957		Melody Maker (London) Critics' Poll November, 1957		Jazz Hot (Paris) Readers' Poll February, 1958		Jazz Echo (Hamburg) Readers' Poll February, 1958		Muziek Express (Holland) Readers' Poll January, 1958	
Louis Armstrong	1995	Louis Armstrong	55	Miles Davis	3804	Chet Baker	3830	Louis Armstrong	36%
Dizzy Gillespie	1596	Buck Clayton	21	Dizzy Gillespie	2586	Miles Davis	3057	Miles Davis	31%
Miles Davis	1272	Miles Davis	17	Louis Armstrong	1621	Louis Armstrong	800	Eddy Calvert	13%
J. J. Johnson	2283	Vic Dickenson	37	J. J. Johnson	4017	Bob Brookmeyer	3484	J. J. Johnson	43%
Jack Teagarden	1236	J. J. Johnson	26	Bob Brookmeyer	1064	Kai Winding	2824	Kid Ory	15%
Bob Brookmeyer	1206	Jack Teagarden	25	Kai Winding	916	J. J. Johnson	1749	Chris Barber	10%
Milt Jackson	5779	Lionel Hampton	58	Milt Jackson	4565	Milt Jackson	4880	Lionel Hampton	43%
Lionel Hampton	2478	Milt Jackson	44	Lionel Hampton	3456	Terry Gibbs	1688	Milt Jackson	41%
Victor Feldman	552	Victor Feldman	6	Terry Gibbs	710	Red Norvo	1412	Terry Gibbs	7%
Dave Brubeck	1875	Earl Hines	38	Bud Powell	2543	John Lewis	3092	Erroll Garner	38%
Erroll Garner	1302	Erroll Garner	29	Erroll Garner	1481	Oscar Peterson	2972	Oscar Peterson	12%
Oscar Peterson	1260	Thelonious Monk	10	Thelonious Monk	1397	John Williams	554	Dave Brubeck	11½%
Barney Kessel	3012	Freddie Greene	32	Tal Farlow	2086	Tal Farlow	4297	Les Paul	20%
Freddie Greene	909	Barney Kessel	22	Jimmy Raney	1868	Barney Kessel	2120	Barney Kessel	19½%
Tal Farlow	861	Tal Farlow	16	Barney Kessel	1826	Billy Bauer	837	Tal Farlow	17%
Percy Heath	1449	Milt Hinton	26	Oscar Pettiford	3320	Red Mitchell	4063	Percy Heath	17%
Ray Brown	972	Oscar Pettiford	23	Percy Heath	2307	Ray Brown	2572	Oscar Pettiford	17%
Oscar Pettiford	855	Walter Page	14	Ray Brown	1532	Percy Heath	1300	Ray Brown	16½%
Shelly Manne	1536	Jo Jones	33	Kenny Clarke	3015	Shelly Manne	3944	Gene Krupa	26%
Chico Hamilton	1316	Sam Woodyard	17	Max Roach	1544	Max Roach	2308	Max Roach	24%
Max Roach	720	Art Blakey	14	Art Blakey	1308	Kenny Clarke	753	Shelly Manne	12%
Category Not Included		Category Not Included (See Miscellaneous Instrument)		Category Not Included		Category Not Included		Category Not Included	
Category Not Included (See Miscellaneous Instrument)		Category Not Included (See Miscellaneous Instrument)		Category Not Included (See Miscellaneous Instrument)		Category Not Included		Category Not Included (See Miscellaneous Instrument)	
Frank Wess (flute)	2277	Frank Wess (flute)	21	Frank Wess (flute)	2282	Category Not Included		Helmutt Zacharias (violin)	22%
Sidney Bechet (soprano Sax.)	807	Sidney Bechet (soprano sax.)	20	Stuff Smith (violin)	1720			Frank Wess (flute)	20%
Bud Shank (flute)	492	Stuff Smith (violin)	12	Sidney Bechet (soprano sax.)	1368			Sidney Bechet (soprano sax.)	17%
Hi-Lo's	4059	Hi-Lo's	13	Category Not Included		Category Not Included		Category Not Included	
Four Freshmen	2313	Four Freshmen	11						
Platters	465	Ward Singers	11						

ABBREVIATIONS

ABC   *American Broadcasting Co.*
ABC-Par.   *ABC-Paramount Records*
acc.   *accompanied, accompanying, accompanist*
addr.   *address*
AFM   *American Federation of Musicians*
Alad.   *Aladdin*
All.   *Allegro*
Amer. Mus.   *American Music*
Ap.   *Apollo*
app.   *appeared, appearing*
A & R   *artists and repertoire*
arr.   *arranged, arranger, arrangements*
ASCAP   *American Society of Composers, Authors and Publishers*
Atl.   *Atlantic*
Audio.   *Audiophile*
Aud. Fid.   *Audio Fidelity*
b.   *born*
Bat.   *Baton*
BBC   *British Broadcasting Corporation*
Beth.   *Bethlehem*
bro.   *brother*
Bruns.   *Brunswick*
ca.   *about*
Cad.   *Cadence*
Cam.   *Camden*
Cap.   *Capitol*
Cav.   *Cavalier*
CBS   *Columbia Broadcasting System*
cl., clar.   *clarinet*
Col.   *Columbia*
coll.   *college*
Comm.   *Commodore*
comp.   *composed, composer, compositions*
cons.   *conservatory*
cont.   *continued*
Contemp.   *Contemporary*
Cor.   *Coral*
Counter.   *Counterpoint*
Crit.   *Criterion*
d.   *died*
Deb.   *Debut*
Dec.   *Decca*
Del.   *Delmar*
Des.   *Design*
dj   *disc jockey*
Dix. Jub.   *Dixieland Jubilee*
Doo.   *Dooto*
educ.   *education, educated*
Elek.   *Elektra*
Em.   *EmArcy*
Eso.   *Esoteric*
Fant.   *Fantasy*
fav., favs.   *favorite, favorites*
feat.   *featured, featuring*
Folk.   *Folkways*
Gold. Cr.   *Golden Crest*
Harm.   *Harmony*
Imp.   *Imperial*

incl.   *includes, including, included*
JATP   *Jazz at the Philharmonic*
Jub.   *Jubilee*
KC   *Kansas City, Missouri*
LA   *Los Angeles, California*
Lib.   *Liberty*
Lond.   *London*
LPs   *Long-playing records at 33⅓ revolutions per minute*
MCA   *Music Corporation of America*
Merc.   *Mercury*
Mod.   *Modern*
mos.   *months*
Mot.   *Motif*
mus. dir.   *musical director*
NBC   *National Broadcasting Company*
NJF   *Newport Jazz Festival*
NO   *New Orleans, Louisiana*
NYC   *New York City*
orch.   *orchestra*
Per.   *Period*
Phil.   *Philharmonic*
pl.   *played, plays, playing*
Pres.   *Prestige*
quart.   *quartet*
quint.   *quintet*
Rain.   *Rainbow*
rec.   *recorded, recordings*
Reg.   *Regent*

Rep.   *Replica*
repl.   *replaced, replacing*
ret.   *returned, returning*
River.   *Riverside*
Roul.   *Roulette*
Sav.   *Savoy*
sch.   *school*
SF   *San Francisco, California*
Sig.   *Signal*
South.   *Southland*
Spec.   *Specialty*
st.   *started*
Star.   *Starlite*
Stin.   *Stinson*
Story.   *Storyville*
stud.   *studied, studying*
symph.   *symphony*
Trans.   *Transition*
tpt.   *trumpet*
trom.   *trombone*
U., Univ.   *University*
Vang.   *Vanguard*
Vict.   *Victor*
vln.   *violin*
w.   *with*
West.   *Westminster*
Wor. Pac.   *World-Pacific*
yrs.   *years*

BIOGRAPHIES

As was pointed out in *The Encyclopedia Yearbook of Jazz* (Volume Two of this series), it is impossible, partly because of space considerations and also on account of the extraordinary degree of expansion in the field, to avoid occasional omissions, but it is still planned to keep the listings as complete and up to date as possible.

In the alphabetical section that follows will be found not only about two hundred biographies of musicians who have risen to prominence in the past two years, or who were omitted from the previous volumes for one reason or another, but also details of important recent developments in the lives of those whose biographies were included in the previous books. In a couple of cases (such as Sonny Clark, Philly Joe Jones, Bessie Smith), biographical details have been added that were either unknown or incorrectly stated in the earlier volumes. Volume Two went to press in the summer of 1956 ; the biographies below cover the period through the summer of 1958.

ABNEY, Don. Left Ella Fitzgerald fall '57 and has since free-lanced in NYC. LPs w. Marilyn Moore (Beth.), O. Pettiford (Beth.), B. Carter (Verve), L. Bellson (Verve).
   Addr: 66 Chase St., Hempstead, L.I., N.Y.

ADAMS, Park "Pepper," *baritone, tenor, alto sax, clarinet*; b. Highland Park, Ill., 10/8/30. Raised in Rochester, N.Y. Began gigging there on tenor and clar. In Detroit, switched to bari. and in 1947 was working in Lucky Thompson's band w. Tommy Flanagan for two months. Then gigs in Detroit while he worked in auto plants. Into Army and to Korea, 1951-3, w. some playing in Spec. Serv. shows. Back to Detroit w. James Richards at the Bluebird working w. visiting stars for two years, then w. Kenny Burrell's group. Came to NYC Jan. '56, w. Stan Kenton briefly that year; later w. Maynard Ferguson, then w. Chet Baker. Gigs and stud. work on West Coast. Won first place in *Down Beat* Critics' Poll on bari. summer '57; came to NYC early '58. Local gigs, incl. stay at Five Spot, and record dates. Plays in a modernish version of most of his favorites: C. Hawkins, Chu Berry, H. Carney, and Detroit pianist Barry Harris. LPs w. L. Vinnegar (Contemp.), S. Rogers (Vict.), Q. Jones (ABC-Par.), A. K. Salim (Sav.), Lee Morgan (Blue Note). Own LPs: Mode, Wor. Pac.
   Addr: 314 E. 6th Street, New York 3, N.Y.

ADDERLEY, "Cannonball." Broke up own combo in late 1957; joined Miles Davis '58. LPs w. D. Washington (Em.). Own LPs: Em., Sav.
Addr: 112-19 34th Ave., Corona, L.I., NY.

ADDERLEY, Nat. After break-up of combo of Adderley brothers, he joined Jay Jay Johnson. LPs w. Cannonball (Em.), Tony Bennett (Col.). Own LP: *To the Ivy League from Nat* (Em.).
Addr: 112-19 34th Ave., Corona, L.I., N.Y.

ALBAM, Manny. Cont. as free-lance writer mainly for record dates in NYC. Own LP: *Jazz Greats of Our Time* (Cor.).

ALLEN, "Red." Appeared at Newport Jazz Festival, July 1957, and on NBC-TV's *The Sound of Jazz* in Dec. 1957. Own LPs: *Ride, Red, Ride* (Vict.), *At Newport* (Verve).

ALLEN, Steve. Emceed first major network jazz television show on NBC, Dec. 30, 1957. Led jazz combo at Roundtable, NYC, June '58. Comp. an album of originals which Gus Bivona recorded on Merc.

ALLISON, Mose, *piano* (also *trumpet, singer*); b. Tippo, Miss., 11/11/27. Started on piano at 6 w. private teacher, later trumpet and had Dixieland group in high school. Stud. Louisiana State U. Early listening was to Armstrong, Nat Cole, and blues singers Sonny Boy Williamson, Tampa Red, John Lee Hooker, and many others. Army, 1946-7. First came to NYC in 1951, again in '56. Played for a year off and on w. Stan Getz, 1956-7, also briefly w. Chet Baker, Al Cohn, G. Mulligan, and recorded his version of country blues. One of the few young pianists infl. by early jazz roots. Favs: Sonny Boy Williamson, Ellington, Monk, Gillespie. LPs w. A. Cohn (Cor.). Own LPs: Pres.
Addr: 4045 75th St., Elmhurst 73, N.Y.

ALMERICO, Anthony, *trumpet*; b. New Orleans, La., 8/16/05. Stud. music in Jesuit high school and started in dime-a-dance hall. Worked various local engagements and toured as far as Memphis and New York. Organized own orch., 1937. First came to prominence accompanying Lizzie Miles on her albums for Cook. Favs: L. Armstrong. LP w. George Girard (Vik).
Addr: 1445 Madrid Street, New Orleans 22, La.

ALPERT, "Trigger." Made own LP for River.: *Trigger Happy*.
Addr: Cedar Gate Road, Darien, Conn.

ALVIS, Hayes. Served as merchant seaman on S.S. *United States* until May '58, when he joined Wilbur De Paris.

AMRAM, Dave. Remained inactive in jazz, but composed music for the New York Shakespeare Festival and various off-Broadway productions.
Addr: 114 Christopher St., New York, N.Y.

ANDERSON, John, Jr., *trumpet, composer-arranger*; b. Birmingham, Ala., 1/31/21. Stud. alto horn and trumpet in high school and later at Los Angeles Conservatory of Music and Westlake College of Music. Four years in Navy band, World War II; worked w. T. Bradshaw '41, free-lanced w. B. Carter, Jerry Fielding, Perez Prado, E. Bostic and others, 1946-57. Led own combos L.A. area which included B. Collette, C. Counce, Britt Woodman. Fav. own solos: *Buzzin' Cool* and *Crow's Nest* on Motif w. Max Albright. Favs: H. Edison, Gillespie, C. Shavers. LP w. B. Collette (Dig.).
Addr: 4101 S. Harvard Blvd., Los Angeles 62, Calif.

ANDRUS, Charles E., Jr., *bass*; b. Holyoke, Mass., 11/17/28. Stud. Manhattan School of Music. Formed jazz group in Springfield, Mass., w. Joe Morello, Phil Woods, Sal Salvador *et al.* Worked w. C. Barnet '53, C. Thornhill '54, '55; T. Gibbs part of '54, B. Peiffer '56. Fav. own solo: *Royal Garden Blues* w. Don Stratton (ABC-Par.). Fav: Ray Brown. LPs w. Peiffer (Em.) and Stratton (ABC-Par.).
Addr: 34-34 77th Street, Jackson Heights, L.I., N.Y.

APPLEYARD, Peter. Formed own quartet, played at the Embers, spring 1958.

ARCHEY, Jimmy. In San Francisco free-lancing.

ARMSTRONG, Louis. In May 1956 Armstrong took his band to Britain for his first visit there in 20 years; immediately after, he pl. on the Gold Coast (Ghana), where he was a guest of the prime minister. In spring '57 the Armstrong unit visited the British West Indies. Appeared at Newport Jazz Festival, July '57. The following Nov. the group undertook a tour of Latin America, where Armstrong was met by the president of each country. A film and record commemorating some of his travels, produced by Edw. R. Murrow and titled *Satchmo the Great*, were released in 1957, the record being a Col. LP. Armstrong also made international headlines in the fall of '57 when, for the first time, he took a strong stand on a political issue, denouncing Pres. Eisenhower's failure to implement racial integration in southern schools. A four-volume album entitled *Satchmo, A Musical Autobiography*, in which Armstrong's spoken narrations introduced newly recorded versions of some of his pre-1935 recordings, was released by Decca in 1957.
During 1956-8 Armstrong was also seen at numerous jazz festivals, concerts and TV shows.

ASH, Victor, *clarinet, saxophones*; b. London, Eng., 3/9/30. Began study w. private teacher in 1945. Worked w. Kenny Baker '51-53 and Vic Lewis '53-55. Won *Melody Maker* Critics' Poll '52 and *MM* Readers'

Poll for Britain's Best in '57. Acc. Maxine Sullivan and Cab Calloway with his quartet on British tours 1954-5. Fav. own solo: *Hoagy* w. own quartet on Nixa EP. Favs: S. Getz, J. Hamilton. LP w. Lauri Johnson (MGM).

Addr: 38 Denver Rd., Amhurst Park, London, N.16, England.

ASHBY, Dorothy Jeanne, *harp, piano*; b. Detroit, Mich., 8/6/32. Father, self-taught guitarist, instr. her in harmony. Stud. Cass Tech. High, Wayne U; mus. educ. major. Gave piano recitals; bought harp in '52; first job on harp in Phila. club, Nov. '53. Tasteful performer with more jazz feeling than most harpists. Favs: O. Peterson, B. Taylor, Shearing. LPs: own group on Savoy.

Addr: 9327 Richter, Detroit 13, Mich.

ASHBY, Irving. After many years of semi-inactivity, he earned renewed recognition as a rock-'n'-roll recording artist in 1958. LPs w. Louis Jordan (Em.).

Addr: 6017 S. Budlong, Los Angeles 44, Calif.

AULD, Georgie. Gave up studio work in Los Angeles and returned to New York to free-lance in 1958. LPs w. B. De Franco (Verve), B. Sherwood (Savoy), own band (Em.).

BABASIN, Harry. Formed own group, "The Jazzpickers," 1956, and recorded w. varying personnels featuring himself on cello, with vibes, etc. LPs on Em., Mode.

BAGLEY, Donald. Own LP: *Basically Bagley* (Dot).

BAILEY, Donald, *drums*; b. Philadelphia, Pa., 3/26/34. Got first musical inspiration from brother Maurice, who played tenor and drums. Largely self-taught. First experience w. Jimmy Smith; various jobs around Philadelphia w. Spanky De Brest. Believes own best work is yet to come. Favs: Blakey, Roach, Philly Joe Jones, A. Taylor. LPs w. J. Smith (Blue Note), Sonny Rollins (Blue Note).

Addr: 3220A McMichael St., Philadelphia, Pa.

BAILEY, Pearl. Appeared on many television shows 1957-8, as well as in night club engagements. In film: *St. Louis Blues*, 1958. Own LPs: Cor., Roulette, Mercury.

Addr: Apple Valley, Calif.

BAILEY, Samuel David, *drums*; b. Portsmouth, Va., 2/22/26. Received first training at home w. musical family; later stud. Music Center Conservatory, New York, under G. I. Bill. First job w. Herbie Jones band '51-53; gigged w. Al Sears, J. Hodges, L. Donaldson, C. Mingus, H. Silver, Mulligan *et al.* Toured Europe w. Mulligan '56; worked w. Ben Webster, New York, Apr. '58. Favs: Blakey, Roach, Ed Thigpen, A. Taylor, Philly Joe Jones, Elvin Jones, Ron Jefferson. LPs w.

Mulligan (Em., Verve, Wor. Pac.), L. Donaldson (Blue Note), B. Brookmeyer (Wor. Pac.).

Addr: 712 E. 175th St., Bronx 56, N.Y.

BAKER, Chet. Toured w. Birdland All-Stars, Feb. 1957 then in Scandinavia and Italy w. own combo. Semi-inactive since then, working from time to time w. quartet of various personnel. LPs w. G. Mulligan (Wor. Pac.), R. Freeman (Wor. Pac.). Own LPs: Wor. Pac.

BAKER, Edward, Jr., *piano*; b. Chicago, Ill., 10/13/27. Stud. piano and comp. American Conservatory, 1937-41, and w. Bill Russo '48-56. Became interested in jazz after hearing M. Roach, Bud Powell, L. Young, D. Gordon. Worked in Chicago w. M. Davis '50, Illinois Jacquet '51, Paul Bascomb, B. Russo, Sonny Stitt, W. Ware *et al.* Toured Germany, France and England '55; Hawaii '56. Wrote *L'Affaire Bugs* for Russo's *World of Alcina* LP on Atl. Favs: J. Lewis, B. Powell, Monk, H. Silver. Fav. arr: Lewis, G. Russell, Russo, S. Rollins. LPs w. Russo (Atl.), *Chicago Scene.* (Argo).

Addr: 314 S. Sacramento Blvd., Chicago 12, Ill.

BAKER, Harold "Shorty." Rejoined D. Ellington, May 1957. LP w. Ellington: *Ellington Indigos* (Col.).

Addr: c/o Duke Ellington, 1619 Broadway, New York 19, N.Y.

BAKER, Kenneth, *trumpet*; b. Withersnea, Yorks, England, 3/1/21. Learned piano at home; took up cornet at 12 in local brass band. Began playing w. Lew Stone in London, 1939; also worked w. Maurice Winnick, J. Hylton, Ambrose, Sid Millward. From 1946-9 was lead trumpeter and arr. for T. Heath. Studio and film work, 1949-51, including sound tracks for *Red Shoes*, *Genevieve*, etc. Won *Melody Maker* Readers' Poll of Britain's Best, 1957. L. Armstrong, B. Berigan were early influences. Fav. own solo: *Dark Eyes* w. Heath (Decca). On all Heath LPs for Decca/London. Own LPs: Nixa.

Addr: 63 Witley Court, Woburn Place, London, W.C.1, England.

BAKER, Lavern. Scored success w. album *Lavern Baker Sings Bessie Smith* (Atl.).

BAKER, McHouston "Mickey," *guitar*; b. Louisville, Ky., 10/15/25. Began playing bass in 1945; switched to home-made guitar. After experience as sideman, leader and studio musician for record dates, he teamed w. Sylvia Vanderpool. As Mickey and Sylvia, they had great success in the rhythm and blues field. Has written several guitar instruction books. Fav: C. Christian. LP w. Louis Jordan (Merc.). Own LP w. Sylvia: Vik.

Addr: 238 W. 101st St., New York 25, N.Y.

BARBER, Donald Christopher "Chris," *trombone, leader*; b. London, Eng., 4/17/30. First pl. violin, sop. sax; stud. trom., bass at Guildhall School of Music. Started first band, 1949; helped org. band w. Ken Colyer '53, took it over himself '54. Barber's position in Eng. is comparable w. Turk Murphy's in U.S.: though attacked by many critics as musically worthless, his band has enjoyed a phenomenal success in the past couple of years and has pl. to packed houses in concert halls all over Europe.

BARCELONA, Daniel, *drums*; b. Honolulu, 7/23/29. Self-taught. Trombonist Trummy Young, then resident in Hawaii, took Barcelona out of high school into his orchestra in 1948. After working with Young for three years, he formed his own sextet, the Hawaiian Dixieland All Stars, and toured the Far East. In 1955 he visited the Far East again as a member of an international revue. He then played club engagements in Waikiki, etc., until Sept. 1957, when he left for the U.S. In Feb. 1958 Trummy Young, now a member of Louis Armstrong's band, recommended him for a job w. Armstrong, whom he then joined, replacing Barrett Deems. Favs: Krupa, Buddy Rich, Max Roach. LP w. Teddy Buckner for Gene Norman, also recent Armstrong dates.

    Addr: c/o Associated Booking Corp., 745 Fifth Ave., New York 22, N.Y.

BARKER, Danny. Returned to NYC, 1957. Appeared on *Sound of Jazz* show, CBS-TV, Dec. '57, and in local gigs. LP w. Lavern Baker (Atl.).

BASIE, Count. Toured European Continent, Sept. 1956. In Dec. the band was feat. on a series of CBS network broadcasts sponsored by Camel Cigarettes. The band left on its first tour of Great Britain, Apr. '57, and was so successful that a return tour took place the following Oct.-Nov.; during the latter, Basie's became the first U.S. band ever to play for a Royal Command Performance for the Queen. After this second British tour, the band spent a week in Paris at the Olympia Theatre. Basie also set a precedent by playing 13 weeks in the roof ballroom of the Waldorf-Astoria Hotel, June 3-Sept. 18, 1957, the first big Negro jazz band ever to play the Waldorf. In the fall of '57 the band switched its record affiliation from Verve to Roulette. In the U.S. Basie enjoyed many appearances at Birdland and toured in the Birdland jazz concert unit. His band appeared at the Newport Jazz Festival, summer '57. He was scheduled to take the orch. on a 3-week tour of South America in Oct. '58. LPs: *A Night at Count Basie's* (Vang.), *April in Paris, Basie Rides Again, Basie in London, Band of Distinction, Basie at Newport* (Verve), *Basie* (Roul.). LP tributes to Basie incl. *Sing a Song of Basie* by Dave Lambert (ABC-Par.).

BATES, Norman. Left D. Brubeck, Feb. '58, to settle down in Calif. LPs w. Brubeck (Col.).

BAUER, Billy. Studio work and occasional appearances w. Lee Konitz *et al.* Joined B. Goodman for European tour, spring '58. LPs w. Konitz (Atl.), C. Parker (Verve), Hackett-Teagarden (Cap.).

BEAN, William F., *guitar*; b. Philadelphia, Pa., 12/26/33. Family musical; mother played piano, father guitar and sax, sister sang professionally. First inspiration was C. Parker. Gigged in Philadelphia, then joined C. Ventura, July '56. LPs w. Ventura (Baton, Tops). Own LP: Decca.

    Addr: 5213 N. 11th St., Philadelphia, Pa.

BECHET, Sidney. Own LPs: *Sidney Bechet Has Young Ideas* (Wor. Pac.), *Sidney Bechet in Paris* (Bruns.).

BECK, Pieternella "Pia," *piano, singer*; b. The Hague, Holland, 9/18/25. No formal study, but family played various instruments. Ran away from home at 18 to play with the Miller sextet as pianist; played U.S.O. shows in Europe. Formed own trio late '49; came to the U.S. in '52. Toured Europe and Africa in '53-4; back to U.S. and Canada in '56. Voted best small combo in Holland. Fav. own record: *I'm Feeling Like a Stranger in This Big Town.* Favs: O. Peterson, E. Garner, Mary Lou Williams, E. Fitzgerald, S. Vaughan. Own LPs on Epic.

    Addr: P.O. Box 502, The Hague, Holland.

BELLETTO, Alphonse Joseph, *alto, clarinet, baritone sax*; b. New Orleans, 1/3/28. Began playing clar. in high school and was jobbing around New Orleans as soon as he had his first sax. Had own group while attending Loyola U. where he obtained Bach. of Music Ed. degree. Also has Master's degree in music from Louisiana State U. Worked w. Sharkey Bonano, Leon Prima, W. Manone, Dukes of Dixieland. Started own sextet Dec. '52; has worked in most major jazz rooms in the U.S. He and his sextet joined Woody Herman's band Jan. '58. Favs: C. Parker, C. Basie, S. Kenton. LPs w. Jerri Winters (Beth.). Own LPs: Cap.

BELLSON, Louis. Free-lanced as drummer, composer and arr., including score for Broadway show in '58. LPs w. E. Fitzgerald-L. Armstrong (Verve), Art Tatum (Verve), B. De Franco-O. Peterson (Verve). Own LPs: *Drumorama* (Verve), *At the Flamingo* (Verve).

    Addr: Apple Valley, Calif.

BENNETT, Max. Joined E. Fitzgerald, fall 1957. LPs w. B. Holman (Cor.), B. Cooper (Contemp.). Own LPs: Beth.

    Addr: 3935 Vineland, N. Hollywood, Calif.

BERNSTEIN, Elmer, *composer, arranger*; b. New York City, 4/4/22. Stud. piano at Juilliard, comp. w. Aaron Copland and several others, incl. Stefan Wolpe. Wrote dramatic background scores for Army Air Force radio shows. Did background for United Nations shows, 1949, as a result of which he was selected by Columbia Pictures to do motion picture work. Has been associated w. such films as *Sudden Fear* '52, *Man with the Golden Arm* '55, *The Ten Commandments* '56, *Sweet Smell of Success* '57. Bernstein states that his aim is the integration of jazz elements in the American idiom in terms of the scoring of pictures and serious comp. Favs: In classical music, Aaron Copland. In jazz: Kenton, Armstrong, Basie. Own LPs: *Sweet Smell of Success, Blues and Brass*, etc. (all on Decca).

Addr: 11747 Canton Place, Studio City, Calif.

BERNSTEIN, Leonard, *piano, composer, conductor*; b. Lawrence, Mass., 8/25/18. Bernstein's non-jazz background will not be dealt with here; however, throughout his career he has had a peripheral association with jazz and a stronger one with popular music. In the late '30s he acted as pianist for a night club act, The Revuers. His music for Broadway shows had included the scores of *On The Town*, 1944; *Wonderful Town*, 1953; *West Side Story*, 1958. Forums on jazz, at Brandeis U., 1953; Hollywood Bowl, 1955, etc. Seen on NBC-TV show *Omnibus*, Oct. '55, he lectured on jazz and cond. premiere of his piece for jazz orch., *Prelude, Fugue and Riffs*. He has commissioned jazz composers to write works for performance by the N.Y. Philharmonic, incl. Teo Macero '57, Bill Russo '58. LP: *What Is Jazz* (Col.).

Addr: c/o Columbia Artists, 113 W. 57th St., NYV 19.

BERRY, Chuck, *singer*; b. St. Louis, Mo., 10/18/26. Majored in music at high school; pl. guitar, saxophone and piano. Popular artist in rock-'n'-roll field. Rec. for Chess.

BERRY, Emmett. Appeared on *Sound of Jazz* CBS-TV show, Dec. 1957. Toured Europe w. B. Goodman, May '58. LPs w. J. Hodges (Verve), C. Basie (Vang.), J. Rushing (Vang.), R. Stewart (Jazz.); *Trumpets All Out* (Sav.).

BIG MAYBELLE—*See* **SMITH, Mabel.**

BIGARD, Barney. Free-lanced in Los Angeles, Calif. in 1957-8. Own LP: Lib.

BIVONA, Gus, *clarinet, alto sax, flute*; b. New London Conn., 11/25/17. Stud. alto in Stamford, Conn., 1934. After working locally w. Frank Dailey's orch., went to NYC in '37. Played w. Hudson-DeLange '37, Bunny Berigan '38, Teddy Powell '39, feat. as clar. soloist. After leading own band in Larchmont, N.Y., he worked for B. Goodman '40, Jan Savitt, and Les Brown '41. In service '42, led own band in Navy Air Force. Played w. T. Dorsey '45, Bob Crosby '46; since '47 on staff at MGM Studios. To NYC, June '58, w. Steve Allen combo at Roundtable. Fav: B. Goodman. LPs w. Glen Gray—all clar. solos (Cap.), all MGM soundtrack albums. Own LPs: *Music for Swingers*—music comp. by Steve Allen; *Hey! Dig That Crazy Band* (Merc.).

Addr: 15902 Gault Street, Van Nuys, Calif.

BLAKEY, Art. During 1957-8 the personnel of his Jazz Messengers varied considerably. The members included B. Hardman, trumpet; J. McLean, alto; B. Golson, tenor; J. Griffin, tenor; S. De Brest, bass; Junior Mance, piano. LPs w. K. Dorham, H. Mobley, T. Monk, L. Donaldson, J. Smith, S. Rollins, C. Jordan-J. Gilmore (Blue Note), T. Monk-S. Rollins (Pres.), S. Stitt (Pres.), R. Weston (River.), S. Stitt (River.). Own LPs: Col., Blue Note, Elek., Vik, Beth., Jub., Wor. Pac.

BLOCK, Sidney Sanford "Sandy," *bass*; b. Cleveland, Ohio, 1/16/17. Moved to Brooklyn, stud. violin, switching to bass in high school, 1934. Worked as sideman in various big bands in the '30s and '40s, including Van Alexander, A. Rey, J. Wald, T. Dorsey. Since then has worked w. various groups, incl. C. Shavers quartet, and currently is mainstay in New York recording studios. Fav. own record: *Then I'll Be Happy* w. T. Dorsey. Fav: T. Dorsey. LPs w. Hazel Scott (Decca), Teddi King (Vict.).

Addr: 1824 E. 15th St., Brooklyn 29, N.Y.

BLONS, Harry, *clarinet, tenor sax*; b. St. Paul, Minn., 11/29/11. Began w. private teacher in St. Paul, 1927. Played w. local groups in 1930; later w. H. McIntyre '37-8; on tour w. Red Nichols '39; Red Dougherty '39-42. Formed own Dixieland combo, 1949; joined Doc Evans, Sept. '54; back w. own group, 1955. Fav. own solo: *Singin' the Blues* on Merc. Favs: Jack Teagarden, B. Goodman, I. Fazola, Ed Hall, O. Simeon. Own LPs: Merc., Zeph., Audio.

Addr: 1471 Grand Ave., St. Paul, Minn.

BOSE, Sterling. In June 1958 the 52-year-old trumpeter was found dead of a self-inflicted bullet wound in St. Petersburg, Fla., where he had played since 1950.

BRAFF, Ruby. Appeared on Timex CBS-TV show, Apr. '58, and free-lanced in NYC w. various combos, 1957-8. LPs w. B. Clayton (Vang.), V. Dickenson (Vang.). Own LPs: Vang., Vict., ABC-Par., Beth., Epic, Verve.

BRICE, Percy. Left B. Taylor trio to join G. Shearing, Oct. 1956. LPs w. Taylor (Pres.).

BRIGHT, Ronnell, *piano*; b. Chicago, Ill., 7/3/30. Began stud. piano at 6, intending to become a concert pianist. Stud. at University of Ill., Juilliard, Roosevelt University. Began playing jazz piano while in Navy band in 1953. Worked in Chicago w. bassist Johnny Pate. Worked w. Rolf Kuhn and own trio around NYC, 1957, repl. Jimmy Jones as acc. for Sarah Vaughan, 1958. Capable modern soloist and expert accompanist. Favs: O. Peterson, N. Cole, E. Garner, J. Lewis. LP w. Rolf Kuhn (Vang.). Own LPs: Vang., Reg.

Addr: 270 St. Nicholas Ave., c/o Miller, New York, N.Y.

BROOKMEYER, Bob. Toured Britain w. G. Mulligan quartet, Apr. 1957. Left Mulligan, Aug. '57, had own group briefly, then joined J. Giuffre, Nov. '57. LPs w. Mulligan (Wor. Pac., Em.), T. Gibbs (Em.). Own LPs: *Traditionalism Revisited, Street Swingers* (Wor. Pac.), own group (Vik).

BROOKS, John Benson, *composer-arranger, piano*; b. Houlton, Me., 2/23/17. Mother had scholarship at Peabody Conservatory. He received instruction on several instruments from neighbors, friends and at school. Attended New England Conservatory and Juilliard. Had own band in Boston, 1939; worked w. Eddie DeLange '40; Boyd Raeburn, T. Dorsey, J. Dorsey, L. Brown *et al.* in '30s and '40s. Introduced a folk jazz combo at a Town Hall concert by the Weavers in 1950 and has recorded similar works for Vik. Wants to unify folk, New Orleans, Kansas City, mainstream and avant garde jazz into a single style. Own LP: Vik.
Addr: 535 Hudson St., New York, N.Y.

BROONZY, Big Bill. Had serious lung operation, summer 1957, in Chicago and was not expected to sing again. A large and successful benefit was held for him in Chicago, Nov. '57, and another in London in 1958. Autobiography, *Big Bill Blues*, as told to Belgian jazz writer Yannick Bruynoghe, was published in the U.S. by Grove Press, 1957. Own LPs: Per., Folk., Em.

BROWN, Lawrence. On staff at CBS in NYC since early '57. LPs w. R. Braff (Epic); *The Big Challenge* (Jazz.). Own LP: *Slide Trombone* (Verve).
Addr: 100 Hirliman Road, Teaneck, N.J.

BROWN, Les. Toured U.S. Army bases in England, July 1957. Many LPs on Cap.; earlier LPs on Cor.

BROWN, Ray. Toured Europe w. JATP, 1957, and in the spring of 1958. Member of the faculty at School of Jazz, Lenox, Mass., Aug. '57. LPs w. O. Peterson, B. De Franco, B. Webster, I. Jacquet, B. Dearie, C. Parker, L. Hampton, S. Smith, A. O'Day, E. Fitzgerald-L. Armstrong, H. Edison, B. Powell, S. Getz-G. Mulligan, S. Stitt (Verve); H. Geller (Jub.); S. Rollins (Contemp) D. Gillespie (Sav.); *The Poll Winners* (Contemp.). Own LP: *Bass Hit* (Verve).

BROWN, Tom, *trombone*; b. New Orleans, La., 1890. Died N.O., 3/25/58. Began with "kids" band at 8 on violin, later switched to trombone; many young white New Orleans players were in and out of his groups. Took the first Dixieland band w. Ray Lopez, cornet; Gussie Mueller, clar.; Bill Lambert, drums; Arnold Loyocano, piano and bass to Chicago in 1915. Worked in vaudeville w. "The Five Rubes" and w. various groups, incl. Yerkes Marimba orch., Happy Six, Ray Miller, Johnny Bayersdoffer, Norman Brownlee and others. During the years before his death he owned a radio and music shop and gigged around New Orleans w. "Red" Bergan, Johnny Wiggs and others. Recorded for Comm. w. J. Wiggs and w. own group for Jazzology.

BRUBECK, Dave. The quartet toured in concert work and occasional night club dates in 1957-8. Appeared at the Newport Jazz Festival, July 1958. Toured w. great success in England, on the Continent, Poland and the Middle East in spring '58. Own LPs: Col.

BRYANT, Ray. Accompanied Carmen McRae, spring 1957; appeared at Newport Jazz Festival, worked briefly w. D. Gillespie's band, then joined Jo Jones' trio early '58. LPs w. A. Blakey (Col.), A. Taylor (Pres.), Miles Davis (Pres.), M. Roach (Em.), A. Blakey (Blue Note), C. Jordan (Blue Note), C. McRae (Decca), C. Hawkins at Newport (Verve), D. Gillespie-S. Stitt-S. Rollins (Verve). Own LP: Pres.

BUFFINGTON, James Lawrence, *French horn*; b. Jersey Shore, Pa., 5/14/22. Self-taught; father played trumpet, piano. Picked up Fr. horn in school, later got Master's degree in theory and performing at Eastman School of Music. Gigged in N.Y. during 1950s, especially w. O. Pettiford. Fav. own record: *A Touch of Modern* w. Stu Phillips (MGM). Was one of first soloists to play jazz Fr. horn. Fav: John Barrows. LPs w. Stu Phillips (MGM), Quincy Jones-Billy Taylor (ABC-Par.), Lou Stein (Epic).
Addr: 245 W. 104th St., New York 25, N.Y.

BURKE, Vinnie. LPs w. G. Melle (Pres.), T. Farlow (Verve).

BURNS, Ralph. Continued recording and free-lance arranging in NYC, incl. work for B. Goodman's *Swing into Spring* television show on NBC, Apr. 1958. Own LPs: *The Masters Revisited, Very Warm for Jazz* (Decca).

BURRELL, Kenny. With B. Goodman, 1957; had own quartet late '57 and early '58; w. T. Scott in May at the Black Pearl, NYC. LPs w. K. Dorham, P. Chambers, J. Smith (Blue Note), F. Wess (Sav.), G. Ammons (Pres.), A. Cohn (Pres.), R. Bright (Reg.), A. K. Salim (Sav.), B. Clayton (Vang.), D. Watkins (Trans.). Own LPs: Pres., Blue Note.
Addr: Apt. 3-c, 11 Wadsworth Ave., New York 33, N.Y.

BURROUGHS, Clark, *singer*; b. Los Angeles, 3/3/30. Att. Powers High Sch., Loyola U. Worked as actor before becoming member of the Hi-Lo's (q.v.). LPs: Star., Col.
Addr: 1626 N. Vine, Hollywood, Calif.

BUTTERFIELD, Billy. Still free-lancing around NYC in 1957-8. LPs w. B. Freeman (Vict.), J. Rushing (Col.), B. Raeburn (Col.), E. Condon (Col.), E. Condon

TV in Hollywood. Stan Kenton, producer Jimmie Baker, host Bobby Troup, and singer Ann Richards (Mrs. Kenton) in a pre-production meeting on *Stars of Jazz*, on KABC-TV (*Sherman Weisburd*).

TV in Hollywood. Teddy Buckner and drummer Jesse Sailes before the *Stars of Jazz* cameras, fall 1957 (*Ray Avery*).

Opposite: Al McKibbon, George Shearing, Percy Brice, Rev. Norman J. O'Connor, Jean 'Toots' Thielemans, Emil Richards in the O'Connor-Shearing educational jazz TV series on WGBH in Boston in the fall of 1957.

Right: Newport Jazz Festival. Sarah Vaughan (*Wolfe*).

Bottom left: Newport Jazz Festival. Carmen McRae (*Wolfe*).

Bottom right: Newport Jazz Festival. Bobby Hackett (*Capitol Records Inc.*).

Opposite: Newport Jazz Festival. Farmingdale High School Band, Marshall Brown directing. Andy Marsala at microphone.

Right: Jazz Concert in Germany. John Lewis (*Hanns E. Haehl*).

Bottom left: Jazz Concert in Germany. Percy Heath (*Hanns E. Haehl*).

Bottom right: Jazz Concert in Germany. Milt Jackson (*Hanns E. Haehl*).

Above: School of Jazz in Lenox, Mass. Dizzy Gillespie
and student (*Warren D. Fowler*).

Below: School of Jazz in Lenox, Mass. Max Roach
and student (*Warren D. Fowler*).

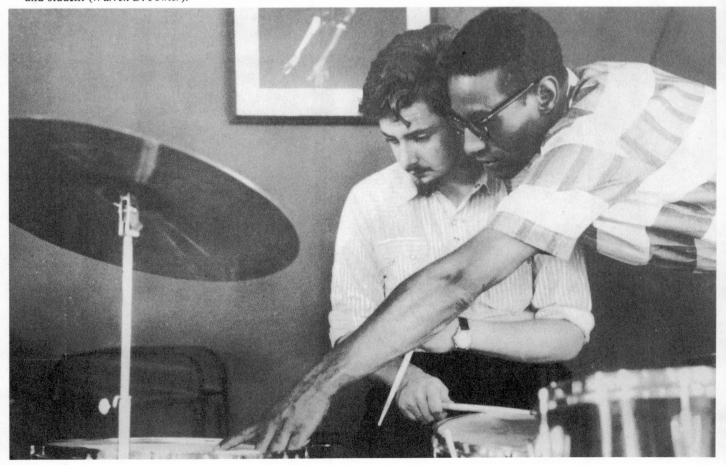

Above: New Faces. John Coltrane (*Esmond Edwards*).

Left: New Faces. Pepper Adams (*Francis Wolff*).

Below: New Faces. Lee Morgan (*Francis Wolff*).

Above: New Faces. Mal Waldron.

Right. New Faces. Mose Allison
(*Esmond Edwards*).

(MGM), Lee Wiley (Vict.), Connee Boswell (Vict.). Own LPs: *They're Playing Our Song, Thank You for a Lovely Evening* (Vict.).

BYERS, Billy. Returned to NYC from France, Nov. 1957, after extensive recording and studio work there. LPs w. K. Clarke (Epic), H. McKusick (Pres.).
Addr: 461 W. 49th St., New York 19, N.Y.

BYRD, Charlie L., *guitar*; b. Suffolk, Va., 9/16/25. Began stud. at 10 w. father, also a guitarist. Began playing for high school dances; later worked w. Sol Yaged '47, Joe Marsala, Barbara Carroll '48, F. Slack '49. Took up classical guitar '50; has played recitals in Washington, D.C., area. Stud. w. Andres Segovia in Sienna, Italy, 1954. Favs: C. Christian, Segovia. Own LP: Sav.
Addr: 1306 Grandin Ave., Rockville, Md.

BYRD, Donald. With Max Roach, summer '56; in 1957 he was part of a group which gigged around NYC and recorded under various leaders, incl. Red Garland, A. Taylor, J. Coltrane or L. Donaldson, and G. Joyner. He also worked w. Gigi Gryce in the Jazz Lab quintet. In early 1958 he was w. Pepper Adams at the Five Spot Cafe in NYC. LPs w. Gryce (Jub., Verve, Col., River.), A. Blakey (Col.), Garland, G. Ammons, H. Mobley, A. Taylor, K. Burrell-J. Raney (Pres.), Sonny Clark, P. Chambers, H. Silver, S. Rollins, L. Donaldson, Jimmy Smith (Blue Note), H. Jones (Sav.), Andre Hodeir (Sav.), K. Drew (River.). Own LPs: *All Night Long, The Young Bloods, All Day Long* (Pres.), *Byrd Blows on Beacon Hill* (Trans.).
Addr: 594 Teasdale Place, Bronx 56, N.Y.

CACERES, Ernie. Spent a year w. Bobby Hackett in a very successful engagement at the Henry Hudson Hotel in NYC, 1956-7. LPs w. Hackett (Cap.), Hackett-Teagarden (Cap.), R. Braff (Epic), J. McPartland (Epic).

CAIN, Jackie. LPs w. R. Kral: Story., ABC-Par., Bruns.

CALLENDER, Red. LPs w. A. Tatum, B. Webster, B. De Franco (Verve), Jerry Fielding (Decca), J. Graas. (Merc.), Rusty Bryant (Dot).

CALLOWAY, Cab. Revived big band periodically for night club revues, 1957-8. European tour, spring, summer '58, opening in Paris in May. LPs: Epic.

CAMPBELL, James L., *drums*; b. Wilkes-Barre, Pa., 12/24/28. Self-taught, he began playing while in the Army in 1947. First prof. job w. Lee Vincent in 1950; later worked w. R. Flanagan '52, T. Tucker, D. Elliott, R. Marterie, S. Salvador, C. Thornhill, Tex Beneke. Rejoined Elliott '56 and was member of M. Ferguson's Birdland Dream Band that year. Free-lanced in many combos in NYC, 1957-8. Favs: D. Tough, Blakey, D. Lamond, M. Roach. LPs w. Bob Corwin (River.),

Don Elliott (ABC-Par.), M. Ferguson (Vik), S. Salvador (Beht.), F. Socolow (Beth.).
Addr: 150-24 75th Ave., Flushing 67, L.I., N.Y.

CANDIDO. Free-lanced in NYC, 1956-7; w. D. Gillespie's combo early 1958. LPs w. D. Elliott (ABC-Par.), Ray Bryant (Epic), A. Blakey (Col.), D. Ellington (Col.), K. Burrell (Blue Note), Dinah Washington (Merc.). Own LP: *Candido the Volcanic* (ABC-Par.).

CANDOLI, Conte. On tour w. Sammy Davis, Jr., spring 1958. LPs w. H. Rumsey (Contemp.), B. Holman (Cor.), Med Flory (Jub.), Bob Cooper (Contemp.), G. Williams (Vict.), Shorty Rogers (Vict., Atl.). Own LPs: Beth., Mode, and w. brother Pete (Dot).
Addr: 1276 Sunset Plaza Dr., Los Angeles 46, Calif.

CANDOLI, Pete. LPs w. Ray Brown (Verve), Shorty Rogers (Vict.), P. Rugolo (Merc.), Bob Cooper (Contemp.). Own LP w. brother Conte (Dot).
Addr: 1276 Sunset Plaza Dr., Los Angeles 46, Calif.

CARLISLE, Una Mae. The songwriter-pianist and singer, best-known for her *Walkin' By the River* and *I See a Million People*, died in NYC, Dec. 12, 1956, after a long illness.

CARTER, Benny. Continued to free-lance as soloist and movie music writer in Hollywood. Operated own jazz theatre in Los Angeles, summer 1957. LPs w. B. Webster, Roy Eldridge, Art Tatum (Verve), Q. Jones (ABC-Par.), Abbey Lincoln (Lib.).

CARY, Dick. With Bobby Hackett, Sept. '56-Nov. '57, both as chief arr. and instrumentalist, in successful engagement at the Henry Hudson Hotel in NYC. Joined Max Kaminsky, Mar. '58, playing trombone, alto horn, and arranging. LPs w. Hackett (Cap.), E. Condon (MGM), J. McPartland (Epic). Own LP: *Dixieland Goes Progressive* (Gold. Cr.).

CASTLE, Lee. Led Dorsey Bros. orch. until Jimmy's death, after which he took Jimmy's band on tour.

CHALOFF, Serge. After being ill for 18 months, during which he had continued to work intermittently (mostly in Boston), the baritone saxophonist, who in the mid-40s had been the first well-known bop soloist on this instrument, died of cancer in Boston, July 16, 1957. His last record session took place in New York, Feb. '57: *The Four Brothers—Together Again* (Vik). Other LP: *Blue Serge* (Cap.); early LPs w. Herman (Cap., Col.).

CHAMBERS, Paul. With Miles Davis, 1956-8. LPs w. Davis (Col., Pres.), Lee Morgan, C. Fuller, J. Griffin, B. Powell, S. Clark (Blue Note), R. Garland, J. McLean, J. Coltrane (Pres.), B. Golson (River.), C. Terry (River.).

Own LPs: *Whims of Chambers, Bass on Top* (Blue Note), *Chambers' Music* (Jazz: West).

Addr: Apt. 2L, 106 Steuben St., Brooklyn 5, N.Y.

CHAMBLEE, Edward Leon, *tenor sax*; b. Atlanta, Ga., 2/24/20. Father gave him a sax on his 12th birthday and during law study at the U. of Chicago he worked as a musician. In Army bands from 1941-6; on leaving Army had own combo, in which Osie Johnson played. Toured Europe w. Lionel Hampton '54. In '57 married Dinah Washington, whom he had known when they both attended Wendell Phillips High School in Chicago. LPs w. Dinah Washington (Em.). Own LP: Merc.

CHARLES, Ray, *piano, singer, arranger, saxophone*; b. Albany, Ga., 1932. Accident left him blind at 6; stud. music at school for blind in St. Augustine, Fla. Left school at 15 and began playing w. various local bands in Fla.; two yrs. later organized a trio in the King Cole style, and played on a sponsored television show in Seattle, Wash. Formed own band in 1954 and its first job was as acc. to singer Ruth Brown. The group gradually acquired a style of its own under Charles' careful planning and rehearsal. Its records not only became rhythm and blues and rock-'n'-roll hits but were greatly admired by many jazz artists. In late 1957 he had his own LP of instrumentals, including jazz standards, pop and gospel melodies in a modified modern jazz style. Charles' vocal and piano style is very strongly influenced by the contemporary gospel idiom. As an arr., he also shows a keen appreciation of modern jazz, even in some of his simple blues recordings, and he certainly broadened the market for such music. He sings blues in an authentic fashion with great energy, emotion, and an often subtle rhythmic sense. Favs: Tatum, B. Powell, N. Cole, O. Peterson. Own LPs for Atl.

Addr: c/o Shaw Artists Corp., 565 Fifth Ave., New York 17, N.Y.

CHARLES, Teddy. Joined Jub. Records as mus. dir. early '58; comp. and participated in concerts of jazz and modern experimental music at Cooper Union, NYC, 1957-8. Joined C. Mingus group, May 1958. LPs w. B. Brookmeyer, Teo Macero (Pres.), Alonzo Levister (Deb.). Own LPs: *Word from Bird* (Atl.), *Vibe-Rant* (Elek.), *Evolution* (Pres.), *Three for Duke* (Jub.).

Addr: 4 W. 93rd St., New York 25, N.Y.

CHEATHAM, Doc. On tour w. Wilbur De Paris in Africa for State Dept., spring 1957. Appeared on *Sound of Jazz* CBS-TV show, Dec. '57. Cont. work w. Machito. LPs w. Machito (Roul), Juanita Hall (Counter.).

CHISHOLM, George, *trombone*; b. Glasgow, Scotland, 3/29/15. Gigged around Glasgow; worked w. Teddy Joyce 1936; w. Benny Carter in Holland '37, Ambrose '38; rec. w. Coleman Hawkins '37; pick-up group and records under own name '37-39; at that time, was

rated first great Brit. trombonist, in Teagarden-infl. style. Joined BBC show band '52. Favs: B. Harris, L. Armstrong, B. Hackett. LPs w. K. Baker (Nixa). Own LP: Decca/Lond.

Addr: 13 Lindal Crescent, Enfield, Middlesex, Eng.

CHRISTIE, Ronald Keith, *trombone*; b. Blackpool, Eng. 1/6/31. Began study at 14 in Blackpool, later at Guildhall School of Music, London. Worked w. H. Lyttleton, 1949-51; own groups w. brother Ian '51-53, then w. J. Dankworth '53-55; T. Whittle's combo '55-6; free-lanced in London clubs '56-7; joined T. Heath '57, and was present on the latter's tours of the U.S. and Canada. Favs: Armstrong, Teagarden, Parker, A. Cohn. LPs w. T. Heath (Lond./Decca).

Addr: 38 Peel St., London, W.8, England.

CHRISTY, June. On tour of the U.S. w. T. Heath package show, Feb. 1957, and Mar. '58; made return tour of Europe (also Africa) w. B. Shank, B. Cooper, C. Williamson *et al.*, spring '58. Own LPs: *Gone for the Day, June Fair and Warmer* (Cap.).

CINDERELLA, Joseph R., *guitar, drums*; b. Newark, N.J., 6/14/27. Father, a music publisher and banjoist, introduced him to music. Stud. at the Essex Conservatory. In '46, while in the special service branch of the Army, pl. w. Warne Marsh, C. Candoli, Don Ferrara. During 1955 gigged around N.Y. w. G. Gryce, D. Byrd. Worked w. Vinnie Burke in '55-6, then w. Gil Melle. Fav. own solo: *Adventure Swing* in *Primitive Modern* w. Gil Melle on Pres. Favs: C. Christian, D. Reinhardt. LPs w. Vinnie Burke (Beth.), Gil Melle (Pres.).

Addr: 174 E. 16th St., Paterson, N.J.

CLARKE, Kenny. Went to France, summer '56, to join Jacques Hélian band and free-lanced w. such visiting Americans as Bud Powell, Miles Davis *et al.* LPs w. M. Davis (Cap., Pres.), R. Sharon (Lond.), K. Burrell (Blue Note), L. Feather-D. Hyman (MGM), M. Mathews (Dawn), S. Bechet (Wor. Pac.). Own LP: *Kenny Clarke Plays André Hodeir* (Epic).

CLARK, Sonny, *piano* (corrected biography); b. Herminie, Pa., 7/21/31. Moved to Pittsburgh at 12, stayed until 19. Played bass and vibes in high school band; went to the West Coast w. his brother in 1951; worked w. Wardell Gray, then was in a band w. O. Pettiford in San Francisco. With B. De Franco quartet late '53-6, incl. European tour, Jan., Feb. '54. Throughout '56 was w. H. Rumsey's Lighthouse All-Stars. Returned East, Apr. '57, as acc. to Dinah Washington, and has since free-lanced in NYC. LPs w. De Franco (Verve), Rumsey (Contemp.), S. Rollins (River.), S. Chaloff (Cap.), C. Fuller, C. Jordan, J. Griffin, J. Jenkins (Blue Note). Own LPs: Blue Note.

CLAY, James Earl, *tenor sax, flute*; b. Dallas, Texas, 9/8/35. Stud. alto in high school; became prof. when school band director took him on gigs. Made first rec. date w. Lawrence Marable for Jazz-West; other West Coast sessions incl. Red Mitchell (Contemp.), own track on *Solo Flight* for Wor. Pac. Fav: Sonny Rollins.

Addr: 113 Cliff St., Dallas, Texas.

CLAYTON, Buck. With B. Goodman's reorganized band, Feb. 1957, for Waldorf-Astoria engagement, NYC; later toured w. Goodman band and from Sept.-Nov. '57 was on nation-wide tour w. T. Wilson. Appeared on *Swing into Spring* NBC-TV show as guest of Goodman, Apr. '58; also on NBC-TV educational series *The Subject is Jazz*. LPs w. J. Rushing (Col.), Boyd Raeburn (Col.). Own LPs: *Singing Trumpets* (Jazz.), *Buckin' the Blues* (Vang.).

CLEVELAND, Jimmy. Joined J. Richards' big band for various engagements during 1957-8. Part of regular group which appeared on NBC-TV educational series *The Subject Is Jazz*, Mar.-June '58; also cont. doing record dates w. own groups. LPs w. Specs Powell (Roul.), Gil Evans (Pres.), L. Feather-D. Hyman (MGM), Q. Jones, O. Pettiford, B. Taylor, Candido (ABC-Par.), as "Jimmy O'Heigho" w. G. Williams and J. Newman (Vict.), Milt Jackson (Atl.); *Trombone Scene* (Vik). Own LP: *Cleveland Style* (Em.).

COHN, Al. Cont. free-lance engagements and playing around NYC, including a group w. Zoot Sims during summer 1957. LPs w. U. Green, Candido, J. Raney (ABC-Par.), Sims (Cor., Vict., Vik), J. Giuffre (Atl.), G. Mulligan (Wor. Pac.), Marilyn Moore (Beth.), J. B. Brooks, B. Brookmeyer, M. Ferguson (Vik), M. Albam, Tommy Shepard (Cor.). Own LPs: Cor., Epic (*The Sax Section*), Dawn, Pres. (*Earthy*).

COLE, Cozy. Successful tour of Britain and Continent w. J. Teagarden, E. Hines, fall 1957. Appeared on CBS-TV Timex jazz show, May '58, and cont. at Metropole, NYC.

COLE, Nat. Abandoned own TV show under protest after 68 weeks in mid-Dec. 1957, complaining that the attitude of the advertising agencies had resulted in his failure to find a sponsor. Cole, who had been the only Negro artist on network TV with his own series, used many guest stars, Negro and white, from the pop music and jazz fields during his broadcasts. In the fall of '57 he played the role of W. C. Handy in the motion picture *St. Louis Blues*. LPs: *After Hours, Just One of Those Things, St. Louis Blues* (Cap.).

COLEMAN, Cy (Seymour Kaufman), *piano*; b. New York City, 6/14/29. Started with private teachers at 4; attended New York College of Music. Gave recitals at 6 in Steinway and Town Halls. Began as single at Stage Door Canteen and Sherry-Netherlands bar. Formed trio, played at Bop City, at which time he decided jazz was

the music he wanted to play. Generally known as a cocktail pianist, he has more and more reflected the influence of the jazz idiom. Favs: Tatum, Garner, B. Taylor, R. Freeman. Own LP: Jub.

Addr: 37 W. 58th St., New York 19, N.Y.

COLEMAN, George, *tenor sax*; b. Memphis, Tenn. Toured with several rock-'n'-roll combos, incl. B. B. King; gigged around Chicago w. Ira Sullivan, John Gilmore, Bill Lee. In NYC pl. w. K. Burrell at Birdland; joined Max Roach, 1958. Favs: C. Parker, S. Rollins, J. Coltrane, S. Stitt, B. Golson. LP w. Lee Morgan (Blue Note).

COLLETTE, Buddy. Cont. gigs in Los Angeles area after having left C. Hamilton (Oct. '56) to form own quart. LPs w. John Graas (Merc.), J. Giuffre (Atl.), B. Kessel, R. Norvo (Contemp.), Q. Jones (ABC-Par.). Own LPs: *West Coast Jazz* (Doo.), *Nice Day with Buddy Collette* (Contemp.), *Tanganyika* (Dig.), *Calm, Cool and Collette* (ABC-Par.).

COLLINS, Lee. Forced to stop playing after serious operation in 1957. Benefit performances were held for him in Chicago and London in which many jazzmen of all schools participated.

COLTRANE, John. Had successful stay at Five Spot Cafe, NYC, in T. Monk quart., summer and fall 1957. Rejoined Miles Davis group, Jan. '58. LPs w. Davis (Col., Pres.), Monk (River.), S. Clark, P. Chambers, J. Griffin (Blue Note), M. Waldron, R. Garland, F. Wess, T. Dameron (Pres.). Own LPs: *Blue Train* (Blue Note), *Interplay* (Pres.), *Coltrane* (Pres.).

CONDON, Eddie. Had successful tour of Britain in early 1957. Moved his NYC club to the upper east side in Feb. '58. LPs w. J. McPartland (Epic). Own LPs: *Condon's Uptown Now* (MGM), *The Roaring Twenties* (Col.), *A Night at Eddie Condon's* (Decca).

COOK, Willie. Left D. Ellington, summer 1957.

COOPER, Bob. Return tour of Europe, Mar. 1958, w. J. Christy, Bud Shank, C. Williamson *et al*. Group also was in North and South Africa. While not on tour, cont. to play w. H. Rumsey's group at the Lighthouse in Calif. LPs w. Rumsey (Lib., Contemp.), J. Giuffre (Atl.), M. Roach-S. Levey (Lib.), P. Rugolo, J. Graas (Merc.). Own LPs: *Flute 'n' Oboe* (Wor. Pac.), *Coop* (Contemp.).

COPELAND, Ray. With Randy Weston combo, 1957-8, gigging in NYC area. LPs w. Weston (Dawn), Monk (River.), A. Kirk (Vict.), Specs Powell (Roul.).

COSTA, Eddie. Was extremely active in NYC recording studios, 1957-8. Appeared at Newport Jazz Festival, July '57; also led own trio for night club engagements.

LPs w. André Hodeir, H. Mann, B. Ver Plank (Sav.), B. Galbraith (Decca), B. Jaspar, H. McKusick (Pres.), J. Puma (Jub.), S. Salvador, R. Sharon, F. Socolow (Beth.), L. Hambro (Epic). Own LPs: *At Newport* (Verve), Mode, Cor.

COUNCE, Curtis. Active in Los Angeles, incl. work w. own quint. which he had formed Oct. '56 feat. Harold Land, tenor, and J. Sheldon, trumpet. LPs w. C. Baker-A. Pepper (Wor. Pac.), C. Brown (Em.), T. Charles (Pres.), R. Norvo (Lib.). Own group LPs on Dooto (*Exploring the Future*), Contemp. (*You Get More Bounce w. Curtis Counce*).

CRABTREE, Richard Arthur "Richie," *piano*; b. Sidney, Mont., 2/23/34. Has worked w. C. Candoli, Scat Davis. Currently w. Monk Montgomery's Mastersounds. Favs: Parker, Gillespie, Miles Davis, B. Powell. LPs w. Mastersounds (Wor. Pac.).

CRAWFORD, Jimmy. Cont. free-lance and studio work around NYC, incl. pit bands in Broadway shows. LPs w. Juanita Hall (Counter.), Hazel Scott (Decca), Rex Stewart, F. Henderson reunion (Jazz.).

CRISS, Sonny. Joined Hampton Hawes' group on West Coast, Feb. 1958. Own LP: *Sonny Criss Plays Cole Porter* (Imp.).

CUTSHALL, Cutty. Joined E. Condon, Feb. 1958. LPs w. Condon (Col., MGM), Wild Bill Davison (Col.).

DANKWORTH, Johnny. Won *Melody Maker* poll in five different categories: Musician of the Year, Band, Alto, Composer, Arranger in Oct. 1957. Married singer Cleo Laine, 1958.

DARENSBOURG, Joseph, *clarinet, soprano sax*; b. Baton Rouge, La., 7/9/06. Father was cornetist-leader of brass band. Stud. clar. w. Alphonse Picou; also violin, piano. Pl. in NO w. Buddy Petit; worked w. Fate Marable on riverboats and many New Orleans-style bands, incl. Gene Mayl, Pete Daily, Teddy Buckner; ten years w. Kid Ory from 1944 repl. Jimmie Noone; in 1958, in Hollywood, had own group, the Dixie Flyers. Has rec. w. Pete Daily (Cap.), Kid Ory (Col., Decca), Dixieland Rhythm Kings (River., Audiophile). Fav. own solos: *Sweet Georgia Brown, Yellow Dog Blues* w. own group on Lark label.
    Addr: c/o Lark Records, 9337 S. Vermont Ave., Los Angeles 44, Calif.

DAVIS, Eddie "Lockjaw." Joined C. Basie, Oct. 1957; left Feb. '58 to form own trio and worked at C. Basie's bar in Harlem. LPs w. Basie (Verve, Roul.). Own LPs on King.

DAVIS, Miles. Early in 1958 was in Paris where w. both American and French musicians did background music for the film *L'Ascenseur Pour L'Echafaud* (*The Elevator to the Gallows*). Previously, after an operation, summer 1957, he had reorganized his quintet and w. various changes in personnel (sometimes making it a sextet) was active in the East, and virtually a mainstay at Cafe Bohemia in NYC. His recording activities incl. a big band date, a reunion w. Gil Evans, listed below. Was also present at most of the major jazz festivals and concerts in the East. LPs w. Gunther Schuller (Col.), Evans—*Miles Ahead* and *Miles Davis Plus 19* (Col.). Own LPs: *Relaxin', Walkin', Cookin', Bags' Groove, Collector's Items* (Pres.), *Birth of the Cool* (Cap.), *'Round About Midnight* (Col.).

DAVISON, Wild Bill. Played w. German bands in Bavaria, Sept. 1957. Gigs around NYC since then. LPs w. E. Condon (Col.). Own LPs: *With Strings Attached* (Col.), *Singing Trumpets*—6 tracks (Jazz.).

DEARIE, Blossom, *singer, piano*; b. East Durham, N.Y., 4/28/26. Worked w. vocal groups in mid-1940s, incl. Blue Flames w. Woody Herman band and Blue Reys w. Alvino Rey; also pl. cocktail piano on many jobs. Went to Paris in 1952, singing in clubs there w. Annie Ross and forming a vocal group, The Blue Stars, for which she wrote some of the arrangements. Their jazz vocal version of *Lullaby of Birdland*, sung in French, was a big hit, both in France and the U.S. While in Paris, married Belgian tenor saxophonist Bobby Jaspar. Returned to NYC, summer '56, worked in night clubs, singing at the piano. LPs: *Give Him the Ooh-La-La* and *Blossom Dearie* (Verve), *The Blue Stars* (Em.).
    Addr: 138 W. 10th St., New York, N.Y.

De BREST, James "Spanky," *bass*; b. Philadelphia, Pa., 4/24/37. Worked locally w. Jimmy De Priest, Lee Morgan; joined Art Blakey, July '56. Favs: P. Heath, R. Brown, Pettiford, Wilbur Ware. Many LPs w. Blakey's Messengers.

DEEMS, Barrett. Left L. Armstrong, Feb. 1958.

De FRANCO, Buddy. Cont. to free-lance mostly on the West Coast w. a quartet or quintet, 1957-8. Feat. in movie *The Wild Party*, 1957. Left Verve Records to free-lance, Apr. '58. LPs w. O. Peterson, A. Tatum, L. Hampton (Verve). Own LPs: MGM, Verve.
    Addr: Apt. 8, 3921 Hillcrest Dr., Los Angeles 8, Calif.

DELANEY, Eric, *drums*; b. London, Eng., 5/22/24. From a musical family, he began pl. piano in school, drums with private tutor in 1934. Stud. tympani at Guildhall School of Music '46-7. Studio recording and concert work '47-54. Appeared w. *Musical Express* Poll Winners' concert, 1955, '56-7. Fav. own solo: *Mainly Delaney* (Merc., Nixa). Favs: Bellson, Blakey, S. Woodyard, Krupa, C. Webb. Own LP: Merc.
    Addr: 13 Alders Close, Edgware, Middlesex, Eng.

DENNIS, Willie. Joined W. Herman, 1957. LPs w. Herman (Verve), R. Ball (Sav.); *Trombone Scene* (Vik), *Four Trombones* (Deb.).

De PARIS, Sidney. Led own group at Jimmy Ryan's, NYC, while brother Wilbur toured Africa for the State Dept., spring 1957. LPs w. Wilbur De Paris (Atl.).

De PARIS, Wilbur. For 15 weeks beginning Mar. 1957, while his brother Sidney maintained a group at Jimmy Ryan's, NYC, De Paris toured Africa under the auspices of the State Dept., after which he returned to Ryan's. Appeared on NBC-TV's educational series *The Subject Is Jazz* discussing early jazz, Apr. '58. Own LPs: *Wilbur De Paris at Symphony Hall*, *Wilbur De Paris Plays and Jimmy Witherspoon Sings* (Atl)

DESMOND, Paul. With D. Brubeck, incl. tour of Europe, Poland, Middle East, spring 1958. LPs w. Brubeck (Col., Jazz.), G. Mulligan (Verve). Own LP: *Jazz at Wilshire-Ebell*, and quartet (Fant.).

DEUCHAR, James, *trumpet, mellophone, arranger*; b. Dundee, Scotland, 6/26/30. From musical family, stud. trumpet and played in local jazz band. First job w. J. Dankworth, 1951. Played w. J. Parnell, R. Scott, Tony Crombie. Toured Continent w. L. Hampton; w. R. Scott to U.S., 1957; then joined Kurt Edelhagen at Radio Station Cologne, Germany. Fav. own record: *Pub Crawling* (Contemp.). Fav: Dizzy Gillespie. LP w. V. Feldman (Contemp.). Own LP: Contemp.
 Addr: A. M. Duffesbach 44, Cologne, Germany.

DICKENSON, Vic. Appeared on NBC-TV's *The Sound of Jazz*, Dec. 1957; joined Red Allen's group at the Metropole in NYC, Feb. '58. LPs w. Jonah Jones (Beth.), LaVern Baker (Atl.), J. Rushing, C. Basie, B. Clayton (Vang.), E. Condon, J. Rushing (Col.). Own LPs: *Vic's Boston Story* (Story.), *Showcase*, Vol. 1 and 2 (Vang.), *Golden Era of Dixieland Jazz* (Des.).

DISTEL, Sacha, *guitar, singer*; b. Paris, France, 1/29/33. Nephew of noted bandleader and producer, Ray Ventura. Stud. piano at 5; guitar from 1948. Started in college band; won amateur contest. Worked w. Bernard Peiffer, 1952; Henri Renaud, Sandy Mosse, Bobby Jaspar '53, also w. Martial Solal, Barney Wilen, Rene Urtreger, Kenny Clarke. Recently featured as singer though best known as outstanding modern jazz guitarist. Favs: Ch. Parker, K. Burrell, J. Raney, Tal Farlow, Ch. Christian. LPs w. Lionel Hampton, Bobby Jaspar (Em.), John Lewis (Atl.); own LP for Fr. Versailles label.

DIXON, Joseph, *clarinet, reeds*; b. Lynn, Mass., 4/21/17. Stud. clarinet at 8 w. local bandmaster in Malden, Mass., later w. symphony clarinetist in Boston. Stud. harmony at New England Conservatory. Had small combos for high school dances; worked w. Bill Staffon, 1934; in

house band at Adrian Rollini's after hours room; T. Dorsey, 1936-7 (feat. w. Clambake Seven); G. Arnheim, 1937 (S. Kenton was in band); Bunny Berigan, 1938. During '40s worked at Condon's; w. Miff Mole at Nick's. Had own quintet in New York area, 1958. Fav. own record: *I'm Coming Virginia* and *Carolina in the Morning* w. Brad Gowans (Vict.). Favs: D. Murray, I. Fazola, Goodman, De Franco, T. Scott. LPs w. T. Dorsey (Vict.).
 Addr: 214 Bayfield Blvd., Oceanside, L.I., N.Y.

DODDS, Baby. Two instalments of his autobiography as told to Larry Gara appeared in *Evergreen Review*, published by Grove Press, NYC.

DODGE, Joe. Left D. Brubeck, July 1957, to sell furniture.

DOMINO, Antoine "Fats," *piano, singer*; b. New Orleans, La., 2/26/28. Father played violin and an uncle had worked w. Kid Ory and Oscar Celestin. Began picking out tunes on piano at home and when he was 10 was playing for pennies in local bars, but during early youth did factory work. Re-learned piano after an accident to his hand. His reputation among musicians led a record scout to a roadhouse where he was playing and he was signed to almost immediate success during the rock-'n'-roll craze. Has toured widely w. own group since, playing in clubs, for dances and in theatres throughout the U.S. Appeared in the film *The Girl Can't Help It*. Even on the pop material he performs, he manages to show himself an authentic blues singer; has also composed several fine blues. Many LPs for Imp.
 Addr: c/o Shaw Artists Corp., 565 Fifth Ave., New York 17, N.Y.

DONALDSON, Lou. Cont. free-lance recording and club dates around NYC, 1957-8, incl. a stay at the Half Note w. own quintet. LPs w. Monk, A. Blakey, Jimmy Smith (Blue Note). Own LPs: *Quartet, Quintet, Sextet, Wailing w. Lou, Swing and Soul* (Blue Note).

DORHAM, Kenny. Repl. the late Clifford Brown w. Max Roach quintet, June 1956, after having disbanded his own Jazz Prophets. LPs w. Roach (Em.), E. Henry, M. Gee (River.), Herb Geller (Jub.), A. K. Salim (Sav.), H. Mobley, S. Rollins (Pres.), C. Payne (Sig.), Monk, L. Donaldson (Blue Note). Own LPs: Blue Note, River.

DOROUGH, Robert Lord, *piano, singer, composer-arranger*; b. Cherry Hill, Ark., 12/12/23. Stud. clar. at Plainview, Texas high school and Texas Tech.; comp. and piano at North Texas State Teachers' College. Two years as accompanist and arr. for Sugar Ray Robinson in U.S., Canada and France, where he left the group and worked as single '54-5. Gigs in New York since 1955. Fav. own solo: *Hushabye* w. Sam Most (Beth. LP). Favs: B. Powell, H. Silver, D. Jordan, J.

Lewis. Fav. singers: Teagarden, Armstrong, Mama Yancey. LPs w. Sam Most (Beth.). Own LP: Beth.
Addr: 333 E. 75th St., New York 21, N.Y.

DORSEY, Jimmy. After the death of Tommy Dorsey in Nov. 1956, Jimmy continued to lead the band, but illness soon forced him to turn it over to Lee Castle. On June 12, 1957, he died in NYC of cancer. Ironically, a single record he had made some months earlier for the Fraternity label, *So Rare*, had risen rapidly in public acceptance and at the time of his death was the first hit record he had had in several years. LPs w. Tommy (Col., Des., Decca). Own LPs: Frat., Decca.

DORSEY, Tommy. On Nov. 26, 1956, Tommy Dorsey died suddenly and unexpectedly at his Greenwich, Conn., home. Death was attributed to strangulation caused by food particles lodged in his windpipe. In the fall of 1957 an orchestra designated as the Tommy Dorsey band, under the direction of trombonist Warren Covington, formerly the leader of The Commanders, was organized and toured dance halls throughout the U.S. LPs w. Jimmy (Des., Decca, Col.). Own LPs: Vict.

DRAPER, Raymond Allen, *tuba*; b. New York City, 8/3/40. Father, Barclay, pl. tpt. w. name bands; mother concert pianist. Got into High School of Performing Arts after auditioning on tuba. Jazz Unlimited sessions with own group at The Pad and Birdland, winter '56-7. Documentary film w. All City High Sch. Symphony, 1957. Comp. *Fugue for Brass Ensemble* played at NYU; working on symphony. Fav: Bill Barber. A youngster with a predictably brilliant future.
Addr: 50 W. 106th St., NYC 25.

DRASNIN, Robert Jackson, *flute, reeds*; b. Charleston, W. Va., 11/17/27. Raised in Los Angeles where he stud. reeds and flute. Had own combo in college at UCLA. During 1950s worked w. L. Brown, A. Rey, T. Dorsey *et al.* Grad. work in comp. at UCLA, 1954-7; associate conductor UCLA Symphony. With Red Norvo quint. '56-8. Fav. own solo: *Get Out of Town* w. Norvo (Lib.). Favs: Goodman, Shaw, Parker, Gillespie, Getz. LPs w. Norvo (Vict., Tampa).
Addr: 1551½ Ellsmere Ave., Los Angeles 19, Calif.

DREW, Kenny. In 1957 Drew moved from Calif. to NYC and made local gigs and record dates. LPs w. J. Coltrane (Blue Note), D. Gordon (Beth.), E. Henry (River.), S. Rollins (Pres.). Own LP: *This Is New* (River.).
Addr: 1534 Nelson Ave., Bronx 52.

DROOTIN, Buzzy. With B. Hackett, 1956-7, at the Henry Hudson Hotel in NYC. Appeared at Newport Jazz Festival w. R. Braff, July '57. LPs w. Hackett-Teagarden (Cap.), Braff (Verve, Epic, ABC-Par., Vict.), V. Dickenson (Story.).

EAGER, Allen. Returned to U.S., Nov. 1957, after two years in Paris and was again active in NYC. LPs w. Fats Navarro (Blue Note), G. Mulligan (Wor. Pac.).
Addr: 1500 Grand Concourse, Bronx 57, N.Y.

ECKSTINE, Billy. Toured w. Birdland All-Stars early 1957; subsequent British tour and various club dates in U.S. LP w. Sarah Vaughan (Merc.). Own LP: *Billy's Best* (Merc.).

EDISON, Harry. Club dates and extensive rec. activity on the West Coast, 1957, also tours w. Pearl Bailey and L. Bellson early 1958. First visit to NYC in several years when he acc. Pearl Bailey in Feb. '58 at the Waldorf-Astoria. Worked regularly w. F. Sinatra on his TV show, records, etc. LPs w. M. Albam (Cor.), L. Feather-D. Hyman (MGM), R. Norvo (Vict.), J. Giuffre, S. Rogers (Atl.), B. Webster, Ray Brown, W. Herman (Verve); *Tour de Force* w. Gillespie and Eldridge (Verve). Own LP: *Sweets* (Verve).

EDWARDS, Arthur, *bass*; b. Ft. Worth, Tex., 2/9/14. Stud. bass in high schools in Ardmore, Okla., Oklahoma City, and Wiley College, Marshall, Tex. Worked in Chicago, Denver, Los Angeles w. Bud Scott '43-5; Horace Henderson '47-53. Was w. T. Buckner '54-8. Fav: O. Pettiford. LP w. T. Buckner (Dix. Jub.).
Addr: 217 W. 54th St., Los Angeles 37, Calif.

ELDRIDGE, Roy. Appeared at Newport Jazz Festival, July 1957; toured w. JATP, fall 1957. Appeared on *Sound of Jazz* CBS-TV, Dec. '57. Gigged around NYC, incl. week ends at the Metropole. Toured Europe w. JATP, spring '58. LPs w. I. Jacquet, O. Peterson, C. Hawkins, C. Basie (Verve); *Tour de Force* w. Gillespie and Edison (Verve). Own LP: *Swing Goes Dixie* (Verve).

ELLINGTON, Duke. Continued the renaissance he had experienced since his appearance at the Newport Jazz Festival, 1956. A television spectacular featuring choreography to his *A Drum Is a Woman* was performed on CBS in May 1957. A few weeks later he premiered at Town Hall, NYC, a suite written in collaboration w. Billy Strayhorn based on Shakespeare characters, entitled *Such Sweet Thunder*, which had been commissioned by the Stratford, Ontario, Shakespeare Festival, where he played summer '56 and '57. Completed rec. his revised *Black, Brown and Beige* featuring Mahalia Jackson. Appeared at Carnegie Hall in concert, Apr. '58, w. Ella Fitzgerald to celebrate release of album they had recorded jointly for Verve. Was invited by both the Newport Jazz Festival and Great South Bay Festival for the summer '58 to appear and present new extended work. Arranged for his first European tour in 8 years, Oct. '58. LPs -w. E. Fitzgerald (Verve), Al Hibbler, (Bruns.). Own LPs: *Duke Ellington Presents* (Beth.), *A Drum Is a Woman, Such Sweet Thunder, Hi-Fi Ellington Uptown, Ellington Indigos* (Col.), *In a Mellotone* (Vict.).

ELLIOTT, Don. Appeared at Newport Jazz Festival, July 1958. LPs w. Billy Taylor (ABC-Par.), L. Feather-D. Hyman (MGM), R. Braff (Epic). Own LPs: *Vibrations* (Sav.), *The Voices of Don Elliott, Jamaica Jazz* (ABC-Par.), *The Mello Sound* (Decca), *At Newport* (Verve).

ERICSON, Rolf. Took own all-star American combo on tour of Sweden, summer 1956; spent most of 1956-8 in Calif., working w. H. James, Les Brown, H. Rumsey's Lighthouse All-Stars, etc. LP: *All American Stars* (Em.).

EUELL, Julian Thomas, *bass*; b. New York City, 5/23/29. Took up bass in '44. Army '45-7. In '47 stud. at 3rd St. Settlement House, pl. w. S. Rollins, J. McLean, Art Taylor; gave up playing, worked in post office '49-52. Gigged w. Benny Harris '52-4. Stud. w. Ch. Mingus, Fred Zimmerman, '53; a year in mus. dept. at Col. U. '54-5. Jobbed w. Joe Roland '55, Freddie Redd trio '56; Gigi Gryce quintet '56-7, later w. Mal Waldron *et al.* Stud. at NYU '51-4, att. Col. U. to receive BS in sociology; active in youth work in Newark, N.J. Fav: Pettiford. Rec: *Mal-1, Mal-2* w. Waldron (Pres.). Addr: 1611 Park Ave., New York 29, N.Y.

EVANS, Gil. Once again active in jazz circles, Evans contributed arr. to a H. McKusick workshop LP on Vict., 1957, and in early '58 wrote arr. for Miles Davis' big band of 19 pieces and had own LP for medium-sized group. LPs as arr. D. Elliott (ABC-Par.), arr. Helen Merrill (Em.), cond. and arr. Miles Davis (Col.). Own LP: *Gil Evans and Ten* (Pres.).

EVANS, William, *piano*; b. Plainfield, N.J., 8/16/29. Stud. piano, violin, flute. Had own group w. brother at 16, incl. Don Elliott. Stud. at Louisiana State; pl. w. Mundell Lowe and Red Mitchell. Six months w. Herbie Fields, 1950, followed by 3 years in Army. After discharge in '54, worked w. Jerry Wald, Tony Scott; pl. w. Miles Davis '58. Favs: L. Tristano, B. Powell, N. Cole, H. Silver. Outstanding modern pianist with clean, incisive style. LPs w. T. Scott, George Russell (Vict.), D. Elliott (Decca), Jimmy Knepper, C. Mingus (Beth.), D. Garcia (Dawn). Own LP: *New Jazz Conceptions* (River.).

FARLOW, Tal. Cont. local gigs in NYC, incl. Stan Getz' group *et al.* LPs w. Artie Shaw, B. De Franco (Verve), Red Norvo (Sav.). Own LPs: Verve.

FARMER, Art. After working w. H. Silver quintet during most of 1957, joined G. Mulligan's new quartet, formed Apr. '58, and was w. him for its first appearance on the Timex jazz show, CBS-TV, May '58. LPs w. E. Costa (Mode), L. Feather-D. Hyman (MGM), G. Ammons, G. Melle, A. Cohn, Mose Allison (Pres.), H. McKusick, George Russell (Vict.), H. Mobley, H. Silver, S. Clark, C. Jordan (Blue Note), Q. Jones, O. Pettiford, Jackie and Roy, Candido (ABC-Par.); *Three Trumpets* w. Byrd

and Sulieman (Pres.), *Trumpets All Out* (Sav.). Own LP: *Last Night When We Were Young* (ABC-Par.).

FEATHER, Leonard. Orig. music for *The Weary Blues* w. Langston Hughes (MGM), *The Swingin' Seasons* w. D. Hyman, Ralph Burns (MGM), *Hi-Fi Suite* w. D. Hyman (MGM). Other LPs: *Oh Captain* w. Hyman, *Hot Vs. Cool, Cats Vs. Chicks,* 48 *Stars of American Jazz* (all on MGM), *The Lion Roars,* interview with and music by Willie The Lion Smith (Dot). Consultant for NBC-TV educational series *The Subject Is Jazz,* Mar.-June 1958.
Addr: 340 Riverside Drive, New York 25, N.Y.

FELDMAN, Vic. Left W. Herman orch., spring 1957, toured w. B. De Franco combo, then settled in Los Angeles, where he became active in club and record dates. LPs w. Herman (Cap.), B. De Franco (Verve), J. Deuchar, Bob Cooper, Leroy Vinnegar (Contemp.). Own LP: *Suite Sixteen* (Contemp.).

FERGUSON, Allyn M., *piano*; b. San Jose, Calif., 10/18/24. Father pianist and trombonist w. dance bands. Stud. trumpet with Loring Nichols (Red's father) at 4 years; piano at 7. Played prof. since 14, working w. various dance bands on West Coast. Holds both B.A. and M.A. in music. Organized Chamber Jazz Sextet in 1956. Acc. Kenneth Patchen's readings on Cad. LP. Favs: Bach, Bartok, F. Waller, R. Burns, L. Young, Tatum, Monk. Own LPs: Cad.
Addr: 30 E. San Fernando St., San Jose, Calif.

FERGUSON, Maynard. Settling in NYC area, he cont. to lead his all-star band, first formed in Aug. 1956, called the Birdland Dream Band, the personnel of which was variable but which made regular appearances at Birdland and jazz festivals, incl. the Randall's Island New York Festival, summer 1957. LPs w. J. Richards (Beth.), P. Rugolo (Merc.). Own LPs: Vik, Kapp, Em.

FITZGERALD, Ella. During an engagement at the Paramount Theatre in NYC in Jan. 1957, she had an emergency appendectomy. Recovering, she went on a European tour w. a JATP unit in Apr. '57. Cont. to earn wider general recognition, she fulfilled such engagements as 3 weeks at the Copacabana in NYC, June '57; also had successful concert at the Hollywood Bowl, July 20, and appeared at Newport Jazz Festival, summer '57. In Apr. '58 she gave a concert at Carnegie Hall w. D. Ellington, celebrating the release of the four-LP set on Verve titled *Ella Fitzgerald Sings the Duke Ellington Song Book;* also on B. Goodman's *Swing into Spring* TV show on NBC in Apr. In May was in England on the first stop of a European tour w. JATP. LPs w. Ellington, L. Armstrong (Verve). Own LPs: *Sings Rodgers and Hart, Jazz at the Hollywood Bowl, At Newport, Like Someone in Love* (Verve), *Ella and Her Fellas, Ella Sings Gershwin* (Decca).

FLANAGAN, Tommy Lee, *piano*; b. Detroit, 3/16/30. Clarinet at 6; piano at 11; prof. debut 1945 w. Dexter Gordon; later w. Lucky Thompson, Milt Jackson, Rudy Rutherford '46-8. Was w. Billy Mitchell before and after Army service, 1951-3. Joined Kenny Burrell '54; to NYC, Feb. '56, worked briefly w. Ella Fitzgerald, then from Aug. '57 spent a year with Jay Jay Johnson quintet, touring Sweden w. him. Later worked w. Miles Davis and again w. Johnson. Favs: Hank Jones, Barry Harris *et al.* Considered one of best of modern school of pianists from Detroit. LPs w. Burrell (Blue Note, Pres.), Johnson (Col.), Thad Jones (Per.), Rollins (Pres.), Salim (Sav.) *et al.*

Addr: Apt. 2-A, 251 W. 101st St., NYC 25.

FOSTER, Frank. LPs w. Basie (Verve), Milt Jackson (Atl.), Tony Scott (Vict.), Thad Jones (Per.), M. Gee (River.). Own LPs: *No Count* (Sav.), *All Day Long, Wail, Frank, Wail* (Pres.).

FOUNTAIN, Pete. Disbanded his own group, spring 1957, to join Lawrence Welk and has since become a permanent fixture as leader of a Dixieland group within Welk's band on his weekly ABC-TV show. LPs w. Geo. Girard (Merc., Vik), Welk (Cor.), Al Hirt (Verve). Own LP: Cor.

FREEMAN, Bud. After usual gigs in the NYC area, Freeman settled down at E. Condon's new club, Feb. 1958, with his own trio. LPs w. Condon (MGM), J. McPartland (Epic); *The Big Challenge* (Jazz.), *A String of Swinging Pearls* (Vict.). Own LPs: *Chicago Austin High School Jazz in Hi-Fi* (Vict.).

FRIEDMAN, Donald E., *piano*; b. San Francisco, Calif., 5/4/35. Began stud. piano in 1940; first job after participating in local jam sessions. Worked briefly w. Dexter Gordon, S. Rogers, B. Collette, 1956; w. B. De Franco '56-7. Came to New York w. Pepper Adams, 1958. Favs: Parker, B. Powell. LP w. Collette (Contemp.).

Addr: 5016 Bakman Ave., San Francisco, Calif.

FULLER, Curtis Dubois, *trombone*; b. Detroit, Mich., 12/15/34. Pl. baritone horn in high school '49, later switched to trombone. In Army, 1953-5, in band w. Cannonball Adderley, Junior Mance. Pl. w. Kenny Burrell, Yusef Lateef in Detroit, 1955-6; to NYC '57, worked briefly w. Miles Davis. Favs: J. J. Johnson, Cleveland, Brookmeyer, Urbie Green. Fluent, promising Johnson-influenced trombonist.

Addr: 251 W. 101st St., NYC 25.

GALBRAITH, Barry. LPs w. D. Elliott, R. Burns (Decca), J. Lewis (Atl.), C. Hawkins (River.), T. Scott, Geo. Russell, H. McKusick (Vict.), J. B. Brooks (Vik). Own LP: *Guitar and the Wind* (Decca).

GARLAND, Ed. After an assoc. which had lasted most of their musical lives, Garland and Kid Ory broke up in the middle '50s and Garland cont. to work w. groups in the Los Angeles area. LP w. Ory (Good Time Jazz).

GARLAND, Red. Has been usually in, though occasionally out, of Miles Davis' quint. since 1957. LPs w. Davis (Pres., Col.), Art Pepper (Contemp.), J. Coltrane, A. Taylor (Pres.). Own LPs: *A Garland of Red, All Mornin' Long* (Pres.).

GARNER, Erroll. Cont. his striking success expanding his career to incl. concert and club dates outside the strictly jazz circuit. Made his first European tour. Dec. 1957, returning to U.S., Feb. '58, w. plans for more concert work and less night club engagements. Own LPs: *The Most Happy Piano, Garner Alone, Concert by the Sea, Other Voices, Soliloquy* (Col.), *Early Garner* (Jazz.), *Modern Jazz Piano: Four Views*—w. other artists (Cam.).

GASKIN, Leonard, *bass*; b. Brooklyn, N.Y., 8/25/20. Stud. piano, then bass in high school and w. private teachers. Worked at Monroe's in Harlem w. D. Jordan, M. Roach in 1943; D. Gillespie '44; E. South, C. Shavers, C. Parker '45-6. Joined E. Condon, Oct. '56; made British tour '57. Still w. Condon; also studio work in radio, TV, recording. Favs: O. Pettiford, G. Duvivier. LPs w. R. Bright (Reg.), B. Freeman (Vict.), Condon (Col.).

Addr: 63 Lefferts Pl., Brooklyn 16, N.Y.

GEE, Matthew. Worked for a while w. D. Gillespie's big band late 1957 before it was disbanded. Own LP: *Jazz by Gee* (River.).

GELLER, Herb. LPs w. M. Albam (Cor.), Q. Jones (ABC-Par.), M. Ferguson (Vik). Own LP: *Fire in the West* (Jub.).

GERSH, Squire (William Girsback), *bass*; b. San Francisco, Calif., 5/13/13. Worked w. various commercial groups; was part of the San Francisco "revivalist" movement when he worked w. Lu Watters, B. Scobey, T. Murphy, Mutt Carey, B. Johnson. With L. Armstrong '56-Dec. '57. Favs: Several New Orleans bassists and Jimmy Blanton. LP w. Armstrong (Decca).

Addr: 230 Jones St., San Francisco, Calif.

GETZ, Stan. Although he had announced in Feb. 1956 after his return from Stockholm that he intended to give up music and fulfil a life-long ambition by studying medicine, he cont. to appear at jazz clubs and in concert w. his own groups and as a single. On tour w. JATP, fall '57 and spring '58. LPs w. Kai Winding (Sav.), Ella Fitzgerald (Verve); *Getz Meets Mulligan in Hi-Fi, For Musicians Only*—w. Gillespie, S. Stitt (Verve). Own LPs: *Lestorian Mode* (Sav.), *Stan Getz and the Cool Sounds, Sittin' In, Stan Getz in Stockholm* (Verve).

GIBBS, Terry. Toured w. Birdland All-Stars, Feb. 1957; subsequently much of Gibbs' activity was on the West Coast and he arrived in NYC spring '58 w. a new group which he had formed in Los Angeles. LPs w. H. Babasin (Mode). Own LPs: Sav., *Mallets-A-Plenty, Swingin'* w. *Terry Gibbs, Vibes on Velvet* (Em.).

GILLESPIE, Dizzy. During 1956-7 Gillespie maintained his large orch., w. interruptions for tours as a member of JATP. The band appeared at the Newport Jazz Festival, July '57, and Gillespie was a member of the faculty of the School of Jazz, Lenox, Mass. in Aug. '57. He broke up the band, Jan. 2, 1958, to adopt a quintet format, w. S. Stitt featured. In Apr. '58 he dissolved the group to go on tour again w. JATP in Europe. LPs w. C. Parker (Verve), C. Christian (Eso.), Stuff Smith, Mary Lou Williams at Newport (Verve); *Tour de Force* w. R. Eldridge, H. Edison; *For Musicians Only* w. S. Getz, S. Stitt; *Norman Granz Jam Session No. 9* (Verve). Own LPs: *School Days* (Reg.), *Dizzy Gillespie Story* (Sav.), *World Statesman, Dizzy in Greece, At Newport, Birks' Works* (Verve).

GIRARD, George, *trumpet*; b. New Orleans, La., 10/7/30; d. N.O., 1/18/57, after long siege of cancer. Began playing prof. after grad. from high school, 1946, first w. Johnny Archer on nation-wide tour, then back in New Orleans w. Phil Zito, Basin Street Six, Joe Mares *et al.* Formed own group in '54 to play at Famous Door in N.O. Pl. the annual Dixieland Jubilee in Los Angeles, fall '54. Was active in music until Jan. '56, when he had operation; played again 4 months, spring '56, before illness forced him to retire permanently. Last rec. date for Dr. Edmond Souchon, who organized Good Time Jazz/New Orleans Jazz Club date, Apr. 14, 1956. LPs: *Jam Session on Bourbon Street* (Vik), *Strictly Dixie* (Merc.), Good Time Jazz.

GIUFFRE, Jimmy. Formed own trio in Calif., Feb. 1956, w. guitarist Jim Hall and bassist Ralph Pena, later Jim Atlas, and came East later in the spring. Appeared in night clubs, concerts and was at Newport Jazz Festival, July '57. On faculty at School of Jazz, Lenox, Mass., Aug. '57. Formed new trio w. trombonist Bob Brookmeyer and Hall on guitar late '57. Drawing inspiration from S. Getz, G. Mulligan and the Modern Jazz Quartet, Giuffre's groups performed an improvisational chamber music, using American folk sources as well as jazz. LPs w. J. Graas (Decca), Mod. Jazz Quart. (Atl.), Shorty Rogers (Vict., Atl.), R. Brown (Verve), T. Charles (Pres.), Brookmeyer (Wor. Pac.). Own LPs: *The Jimmy Giuffre Clarinet, The Jimmy Giuffre 3, The Music Man* (Atl.).

GLAMANN, Betty, *harp*; b. Wellington, Kan., 5/21/23. Mother and father musical; began study of piano at 8, harp at 10 in Wichita, Kan. Holds B.S. in music from Goucher College and Peabody Conservatory. Played harp w. Baltimore Symphony 3 years. With Spike Jones, 1948; radio and TV work in New York '48-54. Formed Smith-Glamann quintet, 1954, w. Rufus Smith. Joined D. Ellington for several weeks '55; w. Oscar Pettiford '57-8. Fav. own solo: *Jeepers Creepers* (Merc.). LPs: *Drum is a Woman* w. Ellington (Col.); K. Dorham (River.). Own LP: Merc.
Addr: 90 Charles St., New York, N.Y.

GOLSON, Benny, *tenor sax, composer-arranger*; b. Philadelphia, Pa., 1/25/29. Began stud. piano at 9, switched to sax at 14. Attended Howard U. in Washington. Worked around Philadelphia; left w. Bull Moose Jackson in 1951 (band incl. Tadd Dameron, who encouraged his interest in arranging). Joined Dameron's group in 1953; later the same year w. L. Hampton; w. J. Hodges, 1954; E. Bostic '54-6. Joined D. Gillespie's big band in '56 and toured S. America. With Gillespie until band broke up in '58 and has since done extensive recording and worked gigs with own group in New York. In addition to playing tenor in a warm style sometimes recalling Ben Webster's, Golson has been called the most promising young comp.-arr. to appear in jazz in the last few years. His most celebrated composition, *Stablemates*, was featured by the Gillespie band and recorded by Miles Davis. Other well known comps. incl. *Whisper Not, I Remember Clifford.* Fav. instrumentalists: D. Gordon, D. Byas, L. Thompson, C. Hawkins, S. Stitt, S. Getz. Fav. arr: Dameron, Q. Jones, G. Gryce, E. Wilkins. LPs w. Gillespie (Verve), Lee Morgan (Blue Note), J. Moody (Argo). Own LP: River.
Addr: Apt. 7H, 1925 Seventh Ave., New York 26, N.Y.

GOODMAN, Benny. In early 1957 Goodman was still on his tour of the Far East. During '57-8 he led bands intermittently for television and concert appearances. For a few months in the fall of '57 a band went out under Goodman's name fronted by Urbie Green but Goodman did not generally appear with it. After app. as star of his own NBC-TV show *Swing into Spring* on Apr. 30, he toured Europe, May '58, ending w. a week at the Brussels World's Fair.

GRAETTINGER, Bob. The former Stan Kenton arranger died at the age of 33 in Los Angeles, spring 1957, after a long illness.

GRAHAM, Bill. In the fall of 1957 left C. Basie and joined D. Ellington for 3 months during Johnny Hodges' absence.

GRAHAM, Kenny (Kenneth Thomas Skingle), *tenor sax, clarinet, flute*; b. London, Eng., 7/19/24. From musical family, began playing banjo at 5, sang in church choir, played w. Ambrose, J. Parnell *et al.* Formed own group called the Afro-Cubists in early '50s and worked in Eng. and on Continent. Favs: Ellington, Gillespie. Own LP: MGM.
Addr: 64 Sarsfield Rd., Greenford, Middlesex, Eng.

GRANZ, Norman. Expanded his European activities in 1958 to send three separate shows on tour of the Continent: one with the JATP instrumentalists; a second starring Ella Fitzgerald and O. Peterson trio; and a third w. B. Goodman's orchestra. By early 1957 he had abandoned Clef, Norgran and Down Home labels to consolidate all his record releases under the Verve mark.

GREEN, Bennie. After a year of inactivity he returned to the jazz scene, spring 1958, gigging first in Chicago and later in NYC, and recording his own LPs for Blue Note. Other LPs: *Three Trombones* (Pres.), *Four Trombones* (Deb.).

GREEN, Urbie. Fronted B. Goodman's band, fall 1957, and was on tour with it through Dec. Much free-lance recording and studio work in NYC. LPs w. B. Galbraith, Toots Thielemans, R. Burns (Decca), T. Gibbs (Em.), H. Mann (River.), T. Scott (Vict.), J. Rushing (Col.); *Session at Riverside* (Cap.), *Manhattan Jazz Septet* (Cor.). Own LP: *All About Urbie Green* (ABC-Par.).

GREY, Albert Thornton, *trombone*; b. Aldie, Va., 6/6/25. From musical family in which trumpet, piano, organ, sax and clarinet were played. During World War II worked in Navy band w. several name musicians who recommended him to B. Carter, whom he joined on discharge. Subsequently w. J. Lunceford, L. Hampton, A. Cobb, L. Millinder, and recorded with all these bands. With D. Gillespie '56-7; joined C. Basie late '57. Fav. mus: B. Carter.
Addr: 2429 N. 27th St., Philadelphia, Pa.

GRIFFIN, John Arnold III, *tenor saxophone*; b. Chicago, Ill., 4/24/28. Mother a singer, father ex-cornetist. Clar. at Du Sable High School, 1941. Pl. w. L. Hampton, 1945-47; Joe Morris, 1947-50; Jo Jones, 1950; Arnett Cobb, 1951; Art Blakey, Mar.-Oct. '57. Fav: C. Parker. Good tenor man of hard-bop school. LPs w. Wilbur Ware (River.), A. K. Salim (Sav.), Blakey (Beth., Vik, Jub.). Own LPs: *Chicago Calling, A Blowing Session, The Congregation* (Blue Note).
Addr: 1201 E. Madison Park, Chicago, Ill.

GRYCE, Gigi. Cont. to play club dates w. a slightly revamped Jazz Lab quint. feat. D. Byrd on trumpet, and appeared at Newport Jazz Festival, July 1957. LPs w. Byrd (Verve, River., Col., Jub.), O. Pettiford (ABC-Par.), M. Waldron (Pres.), T. Monk (River.), Lee Morgan, Thad Jones (Blue Note).

GULLIN, Lars. Own LPs: *Baritone Sax* (Atl.), *Lars Gullin Swings* (East-West).

HACKETT, Bobby. Throughout 1957 Hackett led a sextet at the Henry Hudson Hotel, NYC, which drew on jazz styles from Dixieland to cool in its often ingenious arrangements (most of which were by Dick Cary) and

manner of playing. LPs w. L. Armstrong (Vict.), Jack Teagarden (Cap.). Own LP: Cap.

HADI, Shafi (Curtis Porter), *tenor sax, alto, reeds*; b. Philadelphia, Pa., 9/21/29. Piano lessons from grandmother at 6; worked w. high school orch.; later w. rhythm and blues bands, incl. P. Williams, Griffin Brothers, Ruth Brown. Stud. comp. at Howard U. and U. of Detroit. With C. Mingus' Jazz Workshop since 1956. Fav: D. Ellington. LPs w. Mingus (Beth., MGM).
Addr: 255 W. 108th St., New York, N.Y.

HAIG, Al. With D. Gillespie briefly in 1957. LPs w. C. Parker (Verve, Deb.), P. Woods-D. Byrd (Pres.). Own LP: *Jazz Will O' the Wisp* (Counter.).

HAKIM, Sadik (Argonne Dense Thornton), *piano*; b. Duluth, Minn., 7/15/21. Grandfather was music professor, school-teacher; mother and others in family pl. chamber music. Stud. theory w. grandfather; no piano lessons. Left home 1940, gigged in Peoria, Ill., w. Fats Dudley; to NYC from Chicago late '44, pl. w. Ben Webster for 15 months, then w. Lester Young to '48; later worked w. Slam Slewart; in Canada w. Louis Metcalf, and toured w. James Moody orch. '51-4; for next 2 years jobbed around in N.Y. and New Jersey; had own quartet in Mount Vernon, then pl. w. Buddy Tate orch. '56-8. Hakim, whose name was changed in 1947 for religious reasons, was important as one of the first bop pianists. He played, on the famous C. Parker rec. date for Sav., 8 bars on *Ko-Ko* and all the rest of the date, except *Billie's Bounce* and *Now's The Time*. Also *Dexter's Deck*, etc., w. Dexter Gordon (Sav.), Aladdin dates w. Lester Young, etc. Fav. own solos: *Jumping With Symphony Sid, No Eyes Blues* w. Young. Favs: Tatum, Bud Powell.
Addr: 162 Vernon Ave., Brooklyn 6, N.Y.

HALEN, Carl H., *cornet, trumpet*; b. Hamilton, Ohio, 6/10/28. One of the younger members of the "revivalist" school; first played accordion, then switched to trumpet, 1948. Played w. Dixieland Rhythm Kings, 1948-50; Army band '50-2; formed own group in 1953 known as the Gin Bottle 7. Favs: Bix, B. Hackett, Doc Evans.
Addr: 345 McAlpin Ave., Cincinnati 20, Ohio.

HALL, Ed. Left L. Armstrong, July 1, '58. LPs w. Armstrong (Col., Decca), V. Dickenson (Vang.), J. Teagarden, Jonah Jones (Beth.).

HALL, Herbert, *clarinet, reeds*; b. Reserve, La., 3/28/07. Younger brother of Ed Hall. Started on guitar, then clar., borrowing brother Robert's instrument. Left home 1927 to join band in Baton Rouge; later to New Orleans w. Sidney Desvignes. Worked in Texas w. Don Albert, 1929-45, then came to New York. In '55-6 toured Europe and North Africa w. Sammy Price for Les Jeunesses

Musicales de France. Joined Eddie Condon, 1957. Fav: Ed Hall. LP w. Condon (MGM).

Addr: 251 E. 148th St., Bronx, N.Y.

HALL, Jim. Left C. Hamilton to join J. Giuffre late 1956 and cont. w. him in club and concert dates. LPs w. Giuffre (Atl.), J. Lewis, C. Hamilton, B. Brookmeyer (Wor. Pac.). Own LP: *Jazz Guitar* (Wor. Pac.).

HAMILTON, Chico. Cont. to lead his successful quint. which w. several changes of personnel appeared in concert and club dates throughout the U.S. Feat. in the movie *The Sweet Smell of Success,* incl. brief speaking part for some of the members of the group, 1957. LPs w. J. Lewis, Fred Katz (Wor. Pac.). Own LPs: *Plays South Pacific,* trio date, quintet date (Wor. Pac.), soundtrack *Sweet Smell of Success* (Decca).

HAMLIN, Johnny, *piano, accordion;* b. San Diego, Calif., 5/19/21. Stud. accordion privately, worked in San Diego and Los Angeles w. various groups, switching to piano in 1949. In Air Force during World War II. Formed own quintet, 1950, in San Diego; with various changes in personnel, the group has remained active since and toured widely. Received early encouragement from L. Hampton. His group plays an innocuous brand of modified jazz. LPs: *Polka Dots and Moonbeams, Powder Puff.* Own LPs. (Vict.).

Addr: c/o McConkey Artists Corp., Congress Hotel, Chicago, Ill.

HAMPTON, Lionel. The Hampton orchestra devoted much of 1956-8 to a series of extremely successful tours overseas. After touring France, Spain, Italy and Israel, the band returned to the U.S. in Aug. 1956, remained only 2 months, then left for a long tour of Great Britain and engagements in Germany and Scandinavia. Remaining in the U.S. from Dec. 1957 until the following April, Hampton then took off for Australia. In Dec. 1957 the orchestra left for still another tour of the European Continent, also visiting North Africa, returning home Mar. 1958. During this time, though often recording for Verve, Hampton remained independent, making LPs here and abroad for a number of labels. One LP cut in Spain, *Jazz Flamenco,* was released in the U.S. on RCA Victor. Other LPs: *Travellin' Band, Hamp's Big Four, Genius of Lionel Hampton, Hallelujah Hamp, The High and The Mighty,* all on Verve; *Jivin' The Vibes,* reissues of combo sides from the late 1930s, on Camden; new sessions on Audio-Fidelity.

HANDY, W. C. After a series of honors which included a testimonial dinner on his 84th birthday, Nov. 1957, and the completion of *St. Louis Blues,* a film roughly based on his early life, the "Father of the Blues" died in NYC, Mar. 28, 1958.

HARDMAN, William Franklin, Jr., *trumpet;* b. Cleveland, Ohio, 4/6/33. Uncle plays bass w. James Moody. Stud.

trombone in junior high school, then worked in local groups. With T. Bradshaw from 1953-5; local gigs w. T. Dameron, C. Mingus '56. Member of Jazz Messengers since Sept. '56. Favs: C. Brown, M. Davis, D. Byrd, D. Gillespie. LPs w. Jackie McLean, Mal Waldron (Pres.), Messengers (Beth., Jub., Elek., Col., Vik, Wor. Pac.).

Addr: 133 W. 47th St., New York 36, N.Y.

HARRINGTON, Robert M., *piano, vibes, drums;* b. Marshfield, Wis., 1/30/12. Father plays violin. Stud. E-flat bass in high school; played piano w. C. Barnet, 1951-4; G. Auld, 1955-6; B. De Franco, 1956; Vido Musso, 1949-52; played drums w. Red Nichols and Bud Freeman, 1944-5. Favs: Ellington, Basie, R. Norvo. LPs w. H. Babasin (Em.). Own LP: Imp.

Addr: Paradise Valley Trailer Ct., Las Vegas, Nev.

HARRIS, Barry Doyle, *piano;* b. Detroit, Mich., 12/15/29. Mother, a church pianist, gave him lessons from age 4. Pl. w. jazz band at amateur show '46. From '54 on was house pianist at Blue Bird Club in Detroit, pl. w. such visiting jazzmen as Miles Davis, Sonny Stitt, Max Roach; for a while pl. at Rouge Lounge w. Konitz, Lester Young *et al.* Favs: Powell, C. Parker. Fav. own solo: *Billy Do* w. Thad Jones on Blue Note. Considered a major influence among the newer jazzmen from Detroit. Has developed own theory for teaching jazz and had several pupils in 1958. LPs with Donald Byrd (Trans.), H. Mobley, Art Farmer-Byrd (Pres.).

Addr: 6568 Stanford St., Detroit, Mich.

HARRIS, Bill, *trombone.* LPs w. W. Herman (Verve, Cap.), N. Pierce (Cor.), Chubby Jackson (Argo), B. Ver Plank (Sav.). Own LP: *Bill Harris and Friends* (Fant.).

HARRIS, Willie "Bill," *guitar;* b. Nashville, N.C., 4/14/25. Mother taught him the rudiments of harmony on piano and he later played organ in his father's church. When he was 12, an uncle bought him a guitar, but his progress was so limited that he gave up. Entering the Army at 18 in the Engineers Corps, he limited his musical activities to bugling, while he saw overseas service in England and France. After his discharge in Sept. 1945, he studied guitar in Wash., D.C., gradually becoming a fair jazz guitarist as well as learning to play a few classics with a pick. Later, at Columbia School of Music in Washington, Sophocles Papas, who owned the school, encouraged his studies as a classical guitarist. The problem of making a living precluded any further efforts in this direction. In 1950, after some gigging in Washington with jazz groups and teaching at local schools, he joined The Clovers, a r. & b. vocal group, as accompanist. Has been on the road with them ever since. Guitarist Mickey Baker heard him practicing jazz and classics in his dressing room, encouraged him to make some demonstration records. Result was series of LP solos showing remarkable versatility and range of styles. Favs: Oscar Moore, Barney Kessel, Les Paul, Django Reinhardt, Charlie Christian, J. Collins. Recs. for EmArcy.

Addr: 2021 Hamlin St. N.E., Washington 18, D.C.

HAWES, Hampton. Semi-inactive during large part of 1957. LPs w. B. Perkins (Wor. Pac.), A. Pepper (Sav.), C. Mingus (Jub.). Own LP: Pres.

HAWKINS, Coleman. Cont. free-lance work in clubs, week-end "jam sessions," concerts, dances and in the recording studios in the New York area. On tour w. JATP, fall 1957, after app. at Newport Jazz Festival, July. Seen on *The Sound of Jazz*, CBS-TV show, Dec. '57. A two-LP set of biographical reminiscences of his life in music was released in '57. Toured Europe w. JATP, spring '58. LPs w. T. Monk (River.), L. Feather-D. Hyman (MGM), Red Allen (Vict.), J. McPartland (Epic); *The Big Challenge* and *Fletcher Henderson Reunion* (Jazz.). Own LPs: *The Hawk Flies High* and *A Documentary* (River.), *At Newport* (Verve), *The Gilded Hawk* (Cap.).

HAWKINS, Jelacy "Screamin' Jay," *singer, piano*; b. Cleveland, Ohio, 1929. Adopted from Cleveland orphanage when 18 months. At 6 he began playing a neighbor's piano and in later years continued playing as he pursued a career as a boxer, winning a Golden Gloves contest in 1947, later turning professional. In 1953, after completing Army service, he joined Tiny Grimes as pianist, and later was w. Lynn Hope and Fats Domino. When he went on his own, he began affecting outlandish costumes and a wild stage manner to achieve great success in the rock-'n'-roll field. At base, Hawkins is an authentic blues shouter. Own LP: *At Home with Screamin' Jay* (Epic).

Addr: c/o Gale Agency, 48 W. 48th St., New York 36, N.Y.

HAWKSWORTH, John, *bass, piano*; b. London, Eng., 1/20/24. Stud. in Sheffield, Eng.; Capetown, S. Africa (while in R.A.F.); and in London after the war. Met Buddy Featherstonehaugh while in R.A.F. and joined his group later; then w. Tommy Sampson. Toured Britain, U.S. w. T. Heath; won first place in *Melody Maker's* Readers' Poll of Britain's Best. Good bassist who earned fan acclaim through comedy showmanship. Favs: Ellington, J. Smith, T. Farlow, O. Peterson, Ray Bryant. LPs w. Heath on Lond.

Addr: 22 Crundale Ave., Kingsbury, N.W.9, Eng.

HAYES, Louis Sedell, *drums*; b. Detroit, 5/31/37. Father pl. drums; stud. w. cousin at 11; Wurlitzer Sch. of Mus. in Detroit '51-2. Worked w. own group in local club at 15; w. Yusef Lateef '56; to NYC, Aug. '56; and for the next 2 years toured w. Horace Silver quintet. Favs: Philly Joe Jones, Blakey, Roach, K. Clarke. LPs w. Silver (Blue Note).

HAYNES, George "Tiger," *guitar, bass*; b. St. Croix, V.I., 12/13/07. No formal musical training but father and brother taught him at home. First came to prominence when he joined the Three Flames in Sept. 1945 for very successful night club stints; seen at Bon Soir, NYC, for past few years. Had own NBC-TV series for 39 wks. Favs: D. Reinhardt, C. Christian. Own LP: Merc.

Addr: 587 E. 169th St., Bronx 56, N.Y.

HEATH, Percy. Cont. as member of the Mod. Jazz Quart. LPs w. Quart. (Atl.), J. Lewis, Milt Jackson (Atl.), Thad Jones, K. Dorham (Blue Note), Miles Davis, T. Monk, Sonny Rollins (Pres.).

HEATH, Ted. Toured U.S., Feb. 1957, w. Al Hibbler, June Christy, E. Heywood and again in Oct. w. Hi-Lo's and Carmen McRae. Cont. to enjoy great popularity both in England and U.S. LPs: Lond.

HENDERSON, Bobby "Jody Bolden" (Robert Bolden Henderson), *piano, trumpet*; b. New York City, 4/16/10. Studied from 1923. Acc. Billie Holiday ca. '33; in obscurity in upstate N.Y. for years until John Hammond recorded him in 1956. Very much influenced by Harlem "stride" pianists. Appeared at Newport Jazz Festival, 1957. Favs: Tatum, Ellington, Waller, C. Profit, T. Wilson, Basie. LP w. Basie (Vang.). Own LPs: Verve, Vang.

Addr: The Kerry Blue, 16 Eagle St., Albany 10, N.Y.

HENDERSON, Horace. In spring 1958 he had a group in a night club in Minneapolis, Minn.

HENDRICKS, Jon, *singer, drums*; b. Newark, Ohio, 9/16/21. Has been singing since he was 7 and worked club dates in Toledo at 13. Art Tatum, a friend of the family, accompanied him from time to time. Formed own four-piece combo which played Toledo clubs. In 1958 an LP, *Sing a Song of Basie*, in which he sang his own ingenious lyrics set to famous Basie instrumentals, was released and was very successful. Favs: Tatum, King Pleasure, M. Roach, Blakey, S. Catlett. Arr: Q. Jones, G. Gryce, G. Evans. LP w. Dave Lambert; *Sing a Song of Basie* (ABC-Par.).

Addr: 316 E. 6th St., Apt. 16, New York, N.Y.

HENRY, Ernie. In Dec. 1956 Henry joined D. Gillespie's band repl. Phil Woods. In Dec. '57 he was w. the band during its engagement at Birdland, NYC. On Dec. 29 he went home after playing that night and died very unexpectedly in his sleep. LPs w. K. Dorham (River.), Gillespie (Verve), T. Monk (River.). Own LPs: *Seven Standards and a Blues*, *Presenting Ernie Henry* (River.).

HERBERT, Mort (Morton Herbert Pelovitz), *bass, arranger*; b. Somerville, N.J., 6/30/25. After two lessons on trumpet, taught himself bass in high school and began doing local gigs. Worked w. various swing bands during 1940s and '50s; in charge of music for the Navy in Pearl Harbor area '43-46. From Sept. '55 to Jan. '58 was featured at the Metropole in NYC w. Sol Yaged's group and has also gigged w. Sauter-Finegan, Marian McPartland, Don Elliott. Joined L. Armstrong, Jan. '58. Fav. own solo and arrangement: *I've Got You Under My Skin* in *Night People* (Sav.). Favs: Red Mitchell, P. Heath, C. Lombardi. Fav. arr: E. Sauter, N. Hefti, E. Wilkins. LP w. Don Elliott (Sav.). Own LP: Sav.

Addr: 52 E. 97th St., New York, N.Y.

HERMAN, Woody. Herman remained on tour around the U.S. w. a big band, except for 8-week periods in the fall of '56 and fall of '57, when he disbanded temporarily to lead a smaller group at a Las Vegas night club. In Jan. 1958 the Al Belletto Sextet was incorporated into his band. The State Dept. arranged to subsidize a 10-week tour of Latin America by the Herman band starting in July 1958. Herman remained under contract to Verve Records, 1956-8. LPs: *Blues Groove* (Cap.), *Bijou, Summer Sequence* (Harm.), *Songs for Hip Lovers, Jazz, the Utmost, Early Autumn, Woody Herman '58, Men From Mars* (Verve), *The Swinging Herman Herd* (Bruns.).

HEYWOOD, Eddie. Enjoyed great success on records and in night clubs as pop-music artist rather than as jazzman, 1956-8. LPs: *Eddie Heywood at Twilight* (Epic), *Canadian Sunset, The Touch of Eddie Heywood* (Vict.).

HIGGINBOTHAM, J. C. Appeared during 1957 w. Red Allen group at the Metropole, NYC, and was w. him at the Newport Jazz Festival, July of that year. LPs w. Allen (Vict., Verve); *The Big Challenge* and *Fletcher Henderson Reunion* (Jazz.).

HILL, Alexander, *piano, composer-arranger*; b. Little Rock, Ark.; d. NYC, 2/1/36. Received earliest training from his mother, had own group, 1924. Worked around Chicago from about 1925 on as pianist and arranger for Jimmie Noone, L. Armstrong and others. In 1930 went to NYC where he arranged for Claude Hopkins, Benny Carter, Andy Kirk, Fats Waller, others. One of the better and less recognized arrangers of the early swing era, Hill had planned to start his own band, but his career was ended when he became a victim of tuberculosis. Hill occas. pl. piano on rec. dates, incl. one session w. E. Condon (*The Eel*, etc., 1933).

HI-LO'S. Vocal quartet organized in Apr. 1953, discovered by Jerry Fielding, who arranged their first rec. date for now defunct Trend label. Later rec. for Starlite, Col., seen at Hollywood Bowl and in movies; rapidly rose to become most popular jazz-oriented vocal group of kind. See Clark Burroughs, Bob Morse, Gene Puerling, Bob Strasen.

HINES, Earl. Had very successful tour of Britain and the Continent w. Jack Teagarden, fall 1957, then ret. to his club activities in San Francisco. LP w. L. Armstrong (Decca). Own LP: *Solo* (Fant.).

HINTON, Milt. Cont. activities in broadcasting studios, rec. sessions and in concerts, NYC, 1956-8. LPs w. Z. Sims (Dawn), T. Scott, H. McKusick, Geo. Russell (Vict.), and scores more.

HODEIR, André. Visited U.S. during spring 1957. In NYC rec. some of his own compositions; later on the West Coast and to Mexico before ret. to France. LPs: *American Jazzmen Play André Hodeir, Paris Scene* (Sav.); arr. for Kenny Clarke (Epic.).

HODGES, Johnny. Except for a brief engagement early 1958 in a Florida club, during which he, Billy Strayhorn and Jimmy Grissom worked as the Ellington Indigos, Hodges cont. as a mainstay of the Ellington band. LPs w. Ellington (Beth., Col., Verve), Clark Terry (River.).

HOFFMAN, Jean, *electric piano, singer*; b. Portland, Ore., 9/22/30. From a musical family, she started classical piano at 5, but played largely by ear and started sitting in w. local combos around '53. Working as a single, she added vocals. Married drummer Bill Young and in 1957 they formed a trio. Favs: Bartok, B. Young, C. Parker. Own LP: Fant.

Addr: 245 Bristol Blvd., San Leandro, Calif.

HOLIDAY, Billie. Cont. concert, club appearances on publication of her autobiography co-written by William Dufty, *Lady Sings the Blues*, in 1956. Appeared in a concert at Carnegie Hall reviewing her career. In July 1957 she appeared at Newport Jazz Festival and later at the Music Barn in Lenox, Mass. She was feat. on CBS-TV's *The Sound of Jazz* television show, Dec. 1957, and was part of an all-star concert at Carnegie Hall soon afterwards. LPs: *Solitude, Velvet Moods, Recital, Lady Sings the Blues, Music for Torching, Body and Soul, At Newport* (Verve), *Lady In Satin* (Col.).

HOLMAN, Bill. Was active on the West Coast, chiefly w. Shorty Rogers, 1956-8. LPs w. Rogers (Vict.), Ray Brown (Verve), Richie Kamuca (High Fid.), S. Manne (Contemp.). Own LPs: *The Fabulous Bill Holman* (Cor.), *Mucho Calor* (Andex).

HOPKINS, Claude. Cont. at Metropole, NYC. LP w. Juanita Hall (Counter.); *Golden Era of Dixieland Jazz* (Des.).

HORN, Paul, *clarinet, flute, reeds*; b. New York City, 3/17/30. Began on piano at 4 (mother was Irving Berlin's pianist for many years). Took up sax at 12, flute in college. Bach. of Music at Oberlin College, 1952; M.A.

Manhattan School of Music, 1953. Began w. Sauter-Finegan orch. playing lead tenor and from Sept. '56 until Feb. '58 was feat. w. Chico Hamilton quint. Fav. own solo: *Reflections* w. Hamilton (Wor. Pac.). Favs: Parker, T. Scott, F. Wess, A. Cohn, Z. Sims, L. Konitz. LPs w. Hamilton (Wor. Pac., Decca), Fred Katz (Wor. Pac., Dot, Decca), John Pisano-Billy Bean (Decca). Own LP: Dot.
Addr: 1806 S. Cochran Ave., Los Angeles 19, Calif.

HORNE, Lena. After successful engagement at Waldorf-Astoria, NYC, opened in Broadway musical *Jamaica*, Oct. 1957. LPs: *Stormy Weather, Lena Horne at the Waldorf-Astoria, It's Love* (Vict.).

HORROX, Frank (Horrocks), *piano*; b. Bolton, Eng., 2/15/24. Parents amateur musicians; began piano study at 8 w. private teacher, later at Trinity College of Music, where he won three exhibition prizes. At 17 joined Bertini's band as pianist. Was featured soloist and arranger for 8 years w. T. Heath, later leaving to freelance w. own trio, but continued to arr. for Heath. Fav. own solo and arrangement: *Love for Sale* w. Heath in *Spotlight on Sidemen* (Decca/Lond.). Favs: O. Peterson E. Garner, A. Tatum, T. Wilson, P. Newborn. LP w. Heath (Decca/Lond.).
Addr: 4 Palace Court Gardens, Muswell Hill, London.

HUCKO, Peanuts. Toured Europe w. J. Teagarden group, fall 1957. LPs w. J. McPartland (Epic), L. Armstrong, B. Freeman (Vict.), B. Hackett-J. Teagarden (Cap.); *Session at Riverside* (Cap.), *Mellow Moods of Jazz* (Vict.). Own LP: *With a Little Bit of Swing* (Vict.). Joined Louis Armstrong, July 1958.

HYMAN, Dick. Left his staff job at NBC in fall 1957 to do free-lance studio work, also appearing w. own jazz trio at Cherry Lane Club, NYC. LPs w. L. Feather: *Oh Captain, The Swingin' Seasons, Hi-Fi Suite* (MGM). LPs w. T. Scott (ABC-Par.), Maxine Sullivan (Per.), Sam the Man Taylor (MGM). Own LP: *Gigi* (MGM).

JACKSON, Chubby. Returned to NYC early 1958 after several years of living in Chicago. Appeared on Timex CBS-TV jazz show, May '58. LP: *Chubby's Back* (Argo).

JACKSON, Mahalia. Aside from her regular appearances in churches, Miss Jackson was at the Newport Jazz Festival for the gospel afternoon session, July '57; later that summer she was at the Music Barn in Lenox, Mass., for a concert. In Feb. '58 she and Duke Ellington recorded an expanded version of his *Black, Brown and Beige*. During the session Miss Jackson completed the *Come Sunday* movement and spontaneously broke into *Sometimes I Feel Like a Motherless Child*; the performance was retained intact. LPs: *Bless This House* (Col.), *Gospel Songs* (Grand Award).
Addr: 8358 S. Indiana, Chicago 19, Ill.

JACKSON, Milt. Cont. as member of Mod. Jazz Quart. Was on faculty of School of Jazz, Lenox, Mass., Aug. 1957. On Continental tour, fall and winter '57-8. Back to U.S. for Town Hall concert, NYC, May '58. LPs w. Quart. (Atl., Pres.), T. Monk, F. Navarro, H. Mobley (Blue Note), Q. Jones (ABC-Par.), D. Gillespie (Sav., Reg.). Own LPs: *Plenty, Plenty Soul, Ballads and Blues* (Atl.), *Jackson'sville, Opus de Jazz* (Sav.).

JACQUET, Illinois. LPs: *Groovin', Jazz Moods, Swing's the Thing, Port of Rico, Kid and the Brute* w. B. Webster (Verve).

JAMES, Harry. Toured Europe, Oct. 1957. Appeared on B. Goodman's NBC-TV show titled *Swing into Spring*, Apr. '58. LPs: *A String of Swinging Pearls* w. other artists (Vict.), *Wild About Harry* (Cap.).

JASPAR, Bobby. In Oct. 1957, after their tour of Sweden and the Continent, he left Jay Jay Johnson's quint. Gigs around NYC w. various groups, incl. a stay at Birdland w. Miles Davis. LPs w. B. Galbraith (Decca), André Hodeir (Sav.), Johnson (Col.), J. Raney (Dawn); *Flute Souffle* w. Herbie Mann (Pres.). Own LP: River.

JAZZPICKERS: See BABASIN, Harry.

JEFFERSON, Hilton. Aside from many rhythm and blues dates at Vict. Records during 1957, appeared on *The Big Reunion* of ex-F. Henderson musicians under the leadership of Rex Stewart for Jazztone, other LPs w. Jimmy Rushing (Col.).

JENKINS, John, Jr., *alto sax*; b. Chicago, 1/3/31. Clarinet at Du Sable High under Capt. Walter Dyett. Six months later switched to alto. From 1949 to 1956 appeared at Roosevelt College sessions run by Joe Segal. Appeared with Art Farmer in Chicago and Cleveland in 1955; own quartet at Bee Hive in Dec. 1955. Came to New York in Mar. 1957, working with Charlie Mingus for a short while and then concentrating on recording. Favs: Parker, McLean, Stitt, Rollins. LPs w. own group (Blue Note), H. Mobley (Blue Note), J. McLean, P. Quinichette (Pres.).

JOHNSON, Budd. Free-lanced in NYC, 1957-8, incl. jobs w. B. Goodman. LPs w. M. Ferguson (Vik), J. Rushing (Col.).

JOHNSON, Ella. Own LP: *Swing Me* (Merc.).

JOHNSON, Gus. Joined Ella Fitzgerald, fall 1957. LPs w. Nat Pierce (Cor.), Z. Sims, O. Pettiford (ABC-Par.), Z. Sims (Argo, Dawn).

JOHNSON, Jay Jay. Ended his association w. Kai Winding, Sept. 1956, and formed own quint. Toured Sweden and the Continent, summer 1957. LPs w. B.

Golson (River.), G. Schuller (Col.), Miles Davis (Pres., Cap.); *Four Trombones* (Deb.), *Three Trombones* (Pres.). Own LPs: *J Is for Jazz, First Place, Dial JJ 5* (Col.).

JOHNSON, Osie. Cont. free-lance studio and concert work, NYC. Appeared at Newport Jazz Festival, July 1957. Was on television *Sound of Jazz* show on CBS, Dec. '57. LPs w. L. Feather-D. Hyman (MGM), T. Scott (Vict., Bruns.), H. McKusick, Geo. Russell (Vict.). Own LPs: *A Bit of the Blues* (Vict.), *Happy Jazz of Osie Johnson* (Beth.).

JOHNSON, Richard Brown (Dick), *alto sax, clarinet*; b. Brockton, Mass., 12/1/25. Mother, who holds Master's degree in music, encouraged him to begin study on piano at 5. Started on clar. at 16, alto at 19. Two years at New England Conservatory, Navy band during World War II, gigged around Boston until 1952, then joined C. Spivak and later B. Morrow ('55). Recorded w. own groups, as listed below, as well as w. Morrow. Favs: Parker, D. McKenna. LPs w. Morrow (Merc.), Eddie Costa (Verve). Own LPs: Em., River.
Addr: 22 Milton St., Brockton, Mass.

JONES, Elvin. Cont. playing gigs around NYC, incl. a stay at the Five Spot w. Pepper Adams, 1958. LPs w. Thad Jones (Per., Blue Note), Jay Jay Johnson (Col.), K. Burrell (Pres.), S. Rollins (Blue Note).

JONES, Hank. Worked w. B. Goodman off and on, 1957-8, and took part in at least 100 jazz LPs during this period. Signed solo contract w. Cap. Records, spring '58. LPs w. Milt Jackson, C. Tjader, A. K. Salim (Sav.), Q. Jones, J. Raney (ABC-Par.), Jay Jay Johnson, J. Rushing (Col.) *et al.* Own LPs: *Urbanity* (Verve), *Have You Met Hank Jones* (Sav.), quart., quint. (Sav.).

JONES, Jimmy. Left Sarah Vaughan, Jan. 1958, because of his health to free-lance around NYC. Worked w. Ruby Braff, B. Webster *et al.* LPs w. Joe Williams (Roul.), I. Jacquet, S. Stitt (Verve), S. Vaughan (Merc., Em.). Own LP: Atco.

JONES, Jo. With E. Fitzgerald and O. Peterson on European tour, spring 1957. Formed own trio and pl. club dates, 1957-8, in addition to his appearances at the Newport Jazz Festival in July '57 and on *Sound of Jazz*, CBS-TV show, Dec. '57. With JATP, fall '57. LPs w. P. Quinichette (Pres.), C. Hawkins (River.), Thad Jones (Per.), J. Rushing, Art Blakey (Col.), R. Eldridge, A. Tatum, S. Stitt, T. Wilson (Verve).

JONES, Jonah. Cont. his successful "muted jazz" work at the Embers, NYC, w. a few forays to several other major cities. LPs: *Muted Jazz, Swingin' on Broadway* (Cap.), *Jonah Jones at the Embers* (Vik).

JONES, Joseph Rudolph "Philly Joe," *drums* (amplified biography); b. Philadelphia, Pa., 7/15/23. Mother, a

piano teacher, gave him lessons as child. Played for several years in local combos, backing Dexter Gordon, Fats Navarro and other name jazzmen visiting Phila. With Ben Webster in Washington, 1949. Subsequently free-lanced extensively in NYC, working w. Z. Sims, L. Konitz at Down Beat club, 1952, and w. Miles Davis intermittently since '52 and more or less regularly since '55. First prominently feat. on records w. Tadd Dameron '53; made first LP as leader for River. '58.

"Philly Joe," as he is called among musicians (he is not related to the Jo Jones who played drums w. the old Basie band), has enjoyed increasing prestige in the past couple of years as one of the most dynamic and expert percussionists of the explosive modern school favored by the "hard-bop" jazzmen. He rates Cozy Cole and Sid Catlett as his all-time favorites. LPs w. Dick Johnson, K. Drew, C. Terry (River.), P. Chambers, Lee Morgan, J. R. Monterose, H. Mobley (Blue Note), M. Davis, T. Dameron, J. McLean (Pres.), S. Chaloff (Cap.), A. Pepper (Contemp.).
Addr: 120 Bambridge, Brooklyn, N.Y.

JONES, Quincy. Left for Paris, May 1957, and spent the next year there, arranging and conducting for Barclay Records, etc., and visiting Scandinavia, May '58. LPs w. Milt Jackson (Atl.), Thad Jones (Per.), D. Gillespie (Verve). Own LPs: *This is How I Feel about Jazz, Go West, Man* (ABC-Par.).

JONES, Reunald. Left C. Basie late 1957. LPs w. Basie (Verve), P. Quinichette (Dawn).

JONES, Samuel, *bass*; b. Jacksonville, Fla., 11/12/24. Father played piano and second cousin is bassist Al Hall. Began as drummer in school marching band and was inspired by hearing Lunceford, Basie, B. Eckstine bands on tour and fascinated by early records of Parker and Gillespie. Worked around NYC w. T. Bradshaw, Les Jazz Modes, K. Dorham's Prophets, I. Jacquet, C. Adderley, and recorded with several of these groups. Joined S. Rollins, May '58. Favs: J. Blanton, R. Brown, O. Pettiford, M. Hinton, A. Hall. LPs w. K. Dorham (Blue Note, ABC-Par.), K. Burrell (Blue Note), Nat Adderley (Em.), C. Adderley (Em.).
Addr: 541 W. 150th St., New York, N.Y.

JONES, Thad. LPs w. C. Basie (Verve, Roul.), C. Mingus O. Johnson (Beth.), T. Scott (Vict.), L. Feather-D, Hyman (MGM); *The Magnificent Thad Jones* (Blue. Note), *Mad Thad* (Per.).

JORDAN, Clifford, *tenor sax*; b. Chicago, Ill., 10/2/31. Began on piano when quite young and tenor at 14. Attended Du Sable High with Johnny Griffin, John Gilmore, John Jenkins and other musicians. Gigs around Chi. w. Max Roach, Sonny Stitt, and various r. & b. bands. Left Chi. to go with Roach, then w. Horace Silver's quintet in 1958. Favs: Young, Rollins,

Coltrane, Byas, Mobley. Several records for Blue Note w. John Gilmore and own group.

JORDAN, Louis. Once again active for club and theatre dates w. his Tympany Five. LPs: *Somebody Up There Digs Me, Man, We're Wailin'* (Merc.), *Go Blow Your Horn* (Score).

JORDAN, Taft. LPs w. Sy Oliver (Decca), Fletcher Henderson Reunion (Jazz.). Pl. w. B. Goodman '58.

JOYNER, George Leon, *bass*; b. Memphis, Tenn. 6/21/32. Stud. w. mother, a church pianist. Golden Gloves bantamweight boxer at 15; got first bass at 16, played first gig less than 2 wks. later. At Arkansas State '49-52, led college dance band. Tuba in Army band '53-5; part of time in special services w. Phineas Newborn, Wynton Kelly. Electric bass w. B. B. King '55-Mar. '56, then to NYC with Newborn; stud. w. Michael Krasnapolsky, pl. w. Teddy Charles, S. Rollins, S. Stitt *et al.* Favs: Ray Brown, Mingus, Pettiford.

KAMINSKY, Max. With J. Teagarden in Britain, fall 1957. Led own group at Duane Hotel, NYC, spring '58. LP w. J. McPartland (Epic).

KATZ, Fred. Left C. Hamilton early 1958. Formed own group and began work as A. & R. man on the West Coast for Decca. LPs w. C. Hamilton (Wor. Pac., Decca), Paul Horn (Dot). Own LPs: *Zen: The Music of Fred Katz* (Wor. Pac.), *Soulo Cello* (Decca).

KATZMAN, Lee, *trumpet*; b. Chicago, Ill., 5/17/28. Aunt a concert pianist. Began playing at 13 in various Chicago spots, and starting in 1946 worked w. various big bands, incl. Bob Strong, S. Donahue, C. Thornhill, G. Krupa, J. Dorsey *et al.* From 1955-8 was w. S. Kenton. Fav. own solo: *Devil and Deep Blue Sea* w. Med Flory in *Jazz Wave* (Jub.). Favs: Parker, Gillespie. LPs w. Pepper Adams (Wor. Pac.), Flory (Jub.).

Addr: 14354 Germain, San Fernando, Calif.

KAY, Connie. Cont. work w. Mod. Jazz Quart. LPs w. MJQ (Atl.), Randy Weston (Jub.), Joe Newman (Cor.).

KEATING, John, *arranger, trombone*; b. Edinburgh, Scotland, 9/10/27. Began stud. piano at 8, taught himself arr. at 15. Took up trombone at 17 w. local teacher. After stint w. T. Sampson, played trombone w. T. Heath '52-3, also did some composing. In '54 became staff arranger for Heath, giving up trombone. Quit music business early '58. Fav. own arr: *English Jazz* (Bally), *Swinging Scots* (Dot). Favs: K. Winding, M. Bernhart, B. Harris. Fav. arr: N. Hefti.

Addr: 51 Woodhill Cres., Kenton, Middlesex, Eng.

KELLY, Wynton. Left D. Gillespie to form own trio, Dec. 1957. LPs w. Gillespie (Verve), A. K. Salim (Sav.),

J. Griffin, S. Rollins, Lee Morgan (Blue Note), C. Terry, E. Henry, B. Golson (River.); *Dizzy Atmosphere* (Spec.), *Sittin' In* (Verve). Own LP on Riverside.

KERSEY, Ken. Left Metropole, NYC, 1957, due to illness. LPs w. C. Shavers, Jonah Jones (Beth.), Andy Kirk (Vict.), C. Christian (Eso.).

KESSEL, Barney. Played concert in Caracas, Venezuela, at the annual festival of jazz club there, Aug. 1957. He was the only American jazzman to appear. Worked as A. & R. man for Verve Records, in addition to recording his own sessions for Contemp. LPs w. L. Hampton (Decca), B. Webster, Stuff Smith, W. Herman, B. Holiday, H. Edison (Verve), Red Norvo (Contemp.). Own LPs: Contemp.

KIRK, Andy. Returned to records for first time in many years as director of *A Mellow Bit of Rhythm* (Vict.).

KLEIN, Harold "Harry," *baritone sax, reeds*; b. London, Eng., 12/25/28. Began stud. alto in 1944 and is largely self-taught. Worked for K. Baker '52, J. Parnell '52-3, and in '56 was feat. w. S. Kenton on his European tour. Has recorded extensively w. own group and w. various pick-up bands in Eng. One of the most confident and capable of Brit. jazzmen. Won *Melody Maker* Britain's Best Poll, 1957. Favs: Parker, Hodges, B. Carter. LPs w. V. Feldman (Contemp.).

Addr: 21 Lewis Flats, Amhurst Rd., Hackney, London, E.8, Eng.

KENTON, Stan. In the fall of 1957 formed a dance band which opened at his own Balboa Beach Rendezvous ballroom, but by Apr. '58 had to give up the operation and announced his temporary retirement. Was also feat. in local television series in LA early '58. LPs: *Kenton w. Voices, Cuban Fire, Rendezvous w. Kenton* (Cap.).

KNEPPER, James M., *trombone*; b. Los Angeles, Calif., 11/22/27. Began on alto horn at 5, trombone at 9 w. private teacher and later at Los Angeles City and State colleges. Has worked w. a great variety of big bands: C. Barnet, C. Spivak, W. Herman, R. Marterie, C. Thornhill, S. Kenton, etc., and small groups: Parker, G. Roland, R. Bauduc, A. Pepper, etc. Joined C. Mingus' Jazz Workshop quint. in 1957. Knepper, who has been called by commentator Whitney Balliett "the first original trombonist in the modern idiom since Jay Jay Johnson," lists among his major influences not only C. Parker but such mainstream trombonists as D. Wells, J. C. Higginbotham, L. Brown, V. Dickenson. Fav: Parker. LPs w. Mingus (Beth., Atl.), Langston Hughes (MGM); *Trombone Scene* (Vik). Own LP: Beth.

KOFFMAN, Moe, *alto sax, flute*; b. Toronto, Can., 1928. Stud. vln. at 9, sax at 13. To NYC, 1950; 6 mos. w.

Sonny Dunham band, 9 mos. w. Ralph Flanagan, then 6 mos. w. Buddy Morrow, 4 mos. w. Jimmy Dorsey, after which he settled in NY, free-lancing on records and playing week ends w. Charlie Barnet, Art Mooney, Chico O'Farrill. Later toured for a year w. Tex Beneke's band; spent a year w. Don Rodney at Arcadia Ballroom, NYC; free-lanced again for a while, then ret. to Toronto. Organized jazz group w. best local musicians and they pl. together at after-hours jazz club for a year and a half. Soon landed three local TV shows for revised group. Signed w. Jub. Records, 1957; *The Swingin' Shepherd Blues*, one of the compositions in his album *Cool and Hot Sax*, was released as a single and became a big hit in the pop music market. A second Jub. LP, *The Shepherd Swings Again*, was released June 1958.

Addr: c/o Jubilee Records, 1650 Broadway, New York 19, N.Y.

KONITZ, Lee. Cont. his activities both as teacher and performer around NYC. Among his gigs was a lengthy stay at the Half Note Cafe late 1957-8. Appeared on the "cool" show of NBC-TV's educational series *The Subject Is Jazz*, May '58. LPs w. Miles Davis (Cap.), Gil Evans (Pres.), G. Mulligan (Wor. Pac.). Own LPs: *Very Cool* (Verve), *Lee Konitz Inside Hi-Fi, The Real Lee Konitz* (Atl.).

KOTICK, Teddy. Worked w. H. Silver quint., 1957-8. LPs w. Silver (Blue Note), J. Knepper (Beth.), Bill Evans (River.), B. Brookmeyer, P. Woods-D. Byrd P. Woods-G. Quill, A. Cohn (Pres.); *Four Most Guitars* (ABC-Par.).

KRAL, Roy. LPs w. J. Cain: *Sing Baby Sing* (Story.), *Bits and Pieces, Free and Easy* (ABC-Par.), w. C. Ventura (Bruns.).

KRUPA, Gene. Cont. working clubs w. his own quart. In 1958 plans were set for the production of a movie based on Krupa's life. LPs w. L. Hampton, T. Wilson, R. Callender (Verve). Own LPs: *Driving Gene, Drum Boogie, Drummer Man, Exciting Gene Krupa, Jazz Rhythms; Sing, Sing, Sing; Trio at JATP* (Verve), *Mutiny in the Parlor* (Cam.).

KUHN, Rolf, clarinet; b. Cologne, Germ., 9/29/29. Father was variety artist in Germany. Kuhn began stud. concert piano, 1938, in Leipzig and switched to clar. when he was 12. In 1952 he moved to West Germany to join a jazz group and heard Goodman and De Franco. Was soon broadcasting w. own quartet over American station RIAS in Berlin and winning European jazz polls on clar. Came to U.S. in May '56 and pl. w. Caterina Valente in NYC. Through the encouragement of Friedrich Gulda, John Hammond and agent Willard Alexander, formed own quart.; later worked on alto and clar. w. Goodman. Appeared at Newport Jazz Festival, 1957. Toured w. T. Dorsey memorial band led

by W. Covington, 1958. Favs: De Franco, Goodman. LP w. E. Costa (Verve). Own LP: Vang.

Addr: 161 E. 91st St., New York, N.Y.

LACY, Steve (Steven Lackritz), soprano sax; b. New York City, 7/23/34. Stud. w. Cecil Scott and at Schillinger School in Boston, also at Manhattan School in New York. Also stud. briefly w. L. Konitz and Cecil Taylor. Began working as result of following Scott around on his jobs; gigged in NYC w. various Dixieland and swing musicians (M. Kaminsky, R. Stewart, B. Clayton, C. Shavers, Lips Page, etc.). Joined Cecil Taylor quart. in Dec. '56 until fall of '57, then returned to gigs around town. Only musician who plays sop. sax in the modern idiom. Voted New Star in *Metronome Yearbook*, 1957. Favs: Ellington, Monk, S. Rollins, M. Davis, Parker, Pee Wee Russell, J. Coltrane. LPs w. Tom Stewart (ABC-Par.), W. Mitchell (ABC-Par.), C. Taylor (Trans., Verve), Gil Evans (Pres.). Own LP: Pres.

Addr: 21 Bleecker St., New York 12, N.Y.

LAMBERT, Dave. Wrote arr. in collaboration w. Jon Hendricks for very successful LP in which they and Annie Ross sang lyrics to some famous Basie solos in *Sing a Song of Basie* (ABC-Par.) released Feb. '58.

LA PORTA, John. LPs w. A. Levister (Deb.), C. Mingus (Jazz., Beth.). Own LPs: *South American Brothers, Clarinet Artistry of John La Porta, Conceptions* (Fant.).

LATEEF, Yusef (William Evans), tenor sax, flutes; b. Chattanooga, Tenn., 1921. Started on alto, then tenor while at Miller High School in Detroit in 1937. In NYC in 1946 w. L. Millinder through L. Thompson recommendation. Then w. Lips Page, R. Eldridge and others; toured w. D. Gillespie in 1949. Back to Detroit in 1950 where he formed own group in 1955 and returned to study at Wayne U. In and out of NYC for recordings, 1957-8, on some of which he employed odd instr., incl. argol, rabat, earth-board, etc. Favs: Gillespie, C. Parker, Billie Holiday, S. Stitt. Own LPs: Sav., Verve, Pres.

Addr: 2151 W. Grand Blvd., Detroit, Mich.

LAWRENCE, Elliot. Prod. a series of jazz albums for the Vik label, 1957: *Trombone Scene, Four Brothers—Together Again, Jazz Goes Broadway*; also *Elliot Lawrence Plays for Swinging Dancers* (Fant.).

LESBERG, Jack. Toured Britain w. Jack Teagarden, fall 1957.

LEVISTER, Alonzo H., composer, piano; b. Greenwich, Conn., 11/1/25. Stud. Boston Conservatory of Music, 1946. During early 1950s wrote dance scores for Primitive Dance Group in Mexico, the Modern Dance Group, NYC, worked as acc. at Katherine Dunham school. In 1953 did vocal arr. for Debut Records and in '55 the Interracial Fellowship Chorus performed his work at

Town Hall. His *Manhattan Monodrama* was recorded in '56 and Levister made a city-to-city, house-to-house tour of the U.S. playing his record and discussing his music with housewives and anyone he found at home. Favs: Bach, Bartok. Own LP: Deb.

Addr: 27 W. 15th St., New York 11, N.Y.

LEVY, Lou. Pl. with T. Gibbs, summer 1957; joined Ella Fitzgerald, Oct. '57, and toured U.S. and Europe w. her. LPs w. L. Niehaus (Contemp.), B. Holman, (Cor.), S. Rogers (Atl., Vict.), Q. Jones (ABC-Par.) S. Getz-G. Mulligan (Verve). Own LPs: *Jazz in Four Colors, A Most Musical Fellow* (Vict.).

LEWIS, George. Toured Britain, Mar. '57; appeared at Newport Jazz Festival, July '57. Week end appearances in NYC, Apr. '58. LPs: *Jazz at Vespers, Classic New Orleans Traditions* (River.), *Doctor Jazz* (Del.), *At Newport* (Verve), re-issues on Blue Note.

LEWIS, John. Returning from Paris, spring 1957, Lewis (w. the other members of the Mod. Jazz Quart.) premiered his film score *One Never Knows* (*No Sun in Venice*) at a Town Hall concert. Was director of the first session of the School of Jazz at Lenox, Mass., in Aug. '57 and again in '58. In the winter of '57 the Quart. played 88 concerts in 4 months in the British Isles and on the Continent, particularly in Germany, returning to the U.S. early '58, where their first NYC appearance was a solo concert at Town Hall in May. LPs w. Quart.: Atl., Pres.; w. Miles Davis (Cap.), Sacha Distel (Atl.), C. Parker (Verve). Own LPs: *Grand Encounter* (Wor. Pac.), *The John Lewis Piano* (Atl.).

LEWIS, Vic. Brought band for tours of U.S. in 1956-7, playing first in rock-'n'-roll concert unit, later at U.S. Army camps.

LINCOLN, Abbey (Anna Marie Wooldridge), *singer*; b. Chicago, 8/6/30, tenth of 12 children. Raised in Calvin Center, Mich. While in high school, worked as housemaid, sang and acted at social functions; later, while still in teens, toured Michigan as dance band vocalist. In 1951 moved to Calif., worked local clubs; spent 2 years in Hawaii, singing under name Gaby Lee. Back in U.S. '54, and during next 3 years scored successes at major Hollywood clubs, changing name to Abbey Lincoln in '56 and cutting her first LP, for Lib. In 1957 her first movie, *The Girl Can't Help It*, was released, and she made an LP for River. w. Max Roach and an all-star jazz group. Like many vocalists who have worked in such a setting, she is a superior pop singer who has earned acceptance in jazz circles. LPs: *Affair* (Lib.), *That's Him* (River.).

Addr: 250 W. 74th St., New York 23, N.Y.

LISTON, Melba. With D. Gillespie's band, spring 1956, until Nov. '57, incl. the State Dept. tours of the Near East and Latin America. Left to do free-lance writing and arr. in NYC. LPs w. Gillespie (Verve); *Jazzville* (Dawn).

LITTMAN, Peter, *drums*; b. Medford, Mass., 5/8/35. Very little formal study. Mother is choral dir. for local Temple Beth-El. Began stud. piano at 6; at 16 worked w. H. Pomeroy and C. Mariano, and has been w. C. Baker on and off since the mid-50s, incl. a tour of the NATO countries in '55. Favs: Philly Joe Jones, Blakey, K. Clarke, R. Haynes. LP w. Baker (Wor. Pac.).

Addr: 83 Deau St., Belmont, Mass.

LLOYD, Jerome "Jerry," *trumpet, piano*; b. New York City, 7/17/20. Stud. piano and gave concert when he was 5 at Steinway Hall. Started on trumpet at 13, originally as therapy for collapsed lung. First prof. engagement at 13 and has been a union member since. Worked w. G. Auld, B. Rich, G. Wallington. Out of music for 6 years due to attack of arthritis, but returned w. Zoot Sims' group in 1956, staying for a few months. Favs: L. Young, R. Eldridge, Parker, Gillespie, M. Davis. LPs w. Jutta Hipp (Blue Note), Sims (Dawn), Wallington (East-West).

Addr: 75-40 Bell Blvd., Bayside 64, L.I., N.Y.

LONDON, Julie. Active mainly as a motion picture actress, she went to Britain, fall 1957, to play the lead in a film there. Film appearances in the U.S. incl. *The Great Man* and *The Girl Can't Help It*. LPs: Lib.

LOWE, Mundell. Appeared as regular member of the band on NBC-TV's educational series *The Subject Is Jazz*, Mar.-June '58, in NYC. LPs w. T. Scott (Vict.), J. Guarnieri (Cor.). Own LPs: *A Grand Night for Swinging, This Could Lead to Love* (River.).

LUCRAFT, Howard, *composer, guitar*; b. London, Eng., 8/16/16. Was active during 1940s in England as arranger, bandleader and commentator, broadcasting on BBC, etc. Arrived in U.S., Sept '50, settled in Calif., and has been active mainly as writer and promoter, organizing jam sessions and forums at Hollywood clubs and working closely w. Stan Kenton in the founding and running of Jazz International (see *Jazz Organizations*). Produced radio and TV shows for Jazz International; articles for *Metronome*; West Coast correspondent for London *Melody Maker* and for *The Encyclopedia of Jazz*. Fav. mus: Ellington, Basie, Parker. Own LP: *Showcase for Modern Jazz* (Decca).

Addr: Box 91, Hollywood 28, Calif.

LYTTLETON, Humphrey. Worked w. various American artists on their British tours, incl. L. Hampton and J. Rushing. Was a regular contributor to the *Melody Maker*.

MANCE, Junior. Worked w. Cannonball Adderley quint. during 1957; also briefly w. D. Gillespie and Art Blakey.

LPs w. Wilbur Ware (River), A. Blakey (Beth.), C. Adderley, Dinah Washington, Nat Adderley (Em.).

MANN, Herbie. Combined a honeymoon w. very successful European tour, Sept. '56 throughout Scandanivia and France, then returned to U.S. Active in Cal. during summer '57. LPs w. Mat Matthews (Dawn), A. K. Salim (Sav.), A. Blakey (Blue Note); *Flute Fraternity* w. Buddy Collete (Mode), *Flute Soufflé, Flute Flight* w. B. Jaspar (Pres.). Own LPs: *Great Ideas of Western Mann, Go West, Young Man, Sultry Serenade* (River.), *Love and the Weather* (Beth.), *Yardbird Suite, Mann Alone* (Sav.).

MANNE, Shelly. LPs w. Q. Jones (ABC-Par.), P. Rugolo (Em.), J. Giuffre (Atl.), André Previn, Russ Freeman, Barney Kessel, S. Rollins, Red Norvo (Contemp.). Own LPs: Contemp.

MARKEWICH, Maurice "Reese," *piano, flute*; b. Brooklyn, N.Y., 8/6/36. Began on piano at 8, flute in high school. Formed the Mark V Quintet at Cornell Univ., incl. bar. saxist Nick Brignola, which won a competition and appeared at the New York Jazz Festival concert at Randall's Island summer '57 and subsequently at the Cafe Bohemia in N.Y.C. Favs: H. Silver, T. Flanagan, C. Parker. Own LP: *Modernage.*
Addr: 175 Riverside Drive, New York 24, N.Y.

MARSHALL, Wendell. LPs w. Herbie Mann, Milt Jackson, A. K. Salim (Sav.), Art Blakey (Blue Note), Gigi Gryce (River.).

MARX, Richard, *piano, arranger*; b. Chicago, Ill., 4/12/24. Private study from age 5, later at De Paul Univ. Has worked extensively in Chicago as studio man and played in the groups of Chubby Jackson, Thad Jones, R. Burns, F. Katz. Considers himself most successful as accompanist to singers; also teaches piano and does vocal coaching. Favs: Tatum, O. Peterson, B. Taylor. LPs w. J. Frigo (Merc.), F. Katz (Dot). Own LPs: Cor.
Addr: 7652 E. Prairie Rd., Skokie, Ill.

MASTERSOUNDS—*See* MONTGOMERY, Monk.

MATHEWS, Mat. Appeared at Newport Jazz Festival, July, 1957. LPs w. J. Puma (Dawn), Julius Watkins (Elek.), New York Jazz Quart. (Elek.). Own LPs: *Modern Art of Jazz, Gentle Art of Love* (Dawn).

McCALL, Mary Ann. LP: *Easy Living* (Reg.).

McGARITY, Lou. Suffered a heart attack March, 1957, which kept him incapacitated for some time. Returned to studio work and recording incl. appearance on NBC-TV's educational series *The Subject Is Jazz* in Apr. '58. LPs w. J. McPartland (Epic), Lee Wiley (Vict.); *Session at Riverside* (Cap.).

McKENNA, Dave. LPs w. Dick Johnson (River.), Urbie Green, R. Braff (ABC-Par.), C. Ventura (Tops), P. Woods-G. Quill, A. Cohn-Z. Sims (Vict.).

McKIBBON, Al. Left G. Shearing Mar. 1958 and joined Cal Tjader in San Francisco. LPs w. Tjader (Sav.), Thelonious Monk (Blue Note), Nat Adderley (Em.), C. Hawkins at Newport (Verve).

McKINLEY, Ray. During spring 1957 toured the Iron Curtain countries as leader of the new Glenn Miller orch. LPs: *Borderline* (Sav.), *Swinging 30's* (Grand Award), *Glenn Miller in Hi-Fi* (Vict.).

McKUSICK, Hal. Cont. studio and rec. work in NYC and appeared w. the New Music Society's Cooper Union concerts in the fall 1957. LPs w. D. Elliott (Decca), André Hodeir, Terry Gibbs (Sav.), Urbie Green (ABC-Par.), Geo. Williams, Andy Kirk, Geo. Russell (Vict.), Elliot Lawrence (Vik., Fant.). Own LPs: Cor., Pres., Vict.

McLEAN, Jackie. LPs w. Art Blakey (Col., Wor. Pac., Elek.—as "Ferris Bender" on Vik.), G. Ammons, H. Mobley, R. Draper, M. Waldron (Pres.). Own LPs: *Jackie's Pal, Alto Madness* w. J. Jenkins (Pres.), quint. (Jub.).

McPARTLAND, Jimmy. As a result of his successful foray as an actor in a television fantasy about jazz musicians, he had a speaking role in *Showboat* at the Marine Theatre, Jones Beach, New York, summer 1957. Cont. gigging around NYC w. own groups, w. several brief trips to other cities. His jazz LP of the score of *The Music Man* included some of his histrionics as well as trumpet playing. LP w. Bud Freeman (Vict.). Own LPs: *Dixieland, Music Man Goes Dixieland* (Epic).

McPARTLAND, Marian. Cont. appearances at NYC clubs, The Composer and Hickory House, w. her trio. LPs w. J. McPartland (Epic), Helen Merrill (Em.). Own LPs: *With You in Mind; At the Hickory House* (Cap.).

McRAE, Carmen. LPs: *After Glow, Mad About the Man, Torchy* (Decca).

McSHANN, Jay. Back in Kansas City working w. own group.

MEHEGAN, John. Wrote jazz-colored incidental music for Tennessee Williams' *Orpheus Descending* which opened in NYC March 1957. Late that year left his long stand at NYC Club, The Composer, for a brief engagement at the Weylin Bar, NYC. Cont. teaching jazz piano and reviewing jazz for N.Y. *Herald Tribune.*

MERRIWEATHER, Maceo, "Big Maceo," *singer, pianist*; b. Texas, 3/30/05; d. Chicago 2/26/53. Blues singer and boogie woogie pianist, working chiefly in Chicago w. excursions to Detroit and elsewhere. In 1946 he was left paralyzed by a stroke.

MICKEY AND SYLVIA—*See* BAKER, Mickey, *and* VANDERPOOL, Sylvia.

MILES, Lizzie, (Elizabeth Mary Landreaux), *singer*; b. New Orleans, La., 3/31/95. Began singing hymns in Sunday School at 5. Later worked in New Orleans w. King Oliver, A. J. Piron, *et al.* Toured the South w. the Alabama Minstrels and Cole Bros. Circus; sang in Paris for a while; worked w. Fats Waller at Capitol Palace in Harlem. During the '20s her recordings were successful and her accompanists included Oliver, Jelly Roll Morton, Clarence Williams and others. To NYC for appearance on CBS-TV show *Crescendo* 1957. LPs w. Sharkey Bonano (Cap.), Bob Scobey (Verve).
Addr: 1214 N. Tonti, New Orleans 19, La.

MILLS BROTHERS. Father, John Mills, retired to Ohio after operation which necessitated the amputation of one leg, occasionally coming out for record dates. Otherwise the group cont. its appearances as a trio. *Memory Lane, One Dozen Roses, Souvenir Album, Singin' and Swingin'* (Decca).

MINGUS, Charlie. After a successful stay at the Five Spot, NYC club, w. his quint. feat. J. R. Monterose, M. Waldron and J. McLean, Mingus opened in the late summer of '57 at the Half Note, NYC, w. a revamped quint. incl. J. Knepper, Shafi Hadi, and Horace Parlan. This group also appeared at the Village Vanguard, NYC, after which Mingus worked there in a duo w. Phineas Newborn. In May '58 Mingus was again at the Half Note w. a group incl. two cellos, Hadi on tenor, T. Charles on vibes. LPs w. Q. Jones (ABC-Par.), Red Norvo (Sav.), C. Parker (Verve). Own LPs: *The Clown* and *Pithecanthropus Erectus* (Atl.), *Jazz Experiment* (Jazz.), *A Flight w. Charlie Mingus, At the Bohemia* (Deb.), *Mingus Three* (Jub.).

MITCHELL, Billy. After having been musical dir. of D. Gillespie's orch., he left in late 1957 to join C. Basie. LPs w. Gillespie (Verve), Thad Jones (Blue Note); *Dizzy Atmosphere* (Spec.). Own LP: Sav.

MITCHELL, Red. In Feb. 1957 he had a successful quart., featuring James Clay on tenor, which played in a style quite "hard" for the West Coast. After this group broke up he cont. to be active in the Hollywood rec. studios. LPs w. P. Horn (Dot), H. Rumsey (Lib.), Jim Hall, B. Perkins (Wor. Pac.), B. Kessel, Red Norvo, A. Previn (Contemp.). Own LPs: *Presenting Red Mitchell* w. quart. described above (Contemp.).

MOBLEY, Hank. Was feat. in several groups, 1956-58, particularly w. Max Roach quint. In Apr. and May 1958

was in T. Monk's group at the Village Vanguard, NYC. LPs w. A. Blakey (Col.), J. Smith, C. Fuller, H. Silver, K. Dorham, J. Griffin (Blue Note), K. Drew (River.), Doug Watkins (Trans.). Own LPs: Blue Note, Pres.

MODERN JAZZ QUARTET—*See* LEWIS, John, JACKSON, Milt, HEATH, Percy, *and* KAY, Connie.

MONK, Thelonious. In early spring 1957 opened at Five Spot Cafe, NYC, w. a quart. featuring J. Coltrane and had a successful stay through New Year's Eve '57. Appeared on CBS-TV's *The Sound of Jazz* show Dec. '57. In Apr.-May '58 had an engagement at the Village Vanguard, NYC. LPs w. Miles Davis (Pres.), A. Blakey (Atl.), S. Rollins (Pres., Blue Note). Own LPs: *Brilliant Corners, Thelonious Himself, Monk's Music, Mulligan Meets Monk* (River.).

MONTGOMERY, Eurreal, "Little Brother" *piano, singer*; b. Kentwood, La., 5/17/07. First played in home town, later moved to Chicago where he has been active since, w. occasional returns to N.O. Primarily known as a blues pianist on recordings, he was w. various New Orleans style groups during the '40s and '50s. Joined Franz Jackson's band in Apr. 1958 at the Preview Lounge.

MONTGOMERY, William Howard "Monk," *electric bass*; b. Indianapolis, Ind. 10/10/21. Largely self-taught, he has played w. L. Hampton, G. Auld, and A. Farmer. In the fall of 1957, along with his brother, Charles "Buddy" Montgomery (vibes), Richie Crabtree (piano), and Ben Barth (drums), he formed the co-operative unit, *The Mastersounds*. They were featured in West Coast Clubs and on recordings. LPs: Wor. Pac.

MONTROSE, Jack. LPs w. Red Norvo (Lib.), Shorty Rogers (Vict.), Art Pepper (Sav.), John Graas (Decca), Shelly Manne, L. Niehaus (Contemp.). Own LPs: *Blues and Vanilla, The Horn's Full* (Vict.).

MOORE, Marilyn, *singer*; b. Oklahoma City, Okla., 6/16/31. Parents vaudevillians, and she broke in as part of the act at 3. Didn't sing again until high school, when she worked w. a band, then began in clubs around Oklahoma City; later worked around Chicago. Sang briefly w. W. Herman, then back to Oklahoma City; w. C. Barnet in 1952. Married Al Cohn in 1953 and was in retirement four years. Made record debut in 1957 and was compared to the Billie Holiday of the 1930s. One of the few young singers with a natural jazz timbre and sense of phrasing. LP *Oh Captain!* w. Leonard Feather-Dick Hyman (MGM). Own LP: Beth.
Addr: 32-28 164th St., Flushing 58, L.I., N.Y.

MOORE, Oscar. LP: Trio w. Redman (Tampa). Own LP: *Gallivantin' Guitar* (Tampa).

MORELLO, Joe. Was a prominent member of Dave Brubeck's quart., having left Marian McPartland's trio, fall, 1956. LPs w. McPartland (Cap.), Brubeck (Col.).

MORGAN, Edward Lee, *trumpet*; b. Philadelphia, Pa., 7/10/38. Father pianist for church choir. Stud. trumpet privately and at Mastbaum Tech; worked locally from the age of 15 at dances w. own group which included Spanky De Brest. Sat in with many name bands at Music City, and when A. Blakey needed substitutes he and De Brest joined—De Brest stayed on. Morgan joined Gillespie when the latter returned from his South American tour and stayed with the band until it broke up in Jan. 1958. Style not yet matured, but showed exceptional technical command and promised to develop into important musician. Favs: C. Brown, Gillespie, F. Navarro. LPs w. H. Mobley, Cliff Jordan, J. Coltrane (Blue Note), Gillespie (Verve), C. Persip (Lib.), *Jazz Message # 2* (Sav.), *Dizzy Atmosphere* (Spec.). Own LPs: Blue Note, Savoy.
Addr: 2035 W. Madison St., Philadelphia, Pa.

MORSE, Robert, *singer*; b. Pasadena, Cal., 7/27/27. Musical family; one brother pl. tpt. for Kenton, another arr. for Johnny Richards. Pl. alto at 6; took up bass in '47. Sang w. brother Burton's band in '46. Rec. w. the Encores, Billy May. In 1953 joined Hi-Lo's quartet (*q.v.*). Fav. own solo: *Skylark*. Fav. singer: B. Holiday. LPs: Starlite, Columbia.
Addr: 6470 Deep Dell Pl., Holywood, Cal.

MORTON, Benny. Aside from work in Broadway pit bands, his jazz activities incl. several record dates and appearances on *The Sound of Jazz*, CBS-TV, Dec. '57, and *The Subject Is Jazz*, NBC-TV's educational series, Apr. '58. LPs w. B. Clayton-R. Braff (Vang.), C. Shavers (Beth.), Roy Eldridge (Verve); Fletcher Henderson reunion (Jazz.).

MOSSE, Sanford, "Sandy," *tenor, clarinet, alto sax*; b. Detroit, Mich., 5/29/29. Began on clar. in Detroit, 1939; later took up alto. Attended Chicago Musical College 1947-9 and later stud. arranging w. B. Russo. In 1951, moved to Europe where he toured and recorded for five years in France, Italy, Germany, Belgium, etc. w. D. Reinhardt and own groups. Back in U.S., played w. W. Herman, B. Russo's quintet, Chubby Jackson, R. Marterie. Fav. own solo: *Chubby's Back* w. Jackson (Argo). Favs; L. Young, A. Cohn, Z. Sims, S. Rollins, E. Miller, S. Getz. LPs w. Russo (Atl.), C. Jackson (Argo); *Chicago Scene* (Argo).
Addr: 1320 Columbia Ave., Chicago, Ill.

MOTEN, Benny. Joined W. De Paris group Jan. 1957 for a year, then worked w. house band at the Metropole, NYC. LPs w. De Paris (Atl.).

MOTIAN, Stephen Paul, *drums, guitar*; b. Providence, R.I., 3/25/31. Began on guitar in Providence, 1949.

Upon discharge from service in 1954, gigged around NYC and stud. at Manhattan School of Music. Worked w. G. Wallington, J. Wald, R. Jacquet, T. Scott, Z. Sims *et al.*, in 1956; with Scott early 1958. Favs: K. Clarke, Philly Joe Jones, M. Roach. LPs w. G. Russell, T. Scott (Vict.), B. Evans (River.), D. Elliott (Decca), E. Costa (Mode).
Addr: 14 West 71st St., New York 23, N.Y.

MUCCI, Louis Raphael, *trumpet*; b. Syracuse, N.Y., 1/13/09. Began study of baritone horn at 10, switched to trumpet at 16. Went on road w. Don Gregory's band. With Red Norvo-Mildred Bailey in 1937 when E. Sauter switched to arr. With Glenn Miller '38-9, B. Chester '40-1, Coast Guard band '43-6 (toured Italy). Joined B. Goodman upon discharge, then w. C. Thornhill two years. Has done free lance and studio work since 1951. Fav. own solo: *The Old Man's Touch* w. J. La Porta (Deb.). Fav. arr: G. Evans, La Porta, D. Broekman. LP w. A. Levister (Deb.).
Addr: 325 West 45th St., New York, N.Y.

MULLIGAN, Gerry. Toured Britain April 1957; appeared at Newport Jazz Festival '57, '58. Appeared as a single in two groups on *The Sound of Jazz* CBS-TV show Dec. '57. In Apr. '58 had a new group feat. Art Farmer on trumpet which appeared on Timex jazz show, CBS-TV. LPs w. B. Brookmeyer (ABC-Par.), Miles Davis (Cap.), Manny Albam (Cor.), Stan Getz (Sav.), Paul Desmond (Verve). Own LPs: *Gerry Mulligan Song Book* and quart. (Wro. Pac.), *At Newport* (Verve), *Mainstream of Jazz* (Em.).

MURPHY, Turk. Appeared at Newport Jazz Festival, July 1957; in the fall worked at Bourbon Street Club in NYC, then returned to San Francisco, where he opened his own club called Easy Street. LPs: *At Newport, Music for Losers* (Verve), *San Francisco Jazz*, Vol. 1 and 2 (Good Time Jazz).

NERO, Paul. After suffering from mental illness for several years, Nero died suddenly in his doctor's office in Calif. on Mar. 21, 1958. He was best known as composer of *Hot Canary*.

NEVES, John, *bass*; b. Mansfield, Mass., 10/22/30. Father pl. guitar, vln. Stud. in Revere, Mass. 1955. Got into music bus. through brother, Paul, a pianist and violinist. Worked w. Bobby Scott Trio; Boots Mussulli in Milford, Mass.; three yrs. at Jazz Workshop in Boston w. Herb Pomeroy. While in service pl. in band in Korea, 1953. Joined George Shearing April '58. Favs: Ray Brown, Heath, Pettiford, Chambers, Red Mitchell. LPs: Transition, Roulette.
Addr: 22 Blagden St., Boston, Mass.

NEWBORN, Phineas. Toured w. Birdland All-Stars, spring 1957; then was semi-inactive for the past year owing to illness. Was at Village Vanguard, NYC, in a duo w. C. Mingus Feb. '58. LPs: *Phineas' Rainbow, While My Lady Sleeps, Music from Jamaica* (Vict.).

NICHOLAS, Albert. Remained in Paris, renewed study of his instrument; his latest records showed a more advanced harmonic and technical conception by the veteran New Orleans clarinetist.

NICHOLAS, Wooden Joe. Died Nov. 17, 1957 in New Orleans after a prolonged illness at the age of 74.

NIEHAUS, Lennie. LP w. S. Kenton (Cap.). Own LPs: Contemp.

NOBLE, Ray. Returned to England, summer 1956.

NORVO, Red. Cont. his recording and club activities on the West Coast. Came East as B. Goodman's guest on NBC-TV's *Swing into Spring* show April '58. LPs w. H. Babasin (Em.), Jack Montrose (Vict.), B. Troup (Lib.). Own LPs: *Norvo Naturally* (Tampa), *Vibrations, Ad Lib* (Lib.), *Hi-Five* (Vict.), *Music to Listen to Red Norvo By* (Contemp.).

O'DAY, Anita. Beginning in the fall of 1956 became very active in clubs and on records. Toured as far as Hawaii and throughout the U.S. LPs: *Pick Yourself Up, Anita Sings the Most, An Evening w. Anita O'Day, Lady is a Tramp.*

ORE, John Thomas, *bass*; b. Philadelphia, Pa., 12/17/33. Father played cello and mother piano. Stud. cello at New School of Music in Phila. '43-6, bass at Juilliard, '52. First job w. Tiny Grimes in 1953 for one month and has since worked w. G. Wallington, L. Young '54, B. Webster, C. Hawkins. Chiefly known for work w. Bud Powell trio beginning 1955. Favs: O. Pettiford, R. Brown. LP w. F. Redd (Pres.).
Addr: 6 Bleeker St., New York, N.Y.

ORY, Kid. Ory's activities incl. a tour of Europe and the Continent and an appearance at the 1957 Newport Jazz Festival in July where he joined w. Red Allen, L. Armstrong's group and J. Teagarden. Returned to club work in San Francisco with own ensemble. LPs w. Red Allen at Newport (Verve). Own LPs: *Tailgate* (Good Time Jazz), *Kid Ory in Europe* (Verve).

PAGE, Walter. The veteran bassist, in whose band C. Basie played in 1929, and who himself was a Basie sideman from 1935-43 and again '46-8, died Dec. 20, 1957 of pneumonia in NYC, at the age of 57. LPs w. V. Dickenson, Mel Powell (Vang.), J. Teagarden (Beth.), J. Rushing (Col.), Roy Eldridge (Verve), P. Quinichette (Pres.), Ruby Braff (Vict.).

PARIS, Jackie. During 1957 Paris made several appearances at Cafe Bohemia as an added attraction on week-

ends. LPs w. L. Feather-D. Hyman (MGM), Jazz Lab Quint. (Col.). Own LPs: *Skylark* (Bruns.), *The Jackie Paris Sound* (East-West).

PARKER, John W. Jr. "Knocky," *piano*; b. Palmer, Tex., 8/8/18. First learned about jazz from itinerant cotton pickers in Texas, players in Dallas dives, and from following the keys as piano rolls ground out ragtime. Played w. Light Crust Doughboys while at Trinity University in Waxahachie, Tex. After Army discharge joined Z. Singleton-Albert Nicholas trio in Los Angeles area. Gigged around NYC while stud. English at Columbia University and has since embarked on the dual career of English teacher and jazz concert lecturer. In the latter capacity he demonstrates all ragtime and jazz styles from S. Joplin through Brubeck. Fav: Jelly Roll Morton. Recorded for Audiophile.
Addr: Kentucky Wesleyan College, Owensboro, Ky.

PARLAN, Horace Louis, *piano*; b. Pittsburgh, Pa., 1/19/31. Began piano w. private teachers in 1943. After a childhood attack of polio which left right hand partially paralyzed, Parlan, through the encouragement of his teacher, Mary Alston, and bassist Wyatt Ruther, developed a predominantly left-hand style. Gigged w. local groups in Pittsburgh 1952-7, also brief stint in Washington D.C. w. Sonny Stitt. Became member of C. Mingus' Jazz Workshop in Oct. '57 which worked in New York clubs and on tour. Favs: H. Silver, B. Powell, J. Lewis. LPs w. Mingus (Beth., Vik.), led own quint. accompanying Langston Hughes' *The Weary Blues* (MGM).
Addr: 180 W. 135th St., New York, N.Y.

PAYNE, Cecil. Gigs around NYC incl. own group at Five Spot, and w. Randy Weston. LPs w. M. Gee, R. Weston (River.). K. Dorham (Blue Note), K. Burrell (Pres.), Rolf Ericson (Em.). Own LP: *A Night at the Five Spot* (Sig.).

PENA, Ralph. Left J. Giuffre in Oct. 1957 to return to Calif. LPs w. Giuffre (Atl.), S. Rogers (Vict.), B. Brookmeyer (Wor. Pac.).

PEPPER, Art. Became very active again in clubs in Los Angeles area and on record dates. Also pl. some gigs in Las Vegas, proving himself to be one of the most individual reed soloists on the West Coast. LPs w. J. Graas (Merc.), Joe Morello (Intro), M. Paich (Tampa), S. Rogers (Fict.), Bill Perkins (Wor. Pac.). Own LPs: *Modern Art* (Intro), *Return of Art Pepper* (Jazz: West), *Art Pepper Meets the Rhythm Section* (Contemp.).

PERKINS, Bill. Worked w. Stan Kenton throughout most of 1957. LPs w. S. Kenton (Cap.), L. Niehaus (Contemp.) M. Roach-S. Levey (Lib.); John Lewis (Wor. Pac.), *Tenors Head-On* w. R. Kamuca (Lib.). Own LPs: *Onstage, Just Friends* (Wor. Pac.).

PERKINS, Carl. After a long stay w. Chet Baker's group Perkins died unexpectedly in Calif. 3/17/58. LPs w. Baker-A. Pepper (Wor. Pac.), B. De Franco (Verve), C. Counce, L. Vinnegar (Contemp.), Q. Jones (ABC-Par.). Own LP: *Introducing Carl Perkins* (Doo.).

PERSIP, Charlie. Gigs around NYC in 1958 after D. Gillespie broke up his big band in which Persip had played drums since 1956. LPs w. Gillespie (Verve), Q. Jones (ABC-Par.), H. Mobley, L. Morgan (Blue Note), H. McKusick, P. Woods-D. Byrd (Prs.); *Dizzy Atmosphere* (Spec.), *Double or Nothin'* (Lib.).

PETERSON, Oscar. Toured Europe w. Ella Fitzgerald early spring, 1957; appeared at Stratford Ontario Shakespeare Festival, Newport Jazz Festival, and was member of the faculty of School of Jazz, Lenox, Mass. Worked at the Embers NYC, on tour w. JATP fall '57 and European tour w. JATP spring '58. LPs w. B. De Franco, A. O'Day, L. Hampton, B. Webster, H. Edison (Verve). Own LP: Verve.

PETTIFORD, Oscar. During the spring of 1957 Pettiford had a big band which appeared at clubs both in NYC and Boston. Forced to disband it, he went into the Five Spot NYC w. a small group and in early 1958 opened at a new club, the Black Pearl on the upper East Side, staying several weeks. LPs w. Toshiko (Story.), T. Charles (Jub.), T. Monk, K. Dorham, C. Hawkins (River.), A. Blakey (Col.), *Four Most Guitars* (ABC-Par.). Own LPs: *In Hi Fi* (ABC-Par.), *Bass by Pettiford/ Burke* (Beth.).

PIERCE, Nat. After disbanding the big band he had formed Feb. 1957, Pierce returned to his free-lance arr. and recording work in NYC. Was pianist w. the Ruby Braff group which appeared both at Newport Jazz Festival and Randall's Island Festival in New York, summer '57. Among his other activities he was both arr. and instrumentalist on *The Sound of Jazz* CBS-TV show, Dec. '57. In 1957-8 he pl. frequently w. C. Basie's band as assistant pianist and subbed for him during Basie's illness. LP's with D. Lambert (ABC-Par.), P. Quinichette (Pres., Dawn). Braff (Verve, Vict., Epic), Specs Powell (Roul.). Own LPs: *Kansas City Memories, Chamber Music for Moderns* (Cor.).

PIKE, David Samuel, *vibraphone, drums, piano*; b. Detroit, Mich., 3/23/38. Began on drums at 8, is self-taught on vibes. Has worked w. Elmo Hope, C. Perkins, James Clay, C. Counce, and other West Coast groups. Since April 1957 has been a member of Paul Bley quartet. Fav. own solo: *Birk's Works* w. Bley on *Gene Norman Presents*. Favs: C. Brown, M. Jackson, J. Coltrane. LPs w. Jazz Couriers (Whip.), Bley (Gene Norman Presents). Addr: 1700 N. Lima St., Burbank, Cal.

PISANO, John, *guitar*; b. New York City, 2/6/31. Father an amateur guitarist. Began on piano at 10, guitar at 14 w. private teachers. Decided on musical career while w. "Crew Chiefs" Air Force band, 1952-5. Since 1956 has been feat. with Chico Hamilton. Fav. own solo: *Zen* w. Fred Katz (Wor. Pac.). Favs: C. Wayne, T. Farlow, J. Raney, Segovia. LPs w. C. Hamilton (Wor. Pac., Decca), F. Katz (Wor. Pac., Decca, Dot), P. Horn (Dot). Own LP: Decca.
Addr: 150 Park Ave., Staten Island 2, N.Y.

POLLARD, Terry. After leaving T. Gibbs in 1957, freelanced in Detroit w. Yusef Lateef and others. LPs w. Billy Mitchell (Sav.), T. Gibbs (Em.), Dick Garcia (Dawn).

POMEROY, Herb. Led own big band in Boston and at Birdland, NYC. LP: *Life Is a Many Splendored Gig* (Roul.).

POTTER, Tommy. In summer 1956 went to Sweden and toured w. Rolf Ericson. LPs w. Artie Shaw (Verve), C. Payne (Sig.), C. Parker (Deb.). Own LP: *Tommy Potter's Hard Funk* (East-West).

POWELL, Bud. On tour w. Birdland All-Stars, Feb. 1957; subsequently app. in Paris, often working w. K. Clarke. LPs w. C. Parker (Sav.), Fats Navarro (Blue Note). Own LPs: *Strictly Powell* (Vict.), *Amazing Bud Powell* (Blue Note), *Blues in the Closet, Genius of Bud Powell, Jazz Giant, Moods* (Verve).

POWELL, James Theodore "Jimmy," *alto sax, clarinet, flute*; b. New York City, 10/24/14. From a musical family, he began stud. violin at 7, gave Town Hall recital at 14. Also stud. piano, and harmony and theory at Dewitt Clinton High School. Began gigging w. bands at 17 on alto, first w. Frankie Newton. Subsequently w. Fats Waller, Edgar Hayes, B. Carter (1939-40), Basie ('42-6), and later the small groups of Sid Catlett, E. Heywood, Lips Page, L. Thompson, I. Jacquet, and the large groups of D. Redman and L. Millinder. Was lead alto in Flip Phillips' *Down Beat* All-American band while w. Basie. With Gillespie on State Dept. tour of Near East and South America. Good lead alto. Solo on Basie's *Taps Miller* (Col.). Fav: B. Carter. LP with Gillespie (Verve).
Addr: 112 S. 13th Ave., Mt. Vernon, N.Y.

POWELL, Mel. Worked w. B. Goodman band in its engagement at Waldorf-Astoria, NYC, Feb. 1957. LPs: *Easy Swing, Borderline, Out on a Limb* (Vang.).

POWELL, Specs. Still a staff musician at CBS, Powell returned to jazz intermittently in 1957-8, as a recording bandleader and talent scout. LPs w. E. Garner (Col.), C. Shavers (Beth.). Own LP: *Movin' In* (Roul.).

PRESLEY, Elvis. Inducted into Army, Mar. 1958. LPs: Vict.

PREVIN, André. Except for a trip to Paris in summer 1957 to score music for a movie, Previn remained at MGM Studios, taking an occasional leave of absence to lead a trio in club appearances. His LP of *My Fair Lady* w. Shelly Manne, released early 1957 on Contemp., became a best-seller and led to greatly increased activity as a solo rec. artist on jazz LPs. Other LPs w. D. Pell (Atl.), B. Kessel, Russ Freeman (Contemp.), P. Rugolo (Merc.). Own LPs: *Pal Joey* (Contemp.), *Mad About the Boy* (Cam.), *André Previn Plays Fats Waller* (Zen.).

PRICE, Sammy. Again spent much time in Continental Europe, especially France, 1956-8. LPs w. S. Bechet (Bruns.), J. Rushing (Vang.). Own LPs: *Rock* (Sav.), *The Price Is Right* (Jazz.).

PUERLING, Eugene Thomas, *singer*; b. Milwaukee, Wis., 3/31/29. Worked as disc jockey, free-lance singer in Milwaukee; org. two vocal groups before moving to West Coast, where he got first major break as leader-arranger for Hi-Lo's quartet (q.v.). Fav. singers: Mel Torme, Four Freshmen. LPs Col., Starlite.
   Addr: 1626 N. Vine, Hollywood 28, Calif.

QUILL, Gene. Led own combo intermittently as co-leader w. Phil Woods in NYC night clubs and also was feat. w. J. Richards' orch. LPs w. J. Knepper (Beth.), Richards (Cap.), Woods (Vict., Pres.), Q. Jones (ABC-Par.); *Four Altos* (Pres.).

QUINICHETTE, Paul. Led own combo, NYC, 1957-8. App. on NBC-TV's educational series *The Subject Is Jazz*, Apr. '58. LPs w. F. Wess (Pres.). Own LPs: *The Kid from Denver* (Dawn), *For Basie, For Count, On the Sunny Side* (Pres.).

RANEY, Jimmy. Remained at Blue Angel, NYC, w. Jimmy Lyon trio, 1957-8. LPs w. B. Brookmeyer (Wor. Pac., ABC-Par., Pres.), Aaron Sachs (Rama); *Four Most Guitars* (ABC-Par.), *Two Guitars* (Pres.). Own LPs: *In Three Attitudes* (ABC-Par.), *Jimmy Raney Visits Paris* (Dawn).

REDD, Freddie. To Sweden w. Rolf Ericson, June 1956, later free-lanced, NYC. LPs: *Piano: East/West* (Pres.), *San Francisco Style* (River.).

REDMAN, Don. LP: *Park Avenue Patter* (Gold. Cr.).

REHAK, Frank. After leaving D. Gillespie played w. J. Richards and in Broadway show *Copper and Brass*, 1957; later worked as staff musician at WNEW, NYC. LPs w. Richards (Cap.), Gillespie (Verve), A. Kirk (Vict.), A. Hodeir, A. K. Salim (Sav.), Q. Jones, Candido (ABC-Par.), J. Newman (Cor.).

RENDELL, Don Percy, *tenor sax, clarinet*; b. Plymouth, Eng., 3/4/26. Parents both prof. musicians; started him on piano at 6 but kept him at it only until he was 10. At 16, he took up alto and was at first largely self-taught, doing his first prof. work at that age. Was w. J. Dankworth's Seven, 1950-3, had own group '54-5, w. T. Heath 6 months in '55, toured Europe w. S. Kenton for 6 weeks in '56; own group again in 1957. Won *Melody Maker* Readers' Poll for Britain's Best, 1957. Fav: L. Young. LPs on various English labels and w. J. Keating (Bally).
   Addr: 5 Arlow Rd., London, N.21, Eng.

REYNOLDS, Thomas A., *clarinet, leader, radio producer*; b. Akron, O., 1/17/17. Vln. at 8, concert clar. at 14; stud. at Ohio State U. Pl. w. Isham Jones, 1938-9. Org. band in Cleveland, 1939. Throughout the 1940s led popular swing band, rec. for Col., seen at Meadowbrook, Roseland, New Yorker Hotel, Paramount Th., etc. Gave up touring 1955, became house mus. on WOR-TV, NYC, on Ted Steele show, then became prod. of radio shows, incl. *Bandstand U.S.A.* on Mutual network, two-hour live jazz show, 1956-8. LP: *Jazz For Happy Feet* (King).
   Addr: 901 8th Ave., N.Y.C.

RICH, Buddy. Toured Europe w. Harry James, Oct. 1957. Led various combos and app. on TV as actor, 1957-8. LPs w. L. Hampton, C. Parker (Verve). Own LPs: *Buddy and Sweets, Just Sings, This One's for Basie, Swinging Buddy Rich* (Verve).

RICHARDS, Emil (Emilio Joseph Radocchia), *vibraphone* (also *xylophone, piano, tympani*); b. Hartford, Conn., 9/2/32. Began studying at 6, first on xylophone. Was at Hartford School of Music, 1949-52. Between 1950-54, was percussionist w. Hartford and New Britain Symphonies and Connecticut Pops Orch. In 1954-5 was assistant leader of Army band in Japan, and worked w. Toshiko Akiyoshi during that time. In 1956 gigged around NYC; joined G. Shearing, Sept. '56, and has been with him since. Fav. own solo: *You Stepped Out of a Dream* w. Shearing (MGM). Favs: M. Jackson, L. Hampton. LPs w. Shearing (Cap., MGM).
   Addr: 1240 Woodycrest Ave., Bronx, N.Y.

RICHARDS, Johnny. Led own big band frequently, 1956-8. LP w. D. Gillespie (Sav.). Own LPs: *Something Else* (Beth.), *Wide Range* (Cap.).

RICHARDSON, Jerome. Remained on staff at Roxy Theatre until Mar. 1958, then free-lanced in New York. LPs w. P. Newborn (Vict.), O. Pettiford (ABC-Par.), L. Feather-D. Hyman (MGM), Maxine Sullivan (Per.), Hank Jones (Sav.).

ROACH, Max. On faculty School of Jazz, Lenox, Mass., Aug. 1957. Cont. to lead own combo. LPs w. B. Golson (River.), Jay Jay Johnson (Col.), C. Parker (Verve, Sav.), S. Rollins, T. Monk, Thad Jones, J. Griffin (Blue Note), S. Rollins (Pres.); *Drummin' the Blues* w. Stan Levey

(Lib.). Own LPs: Deb., *Max Roach Plus Four, Jazz in 3/4 Time* (Em.).

ROBERTS, Charles Luckeyeth "Lucky," *piano*; b. Philadelphia, 8/7/1895. To NYC at 3 as actor in *Uncle Tom's Cabin*. Worked as child acrobat; pl. piano in Baltimore clubs. During the 1920s he was a favorite bandleader in high society, catering to millionaire clientele with his orchestras in New York, Newport, Palm Beach, etc. An early ragtime soloist, he published a number of orig. piano rags from 1913 (*Junk Man Rag, Pork and Beans*) through 1923. In later years he became owner of the Rendezvous, a bar on St. Nicholas Ave. in Harlem, but remained active in music: he had a successful Carnegie Hall concert appearance in 1939, another at Town Hall in '41; one of his more ambitious works, *Whistlin' Pete— Miniature Syncopated Rhapsody*, for piano and orch., was presented at Robin Hood Dell in Phila.

During the 1940s Roberts went in for popular songwriting, enjoying some success with *Moonlight Cocktail* ('41) and *Massachusetts* ('42). One of the most versatile and energetic of all the ragtime pianists of his day, he wrote music for 14 musical comedies, produced before and after World War I. As a society pianist, he was a great favorite of the Duke of Windsor (then Prince of Wales), playing for him frequently and helping to choose his collection of jazz records. He was an important early influence on Duke Ellington, James P. Johnson and many other Harlem pianists of the early 1920s. Rec. LP 1958 for Contemp.

Addr: 270 Convent Ave., New York 31, N.Y.

RODIN, Gilbert A., *reeds, trumpet, flute*; b. Chicago, Ill., 12/9/06. Began study of reeds, flute and trumpet while attending school in Chicago. Joined B. Pollack's orch. in 1927 and was with him until 1935. Helped organize group which became the Bob Crosby orch. in '35 and was long associated with it on alto and as arranger and musical director. Inactive as musician in recent years, working w. Crosby as radio and TV exec. Favs: Eddie Miller, M. Matlock, B. Goodman, I. Fazola. LPs w. Crosby (Cor.).

Addr: 445 N. Laurel Ave., Los Angeles, Calif.

RODNEY, Red. Released from Lexington, Ky., June 1957, after serving a narcotics sentence, he worked w. Sammy Davis, Jr., O. Pettiford and others. In 1958 had own quart. in Phila. LPs w. C. Parker (Verve, Deb.), Al Hibbler (Bruns.).

ROLAND, Gene, *trumpet, trombone, arranger*; b. Dallas, Tex., 9/15/21. Began stud. at North Texas State Teachers' College, where he majored in music from 1940-2 and roomed w. J. Giuffre and H. Babasin. Later, joined Air Corps, where he and Giuffre formed Air Force band which grew into the Eighth Air Force Orch. Joined S. Kenton, summer '44, as trumpeter-arr.; remained until 1955, except for brief stints both as free-lance arr. and

w. L. Hampton, C. Barnet, C. Thornhill, A. Shaw, H. James. Joined W. Herman, Nov. '56; wrote 65 arrangements by Feb. '58, when he left to write and arr. for Dan Terry's big band. Fav. own arrangements include several recorded by Kenton (Cap.) and Herman (Verve), especially *Are You Livin' Ol' Man* (Anita O'Day w. Kenton), *Tampico, Sittin' and A-Rockin'* (J. Christy w. Kenton). Names Giuffre as early personal influence; Basie and Lunceford as first big band inspirations. Then Ellington became his lasting favorite. Likes Armstrong, Eldridge, Gillespie, but H. Edison is present influence; Bill Harris fav. trombone. LP w. J. Knepper (Beth.).

Addr: 215 W. 75th St., New York 23, N.Y.

ROLLINS, Sonny. Left Max Roach, summer 1957; led own combo '57-8. Enjoyed a great rise in popularity among musicians and fans. LPs w. Roach (Em.), T. Monk, K. Dorham, Abbey Lincoln (River.), Monk, Miles Davis (Pres.); *Tour de Force* (Pres.). Own LPs: *Night at the Village Vanguard* (Blue Note), *Way Out West* (Contemp.), *Rollins Plays for Bird, Movin' Out, Rollins Plus 4, Saxophone Colossus, Work Time, Tenor Madness* (Pres.).

ROSOLINO, Frank. LPs w. R. Kamuca (High Fid.), Bob Cooper (Contemp.), H. Rumsey, M. Roach-S. Levey (Lib.), P. Rugolo (Merc.), S. Rogers (Vict.). Own LPs: *Frankly Speaking* (Cap.), *I Play Trombone* (Beth.), sextet (Mode, Cap.).

ROSS, Annie. App. in musical comedy *Cranks* in England 1956 and U.S., 1957. Later worked as single in NYC night club and in vocal group on Patrice Munsel TV series '57-8. Prominently feat. w. Dave Lambert on *Sing a Song of Basie* LP (ABC-Par.). Other LPs: *Annie Ross Sings* (Pres.), one track w. André Hodeir (Sav.).

RUSHING, Jimmy. Had a very successful appearance at the Great South Bay Jazz Festival after app. at NJF, summer 1957. Toured England in Sept. '57; feat. on *The Sound of Jazz*, CBS-TV, Dec. '57, and *The Subject Is Jazz*, NBC-TV's educational series, Apr. '58. Toured Europe w. B. Goodman, May '58. LP w. C. Basie at Newport (Verve). Own LPs: *If This Ain't the Blues, Goin' to Chicago, Listen to the Blues* (Vang.), *The Jazz Odyssey of James Rushing Esq.* (Col.).

RUSSELL, Pee Wee. Worked w. Ruby Braff group in NYC area, summer 1957, incl. app. at NJF. Appeared on *Sound of Jazz* show, CBS-TV, Dec. '57. LPs w. J. McPartland (Epic), Ruby Braff (Verve, Vict.).

RUSSO, Bill. On faculty at School of Jazz, Lenox, Mass., Aug. 1957. Left Chicago and moved to NYC, Nov. 1957, to do free-lance arr. LP: *The World of Alcina* (Atl.).

SADI (Lallemand Sadi), *vibraphone*; b. Andenne, Belgium, 10/23/26. Started in Belgium ca. 1937 on xylophone, playing in circus. Worked w. Bobby Jaspar in the Bob Shots in Liège '46, Don Byas combo '47; w. Lucky Thompson at Nice Jazz Festival '48, later w. Jack Diéval and at Ring Side in Paris w. Django Reinhardt, with whom he made a short movie. Played w. Aime Barelli '53, Martial Solal quart. '54; had own band in Paris '55 w. B. Jaspar, David Amram *et al.* Concerts w. André Hodeir's Jazz Groupe de Paris '55, '56, '57; worked w. Jacques Helian '56-7. Fav. own rec: LP w. own group released in U.S. on Blue Note; also rec. w. Jaspar, D. Byas, Hodeir, Reinhardt. Favs: Originally L. Hampton, later Milt Jackson.

Addr: 22 Rue du Moulin, Paris, France.

SAFRANSKI, Eddie. Member of the group that app. on *The Subject Is Jazz* on NBC-TV, Mar.-June 1958. Own LP: Sav.

SALIM, Ahmad Khatab (A. K. Atkinson), *composer-arranger*; b. Chicago, 7/28/22. Att. DuSable High Sch. w. Bennie Green, Dorothy Donegan, Gene Ammons. Pl. alto w. King Kolax, 1938-9; Jimmy Raschel '41-2; Tiny Bradshaw '43. Jammed at Minton's w. Lester Young, C. Parker *et al.* Stopped playing in '44; wrote for L. Millinder band for 2 years, later for C. Calloway, J. Lunceford, L. Hampton, Basie. His *Normania* for Basie on Vict. later became famous in new treatment as *Blee Blop Blues.* Inactive 1949-56, in real estate, etc., then returned to write for Tito Puente *et al.*, and in 1957-8 became one of the more important bop-derived arrs. in New York scene. Fav. arrs: Tadd Dameron, Neal Hefti, Ernie Wilkins. LPs: *Flute Suite* (Sav.), arrs. for Machito (Roul.), Herbie Mann (Epic), Phineas Newborn's *Jamaica* (Vict.), etc.

Addr: 323 W. 74th St., New York 23, N.Y.

SASH, Leon. App. NJF, July 1957. LPs: Story. and *At Newport* (Verve).

SAUNDERS, Theodore "Red," *drums, tympani, vibraphone*; b. Memphis, Tenn., 3/2/12. Began stud. drums in Milwaukee at St. Benedict The Moor School. Own band in 1937 and has worked w. Ellington, Herman, Armstrong. Popular bandleader in Chicago for many years at Club De Lisa. Encouraged J. Williams as a blues singer and has worked w. Lurlean Hunter and African drummer Guy Warren. Fav. own solo: *Duet* in *Africa Speaks, America Answers* w. Warren (Decca). Favs: Z. Singleton, S. Catlett. LP w. Warren (Decca).

Addr: 7332 S. Calumet, Chicago, Ill.

SAUTER, Eddie. In Mar. 1957 broke up the Sauter-Finegan band and left for Baden-Baden, Germany, for job as bandleader-arranger at radio station Sudwestfunk. LPs w. Finegan: *Under Analysis, Straight Down the Middle* (Vict.).

SCHULLER, Gunther. Besides his work w. the Metropolitan Opera orch., conducted a recital of jazz and contemp. music at Cooper Union. Began a series of jazz programs on New York radio station WBAI w. critic Nat Hentoff. LP: *Music for Brass* (Col.).

SCOTT, Hazel. Spent most of 1956-8 in Paris, where she app. in vaudeville and on dramatic stage. LP: *Round Midnight* (Decca).

SCOTT, Tony. Toured Europe and Africa for 7 months during 1957, incl. forays behind the Iron Curtain. App. on television show *The Mythical Bird* on CBS's *Camera Three*, Feb. '57, and was part of the regular group featured on *The Subject Is Jazz*, NBC-TV's educational series, Mar.-June '58. Had own group at Minton's briefly, winter '57, and at the Black Pearl, spring '58. LPs w. Billie Holiday (Verve), L. Feather-D. Hyman (MGM). Own LPs: *South Pacific Jazz* (ABC-Par.), *The Touch of Tony Scott, The Complete Tony Scott* (Vict.), *Tony Scott in Hi-Fi.* Often pl. bar. sax '57-8.

SELLERS, John "Brother John," *singer*; b. Clarksdale, Miss., 5/27/24. Raised in Greenville, Miss., by grandmother, who used to let out plot of land to travelling tent shows. There he heard Ma Rainey, Ida Cox, and other blues singers of the '20s. Sang in church and was particularly influenced by Leroy Carr's recordings. Moved to Chicago at 10 w. an aunt and did gospel singing, largely under the inspiration of Mahalia Jackson, with whom he toured. During the '50s he became acquainted w. Josh White, Sonny Boy Williamson, S. Price, Tampa Red, and w. Bill Broonzy, who encouraged him. Repl. Broonzy at the Blue Note in Chicago when the latter toured Europe in 1950, and has toured the South and West widely since. Toured and recorded in England in 1957. Own LP: Decca/Lond.

SHANK, Bud. In Mar. 1958 did a reprise of his European tour of 2 years previous, visiting Scandinavia and also North and South Africa, w. Bob Cooper, June Christy, C. Williamson *et al.* LPs w. H. Rumsey (Contemp.), Bill Perkins, Chet Baker (Wor. Pac.), J. Giuffre, S. Rogers (Atl.), P. Rugolo (Merc.). Own LPs: *James Dean Story, Jazz at Cal-Tech, Flute 'n' Oboe* (Wor. Pac.).

SHARON, Ralph. Toured as acc. to Tony Bennett, 1957-8, incl. visit to England. LPs: *Easy Jazz* (Lond.), *Mr. and Mrs. Jazz* (Beth.), *Around the World in Jazz* (Rama).

SHAW, Arvell. With B. Goodman band, incl. its *Swing into Spring* NBC-TV show, Apr. 1958, and its European tour in May. LPs w. L. Armstrong (Decca), Vic Dickenson (Story.).

SHAW, Joan (Joan DeCosta), *singer*; b. Newport News, Va., 1/29/30. Uncle, Bootsie Swan, was famous comic, singer, dancer. Began singing in local night clubs when 15; w. Paul Williams, 1948-9. Has worked many club dates and recorded for MGM, ABC-Par., Sav., and other labels. Has written and recorded many original tunes. Though often limited in her work to rhythm-and-blues and pop performances, she is an excellent jazz-oriented singer. Favs: E. Garner, B. Booker.

Addr: 2480 N. W. 55th Terrace, Miami, Fla.

SHEARING, George. App. on educational television series in Boston w. Father Norman O'Connor in fall 1957, and was also on second Timex all-star jazz show in Apr. '58 on CBS. LPs: *Latin Escapade, The Shearing Piano, Night Mist, Black Satin, Velvet Carpet* (Cap.).

SHERMAN, Richard Anthony, *trumpet, arranger*; b. New York City, 11/13/27. Stud. at Juilliard and w. Sammy Silen. On road w. Johnny Richards, B. Goodman, C. Barnet, Kenton; writing for Elliot Lawrence. House band at Roxy, 1956-8. LPs w. Al Cohn-Zoot Sims (Vict.), *Jazzville No. 1* (Dawn).

Addr: 4530 Broadway, New York, N.Y.

SHERRILL, Joya, *singer*; b. Bayonne, N.J., 8/20/27. Worked briefly w. D. Ellington, fall 1942; joined band in 1944 while still in high school after she wrote words to Strayhorn's *Take the A Train*. Remained w. Ellington for 4 years and then went out as a single. Rejoined Duke for his CBS-TV spectacular and recording of *A Drum Is a Woman*. Favs: E. Fitzgerald, L. Horne, P. Bailey. LPs w. Ellington (Col.). Own LP: Des.

Addr: 18 Spinney Hill Dr., Great Neck, L.I., N.Y.

SHREVE, Richard G., *piano, bass, trombone*; b. 8/16/28, Kansas City, Mo. Father, a doctor, played Dixieland trombone in K.C. area. Began working in father's band on piano in 1945. Stud. music 6 years at Oklahoma City U. Sat in w. L. Brown in July '56 and stayed several months, settling in Los Angeles. With Buddy Childers, B. Collette '56, and joined H. Rumsey's Lighthouse group in '57. Fav: Tatum. LPs w. Collette (ABC-Par., Contemp.), Rumsey (Lib.), M. Roach-S. Levey (Lib.).

Addr: 604 25th St., Manhattan Beach, Calif.

SHULMAN, Joe. Best known as bassist w. his wife, Barbara Carroll, in her trio, he died unexpectedly of a heart attack, NYC, 8/2/57. LPs w. B. Carroll (Atl., Vict., Verve).

SILVER, Horace. With several changes in personnel, cont. to work in the East, especially NYC clubs w. a quint. he had formed, Sept. 1956. LPs w. Miles Davis, Milt Jackson (Pres.), A. Blakey (Col., Blue Note), P. Chambers, L. Morgan, H. Mobley, K. Dorham, S. Rollins (Blue Note). Own LPs: *Six Pieces of Silver, Stylings of Silver* (Blue Note), *Silver's Blue* (Epic).

SIMEON, Omer. With Wilbur De Paris (q.v.) on its tour of Africa under the sponsorship of the State Dept. LPs w. W. De Paris (Atl.), Kid Ory (Good Time Jazz).

SIMS, Zoot. Toured w. Birdland All-Stars early 1957, then formed a group w. Al Cohn that summer; also gigged w. own group, then to Europe w. B. Goodman, May '58. LPs w. G. Mulligan (Wor. Pac., Em.), Cohn (Vict.), M. Albam (Cor.); *Tenor Conclave* (Pres.), *Four Brothers—Together Again* (Vik). Own LPs: *Modern Art of Jazz, Zoot Sims Goes to Jazzville* (Dawn), *Zoot* (Argo), *Zoot* (River.), *Zoot Sims Plays Four Altos* (ABC-Par.).

SINATRA, Frank. Began own TV series on ABC network, fall 1957. LPs: *This is Sinatra, Close to You, A Swingin' Affair, Where Are You, Come Fly with Me* (Cap.), *The Frank Sinatra Story* (Col.).

SMITH, Bessie (Note: corrected birthdate 4/15/1894). In the spring of 1958 four LPs of songs made famous by Bessie Smith were released: *Dinah Washington Sings Bessie Smith* (Em.), *Lavern Baker Sings Bessie Smith* (Atl.), *The Legend of Bessie Smith* sung by Ronnie Gilbert (Vict.), *Juanita Hall Sings the Blues* (Counter.). The last was a stereophonic disc. Bessie Smith herself was feat. on one track of *Famous Blues Singers* (River.), released Apr. '58.

SMITH, Edward Louis, *trumpet*; b. Memphis, Tenn., 5/20/31. Began stud. trumpet 1944, later pl. in high school band. Scholarship to Tennessee State U. where he majored in music. Pl. with the Tennessee State Collegians in Carnegie Hall concert. Postgrad. work at U. of Michigan, where he stud. trumpet under Prof. Clifford Lillya. In Army, Jan. 1954-5; played in the Third Army Special Services unit. In 1955 he began teaching instrumental music at Booker T. Washington High School in Atlanta, Ga. Was praised by some critics as promising new star in neo-bop style on release of his first record. Favs: F. Navarro, Clifford Brown, C. Parker. Own LP: Blue Note. Joined H. Silver '58.

SMITH, Floyd "Wonderful," *electric guitar*; b. St. Louis, Mo., 1/25/17. Son of a drummer, he stud. music locally at the Victor Hugo School after early instruction on ukelele in 1932. Played banjo w. Eddie Johnson and Dewey Jackson for 2 years, then w. Jeter-Pillars orch., with whom he made first records for Bruns. After an appearance w. Sunset Royal Entertainers at Harlem's Apollo Theatre, joined Andy Kirk's band, Jan. 1939, rec. w. Kirk *Floyd's Guitar Blues*, first jazz elec. guitar record of note, and stayed until May '42, when he entered the service. Worked w. Wild Bill Davis, Ravens, and w. various St. Louis groups. Most recently w. drummer Chris Columbus' group. Rec. w. Kirk (Decca), Davis (Epic). Fav: Segovia.

Addr: 1701 Pendleton Ave., St. Louis, Mo.

SMITH, Henry "Buster," *alto sax, clarinet*; b. Ellis County, Tex., 8/26/04. Largely self-taught, he began working w. local bands in Dallas. In 1926 he joined Walter Page's Blue Devils and when Page, Jimmy

Rushing and Hot Lips Page left that group to join Bennie Moten, he kept leadership of the Blue Devils, took it on the road, but was soon back in Kansas City, joining Moten. When C. Basie took a small group from the remnants of this band after Moten's death, Smith was part of it at Reno Club, KC, 1936, and contributed a portion of the book. However, when Basie went North, Smith had no faith in the enterprise and remained in KC and the Southwest playing w. Andy Kirk, Claude Hopkins and various other groups; later came to NYC as arr. for Basie, B. Carter *et al.* According to the testimony of many musicians, C. Parker's idol was Buster Smith. He once said, "Buster was the guy I really dug." In 1937 Parker was a part of Smith's group in KC. In 1941 Smith returned to Dallas and has been there since w. his own small group. Has been inadequately recorded so far but some solos can be heard on records led by Pete Johnson, Eddie Durham and Snub Mosley. Fav. own solo: *Moten Swing* w. Durham (Dec.). Favs: C. Parker, Hawkins, Webster and Art Tatum.

SMITH, Jimmy. LPs: *A Date w. Jimmy Smith*, Vol. 1 & 2, *Plays Pretty Just for You, At Club Baby Grand* (Blue Note)

SMITH, Mabel "Big Maybelle," *singer*; b. Jackson, Tenn., 1924. Sang blues as a child; also was member of Sanctified Church choir. Won vocal contest at 9 in Memphis Cotton Carnival. First sang w. Dave Clark in Memphis; later w. T. Bradshaw, 1947-50, then as a single. Does a great deal of pop material as well as blues, but whatever she does comes out in the traditional blues shouting style. Is very successful in rock-'n'-roll concerts and on records, first for Okeh, currently with Sav. Sang at Newport Festival, July '58.

Addr: c/o Associated Booking Corp., 745 Fifth Ave., New York 22, N.Y.

SMITH, Stuff. Toured Europe w. O. Peterson trio and Ella Fitzgerald, Apr. 1957. LPs w. Nat Cole (Cap.), D. Gillespie (Verve). Own LP: Verve.

SMITH, Willie The Lion. His 40th year in jazz was celebrated, Nov. 1956, at the Central Plaza, NYC, where he app. week ends, 1956-8. LPs: *The Lion Roars* (Dot), *Accent On Piano* (Urania). Was at Newport Festival '58, also on several TV shows.

SNOWDEN, Elmer Chester "Pops," *saxophones, guitar, banjo*; b. Baltimore, Md., 10/9/00. Started locally w. Eubie Blake. Had own combo in Washington, D.C., in 1921 w. Sonny Greer, Otto Hardwicke, which travelled to NYC in '23 on the promise that F. Waller would join them. When he did not, D. Ellington was sent for and the group became "The Washingtonians." During the late '20s and early '30s, in NYC, he led successful groups w. many famous jazzmen. At the Bambille in Harlem ('27), he had Count (then Bill) Basie, Claude Hopkins,

J. Lunceford, Bubber Miley, Frankie Newton, "Tricky Sam" Nanton, C. Webb and B. Carter. At the Hot Feet Club in Greenwich Village ('28-9), he had Waller, Garvin Bushell, Hardwicke, Webb and others.

During 1930 at The Nest, he feat. Rex Stewart, Jimmy Harrison, Prince Robinson, Joe Garland, Freddy Johnson. From '31-33 he led a very famous band at Smalls Paradise, which feat. S. Catlett, R. Eldridge, Gus Aiken, D. Wells, Bushell, Al Sears, Hardwicke. This group made several short films for Warner Bros. He was also in the band of Ford Dabney for *Keep Shufflin'* in '28 and w. Eubie Blake for *Blackbirds of* 1930.

From 1923 on he rec. for almost every label in NYC under a variety of pseudonyms: "Sepia Serenaders" for Vict. and Bluebird, "Red Hot Eskimos" for Col., for the Canadian label Ajax. w. a variety of blues singers, etc. He is still active; visited Canada in '56 and has appeared at the Central Plaza, Jimmy Ryan's and The Metropole in NYC. Fav. own records: *West Indian Blues* (Viola McCoy, Vocalion), *I Ain't Got Nobody* (Bessie Smith, Col.), *Breaking the Ice* (Sepia Serenaders, Bluebird). Favs: Eddie Peabody, banjo; J. Smith, T. Farlow, O. Moore, guitar.

Addr: 699 N. Broad St., Philadelphia, Pa.

SOLAL, Martial, *piano* (also *clarinet, saxophone*); b. Algiers, N. Africa, 8/23/27. Started on piano in Algiers at 7 and decided in 1940 to take up jazz. Settling later in Paris, he pl. at the Club St. Germain for several years, working w. Jay Jay Johnson, K. Clarke, L. Thompson, Don Byas and other visiting American stars. Has won several awards, incl. the Prix Django Reinhardt, Grand Prix du Disque, and Prix Jazz Hot. With Bernard Peiffer's departure to the U.S., Solal immediately earned the position of outstanding pianist in Paris. Favs: A. Tatum, Bud Powell. LPs w. S. Bechet (Wor. Pac.), L. Thompson (Dawn), K. Clarke (Epic); *Jazz on the Left Bank* (Epic).

Addr: 201 Rue du Temple, Paris 3, France.

SPANIER, Muggsy. Teamed briefly w. Earl Hines in 1957 before the latter's European tour w. J. Teagarden. LPs: *Dixieland at Jazz Ltd.* (Atl.), *The Great* 16 (Vict.), Merc.

STEIN, Harold Jerome, *alto, tenor saxes*; b. Weehawken, N.J., 9/5/28. Clarinet at 11, tenor at 15; Town Hall concert w. Don Byas, Specs Powell at 15. Worked w. Rudy Williams, Roy Haynes, 1946. Stud. at Juilliard, 1950-1; Army '51-4, during which time he pl. w. Toshiko in Japan for 7 months. Switched from tenor to alto while in Korea; pl. w. Teddy Charles '55, Les Elgart '56, Larry Sonn '57. Favs: C. Parker, J. Coltrane, S. Rollins. Att. Manhattan Sch. of Music, 1958.

STEWART, Rex. In Dec. 1956 returned to NYC and was again active. Org. and dir. the reunion of F. Henderson's sidemen for the Great South Bay Festival, summer '57. App. on *The Sound of Jazz*, CBS-TV, Dec. '57; joined

E. Condon, Feb. '58. Feat. on *Art Ford's Jazz Party*, WNTA-TV, spring '58. LPs w. D. Ellington (Vict.), E. Condon (MGM); *The Big Challenge, F. Henderson Reunion* (Jazz.).

STITT, Sonny. In Jan. 1958 gave up his own group to join D. Gillespie combo after the latter broke up his big band. On European tour w. JATP, spring '58. LPs w. Gillespie, S. Rollins, O. Peterson (Verve); *For Musicians Only* (Verve). Own LPs: *Jazz Kaleidoscope* (Pres.), *New York Jazz* (Verve).

STRAND, Les (Leslie Roy Strandt), *electric organ, piano, pipe organ*; b. Chicago, Ill. 9/15/24. Father was theatre organist and Strand began teaching self piano, then organ at 5. At 18, he was introduced to A. Tatum by a friend. Stud. formally beginning 1944, at Baldwin-Wallace Conservatory in Ohio and Augustana College in Rock Island, Ill. In late '47 was introduced to the work of D. Gillespie and Parker and began using modern style on organ. Jobs in Chicago area; first recordings w. C. Hawkins on Peacock. Fav. own solo: *If I Had You* (Fant.). Favs: Tatum, Gillespie, Parker, Tristano, Jimmy Smith. Own LPs: Fant.
Addr: 917 Diversey Pkwy., Chicago, Ill.

STRASEN, Robert M., *singer*; b. Strasbourg, France, 4/1/28. Raised in Milwaukee. Sang in choirs for many years. Led male chorus in Army while stationed in Japan. Got into pop music through Gene Puerling and joined Hi-Lo's (q.v.), Apr. 1953. Fav. singers: Jackie Cain, Roy Kral. LPs: Starlite, Col.
Addr: 1626 N. Vine, Hollywood 28, Calif.

STRAYHORN, Billy. Chief contribution to the Ellington book was sections of *Such Sweet Thunder* written especially for the Stratford, Ontario, Shakespearean Festival. Led own trio w. J. Hodges and Jimmy Grissom called Ellington Indigos, spring 1958, in Florida. LPs w. Ellington (Col.), C. Terry (River.), Al Hibbler (Bruns.).

SULLIVAN, Ira Brevard, Jr., *trumpet, saxophones*; b. Washington, D.C., 5/1/31. From a musical family, he received his early training on trumpet from his father, on sax from his mother. Started jobs when still in high school. In 1952, for 2½ years, he was part of the house band at the Bee Hive in Chicago, and there worked w. B. Green, P. Quinichette, S. Stitt, H. McGhee, W. Gray, L. Young, R. Eldridge and C. Parker. Later worked w. Bill Russo's group. Was w. A. Blakey briefly in 1956. Favs: Gillespie, M. Davis, Navarro, H. Edison, C. Terry, C. Parker, C. Hawkins, L. Young and Sonny Rollins. LPs w. Blakey (Col.), J. R. Monterose (Blue Note). Own LP: ABC-Par.
Addr: 5246 N. Ashland Ave., Chicago, Ill.

SUTTON, Ralph. Took over the group at the Hangover Club in San Francisco during Earl Hines' British tour.

LPs w. Bob Scobey (Vict., Verve). Own LPs: *Classic Jazz Piano* (River.), *Ragtime Piano* (Verve), *Salute to Fats* (Har.).

TAKAS, William J., *bass, trumpet*; b. Toledo, Ohio, 3/5/32. Began on piano, then trumpet, finally bass. With B. May in 1955; came to NYC in '56 and has worked w. various groups, incl. S. Salvador, Z. Sims, Jutta Hipp, N. Pierce, and chiefly T. Farlow's and E. Costa's groups. LPs w. Bob Dorough, F. Socolow (Beth.).
Addr: 137 Thompson St., New York 12, N.Y.

TATE, Buddy. Working as leader of own group in New York area. LPs w. J. Rushing (Col., Vang.), B. Clayton-R. Braff (Vang.).

TATUM, Art. After about a year of ill-health, Tatum became seriously ill during a tour late in Oct. 1956 and died in LA, Nov. 4, 1956, of uremia, at the age of 46. His passing was mourned as a severe loss to jazz; a typical comment was that of Art Blakey, who said: "He was the greatest pianist that ever lived. I have known Art Tatum all my life and loved him as a musician and human being." LPs: *Concert* (Harm.), *Encores* (Cap.), *Makin' Whoopee, The Genius of Art Tatum, Trio*; w. Buddy De Franco; w. Ben Webster (Verve).

TAYLOR, Billy. Cont. working in New York clubs, mainly the Embers and Composer. Was mus. dir. for NBC-TV's educational series *The Subject Is Jazz*, Mar.-June 1958. LPs: *New Billy Taylor Trio, My Fair Lady Loves Jazz, Presents Ira Sullivan* (ABC-Par.), *At Town Hall, Cross Section, Let's Get Away from It All* (Pres.).

TAYLOR, Cecil, *piano*; b. New York City, Jan. 1933. Stud. privately, then at New York College of Music and 4 yrs. at New England Conservatory. Later gigs w. Hot Lips Page, Lawrence Brown, J. Hodges *et al.* In the late '50s began to be heard around NYC with, first, a quart. consisting of Steve Lacy, sop. sax; Buell Neidlinger, bass; and Dennis Charles, drums; for a long stay at the Five Spot, and app. at NJF, July '57. Late '57 had revamped quart. featuring vibes in place of sop. sax and app. in concert at Cooper Union. Accused of making a pastiche of Bartok, Stravinsky and jazz, Taylor has also been called acutely aware of the specific techniques of jazz and its folk heritage and a member of the advance guard of the music of Duke Ellington and T. Monk. Favs: Many older musicians like S. Bechet, L. Armstrong, C. Hawkins, but as direct influences: Monk, Ellington. LPs: *Jazz Advance* (Trans.), *At Newport* (Verve).

TEAGARDEN, Jack. App. NJF, July 1957; toured Britain, fall '57, in all-star group w. Earl Hines. App. on Timex jazz TV shows in Dec. '57 on NBC and Apr. '58 on CBS. LPs w. Bud Freeman, L. Armstrong (Vict.), Bobby Hackett (Cap.), E. Condon (Decca), Red Allen

Verve); *Escapade Symposium* (Lib.), *String of Swinging Pearls* (Vict.). Own LPs: *Jack Teagarden—Jazz Great* (Beth.), *This Is Teagarden, Swing Low Sweet Spiritual, Big T's Jazz* (Decca).

TERRY, Clark. LPs w. Ellington (Col.). Own LPs: *Out on a Limb* (Argo), *Duke with a Difference, Serenade to a Bus Seat* (River.).

THARPE, Sister Rosetta. Toured England and Continent, Nov.-Dec. 1957, acc. by Chris Barber.

THIGPEN, Ed. Worked w. Billy Taylor trio, 1956-8. LPs w. Taylor (ABC-Par.), B. Peiffer (Em.), Toshiko (Story.), P. Quinichette, A. Cohn (Pres.), D. Ashby (Reg.).

THOMPSON, Lucky. Spent much of 1957-8 in Europe. LPs w. Ralph Sharon (Rama), T. Monk (Blue Note), Q. Jones, O. Pettiford (ABC-Par.), Miles Davis (Pres,.) Milt Jackson (Atl.). Own LPs: Dawn; *Accent on Tenor* (Urania).

THORNE, Francis Burritt, Jr., *piano*; b. Bay Shore, L.I., N.Y., 6/23/22. Stud. piano from age of 7; majored in theory and comp. at Yale (grad. in '43); stud. w. Hindemith for 2 years and 4 years w. Richard Donovan. D. Ellington heard and encouraged him in 1955 after he had spent several years in stockbroking. Worked as single at Hickory House in NYC, fall '55 to mid-'56. Was associated w. producing the Great South Bay Jazz Festivals in 1957-8. Favs: O. Peterson, H. Silver, T. Wilson, J. Lewis. Own LP: Trans.
Addr: 39 E. 79th St., New York 21, N.Y.

TJADER, Cal. LPs: *Vibrations* (Sav.), *Latin Kick, Jazz at the Blackhawk, Mambo, Mas Ritmo Caliente* (Fant.).

TORME, Mel. Visited England, summer '56, and again in '57. LPs: *Mel Torme Sings Fred Astaire, California Suite, At the Crescendo* (Beth.).

TOUFF, Cy. Joined group formed by Chubby Jackson, Mar. 1957, in Chicago. LPs w. C. Jackson (Argo), Woody Herman (Cap., Verve).

TROUP, Bobby. Beginning in July 1956, moderated a successful television series titled *Stars of Jazz*, which originated over KABC-TV in Hollywood, locally until 1958, after which it was seen on ABC network. LPs: *Bobby Swings Tenderly* (Mode), *Do-Re-Mi, Here's to My Lady* (Lib.).

TUCKER, George Andrew, *bass*; b. Palatka, Fla., 12/10/27. Moving to NYC in 1948, he began study at New York Conservatory of Modern Music. Had become interested in music (through a record by Ellington w. O. Pettiford) in the Army. Worked w. various groups and instrumentalists, incl. E. Bostic, S. Stitt, J. Coltrane, and became

house bassist in Continental Lounge in Brooklyn, playing w. many famous musicians there. Stud. privately w. Fred Zimmerman of Juilliard, 1957-8. Favs: M. Davis, C. Parker, O. Pettiford. LPs w. F. Redd (River.), Curtis Fuller (Pres., Blue Note), J. McLean (Jub.).
Addr: 1800 7th Ave., New York, N.Y.

TURNER, Joe. LP: *Boss of the Blues* (Atl.).

VANDERPOOL, Sylvia, *guitar, singer*; b. New York City, 5/29/35. Stud. piano as a child. Was singing w. bands at 14 and recording as "Little Sylvia." Met Mickey Baker, took up guitar, and as "Mickey and Sylvia" they had wide popularity beginning in 1957 in the rhythm and blues field. Fav: Mickey Baker. Own LP (w. Baker): Vik.
Addr: 461 Central Park West, New York, N.Y.

VAUGHAN, Sarah. Toured w. Birdland All-Star troupe, Feb. 1957. Had a very successful stay at Waldorf-Astoria, NYC, w. Count Basie, summer '57. LP w. B. Eckstine (Merc.). Own LPs: *Swingin' Easy, Sassy* (Em.), *Linger Awhile* (Col.), *Wonderful Sarah, In a Romantic Mood, At Mr. Kelly's, Sings George Gershwin, Great Songs from Hit Shows* (Merc.).

VENUTI, Joe. Appeared on Tommy Dorsey memorial TV show on CBS, Dec. 1956. LP: *Fiddle on Fire* (Grand Award).

VINNEGAR, Leroy. Had serious auto accident, Jan. 1957. Left Chico Hamilton and had own group on West Coast. LPs w. S. Rogers (Atl.), B. De Franco (Verve), S. Chaloff (Cap.), Dexter Gordon (Beth.), S. Manne (Contemp.). Own LP: *Leroy Walks* (Contemp.).

WALDRON, Mal. Worked as acc. for Billie Holiday in 1957 and intermittently led own groups chiefly in New York clubs. LPs w. Jackie McLean (Jub., Pres.), P. Quinichette, John Coltrane, Teo Macero, Thad Jones, Teddy Charles, Frank Wess (Pres.). Own LPs: *Mal-1 Mal-2* (Pres.).

WALLINGTON, George. LPs w. Thomas Talbert (Atl.), Bobby Jaspar (River.). Own LPs: *Variations* (Verve), *Knight Music* (Atl.), *Piano* (Sav.).

WARD, Clara, *singer*; b. Philadelphia, 4/21/24. Sang sacred songs from age of 5 at Baptist Church under tutelage of her mother, a choir leader. Stud. piano at 8. By age 10, was appearing with sister and mother in local church events. Two new members, Henrietta and Marion Waddy, were added to the group, which by the time she had finished high school was well known locally. The Ward Singers first became nationally known in 1943 after appearing at a Baptist convention. Since then, they have been in constant demand, seen by audiences of up to 25,000 in stadiums, armories, etc. During the past decade, the gospel group has also been heard on records for the Duke, Savoy, Gotham and Peacock labels. They toured nationally in such shows as The Big Gospel Cavalcade of 1957, and in 1957 were heard at the Newport Jazz Festival.

The work of the Ward Singers, though not directly related to jazz, has common roots with it and, like that of many Negro gospel groups, has a strong emotional appeal akin melodically and rhythmically to that of earlier jazz forms. LPs and singles on Savoy.

WARE, Wilbur Bernard, *bass*; b. Chicago, Ill., 9/8/23. First became interested in music in church run by foster father who played drums, guitar, bass, trombone, sax. With his help, Ware taught himself first banjo then bass from childhood and was soon playing in amateur string groups in Chicago, later prof. gigs locally and elsewhere in the Mid-west w. Stuff Smith, R. Eldridge, S. Stitt and others. In 1953 had own groups at the Bee Hive and Flame Lounge in Chicago playing w. Monk, J. Griffin and others; w. E. Vinson '54-5. Toured w. A. Blakey in '56, ending in NYC w. B. De Franco and Monk during 1957. Own trio at Bohemia, w. Monk, other local gigs '58.

Ware plays in a percussive-lyric style, in contrast to the virtuoso manner of most bassists in the modern idiom, and sometimes makes remarkable use of double-stops. Favs: J. Blanton, Israel Crosby. LPs w. E. Henry, T. Monk, J. Griffin and others (River.), L. Morgan, H. Mobley, S. Rollins and others (Blue Note). Own LP: River.

Addr: 553 W. 51st St., c/o Riverside Records, New York, N.Y.

WARREN, Guy, *drums*; b. Accra, Ghana, W. Africa, 5/4/23. Despite family opposition, he stud. jazz through records, and theory at Achimota College and by mail from U.S. School of Music, Port Washington, N.Y. Until 1953, he worked in Accra off and on w. own groups, meanwhile working in England w. Kenny Graham's Afro-Cubists and other groups and free-lancing for a while in Paris. In 1954 he worked in Monrovia. On the Gold Coast (Ghana) he was disc jockey and newspaper editor. Came to the U.S. and Chicago in 1955, working with and meeting such former idols as D. Gillespie, C. Parker and L. Young. Moved to NYC in July 1957 and had own trio at the African Room. Has a detailed authentic knowledge of African music (and dance) which he uses in his playing. Fav. own solo: *Guy's Chant* in *Africa Speaks, America Answers* w. R. Saunders (Decca). Favs: J. Costanzo, K. Clarke. Own LP: Decca.

Addr: 56 W. 95th St., New York, N.Y.

WARWICK, William Carl "Bama," *trumpet*; b. Brookside, Ala., 10/27/17. To N.J. at 13. Att. mus. sch. w. C. Shavers. Met D. Gillespie when they worked in Frank Fairfax band in Phila. Pl. w. Hardy Bros., NYC, '33, then w. Millinder, Bradshaw, T. Hill, R. Eldridge, B. Berigan; to Army '41 for 3½ years, in charge of

60-piece military band in Boston. Later worked w. many pop bands (Milt Britton, Abe Lyman, etc.); also w. Woody Herman, 1944-6, Buddy Rich '47 (feat. on rec. *Baby, Baby All The Time*, Merc.) and several Latin bands. Own combo w. Brew Moore in San Francisco, 1954-5; toured w. D. Gillespie '56-7. Though never considered a jazz soloist, Warwick at one time has worked in most of the name jazz bands and is a dependable all-round section man.

WASHINGTON, Dinah. LPs on Em. and Merc., incl: *In the Land of Hi-Fi, The Swingin' Miss D, The Best in Blues, Dinah Washington Sings Bessie Smith, Dinah Washington Sings Fats Waller, Dinah Jams, Music for a First Love.*

WATKINS, Doug. LPs w. Thad Jones (Per.), Pepper Adams (Wor. Pac.), Art Blakey (Col.), Frank Wess, Gene Ammons, H. Mobley, S. Rollins, J. McLean, P. Quinichette (Pres.). Own LP: *Watkins at Large* (Trans.).

WAYNE, Chuck. Played solo score for Tennessee Williams' play *Orpheus Descending* on Broadway, spring 1957. LP w. George Shearing (Sav.); *Four Most Guitars* (ABC-Par.). Own LPs: Sav., *String Fever* (Vik).

WEATHERFORD, Teddy, *piano*; b. Bluefield, W. Va. 10/11/03; d. Calcutta, India, 4/25/45. Moved to New Orleans when he was 12 and began on piano 2 years later. In Chi. in early '20s w. Erskine Tate and others, where he was considered one of the most advanced pianists of the time, sometimes compared w. Earl Hines. Beginning in 1926, he went to California and subsequently to China w. Jack Carter's band (which incl. Albert Nicholas). Then Japan, India and the East Indies. He remained in the Far East the rest of his life, except for a European tour in 1937 w. several mos. in Paris.

WEBSTER, Ben. Returned to NYC for club dates, Oct. 1957. App. on *Sound of Jazz*, CBS-TV show, Dec. '57, and on *The Subject Is Jazz*, NBC-TV's educational series, Apr. '58. Led own quart. at Village Vanguard, spring '58, and app. on Art Ford's WNTA-TV *Jazz Party*, May '58. LPs w. Red Norvo (Vict.), *F. Henderson Reunion* (Jazz.), W. Herman, Billie Holiday, Harry Edison, Buddy Rich, Art Tatum (Verve). Own LPs: *King of Tenors, Sophisticated Lady* (Verve).

WELLS, Dickie. App. at Great South Bay Festival, New York, summer '57; on *Sound of Jazz*, CBS-TV show, Dec. '57. LPs w. J. Rushing (Col.), *F. Henderson Reunion* (Jazz.).

WESS, Frank. LPs w. Thad Jones (Pres., Per.), Count Basie (Roul., Verve), Tony Scott (Vict.), L. Feather-D. Hyman (MGM), A. K. Salim, Frank Foster (Sav.). Own LPs: *Wheelin' and Dealin'* (Pres.), *Opus in Swing, Jazz for Playboys* (Sav.).

WETTLING, George. Toured Britain beginning Jan. 1957 w. Eddie Condon. LPs w. J. McPartland (Epic), Bud Freeman (Vict.), Condon (Col.); *Golden Era of Dixieland Jazz* (Des.), *Dixieland in Hi-Fi* (Harm.).

WILBER, Bob. With B. Hackett's group doubling on reeds and vibes late 1957. Joined Max Kaminsky, Mar. '58. LPs w. J. McPartland (Epic), R. Braff (Beth.), Wild Bill Davison, E. Condon (Col.); *Dixieland Goes Progressive* (Gold. Cr.).

WILDER, Joe. LPs w. Hank Jones, A. K. Salim, Billy Ver Planck (Sav.), Tony Scott (Vict.), Urbie Green (ABC-Par.), J. Giuffre (Atl.), Gunther Schuller (Col.), Don Redman (Gold. Cr.).

WILKINS, Ernie. Cont. in NYC as free-lance arr. for C. Basie, H. James *et al.* and many rec. sessions, incl: N. Adderley (Em.), M. Ferguson, Lurlean Hunter (Vik), Candido (ABC-Par.).

WILLIAMS, Alfred, *piano, organ, arranger*; b. Memphis, Tenn., 12/17/19. Began study in Chicago at 8, playing first prof. engagement at 16. Led own 12-piece dance orch. in Chicago, 1937. In '43 he joined Red Allen's combo at the Down Beat Room in Chicago and has been w. Allen off and on since, incl. a trip to Bermuda in 1953, and at the Metropole in NYC in 1958. Has also recorded w. Haywood Henry and S. Stitt. Good blues pianist. Favs: Ellington, Tatum. LPs w. Allen, *The Weary Blues*, w. Langston Hughes (MGM).
Addr: 242 Bradhurst Ave., Bronx 56, N.Y.

WILLIAMS, Clarence. During early 1957, recovered from serious illness.

WILLIAMS, Cootie. Although Cootie's small group cont. to play mostly rock-'n'-roll and chiefly at the Savoy Ballroom, NYC, he played jazz on some records. LPs w. D. Ellington (Vict.), *Ronnie Gilbert Sings Bessie Smith* (Vict.), *The Big Challenge* w. Rex Stewart (Jazz.).

WILLIAMS, Joe. Aside from his work w. Basie, app. on records under his own name as follows: *Joe Williams Sings* (Reg.), *A Man Ain't Supposed to Cry* (Roul.), *A Night at Count Basie's* (Vang.).

WILLIAMS, Mary Lou. Came out of retirement for app. at NJF, July 1957. Subsequent club dates, NYC (Cherry Lane, Composer *et al.*). LPs: *Women in Jazz* (Story.), *Modern Jazz Piano: Four Views* (Cam.), w. D. Gillespie at Newport (Verve). Own LP: Atl.

WILLIAMS, Sandy. In late 1957 he recovered from a serious illness, NYC.

WILLIAMSON, Claude. Toured Europe, N. and S. Africa w. Bud Shank, Bob Cooper, June Christy group, spring 1958. LPs w. Shank (Wor. Pac.), H. Rumsey (Contemp.),

Tal Farlow (Verve. Own LPs: *Claude Williamson Mulls the Mulligan Scene* (Crit.), *Round Midnight* (Beth.).

WILSON, Shadow. Worked w. T. Monk during the latter's long stay at the Five Spot, NYC, beginning summer 1957. Subsequently w. him at the Village Vanguard. LPs w. Monk (River., Blue Note), Joe Puma (Dawn), P. Woods-G. Quill (Vict.), L. Konitz (Verve).

WILSON, Teddy. Toured w. own concert unit, fall 1957, playing many college dates. Had own trio for night club, concert and TV appearances, 1956-8. LPs: *At Newport, I Got Rhythm, For Quiet Lovers, Intimate Listening* (Verve).

WINDING, Kai. With various changes of personnel, cont. leading the septet he formed after parting w. Jay Jay Johnson, Oct. 1956. LPs w. Johnson (Col., Pres.), Miles Davis (Cap.), Don Elliott (Sav.). Own LPs: *The Trombone Sound, Trombone Panorama* (Col.).

WOODS, Phil. Left D. Gillespie to form own unit w. Gene Quill, Dec. 1956; subsequently free-lanced, NYC. LPs w. Gillespie (Verve) Quill (Vict., Pres.), Q. Jones, J. Cain-R. Kral (ABC-Par.), Joe Newman (Vict.). Own LPs: *Warm Woods* (Epic), *The Young Bloods, Woodlore* (Pres.).

WRIGHT, Charles "Specs," *drums*; b. Philadelphia, Pa., 9/8/27. Pl. in band at S. Phila. High, then Army band; discharged 1947, pl. w. Jimmy Heath's 17-piece band; 6 months w. Howard McGhee, incl. trip to France, 1948. Joined D. Gillespie, pl. in his big band and sextet, 1949-50. Worked in Phila. until '56, except for tours w. Earl Bostic; joined C. Adderley '56 and stayed for almost a year, then joined Carmen McRae's acc. trio. Pl. drums and tympani on Art Blakey's *Orgy in Rhythm* (Blue Note).
Addr: 764 S. 16th St., Philadelphia 46, Pa.

WRIGHT, Gene. Joined D. Brubeck, Feb. 1958. LPs w. B. De Franco (Verve), C. Tjader (Fant.), Gerald Wiggins (Spec.).

WRIGHT, Specs. With Carmen McRae, 1957-8. LPs w. R. Bryant (Pres.), Nat Adderley (Em.), Art Blakey (Blue Note, Col.).

WYNN, Albert, *trombone*; b. New Orleans, La., 7/29/07. Was prom. in Chicago during the twenties w. various groups, incl. Earl Hines. Toured Europe w. Sam Wooding in 1928. Back in Chi. was active in the thirties w. Carroll Dickerson and at the Apex Club w. Jimmie Noone. With Fletcher Henderson during 1937-8. Still active in Chi. w. local groups. Like Preston Jackson, did not use the percussive "tailgate" style but one more like that associated w. Teagarden and Jimmy Harrison. LP w. Franz Jackson (Replica).

YOUNG, Eugene Edward "Snookie," *trumpet*; b. Dayton, Ohio, 2/3/19. First instruction came from parents and private teacher. His first important engagement was w. Chick Carter in 1937. Subsequently he was w. J. Lunceford '39-42, C. Basie '42, L. Hampton '43-4, B. Carter '44, Gerald Wilson '45, Basie again '45-7. Returned to Dayton in '47 and had own group there until Oct. '57, when he rejoined Basie. Appeared in several films during '40s, incl. *Blues in the Night* as the off-screen trumpeter for Jack Carson in one sequence. Fav. own solos: *Uptown Blues* and *Time To Jump and Shout* w. Lunceford (Col.). Favs: The young Armstrong, M. Davis, R. Eldridge, C. Shavers, C. Spivak.

Addr: 1502 Hockwalt St., Dayton, Ohio.

YOUNG, Lester. Toured w. Birdland All-Stars, Feb. 1957. App. NJF, July '57, incl. session w. C. Basie. App. on *Sound of Jazz*, CBS-TV show, Dec. '57. Suffered breakdown late Dec. '57 but was active again early '58. LPs w. Basie (Verve, Sav.), H. Edison (Verve). Own LPs: *Blue Lester* (Sav.), *It Don't Mean a Thing, Lester's Here, Lester Swings Again, Pres* (Verve), *Aladdin*, Vol. 1 & 2.

YOUNG, Webster, *trumpet*; b. Columbia, S.C., 12/3/32. Raised in Washington, D.C., played in Army band w. Hampton Hawes, later gigs in Washington w. local groups. Came to NYC, June 1956. Favs: M. Davis, Gillespie. LP w. R. Draper (Pres.). Own LP: Pres.

YOUNG, William, *drums, flute, piano*; b. Salt Lake City, Utah, 2/11/28. Started playing drums in 1949 when he heard M. Roach on a C. Parker record. Played w. Salt Lake City Symphony. In 1950 was w. Gene Mayl's Dixieland Rhythm Kings; in '52 was w. D. Gordon in San Francisco, later w. Brew Moore. Formed trio w. wife Jean Hoffman (q.v.) in 1957. Favs: Roach, Parker, Bobby Donaldson. LP w. Jean Hoffman (Fant.).

Addr: 245 Bristol Blvd., San Leandro, Calif.

ZIEFF, Robert Lawrence, *composer-arranger*; b. Lynn, Mass., 6/4/27. Stud. music at Boston U. Has written for Chet Baker, Bill Harris and others, but favors the Viennese school of composers. LPs: comp. for D. Wetmore (Beth.), C. Baker (Wor. Pac.), J. Nimitz-Bill Harris (ABC-Par.), A. Ortega (Beth.).

Addr: Apt. 5-D, 142 W. 62nd St., New York, N.Y.

JAZZ AND THE PHONOGRAPH

Charles Graham has written numerous technical and lay articles on electronics and high fidelity during the fifteen years he has been connected with prominent manufacturers of recording and hi-fi equipment in capacities ranging from technician to sales manager. His articles on jazz music and musicians have appeared in the American Record Guide *and* Hi-Fi Music *magazine.*

Survey articles on jazz history often start off with a reference to the Original Dixieland Jass Band of Nick LaRocca, Larry Shields *et al.*, familiarly known as the ODJB. It is particularly appropriate here because they made the first jazz recording we know about. Listening to Victor 18255, *Livery Stable Blues* and *Dixieland One Step*, made during the ODJB's first engagement in New York (where they were crowding the floor and tables at Reisenweber's Restaurant in early 1917), some people claim that sound recording and reproduction have come further since then than has jazz!

Actually, in 1917, the phonograph had been around in various forms for almost forty years although there were few records available until about 1895, twenty-two years before LaRocca pointed his trumpet at the recording horn. Edison's first phonograph, a primitive voice-only, hand-driven cylinder machine much like the early dictaphone of the twentieth century, appeared briefly in the late 1870's. The first musical recordings were made by Edison before 1890, still on vertical-cut cylinders which played for about two minutes. At about that time, in 1887, Emile Berliner invented the lateral-cut flat disc which is basically what we still have. Berliner's machine was called a gramophone, and its discs were gramophone records. Edison's dictaphone-like machine was called a "phonograph." There was also a machine developed by Chichester Bell and Charles Tainter, based on Edison's first phonograph, but materially improving on it in several ways, called the "graphophone." Ultimately the other words disappeared, and the word phonograph came to describe what evolved from Berliner's gramophone.

In 1891 Bettini cylinders carried the first real music, recorded by numerous prominent operatic stars, on as many cylinders as these stalwarts could cut, making up to perhaps a dozen cylinders every time they shouted into the horn. By 1910 there were several different types of commercially available records, in various forms which included different sizes of cylinders, and both lateral and vertical-cut discs. The disc was beginning to replace the cylinder, since it could be duplicated readily. The cylinders, on the other hand, had to be cut individually by a pantographic copying system with one recording machine cutting each of ten to twenty copies while a master played from the original. At this time, no jazzmen were known outside their home-towns, except to a few other jazzmen through word-of-mouth. And no jazz had been recorded.

Because the science of recording music has progressed at about the same rate and in the same period with that of reproducing it, hi-fi and recording are inextricably intertwined. And jazz has been so strongly affected by the phonograph and its progress that no story of jazz is complete without recognition of the phonograph, or today, of " Hi-Fi." The phrase, a contraction of "high-fidelity" (coined probably in the middle 1930's by English speaker-designer H. A. Hartley), was yet to be thought of, but the search for fidelity was on.

The cylinder phonograph (and flat disc gramophone) started going places after 1910, with numerous companies making machines, symphony orchestras recording, and millions of records being sold within a few years. (Victor and Columbia record sales in 1920 totalled 100 million dollars.) After the ODJB discs, jazzmen started hearing each other through the medium of the ten-inch 78 RPM disc we know so well.

The most obvious impact of reproduced jazz, despite the fact that it was recorded badly by present hi-fi standards, was that even without radio broadcasts of jazz, which came later, jazzmen all over the country started hearing King Oliver's Creole Band (including Louis' second trumpet) on Okeh, Bix and the Wolverines on Gennett, and Fletcher Henderson's Orchestra on Emerson, Black Swan, Vocalion and other labels. When they heard these men playing JAZZ, and when every jazzman started hearing all the others, things started cooking! These musicians had always spent every spare minute digging up other sessions to listen to when they were not actually working. Now the phonograph (the word gradulaly came to mean all recorded cylinder *and* disc machines) let them not only hear each other, but play and replay, study, copy, adapt, or build on what others were doing. In short, the interaction of musicians' ideas and styles on each other was speeded up enormously. It was not doubled or tripled, which is multiplication; it was stepped up at a mathematically increasing rate—algebraically. And it has never slowed up since. Today all musicians listen to the phonograph: there are actually some who go out of their way not to listen too much! There is such an outpouring of jazz records that it is safe to say that there is no jazzman alive today who has not been recorded far beyond the dreams of jazz collectors of even a few years ago, before the avalanche that came with LP.

When Billie Holiday was learning about singing in her early teens through listening to Bessie and Louis on the parlor phonograph of an East Baltimore madam, she was doing in effect what every other jazz musician has done since 1925: she was listening, loving and learning. It became her life, this listening, and of course it greatly affected the rest of her life. Young Roy Eldridge had a trumpet specialty at the age of sixteen—the Coleman Hawkins tenor sax take-off from the 1926 Columbia record of Fletcher's *Stampede*. Though he "couldn't read a note the size of a house," he could listen and imitate and learn and grow; and he did, adding a totally new dimension to trumpet playing and jazz. Records have been and are the life blood of communication between jazzmen and their audience. The examples of contributions by one musician to another which any jazz amateur runs across when he starts listening seriously to records are so obvious and numerous as to be beyond further comment.

A second effect produced by the impact of the phonograph record on jazz was the $2\frac{1}{4}$ to $3\frac{1}{2}$ minutes (depending on tempo) limitation which the ten-inch 78 RPM disc imposed. This limitation was almost universally accepted until the LP record, with, however, some exceptions. These exceptions were due in most part to the clamor from jazz fans for on-the-spot recordings. Columbia recorded Duke Ellington's *Reminiscing in Tempo*, the first of his extended works to be recorded, on four ten-inch 78 records in 1935. Other early discs to exceed three minutes were the four 78 RPM twelve-inchers which RCA issued in the late 1930's under the album title *A Symposium of Swing*. This album included eight sides by Tommy Dorsey, Fats Waller, Bunny Berigan, and Benny Goodman. The BG disc was a two-sided affair lasting ten minutes, parts 1 and 2 of *Sing, Sing, Sing* which the band had been playing up to as much as twenty minutes or so on one-night stands. Sales of this album, and especially of *Sing, Sing, Sing* even in later abbreviated versions dubbed on to ten-inch records, helped pave the way for other part 1 and 2 records of specialties that just would not fit the $3\frac{1}{2}$ minute-or-less format. It is also true that the repeated pattern of thirty-two bars for a pop tune worked out well in the familiar dance band (fox trot) number. Since little jazz before World War II paid very well unless it doubled as popular dance music, this helped keep the three minute limit in force.

It was only with the spread of chamber jazz, sparked by the small Goodman trio and other groups, semi-public jam sessions, jazz concerts and the recording of all these, at first by dedicated amateurs, later by the small record companies, that the pattern of three minutes was broken. Now, except for pops and dance music, nobody pays much attention to the old dimensions any more. An LP can handle up to almost sixty minutes with only one break for flipping it, and tape and the 16 RPM disc, just released in small numbers for jazz early in 1958, have abolished even the minimal limitations of two sides at 33 RPM microgroove.

Before LP the 78 RPM disc carried 85 to 115 or so lines per inch. Modern LPs have their grooves spaced at from 200 to 300 plus lines per inch, and often the grooves are unevenly spaced, using the variable groove spacing technique developed in the 1940's by recording engineer Robert Fine and Fairchild Recording. This method allows cutting the grooves farther apart when heavy bass notes are being recorded, and much closer together during, say, quiet piano passages with little bass. In this way maximum space on an LP can carry music, instead of unused "land" (the space between the grooves). Another way in which LP gets its long playing time is through the use of the microgroove, which has a width of less than two one-thousandths of an inch (needle is one mil radius maximum). This contrasts with the five- to six-thousandths of an inch of the old-fashioned 78 record (stylus tip about three mils).

In 1894 the cylinder *Graphophone*, which had a spring-driven motor, was advertised as reproducing music "as though the artists are present right in your living room." Today's advertisements for high fidelity instruments still say the same thing, though admittedly with somewhat more justification. Early commercial cylinders and flat vertical cut discs transmitted a frequency range of about 200-300 at the low end, up to perhaps 3,000 cycles at the high end. The giant steps toward realism, first of LP, and now of stereophonic recordings, much closer to complete reproduction of musical performances, carry frequencies from the lowest produced, say 30 cycles, to 18,000 and more, though many of us cannot hear the top end. Even today's cheapest "hi-fi" (which has become a synonym for the word "phonograph" to many people) is far ahead of the pre-electric Victrola of the 1920's.

The early jazz recordings were made using mechanical recording equipment which rather poorly captured most sounds between 200 and 3,000 cycles.

The reproducing equipment was capable of even less. At that time the rhythm section did not include a bass violin. Later when it had been added, replacing the tuba, and the bass drum had come into common use, they still were not used for recording sessions because the cutting stylus would have jumped the groove and ruined the recording. The reason is that in the system of cutting used then (and to this day) the greatest excursion of the cutting stylus is caused by low frequency and/or loud notes. Only after electrical recording became universal, in the later 1920's, was the bass drum heard in its rightful place in jazz recordings. Until then, when drums were recorded they were placed way back from the recording apparatus. When the ODJB made *Livery Stable Blues*, LaRocca, on trumpet, stood farthest from the pickup horn, some twenty feet back, with Larry Shields and his clarinet much closer.

This was changed in December, 1927, when Gene Krupa appeared in a Chicago recording studio with a bass drum for an Okeh recording of the McKenzie and Condon Chicagoans. On this historic session *Sugar* and *China Boy* were cut by Jimmy McPartland (trumpet), Teschmacher (clarinet), Bud Freeman (tenor), Joe Sullivan (piano), and Jim Lannigan (tuba and bass) with Condon (guitar) and Krupa. Since the Okeh engineers were using electrical recording equipment they were able to restrict the width of the swing made by the cutting needle on bass notes. In present playback systems we electronically expand the bass notes after they have been picked up by the playback needle. But at that time, since playback instruments continued to be largely the mechanical type (called, correctly, acoustical system), with an·acoustical horn driven by a small tin diaphragm in turn moved by the needle which was wiggled by the groove, the bass sound was pretty thin, when present at all. Before 1930 Brunswick brought out a large phonograph cabinet with an electrical (vacuum tube) amplifier, calling it the Brunswick Panatrope. But it cost over $350 and few people could afford it. Slowly other companies also brought out electrical playback instruments, but until RCA marketed an inexpensive player for attachment to any radio in 1934, acoustical phonographs were used in most homes.

This restricting of the swing of the cutting stylus by electrical means during recording, and restoring it during playback is called *bass equalization* in hi-fi and electronics. It is half of the story involved in the *equalization curves* which for several years have complicated hi-fi for mere music listeners. Happily the recording industry has standardized on one method of equalizing all recordings, called the RIAA curve, and most equipment is now readily set for that curve. The other part of equalization has to do with the high notes and is called *rolloff*, or *de-emphasis* (and in recording, *pre-emphasis*). It is a means for over-riding surface noise. The upper register contains all the *overtones*, also called *harmonics*, which lend richness and specific character (timbre, tone) to various instrumental sounds. The difference in the sound of a clarinet and a trumpet on the one hand, or a flute on the other, lies in the variety of overtones which each instrument produces in addition to the fundamental ones we hear, and which determine the nominal pitch of any musical note. Of these three the trumpet of course has the most harmonics; the flute the least. Since the better hi-fi system reproduces the high notes more faithfully, fully, and with the least possible *distortion* (or additions of its own), the characteristic sound of one hornman can be more easily distinguished from the sound of another, the better the hi-fi equipment.

Thus on the famous *Charlie Parker Story*, Savoy MG 12079, there are spots which may be either Dizzy Gillespie or Miles Davis, both of whom participated. Without good listening equipment it is difficult, if not impossible to tell, at times, which is which. Another recording of special interest, made on portable equipment in 1941 on location in night clubs is *The Harlem Jazz Scene* featuring Gillespie and Charlie Christian. This recording, Esoteric 548, is one of the most obviously *real* jam sessions on record, entirely apart from its musical significance. It is one of the few recordings of Christian away from the Goodman groups, with Dizzy and others beginning to work out the birth pangs of modern jazz, at that time still unrecognized by most of us.

By 1930 electrical recordings included frequencies as low as 100 or so cycles, which is near the second C down from middle C on the piano. (Middle C=440; one octave down=220; two octaves down=110 cycles per second.) There were few loud-speakers which would deliver below about 150-180 cycles. But in the treble any instrument could be at least partially recorded since the highest notes of piano, piccolo, etc., are usually sounded below 5,000 cycles. (High C, two octaves up from middle is 1,760 and C above C is only 3,520.)

Those recordings went up to about 6,000 cycles. But this left out the over-tones of much violin, trumpet, piano and other music. By 1934 the range on records extended from 30 cycles to about 8,000 or 9,000, and reproducing instruments, now electric, were improving all the time. The better radios of that time could play back the upper end of this range fairly well, though their response at the bottom still cut off usually at around 100. Phonograph pickups were beginning to get lighter, although the most popular in radio broadcast and studio work was a massive affair called the Brush-B-19 which put over five ounces on the tip of the replaceable steel needle.

Only Capehart made really top grade phonographs, and AM radio, with its technical limitations set the upper useful limit at 8,000 cycles anyway. FM radio, which would ultimately extend the radio sound spectrum to a good 15,000 cycles (and be used universally for the sound portion of TV programming) was still a novelty. It was to take many years to catch hold, due to an almost incredible series of misfortunes which included a war, one of the longest patent litigations in history, and the coming of age of an even more spectacular electronic marvel, television.

The jukebox caught on in time to help Benny Goodman capture the country in 1936, and set the taste of millions of people in dance music. A big seller was *The Music Goes Around and Around* played by the Reilly-Farley Combo, with over 100,000 copies sold; by 1939 Ella Fitzgerald's first big hit, Chick Webb's *A-Tisket, A-Tasket* passed 300,000 copies at 35 cents each.

Echo chambers were not in use yet, but some of the companies started using big halls for recording dance bands, finding that the added reverberation gave a "live" sound which listeners liked. This was one of the first steps on a long road towards aiding the illusion of reality. Multiple microphones began to be used more commonly. The frequency range of recordings was extended ever upwards, and by 1941, at the beginning of the war, was above 10,000 cycles. This was, of course, low compared to the fantastic sound that is on today's best stereophonic tapes, but nevertheless, it sounded good. The proof is easily found by listening to many of those records on today's equipment, which does them more justice than did playback systems of the early 1940's.

On August 1, 1942, the American Federation of Musicians went on a recording strike for the purpose of getting a larger share of the profits from recorded music, which James Petrillo saw as a threat to live music. There was a wartime limitation on shellac, so recorded jazz went under for the duration except for a lot of fine V-Discs made for the armed forces on vinylite records with the best of recording equipment. Few have come to light, however, in particularly playable shape! The recording ban ended when Decca signed back with AFM in 1943, followed by many smaller companies. By the end of the war, tape, with its enormous impact on recording, was just around the corner, having been developed by the Germans in the late '30s and early '40s. American firms were able to produce practical recording machines, and tape was here by 1948, the year the LP microgroove record broke.

Before tape there had been some interesting recording experiments, like the one-man-band record of Sidney Bechet on Victor 27485, in 1941. At this session the great soprano saxophonist played soprano, tenor, clarinet, piano, bass and drums. Each time he listened through headphones to what he had done before, via the disc recording his engineers had cut. The session was little more than a technical curiosity, however, though his *Sheik* and *Blues* were hardly dull. A more modern example of this technique may be found on Verve 8202, *Urbane*

Jazz, on which Roy Eldridge recorded a honky-tonk piano with drums backing him, then built a crackling trumpet solo over the resulting track, called *Wailin'*. For some reason Norman Granz passed up the opportunity to include Benny Carter who was present at this session. This could have resulted in something spectacular, for Benny is a good pianist and a fine trumpeter, in addition to his mastery of the alto. And Roy is a good drummer, though he merely plays around with the piano.

On a number of recent Armstrong records, notably Columbia CL 1020, *Jazz Omnibus*, and the Verve *Louis and Ella Again*, Louis vocalizes and then records again filling in horn obligatos and counter-melodies. Les Paul has probably carried this as far as it can go and still pretend to be jazz. He has done some amazing things through doubling (and even quadrupling) the speed of his tape recorder. Now Ampex has built for him a special tape recorder which can make up to eight tracks on one tape without dubbing, mix them in any proportions, and copy any or all of them again for additional mixes or dubs in any sequence or number.

Present-day recording techniques vary all the way from taking one microphone (two of course for stereo, which means almost all studio sessions nowadays) and hanging it high over a huge orchestra, to the other extreme of up to nine microphones for a trio. One philosophy behind the many-mike idea seems to be that each will pick up only the sound of one horn through being very close to it. Then the engineer puts them all together in the mixing console. This is believed by some to eliminate the acoustics of the recording room. Then the sound produced during playback in the listener's room is colored only by the acoustics of his playback situation—it is hoped. Other engineers, of the as-few-as-possible-mikes school, call the former method "telephone booth sound," because telephone booths are lined with acoustical absorbent material to eliminate reverberation. Despite the fact that we have engineers recording at both of these extremes, as well as in between, the worst of today's recordings are usually pretty good. The greatest deficiences today are usually found in the playback system.

Much of the superiority of today's recordings comes from almost thirty years of accumulated experience of electrical recording. More is due to the miracle of magnetic recording tape which not only has, if required, virtually unlimited frequency response (at the 30 inches per second which some purists among recording engineers still insist on, though most feel that 15 inches per second is adequate even for masters) but can be so easily edited, cut and patched. Much of this superiority is also due to the fine disc cutters now widely used, which with their cutting styli heated can approach, on wax masters, good tape. Most companies producing LP records today state that their discs carry everything from the lower limit of hearing to 18 or 20 kilocycles (20,000 cycles per second). Beyond this some even talk about 25 kilocycles (KC) or more, but it is almost academic at that point since the difference between 18 and 25 KC is something like four whole tones, or half an octave. In this range lie only extreme upper harmonics of musical tones.

The lower limit of human hearing is usually stated for convenience at 15 to 30 cycles per second (cps). Below that sounds seem to become individual vibrations, and often are felt rather than actually heard. The upper limit of hearing depends upon one's age and condition (some even claim upon sex—that women can hear higher notes than men!) and also of course on the altitude and strength of the notes. Most of us can hear to between 12 and 18 KC, though at age 60 we may drop off to 10 KC or lower. An easy test which anyone can administer may be taken by listening to a TV set with the sound volume off but the picture on, in a very quiet room. Every TV set (U.S. standard; 30 pictures, 525 lines) produces a high pitched note at exactly 15,750 cps, just under 16 KC, in its horizontal output circuit.

Reproducing equipment has steadily improved and has lately made more rapid gains perhaps than recording techniques. These improvements in playing systems have helped bring about improvements in the vinylite on which LPs are pressed. Today the quest for ever-increasing frequency range in hi-fi system components is abating somewhat, and progress is in system refinements such as smaller loudspeakers which produce as good or better bass than their larger predecessors.

Another step lies in the lowering of distortion contributed to the overall system by phonograph pickup cartridges and lowering the disc wear they produce through greater compliance and lower pressures. There has also been some simplification of the controls on hi-fi amplifiers due to the standardisation of recording equalization on the RIAA curve. Internal noise of the electronics has been lowered too, with more progress in this direction to come, through the use of transistorized circuitry. Most important of all, amplifiers and other components are now supplied so that mere musicians or music listeners can assemble them with only a screwdriver.

Record companies are getting louder passages on discs and tapes, all the while lowering the distortion content of the loud passages. Tape hiss and groove noise (scratch), vinylite pops and crackles are lowering so that there are wider dynamic ranges recorded between *pp* and *fff*. And most of us have learned to handle LPs by their edges, keep them in dust jackets, and to occasionally wipe them lightly with a damp cloth or anti-static preparation. Diamond needles are widely available, and widely used, of course.

Finally, the search for more playing time is bringing us recorded tapes at half-speed. This year it is a tape cartridge at $3\frac{3}{4}$ inches per second. This seems unlikely to displace $7\frac{1}{2}$ inch stereo tape for some time, for it cannot compete noisewise or frequencywise with $7\frac{1}{2}$, though it has other advantages. The first releases of slow speed LPs carrying jazz, at $16\frac{2}{3}$ RPM, have been sent out by Prestige Records, with more to come before long.

The big news of 1958 is stereo discs. It seems likely that these new records, which at this writing are just beginning to come from the companies, are the coming mass hi-fi medium. Only slightly more expensive than regular LPs, they look the same, and work very well indeed. Most companies are listing stereo discs at just one dollar more than regular LPs. There seems little doubt that most of the studio recordings made in the past couple of years, since they are available to the companies on master stereo tapes, will gradually be issued on stereo discs, in even greater profusion than the stereo tapes of the past two years. Within a year or two stereo installations will be the goal of most hi-fi music listeners and a great percentage will already have converted their hi-fi rigs to stereo. Monaural will more and more be used only for playing historical recordings and for simple communication. With this in mind we have listed below the basic facts regarding stereo playback equipment to aid those considering it in the near future.

Reproduction of stereophonic sound requires: (a) at least *two* separate signals picked up by at least *two* microphones; (b) a device for reproducing these *two* signals, either a stereo tape head or a stereo phono pickup cartridge; (c) *two* amplifiers, and (d) *two* separate loudspeakers. We have stereo tapes, stereo discs and stereo radio broadcasts. Unfortunately there is no standardization yet on the method of transmitting the two stereo radio signals, so most people will have to wait some time for that. There is no reason to wait on stereo tapes or discs, however. Claims by some manufacturers for devices that will "provide stereo sound from ordinary recordings" through the use of special added phase shifting, delay or reverberation devices just are not true, although these devices may in some cases provide slight increase in the illusion of reality.

Musicians are among the most avid hi-fi enthusiasts today, since interest in hi-fi usually stems from the desire to improve one's listening setup. Typical of this trend is the hi-fi system set up earlier this year by Louis Armstrong, which includes a record changer with a magnetic cartridge, tape recorder, amplifier, and two speakers, one remote in his bathroom. Gene Krupa installed an elaborate hi-fi system in his home several years ago, with an outdoor speaker for summer listening. Benny Goodman has progressed through a number of improvements in his excellent hi-fi setup. And Roy Eldridge is becoming a real hi-fi expert, having completely wired a 50 watt amplifier, designed and built an enclosure for his loudspeaker system; he was recently engaged in building a control room in his cellar from which to record music from his large basement room.

Many musicians ask, "Shall I buy hi-fi components or a packaged hi-fi set?" This is particularly important for those who are on the road a great deal. They tend naturally to select small portable phonographs, though they may prefer more elaborate setups at home, often with facilities for tape recording off the air and playback through extra speakers in various places through the house. Packaged sets are better than ever before, but by now almost everyone realizes that simply applying the adjective "hi-fi" to a small phonograph does not guarantee concert hall realism.

If cost is no object, a hi-fi system can easily be assembled which will have only two weak links in the reproducing chain. They are the phonograph pickup and the loudspeaker. The pickup is less an offender now than the loudspeaker, which is undergoing continual improvement. The new electrostatic loudspeakers which handle most frequencies above middle C (often called "tweeters") are surprisingly natural sounding, though still expensive. And numerous bass (woofer) speakers do well by the rhythm section. An especially noteworthy development of recent years is the acoustic suspension system developed by Acoustic Research, Inc. of Cambridge, Massachusetts, and emulated in varying degree by others.

True corner horn loudspeakers have been with us since Paul Klipsch made known his famous design in the 1940's. Variants of this can be built from plans by any carpenter or from kits by anyone who can use a screwdriver. The better ones provide extremely good bass response. Excellent amplifier kits rivalling the best finished units obtainable from the factories can be wired from scratch by anyone who can read and use simple hand tools. These kits are supplied complete with screws, wire, solder and thorough instructions.

Today a phonograph should have, if it is to be part of a high fidelity setup in the home, separate bass and treble controls, push-pull output, diamond stylus for LP records, and at least a heavy eight-inch speaker in a good baffle. This is minimal, and these details alone are no guarantee of concert hall sound. With stereo discs coming on the market most listeners will want sets which can have another speaker and amplifier added later for stereo playback.

There are scores of companies today issuing jazz records. Hundreds of labels have appeared and passed into oblivion since the mushrooming of the small companies in the late '30s and early '40s. In 1948 DeLaunay's *New Hot Discography* listed almost 300 jazz labels, all of them pre-LP. Hi-fi alone (of which LP is an important part) has not made this possible, but it has helped a lot. Custom pressing of discs by the large companies for the small ones has made it profitable, or at least potentially so, to cut a session and issue as few as 500 copies. If sold, fine, press more. If not, cut something else. In this way musicians who might otherwise not have been heard got their work around for other musicians, agents, critics and record buyers to hear.

One critic noted recently that he received 72 jazz LPs in one four-week period, not counting semi-jazz, half-pops, or 45 RPM discs. It has been conservatively estimated that records at least nominally qualifying as jazz on LP were issued at a rate between 1,000 and 2,000 a year in 1957 and early 1958! Fortunately there are strong indications that this is letting up. One major recording executive last week said that his company, a leader in the field who has been issuing six or seven discs every month, is cutting back to one or two jazz LPs for the foreseeable future. And there is the prospect of another recording ban by the American Federation of Music when the ten year old contract between the Musicians' Union and the record companies expires in December 1958. Perhaps that will solve some of the problems of the flood of jazz on LPs.

CHRONOLOGY OF PHONOGRAPH RECORDING

1877 Edison's tin-foil cylinder "phonograph" invented—hand cranked.

1885 Bell & Tainter patent wax cylinder "graphophone."

1887 Berliner invents lateral-cut flat disc "gramophone."

1890 Cylinder phonographs in public places; nickel-play a la jukebox. First commercial cylinders on sale. (Vertical-cut; play two minutes.)

1894 Berliner starts producing Gramophones and hard rubber discs. Pathe Bros. in France ditto cylinders. (Until now all machines hand-cranked).

1896 Eldridge Johnson, later head of Victor Talking Machine Co., develops a spring motor for players.

1897 Shellac introduced in place of hard rubber for discs.

1899 Poulsen (Denmark) invents rudimentary magnetic recording.

1902 Caruso and others start recording.

1906 Victor markets horn-enclosed phonograph. Pathe switches from cylinders to discs. (Mechanical recording now about 200-3,000 cycles.)

1908 Edison tries a four-minute cylinder (previously only 2 minutes).

1912 Columbia switches from cylinders to discs.

1913 Odeon (Germany) issues first symphonies; Edison starts producing vertical-cut discs. (Continues with cylinders.)

1917 Original Dixieland Jass Band makes first jazz record.

1925 Beginning of electrical recording (electronic); about 100-5,000 cycles. Playback machines still mechanical. Soon to start switching to electrical.

1926 RCA releases first electrical recording.

1926 All companies switch from vertical cutting to lateral (present-day) cut.

1929 RCA converts Victor phonograph plant to radio production; Edison goes out of phonograph and record business.

1934 Decca (U.S.) formed—35 cent label with Glen Gray, Crosby, Fletcher Henderson, Louis and other first rank artists to compete with other 75 cent labels. RCA brings out inexpensive player attachment for radios. People start throwing out mechanical phonographs.

1940 Columbia cuts Red Seal prices from $2.00 to $1.00. RCA follows suit soon. Germany produces high quality broadcast tape recorders.

1942 AFM recording ban.

1947 Magnetic tape recording starts in U.S.A.

1948 Columbia introduces 33 RPM, long playing microgroove disc. Second AFM recording ban.

1949 RCA ditto 45 RPM disc.

1950 High-fidelity starts to spread—assembling of heavy amplifiers, large loud-speakers for use in home listening.

1954 Stereo taping of most studio recording sessions starts.

1956 Stereo tape for home use.

1958 Stereo discs introduced commercially for home use.

1959 Stereo disc and tape playing equipment widely manufactured and sold.

WHERE TO FIND JAZZ ON STEREOPHONIC TAPES

The following companies have issued jazz on stereophonic tapes :

Bel Canto, 2919 S. LaCienega Blvd., Culver City, Cal.

Capitol Records, Hollywood & Vine, Hollywood, Cal.

Columbia Records, 799 Seventh Ave., New York 19, N.Y.

Concert Hall Society, 71 Fifth Ave., New York 3, N.Y.

Counterpoint Records, 333 Sixth Ave., New York 14, N.Y.

Fantasy, 654 Natoma St., San Francisco.

Manhattan Recording Corp., 1650 Broadway, New York 19, N.Y.

Mercury Records, 35 E. Wacker Drive, Chicago 1, Ill.

Livingston Tape Library, Box 202 Caldwell, N.J.

Riverside Records, 553 W. 51st St., New York 19, N.Y.

Stereo Age Recordings, Box 144, Upper Montclair, N.J.

Urania Records, 233 Main St., Belleville, N.J.

Verve Records, 451 N. Canon Drive, Beverly Hills, Calif.

Vanguard Recording Society, 256 West 55th St., New York 19, N.Y.

New Faces. Yusef Lateef (*Austin Chevou*).

Top left: New Faces. Charles Baird Parker, age 5.

Top right: New Faces. Sonny Rollins.

Cootie Williams at W. C. Handy's casket (*James C. Campbell*).

Above: Leonard Feather, W. C. Handy, Dizzy Gillespie, Mrs. Handy, at Handy's 84th birthday banquet given by ASCAP at the Waldorf-Astoria, Nov. 1957 (*Cecil Layne*).

Left: Tommy Dorsey and his vocalist Frank Sinatra, 1941.

Left: Jimmy Dorsey (*Decca Record Co.*).

Below: Art Tatum.

Above: 'The Four Brothers' of Woody Herman's 1948 band, reunited on Serge Chaloff's final record session, Vik Records, Feb. 1957: Herbie Steward, Al Cohn, Zoot Sims, Serge Chaloff.

Bottom left: Ernie Henry (*Lawrence*).

Bottom right: Jazz on British TV. Johnny Dankworth and Sarah Vaughan (*Associated-Rediffusion Ltd.*).

Above: Jazz on British TV. The Steve Race Five. Steve Race (piano), Terry Walsh (guitar), Roy Davey (vibes), Frank Clarke (bass), Geoff Lofts (drums) (*Teddy Fader*).

Opposite: Jazz on British TV. Ted Heath and his Music. (In the Commercial Television series, *The Ted Heath Story*) (*Associated-Rediffusion Ltd.*).

Jazz on British TV. Humphrey Lyttelton and his Band.
(Alto Sax: Bruce Turner) (*Associated-Rediffusion Ltd.*).

NEW FACES,
NEW HORIZONS

*T*he only constant factor observable in jazz at all times is its inconstancy. Perhaps because of the rapidity of its artistic evolution, possibly because of the fickleness and ceaseless turnover among its supporters, the new idols of musicians, fans and critics rise to fame suddenly and the old depart sometimes with alarming haste.

A telescopic and significant view of these shifting sands could be found in the results of the Sixth Annual *Down Beat* International Poll of Jazz Critics, announced in August 1958. Miles Davis took over Gillespie's chair as the critics' first choice on trumpet; Duke Ellington replaced Count Basie in the big band category; Thelonious Monk replaced Erroll Garner in the piano voting; Ray Brown usurped Oscar Pettiford's bass crown; Freddie Green was the No. 1 guitarist instead of Tal Farlow; and a jazz singer, Jimmy Rushing, replaced a pop singer, Frank Sinatra, as the preferred male vocalist.

The remainder of the winning categories found the leading occupants unchanged: the Modern Jazz Quartet for No. 1 combo, Jay Jay Johnson on trombone, Lee Konitz on alto saxophone, Gerry Mulligan on baritone, Stan Getz on tenor, Tony Scott on clarinet, Max Roach on drums, Milt Jackson on vibes and Ella Fitzgerald as female vocalist. But in the "New Stars" section of the voting, where previous winners are ineligible, the results offered a valuable indication of the areas in which jazz is drawing its most important new talent. As will be seen in the listings below, the results implied that the critics are tending toward the more extrovert school of jazz in their choices for most instruments, though their concurrent acceptance of softer and oblique statement is to be observed in a few selections.

In order fully to illustrate the paths of preference followed by the experts through the years, the following listings have been arranged so that the progress of the critics' polls can be seen chronologically, instrument by instrument. The first poll was conducted in 1953. Starting in 1957, no musician was declared a winner unless he received a total of five votes (including split votes *pro rata*).

On trumpet: Chet Baker won in 1953, the late Clifford Brown in 1954, Ruby Braff in 1955, Thad Jones in 1956, Donald Byrd in 1957 and Art Farmer in 1958.

On trombone: Bob Brookmeyer, Carl Fontana and Frank Rosolino tied for first place in 1953, Urbie Green won in 1954, Jimmy Cleveland in 1955, Benny Powell in 1956, Frank Rehak in 1957 and Jimmy Knepper in 1958.

On alto saxophone: the winners were Paul Desmond, 1953; Bud Shank, 1954; Herb Geller, 1955; Phil Woods, 1956; Art Pepper, 1957; the 1958 voting was declared no contest, as no musician received the required minimum number of votes.

On tenor saxophone: Paul Quinichette, 1953; Frank Wess, 1954; Bill Perkins, 1955; Bobby Jaspar, 1956; Sonny Rollins, 1957; Benny Golson, 1958.

On baritone saxophone: Gerry Mulligan, 1953; Lars Gullin, 1954; the late Bob Gordon, 1955; Jimmy Giuffre, 1956; Pepper Adams, 1957; Tony Scott, 1958.

On clarinet: Tony Scott, 1953; Sam Most, 1954; Jimmy Giuffre, 1955; Buddy Collette, 1956; no contest, 1957 and 1958.

On piano: Billy Taylor, 1953; Horace Silver, 1954; Randy Weston, 1955; Hampton Hawes, 1956; Eddie Costa, 1957; Bill Evans, 1958.

On guitar: Johnny Smith, 1953; Tal Farlow, 1954; Howard Roberts, 1955; Dick Garcia, 1956; Kenny Burrell, 1957; Jim Hall, 1958.

On bass: Charlie Mingus and Red Mitchell tied in 1953; Percy Heath, 1954; Wendell Marshall, 1955; Paul Chambers, 1956; Leroy Vinnegar, 1957; Wilbur Ware, 1958.

On drums: Art Blakey, 1953; Osie Johnson, 1954; Joe Morello, 1955; Chico Hamilton, 1956; Philly Joe Jones, 1957; no contest, 1958.

On vibes: no category in 1953; Teddy Charles in 1954; Cal Tjader, 1955; Terry Pollard, 1956; Eddie Costa, 1957; Victor Feldman, 1958.

Male vocalist: Jackie Paris, 1953; Clancy Hayes, 1954; Joe Williams, 1955; Joe Turner, 1956; no contest, 1957; Ray Charles, 1958.

Female vocalist: Annie Ross and Jeri Southern tied, 1953; Carmen McRae, 1954; Teddi King, 1955; Barbara Lea, 1956; no contest, 1957 and 1958.

Out of a total of more than seventy musicians who thus earned the right to call themselves *Down Beat* poll winners, about fifteen have lapsed into comparative obscurity, or have (in the vocal categories) departed from the field of jazz; two have died; the rest may be considered to be at least as well known as when they won, but more often than not, as should be the case, are now considerably more prominent and are enjoying fairly substantial success working strictly within jazz.

It is important that jazz has proven itself capable, in recent years, of providing enough outlets for these new talents and of enabling them to hold on firmly to the acclaim accorded them by the critics. It can safely be predicted that on looking over the above lists in 1970, the jazz fan will be able to find a healthy percentage of names that will still be familiar, and in some instances world-famous.

It will be observed that, despite the international nature of the poll, only three foreign-born instrumentalists were elected during the first six years of balloting: Lars Gullin on baritone sax in 1954, Bobby Jaspar on tenor saxophone in 1956 and Victor Feldman on vibes in 1958. (Gullin has never been to this country; Jaspar and Feldman have been U.S. residents in recent years.) Nevertheless, there has been an accelerating awareness, among fans and critics as well as musicians, of the contributions now being made to jazz by performers who have learned all they know of it either through the careful study of records imported from America, through personal contact with visiting U.S. musicians, or a combination of both allied with general music studies.

The interest in foreign jazzmen reached a peak in July 1958 with the appearance at the Newport Jazz Festival of the International Band assembled by Marshall Brown and mentioned briefly in an earlier chapter.

BAND OF THE YEAR:
THE NEWPORT INTERNATIONAL BAND

The two most remarkable events in jazz during the period covered by this volume (summer, 1956 to summer, 1958) both were the work of the same man, a musician and educator named Marshall Brown. Both involved the creation of a large orchestra, each unique in concept, and both were presented at the Newport Jazz Festival.

In 1957 Brown managed to *épater* the musical *bourgeois* by producing an 18-piece jazz band composed of boys and girls in their middle teens, from a high school at Farmingdale, Long Island, near New York City. In 1958, after a tour of eighteen countries made jointly with Newport producer George Wein, he assembled a band in which each member came from a different country. The important difference between these two bands was that in the second all were experienced adult musicians. The Farmingdale band was an academic triumph, demonstrating Brown's ability to whip a bunch of youngsters into presentable shape; by high school standards they were admirable, but judged subjectively (as was shown by the use of their records in blindfold tests) their work naturally could not be ranked with that of a professional band. It is an ironic reflection on the tortuous psychology underlying music criticism that while the Farmingdale band earned unanimous panegyrics in the press, the International Band, which in terms of intrinsic esthetic merit and completely subjective musical reaction was beyond the slightest doubt immeasurably superior, met with qualified endorsements and carping criticisms from most of the same experts.

Most of the writers' reservations involved the music written for the band. Yet Brown had sought out such highly individual composers as Bill Russo, John LaPorta, Jimmy Giuffre, Adolphe Sandole and the Belgian Jack Sels, and with their work, augmented by a jump blues from Brown's own pen, the band had a broad canvas of material on which to demonstrate its teamwork and solo talents. The works performed at Newport ranged all the way from Brown's *Don't Wait for Henry* and LaPorta's bristling treatments of *Perdido* and *Swingin' The Blues* to an extended three-part composition by Giuffre, *The Pentatonic Man*.

The fact is that the International Band proved exactly what its originators set out to prove; indeed, it did better than that, turning in a performance superior by far to that given at Newport by a band of American musicians of far broader experience, presented under the directorship of a man who had been a leader for twenty-four years, Benny Goodman.

The story of the birth and short life of the Newport band is extraordinary enough to deserve permanent documentation in the annals of jazz. Marshall Brown, writing of it in the festival program, stated: "The idea of creating an international youth jazz band had been in George Wein's mind for some time before I was elected to the Newport Jazz Festival board of trustees. The idea was to dramatize that music in general, and American jazz in particular, is an international language."

Brown sat down with Louis Lorillard, president of the Festival, and pored over a map of Europe. It was decided to explore countries on either side of the Iron Curtain. (This led to only one disappointment: at the last minute the Czech musician selected was refused a visa to leave his country.) A $30,000 budget was allocated out of the Newport funds to enable Brown and Wein to make their tour, bring the men over, lodge and rehearse them.

Then, says Brown, "We contacted scouts in each country to start sifting through their jazz musicians in preparation for auditions. Among the scouts were editors, critics, recording executives, impresarios . . . We set up an itinerary that allowed us two or three days in each country . . . Our auditions were greeted with tremendous press, radio and TV coverage."

Being an old schoolmaster, Brown added, he carried report cards with him, and by the time he returned home he had dossiers on some 700 musicians— solo talent, reading ability, appearance, deportment, every relevant qualification. "I switched back and forth . . . my report cards spread out in front of me, along with a score, and tried to sing to myself how this alto man would play this part and whether we would be stronger with an Austrian or a Spaniard playing lead alto."

When he had the band set in his mind, Brown convoked the men to a meeting in Paris, June 12, and brought them to New York for ten days of rehearsal, sightseeing and socializing with American jazzmen.

While in the United States, in addition to playing twice at Newport (the matinee on July 4 and the evening session on July 6), they made TV appearances on the Arthur Godfrey and Bob Crosby shows. Two weeks after the festival they left for Europe, playing in Amsterdam, July 27, and at the Brussels World's Fair, July 29, through to August 3. Soon after, they had to disperse to their various jobs and countries, but in their few weeks together they had accomplished more for jazz than most orchestras could hope to achieve in a lifetime.

Before they left the United States I asked the members of the band (excepting two who were already U.S. residents) a couple of questions concerning their reactions to the visit.

1. What music has excited or impressed you most during your visit to the U.S.?

In answering this question the musicians tried to limit their choice to one musician, but most were impelled to name two, three or even four. The musician mentioned most frequently was Thelonious Monk, named by seven of those who had heard him at Newport. Ellington was named five times, as was Miles Davis; the Maynard Ferguson band was the selection of two trumpeters (Palle Bolvig, Jose Magalhaes) and a saxophonist (Hans Solomon). Mentioned twice each were the organist Jimmy Smith, whom Dusko Gojkovic and Rudolf Jacobs heard one night at Smalls in New York; and Gerry Mulligan, selected by fellow-baritonist Ronnie Ross and by Solomon. Mahalia Jackson was the sole choice of trombonist Kurt Jaernberg and was also mentioned by Vlady.

Mentioned once each were Johnny Griffin, whose tenor was cited by Albert Mangelsdorff; Art Blakey, whose group excited Erich Kleinschuster; Ram Ramirez, the organist, heard by Christian Kellens at Smalls in New York; Louis Armstrong, whose work at Newport impressed Hans Solomon; Dave Brubeck, selected (along with Miles Davis) by Jan Wroblewski; and Art Farmer, the other choice of Ronnie Ross.

In examining these choices one must bear in mind that during almost a month in this country the musicians had an opportunity to hear a large proportion of America's leading jazz soloists, bands and combos, either at Newport or in New York. Clearly, their enthusiasms stretched beyond the area of their own strictly modern solo styles.

2. Who in your opinion is the greatest living jazz artist?

With understandable diffidence, the European musicians limited their choices to one apiece. The results were as follows:

Louis Armstrong	4
Duke Ellington	3
Count Basie	3
Bud Powell	2
Lester Young	2
Thelonious Monk	1
Sonny Rollins	1

Aware that the Charlie Parker spirit was strong in the band, I asked whether any of the musicians would have preferred to name Bird had the word "living" been excluded from the question. Ten men raised their hands.

3. Would you like some day to come to the United States to live?

The answers in several cases were arrived at after a prolonged pause for thought. Following were the results:

Yes …	…	…	…	2
Qualified yes…	…	…	6
No …	…	…	…	6
Don't know …	…	…	2

The only outright affirmatives came from Gojkovic and Vlady. The qualified-yes replies included "for a short time only" (three), "to study but not to live" (one) and "yes, but not as a musician" (two).

With the answers to this question the illusion that every foreign jazzman yearns eventually to settle in America was effectively destroyed. The majority are aware of the innumerable problems—economic, social, racial, professional, psychological—that might be an inevitable concomitant of a life spent in the homeland of their musical idols.

Biographical details of the men involved in the memorable mission to Newport are appended below. In the next revised edition of the complete *Encyclopedia of Jazz* they will be included in the main body of the biographical text, since their places in jazz seem permanently assured.

BROWN, Marshall Richard, *leader, composer-arranger, educator, valve trombone*; b. Framingham, Mass., 12/21/20. Father a vaudeville magician; mother pl. piano in silent movies. Pl. guitar at nine, valve trombone at 16, self-taught. BS *cum laude* in mus. at NYU, 1949; MA at Col. U. '53. Org. own band while in high sch. '37. While in Army '42-5, pl. and arr. w. Bernie Leighton. Staff arr. at Adirondacks summer hotel '49; band dir., East Rockaway High Sch. '49-51; Farmingdale High Sch. '51-7. Org. & dir. Farmingdale band, heard at NJF '57; International Band, NJF '58.

Brown has enjoyed great success as a pop. songwriter, his hits incl. *Seven Lonely Days, The Banjo's Back In Town* and a big success in France, *Tout au Bout de la Semaine*. He wrote the score for a U.S. Steel Hour music drama in '56. Named "outstanding educator of the year" by Westlake Coll. of Mus. '57. Brown's main infl., he says, were Charlie Parker in jazz, John Dewey in education.

Addr: 103 East 86th St., New York 28, N.Y.

BOLVIG, Palle S. P., *trumpet, arranger*; b. Copenhagen, Denmark, 11/25/32. Formal training, 1949-51; since '51 has been w. Ib Glindemann Orch. as lead trumpet & arr. Was in staff orch. for *Hidden Fear*, John Payne movie filmed in Copenhagen. Fav: Maynard Ferguson. Fav. arr: Bill Holman.

Addr: Vermundsgade 10, Copenhagen.

CUPPINI, Gilberto, *drums*; b. Milan, Italy, 6/6/24. Stud. piano, harmony from 1939; medicine, surgery at U. of Milan. Took up drums '46; prof. debut '47 in Switzerland. Pl. w. Hazy Osterwald around Europe '49; Gorni Kramer '50; own group at Taverna Mexico, Milan '55; on radio-TV Italiana '56; was w. Armando Trovajoli's big band '57. Has pl. annually at San Remo jazz festival and has made hundreds of Italian jazz records w. own and other combos. Fav. mus: Ellington, Parker, Roach, M. Davis, Mulligan.

Addr: 43 Viale Piave, Milan.

GOJKOVIC, Dusan "Dusko," *trumpet*; b. Jajce, Yugoslavia, 10/14/31. Stud. at mus. sch. in Belgrade '48-53; pl. w. Radio Belgrade dance orch. '51-5. To Germany: rec., concerts, tours w. German All-Stars; named by critics as best of year at '56 Frankfurt Jazz Festival. Since Apr. '57 w. Kurt Edelhagen band at Radio Cologne. Worked briefly w. Chet Baker in Storyville Club in Frankfurt. Has made movies w. Caterina Valente and Edelhagen. Favs: Gillespie, Armstrong, M. Davis, Clifford Brown, Eldridge.

Addr: Maybachstr. 28, Cologne, Germany.

GRUNTZ, George, *piano*; b. Basel, Switzerland, 6/24/32. Stud. at conservatory in Zurich at 14. Won several first prizes at Swiss amateur jazz festivals. Pl. for 6 months in Scandinavia; back home, had to make living as auto salesman, but since '56 has been doubling as pianist & arr. on Basel radio. Seen at San Remo Jazz Festival annually since '56. Favs: Tatum, Bud Powell, H. Silver.

Addr: Amerikanerstr. 16, Basel-Binningen, Switzerland.

GUERIN, Roger, *trumpet*; b. Sarrebruck, Saar, France, 1/9/26. Stud. vln. 8 yrs., tpt. 12 yrs.; first prize tpt. and cornet at Paris Cons. Prof. debut w. Aimé Barelli band, 1947. Pl. w. Don Byas and Django Reinhardt combos '51; Michel LeGrand band '56; also pl. and rec. w. James Moody, Bernard Peiffer, Christian Chevallier, Fats Sadi, Jimmy Raney, B. Jaspar, Kenny Clarke, Lucky Thompson; sang for a year w. Blossom Dearie's Blue Stars. Heard on *The Paris Scene* w. André Hodeir (Savoy). First place on tpt. in *Jazz Hot* poll for three years. Fav: Armstrong.

Addr: Ruelle du Clos, Beynes, Seine-et-Oise, France.

JACOBS, Rudolf, *bass*; b. Hilversum, Holland, 5/3/38. Also plays tenor, clar., piano. St. on alto at 16; soon after bought bass, stud. for 6 months, pl. in trio w. brother on piano. Concerts in Amsterdam w. Herbie Mann, Tony Scott, Bud Shank, Bob Cooper, Lucky Thompson. Does regular radio-TV work w. Rita Reyes; rec. w. H. Mann, Wes Ilcken. Favs: Blanton, Pettiford; also Charlie Parker, Bud Powell.

Addr: Wernerlaan 22, Hilversum, Holland.

JAERNBERG, Kurt, *valve and slide trombone*; b. Gävle, Sweden, 6/8/32. Father, brother pl. tpt. Started as Army musician, 1946. Pl. in big band at dance hall, the Tivoli in Copenhagen '54. Rec. w. Lars Gullin, Goesta Theselius, Eric Moseholm. Pl. w. Ib Glindemann band, Copenhagen, June '56-Dec. '57. Scholarship to Berklee Sch. in Boston from Sept. '58. Biggest ambition is to compose, arrange and play w. Count Basie and Bill Harris. Favs: Bill Harris; also Fats Navarro, Lee Konitz.

Addr: Box 3605, Gävle, Sweden.

KELLENS, Christian, *trombone*; b. Andenne, Belgium, 1/18/25. St. on harmonica; tbn. self-taught from 1944. Prof. debut w. Fats Sadi. Has pl. w. many bands in Belgium (Franz Lebrun, Jack Sels, the Bob Shots *et al.*); Germany (Kurt Edelhagen); France (Jack Diéval, Henri Renaud, Tony Proteau, Martial Solal); Holland and Scandinavia. Pl. bass tbn. w. Christian Chevallier, euphonium w. Fred Bunge. Has rec. w. most of these groups. Foreign languages are his hobby; he once quit music for four years to work as an interpreter. Fav. mus: Armstrong, Ellington, Basie.

Addr: 2 Boulevard Cauchy, Namur, Belgium.

KLEINSCHUSTER, Erich, *trombone*; b. Graz, Austria, 1/23/30. Stud. piano, 1946, and tbn. '53 at Cons. in Graz. Prof. debut in radio dance band; featured since 1954 in Kleiner Tanzorchester von Radio Graz. Not a full-time musician, he is a lawyer by profession. Favs: Brookmeyer, Jay Jay Johnson.

Addr: Schoeckelbachweg 39, Graz.

MAGALHAES, Jose Manuel, *trumpet*; b. Lisbon, Portugal, 1/31/29. First pl. Fr. horn. Worked in Navy band, 1946-52, playing trumpet and tympani. Two years w. symphony orch. on tympani to '54; for several years has been in tpt. section of band at national radio station, also leading dance band w. three of his brothers playing trumpet, saxes and bass. Fav. mus: Basie, Ellington, M. Ferguson, Armstrong, Gillespie.

Addr: Rua Candido Figueiredo 70-2, Lisbon.

MANGELSDORFF, Albert, *trombone*; b. Frankfurt am Main, Germany, 9/5/28. Brother Emil is well known alto man. Vln. from age 12, then guitar w. local bands. Started on tbn., 1951, w. Joe Klimm, later working w. Hans Koller, Jutta Hipp and several combos of his own. More recently has been w. Frankfurt All-Stars, Joki Freund Quintet, and led own band on Frankfurt radio station. Has won German *Jazz Echo* poll every year since 1954. LPs available in U.S. incl. *Dass Ist Jazz!* (Decca), *Cool Europe* w. Jutta Hipp (MGM), Hans Koller (World-Pacific), Joki Freund (Jazztone). Made movie, *Jazz Gestern und Heute*, w. Hans Koller, 1953. Fav. mus: Jay Jay Johnson, Miles Davis.

Addr: 6 JM Sachsenlager, Frankfurt am Main.

MARSALA, Andrew, *alto sax, clarinet, flute, oboe*; b. Brooklyn, N.Y., 6/30/42. Stud. clar. at 9; alto w.

Marshall Brown at 12; later arr. & comp. w. John La Porta. Marsala, who is not related to veteran jazz clarinetist Joe Marsala, scored the major sensation at NJF in '57 as member of Marshall Brown's Farmingdale High School Band, appearing there again the following year as extra attraction w. Newport International Band. The Farmingdale band made three LPs, circulated privately but not released to the public. Favs: Charlie Parker, Paul Desmond.

Addr: 3 Chapin Road, Farmingdale, N.Y.

ROSENGREN, Bernt Aake, *tenor saxophone*; b. Stockholm, Sweden, 12/24/37. Accordion at 10, tenor at 15. Since early 1957 has toured and rec. w. combo known as Jazz Club '57. Stud. harmony for 2 years and has written arrangements. Fav: Charlie Parker.

Addr: Skansbergsvägen 31, Segeltorp, Sweden.

ROSS, Ronald, *baritone saxophone*; b. Calcutta, India, 10/2/33. To England at 12. Clar. in Grenadier Guards Band, 1951; later toured w. Don Rendell sextet, incl. jazz festivals at San Remo and Lyons. Many rec. w. Ken Moule, Ted Heath, Don Rendell, Tony Crombie, Tony Kinsey, Annie Ross, Engl. Decca; while in Stuttgart, Germany, made session w. John Lewis and a symphony orch., Feb. 1958, for RCA Victor release in U.S. Favs: Lester Young, Gerry Mulligan.

Addr: 234 Crofton Road, Orpington, Kent, England.

SOLOMON, Johann "Hans," *tenor and alto saxes, clarinet*; b. Vienna, Austria, 9/10/33. Stud. clar. w. Hans Koller, Karl Kowarik, then played in American-sponsored youth club in Vienna. Later pl. w. Dr. Roland Kovacs, Friedrich Gulda; guest soloist w. Lionel Hampton at concert, 1954; also jammed w. many visiting U.S. jazzmen. Feat. in concert of modern music w. Vienna Symphoniker, 1958. Won poll on alto in German magazine *Podium* for past 3 years. Rec. w. Hans Koller, Johannes Fehring. Sound tracks for many Austrian movies; 12 jazz shows w. Gulda for Vienna Radio; several TV shows in Vienna, one w. Johnnie Ray. Fav. mus: Konitz, Parker, Getz, Mulligan, Davis.

Addr: Vienna 9, Sechsschimmelgasse 4/19, Austria.

SZABO, Gabor I., *guitar*; b. Budapest, Hungary, 3/8/36. Guitar at 15; stud. only 3 months. Learned jazz via Voice of America; developed own fingering technique. Rec. w. many local groups, backed singers, did radio, movie sound tracks; cut a tape for Voice of America that was broadcast the night he left Hungary, 11/22/56. A Freedom Fighter, he arrived in U.S. as a refugee and was at Camp Killmer before settling in Boston, where he has been studying at the Berklee School, app. on TV w. Toshiko. Favs: J. Smith, T. Farlow, S. Salvador.

Addr: c/o Berklee School, 284 Newbury St., Boston, Mass.

VLADY (Wladimiro Bas Zabache), *alto sax*; b. Bilbao, Spain, 2/2/29. Stud. w. father, who plays viola in symphony, saxophone in dance bands. Extensive studies at Bilboa Cons., until economic difficulties forced him to start making living as jazzman and dance band musician. Moving to Madrid, pl. in leading hotels, clubs and in jam sessions w. drummer Jose Farreras and other top Spanish jazzmen. Many commercial rec. w. Rafael Cardona, Blue Stars of Madrid, Perez Prado *et al.*; TV in Bilbao and Madrid. Zabache is known professionally by the single name Vlady. Fav. mus: J. S. Bach, Ellington, Basie, Kenton, Mulligan, Tristano, Konitz.
Addr: Virgen de Africa 6, Madrid.

WROBLEWSKI, Ptaszyn "Jan," *tenor sax*; b. Kalisz, Poland, 3/27/36. St. on piano, then clarinet, baritone, tenor. Had own student dance group, 1954; bari., clar. w. Sekstet Komedy '56-7, then tenor & arr. w. Jazz Believers. Former group pl. jazz festivals at Sopot, Poland, and at world youth festival, Aug. '57, in Moscow, where he rec. silver award. Has broadcast often on Warsaw radio since '56; TV in Lodz, Poznan, Warsaw, Katowice. Wroblewski, who had to make all his contacts w. jazz via radio, says he prefers working in small combos but cannot find in Poland the kind of musicians he would like to work with. Favs: Getz, Z. Sims, B. Perkins; overall fav. mus: Miles Davis.
Addr: Pukaskiego 1, Kalisz, Poland.

These are the men who, in the summer of 1958, added a brief but memorable chapter to jazz history. Though most of them returned to comparative obscurity after the spotlights of Newport and Brussels had faded, it seemed probable that the unique honor of having taken part in the venture would prove to be of durable value to the members of the International Band long after their short, fast weeks of transatlantic glory.

The work of the orchestra at Newport has been preserved on a Columbia LP. The record will serve as a pleasant and constructive reminder not only of the immeasurable value of music as a common language and source of mutual understanding among peoples of starkly different backgrounds, but also of the phenomenal strides made in the past few years in the propagation and sensitive interpretation of our native art form. American jazz is American jazz no longer; today it is a music of the world.

JAZZ ORGANIZATIONS, SCHOOLS and RECORD COMPANIES

THE INSTITUTE OF JAZZ STUDIES
Marshall W. Stearns, Exec. Dir., 108 Waverly Place, New York 11, New York.

JAZZ INTERNATIONAL
Howard Lucraft, P.O. Box 1616, Hollywood 28, Calif.

NATIONAL JAZZ FRATERNITY
Dave Martindale, 40 E. 40th Street, New York 16, New York.

GREAT SOUTH BAY JAZZ FESTIVAL
Fran Thorne, 39 E. 79th Street, New York 21, New York.

NEWPORT JAZZ FESTIVAL INC.
Louis L. Lorillard, Newport, Rhode Island.

BERKLEE SCHOOL OF MUSIC
Lawrence Berk, 284 Newbury Street, Boston 15, Massachusetts.

SCHOOL OF JAZZ
Jule Foster, Dean, Room 1510, 270 Madison Avenue, New York 17, New York.

WESTLAKE COLLEGE OF MUSIC
7190 Sunset Boulevard, Hollywood 46, California.

RECORD COMPANIES

ABC-Paramount, 1501 Broadway, New York, N.Y.
Ad-Lib, 20-43 19th St., Long Island City, N.Y.
Aladdin, 451 N. Canyon Drive, Beverly Hills, Calif.
Allegro, 510 22nd St., Union City, N.J.
American Music, 600 Chartres St., New Orleans, La.
American Recording Society, 100 6th Ave., New York, N.Y.
Andex, c/o Rex Productions, 847 Higuera Rd., Culver City, Calif.
Angel, 38 W. 48th St., New York 36, N.Y.
Apollo, 457 W. 45th St., New York 36, N.Y.
Argo, 4750 Cottage Grove Ave., Chicago, Ill.
Atlantic, 157 W. 57th St., New York, N.Y.
Atco, see Atlantic.
Audiophile, Saukville, Wisc.
Audio Fidelity, 770 11th Ave., New York 19, N.Y.
Baton, 108 W. 44th St., New York, N.Y.
Bethlehem, 1650 Broadway, New York 19, N.Y.
Blue Note, 47 W. 63rd St., New York 23, N.Y.
Brunswick, 50 W. 57th St., New York 19, N.Y.
Cadence, 119 W. 57th St., New York, N.Y.
Camden, see RCA Victor.
Capitol, Sunset and Vine, Hollywood 28, Calif.
Cavalier, 298 9th St., San Francisco, Calif.
Chess, see Argo.
Checker, see Argo.
Columbia, 799 7th Ave., New York 19, N.Y.
Commodore, 147 E. 42nd St., New York 17, N.Y.

Contemporary, 8481 Melrose Pl., Los Angeles 46, Calif.
Cook, 101 2nd St., Stamford, Conn.
Coral, 50 W. 57th St., New York 19, N.Y.
Counterpoint, 333 6th Ave., New York 14, N.Y.
Criterion, 1491 Vine St., Hollywood, Calif.
Crown, see Modern.
Dawn, 39 W. 60th St., New York 14, N.Y.
Debut, 331 W. 51st St., New York, N.Y.
Decca, 50 W. 57th St., New York 19, N.Y.
Delmar, 5663 Delmar Ave., St. Louis, Mo.
Design, 33 34th St., Brooklyn 32, N.Y.
Dig, 2180 W. Washington Blvd., Los Angeles, Calif.
Dixieland Jubilee, see GNP.
Dooto, 9512 S. Central Ave., Los Angeles 2, Calif.
Dot, 157 W. 57th St., New York, N.Y.
East-West, see Atlantic.
Elektra, 361 Bleecker St., N.Y.C.
EmArcy, 745 5th Ave., New York 22, N.Y.
Empirical, P.O. Box 52, Yellow Springs, Ohio.
Epic, see Columbia.
Esoteric, see Counterpoint.
Euterpean, 506 S. Coast Blvd., Laguna Beach, Calif.
Fantasy, 654 Natoma St., San Francisco, Calif.
Folkways, 117 W. 46th St., New York, N.Y.
Fraternity, 413 Race St., Cincinatti, Ohio.
GNP (Gene Norman Presents), 8600 Lookout Mt. Ave., Hollywood 6, Calif.
Golden Crest, 220 Broadway, Huntington Station, N.Y.
Good Time Jazz, see Contemporary.
Grand Award, 8 Kingsland Ave., Harrison, N.J.
Harmony, see Columbia.
Herald, 1697 Broadway, New York, N.Y.
Hi-Fi Record, 7803 Sunset Blvd., Hollywood 38, Calif.
Hip, Box 2337, Van Nuys, Calif.
Imperial, 6425 Hollywood Blvd., Los Angeles 28, Calif.
Intro, see Aladdin.
Jazzman, 6420 Santa Monica Blvd., Hollywood 38, Calif.
Jazzology, 3918 Bergenline Ave., Union City, N.J.
Jazztone, see American Recording Society.
Jazz: West, see Aladdin.
Jazz Workshop, see Debut.
Josie, see Jubilee.
Jubilee, 1650 Broadway, New York 19, N.Y.
Judson, see Riverside.
Kapp, 119 West 57th St., New York, N.Y.
King, 1540 Brewster Ave., Cincinnati, Ohio.

Liberty, 1556 N. La Brea, Hollywood 28, Calif.
London, 539 W. 25th St., New York 1, N.Y.
Mercury, 35 E. Wacker Dr., Chicago, Ill.
MGM, 1540 Broadway, New York 36, N.Y.
Modern, 9317 W. Washington Blvd., Culver City, Calif.
Mode, 8295 Sunset Blvd., Hollywood, Calif.
Motif, 6269 Selma Ave., Hollywood 28, Calif.
Music Minus One, 719 10th Ave., New York, N.Y.
Opus, P.O. Box 106, Forest Hills 75, N.Y.
Period, 304 E. 74th St., New York 19, N.Y.
Prestige, 203 S. Washington, Bergenfield, N.J.
Rama, see Roulette.
Rainbow, 767 10th Ave., New York 19, N.Y.
RCA Victor, 155 E. 24th St., New York 10, N.Y.
Regent, see Savoy.
Replica, 7210 Westview Dr., Besplanes, Ill.
Riverside, 553 W. 51st St., New York.
RKO-Unique, 1440 Broadway, Rm. 1972, New York 36, N.Y.
Rondo, 220 W. Locust, Chicago, Ill.
Roost, 625 10th Ave., New York 36, N.Y.
Roulette, 659 10th Ave., New York 36, N.Y.
San Francisco Jazz, 217 Kearny St., San Francisco, Calif.
Savoy, 58 Market St., Newark, N.J.
Score, 5352 W. Pico Blvd., Los Angeles, Calif.
S-D, 1637 N. Ashland Ave., Chicago, Ill.
Seeco, see Dawn.
Signal, 762 10th Ave., New York 19, N.Y.
Soma, 29 Glenwood Ave., Minneapolis, Minn.
Southland, 58 St. Louis St., New Orleans 16, La.
Specialty, 8508 Sunset Blvd., Hollywood 46, Calif.
Starlite, 6671 Sunset Blvd., Hollywood 28, Calif.
Stinson, 27 Union Sq. W., New York, N.Y.
Storyville, 75 State St., Boston, Mass.
Sunset, 6671 Sunset Blvd., Hollywood 28, Calif.
Tampa, 117 N. El Centro Ave., Hollywood, Calif.
Tempo, 8540 Sunset Blvd., Hollywood 46, Calif.
Tops, 83 Crosby St., New York, N.Y.
Transition, 6 Ashton Pl., Cambridge, Mass.
Urania, 625 8th Ave., New York 18, N.Y.
Vanguard, 256 W. 55 St., New York, N.Y.
Verve, 451 N. Canyon Dr., Beverly Hills, Calif.
Vik, see RCA Victor.
Westminster, 275 7th Ave., New York 1, N.Y.
Wing, see Mercury.
World-Pacific, 8255 Sunset Blvd., Hollywood 46, Calif.

HOW TO REACH THE STARS

*F*ollowing are the principal booking agencies that specialize in the handling of jazz talent, or of artists in closely related fields.

WILLARD ALEXANDER, INC., 425 Park Ave., New York, N.Y., Plaza 1-7070; 333 North Michigan, Chicago, Ill., CEntral 6-2395; c/o Harold Jovien, Premiere Attractions, 1046 North Carol Drive, Hollywood, Calif., CRestview 4-5488.

Artists: Louis Armstrong, George Auld, Henry Franco, Tal Farlow, Bud Freeman, Urbie Green, Peanuts Hucko, Rolf Kuhn, Ray McKinley (directing Glenn Miller band), Hal McKusick, Charlie Mingus, Phineas Newborn, Oscar Pettiford, Boyd Raeburn, Jeri Southern, Sarah Vaughan, Joe Venuti, Mary Lou Williams, Kai Winding.

ASSOCIATED BOOKING CORP., 745 Fifth Avenue, New York 22, N.Y., PLaza 9-4600; 203 North Wabash Ave., Chicago, Ill., CEntral 6-9451; 8619 Sunset Blvd., Hollywood 46, Calif., CRestview 1-8131.

Artists: Louis Armstrong, Georgie Auld, Henry "Red" Allen, Nat Adderley, Julian "Cannonball" Adderley, Australian Jazz Quintet, Dorothy Ashby, Lillian Armstrong, Les Brown, Dave Brubeck, Chet Baker, Basin Street 6, Pia Beck, Al Belletto, Bob Brookmeyer, Benny Carter, Barbara Carroll, Jackie Cain, Conte Candoli, Eddie Condon, Joe Castro, Dixieland Rhythm Kings, Dorothy Donegan, Dukes of Dixieland, Duke Ellington, Billy Eckstine, Don Elliott, Herbie Fields, Ella Fitzgerald, Frances Faye, Maynard Ferguson, Slim Gaillard, Terry Gibbs, Erroll Garner, Dizzy Gillespie, Lionel Hampton, Woody Herman, Bobby Hackett, Billie Holiday, Earl Hines, Art Hodes, Neal Hefti, Chico Hamilton, Lurlean Hunter, Eddie Heywood, Ivory Joe Hunter, Jutta Hipp, Jon Hendricks, Pee Wee Erwin, Chubby Jackson, Mahalia Jackson, Ahmad Jamal Herb Jeffries, J. J. Johnson, Pete Jolly, Calvin Jackson, Beverly Kenny, Lee Konitz, Roy Kral, Morgana King, Gene Krupa, Alex Kallao, Max Kaminsky, Marie Knight, Nappy Lamare, Elliot Lawrence, Big Maybelle, Joe Loco, Carmen McRae, Marian McPartland, Jimmy McPartland, Wingy Manone, Joe Marsala, Helen Merrill, Lizzie Miles, Gerry Mulligan, Charlie Mingus, Vido Musso, Audrey Morris, Red Nichols, Red Norvo, Anita O'Day, Kid Ory, Dave Pell, Lucy Reed, Max Roach, Sonny Rollins, Frank Rosolino, Riverboat 5 plus 2, Salt City Five, Bobby Scott, George Shearing, Muggsy Spanier, Bud Shank, Hazel Scott, Lou Stein, Stuff Smith, Eddie South, Ralph Sutton, Sylvia Syms, Tony Scott, Zoot Sims, Joe Sullivan, Sal Salvador, Billy Taylor, Jack Teagarden, Sister Rosetta Tharpe, Dinah Washington, Teddy Wilson, Josh White, Frances Wayne.

GALE AGENCY, INC., 48 W. 48th Street, New York 36, N.Y., PLaza 7-7100; Milton Deutsch, 9157 Sunset Blvd., Hollywood, Calif., CRestview 4-7321.

Artists: Lavern Baker, Chuck Berry, Rusty Bryant, Savannah Churchill, The Clovers, Eddie "Lockjaw" Davis, Wild Bill Davison, Ella Fitzgerald, Golden Gate Quartet, Tiny Grimes, Roy Hamilton, Ace Harris, Screamin' Jay Hawkins, Clarence "Frogman" Henry, Al Hibbler, John Lee Hooker, Illinois Jacquet, Bullmose Jackson, Buddy Johnson, Little Richard, Clyde Mc-Phatter, Amos Milburn, Turk Murphy, Art Pepper, Bud Powell, Lloyd Price, Red Prysock, Della Reese, Solitaires, Lester Young.

GENERAL ARTISTS CORPORATION, 640 Fifth Avenue, New York, N.Y., CIrcle 7-7543; 8 South Michigan, Chicago, Ill., STate 2-6288; 9650 Santa Monica Blvd., Beverly Hills, Calif., CRestview 1-8101.

Artists: Connee Boswell, June Christy, Four Freshmen, Art Hodes, Louis Jordan, Stan Kenton, Reese Markewich.

WILLIAM MORRIS AGENCY, INC., 1740 Broadway, New York, N.Y., JUdson 6-5100; 919 North Michigan Ave., Chicago, Ill., WHitehall 3-1744; 151 El Camino Drive, Beverly Hills, Calif., CRestview 4-7451.

Artists: Sammy Davis, Jr., Billy Eckstine, Eartha Kitt, Elvis Presley, Louis Prima and Keely Smith, Bobby Scott.

MUSIC CORPORATION OF AMERICA, 598 Madison Ave., New York 22, N.Y., PLaza 9-7500; 430 N. Michigan Ave., Chicago, Ill., DElaware 7-1100; 9370 Santa Monica Blvd., Beverly Hills, Calif., CRestview 6-2001.

Artists: Ray Anthony, Charlie Barnet, Tex Beneke, Billy Butterfield, Lee Castle (Jimmy Dorsey orch.), Les and Larry Elgart, Ralph Flanagan, Harry James, Conrad Janis, Shelly Manne, Perez Prado, Stan Rubin, Charlie Spivak.

SHAW ARTISTS CORP., 565 Fifth Ave., New York 17, N.Y., OXford 7-7744; 203 North Wabash Ave., Chicago, Ill., RAndolph 6-0131; 8923 Sunset Blvd., Hollywood, Calif.

Artists: Sidney Bechet, Art Blakey and Messengers, Milt Buckner, Candido, Benny Carter, Chris Connor, Curtis Counce, Wild Bill Davis, Miles Davis, Bill Doggett, Lou Donaldson, Roy Eldridge, Stan Getz, Hampton Hawes, Coleman Hawkins, Jo Jones, Dave Mackay, Herbie Mann, Mat Mathews, Howard McGhee, Modern Jazz Quartet, James Moody, Thelonious Monk, Sam Most, Oscar Peterson, Flip Phillips, Sahib Shihab, Horace Silver, Jimmy Smith, Dakota Staton, Sonny Stitt, Jean Thielemans, Ben Webster.

UNIVERSAL ATTRACTIONS, 2 Park Avenue, New York 16, N.Y., MUrray Hill 3-3282; 3849 S. Western Ave., Los Angeles 62, Calif., AXminster 2-0517.

Artists: Dud Bascombe, Earl Bostic, Tiny Bradshaw, Nappy Brown, Arnett Cobb, Dexter Gordon, Wynonie Harris, Erskine Hawkins, Etta James, Little Willie John, Roy Milton, The Ravens, Tab Smith, Eddie "Cleanhead" Vinson, T-Bone Walker, Jr., Cootie Williams.

BIBLIOGRAPHY

RECENT CRITICISM AND HISTORY:

Broonzy, Big Bill (with Yannick Bruynoghe), *Big Bill Blues*. Grove Press.
Chartres, Samuel, *Jazz: New Orleans*, 1885-1957. Walter C. Allen.
Condon, Eddie, and Richard Gehman, *Treasury of Jazz*. Dial. Anthology.
Feather, Leonard, *The Book of Jazz*. Horizon.
Gleason, Ralph, *Jam Session*. Putnam. Anthology.
Grossman, William, *The Heart of Jazz*. New York University Press.
Harris, Rex, *Recorded Jazz: a Critical Guide*. Pelican.
Hentoff, Nat, and Nat Shapiro, *The Jazz Makers*. Rinehart. Anthology.
Horricks, Raymond, *Count Basie and His Orchestra*. Citadel.
Jazz 1957 (*Metronome* Yearbook).
Jazz 1958 (*Metronome* Yearbook).
Jazz Record Reviews (*Down Beat*). Vol. I (1956) and Vol. II (1957).
Longstreet Stephen, *The Real Jazz, Old and New*. Louisiana State University Press.
Music '57 (*Down Beat* Yearbook).
Music '58 (*Down Beat* Yearbook).
Paul, Elliot, *That Crazy American Music*. Bobbs-Merril.
Terkel, Studs, *Giants of Jazz*. Crowell.
Ulanov, Barry, *A Handbook of Jazz*. Viking.

FICTION:

Flender, Harold, *Paris Blues*. Ballantine.
Holmes, John Clellon, *The Horn*. Random House.
Hunter, Evan, *Second Ending* (*Quartet in H*). Pocket Books.
Lea, George, *Somewhere There's Music*. Lippincott.

CRITICISM, HISTORY AND FICTION IN RECENT PAPER-BACKED REPRINTS:

Armstrong, Louis, *Satchmo: My Life in New Orleans*. Signet.
Baker, Dorothy, *Jazz: New Orleans*. Signet.
Hodeir, André, *Jazz: Its Evolution and Essence*. Evergreen.
Holiday, Billie, *Lady Sings the Blues*. Popular Library.
Lomax, Alan, *Mister Jelly Roll*. Evergreen.
Stearns, Marshall, *The Story of Jazz*. Mentor.

NEW PERIODICALS:

Jazz Review, monthly: edited by Nat Hentoff and Martin Williams. Box 128, Village Station, New York 14, N.Y.
Jazz: a Quarterly of American Music: edited by Ralph Gleason. 2110 Haste St., Berkeley 4, Calif.

Other DA CAPO titles of interest